April

Vegetables

Sow onions, beet, winter cabbage.
Plant out cauliflowers at the end of the month.
Make a first sowing of main carrot crop.
Start successional sowing of peas, beans, lettuce, radish etc.
Finish planting of late potatoes and earth up earlies.
Plant out onions raised under glass.

Fruit

Net bush fruit against birds.
Ventilate strawberries under cloches and give the strawberry some strawy manure.
Spray peaches with water to help fruit set.
Important to continue using insecticides and fungicides, but do **not** spray open flowers.
Cut back newly planted raspberries.

Flowers

Sow hardy annuals in situ.
Remove the dead heads of daffodils and other spring flowers.
Divide and replant perennials such as michaelmas daisies.
Hoe weeds.
Plant out violas, paeonies, calceolarias, hollyhocks, etc.
In the middle of the month plant up the rockery.
Put summer bedding plants to harden off.
Sow polyanthus and wallflowers for next spring.

Shrubs

Plant coniferous and evergreen trees and shrubs and bamboos.
Prune flowered shrubs, e.g. forsythia and evergreens.
Finish pruning roses.
Trim winter flowering heathers.
Stop side shoots on fuchsias to produce bushy plants.

Lawns

Mow lawns and weed and feed.
Trim edges and if you dislike chemical weed killers grub out dandelions and plantains.
Sow grass seed on bare patches after roughly raking the surface.

Greenhouse

Sow seeds of outdoor tomatoes, melon and marrows.
Remove flower heads of winter flowering plants, such as azaleas.
Top dress pots and hanging baskets and tubs.
Increase ventilation and towards the end of the month start to shade.

House plants

Increase watering and light.
Watch for pests and spray when necessary.
Re-pot ferns and aspidistras.
Top up tubs and containers with fresh soil.

General

Use simazine on paths.
Watch out for bird damage in any part of the garden and net if necessary.

May

Vegetables

Sow beans.
Continue with successive sowings of lettuce, French beans, carrots, turnips, beets etc.
Plant Brussels sprouts.
If early potatoes are through protect them against frost by earthing up.
Thin lettuce, onions and turnips.
At the end of the month plant out tomatoes, marrows, cucumbers, spring cabbage, celery, cauliflower.
Pinch out the tips of broad beans.
Stake peas and beans.

Fruit

If necessary fruit should be watered and as the fruit is swelling a light feed can be given.
Thin gooseberries and spray against insect and fungal pests, but not on open blossoms.
Put straw down for strawberries.
Watch for gooseberry saw fly and spray if it appears.
Towards the end of the month thin vines and net against birds.

Flowers

Harden off bedding plants.
Sow hardy annuals for the autumn and perennials, such as wallflowers.
Thin early sowings.
Dead-head spring flowers and if necessary lift and heel in a spare part of the garden.
Divide and replant polyanthus, aubrietia, Christmas roses.
Plant lilies, stocks, asters outside and start bedding out.
Stake and tie tall herbaceous plants.

Shrubs

Watch roses for pests and disease and spray at once.
Mulch newly planted shrubs and remove weak or surplus shoots.
Pay particular attention to wall shrubs when mulching.
Prune laurels and spring flowering shrubs, such as lilacs, forsythia, flowering currant etc.

Lawns

Lower blades of mower and cut frequently in different directions.
Apply weed killer.
If dry water newly turfed and sown lawns.

Greenhouse

Sow seeds of rockery plants in pans.
Remove side shoots of tomatoes.
Keep a close watch on ventilation especially towards the end of the month both in greenhouse and in cold frames.
Take cuttings of geraniums for autumn flowering.

House plants

Plant out spring bulbs to naturalise.
Increase watering and feed growing plants.
Once risk of frost is over put out azaleas, lilium, etc.

General

It is very important to keep weeds down this month.
Staking and tying of all trees and shrubs should be done.
Remember to mulch after rain.

Vegetables

Continue successive sowings.
Asparagus can be cut until the end of the month, then left alone.
Plant out sprouts, cauliflower, marrows, tomatoes, leeks.
Stake and pinch out runner beans and tomatoes.
Earth up late potatoes.
Watch out for carrot fly and cabbage root fly and dust with calomel.
As rows get crowded, thin.

Fruit

Weed, water and thin surplus fruit.
Propagate strawberries from unwanted runners, and if slugs appear put down slug bait.
Spray against raspberry beetle, apple scab, codling moth.
Mulch raspberries and currants.
Begin summer pruning of apples and pears.
Thin peach fruits.

Flowers

Continue dead-heading.
Cut back early flowering herbaceous subjects in order to produce a late crop of flowers.
Take cuttings of pinks and rock roses.
Finish planting out half hardy annuals, e.g. dahlias.
Divide May flowering perennials.
Pinch out early flowering chrysanthemums.
Sow Canterbury bells for next year.
Sweet peas should be carefully staked and tied.
Biennial seedlings can be set out in rows.

Shrubs

Spray roses to protect against black spot and mildew.
Prune philadelphus, deutzia, spiraea after flowering.
Remove rhododendron seed pods and mulch after rain.
Plant out standard fuchsias.

Lawns

Continue cutting and weed killing.
If weather is dry leave cuttings on the lawn, otherwise use a grassbox.
A little feed would help old lawns.

Greenhouse

Shade house and improve ventilation.
Water night and morning.
Final potting of late chrysanths.
Peaches and grapes should be thinned.
Winter flowering bulbs should be allowed to dry off and rest.
Tub roses can be pruned and tied up for next year.

House plants

Keep eyes open for wilting or the appearance of pests and act appropriately.

General

Most indoor plants can be plunged outside.
Continue with weed killing and watering where necessary.

The

PRACTICAL
GARDENER'S

ENCYCLOPEDIA

The
PRACTICAL
GARDENER'S
ENCYCLOPEDIA

edited by

Professor Alan Gemmell

TREASURE PRESS

First published in Great Britain 1977 by
William Collins Sons & Co Ltd
This edition published in 1984 by
Treasure Press
59 Grosvenor Street
London W1
Reprinted 1985, 1986
© 1977 William Collins Sons & Co Ltd
ISBN 0 907812 69 4
Printed in Czechoslovakia
50542/3

CONTENTS

This book is dedicated to the great British public
in gratitude for what they have taught me over many years
and in the hope that the wisdom and knowledge which it contains
may prove of continuing help and inspiration.

ACKNOWLEDGEMENTS

The publishers wish to thank all those who helped
in the provision of illustrations

ALTON GLASSHOUSES LTD. 214; 215a,b,c.
A. BILLITT 55c; 61a,b,c; 62a,b; 63; 64a,b,c; 65a,b,c.
R. J. BISGROVE 43a,b; 141b.
ELECTRICITY COUNCIL 216a,b.
ELECTROLUX 206b.
V. FINNIS 11; 42a; 44a; 91; 129c; 181; 185b,c;
187; 188a; 191b; 199a; 211a,b.
B. FURNER 29a; 47a,b; 50d; 53a; 55a,b; 77a,b,c;
80c,g; 82a,b; 83; 85b; 86; 87a,b; 88b; 95; 96a,b; 100;
101b,c; 105c,d; 107a,c,d; 108c; 109; 111a; 112a,c;
113b,c; 114a,b,e,f,g; 116e; 117b,c,d; 123b,c;
125a,c; 126c; 129a,b; 149a,b,c,d,e,f;
150a; 151b,c; 152a; 153b,d; 155a,b; 160; 161;
164; 165; 166; 167b; 168a,b,c; 169a,b;
170a,b,c; 171a,b; 173a,b,c; 174b; 175a,b;
176a,b; 177a,b,c; 178a,b; 188b; 190a;
193a,b,c; 194a,b; 195; 196; 197a,b; 199b;
201a,b,c,d; 202a,b,c; 203a,b,c,d; 204a,b,c,d;
205a,b,c; 210a; 221a,b,d; 222a; 226a; 233a,b,c,d,e,f;
234d; 235a,c; 236a,b; 245c; 246a,b,c; 248.
A. R. GEMMELL 9a; 12a,b; 13a,b,c,d; 14a,b; 15a,b; 16; 17; 18a,b,c;
19a,b; 20a,b,c; 21a,b; 22a,b,c,d,e,f;
23a,b,c,d,e,f; 24a,b,c,d,e,f; 25; 27a,b,c,d;
28a,b,c,d; 29b; 30a,b,c; 31a,b,c,d; 32a,b,c;
33a,b; 34a,b,c; 35a,b; 36; 38; 67;
69; 70b; 79d; 85a; 88a; 98b; 107b; 111b,c,d;
114d; 116b,c; 119f; 122a; 123d; 126b;
137; 151a; 152b,e; 153c; 221c; 222c; 223a,b,c;
225c; 243b; 245a,b; 247.
R. GENDERS 97a,b; 98a; 101a; 102; 106; 107e; 108a,b;
110a,b,c; 119a,b,c,d; 150c; 152c; 172a,b,c,d; 209a,b; 220.
P. HEMSLEY 39; 45a; 49a; 115a,b; 120d; 121a; 122b,c; 123a; 124b,c; 131a;
134; 136; 138; 140a,b; 141a,c; 142a,b; 143a,b,c,d,e;
144a,b,c; 153a; 154b.
J. A. HINGSTON 49b; 120a,b,c; 121b; 124a; 125b,d;
126a; 131c,d; 154a.
I.C.I. LTD. 218.
R. KAYE 44b; 45b; 68b; 73; 74; 77d; 78a,b,c,d,e; 79a,c,e; 80a,b,d,e,f,h;
81a,b,e,f; 84a,b; 87c; 88c,d; 105b; 155d; 234a.
F. W. LOADS 70a; 71b; 90; 92a,b,c; 185a; 224; 231a; 237;
240a,b; 241a,b; 242b.
LONG ASHTON RESEARCH STATION 210b.
G. NIGHTINGALE 66; 222d; 223b; 226b; 227c,e; 230; 231b; 234e; 235d,e;
236c; 239a,b,c; 240c; 243a,c.
PAN BRITANNICA INDUSTRIES LTD. 219.
E. POOLE 146; 147a,b.
T. ROCHFORD & SONS LTD. 155c; 225a,b,d,e; 227a,b,d; 228c;
229; 238; 242a,c.
ROYAL NATIONAL ROSE SOCIETY 48; 132a,b,c,d,e; 133a,b,c.
W. E. SHEWELL-COOPER 46a,b,c; 47c; 51; 52a,b; 53b; 54a,b.
J. C. SHORTLAND 131b.
HARRY SMITH 40; 72; 93a,b; 103; 158; 213.
THERMOFORCE LTD. 217.
THOMPSON & MORGAN (IPSWICH) LTD. 50c; 79b;
81c,d; 112b; 113a; 114c; 116a,d; 117a; 148c,d; 150b;
152d; 154c; 162a,b,c,d; 167a; 174a; 228a,b; 234b; 235b.
TUPPERWARE 206a.
B. WALKDEN 56a,b,c; 57a,b,c,d,e; 58a,b,c,d; 59a,b,c.
DON WILDRIDGE 42b; 50a,b; 68a; 71a; 105a; 114h; 119e; 124d;
148a,b; 154d; 182; 184a,b; 190b,c; 191a; 222b; 234c.

INTRODUCTION

There is always a place for knowledge and information especially if it is well presented, clear, and neatly packaged so that the reader can find what he wants to know with the minimum of difficulty. I hope readers will find this book fits this category, for it has been designed to have the following form:

1 It will try most of the time to be practical, so that if you want to make, say, a rockery, then the appropriate chapter will start from the bare earth, go through the construction, the planting, and the growing. It will end up with a list of plants you can grow, and give you cultural hints about each and good coloured illustrations of many of them. Space prevents a description of all the available plants for each situation, but the authors have tried to choose the most reliable as well as the best species and varieties. The bulk of the book is composed of chapters each of which deals in some detail with different aspects of gardens and gardening, ranging from making a lawn, to using hanging baskets, from designing your garden to deep freezing the products. Different authors contribute different chapters, each retaining his or her unique style and manner of presenting the knowledge. This means the book will contain many different styles of writing, but will keep the freshness and originality of each individual author.

2 The first part of the book is called 'Look at Plants' for it is amazing how much the ordinary gardener misses by not looking and noticing what is going on under his nose. In this section I hope to look at each part of the plant separately, and to try to stress the points which are of significance to the gardener. This approach allows me to try to put across some basic plant science, which, if read with a little care, will make the gardener appreciate, so very much more, the wonder and magic of the ordinary garden. Many times I take people round my garden, and on pointing out something in a very ordinary plant I hear them say 'Do you know, I've never noticed that before'.

Such knowledge of plants enables the gardener to understand the science of gardening, and so to use scientific aids with understanding and care. Gardening is both an art and a science. It was an art or a craft long before science came on the scene, and many gardens are a tribute to the sensitivity, experience, and creative artistic talents of the owners; but now that science is here it should be used wisely and well, and when the craft and the science are used together then the man becomes a real gardener.

3 The book also contains a glossary in which I have tried to define in as simple and clear a way as possible all the gardening terms used in this and subsequent chapters. No claim is made for this as a gardening dictionary; the aim is simply to help the reader understand the book. In addition there is what I have called a gardening almanack in which hints for the cultivation of a number of the more common garden plants are given in a brief form. This is not meant to be a complete guide but rather to give the reader an idea of the appearance and the demands made by any particular plant for soil, water, care, etc.

VALUING THE GARDEN

What is the value of a garden? Well, there are some immediate financial advantages, for the garden will provide fruit, vegetables, and flowers for the house and so save money on household bills. It will also add to the market value of a house by 'setting it off' like a picture in a good frame.

But the garden has many other values. For example, it can be a place of relaxation and pleasure where you can sit and the children play, where you can sun-bathe or sleep, or even eat in the good weather. But relaxation takes many forms and after a hard day's work in the factory, shop, or office, it is very relaxing to go out into the fresh air and work hard or even just potter about in the garden. My wife always says that when I'm worrying about the garden, I'm not worrying about anything else! So we should never underrate a garden as a place of relaxation.

There is a great value in the knowledge you accumulate, and in the friends you make at local shows, at gardening club meetings, and literally over the garden wall. You can get lots of real pleasure by running your own experiments with fertilisers, varieties, etc., but if you start to do any experimental work, be sure to make good and full notes of what you have done, and, even more important, see how many different ways you can explain the results you get. Many gardeners immediately leap to the conclusion that fits their particular prejudices and so may be drawing wrong lessons or even more likely, may be missing the most important point of the experiment.

More and more gardeners are beginning to label their plants, for there is nothing more annoying than to be unable to name all the plants in your garden. A good label lasts for years, and you can refresh your memory at any time. People buying houses with established gardens will bless you if the trees, shrubs, etc. are clearly labelled.

A garden therefore brings you a return in financial, aesthetic, and physical terms, but you have to make an investment in order to get a return, and the capital and the kind of investment you make determine the returns.

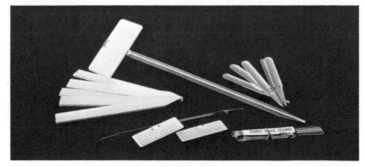

A variety of labels

BUYING FOR THE GARDEN

As in all other situations money has to be spent on what we can loosely call 'Capital' things and on 'Running' expenses, and we must never forget that the running costs may depend on the capital, and carefully chosen but relatively expensive subjects may prove a real economy in the long run.

What is capital expenditure used for in a garden? First of all there are tools. In the garden you use hoe, spade, barrow, fork, secateurs, mower, and maybe many others, if not every day at least very frequently. You should go to the limits of your purse to buy the best possible tools, preferably stainless steel, for it cleans easily and produces a good finished job. Never buy tools which are too heavy for you or feel awkward in the hand. If a spade feels heavy in a shop, think of the additional weight when you are digging heavy clay, and get a lighter one. Remember good tools will last for many years, so that although the initial outlay seems high, it is worth it in the end.

The other equal first in the way of expense in the garden should be the soil. If you are lucky you may be on good land, but most people have to settle for what they get, and it is of immense future value to pay at the outset to have your drainage checked, to level if it is a bumpy area, and even to have it well dug using a hired cultivator-type piece of machinery.

The final major piece of expenditure is plants. Here I do not mean seeds for annual vegetables and flowers, but longer-lasting plants such as shrubs, trees or perennials. Here you should always buy from a good and reputable dealer, and although a rose bush may seem expensive you will enjoy it for years, so the cost per year is very low. I have found it good policy to concentrate my buying on unusual and relatively expensive things, for the ordinary shrubs and trees can usually be raised from cuttings obtained from a friendly neighbour or colleague, and if you want your garden to have a character of its own, then buy the best.

Finally, although I say 'buy the best' do remember to be sensible about it, and take advice before you embark on a £5 shrub. To grow it successfully may require special conditions that you cannot fulfil, and it could be a waste of money to buy it.

Running expenses are the ordinary seeds, fertilisers, etc. and here as in all things try to go for quality as well as quantity. Study the chapters in this book carefully, and then buy on the basis of that advice tempered by local knowledge.

WORK IN THE GARDEN

At the risk of teaching my grandmother to suck eggs let me lay down a few simple rules to govern garden work.

1 Never bite off more than you can chew. This is especially true in planning the garden, as you should never create work for yourself that is not strictly necessary. And remember that the longer you live, the older you get, and jobs which were easy in the thirties are difficult in the forties and fifties and may be impossible in the sixties and seventies.

2 Take the jobs slowly and you will find they get done more easily. If you rush them you are likely to tire too quickly. This is especially true in the spring when so many jobs are calling out to be done that you feel under continual pressure. It is a bad gardener who is rushed by his garden. Remember, gently does it.

3 Try to vary your work at each session in the garden. Digging becomes a hard back-breaking job if there is too much of it. So, when you are tired with digging, you should maybe do a bit of staking or pruning or even just tidying up. If you have a range of jobs available at any time, you will never become bored or exhausted by one.

4 In the same vein take your wheelbarrow with a selection of tools wherever you go. It is maddening to find when you are digging, and you want to change to staking, that you have left scissors, twine, stakes, hammer all back in the garden shed and you have to trek to-and-fro many times.

5 Don't be afraid to ask advice from neighbours or friends, but before you adopt the advice think about it a bit to be sure that it is suitable for your particular garden. Each garden has its own special problem and so you must be willing to *adopt* ideas and then *adapt* them to your own situation.

6 In gardening, as in many other things, experience is a very good teacher, so be willing to try out new things. If they fail, then they fail, and you know a bit more than you did when you started.

7 Don't be afraid to visit garden centres in your area and see what the local professional growers are doing, and how they do it. Many people are amazed at what can be done in someone else's garden, but should remember that if they were willing to put in the same amount of thought and work, their own garden also would become a thing of beauty.

8 Finally, if you are going to be a good gardener be prepared to learn about your subject. Don't be put off by the fact that it seems scientific and may be difficult at first reading or hearing. Gardening enjoyed cannot be simply reduced to rules of growing or to lists, e.g. do-this and do-that. It contains science, folk-lore, history, dietetics, many different sides of human knowledge, all of which contribute to make gardening the most popular hobby in most countries.

I once met a railway porter in the train and we started talking about hobbies. When I asked him what his hobby was he replied 'Megalithic clocks'! It brought me up short, for this is a very 'way-out' study, but he had become interested in Stonehenge and in the ways in which Stone Age man told the time and kept track of the seasons. From knowing nothing he had in a few years become well versed in his subject.

So if you are interested in gardening, all things are possible, for by it you gain knowledge, health, beautiful surroundings, and help save a few pounds at the same time.

A.R.G.

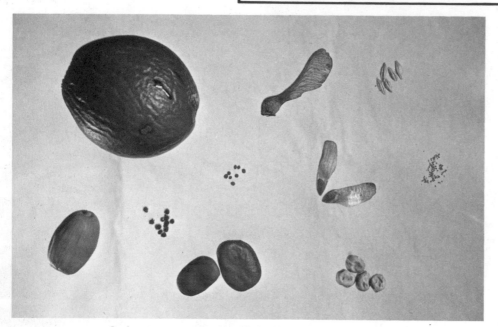

Seeds can vary very considerably in size, as this selection shows

A LOOK AT SEEDS

Every gardener must at some time or other, have sown seeds or at least handled them. Yet if you asked him to describe a seed he would say 'Well, small, usually hard, often black, or green, or brown . . .' and at that point he would stick and start talking about what you do with seeds and how they grow, etc. All of it might be absolutely true, but he would scarcely have answered the question.

The reason is simple. He has never really looked at a seed, much less taken it apart to see how it ticks, and it is the purpose of this chapter to do this 'before your very eyes' as Arthur Askey used to say. I hope that you will find this process interesting and informative, for by the end of the chapter you should see why you do certain things and how the way you deal with seeds in the garden is linked very closely to the actual structure of a seed.

Of course seeds come in many different sizes, from the large broad bean and pea seeds, through the medium-sized cabbage or nasturtium seeds, down to the powder-fine seeds of such plants as begonia or orchid. But no matter the size they have a common structure, and if you would like to follow me in a practical way, use a pea or broad bean for ease of observation.

Seeds are more easily dealt with when they have been soaked in water, so put a few seeds in a cup of water, let them soak overnight, and away we go.

Structure of a Seed

It never ceases to surprise people how much a seed resembles an ordinary hen's egg; but this is only reasonable, for basically they are designed to do the same job, namely to pro-

tect and nourish the young chicken or plant until it is able to care for itself. For this purpose there has to be an outer covering to keep out other organisms and to prevent the seed/egg from completely drying out. This is the seed coat, and in most plant seeds it is a thin tough skin which is easily peeled off the partly germinated soaked seed.

The coat is virtually waterproof, and the water necessary for seed germination usually gains entry to the interior through a small opening in the coat. Once the water

gets in it causes the material of the seed to swell, and as a result the seed coat is burst open and water can then get in and out very freely. It is interesting to note that the pressure exerted by seeds as they swell can be very great, capable of lifting stones and breaking strong earthenware jars. An ancient torture was to force the victim to swallow dry peas and then drink water in great quantity. The pain caused to the victim as the peas swelled in the stomach must have been excruciating.

The seed coat is also nearly gasproof. This seems rather unimportant, but its value lies in the fact that it seals gas *in* and not that it keeps gas out. The seed is a living thing and like all living things it produces the gas, carbon dioxide. This gas, in high concentration, slows life down, and as there is a gradual build-up of carbon dioxide within the seed coat, the life of the seed is slowed down. It can then go into a state of what is virtually suspended animation or dormancy, and this has significance in ensuring long life to many seeds.

Despite the low rate at which a seed is living, it *is* nevertheless alive, and to stay in this state it requires food. It is only reasonable therefore that the greater part of any seed is stored food, to nurture the embryo plant during its long resting period, and to feed the plantlet as it grows until it is capable of feeding itself. This food supply, which corresponds to the yolk of an egg, is called the 'endosperm'. It is the part of the seed which not only keeps the plant alive, but which we also use as food to keep us alive. Thus flour is the ground-up endosperm of wheat. We eat the stored food in peas, beans, cereals, etc.

However, the seed coat and the endo-

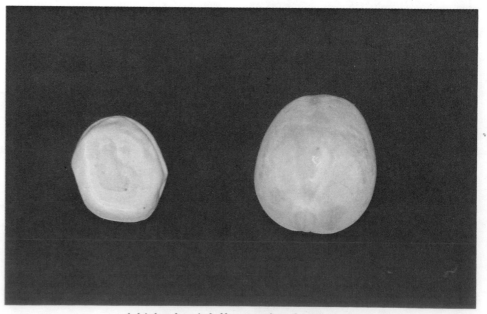

A dried seed cut in half so as to show the embryo root

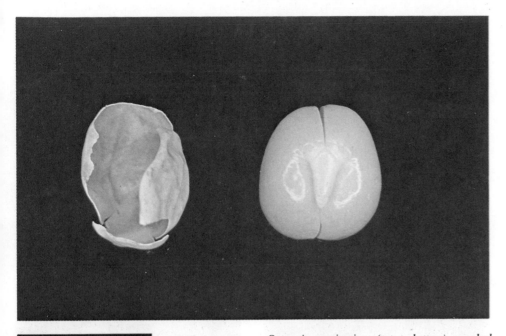

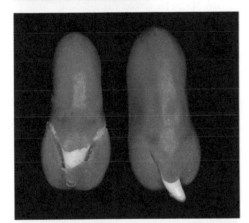

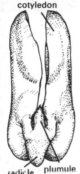

cotyledon

radicle plumule

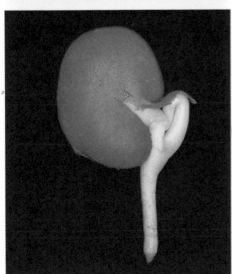

Stages in germination: (top to bottom) a soaked seed with seed coat removed (on the right); seed with young root (radicle) and burst seed coat; a further stage with radicle well through and young shoot beginning to unfurl.

sperm are not the essential parts of a seed, in the same way that the egg shell and the white and yolk are not the essential parts of an egg. The heart of the matter is the embryo plant in one case, and the chick in the other, and in both seed and egg, the embryo is well protected, for it is surrounded by the seed coat/shell and is partly enclosed in endosperm/egg yolk.

The plant embryo is small, but it contains in very rudimentary forms a young root and a young shoot, which bears the seed leaves or *cotyledons*. The latter can be thin and papery, in which case the seed will contain lots of endosperm, or the seed leaves may be green and swollen, and are then filled with the stored food and act as if they were endosperm.

So there we have it, a simple seed with seed coat, endosperm, embryo with seed leaves, and we sow it in the ground to wait for germination to occur and the seedlings to appear.

Germination
It is very easy to show that as a seed starts to germinate there is a sequence of events as follows:
1) water is taken in and the seed swells,
2) the seed coat bursts,
3) the young embryo begins to grow and the seed loses weight.

It must be obvious that the process of seed germination is complex, but the complexity makes a logical story. The speed of germination depends on the conditions in the soil in which the seed is sown. Obviously the soil must contain water otherwise the bursting of the seed coat would not happen, but the necessity for water has a greater significance than that, for it is the medium in which chemical and physical reactions take place.

Let me try to explain that in simpler terms. It is only on very rare occasions that dry chemicals will react when mixed together. Normally they are dissolved in water before a reaction will occur. Although the analogy is not exact, it is rather like sweetening tea with very hard crystalline

sugar. When you first add the sugar there is no sweetness of taste at all, and it is only as the sugar dissolves that the tea becomes sweet and more palatable. So it is, that when the water gains entry to the seed, chemical reactions can begin which yield energy.

Here again the likeness of a seed to any other living thing is noteworthy, for in the same way as we digest food and turn it into energy for work and play and growth, so the food stored in the endosperm is similarly changed. Thus energy becomes available to the embryo, and is used for growth.

There is another parallel between a simple chemical reaction and the changes in a seed, namely they are both affected by temperature. If we want a chemical reaction to go quickly we heat it and if we want materials, e.g. food, drugs, milk, etc., to stay unchanged we put them in a fridge at a low temperature. If we want a seed therefore to germinate quickly we put it in a hot bed, or a frame, or sow it in a seedpan in a heated greenhouse. We even sow it outside in the warmer weather of spring or early summer but *not* in winter.

If we sow seeds when the temperature is low and the soil cold, it does not matter if plenty of soil moisture gains entry to the seed, the vital chemical reactions will not take place. So the seed will lie dormant in the soil where it can be destroyed by insects, slugs, bacteria, fungi, and a host of other food-seeking organisms.

As well as water and temperature there is a third factor necessary for good seed germination, namely oxygen. Human beings need oxygen (O_2) for almost exactly the same reasons as the seed, because it is one of the most important chemicals involved in our life processes. We get our O_2 from the air, but the seed gets it from the soil air. There is usually a good supply of O_2 in the soil, but there is one circumstance which can reduce the quantity very greatly, namely if the soil is flooded, for then the soil air is displaced by water, and the seed can experience a shortage of oxygen.

The soil factors necessary for germination are therefore three in number:
1) a good supply of soil moisture,
2) a suitable soil temperature, and
3) plenty of soil air.

For these reasons all seed beds and seedling composts should be open and well-drained to allow plenty of O_2 into the soil, should contain humus to store and supply adequate quantities of water, and should be in a part of the garden which will warm up quickly, or in a cold frame or greenhouse. Alternatively, seed sowing should be delayed until the soil has heated up a bit after the cold of the winter.

Depth of Planting
It is common knowledge that seeds should be sown at different depths, but the 'why' is not always obvious. For reasons which will be clear later, plants require light before they can manufacture their own food. This means that in the darkness of the soil the growth of a seedling is totally dependent on its stored food until it gets above the soil surface. Now by far the greater part of most seeds is the food store, so that in large seeds there is much stored food, whereas in tiny seeds there is very little. If you sow small seeds deep in the ground they may germinate and grow, but if the food is finished before they reach the surface they will just die and you will never see them.

On the other hand large seeds can be sown 2 ins. or more down, and the young plants will reach the surface easily.

You can therefore generalise that the

smaller the seed the nearer to the surface it must be sown, until with powder-fine seed you simply scatter them thinly on the surface and cover with a sprinkling of sand to help retain a little moisture around them. The usual rule, which is quite good, is that you plant seeds at roughly the same depth in the soil as the size of the seed. Thus a large bean seed could go down 1–2 ins., a carrot seed $\frac{1}{4}$–$\frac{1}{2}$ in., and begonia you simply dust on the surface and thinly cover.

Storage of Seeds

Seeds have to be kept dry or they absorb water and start to swell and germinate. The essential therefore in storing seeds is dryness, and all our efforts must go into the general attempt to keep them away from moisture. Seeds should never be stored in paper packets in damp conditions, for the paper and then the seeds will absorb moisture and when enough is taken up the seeds will begin to germinate. If a seed starts to germinate and then is dried out, due maybe to a change in the weather, it will die. In fact a common cause of inviable, or dead seed, is premature germination followed by drying out.

Seed packets nowadays are designed to keep damp out, and the special foil and plastic packets are ideal for this purpose. But once they are opened damp air can get in, and if we sow half the seeds say in a foil pack and then try to store the rest in the pack for next season, we may be in for a disappointment, for we may innocently seal moisture *into* the pack which, because it keeps dampness out, by the same token must keep moisture in. Try wearing a raincoat on a dry hot day and you will soon see how the material, which keeps rain out, also keeps the perspiration from escaping from your clothing and the *inside* of the coat becomes quite wet.

So unless you can be sure of good dry conditions of storage it is unwise to store seed from year to year, or you may find many gaps in the row of seedlings. It is easy to see also why seed needs to be thoroughly dried before it is put in packets, and amateurs who are interested in saving seed from their own plants must take great care about this point.

The other enemy of stored seeds is mould. Just a little surface dampness is enough to give mould a start and as the mould (which is a fungus) grows it produces antibiotics which can act against the life of the seed. Any farmer knows that mouldy seed means poor germination.

Dormancy and Longevity

When dry and seemingly lifeless, the seed is said to be dormant or in a state of dormancy. This word means 'asleep' and the implication is that the seed can be wakened and brought back to life. But what value has dormancy to the plant and what mechanism produces it?

The value to the plant species is easy to see, for dormant seeds can lie in the soil from one autumn to the following spring and only germinate when the soil conditions are right for growth. Some seeds may stay dormant for years even when buried deep in the soil, and only germinate when brought up near the surface where oxygen and the proper temperature are available.

Thus dormancy has what is technically called a 'survival value' enabling the seed to survive unfavourable conditions without germinating and exposing the tender young plant to frost or drought or any other vagaries of the weather.

There are many mechanisms which pro-

Rosebay willowherb seeds are dispersed by wind

Twisted gorse pods after seeds have been ejected

duce the dormancy, and one of the commonest is a thick hard seed coat which is tough and will not break easily as water is absorbed. Sweet pea seeds are of this type, and to get them to germinate, old gardeners used to 'nick' them with a knife or give them a rub with a file to produce a weak spot in the seed coat where the break would occur. Seeds of clover have very thick coats and may lie in the soil for years before they germinate.

Under natural conditions these tough-coated seeds are attacked by soil bacteria or eaten by animals, and the coat is weakened by bacterial action or by the chemicals in the gut of the animals. Only when this has occurred (and it usually takes all winter) will the seed germinate.

Another common mechanism to produce dormancy is the presence of specific chemicals either in the seed, or in the fruit which contains it. These chemicals are called dormins, and their action can be appreciated when you think of a tomato or gooseberry which is filled with seeds in a moist, often warm situation, yet you practically never see a tomato seed or an orange pip germinate inside the fruit. But if you take the seeds out of the fruit, wash and then plant them, they grow very readily. This is because you have washed away the dormancy-inducing chemicals. Under natural conditions in the soil this is done by soil moisture and/or bacterial action.

There are other techniques for destroying these dormancy-inducing chemicals, including a cold shock, e.g. freezing, heat shock, light (some seeds will only germinate if they are given light), etc.

There are many such mechanisms of dormancy but I will limit myself to one more, for it too is quite common, and that is the immature embryo. I have already said that the embryo is the young plant, but it takes a period of time before this plant is ready to grow, and until it is mature the seed just simply will not germinate. An analogy is the presence of the child within the mother, where, although the child is developing, it is unable to lead a separate life until 9 months elapse. This period between the time when the seed seems ripe and the time when the embryo is ready to grow will also be a

'dormant' period, and this type of dormancy can only be broken by the passage of time.

It is impossible to discuss dormancy without also bringing in longevity, for every sensible gardener (and most gardeners are sensible) will ask 'Well, how long will dormancy persist and the seed remain alive?' The answer to this question must be 'It depends on the conditions of storage'. Under good conditions some seeds will stay alive for many years, although the story of wheat from Egyptian tombs being able to germinate and grow has been disproved long ago. The most careful tests of longevity have been done by taking seeds from plant collections stored under ideal conditions in museums and seeing if the seed would germinate.

The results of these experiments show that longevity depends very much on the species of plant. Thus out of 107 species buried in 1905, 50 species had at least 1% germination after 20 years, and a species of lotus, Nelumbium, germinated after 400 years. In nature, although the position is simple, an exact answer is impossible, and one can only say that in a sample of say 100 seeds most of them will germinate in the first year of sowing, but some will delay until the second year after sowing, and a very few will only grow in a third year. In other words there is a spread in the time of germination or, to put it another way, in the depth of the dormancy. This spread is good for survival of plant species, because it means that if all the plants are killed in the first year of growth, the species does not die out, for there will be a few seeds which germinate the following year and so carry on the species.

Seed Dispersal

Every gardener knows that if you sow seed too close together the resultant plants will be crowded and weak. They compete with each other for food in the soil, for light, for water and as a consequence are thin, spindly and leggy, requiring to be thinned in order that single plants may grow sturdy and strong. Carrots are a good example of this, for you sow a row as thinly as possible, but you still require to thin them further to single plants if you hope to get a crop of good edible carrots. In exactly the same way seedlings are pricked out to give each individual plant room to develop fully and well.

But in nature there is no one to do this thinning job so mechanisms have evolved which ensure that seed is scattered and each seed has a chance to grow unhindered by others. These are called 'seed dispersal' mechanisms and have two results:

1) the young plant does not grow in the shade of, or compete with the mother plant, and

2) the species is spread over a wider area and gets the opportunity to colonise new ground.

This is the reason for the spread of weeds, and everyone at some time must have acted as an unwitting agent of seed dispersal by trying to tell the time by blowing a dandelion clock, thus dispersing the seeds.

The natural mechanism of dispersal in the case of dandelion is clearly the wind, and the wide-spread colonisation of waste land by willow herb shows how effective wind dispersal can be. Similarly water dispersal will spread water and especially sea plants. But animals including man are very important agents of seed dispersal. Many seeds are enclosed in juicy fruits which are attractive to birds and humans. Such berries as holly, elder, rosehips, berberis, etc., and juicy fruits like raspberries, blackcurrants, apples, cherries, etc., all attract animals which eat the fruit, the seeds pass through the intestines of the animal as it moves around and are excreted usually undamaged at some distance from the parent plant. It is obvious that in the case of man or birds this distance can be many miles.

Some plants have explosive devices to spread their seed, and if you sit quietly by a gorse bush on a still hot summer day you can hear the pod bursting and throwing out the seed in a kind of quick jerk catapult movement.

Saving Your Own Seed

As seed becomes more expensive many gardeners are asking 'Is it all right for me to save seed from my own garden?' The answer to this question is 'No, unless . . .', and the rest of this section explains the 'unless'. Because most seed is produced as a result of one plant being pollinated by another, there is a good chance that the second generation will not be exactly like their parents. This is certainly true of the modern F1 hybrids, which are so colourful and fruitful in our gardens. Unless, therefore, you are sure of the parentage of your seeds you may be preserving a bad variety.

Secondly, it is not easy for the amateur to collect and store the seed under ideal conditions, for seed must be carefully dried or it will go mouldy in storage, and must also be carefully stored or the same fate may befall it. In nature, and that is where we must turn for the confirmation, the problem of storage is partly solved by dormancy, but it is more usually solved by sheer waste. Thus a single poppy, the result of the growth of one seed, will produce thousands of seeds in a year, and it does not matter if all die except one, for that one can conserve the species. But the gardener cannot afford this degree of waste.

If you want to try your hand at the fascinating hobby of plant breeding, then of course you must save your own seed, but until vegetable and flower seeds become much more expensive than they are now, it could be a waste of time, and in the end money, to try to keep seed from year to year and to take seed from your own crops.

Seed Treatment

Two types of seed treatment are widely used and it is worth looking at their value. The first is the use of 'pelleted seed'. In the beginning, pelleted seed was coated with fertiliser and a water-absorbing material, but it was found that the concentrated fertiliser could damage the young root, so they are now coated only with the water absorbing material. The theory behind pelleting has two arguments to put forward. Firstly by absorbing water from the soil the coating helps the seed to obtain a quicker, surer water supply and so aids germination. Secondly, the coating is fairly thick, so that single seeds can be handled easily and sown at single stations. This eliminates the need for thinning, as in the case of carrot or fine flower seedlings, so reducing labour and becoming more economic.

These arguments are valid, but some gardeners are finding a reduced germination from pelleted seed as a result of the coating attracting water from the soil so that germination starts normally. But if the soil is at all dry, most of the moisture has been taken out of it by the seed coating, and there is too little left for the continued growth of the seedling which therefore dies. Such a situation would not occur in a cold frame or greenhouse, where the grower has a much greater command of the situation and can add water as he pleases.

The other seed treatment is done by shaking up the seed with a fine dust of a fungicidal chemical. This substance is available to the amateur in the form of a 'puffer pack' which can be used to blow some of the fungicide over the seed in a container, such as a tin can with a lid or even a polythene bag. The lid is then closed and the tin or bag violently shaken with the object of coating each seed with a fine layer of the powder. The chemical has no effect on germination as such, but it kills fungi and moulds which might start to grow on the seed surface, and helps to sterilise the layer of soil immediately around the seed. It is therefore wise to treat early-sown seed, for the danger from fungal attack on the seed or even the young plant is greatest when germination is slow, and the seed lies inert in the soil for a few weeks.

The Process of Germination

I have described what happens in the early stages of germination, but now I have to finish the process so that we can move on to the mature plant. You will remember that the seed swells, the seed coat bursts, and life is on the move. This is especially true in the case of the young embryo whose various parts begin to elongate and emerge from the seed into the soil. Normally the first part to appear is the young root or *radicle*, which begins to grow down into the soil anchoring the seed. This is followed by the young stem

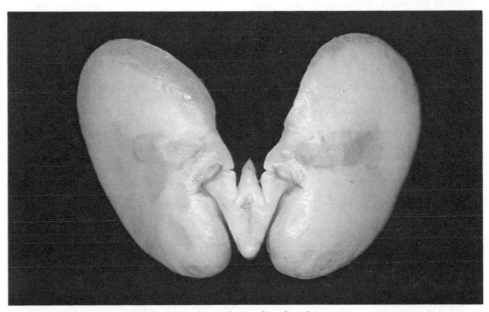

A germinating seed opened to show its parts

A young melon plant bearing two cotyledon leaves and two true leaves

or plumule, which forces its way up through the soil until it reaches the light.

In most cases there are either one or two seed leaves (cotyledons), and if these are thick and fleshy they stay underground – the food they contain is absorbed by the young plant. Such a plant is the pea or the bean. In other cases, e.g. tomato, the cotyledons are the first leaves to appear above ground, when they function as normal leaves but soon wither away and die as the true leaves (sometimes called the 'rough' leaves) get on with their job.

Many a grower will say that the plant grows up 'in order to reach the light' and the radicle grows down 'in order to seek for water and food', but this is not so. You see this is a kind of logic which assumes that plants can think and know in the darkness of the soil where the light is. It is easy to demonstrate that the stem grows up and the root down in response to the force of gravity, which affects the distribution of growth hormones in the plant in such a way that growth of cells and tissues occurs at greater rates at some points than at others. The net result is that the root grows down and the stem up as if they were seeking water and light respectively. Seeds growing in spacecraft, in a state of weightlessness where there is no gravity, just grow on in the direction the radicle or plumule happened to be facing when the seed germinated.

Once the plumule reaches the light the root and the shoot system of the plant can become fully established, so we are now in a position to look at the implications of root and shoot to the gardener.

A LOOK AT SOIL

Every gardener knows the importance of the soil. After all, it is the stuff in which plants grow, and we want to grow plants well. It is obvious that different kinds of soil affect plants differently, and so it is the purpose of this section to look at soil a little more closely to see if there are lessons to be learned by the gardener from this closer examination.

What is Soil Made of?

1) ROCK PARTICLES The basic material of soil is particles of rock. Sometimes the particles are quite large, in which case we have a sandy or even a gravelly soil; on the other hand the rock particles may be very small, and if so, we will then have a clay soil. The difference in size of the particles affects many of the properties of a soil. For example water will drain quickly through a coarse sand, but it will be lost only very slowly from a clay soil. In its turn this means that clay soils will tend to be wet, even waterlogged, cold, and slow to warm up, and very difficult to dig. A sandy soil will be just the opposite. It easily dries out, is quick to warm up, and is easy to cultivate. So far the sandy soil is winning!

2) HUMUS But there is much more to soils than rock fragments, for there is this 'magic' material called *humus*. Humus is not a single chemical compound. It is a mixture of substances formed by the gradual decay of organic material under the influence of bacteria, fungi, earthworms, etc. Humus has many and varied powers, for example it can act as a kind of cement which sticks the particles of rock together. So if you add humus to a clay soil, it will stick lots of the tiny rock fragments together to make a larger particle or 'crumb'. The soil is thereby improved, for the larger crumbs have larger passages between them, and drainage is improved. That is why we say that you should add as

Chickweed growing in a range of soils from very fine silt to almost pure humus

much humus as you can to a heavy clay soil to 'open it up' and to 'lighten' it.

Humus has another and equally important property, for it will soak up water like a sponge. Thus, if you apply humus to a sandy soil, it will enable the soil to hold water which would otherwise just drain through, so ensuring a constant supply to the plants.

It is strange that humus should at the same time have two such opposite qualities as storing water in dry soil and improving drainage in wet soils. Every gardener should try therefore to incorporate lots of humus into his garden for it can do nothing but good.

3) SOIL WATER You can do a very instructive experiment with a milk bottle of dry sand. Pack the sand down fairly tightly and then add a little water to the surface. You will see that the *top* of the soil gets wet but the bottom stays dry. If you want to wet all the soil you have to keep on adding water, and you will see the wet line gradually getting deeper as you add more water until it reaches the bottom, where, if you have added too much, the water will accumulate as visible liquid water.

This simple experiment makes three important points. Firstly, water only passes down in the soil as the upper layers are saturated. Thus if you water plants in dry weather, the water will get nowhere near the roots unless the layers of soil above the roots are absolutely saturated. So don't splash it, soak it.

The second point is that the water accumulates at an impermeable surface such as glass (in the bottle) or rock, or hard clay (in the garden). When this happens roots may actually be under water, although the surface may seem all right, and in this case the plant will die. So always make sure that excess water can drain away, either by breaking up any hard layers below the surface, or by ensuring good drainage in other ways.

The third point is not so obvious, but you can see it nevertheless, and it is the fact that as a soil becomes waterlogged, the water in the spaces between the soil crumbs or sand particles forces the air out of the soil. A waterlogged soil is therefore an air-less soil, and without air the roots of a plant soon die.

This is why composts should be light and open, able to let water pass through and air flow in. This is why more house plants die

of over-watering than of any other single cause. In fact they drown as a result of all the soil air being displaced by water.

4) SOIL MICRO-ORGANISMS The soil is a world in miniature, and in this world a very important role is played by the agents of rotting and decay, the micro-organisms. It is hard for many gardeners to appreciate the part played by soil bacteria and fungi, but if they were not present in astronomical numbers in the soil then nothing which died would ever decay. The surface of the earth would be covered with the corpses of dead plants, trees, and animals, and all the food in each organism would be locked up inside it never to be released.

But because of micro-organisms, decay occurs, and the nitrogen, phosphorus, etc., in each dead plant or animal is liberated to be used to form part of the structure of another living creature. Thus we have great cycles of exchange whereby soil chemicals are absorbed by plants which may be eaten by animals. The animals die, their bodies decay and the chemicals are available for re-use. We live in a closed system and it is imperative that this life in the soil does not disappear.

How can we do this? I have talked glibly about decay, but decay really is the utilisation of dead organic material as food by living organisms. Thus if we want to keep the soil micro-organisms alive we must supply them with food in the form of compost, sewage sludge, manure, peat, etc., all of which will yield their storehouse of chemical foods for further generations. This is another good reason for the addition of organic fertiliser to the soil.

5) SOIL CHEMICALS We will see when we look at roots how it is possible to discover which soil chemicals are essential for plant life and in what quantities. The results of such work show that plants can grow normally if supplied with nitrogen, phosphorus, and potassium, in fairly large quantities. These are the macro-nutrients. But a much larger number of elements is needed in very small or 'trace' quantities, and these include iron, boron, manganese, zinc, molybdenum, sulphur, copper, etc. These are the trace elements or micro-nutrients, whose absence results in deficiency diseases of plants (see section on Leaves, p. 25).

Under completely natural conditions, as in a tropical rain forest or on a peat moor, the plants are in a closed system, and everything that grows is eventually returned to the soil. So the chemicals present in the original rock particles supply the nutrient needs of plants. But modern horticulture and agriculture are very different, for the crop is grown in one part of the country, is shipped and eaten in the cities, and the resultant sewage, after purification, is usually disposed of into rivers and the sea. Thus in heavily cropped farms there is no longer a closed system but an open one, and there arises a need to replace the lost soil chemicals. These can be replaced to some extent by compost, but if cropping is heavy and compost scarce, then the gardener is wise to use the so-called 'artificials'.

It should be made quite clear that artificial fertilisers supply exactly the same chemicals to the plants as humus does and they cannot be faulted on that score. If they have disadvantages they are:

1) so easy to apply that gardeners forget about humus and think artificials can do everything, and

2) applied in the wrong quantities, or at the wrong time, they can scorch or do harm to the plant, but by following the makers' instructions you will not go far wrong with 'artificials'.

Nowadays you can buy ready mixed fertilisers containing appropriate quantities and proportions of the necessary elements, and these can be either the usual types or in the 'slow release' forms. This latter type of fertiliser is manufactured as fairly large granules each of which is composed of many layers like an onion. When the outside layer has been washed away to feed the roots of the plant, a rather tougher layer is left, made of a slow-dissolving chemical. Only when this layer is washed away will the next layer of fertiliser be reached, dissolved, and made available to the plant. Then another slow-to-dissolve layer appears, and so on. This means that the granule will release its fertiliser value slowly over a season, so reducing the chance of all the food value of the fertiliser being washed out by heavy rains.

A third recent advance in fertiliser techniques is the development of foliar feeds. It is based on the discovery that plants can absorb many chemicals through the leaves, and so mixtures are made up to spray on plants and thus feed them. You may ask 'Why feed the plant through the leaves and not the normal way via the roots?' The answer is simply that some trace elements are quickly locked up in certain soils and made unavailable to the plants. To add these micro-nutrients to the soil would just be a waste of materials for they too would be locked up. You therefore spray the leaves and give the plant a foliar feed containing many of these trace elements, and the benefits can be quite spectacular.

Which fertilisers to use is a very complex problem, and the ordinary gardener is well advised to stick to the compound types made up by manufacturers. These show the mixture on the bag expressed in percentage of nitrogen, phosphorus and potash, and if you remember that nitrogen grows leaves, phosphorus grows roots, and potash helps produce fruits and seed you will not go far wrong. For the expert there are special mixtures for roses, tomatoes, turf, etc. Quite a number of growers make their own mixtures of differing quantities of sulphate of ammonia (nitrogen), superphosphate, and sulphate of potash, but this is tricky and requires much experimenting, so it is not for beginners.

6) LIME The role of lime in soil deserves a book of its own for it plays many parts. For

The importance of trace elements is illustrated by this controlled experiment showing the effect of no copper, medium copper, and high copper on Exacum growing in Levington compost

example, it causes clay particles to flocculate or stick together, thus improving the drainage of heavy clay soils. It also reduces the acidity of the soil and makes it 'sweeter'. Soil acidity is expressed in terms of the pH scale which runs in soils from 3 to about 14, being very acid at pH3 and alkaline at pH14, with neutrality around pH6·8. Plants grow best around pH6, and a very acid, sandy, or peaty soil can be made suitable for growing just by adding lime. There are do-it-yourself kits for testing soil pH which can be bought cheaply.

Another part played by lime is the release of chemicals in soil, and it has been said that all soils need treatment with lime about every third year. In the usual way there is a grain of truth in this generalisation, but if the lime is overdone then there is a very real danger of it linking with trace elements in the soil, such as iron, and producing deficiency diseases. So true is this, that in limestone and chalky soils, these deficiencies are widespread, usually showing themselves as yellow chlorotic leaves, and the application of foliar feed becomes standard practice.

The last point about lime is that some plants hate it. These are the calcifuges such as rhododendrons, azaleas, erica, callunas, camellias, etc., and it is giving yourself

trouble and grief if you try to grow such plants in a chalk or limestone area. Most other plants do very well in such areas, and there is no need to think your garden will be deprived of all the good things, for clematis, carnation, viburnum, etc., all love lime, and most other plants are quite neutral about it.

If you have to apply it, use hydrated lime or else crushed limestone at ½ lb. per sq. yd. every 3–5 years and you won't be far wrong.

To Dig or Not to Dig

Part of the ritual of a gardener's life has been digging the soil in the autumn, letting it lie rough through the winter to allow frost to break down the lumps, and in the spring, raking and fining it down to form a seed bed. Recently this has been challenged by a school of thought which says that by turning the soil over and so burying the weeds you are exposing the soil to the rain and the weather, which not only washes the food materials out, but the constant patter of the raindrops helps to destroy the soil crumb structure. These are the 'no-diggers', who simply cover the soil surface with about 6 ins. of humus and sow or plant directly into this.

I wish it were possible to give a firm answer as to which is better, but they both

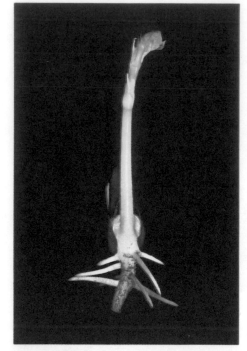

The development of a taproot

The development of lateral roots

The development of adventitious roots

have merits, and the modern farming technique of minimum cultivation could be easily applied to the garden if you are prepared to see your soil covered either with weeds, or a mulch (if you can get the materials!) all year round. There is no doubt that heavy winter rain destroys and puddles the soil surface which is usually protected by surface vegetation, but in the end the weeds must be killed or the crop suffers. This can be done by chemicals or by thick layers of peat or compost, or by digging them under. You can try experiments on this in your own garden, and settle for the one which best suits your soil *and* tired back.

A LOOK AT ROOTS

An old gardener of my acquaintance used to say 'If the roots are all right, then the plant's all right'. This is a vast oversimplification and on the whole is false, but it does contain this grain of truth, that if the roots are *not* all right, then the plant also is *not* all right. He was trying to make the very good point that the root is of great importance, but because we don't see it every day when we walk down the garden, we tend to forget about it, and what we forget about we think is of little or no importance. So to get things truly in perspective let's just say that good roots are essential for good plants.

The important thing about roots is that they are one of the two main contacts the plant has with the world around from which it draws its food and water. Further, roots live in a strange place of darkness, and tiny animals and bacteria, of changing levels of water and chemical nutriment, and of stresses and strains as the stem and leaves of the plant are tossed about by high winds. Roots have to cope with a variety of situations and perform a number of jobs, which they do very well, but they can be helped in their task by creating conditions in the soil which will allow the roots to operate to their maximum effect, and so give the greatest benefit to the rest of the plant.

What do Roots Do?

1) ROOTS AS ANCHORS Roots perform two primary functions, and their growth and structure are related to these. The first

function is that of anchoring the plant in the soil so that it may stand erect and withstand the forces which are exerted on the aboveground parts of the plant. These can be very considerable if you think of the pressure exerted by a 60 mph gale on an oak tree; yet only very rarely is the tree blown over, so that the roots must be effective anchoring organs. How then is this done?

Roots often penetrate very deeply into the ground so that they have a firm hold on the soil. The main penetrating root is known as the 'tap' root, and is usually the result of the continued growth of the radicle of the seed. But a simple root, no matter how deep it penetrates, would have difficulty holding a tree erect, so the plant develops another root system which extends widely around the base of the plant and acts as if it were a system of underground guy-ropes. This is the 'lateral root system' and a lateral root is simply a branch of the tap root. Each lateral will branch again and again to give in the end an enormous mass of roots, each clinging to the earth and helping to support the tree.

In many cases roots will even be formed by the stem where it is underground, or where it runs horizontally along the surface of the soil. These are 'adventitious roots'. Such roots are commonly formed by grasses, and by plants such as potatoes, which are continually earthed up to encourage tuber production.

Finally, each root bears millions of tiny protrusions called 'root hairs'. These play an important part in anchoring the plant, for the strength of vast numbers of root hairs is very great, although they have another and more important function as we shall see soon.

It is said that there is more of the plant below the soil than there is above it, and where plants have been carefully excavated so that the roots are got out intact this has been shown to be largely true. This mass of roots is wide-ranging and spreads out from the base of the plant almost horizontally, so that the anchorage is both deep and extensive rather like a telegraph pole which is sunk in the soil and is supported by guy-ropes.

2) ROOTS AS FOOD AND WATER GATHERERS

The second function of roots is to absorb food and water from the soil and pass it up into the stem and leaves. This is their absorptive function, and a moment's thought will convince you that the type of root system described above is well designed for this purpose. Of course the tap root is not very useful in this connection but the laterals and the root hairs which spread all through the soil, burrowing and penetrating between stones and soil particles, are ideal, for they tap a very great volume of soil and can extract all the necessary food from it.

But roots have no mouths or openings so how do the water and the food get into the plant? This is the function of the millions of root hairs which in the last analysis are the actual absorbing organs. The structure of a root hair is simple, for it consists of a long, often curved or twisted single plant cell which grows out near the tip of the root. This hair not only gets into close contact with soil particles, but also almost fuses with them as a result of its gelatinous wall. It is the minerals in the particles which form the food of the plant, and these minerals dissolve in the soil water which passes through the wall of the root hair and so into the plant. It has recently been demonstrated that root hairs can absorb very tiny *solid* particles, so that the plant can tap the soil for both soluble and insoluble materials. Thus food is extracted from the soil and is then transported to where it is needed at the growing areas of the plant.

Roots have very well marked selective powers. They usually absorb from the soil the types of mineral salts they require in the appropriate amounts, and they have the capacity also to reject other substances. Having said that however, plants are not by any means perfect, and many of them absorb materials which they cannot use. Thus some plants will take up quite large quantities of silica, or gold, or iodine to such an extent that they require to have special storage areas in which these useless materials can be kept, without harming the growth or the economy of the rest of the plant.

Requirements for Root Growth

Like all other living things, plants are composed of relatively few minerals plus a much

Adventitious roots developing from ivy stems

Root hairs (compare diagram below)

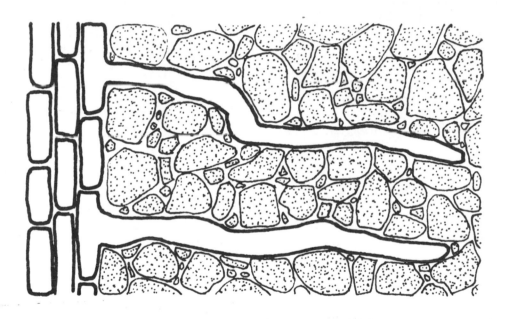

Roots and Other Soil Inhabitants

There is a vast complexity of living organisms in the soil ranging from relatively large animals such as badgers, moles, mice, and rats, through the medium-sized insects and earthworms, down to the microscopic fungi, bacteria, and protozoa. It is a strange but true fact that the character of the soil, and the growth of roots of the plant, are much more affected by the presence of the tiny microscopic organisms than by the large or even the medium-sized ones.

Of all the elements needed by plants, nitrogen is the one used in the greatest quantity. In the soil, nitrogen (which is a gas) is found in chemical combination with other elements, usually in the form of nitrates, nitrites, and ammonium salts. Unfortunately these salts are very easily dissolved in water and so they are quickly washed out of the soil by floods or heavy rains. You may well ask 'Why then doesn't all the nitrogen disappear from the soil very quickly?' and the answer lies in three words: *nitrogen fixing bacteria*.

Many of the bacteria in the soil have the power to use atmospheric nitrogen in the manufacture of their own 'bodies', and although each bacterium is very small, when there are millions and millions in a handful of soil, the total nitrogen captured and 'fixed' by these bacteria is quite large. Most of the nitrogen fixed will be locked up in chemical combinations inside the bacteria, but as they die and are destroyed, the nitrogen then becomes available for use by other organisms, and one of the main users is the plant. In many developing countries there are no artificial fertilisers, and the practice there is to let the land lie fallow and uncropped each alternate year. This allows the nitrogen fixed by bacteria to accumulate in the soil during the year's fallow and a reasonable crop can be obtained the following year.

Among the most active of nitrogen fixers are the bacteria which live in the roots of plants of the pea family, which is called the Leguminosae, and includes peas, beans, clovers, vetches, lupins, broom, etc. If you examine the roots of a pea plant you will find swellings or nodules on the roots and when these are cut open and examined

larger number of carbon-containing organic substances which the plant manufactures from basic materials. Different sorts of plants however require minerals in different quantities, and by using special purified mineral salts in culture solutions it is possible to discover which elements are essential for plant growth and which are not needed at all. The method is simple. A number of salts are dissolved in pure water and plants grown in this culture solution. At the same time an identical solution is made up with one of the salts omitted. It can be seen if this omission affects the growth of the plants adversely, and if it does, then we know that that particular chemical is necessary for maximum plant growth, and we also know the kind of symptoms produced by its absence. In a similar way the relative quantities of essential substances can be found out.

Such experiments show that nitrogen, phosphorus, and potash are needed by plants in relatively large quantities, and other elements of which I shall write later are needed in small quantities, or traces.

Of the three major plant foods, phosphorus in the form of phosphates is demanded more by roots than by any other part of the plant, so that when gardeners are growing root crops such as carrots or swedes, they should be certain that the fertiliser they apply has an adequate phosphate content to ensure a healthy and reasonably-sized root.

Most of the phosphorus needed by annual crops is taken up during the first few days after germination, and to ensure a proper supply, seedling composts are made up with plenty of phosphorus, and superphosphates are often dusted along the seed drill before sowing.

But if roots are to absorb the necessary foods, not only must the materials be in the soil but also there should be an ample supply of oxygen in the soil and a reasonable soil temperature. The absence of O_2 and the low temperature of cold, waterlogged and badly draining soils can depress growth, and turn what should be healthy plants into miserable specimens. Good drainage and aeration are therefore essential for good root growth.

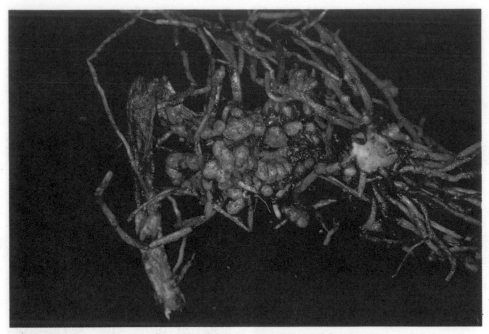

Bean roots showing masses of root nodules

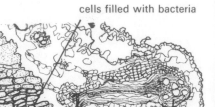

cells filled with bacteria

root

water and food conducting cells

A root nodule in cross-section

under a microscope, the cells of the nodule can be seen to be packed with bacteria. These bacteria fix nitrogen from the air, use it, and then it is passed to the plant which benefits accordingly. Leguminous crops therefore can be said to enrich the soil, and when growing peas and beans there is little or no need to add nitrogenous fertilisers.

There are other organisms which live in the roots of plants and which can fix nitrogen. Many of these are fungi, organisms whose typical form is a much branched and very long thread, but whose fruiting bodies are the mushroom and toadstool, and they are associated with the roots of many plants living either inside the cells of the root or else closely attached to it. This very close association of two organisms, called symbiosis, can take many forms (such as the bacteria which inhabit our intestines and help us to digest our food), and in the case of the plant and the fungus the association is termed a *mycorrhiza*.

Very many more plants have mycorrhiza than have root nodules, but the ability of the fungal partner to fix nitrogen has only been conclusively shown in a few cases. It may be that some mycorrhizas play different roles, such as helping the plant absorb food from the soil, or passing complex chemicals manufactured by the mycorrhiza to the plant. Many trees have mycorrhiza, so too have ericas, rhododendrons, many grasses, leeks, potatoes, etc., etc. In fact when diligently sought, a fungus can be found living in the roots of many plants, but claims that the plants *must* have the fungus present are very much exaggerated, for most plants can be grown perfectly easily in sterile fungus-free culture. It is easy to dismiss mycorrhiza as an interesting and useless phenomenon, but the fact that it is so widespread would seem to indicate that there is some virtue in the association of fungus and plant root, although the whole benefit need not necessarily accrue to the plant.

Most gardeners can forget about mycorrhiza, for most soils contain the appropriate fungi and bacteria and the plants just automatically become infected. When planting trees, however, a number of growers make sure that there is a good ball of soil around the roots when the tree comes from the nursery in order to be certain that the fungus is present. Farmers in the United States sometimes apply a culture of root nodule bacteria to the seed of legumes, or to the soil, to ensure that good and effective nodulation will occur.

Root Parasites

As roots grow through the soil they are often attacked by disease-causing organisms, for if the roots can be invaded by the friendly fungi in mycorrhiza, they can also be in-

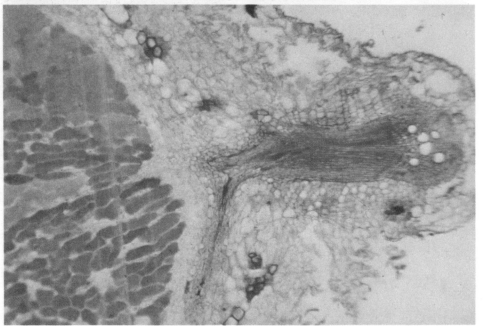

Cross-section of a bean root, showing a large root nodule (compare diagram top right)

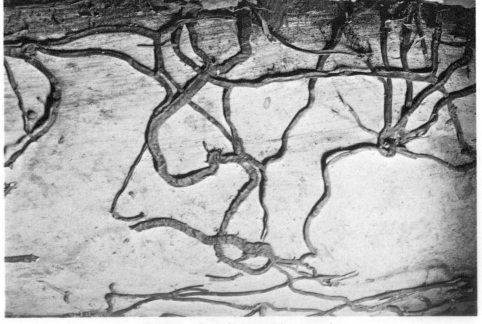

Bootlace or honey fungus growing on wood

vaded by enemies. In fact given the appropriate conditions many so-called friendly fungi and bacteria can become parasitic and cause damage to the roots. The result of root damage is usually seen as wilting first in the heat of the day, then all the time.

If this occurs the sensible thing is to pull the plant up and destroy it, for recovery is rare and the infected plant could act as a centre or focus of infection which would spread to other plants. This is very likely to happen in the case of trees and shrubs attacked by the bootlace fungus, *Armillaria mellea*, which slowly but surely will kill infected trees and then grow through the soil to infect other plants by means of long black strands, technically named rhizomorphs, but in general parlance, called 'bootlaces'. This root invader is responsible for the death of many shrubs and trees, being especially severe on lilacs, privet hedges and apple trees, but it is so omnivorous that it will even attack potatoes.

In a parallel fashion roots are attacked by many voracious soil animals such as cabbage and carrot root fly, potato root eelworm, slugs, earwigs, etc., etc. The great safeguard about roots lies in the fact that if part is damaged, fresh roots will be produced at another part of the root system and even from the base of the stem as adventitious roots. In fact one of the recommendations to reduce the damage caused by cabbage root fly is to plant in the bottom of a V-drill and as the plant grows to fill in the V to encourage the development of stem rooting.

Root Growth

As it grows through the soil, the root has literally to force and worm its way through a dense medium. The soil may be very compacted, full of large stones or sharp gritty particles, yet the roots manage to extend in all directions even to the point of getting into the cracks in rocks and actually splitting them. How is this done without great damage being done to this not very robust part of the plant?

The answer lies in the structure of the root and especially in the actual growing area. If you look closely at a young fine root you will see that it tapers to a narrow tip and if you mark a young root with dots of indian ink spaced at equal intervals, and then leave the root to grow for a few days, it is possible to see where the root has grown most by the change in the distance between the dots. This experiment shows that growth in length of the root takes place just a very short distance behind the tip, and that the area more than about 2–3 ins. behind the root tip is no longer capable of elongating. In fact this area is the region from which the root hairs develop, and if it were also growing in length, the root hairs would be torn and destroyed as the root forced its way through the soil.

But the very tip of the root is not elongating either, and so the picture of root growth which emerges from this simple experiment is of a tip leading the way and slowly being forced through the soil by the extending area behind it, while the necessary pressure – and it must be considerable – is maintained by the root being firmly anchored in the soil by the root hair area.

Of course the tip of the root, the root cap, is constantly running up against hard soil particles and stones, so that it can be damaged or at very least easily worn away. This happens, but the root cap is self-perpetuating and as quickly as it is worn away by its constant abrasion in the soil so new cells are produced which replace those which have

The black lines were painted on equally spaced. Their spacing now shows where the root has grown.

been lost. The cells of the root cap are also fairly loosely connected to each other, and the outer cells almost act as a lubricant being rubbed off and allowing the inner cells to glide past them in the wake of the advancing tip.

Naturally the root grows best in a relatively loose stone-free soil, but roots are so tough and so well adapted for forcing their way through the soil that they can grow in almost any medium provided food and water are available.

Once the tip of the root penetrates say a crack in a rock, the root cap grows on and the area of the root behind the root hairs begins to swell and thicken. It is this swelling and thickening which exerts great physical pressures slowly over a period of many years, and in the end can not only block drains but can crack walls and the foundations of houses. Apart from the problems of shade which may be cast by a tree near a house, one should always remember that under your feet the roots are lengthening and expanding, and may be a danger to the brickwork and the foundations of the house itself.

Roots as Storage Organs

Although the soil can be a very difficult medium for the roots to penetrate, it has many advantages, for it stays at a fairly constant temperature and it has to be a very severe frost indeed which penetrates more than 2 ins. into it. Roots therefore are well protected against the climate, and in countries with a moderately severe winter, all the above-ground parts may die but the plant will survive the winter snugly underground in the form of a number of buds all ready to grow in the spring.

But although the awakening of plant life in the spring is beautiful and often dramatic, a great deal of energy has to be available to allow the formation of new leaves and stems, and to maintain them until they become self-sufficient and can feed themselves. This energy is stored as food materials in the over-wintering roots and many plants have developed roots as food storage organs which in nature are used for regrowth, but also act as a good food crop for man. Such roots as carrots, beetroots, swedes, turnips,

A root as a storage organ

and mangolds are very useful in this country, and in tropical countries yams, cassava, etc. also act as food reserves.

If you think logically about root storage organs you can deduce how they should be kept. Clearly frost is their greatest enemy (it was to escape winter that they evolved in the first place), so they should be stored in a frost-free clamp or room. Then if we can use them as food so too can rats, insects, moulds, etc., and to stop these attackers we set traps, we can dust with insecticide powder and we can try to keep the store or clamp well ventilated to allow lots of oxygen in and so reduce the amount of dampness.

It is not for nothing that we talk about the 'root of the matter' or 'getting to the root of the trouble' for as has been shown, the root is the little-seen but vitally important part of good plant growth.

A LOOK AT STEMS

Although they are the bearers of the leaves, flowers, and fruits, stems are not obvious parts of most plants for they tend to be half hidden by foliage, to be of a dull or neutral colour, and with a few exceptions to have little of beauty to make them noticeable. But a second's pause will bring a few thoughts quickly to mind; for example it is the stem which is the main supporting part of the plant holding the leaves and flowers high in the air where they are easily accessible to light, insects, etc. It is the stem which contains the main conducting channels for food passing from the root to the rest of the plant, and it is the stem which in many cases is the strong part of the plant enabling it to withstand the force of the wind and the rain.

Stems are therefore of considerable importance and certainly deserve a closer scrutiny than they usually get.

General Stem Structure

By far the most obvious type of stem is the tree trunk. These massive structures develop over many hundreds of years, and possess strength and resistance which are still used as timber in our houses and furniture long after the tree is dead. This structure, which seems so complex and huge, is a

A twisting stem – some plants twist to the right and some to the left

Runners on a potentilla – some are welcome, some are pests

A twining stem

Axillary buds on a tomato plant

An apical bud on a chestnut twig in winter

Axillary buds on privet growing out into branches

simple development of the stem of plants such as peas, lupins, wallflowers, etc. The main difference is that some stems are perennial and keep on growing for years, while others die down each year and the plant either continues in the form of a seed, or as an underground storage organ such as a bulb or tuber.

But within these two classes of stem there are all sorts of variation. Some stems twist and climb and so we have bindweed, clematis, and sweet pea, others scramble along the ground or on supports, exemplified by rambler roses. Still others appear as runners (strawberries), rhizomes (many grasses), tubers (potatoes), etc.; in fact for a very uniform and seemingly uninteresting structure, the range of behaviour of stems is great indeed.

How then do we distinguish a stem from a root or a leaf, or even a leaf stalk or petiole? Take a piece of privet or any easily obtained piece of stem, look at it closely, and you will see some critical points. The most obvious things are the leaves which are arranged in a spiral pattern on the stem. If you look a little more closely you will see that in the angle which the leaf makes with the stem there is a tiny bud, known as an axillary bud. Very often this bud never develops, but every tomato and chrysanthemum grower knows that the axillary buds can grow and become axillary shoots, which have to be removed to allow the plant's food to be used in the production of fruit and flowers and not in the production of new leaves. Where a leaf joins the stem is called the 'node' and the length of stem between nodes is the 'internode'. These words are used when we talk about taking cuttings.

In a nutshell therefore, a stem can always be distinguished by the fact that it bears leaves which have axillary buds. This is why we also talk of 'leaflets' and 'compound leaves', for if you look at a tomato or potato leaf, which is a compound structure, you will see that there is only an axillary bud where the leaf joins the stem, but there is no bud where the small leaflets join the main leaf stalk or petiole.

There are two other features worth noting in our piece of privet and the first is at the tip. You will see that as leaves get closer to the tip they become smaller until at the very tip they are so close together that they form a bud, the apical bud. This is a very significant structure, for it can elongate and so the twig will grow in length. The second feature to note is that the stem has two colours. The length nearest the apical bud is light brown or green and is 'this year's wood' or the 'new' wood, whereas that

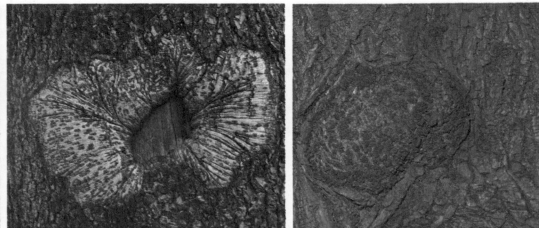

Stages in the healing by special cambium of a pruning wound on a cedar tree

further back is the 'old' or 'last year's' wood. To distinguish these is important, for some plants flower and fruit on old wood, and others on new wood, and to cut off or prune the wrong type of wood can do serious harm.

In many cases the old and the new wood are separated by a series of concentric ridges on the stem, which are the scars left by the scales which covered the apical bud, and protected it from damage during the winter frosts when it was resting.

The final piece of simple observation from the piece of privet is that if the axillary buds are permitted to grow out they will eventually become branches. The leaves which have sheltered or subtended the buds will wither and die, but the buds will grow and appear first as small and then as thicker branches as they age. Each branch will bear leaves which have axillary buds which may grow in their turn, and so the whole branching system of a tree is built up.

Inside a Stem

As has been said above, the stem is the main channel of food conduction through the plant. This means it carries a two-way traffic of materials. Chemicals from the soil are passed up to the growing parts of the plant, and elaborate materials made in the leaves are passed down to feed the rest of the plant, or to be stored for the winter in the roots or even in specially designed bits of stem, e.g. tubers or rhizomes.

A conducting system to do such a varied job is, of necessity, very complex but it can be simplified to this extent. Food from the roots to the rest of the plant travels in the inside of the stem in a tissue known as the xylem. The xylem is composed of large numbers of dead cells with thick walls placed end to end and side by side, and the end or cross walls dissolve. It is most easily pictured as a group of drinking straws held in a tight bunch with the liquid moving upwards. Xylem is very useful to man, for all wood is xylem whose thick hard walls are a very valuable raw material combining strength, flexibility, and lightness, and is often attractive in appearance.

Each tiny xylem cell (vessel) in the leaf, is connected by many similar vessels to a xylem cell in the root. In other words there is a continuous system of xylem cells throughout the plant.

Similarly, there is a continuous system of phloem cells through the plant, which form the channel through which the leaf-made food passes. Phloem differs from xylem, not only in detailed structure (which need not concern us here), but also in the fact that it is a living tissue lying to the outside of the

xylem and able if necessary to pass sugars, proteins etc., in two directions simultaneously.

Xylem and phloem are separated by a thin band, or zone, of living cells named the cambium, which is vital to the gardener. This is a zone which is continually growing and dividing and in which the cells are very active. Thus the increase in girth of a tree is due to the cambium producing more xylem and phloem cells, and all wood is the result of cambial activity. Further, when a shoot is grafted on to a scion, it is the interaction of the cambium of the two separate parts which produces the union and therefore the grafted plant; and when you prune a tree the wound is healed over by the gradual growth of the cambium. It is a very vital tissue indeed.

As a tree expands through cambial growth, there is an increasing strain on the outside or bark, which could easily split or burst. Alternatively the 'skin' of the tree could get so tight that it could compress and maybe shut the fine conducting tubes of the xylem and phloem. To avoid this the bark is constantly being split and shed as a new bark forms inside the old one, and once again this is the result of activity by a special cork or bark cambium.

So there we have the functioning stem, as a structure growing both upwards (by the apical bud) and outward (by the cambium), and acting as the main channel of communication and of food transport.

The Apical Bud

If you pull an apical bud apart in winter you will find that it contains a large number of miniature leaves, and in some cases flowers, which are only waiting the onset of spring to burst open and start new growth. As growth proceeds the tiny leaves expand and the flowers develop, and it is thought by many authorities that nearly the whole of the next season's leafy growth is compressed into the small apical bud.

In some plants, of which apple trees and rhododendrons are good examples, two different types of apical bud can be seen, a rather long pointed type which on dissection will show only leaves, and a much rounder plump bud, which examination will show to contain flowers. These are respectively a leaf bud and a fruit bud, and if you are interested in growing fruit it is essential to be able to differentiate these two types, so that you will not prune away all the fruit buds. Usually, but not always, fruit buds are produced on old wood, whereas the buds on the new wood will develop as leaves.

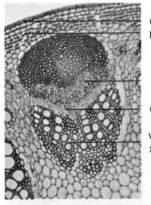
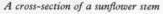

cuticle of stem
protective fibres

food conducting
phloem

cambium

water conducting
xylem

A cross-section of a sunflower stem

Cross-section of a 2-year old lime twig showing increased amount of xylem formed by cambium activity. The growth ring is clearly visible.

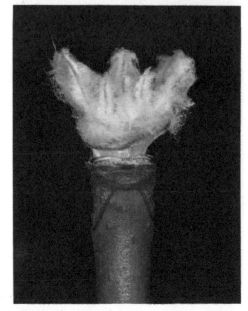

Apical bud of chestnut pulled apart to show the very young leaves

Apical bud on a rhododendron showing development in spring

Removal of the apical bud stimulates the growth of axillary branches

Tomato plants growing to face the light

Bean plants of the same age. The one on the right has been treated with a growth-promoting hormone.

Disorganised growth resulting from the application of hormone weedkiller. This usually leads to the death of the weeds.

The best known of storage organs – the potato

The apical bud unfolds in spring, expands its leaves and maybe flowers, and then as the summer comes and autumn approaches, a new apical bud is formed in which new mini-organs will be enclosed and protected, usually by thick brown scales, during the winter, and so the cycle goes on.

But the apical bud has a peculiar power over its shoot or twig, which can again be seen by looking at privet. Privet usually is grown as a hedge which requires clipping each year, not only to keep it neat and tidy but also to cause it to thicken and branch out. Look at a twig which has had its apical bud cut off during clipping or pruning, and you will see that most of the axillary buds have started to grow and are becoming new branches. This will not be seen in an un-clipped twig which still has its apical bud, although if your twig is long enough to show old wood, the axillary buds may be growing down there.

This rather strange effect is known as 'apical dominance' which simply means that the apical bud is dominating or governing the shoot. This it does by producing chemicals which move back down the twig, which inhibit or prevent the growth of any other buds in reasonably close proximity to the apex. As this inhibition moves down the twig it gets weaker, until by the time last year's old wood is reached the check on growth has disappeared, and axillary buds will grow out normally to form new branches.

It is often asked 'How do you know that an inhibitory chemical moves down the stem starting in the apical bud?'. Well, you can do a simple experiment. Take a growing twig or shoot and cut off the apical bud with a sharp razor. Then replace the bud, attaching it to the twig by a layer of gelatine, and you will find that the inhibition still remains and has therefore passed through the gelatine. It is a simple matter to arrange this kind of experiment and trap the inhibitory substance in the gelatine, which can be analysed chemically. When this is done the substance proves to be the kind of substance which is called an auxin or a growth hormone.

Auxins are substances which regulate the growth of all plants. What they do depends

This green and pleasant land – this corner of it shows the unobtrusive hand of man at work

on their concentration or strength. For example at certain strengths they will cause cells to divide, at different concentrations they will prevent cell division, and at other concentrations they will cause cell expansion and growth movements. So growth of the plant is regulated by the subtle interaction of these substances, and when this interaction is disturbed the plant goes into disorganised growth and usually dies.

This is the principle behind the use of hormone weedkillers which upset the growth balance of weeds and cause their death. They have a selective action, i.e. you can kill daisies in a lawn without harming the grass, because the particular hormones used may not gain entry to the grass leaves and so they stay unharmed, or the concentration may be such that grass is scarcely upset, but daisies, dandelion, and plantains, are severely affected and die.

So not only is the apical bud the site of growth, it is the seat of plant government, and when you prune a hedge you are releasing many axillary buds from the dominance of the apex, and so they grow and the hedge gets thicker. This is the reason for the inwardness of the old garden saying that 'growth follows the knife', for the knife removes apical buds.

Apical Meristem Cuttings
At the core of every apical bud is the very tip of the twig or stem where growth is actually taking place. This is a very, very small area known as the apical meristem, and it contains highly active cells, rapidly dividing, forming more new cells, and plant-building chemicals. Such an area has several peculiar properties of which its relative immunity to virus disease is used commercially.

Virus diseases are common and while they rarely kill the plant, they do weaken it, reduce the yield or the size of the flowers, and in some crops such as potato, dahlia, strawberry, and chrysanthemum, can become very important causes of financial loss. Because viruses are inside the cells of the host, it is very difficult to attack the virus with chemicals without damaging the plant you are trying to save, so that other control measures have to be adopted.

One of the commonest is heat treatment,
which means that you heat the infected plant to a given temperature for a specific time, as a result of which the virus should be destroyed and the host plant left undamaged. In theory this is all right, but the practical difficulties are immense, because a small error of temperature could kill the host plant or leave the virus unharmed. This is where the apical meristem comes into its own, for here is an actively growing area which is virus free.

It is possible therefore to use surgical techniques and remove the minute meristem, grow it in a sterile culture where it would be free from virus infection and let the cells multiply. From this small tip it is possible to obtain hundreds of virus-free plants which, although expensive, are completely disease free and are increasing productivity greatly.

The same techniques can be used, not to clean up a stock from virus infection, but simply to increase a stock of some plant which is sterile and so cannot produce seed, or of which seed production is very slow and unreliable. New varieties of vegetables such as cauliflowers can be multiplied rapidly by this method, and so the growers have access to good stock in a few instead of many years.

Stems and Light
One of the phenomena we will certainly see if we look at stems closely is the way in which they bend towards a source of light. This is most evident in house plants growing on a windowsill. Such plants should be turned regularly to stop them becoming one-sided and unattractive. The mechanism for this movement lies once again in the apical bud, and depends on the fact that light not only destroys auxins but also affects their movement within the plant.

Thus we have a situation where the apical bud is producing auxin which is diffusing back from the tip of the stem causing cell division, expansion, etc. equally all round the stem. If we expose the plant to one-sided light it means that the side of the stem nearest the light is much more brightly lit than the other side, which is in comparative shadow. This differential lighting affects the growth hormone in two ways: firstly,
since auxin is destroyed by light the amount of hormone on the lit side is reduced, and secondly the hormone is moved away from the light by forces which arise in the plant, and so the lit side finds that the little hormone it has left is forced away to the unlit side.

A difference in concentration is produced between the two sides of the stem and, as you would expect, this produces a difference in growth. The side in shadow because it has more auxin grows faster than the brightly lit side, and the result of such a set-up where an object has one side elongating more rapidly than the other side is to cause the object, in this case the stem, to bend towards the light.

Exactly the same system works in roots, but because the concentration of auxin acts in root cells in the opposite manner to the action in stems, the consequence is that root tips exposed to light will bend away from the light thus putting the root into a darker, more shaded situation.

In the same way that plants react to light so they react to the force of gravity, with auxin distribution being affected in such a way as to ensure that under natural conditions the stem will mechanically grow upwards, while the roots will grow downwards into the soil.

The Stem as a Storage Organ
As we saw when we looked at seeds, they are one means whereby the plant can spend the winter in a safe state with a lot of stored food ready for use when spring comes and the seed germinates. But many plants, of which trees are the most obvious examples, live for many years and spend the cold winter above ground having shed their leaves first in many cases. When spring comes growth begins again, but before the plant can manufacture food of its own, leaves must be produced, and this demands food from a food store which has lasted through the winter.

The hard woody stem is an ideal storage area, and as summer moves into autumn, you can show that the cells of the trunk of the tree are being packed with stored food usually in the form of starch grains. This is why trees felled in winter are often more easily attacked by wood-rotting fungi, because the starch and sugars with which the trunks are packed form an ideal diet for these destructive organisms.

Man in his usual way has used this propensity for food storage in stems to his own advantage, and there are many examples of it. For example sugar cane is simply the stem of a plant where sugars and not starch are stored, and in a potato tuber we have a highly modified stem packed with starch. So plant storage becomes useful, and in many parts of the world, essential for man's food supply.

A LOOK AT LEAVES
Blake writes about 'England's green and pleasant land' but what he is really saying is England's *leafy* land, for the bright green of the landscape is the result of the presence of literally millions of green leaves.

Very often the colour of things is unimportant. A pleasant colour may give us greater satisfaction than a crude colour, but that is as far as it goes until we talk about the green of leaves, for *that* green colour is essential to all life and we literally could not exist without it.

There are many simple plants which are not green (a mushroom is a good example), but that kind of plant is dependent (in the same way as we are) on the green plants

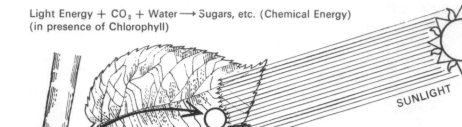

Light Energy + CO₂ + Water ⟶ Sugars, etc. (Chemical Energy)
(in presence of Chlorophyll)

SUNLIGHT

CO₂ IN AIR

H₂O from soil

The mechanism of photosynthesis, which, with the help of chlorophyll, converts carbon dioxide and water into essential energy-giving starches or sugars.

which are the basic producers of all food-stuffs. To put it briefly before we look at it in more detail, the green colouring matter (the chlorophyll) in leaves, is able to use the sun's rays to bring about a series of chemical reactions involving carbon dioxide (CO_2) from the air and water. This chemical reaction finally results in the formation of starches and sugars, which are the basic food on which all life depends. This long chain of chemical reactions is called photosynthesis, because it uses light (photo) to cause the chemical reactions (the synthesis) and it is worthy of a much closer look.

words of Shakespeare we 'eat the air – promise crammed – '!

But if photosynthesis is going to be efficient, two things must happen. Firstly, the carbon dioxide has got to reach the chloroplasts, and secondly, the leaves must be exposed to as much light as possible. Each of these creates problems which the plant solves rather neatly.

The chlorophyll is inside the cells of the leaf, and the air is around the leaf, therefore, there has to be a mechanism by which CO_2 can get inside the leaf. This mechanism resides in the possession by plants of large

duces the plant's need for water. To give some idea of the quantities of water needed by plants as a result of this transpiration, it has been calculated that in one season a maize plant transpired 54 gallons of water, and an acre transpired the equivalent of 11 inches of rain between May and September. Two potato plants lost 12·5 gallons, and a tall sunflower some 120 gallons.

In dry weather therefore we may have to water the soil, but in wet or cold weather when transpiration is very low, there will be little or no demand for water at all.

Because photosynthesis requires light, it is obvious that it will cease at night, and if the stomata stayed open during the hours of darkness precious water would be lost for no gain in photosynthesis. A mechanism for closing stomata has therefore evolved which depends on photosynthesis itself, and so long as this takes place (only in the light) the stomata will stay open, but as soon as photosynthesis stops the stomata will close. The closing is brought about by two guard cells expanding in such a way that their walls touch and close the stoma. In a similar way if water is in short supply and the leaf begins to wilt, the guard cells will shut the stoma and conserve what little moisture is still available.

This movement of water from the soil up through the plant is the transpiration stream, and as we have seen it takes place in the xylem of the stem. The forces involved are very great. Imagine raising water the height of a giant redwood, or even a tall pine, and you have some idea of the energy necessary. The mechanism is still not fully understood, but we do know it is not simple suction by creating a vacuum, for this would only raise water to a height of 32 feet. Most experiments indicate that in the early spring there is an upward pressure exerted by the roots to lift water to the developing leaves, but once the leaves are expanded they draw the water up, not by suction, but rather by a force which is best likened to the pulling up by leaves of fine wires, made of water in this case, from the root hairs to the surfaces of the cells around the stomatal openings.

The second factor about photosynthesis that was mentioned was the exposure of leaves to light. Clearly the maximum light will be received by a flat surface and especially by a large flat surface. Accordingly leaves are flat and thin, and are held out by the plant to the rays of sunlight. Every housewife knows that unless you regularly turn a plant on a windowsill it will become one-sided and grow towards the light. But plants have to make a compromise between very large leaves which are difficult to hold in the correct position and easily torn by wind and rain, and very small leaves which would be easy for the plant to maintain, but would not be very efficient structures for photosynthesis. So most plant leaves are of moderate size. Those plants with small leaves, e.g. broom, grow in sandy and dry areas, while those with large leaves prefer wet shady areas where there will not be a shortage of water, e.g. *Gunnera* and *Petasites hybridus* (the butter-bur).

Another feature of leaves and light is called the phyllotaxy, which is simply the arrangement of leaves on the stem. If you look closely and follow the sequence of leaves up the stem you will find that they occur in a spiral or spirals, which wind up the stem in such a way that leaves do not shade the leaves closest to them but are positioned round the stem to allow the maximum light penetration. There is always a considerable vertical gap between a given

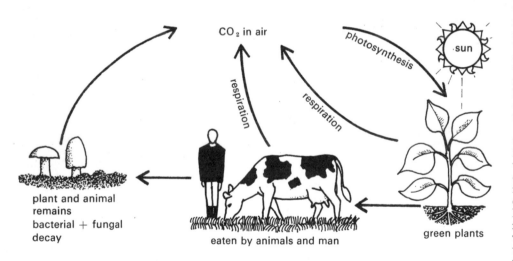

CO₂ in air

photosynthesis

sun

respiration

respiration

plant and animal
remains
bacterial + fungal
decay

eaten by animals and man

green plants

The carbon dioxide cycle is the basis of life as we know it on earth. Sunlight, plants, and animals combine in a ceaseless production line.

Photosynthesis and Transpiration

The process of photosynthesis takes place inside the cells of the leaves, where the chlorophyll is found in little disc-shaped structures called chloroplasts. The atmosphere contains about 3 parts of carbon dioxide in every 10,000 parts of air or 0.03% CO_2. This seems a minute quantity until we remember the vast quantities of air around us, and the fact that we breathe out CO_2, every fire we burn produces CO_2, and that as bacteria destroys dead material in the soil CO_2 is liberated. In fact there is a carbon dioxide cycle, which starts with plants taking CO_2 from the air, the plants being eaten, say, by cattle, the cattle by us, and we breathe back the CO_2 into the air. When we die, the CO_2 in our bodies will eventually be released back into the air to be used again. Thus there is little or no loss, and in the

numbers of tiny openings into the leaf. Each opening is a stoma (the plural of this word is stomata). These are not simple holes in the leaf surface but are rather complex things with a method of opening and closing by means of guard cells. Thus there is also an atmosphere *inside* the leaf, and as the CO_2 in the leaf is used up in photosynthesis, so fresh CO_2 from the ordinary atmosphere will flow in. The internal leaf atmosphere, containing CO_2, dissolves in the moist cell walls lining the inside of the stomatal aperture, and from there goes to the chloroplasts where the chemical changes take place.

But the leaf has to pay a price for the useful stomata, for just as easily as CO_2 can move *into* the leaf so water vapour can move *out* if the air is at all dry. Consequently every leaf loses quantities of water to the air during a dry day, and it is this loss which pro-

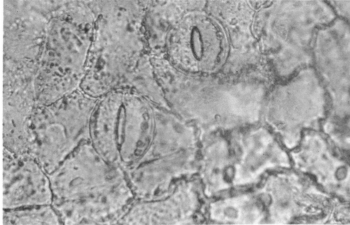

Two stomata on the surface of a leaf

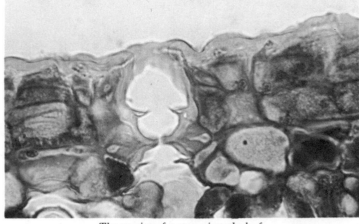

The opening of a stoma into the leaf

leaf and the one which is positioned directly above or below it.

Phyllotaxy is most easily seen in stems which are short and if you look down on a sempervivum, or even a pine cone, you will see this feature beautifully displayed.

For maximum photosynthesis, therefore, you must provide your plants and especially your food crops, with the maximum light and adequate water, for the size of your potatoes, carrots, apples, cabbages, etc., etc., depends on photosynthetic efficiency.

One further point about the relation of leaf structure to photosynthesis and transpiration is worthy of a little comment. If you hold a leaf up to the light it is easy to see that it contains an intricate network of interconnecting veins. In fact you can find leaf skeletons in which the softer parts of the leaf have been rotted away by bacterial action leaving the veins as the skeleton.

This network of veins is necessary, for the food manufactured in the leaf has to be transported out of the leaf to areas of growth, such as the stem or root apex, where it can be used to produce new cells and tissues. The veins are the arteries of food movement, and contain phloem which joins to the phloem of the stem and so to the rest of the plant. Similarly the veins contain xylem, whose function it is to bring the water up to the leaf cells where it is used in photosynthesis, or lost in transpiration.

Finally, the surface of each leaf is covered with a thin waxy coating named the cuticle. This helps to reduce evaporation of water which would occur if the cells were simply exposed to the air. The cuticle also enables stomata to be really efficient controllers of water loss. For a long time the cuticle raised a number of problems for the gardener and botanist, but from these came the discovery of foliar feeding.

Foliar Feeding

It has been known for centuries that if you sprayed plants with a weak solution of certain foods the plants would benefit. Thus in the Middle Ages (and much more recently too) manure water was made by suspending a bag of cow manure in a bucket or barrel of water, and as the manure gradually dissolved, the water could be used to spray plants, which could cause them to perk up.

All this is very well but if the leaves are covered with a cuticle which keeps water *inside* the plant, the cuticle ought also to keep water *out* of the plant. This is the principle of the oilskin which although it keeps rain out, also keeps perspiration in, and on a hot wet day the inside of an oilskin can be absolutely soaking because water vapour cannot get through in either direction. How then do foliar feeds get in?

The answer lies in the microscopic structure of the cuticle which is *not* a simple waterproof layer covering the leaf, but is really a large number of tiny overlapping wax scales which have minute spaces between the overlaps. We now know that there is a small loss of water through the cuticle, but also that certain chemicals such as urea can gain entry to the leaf via the spaces between the overlaps, hence foliar feeding.

Foliar feeding can be a very useful tool to the gardener, for trace elements when applied to the soil might not be easily available to the plant, but when applied to the leaf are immediately taken up and used to good advantage.

A word of warning is necessary here, for if foliar feeds are too strong or concentrated they can cause leaf scorch, so do not make up your own, and those you buy should be used strictly according to the instructions on the container.

Photoperiodicity

Many plants are strongly affected by the length of the day, which can act as a trigger to set off the mechanism which produces flowers. I will discuss this more in the section on Flowers and Fruits, but it is appropriate to mention it here for it is the *leaves* which are the light-sensitive parts of the plant, and which produce substances which bring about the flowering process.

Two experiments can make this clear. Firstly, if you take a plant which is strongly light influenced, e.g. chrysanthemum, and remove the leaves, the influence of the light ceases. But you may say the plant has been injured and so would be upset anyway. The experimenter will then simply shade the leaves and allow the rest of the plant full light and it will still be non-sensitive. Finally he can shade all the leaves except one or two and he will find that the action of light on the exposed leaves is enough to stimulate the whole plant. Thus we connect the leaf with the ability to sense light.

The second type of experiment is more vivid, namely to keep a plant, shall we say, in light which would prevent flowering, then to graft on it a leaf or two which have been exposed to a light which would induce flowering. The result is the plant forming

A leaf skeleton

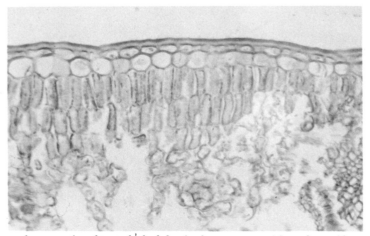

A cross-section of part of a leaf showing brown waxy cuticle on the outside

(Above) Brightly coloured bracts on a Poinsettia   *(Right) Sweet pea leaflets modified as tendrils*

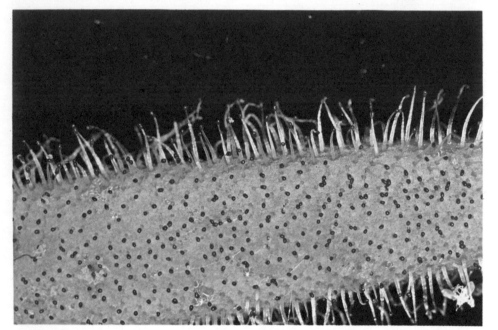

Glands on the leaf of an insectivorous plant (Sundew)

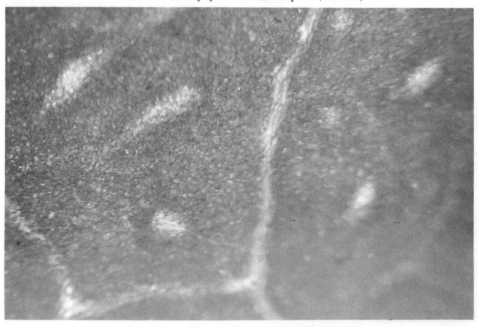

Glands in a leaf of Hypericum, seen when held to the light

flower buds. This simple experiment shows that not only is the leaf the sensitive part, but also that the effect the light has on the leaf can be transmitted to other parts of the plant or, by grafting, to a different plant.

This of course is not a surprising finding, for since the leaves have evolved as photosynthetic organs it is only appropriate that other reactions involving light should also be located in the leaves.

Modifications of Leaves

Leaves are so essential to plants it is not surprising that they have been modified in many ways to perform other and additional functions. For instance some leaves have become brightly coloured and act almost as flowers. The best example of this is the *Poinsettia* with its vivid red floral bracts. Most households either have or have had one of these, for it is probably the most popular house plant, and many housewives have been disappointed, for what should have been bright red bracts have turned out to be like ordinary green leaves.

This colouring of the bracts is also a photoperiodic effect which depends on short day length in the winter. Under the appropriate conditions the green leaves near the flower (the bracts) will form a bright red chemical which will mask the chlorophyll and turn the bract a vivid red, but given the wrong conditions the leaves will stay green and the housewife be disappointed.

Other plants may have highly modified leaves, which appear as tendrils in sweet pea, or as thorns in gorse, but the most elaborate variation on the theme of leaf is the insect-eating plants. Such insectivorous plants are not common all over Britain, but can be found in fair profusion in any upland moor or bog. Our insectivorous plants are small and dainty but there are quite large pitcher plants and Venus fly traps to be found in tropical and sub-tropical areas, which can trap fairly large insects.

The two most common insectivorous plants in Britain are the sundew (*Drosera*) and the butterwort (*Pinguicula*). In each case the leaves are covered with sticky stalked glands to which insects adhere. Once this happens the leaf slowly rolls up in the case of the butterwort, or many other sticky glands bend over the captive insect in the sundew. There are other glands on the leaf surface which are then stimulated to produce enzymes, which kill the insect and slowly dissolve it. As the insect dissolves, the nitrogen and other chemicals which it contains are absorbed by the leaf surface and help to feed the plant. Most of these surface glands are highly modified stomata or surface hairs, and play a vital part in the plant's economy.

It is not only insectivorous plants which have glands on the surface. Practically all herbs have oil glands which produce the lovely scent of thyme, mint, or marjoram, while we all know to our cost that the ordinary stinging nettle carries many glandular stinging hairs.

All of these modifications have evolved from the simple leaf and enable plants to survive, or even thrive, under conditions which they might otherwise find difficult. Consider the sweet pea, which is a tall plant with a weak stem. Without tendrils to attach to a support it would just sprawl on the ground and so get very little light, but because of the tendrils it can climb up almost any support, and allow the leaves to get light from all sides which enables the plant to conduct an efficient photosynthesis system.

Evergreen and Deciduous Trees

In the garden, we often classify shrubs and trees on the basis of whether they shed their leaves in the autumn or at some other time of year. In fact the brilliance of autumn colours is a sign that the deciduous trees are getting ready to shed their leaves, and will remain bare all winter.

The first question is the one about the mechanics of leaf shedding. How does it occur? The answer lies in a layer of cells which form at the foot of the leaf stalk. These cells, instead of having flat sides, like bricks, have a rounded shape, so that they only touch the cells around them at a single point. They are therefore very easily separated from each other, and this separation can be caused by wind shaking the tree or more often by frost, which will freeze a thin film of water around these spherical cells. This water as it freezes will expand and so separate the touching cells, and in the morning the thaw will bring the leaves pattering down in the slightest breeze. You can often tell when the first frost

A stinging hair of a nettle

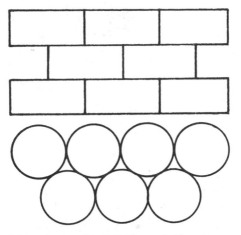

The mechanism of leaf-shedding in deciduous trees — round cells (deciduous) are more easily split off than rectangular cells (evergreen).

has occurred by the ground being carpeted with fallen leaves.

So the mechanism is clear, but the question remains of what sets the mechanism going, or in terms of the leaf, what causes the stalk to produce rounded instead of flat cells. Here, as in so many other phenomena involving plants, the factor which operates is day length, and as the days get shorter in the autumn the plant changes its type of cell production. This can be shown by keeping plants in a heated greenhouse and they will still shed their leaves in the autumn, or, by keeping a cool greenhouse continually lit, and the leaves will not be shed at the usual time.

This shedding of leaves is another device evolved to conserve water. In winter the temperatures are too low for many plants to photosynthesise, and unless the leaves were shed, they would lose water much of the time (even if the soil were frozen) for no compensating photosynthetic gain.

But there are many evergreen plants such as all the pines, rhododendrons, laurels, skimmia, erica, etc. How do they survive the winter? You will notice two things about most evergreens, either the leaves are small, or else they are thick and glossy, well able to withstand the drying out of cold east winds. They are not truly evergreens as every gardener with a holly tree knows, for it sheds its leaves in late spring when the new buds open and growth is under way. Thus although the tree is always green, the leaves are still shed, but not in the autumn before the new ones are formed.

When deciduous shrubs and trees shed leaves, they are losing all the food material which went to make up the structure of the leaf. This loss is minimised by breaking down a lot of the leaf's chemicals in the early autumn, and shipping them back into the stem to be stored. The bright autumn colours are the tell-tale signs of these changes in the leaf chemistry, and a marvellous sight they can be on a fine clear crisp autumn day.

Growing Leaves to Eat

Man eats a lot of plant leaves and from them can obtain some very essential parts of his diet, especially vitamin C. Leaves are also cool and attractive to look at, so that a well-made salad with its background of crisp green lettuce is a delight to the eye as well as to the taste-buds. We also eat cabbage and spinach, and many people get pleasure from the leaves of wild plants such as dandelion, Good King Henry, etc. But undoubtedly lettuce and cabbage are the main types of leaf eaten in Britain, and the fact that we eat

Man needs green leaves; green leaves need chlorophyll; chlorophyll needs nitrogen, iron, and magnesium.

one raw and the other cooked makes little difference to their production.

We must never forget either that unless all our plants have good and efficient green leaves they will not grow well, and the crop, be it fruit, root, or seed, will be poor. How then to ensure good leaves?

We need leaves because they contain chlorophyll, so we must provide the elements essential for its production. These are nitrogen, iron and magnesium. Normally there is enough iron and magnesium in the soil but, if there is any doubt about this the appropriate steps can be taken (see p. 16).

A shortage of nitrogen shows itself by the plant being stunted and having a pale green, almost a yellow colour. Here a quick-acting nitrogen fertiliser is called for, either organic, such as dried blood, or non-organic, such as sulphate of ammonia or nitrate of soda.

Any gardener therefore should pay careful attention to his 'greens', and provide a little extra nitrogenous feed in the autumn or early spring to give them that lift which often means so much. Since nitrogen is quickly washed out of the soil, the golden rule should be to use the slow-release fertilisers, or apply ordinary fertilisers a little and often, and do remember that sandy soils which quickly drain, can easily become short of nitrogen.

Leaf Colour

Most leaves are green, but there are many well-known plants with leaves of other colours. For example there are golden varieties of many shrubs and trees, there are red maples, copper beeches, and very many strains which are variegated, with part of the leaf one colour, usually green, and other parts of the same leaf, white or yellow. The gardener who looks, will wonder how all this squares with the stress I have laid on chlorophyll and the necessity for it.

If we take the coloured leaves such as copper beech first, it is not very difficult to extract the red colour and show that the green chlorophyll is there all the time, but is masked and hidden by the red. In fact some plants do this trick themselves, and a shrub such as *Pieris forrestii* has bright red young leaves which change to green as the leaf ages.

The variegated leaves are a very mixed lot for there are a number of causes for the yellow patterning of the green leaves. In some cases, such as *Abutilon*, the yellow areas are actually due to a virus disease which scarcely harms the plant at all, and in fact produces only this rather unusual mottled effect. This is one of the very rare cases where the presence of a disease on a

(Above) A leaf of Abutilon showing the results of virus infection
(Right) Highly decorative leaf of a Maranta plant

A selection of variegated leaves grown for their decorative effect

plant actually increases the value of it.

Plants such as ivies, tradescantia, hollies, and many others, have light yellow or white stripes on the leaf, or even a bright coloured edge to the leaf. Many of these are examples of a strange phenomenon called chimaera, in which two different types of cell are incorporated in the same plant. A good example is the ordinary *Pelargonium* which can be bought with a silver edge to the green leaf. If you examine this leaf microscopically, you will find that the outer layers of cells do not possess any chloroplasts, but there are plenty in the inner layers. This means that when you get to the edges of the leaf and it becomes only a few cells thick, those will be the outer chlorophyll-free cells which appear as the silver band around the edge.

In many cases buds will form in an inner layer of the plant. This bud will not have the outer layer of chlorophyll-free cells and if allowed to develop will be a perfectly ordinary shoot or leaf. Such ordinary shoots on a variegated or golden variety (e.g. privet) should be cut out, otherwise they will outgrow the rest of the plant, swamping and eventually eliminating the attractive golden bits.

A LOOK AT FLOWERS AND FRUITS

Flowers and fruits are surely the culmination of every gardener's annual work. Vegetables are excellent, and make gardening a healthful and in many cases a valuable economic hobby, but the production of beautiful flowers and luscious fruits is something every gardener seeks, for the house is more beautiful when the garden around it contains many colourful, scented, and lovely flowers, and the pleasure of picking an apple or strawberry and eating it at once, fully fresh and flavoursome, adds a new zest to life.

From the point of view of the scientist, flowers are almost inseparably linked with fruits, for the flower only justifies its biological existence when it results in the production of fruit.

Structure of a Flower

Almost any flower will repay careful study, but for the beginner in looking at plants, a simple uncomplicated flower is best, for example in spring, a daffodil or tulip will show all there is to see, and in the summer or autumn, flowers such as Canterbury bells, nasturtium, poppies, and a host of others

will be more than adequate. If you know very little at all about flowers don't choose a rose, or any flower with a large number of showy coloured parts, choose a regular flower with a single ring of coloured petals.

For the sake of simplicity let us say you choose to look at a primrose or a poppy. You will obviously see the coloured outer ring of petals which has outside it a ring of smaller green leaf-like structures called the calyx. Inside the petals, two different types of structure can be distinguished, the first being a ring or rings of stalked structures, which are the anthers, and in the very centre of the flower, the green style or stigma at the base of which are the carpels.

All this is a complex piece of sexual mechanism, the details of which are very intricate and will be omitted here. Suffice it to say that the anthers produce the yellow powdery pollen which is equivalent to male sexual cells, and the style and stigma give access to the female reproductive structures, the ovules and ova. If an ovum is fertilised by the products of a pollen grain, then an embryo plant is produced inside a seed and a fruit. Having thus given the general gist of the process let's look at it in a little more detail.

The colour and form of the flower is largely determined by the petals which are the big showy part. This is not a happy accident, for nature rarely works that way. The brightness of the petals has a very definite biological role to play in attracting insects. It is a very interesting thing that the evolutionary rise of the insect kingdom occurs at the same time as the upsurge in the number of flowering plants, when the great forests of horsetails and conifers gave way to the bright colours of the flowering plants.

One may know this connection of insect and flower without appreciating the significance of it and simply say 'Oh, the insects carry pollen from flower to flower and so ensure pollination'. But the important thing in this sentence is the 'from flower to flower' bit. We all know that there are rules in societies, even of the most primitive tribes where they are called taboos, which state whom you cannot marry. For example only in Ancient Egypt was a man allowed to marry his sister, and in the Church of England today the marriage of first cousins is discouraged. The reason for this is to prevent inbreeding, and the possible production of abnormal children which often result from such a union. In science we talk about out-breeding as opposed to inbreeding.

In flowers there is at first sight no reason at all why the pollen in any flower should not fertilise the ovules of the same flower, which would be very easy since the anthers and stigma are so close to each other. But from an evolutionary point of view this would be the closest of inbreeding and could be bad for the species, so a number of systems have been evolved which effectively prevent this, and most of these systems depend on insects carrying pollen from flower to flower. One such system may serve to illustrate the general principle.

In many cases flowers have developed a genetic barrier, such, that if the pollen from a given flower lands on the stigma of the same flower, the pollen will die without causing fertilisation and seed production. This type of genetic barrier is only of value if it can be reasonably assured that pollen from another flower of the same species *will* be available to ensure seed production, and this is done by the plant producing coloured petals which the insect can see and distinguish, and at the same time producing nectar which will provide an incentive for the insect's visit.

Thus as an insect goes from one flower to another collecting nectar (and in many cases pollen too) for honey, it transfers pollen as

The coloured petals of a primula

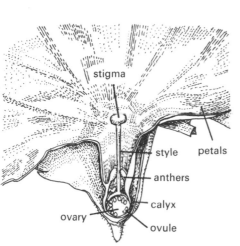

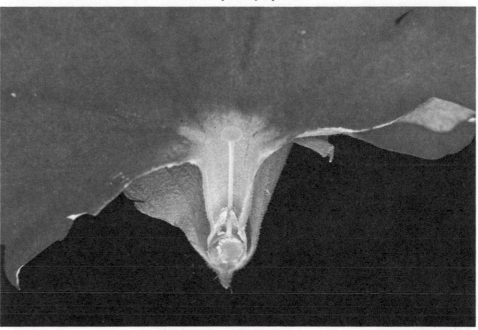
A primula flower cut through the centre to show the floral parts. (Compare diagram.)

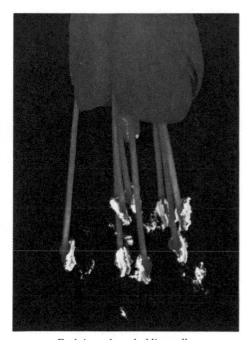
Fuchsia anthers shedding pollen

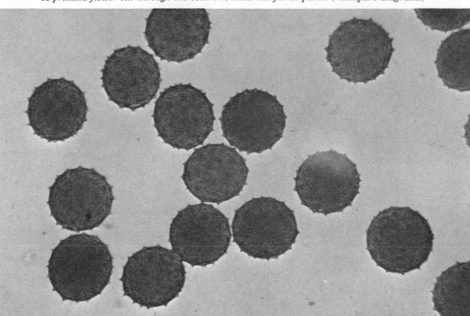
Pollen grains greatly magnified

31

Hellebore flower showing the green nectar-producing organs at the base of the anthers

No insect can visit this Hypericum flower without coming into contact with the anthers

An orchid flower showing a structure adapted for insect pollination

it goes, albeit unintentionally, and so ensures cross-fertilisation.

This is a simple method, but there are many much more elaborate ones in which the structure of the flower is modified in many ways to ensure that the pollen from one flower will be deposited on a part of the body of the insect, which will be rubbed by the stigma of the next flower it visits. In some cases, flowers have grown to resemble insects to such an extent, that an insect will try to mate with the flower and so transfer any pollen sticking to its body.

To fruit growers these, and similar mechanisms, are of great importance, for many of our modern varieties of fruit are self-sterile, and will not set seed and so fruit with their own pollen. These are what are called inter-compatible groups in which all the members of one group of apples (say) are sterile with their own pollen, and on their own will bear no fruit, but there are other groups of apple with which they are fertile. In many, if not most cases therefore, you should never plant a single fruit tree without being very sure that it is self-fertile, and if it is not, to be certain that close to it you plant a tree of a compatible variety to be sure of getting fruit. These limitations apply to apples, pears, plums, cherries, and damsons.

It is also possible that the scent of flowers has attractive powers, and borne on the wind, the scent will help to guide the insect to the source of nectar and so bring about pollination.

There is a further point about pollen which has great economic importance, namely the fact that in certain varieties of fruit the pollen is always sterile. This may seem a great disadvantage until we realise that pollen does two jobs; firstly, it fertilises the ovum which produces a seed, and secondly, it carries hormones to the style and stigma, which set in train the series of events which result in fruit formation. Normally we think of seed production as the most important role of pollen, and this is so, *but*, if we can develop strains of plants the pollen of which will stimulate fruit production without the formation of seed, then we are on a good line, for this is the origin of seedless fruit.

The most common type of seedless fruit is the banana, and there will be few readers who have ever seen a banana seed which is hard, black, and as big as a marble. But as well as seedless bananas we now get seedless oranges and grapes, whose origin lies in this separation of seed formation from fruit formation. In some cases, the hormones carried by the pollen can be produced synthetically, so that by simply spraying the tree at the correct time we can ensure a good set of seedless fruit.

Such chemicals are available to the amateur and can be used on tomatoes and winter cherries (*Solanum*), which produce quite spectacular results in the way of fruit set. The only snag in the case of the tomato is, that the absence of seed subtly alters the flavour of the fruit, and to many people they are not so attractive to eat.

The Flower as the Basis of Classification

When the ancient Greeks started thinking in a scientific way about living things, they realised that the basis of biology must be a system of classification which would allow them to name plants and animals. Accordingly they divided plants into groups corresponding to trees, shrubs and herbs.

This was very soon realised to be an inadequate system, as it lumped pines along

(Above) Seeded and seedless grapefruit. Seedless varieties are usually smaller. (Right) A collection of members of the Compositae family.

with laburnum and apples, and it was difficult indeed to draw a sensible line between a tree and a shrub. The problems of plant classification proved too difficult for easy solution for many hundreds of years until the 18th century, when Linnaeus proposed a system of classifying plants based on the reproductive parts, the flower. This is the system (with modern modifications) which we use today, and practically all research on the biochemical or immunological reactions of plants goes to confirm the soundness of the Linnaean system.

It would be pointless to go into the details of the Linnaean system here, for it demands a more detailed knowledge of floral structure than I have given, but it is not difficult and can quickly be learned and appreciated by a keen gardener. The fundamental unit in the classification of plants is the *species*, and this we would recognise as, say, a dandelion. Scientifically a dandelion is *Taraxacum officinale*.

This is rather like saying that my name is Gemmell Alan, and as there are other Gemmells so there are other Taraxacums. We therefore say that Taraxacum is the name of the genus and the second name 'officinale' is the name of the species.

But once again there are many yellow-flowered plants which resemble dandelions, but not too closely. One can think of dahlias, asters, daisies, hawkbit, ragwort, coltsfoot, etc., a vast number which are obviously related to our dandelion. So they are all gathered together in a family, in this case the Compositae.

The Linnaean system describes the family as the large group, then the genus (Genera) as the smaller group, and then the separately identifiable members of the genus as a species. So here it is laid out:

Family — *Compositae*
Genus — *Taraxacum*
Species — *T. officinale*

The use of Latin names often confuses beginners, but with a little perseverance they are quickly learned, and they are of great value for they form an international language. Anyone who was interested in gardening or botany would know immediately which plant you were referring to when you said *Taraxacum officinale* but if you tried 'dandelion' on a Chinaman or a Russian, he would have no idea what you were talking about.

There is however a complication which has arisen in more recent years, for plant breeders and explorers have discovered that many plants may have virtually the same flower structure, but be so different from the standard species in habit and colour that they deserve a special name. Such plants are called varieties and are extremely important to gardeners.

For example there are dwarf varieties of many trees and shrubs, and they are designated by a further Latin word meaning small or dwarf after the species name. Such a one is *Picea glauca*, the white spruce, which has a dwarf variety called *P. glauca nana*. In a similar way there are golden varieties of many species which usually add '*aurea*' to the species name, and variegated varieties which add '*variegata*'.

You will notice that in many cases the Latin word used describes the plant, and this can prove most helpful if a gardener is not sure of the conditions which suit a plant best, or even what growth habit the plant has. Thus '*procumbens*' and '*repens*' mean sprawling or creeping, '*argentea*' generally means with silver leaves, '*tortuosa*' means with a twisted or tortured stem, and so on. Even varieties may vary a bit, and when this happens some plants may be called a 'strain' or, if maintained in cultivation only, may be called a 'cultivar'. These are however refinements which in most cases will only affect the specialist in a particular species or a group of species, who wishes to have a complete collection of the range of variation within the plant in which he specialises. The ordinary gardener need only know that they exist, until he too becomes a fanatic on some particularly well-loved plant.

Occasionally the name will change as fresh discoveries are made, and plants that were once thought to be related, are found to be quite distinct. A good example of this kind of change is the Cydonia or Quince, which became Japonica, and has now become Chaenomeles. This is very disconcerting and annoying, but in the end it helps keep related plants together, and that is the prime purpose of classification.

Finally, why use the sexual structure, the flower, as the basis of classification? The answer to this question is logical and very important. It is because the size of a plant may vary with feeding or soil, the colour may change, and the shape of the leaves can be altered by age and feeding, but the flower, because it is the basic structure on which the future of the species depends, hardly varies at all, and is passed on intact from generation to generation. It is therefore the most reliable criterion.

Timing of Flowering

Everyone has seen that plants, generally speaking, have a definite season in which they flower. A few plants, especially weeds, can flower more or less all the year round, and you will find daisies and chickweed in good bloom in any month of the year, but, on the whole, we think of flowers associated with seasons as spring flowers or summer or autumn flowers, and even winter-flowering subjects, such as Christmas rose, *Viburnum tinus*, and so on.

This raises the problem of what brings about this reasonably predictable date, or at least season, of flowering. At one time it was thought to be a question of temperature, so that roses would not flower in February because it was too cold, but snowdrops being hardy could flower then with impunity. In a way, temperature does play a part, but mainly in bulbs, which will not usually flower unless they have a period of cold treatment. In fact the treated bulbs which are on sale for Christmas flowering are treated by being exposed to very low temperatures before you buy them.

Generally, too, flowers which are affected by temperature are usually formed in the bud stage the previous summer. They lie dormant all winter, getting a cold treatment, and flower in the warmer days of early spring. This is why you should never prune spring-flowering plants in the winter, for if you do you will simply cut away the flower buds formed the previous summer and you will get no flowers at all. Spring-flowering shrubs such as forsythia, chaenomeles, and some clematis, should be pruned as soon as flowering stops in late spring, and so allow plenty of time for new flower buds to be formed for the next year.

On the other hand most plants which

Flowering two-year old cabbage

Fruits come in a variety of shapes and sizes.

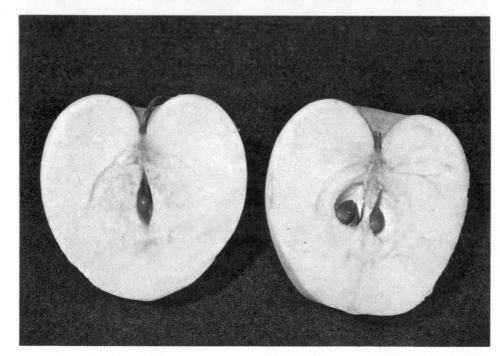

A typical fruit (apple), showing skin, fleshy food store, and seeds.

flower in summer or autumn are under the control, not of temperature, but of the length of day. Thus plants, such as chrysanthemum, will only flower if the day is less than 10–12 hours long. They are called short-day plants. Others, such as carnation, will only flower if the day is more than 12 hours, and these are called long-day plants. There are a number of plants which are unaffected by day length which are called day-neutral.

What happens is that there is a pigment in the leaves which is sensitive to light waves, and so a long day, which is the equivalent of a short night, causes a change in the proportions of this pigment. This affects the production of hormone-like substances which migrate from the leaves to the growing points of the plant. There, the hormone can change a leaf bud to a flower bud, and so about 6 weeks after exposure to the appropriate day length, the plant will come into flower.

Modern growers use this knowledge to induce plants to flower at a specific time, and by skilful manipulation of lights and darkening blinds, almost any photo-sensitive plant can be induced to flower at any time of year when the market for these flowers is at its best.

There is another aspect of flowering which deserves mention, namely the division of flowering plants into annuals, biennials, and perennials. An annual plant grows from a seed, flowers, and dies in one season, whereas a biennial plant, such as a cabbage, grows from a seed, forms a heart, spends the winter in this vegetative stage, and then flowers the following summer. That is, it takes two years to go from seed to seed. Many of our vegetables such as cabbages,

carrots, lettuce, etc., are biennials, and if they receive a check while they are growing they will 'bolt' which means they flower in the first instead of the second year.

Actually, under natural conditions, winter frosts act as the check which induces flowering in biennials, but any check will do. It can take the form of a frost, drought, insect damage, bad planting, and so on. For good results therefore, biennial vegetables and flowers should be kept growing steadily without check all through the first year.

The final group, the perennials, are planted as seed, come into flower, and then continue to flower all through their life. Clearly shrubs and trees are all perennials, but there are also perennial plants, such as michaelmas daisies, which are ordinary herbaceous types.

Structure of a Fruit

There is a very understandable confusion in the mind of ordinary gardeners about what to conceive of as a seed as opposed to a fruit. For example everyone would call an apple a fruit which contained the seeds, but might be a little reluctant to call a hazel nut a fruit, and still more reluctant to call a pea pod a fruit. But they are all fruits of different types, some dry, some juicy, some many-seeded (tomato), some one-seeded (a peach), but all providing some measure of protection for the vital structure – the seed with its embryo plant.

In the vast majority of cases the fruit is produced by the parent plant after receiving the stimulus from the pollen, whereas the seed is the structure arising from the fusion of pollen and ovule elements. The fact that the fruit is a parental structure is important in fruit, and especially in apple and pear growing. As we have seen, the female parts of one variety frequently can only be pollinated by another variety. Such a situation would and does produce a hybrid seed or, as we might say, apples don't come true from seed, and the offspring will vary according to which variety is the male parent. But because the fruit is a parental structure, it makes no difference which plant pollinates a given variety of apple, a Laxton Superb or a Cox's Orange apple will always have the flavour typical of the variety which bears the fruit.

In an earlier section it was shown how the seed had a protective coat, a food store, etc., and these features are duplicated by the fruit. What we call the skin, or the peel, or the shell, of the fruit, is simply the outer covering which in many cases surrounds a mass of food storage tissue which helps to nourish the seed. Most of the fruits we eat have a considerable food value and high flavour (such as apples, oranges, bananas, nuts, raspberries, peaches, etc.), but in many cases we eat the seeds and discard the fruits because they are not so flavourful. Peas and beans come to mind in this category, although we do eat the pods of green runner beans.

Although man has selected and bred fruits of high quality and good flavour, we must remember that the fruits are not put there for our benefit only. They play an important part in the continued life of the plant, and would do so even if there were no human beings at all. I say this because fruits are attractive to animals, and especially birds, who eat them. The fruit is then digested, but the seed, having a tougher seed coat, is resistant to digestive juices and will pass unharmed through the intestine of many animals to be excreted intact, and then will germinate and grow. This is one of nature's methods of seed dispersal, for the animal eats the fruit from the parent plant, then moves on to graze, or to other trees to nest, where the seed is then excreted. Thus seeds do not just drop around the parent, but are dispersed widely by animals and birds as a result of the fruit being attractive as food.

It will also be obvious that the bright colours of many fruits act as signals to the birds to 'come and get them', in fact the colours of both fruit and flowers play the same biological role as signals to attract attention.

Not all fruits are eaten, many are unpalatable, and the seeds they contain are dispersed in other ways. If you sit by a gorse bush on a hot summer day, you will hear lots of tiny pops and crackles caused by the seed pods (the fruit) bursting open in a kind of twisty explosion, which scatters the seeds fairly widely from the parent plant. Some seeds and fruits are dispersed by water and a considerable number by wind. On a fresh windy day in summer you can sit in your garden and watch the seeds of the rosebay willow herb go floating by on the wind, spreading weed problems everywhere they settle down.

But certainly the chief agent of long-distance fruit and seed dispersal is man himself, for every western country imports fruits from far distant parts of the world, the seeds of many of which can settle here and grow in favourable areas. In fact the tomato was originally confined to the New World but is now one of the most widely-grown crops in Britain. It is in man's ability today to move at great speed over vast distances that lies the success of many of his

Fruits dispersed by animals (on the right) and by wind (on the left).

Another, and proverbial, wind-blown seed – thistledown.

Bananas at different stages of ripeness

plant introductions, for in the days of sailing ships, fruits from distant places had largely gone rotten and been discarded by the time they reached land in Europe.

Fruit Ripening and Storage

In a peculiar way a fruit is a law unto itself, for it behaves biochemically very differently from the plant which bears it, or from the seed it contains. Schoolboys have a weakness for stealing apples, and they usually do so when the apples are green and unripe. They pay for this act in a roundabout way, for green apples are hard and sour, and tend to produce tummy upsets in any boy who consumes a quantity of them.

Stop and think for a moment about what I have just written and you will realise that fruit – and it does not matter what type – goes through a series of events starting with being small, green, and usually acid and sour, becoming progressively sweeter, softer, less sour, more full of flavour and gradually changing colour to red, yellow or black until they become soft, the flavour goes, the fruit rots and falls apart.

On the bush or tree it is in this last stage that the seeds may be shed, but it is in the earlier stage of what we would call the ripe fruit, that they are at their most palatable and are therefore most sought after as a source of food.

This series of events has an inevitability about it which we cannot avoid, and if fruit is being brought long distances by sea or is being stored for consumption out of season, then our chief aim should be to delay this series of events to suit our convenience. An important finding is that in most fruits the three stages I have described above are not of equal length, and the process is a gradually accelerating one. The process of ripening takes a long time, the period of perfect ripeness is relatively short, and the decay post-ripeness period is as short or even shorter. Thus we try to interfere with the ripening process.

On the tree this is very difficult indeed and scientists have had little success in this matter. In fact the problem is avoided by

breeding varieties of fruit which ripen naturally at different rates, and which do not go into the after-ripening stage so quickly. But many varieties of fruit we like to eat out of season, and in order to get tropical fruit to our tables in prime condition demands scientific knowledge of fruit physiology.

As fruit ripens, it takes in oxygen and gives off carbon dioxide in a process called cellular respiration. This process is influenced by temperature, and by the atmosphere around the fruit. For example, low temperatures, as in a refrigerator, slow down the rate of respiration and therefore delay ripening. Many companies use cold storage compartments in ships and trains for the movement of fruit, which is picked while still unripe and kept at low temperatures until it is at its market. The temperature is then allowed to rise and the fruit ripens quickly, and is put on the market in prime condition.

A probably cheaper and more widely-used method is called gas-storage. This depends on the fact that the rate of respiration is slowed down if there is high concentration of carbon dioxide in the atmosphere. This is a very harmless gas and it is easily extracted from the air. It is not difficult therefore to design and build chambers within which the fruit can be stored in a controlled atmosphere, and the rate of respiration slowed down greatly. Since it has also been found that the gas ethylene will increase the rate of ripening of fruit, by careful juggling with the gases in the storage compartments, fruit-ripening can be slowed down or speeded up, all to our great advantage.

A LOOK AT THE ENVIRONMENT

What is the 'Environment'?

One of the most over-used and least understood words today is the 'ENVIRONMENT'. To many people it is what other people are destroying and which they are trying to preserve, but to the ecologist the concept of the environment is at the same time both easy

and difficult. In terms of a simple definition the environment of any plant or animal is everything which influences that plant or animal, and that includes men, mice, machinery, and nearly everything else you can think of. Consequently, the environment has to be appreciated as a very intricate thing, for if everything is influencing everything else around it then you have a vast complicated web of interacting forces.

Thus a gardener can look at a plant and say 'What is the environment of this cabbage?' but he has to realise that the cabbage he is looking at is part of the environment of the weeds and the other cabbages around it, of the insects and diseases which may destroy it, and of all the myriad of living things associated with it, even at a great distance. For example that cabbage can become part of the environment of a car worker in Coventry when it appears on a market stall, or even of the fish in the rivers when the sewage of Coventry gets discharged into a river. It may eventually affect another cabbage if the sewage is recycled and is used in another garden.

Any simple approach to the environment is bound therefore to be misleading. But it is possible to subdivide the concept into a number of different parts and to look at them separately, and that's what I propose to do. You must remember however that each part will interact with all the other parts, so that my separation is artificial, and the parts should never be thought of in isolation but as fragments of a vast interacting whole.

For convenience' sake I intend to subdivide the environment into four sets of factors, namely:

1) climatic,
2) geographical,
3) biological,
4) soil (edaphic factors).

Although these are not neatly packaged as separate entities they will do for our purpose.

Climatic Factors

So far as the gardener is concerned these include such things as temperature, rainfall, sunshine, wind, frost, light, etc., or if you like the factors of the weather. It is easy to see how they interact, for an area of high temperature usually has sunshine (but not necessarily so), but it depends on the rainfall whether we have a desert or a lush tropical forest. Even in Britain there is a wide range of rainfall from 80 + ins. per year in the Lake District and the West Highlands, to some 10 or 15 ins. in East Anglia. So climatic factors can vary dramatically even in a small country.

How then should the gardener cope with this section of the environment? Well, as we have seen, plants need light for photosynthesis, so we arrange for maximum light by reducing overhanging trees and shade. If he is in a dry area he arranges for maximum water conservation, by getting lots of humus into the soil, by using mulches, by growing crops and varieties suitable for his district, and by eliminating weeds which compete with his crop for water, light, etc.

It is essential to consider the climatic factors when planning, not only the layout of the garden, but also the crops and varieties it is hoped to grow. In a cold frosty area, say in a Pennine or Highland village it is pointless to try to grow early potatoes or strawberries, for the risk of frost damage is too great, and to get a crop once every 4 or 5 years is bad gardening as well as bad economics.

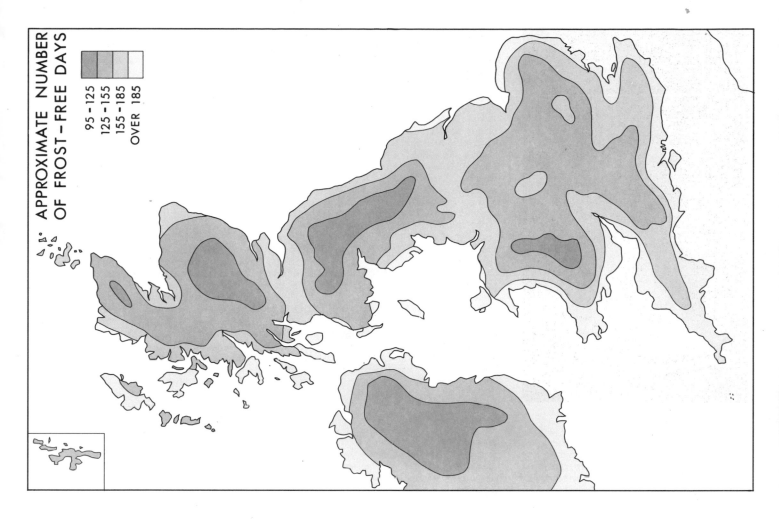

APPROXIMATE NUMBER
OF FROST–FREE DAYS

95 – 125
125 – 155
155 – 185
OVER 185

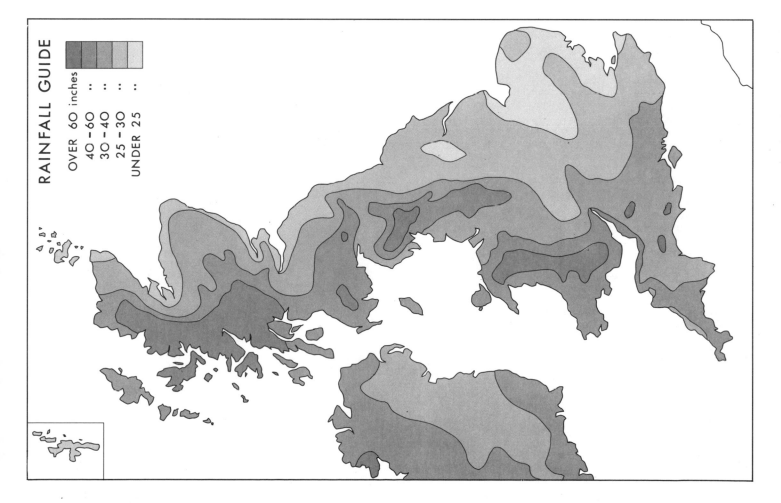

RAINFALL GUIDE

OVER 60 inches
40 – 60 ::
30 – 40 ::
25 – 30 ::
UNDER 25 ::

A frosted geranium

Frost is a special problem, and here, the old adage of 'horses for courses' is a good one, for it means that you should not try to grow tender subjects in frosty areas, but rather settle for what you can do well. Frost surprisingly enough is heavy, and the cold frosty air will run down a slope like water and collect at the bottom to form a frost pocket. Cold air can even be dammed like a river, and a dense hedge can act as such a dam. This is an additional reason why windbreaks should not be solid barriers, for if they are impassable by wind they will be equally so by freezing air, so that the amount of frost can be much increased by a dense barrier on the down-hill side. If you have frost pockets in the garden it sometimes pays to grow tall subjects there which, by virtue of their height, may be above the frosty air next to the ground.

The concept of 'frost-free days' is getting a lot of publicity these days and this is simply the number of days between the last frost of spring and the first one of the autumn. To my mind this is a useful idea, but in a country such as Britain, where climatic areas are not clear cut, it is a mistake to follow the idea too slavishly. Nevertheless if your number of frost-free days is limited to June, July and August then you have 92 days in which to grow your tender subjects to maturity in an average year, and so you should select 'early' (which usually means short season) varieties of vegetables and annuals.

In windy areas, some form of windbreak should be built or grown, remembering all the time that the best windbreaks filter and slow down the wind, rather than stop it absolutely. To use a solid fence or wall as a windbreak can create special problems, for insect pests and fungi will flourish in still damp areas, and there will be all sorts of turbulence at some distance from the windbreak which may be more dangerous to your plants than the initial wind. Many gardeners worry about the degree of protection given by windbreaks, and naturally this varies with the type of shelter provided. You can reckon, however, that the protec-

tion will extend some 8–10 times the height of the barrier, so that if your hedge or area of shrubs is 6 ft. high, there is a reduction in wind speed for about 60 ft. on the sheltered side. Very wet rainy areas will need special attention paid to drainage.

Finally, there is the concept of the 'microclimate'. It is easy to show that even in a single garden there can be quite a variety of climates. For example a tree will produce shelter for plants under it, but at the same time, it is keeping rain off them, depleting the soil of food, shading them from the sun and light, and so reducing the temperature, and so on. Microclimates are very localised areas with a little climate of their own, but apart from the trees, the average gardener is most affected by the microclimate *inside* the crop. Thus if your plants are too close together, they will shade each other. Each will act as a windbreak for all the others and you can get an area of still, damp, cold air inside a thick crop of, say, carrots. Here there could be a shortage of light, high humidity, low temperatures, and a comfortable place for pests to hide. So although each plant may benefit a little from shelter, a garden planted too closely may not be as healthy as one in which the plants have room to develop properly.

Geographical Factors
Generally speaking there is little one can do about the large-scale geographical element in the environment. By this I mean that if you live in Norfolk then no amount of tampering can move your garden to Devon. Once this fact is recognised and the limitations set by geography are accepted, then a great deal can be done to make the best of your situation.

Geographically we are north of the equator, which means that the sun is always to the south of us. It moves in a great arc across the sky from the south-east where it rises, to the south-west where it sets. In the summer it is much further north than it is in the winter. In summer therefore the arc is greater and passes nearly overhead, while in winter it is low and is further to the south.

For this reason shade, cast from the south side of a plot or garden, is a bad thing, whereas buildings or trees to the north side of the garden do little harm, and in many cases may be a blessing.

In the same way a south-facing slope gets the sunlight more directly, and in a more concentrated fashion, than a flat area of land. Thus in Britain a gently sloping south-facing garden is ideal. But only a few gardens have this, and so we must make the best of what we have by allowing the maxi-

mum of light, e.g. by running our cold frames or greenhouses in an east:west direction. This means the long sides get the sun from the south and also plants do not shade each other.

So far as is consistent with good cultivation, crops, and especially vegetables, should be grown with the sun's rays following along the length of the rows instead of across the ends of the rows. Similarly the tallest vegetables should where possible be on the north side of the plot, so that they won't shade the smaller plants.

Biological Factors
This is an enormous field, for it includes all the pests and diseases, the bacteria and fungi in the soil, the beneficial insects, and the harmful birds. It even includes man, for he has a profound effect on the environment. In fact a garden is an artificial man-made thing, so that the idea of a purely natural garden is a nonsense, although we can try to minimise the artificiality of the situation if we think that is desirable.

Of course, man is also the prime agent of what we call pollution, but I shall deal with that aspect separately.

All living things interact, and just as plants are dependent on insects and bacteria, so insects and bacteria are dependent on plants. In Darwin's day this interaction was called the 'struggle for existence' and largely this is still a valid concept, with crops competing with each other, and with weeds for food, light, etc., with insects eating plants and other insects, and at the same time being useful in causing pollination and fruit set. Soil bacteria and fungi cause humus production from dead plant material, but they will also attack living plants causing club root, Dutch elm disease, and a host of other plant diseases. This interaction of organisms has therefore its good and bad sides for the gardener.

If things are left alone and 'nature' allowed to take its course, then, in a few years' time, a natural balance will be reached of pests, crops, birds, insects, etc., and this 'balance of nature' has been suggested as the culmination of all good gardeners' endeavours. But a few moments' thought will convince you that the absolute balance of nature will lead to very unrewarding gardening, for pests, weeds, diseases, will all have a place in the garden, and in some years may gain complete control and ruin a crop. One has only to think of the balance of nature in relation to, say, Dutch elm disease, to realise that it is a balance which is really a see-saw, and in some years the disease may win until it kills nearly all the elm trees.

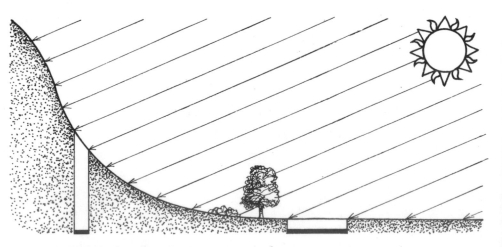

Local geographical factors that affect the gardener include aspect and slope. Note how the sunshine is concentrated on a small area of the hillside, but is spread over a larger area on the flat.

Then, with a shortage of trees to attack, the disease will subside for a time, until the elm population builds up again, then the disease will attack again and we have another epidemic. The same goes for club root, potato blight, and other diseases.

The reason why the 'balance of nature' does not work out for the gardener is that a garden is an un-natural thing in the first place, and we are usually trying to get the optimum yield from a few crops in a fairly large area. Remember nature never grew a row of beans, or a greenhouse-full of tomatoes, or even an apple orchard, and so you can see the lack of applicability of the balance of nature concept.

But, and there is a very great 'but', in the wild a kind of see-saw balance of nature *does* exist, and in it are all sorts of balances and checks which tend to maintain the biological status quo. Thus aphids have ladybirds which feed on them, and so aphids practically never get out of hand in the wild. As plants die and return humus to the soil, there is a constant recycling of minerals, and so soils don't get deficient or eroded. In effect, nature provides many buffers which usually prevent anything going completely off the rail. The gardener should therefore try to work with nature as far as is possible, by doing the kinds of things at a time which will not affect the natural forces. Thus, he should spray against insect pests when the bees and pollinating insects are not active. So far as possible, he should try to recycle as much natural material as he can by way of a compost heap, although this can be very difficult in a small garden in suburbia.

Finally the gardener should study nature, and try to use the knowledge he gains to work more effectively in the garden, and to keep it as close to nature as is consistent with good yields and good husbandry.

Soil (Edaphic) Factors

In this final section I am going to talk about pollution, for the section when we looked at soils, covers much of the basic science of this section of the environment. The point we really have to consider is the long-term effect of all the chemicals we use to help the cultivation of plants. It does not really matter how we apply the chemicals, and a few examples may make this clear. If we apply artificial fertilisers to the crop, we are usually applying them to the soil, and the plant will absorb them in what is usually called the 'ionic' form. The sulphate of ammonia, dried blood, nitrate of soda, farmyard manure, will all in the end be broken down and release nitrates and nitrites, and the plant absorbs the nitrogen in that form. Residues will be left in the soil and used as food by other organisms, or will just be washed out in drainage water and eventually end up in the rivers, lakes, and seas. Part may become CO_2 and end up in the air.

A suitable hedge makes an efficient wind-break – it doesn't blow down and its flexibility creates less turbulence than a wall or solid fence.

In another way, we spray a crop with an organic insecticide, say, derris. This kills the insects which fall on the soil, are broken down by bacteria, some of the chemicals produced are used by plants and the remainder either return to the air as CO_2, or are washed into the rivers, etc.

Alternatively birds may eat poisoned insects and be poisoned themselves, or be eaten by other birds or foxes. Chemicals may get into fish and we will eat them and absorb some of the chemicals ourselves.

What I am saying again, is that all parts of the environment interact, and if we apply poisonous chemicals at one end we must expect to see them in other strands of the web of life. Man is one such strand and he is dependent on everything else. It is vital therefore that in our efforts to achieve higher yields to feed the starving millions of the world, we do not so destroy parts of the environment that the rest begins to suffer.

It is very easy to cry 'Woe, Woe!' and say we should not use this or that spray, or this or that chemical, but if we don't use them, our yields go down and people starve to death. Surely the answer to the problem lies in a few simple ideas, such as using materials when they are needed, in minimum quantities to produce the effect, and at the right time and the right place. To say 'I

shall never use chemicals' is praiseworthy in a small land area but is unrealistic if we are trying to feed three thousand million people from a limited Earth.

Another facet is that of knowledge, for as our understanding of the environment grows so we are able to use methods and techniques which may avoid some of the dangers inherent in chemicals. For example, in greenhouses, whitefly can be eliminated by introducing a chalcyd wasp which eats whitefly. Of course once the whitefly go, the wasp has no more food and so dies. A fresh re-introduction is necessary every season. Methods of trapping insects are improving and so also is the development of immune and resistant varieties of crops, but of course, as we breed new strains of plant, so nature breeds new strains of pest and disease, and this sort of race is never-ending. Nevertheless a fuller understanding of the environment could help to avoid the worst excesses of any gardening practice.

Instead of a short chapter I really need a book simply to introduce the problem of the environment, for it is so complex and wide-ranging in its implications that in the end we will live or die by the way in which we use it, and by the extent of our understanding of it. The moral is 'treat it sensibly and carefully' and you will not go far wrong.

DESIGNING

YOUR GARDEN

R.J. Bisgrove

You are the best person to design your garden, because only you can decide exactly what type of garden you want. You must study the garden plot throughout the seasons and make the gradual adjustments necessary as the family increases, grows up, and leaves home. Even if you seek professional advice, a good professional consultant will spend time finding out about your tastes and your garden, and use his experience to suggest the best way of creating the garden *you* want. Beware of garden books and garden consultants offering a finished design for five pounds or so: it will be their garden, not yours.

However, it may be difficult, in your own garden, to see the wood for the trees: there are so many things to be done, and so much of the present garden layout is taken for granted that the main problem is where to start. This chapter is intended to help you decide what is wanted. Once you know what you would like, the rest of the book is available to tell you how to do it.

WHAT IS THERE NOW?
Why is your garden not satisfactory as it is? It may have developed haphazardly with a scrappy characterless result. Are the plants too overgrown, or is the jungle exciting enough to be made more of? Is the paving cracked and uneven? Is the grass tufty, weedy, and in need of edging? Is the garden full of unwanted sheds, bicycles, untidy compost heaps, gappy or thin hedges? Does it present a generally uncared-for and dusty appearance?

It is amazing how much can be done to a garden by thorough spring-cleaning. Get rid of the rubbish (but NOT in a country lane – the local authority will arrange to take it away for you!). Four stout posts and some plastic mesh will contain the compost. Derelict paving can ruin a garden. Can it be re-surfaced or should it be taken up for a fresh start? Hedges are living plants. A neglected hedge will often require severe cutting back in early spring to restore its shape, and a generous application of fertiliser to restore its vigour. Lawns respond more slowly, but regular cutting, trimming of edges, and one or two applications of combined fertiliser and lawn weedkiller, can make a miraculous difference in one growing season.

It is amazing, too, how often people who dislike gardening create extra work for themselves. The grass is cut once a month instead of once a week, usually with a badly adjusted mower, so it is a struggle to make the grass look bedraggled instead of a simple task to make it look attractive. Shrubs are sheared to tight little lumps with thin twigs, few flowers, and ugly shapes, instead of being left to assume their natural form and to flower abundantly. Plants and bulbs are lifted, divided, and re-planted as sparsely as before, simply out of habit, to create a barren, desolate appearance with lots of bare ground to weed. It is no wonder, when so much effort produces so little in return, that some people dislike gardening.

If, then, you acquire a garden which has received such treatment, it is wise to spend the first year looking at it. A good spring-cleaning, often no more than a weekend's work, thinning any overpruned shrubs to a few strong stems, then leaving them to grow and perhaps filling any major gaps with annual flowers, will enable the garden to achieve more maturity, and will give you time to reflect on the good and bad points of the garden.

A tidy garden, however, is not necessarily a satisfactory one, and the year of reflection can be fully occupied in planning alterations.

HOW MUCH WORK DO YOU WANT?
Some people are happy to spend every available moment in the garden. Others love their gardens but would like to have time for other interests. Still others find everything to do with the garden an absolute chore, usually because they garden badly. These people, however, are unlikely to read gardening books, so we can only feel sorry for them in their absence.

If you want to be kept busy in the garden, grow annuals which require soil cultivation, seed sowing, thinning, weeding, and staking, in large measure. Bedding, too, using annuals or tender perennials (dahlias, fuchsias) in the summer, and bulbs with wallflowers or other biennials in the spring, keeps a gardener busy not only in the raising and cultivation of plants but in the weeding necessitated after each disturbance of the soil. In small gardens even this may not be enough so a greenhouse creates additional scope for sowing, taking of cuttings, growing of grapes, tomatoes, melons, and so on, with constant side-shooting, training, tying in, and thinning. Rock plants (only some of which should truly be called 'alpines') are further sources of work. The hoe is lethal, so each weed must be extracted by hand from among diminutive plants, and the wars waged between more and less vigorous plants require the presence of an ever-vigilant referee.

If your main interests lie elsewhere (and not everybody is fortunate enough to be a gardening fanatic!), there is no reason whatsoever why your garden should not be attractive, but you would be advised to omit from the garden the plants mentioned above. Concentrate instead on shrubs, permanent herbaceous plants, and the many in-between semi-shrubby plants, such as santolina, sage, lavender, hellebores and bergenias.

The shape of the garden will be partly determined by the type of planting. If mainly temporary plants are to be used, the garden must have simple lines preferably emphasised with an edging of low evergreens, such as thrift, pinks, or London pride in small gardens, box, yew, rosemary, or lavender in larger gardens.

HOW SOON MUST YOUR GARDEN BE FINISHED?
What a silly question. Gardens are never finished: they continue to grow and change. However there is a difference between the stark appearance of a newly planted shrub border and the comfortable fullness of a mature garden, and there are ways of hastening the latter. Shrubs, and perhaps trees, provide the backbone of most gardens but are slow to mature. They can be interplanted with herbaceous plants, and even the faster-growing shrubs, to create a furnished appearance in 2 or 3 years.

Plants are usually good value as they are long lived and increase in beauty each year, but the cost of completely refurbishing even a small garden can be very high. There is much to be said for turning a small part of the garden into a nursery area, well manured and generously watered, so that a few plants can be bought in and multiplied for eventual use. If the garden plan is prepared early in the life of a new garden, it is even possible to put all the new plants into a small border, and gradually fill out the lines of the design as these initial plants are increased. An additional advantage of this approach is that the few original plants will be used throughout the garden creating an harmonious effect, with only a few distinct plants for important positions, but of course such economy will delay the fulfilment of the mature design.

For those poor people who move regularly and can never expect to own a mature garden the emphasis must be on (1) adaptation of other people's creations for their own use and (2) on annuals or, more expensively, quick-growing herbaceous perennials for immediate effect. In such circumstances, climbers are especially valuable for giving height to a new garden.

WHAT SHAPE SHOULD YOUR GARDEN BE?
You may think that there is no choice in the matter, but do not confuse the *plot* with the *garden*. The building plot is the piece of land sold or rented with the house, and other than by selling off pieces or begging adjacent fields, its shape is unaltered. The garden, however, is the open space remaining when sheds, walls, tall plants and similar large features have been scattered around on the plot, and the garden's shape need bear no resemblance to the shape of the plot.

The two extremes of garden type are the very open and the heavily planted garden. The former usually consists of a lawn (more rarely paving), surrounded by thin plant borders. It allows maximum room for children to play, for parents to relax, and for pets to romp, but because it is so open to view it usually lacks excitement. If the open space is a lawn it *must* have regular attention to keep it attractive, but the work is not difficult nor necessarily strenuous. The other type of garden is almost filled with plants, leaving only narrow walks for in-

The traditional border is an essential element in most gardening designs. Here a grass path is flanked by two borders, but not all gardens can be as grand as this.

Circular lawns, urns, and brick paths make an effective semi-formal layout. Dividing the garden so that it cannot all be taken in at one glance can add greatly to the interest.

specting them at close range. There is little room for lounging or for ball games but, because much of the garden is concealed, it is exciting, mysterious, and appears to be much larger than the more open type of garden. The extensive areas of plants do not require frequent attention, but occasional more skilled care in thinning, pruning, or replanting of overgrown areas.

Even in relatively small gardens it is possible to have both types, and it is infinitely better to emphasise the openness and the secrecy in turn, than to make the whole garden an area which is not sufficiently open to be expansive yet insufficiently planted to be exciting.

The parts of the garden – the paths, beds, borders and lawns – can be made of straight lines, of strong geometrical curves, weak informal curves, or of no definite lines. On most small rectangular plots straight lines are by far the most satisfactory for the garden. A garden of initially straight lines quickly becomes softened by informal planting and is not necessarily a formal garden. It certainly need not be dull! Circles or arcs can be used in small gardens *if* they are used to outline the open areas rather than the planted areas. Semicircular beds along a rectangular plot leave a very unsatisfactory scalloped lawn, but a circular lawn surrounded by planting can be most attractive. Weak curves, which so many people think are necessary to create an informal effect, look dreadful in small gardens. If, after looking at rectilinear or circular gardens you still think an informal garden needs wiggly edges, then the promontories of the wiggles *must* be planted with permanent and preferably evergreen plants.

The fourth type of garden shape, the 'no-shape' is seldom fully developed in Britain, but is of great value for small gardens. Many have areas of crazy paving with plants growing in the chinks, but in few gardens does the paving extend to cover the whole area, or the chink-planting extend to include large herbaceous plants, shrubs or small trees. The casual grouping of plants in a large expanse of paving to create large and small, open and shady areas, has delightful results. The difficulties of maintaining small areas of irregular lawn, and the unsatisfactory appearance of the areas when maintained, mean that lawns are incompatible with such schemes, but this prompts a series of questions which, in a book designed for keen gardeners, may seem revolutionary.

DO YOU *NEED* A LAWN?

What does your lawn *do* for your garden? Grass is an inexpensive cover for large open areas, provides an easily maintained uniform green sweep which can be an excellent foil for other plants. It can be walked on, rather like paving, but is soft and cool to the touch like other plants. Grass has many advantages.

Lawns, however, require constant mowing, edging, and other care. If walked on excessively they wear out, create muddy tracks and look bedraggled. Lawn grasses are difficult to maintain in the shade of trees or buildings, or on heavy soils. The smaller the lawn the more care it requires to stand up to closer inspection, and the slight yellowing and unevenness of growth of even a well-kept lawn, although scarcely noticed as such by the casual observer, detracts substantially from the appearance of a small garden in winter and in a dry summer. Grass remains cool and damp, not always an advantage in temperate climates, and the sun-trapping season is much longer in a paved garden especially if light shade from a tree offers the choice of sun or shade in midsummer.

In a large garden a lawn is almost inevitable if only for economy; in a small garden its value is questionable, and in tiny gardens mown grass is usually unsatisfactory.

What can replace grass? For walking, sitting, and playing, the only substitute for grass is paving: no other plants will tolerate constant traffic. Paving, however, includes a vast range of materials from stone to variously-coloured or textured concrete mixes, asphalt, wood, foam rubber, or even plastic grass. All paving materials are more expensive than grass but are largely maintenance free, and an infinite number of patterns and finishes of materials can be devised. The other substitute for grass, where traffic is not expected, is low planting, either a uniform cover of ivy, periwinkle, deadnettle, etc., or a rich tapestry of low carpeting plants such as helianthemum, thyme, acaena, and tufty grasses.

If a lawn is required it should be of a simple shape. The shape of a lawn is much more important than the shape of plant beds or borders, which are only seen from one side at a time. If possible the lawn and beds should be separated with paving materials, brick, concrete, or stone. This edging creates an enormous difference in the garden. Instead of border plants being trimmed back to avoid encroaching on the lawn, thus creating a narrow ragged 'no-man's-land' ideal for weed invasion, the plants can flow forward to soften the edging, and the border looks broader and more generous. By adding both to the border and to the neat finish of the lawn even a narrow edging, perhaps 2 or 3 rows of bricks, make the garden appear more spacious.

DO YOU *NEED* A ROCKERY?

Most notes on garden design, written by gardeners, end with a list of features to incorporate including, inevitably, the rockery. This set of notes is different in trying to persuade you to abandon features often taken for granted but which are sometimes inappropriate in small gardens – even to the extent of abandoning a lawn in some cases. Rockeries are seldom appropriate. Somehow a miniature Matterhorn in a small suburban or town garden looks silly, and degrades both the garden and the idea of a rock garden. If the garden is larger, and is not hemmed in by houses, and especially if it incorporates changes of level, then a rock garden can be an interesting, if expensive, feature. In less favourable surroundings a dry wall might be appropriate, but in most small gardens rockwork of any type is simply out of place.

This is not to say that the owner of a small garden need be deprived of an opportunity of growing many very beautiful alpine and rock plants. Some of the more robust, such as *Phlox subulata*, helianthemum, aubrietia, most of the dwarf campanulas, and even *Gentiana acaulis*, make excellent edging plants for small borders. For more demanding plants special areas can be set aside either on a terrace or in raised rectangular beds, perhaps with a small rock or two to break the surface. In Savill Gardens, Windsor, a series of raised rectangular beds, surrounded by low dry walls, houses a great variety of excellent plants, and looks far more pleasing than a rock garden in the usual sense of the word. In smaller gardens brick-edged beds, large sinks, or other rectangular containers, would be even more suitable.

Two contrasting styles – (above) a formal design is softened by the graceful lines of birch trees; (below) an informal design can suit either town or country.

DO YOU *NEED* A GREENHOUSE?

Most keen gardeners would reply 'yes'. The greenhouse offers an excuse to work in the garden in winter, and extends the range of plants which can be grown, including resuscitation of house plants and the cultivation of tomatoes, cucumbers, and other profitable plants. If a greenhouse is required there is no reason to hide it from view. Most greenhouses are attractive structures, the contents, also on full view, are equally attractive, and the greenhouse provides useful height in the garden. Use it to terminate a small terrace extending from the house. Grow more tender plants in borders around the greenhouse where they can benefit from the additional warmth and shelter. If greenhouses (and sheds, garages, and other small buildings) offend the eye, it is because of their hard outlines, not because of their appearance as such. The best way to integrate them with the garden is to soften the outline by planting trees or shrubs beyond the greenhouse, rather than attempting to conceal it with equally hard-outlined fences or trellis.

WHAT ABOUT TREES?

Contrary to popular opinion, *a* tree does not completely fill a garden and envelop it in dense shade. A small tree takes less room on the ground than a large flower pot, its shade moves across the garden so that part of it will still be in sun, and trees add immensely to the character of a garden. The pattern of trunk and branches, the leaves, flowers, and often fruit, add interest; the dappled shade intensifies the colours of plants growing beneath, and the height, partial screening of surroundings and overhead canopy, emphasise the comfortable seclusion of any garden. All of this can be gained with no loss of room in the garden as other plants can be grown beneath the branches.

Of course there are suitable and unsuitable trees. Horse chestnut, sycamore, and plane, grow very large and cast too dense a shade; willows and poplars are notorious for blocking drains and shedding branches in middle age; Japanese cherries, although very popular, are stiff in habit for many years and also cast deep shade. There are many other small trees such as mountain

Another effective asymmetrical layout. Care must be taken to preserve ease of mowing in such irregular designs.

Juniperus chinensis aurea is the sort of decorative, long-lasting subject that makes a good focal point in some part of a garden layout.

ash, laburnum, the small maples, and of course apple, pear, or plum, which are ideal.

WHAT NEXT?
Having thought about the type of garden you want, what you want to grow, and what you find pleasant or unsatisfactory about other people's gardens, design can begin in earnest.

Some design must be made on paper and some inevitably on the ground. With gardens of straight lines, and especially with brickwork and paving patterns, it is important to work out the complete design on paper to ensure that joints line up properly, and that the paths, planters, pools, terraces, and other features align with doors, gables, or other parts of the house. Drawing in each paving slab may seem tedious, but it can save much effort in cutting or manoeuvring heavy materials on the site. The general grouping of plants for seasonal effect can also be done – as a first approximation – on paper, but there are always refinements to be made. If the design is to be informal and especially if the garden is undulating then most of the design will be done on the ground. A quick plan and a few notes on the general disposition of the parts of the garden form a valuable beginning, but pegs and string, viewing the outlines from all directions, and making adjustments to shapes, are easier and more satisfactory alternatives to pencil and paper after the preliminary scheme. This is even more true when the garden is being revised and many existing plants retained.

OPEN SPACE FIRST
To a very large degree the open space *is* the garden, so paths, patios, lawns, and low planting, should be marked out first, to fit neatly together and provide as much or as little open space as is required. Obviously in an existing garden, with fences, sheds, shrubs, and other large items already present, the open space will to some extent be shaped by their position, but the open space is most important, and it is sometimes necessary to remove large plants or even to re-site garden buildings for the sake of the overall effect.

Having designated open areas, some screening is usually necessary for shelter, to conceal unsightly views within or beyond the garden, and for privacy. Screening can be achieved by fences and walls (which are expensive but take up very little room), or by tall plants, or by suitable siting of sheds, garages, and other necessary garden structures. Further high planting may be required to balance the scheme, to unite the house with the garden (usually by linking walls and buildings with trellis, hedges, or overhead beams), and to provide a suitable degree of visual enclosure. Any part of the garden not used in one of these various ways is planted to emphasise or to soften the transition between the horizontal lines of open space and vertical lines of the enclosure.

AVOID SEGMENTED THINKING
Throughout the designing of your garden, ideas should develop from the general to the particular. That is why the emphasis thus far has been on paving, planting, and screens, rather than on paths, patios, herbaceous borders, and rose gardens. We tend to ignore the drive, the vegetable patch, the oil tank or coal bunker, and the washing line, because we have got to have them. Instead we tend to concentrate our efforts on designing the flower beds and borders. However, especially in small gardens, the drive and so on can occupy a very large part of the garden, requiring just as much thought as the flower beds.

In small gardens the drive can often serve as a patio if it is well made. The vegetable garden must be fitted in to be attractive or inconspicuous, and the area around the dustbin, the fuel store, or other utility corner, should not be allowed to become an unsightly rubbish tip.

If you begin, then, by deciding where

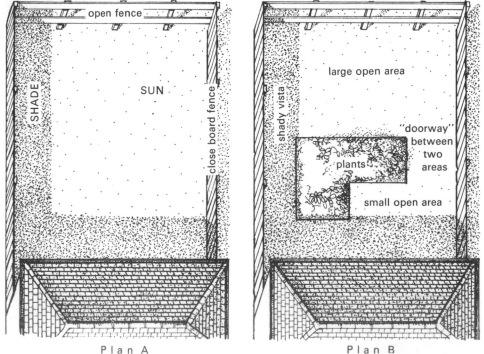

Plan A   Plan B

Variety of space is easily achieved in a small garden and is more permanently satisfying than variety of plants.

Another element in garden design is the border laid out to produce a special effect – in this case it is a 'white' border.

Yet another possible design element is the heather garden, which can be made to yield colour almost all the year round.

open space is required – to walk to the front door, to drive into the garage, to sit in the sun, and for any other reason – you can design a pleasant paved area which incorporates all these requirements, rather than building six little bits of paving, probably in six different materials. The lawn, low planting, high planting, and other screens, can all be planned in the same way, and their shapes adjusted to fit one with another. As a result the garden plan emerges as a unified composition instead of a jumble of bits and pieces.

VARIETY CAN EASILY BE LOST

Variety is important in a garden to maintain interest, but variety is very easily lost. Most garden books suggest that you can achieve variety by using many different plants but this is quite wrong. To draw an analogy, if you see four or five people in a family photograph it is easy to pick out each person: the young and old, men and women are distinct, and the variety is easily noticed. In a wedding photograph or a school photograph, with dozens or hundreds of people, the individuality of each is submerged in a sea of faces, and you have to look very hard to appreciate any differences. It is exactly the same in the garden. It is very difficult to create variety with lots of different plants. Unless you are particularly keen to collect lots of different plants, more variety can be achieved by using simple planting schemes, in which the character of each of the few species used can be appreciated.

In either case, whether you choose a simple composition or a uniform muddle of plants, much more variety can be achieved by concentrating on variety of space, rather than variety of plants. Imagine, for example, a small rectangular garden with a house on one side and walls on two other sides (see plan A). Already there is variety in the pattern of sun and shade. Add an 'L'-shaped plant group and the garden consists of a small open space, a large open space, a long narrow space, and a short narrow space (see plan B).

Both may be in sun and shade during the day and each surrounded by walls or plant-

ing, partially, completely, or scarcely concealed from other parts of the garden, self-contained, or with views beyond the garden. All these variations are not immediately noticed by gardeners accustomed to looking for lots of different plant labels for interest, but the variety is there; it is permanent and it is pleasing, even if subconsciously. The garden looks good although the observer is often not aware of *why* it looks good.

Furthermore the interest is due as much to the *shape* as to the *materials*. The various rectangles on the plan could be sheds, greenhouses, raised alpine beds, rose gardens, or shrub borders. The flat areas could be of paving, grass, or water, so the variations on even a simple theme are innumerable, and the garden can be tailored to suit *your* requirements exactly.

PLANTS MATTER TOO!

From all that has been said above about spaces and variety, shape and proportion, it might appear that plants are unimportant, but this, of course, is not so. In many modern sculpture exhibitions and in creative playground equipment, these ideas may be expressed in wood or metal or plastic, and the results are interesting, amusing, attractive – but they are not gardens. Gardens need plants for greenness, softness, colour, fragrance, texture, and seasonal interest.

Foliage is especially important in small gardens, because it is so much more lasting than flowers. It ranges from the very pale green of *Epimedium* and *Rodgersia tabularis* through the bright green of *Podophyllum* and *Polemonium* to the dark green of *Viburnum davidii* and *Taxus*, extending to purple, gold, silver, striped and spotted, hairy and smooth, large and small. Gardens of good foliage plants can be delightful, even without a flower to be seen, and for a very large part of the year.

Evergreen plants are important to furnish the garden in winter, but plenty of room should be left for the early spring bulbs – the snowdrops, aconites, crocus, and scillas. Heathers, hebes, and low-growing conifers, are especially useful for their variety of evergreen foliage and form, with yucca,

bergenia, *Phormium tenax* and fatsia providing more striking foliage. Rhododendrons, too, are invaluable if the soil is suitably acid.

As the spring bulbs fade their place can be taken by herbaceous plants, growing up to conceal the dying leaves of the bulbs. Some of the later-flowering narcissus and tulip can be interplanted with summer annuals or tender perennials to extend the season of interest. Most of the brighter herbaceous perennials have a short flowering period of 2 or 3 weeks, so one's choice should be directed at providing a series of plants which flower at different periods.

Shrubs are more permanently satisfying, because their form continues to furnish the garden throughout the year. If, in selecting shrubs, you bear in mind not only those with attractive flowers but with good autumn colour or winter stems, then each plant will fully earn its place in the garden.

The range of plants from which to choose is enormous, and there is little to be gained by attempting to deal with it here as other parts of this book have been written with this topic in mind.

WHAT WAS ALL THAT ABOUT?

Your garden is unique. It should suit your family's way of life and fit in with its surroundings. Because the range of materials, and especially of plants, is so vast, actually making a choice can be exceedingly difficult. If, however, you first sort out in your mind – and on paper – the more general points about how the garden is to be used, it will slowly take shape and the more detailed considerations become progressively easier to deal with.

Do not forget to deal with every part of the garden – there is no reason why the dustbin should not have an attractive setting! Never be afraid to adopt, or adapt, other people's ideas so long as they are appropriate in your garden. No garden was created in an instant, and no perfect garden stayed perfect for very long. By observing, adapting, and caring, your garden will soon grow to suit you. It should be a joy to maintain and a joy to use. If it is not then it is badly designed – so carry on trying!

A COMPOST GARDEN

W.E.Shewell-Cooper

Readers may not fully appreciate what a true compost garden is like. So at the outset, I had better explain that a compost garden is one in which no digging is done, no forking is done, a minimum of raking is done, and no chemical fertilisers or poisonous sprays are used. A compost garden is in fact nature's garden – it is a peaceful garden, an anti-pollution garden and a garden from which health is provided free for its owner.

In case there are readers who would claim that I am a fanatic, I would say that I have been practising what I preach for 25 years, and in my present 8-acre garden at Arkley Manor, I have been able to grow beautiful flowers, delicious vegetables and first-class fruits, without cultivations and with the use of compost alone.

Now for the plans and methods.

THE COMPOST BINS
Of course you cannot make a compost garden without compost, and so the start must always be with the wooden bins necessary to produce the dark brown powder which is going to be applied as a top dressing for the worms to pull into the soil. When they pull it in the living creatures will soon convert it into humus – and humus is the 'blood' of the soil. A soil with no 'blood' is a dead soil – and many soils have been eroded in the last fifty years because all the humus has been used up.

Even for the small garden the minimum requirement is two wooden 3-sided bins, 4 ft. square. When made, the planks must have a 2-in. space between them, in order that the bacteria that are going to do the work may breathe. The wood should be treated with Rentokil preserving fluid to make it last – my boards have lasted 14 years and are still fine. The bin must have an earth base so that the worms, which do the job, can work their way up into the heap, and

then go down again when the temperature of the heap rises to 180°F.

The compost gardener has two mottoes:

1) everything that has lived can live again in another plant;

2) only a plant really knows all that another plant needs.

So once the bin is made, everything that has lived must go in – lawn mowings, weeds, leaves, coffee grounds, banana peel, an old cotton shirt, newspapers, hair, egg shells – in fact if 'it' has lived, then it goes in. When the organic material has reached a thickness of 6 ins., then an organic activator is applied at no more than 3 oz. per sq. yd. The best activators are fish manure, seaweed manure, dried poultry manure, and dried farmyard manure. It is *never* advisable to use chemical fertilisers or advertised chemical activators. The bacteria and the worms prefer the natural activator, and give the best results when this is used.

The heap rises 6 ins. by 6 ins. (the activator is applied regularly at each 6-in. layer) until it reaches a height of 6 ft., and then it is capped with 1 in. of soil. Mind you, it is important to tread the 6-in. layers level, so that by the time the heap reaches 6 ft., it is quite flat at the top and the soil can go on absolutely level. Those who are not strong enough to throw on soil to this height may use an old blanket or carpet instead, to cover the heap.

Now leave the heap for 6 months if it is summer, or 8 months if the heap is started in the early winter. If the weather is particularly dry in the summer it may be necessary to water the heap, to make sure the bacteria have the 'drink' they need. In the normal British summer this, however, is seldom necessary. Do not be afraid of putting on to the heap diseased material or pernicious weeds because the heat engen-

dered in the compost heap will kill the weed seeds, the diseases, and the pests.

The brown powder that will be produced will not only contain all the macro-nutrients like nitrogen, phosphates, and potash, but also all the micro-nutrients needed by the plants. In addition of course, it contains the necessary vitamins, the enzymes and antibiotics.

The Alternative
Until the garden owner has made sufficient compost for his garden he must rely on the ideal substitute, i.e. sedge peat. It must be sedge peat and NOT sphagnum peat or moss peat. Sedge peat has been produced by nature from the sedges and works with the natural activator of animal and bird manure. It is of the same texture and colour as true compost, and can do excellent work in the garden.

Inspecting compost at Arkley Manor to ascertain its state of readiness

The raw compost, placed in layers in the bin, is non-homogenous and retains something of its original colour.

The finished compost, in contrast, is a dark, rich colour, fairly even in texture, and should be quite odourless.

Sedge peat always gives better results than sphagnum peat. It contains nearly five times the quantity of available humus – it has 70% more additional humus – the protein content is high, whereas in sphagnum peat it is low. The pH of sedge peat is 5 where in the case of sphagnum peat it is only 4. One hundredweight of medium-grade sedge peat will cover a bed of 11 sq. yds. to about 1 in. deep.

WEEDS

Perennial Weeds

If the garden is pestered with perennial weeds they must be got rid of, either with a strong hormone or with dry powdered sodium chlorate. The idea is to apply the 'killers' to the leaves of the plants and NOT to the soil. If the I.C.I. powdered sodium chlorate is bought, it has in it a depressant so that there is no fear of any fire hazard.

With most weeds, nettles, thistles, docks, and ground elder, for instance, the plan is to dust the leaves with the powdered sodium chlorate – preferably early in the morning. The sodium chlorate is taken in by the leaves and is passed down to the roots to kill them.

In the case of bindweed, it is better to paint the tips of the climbing growths and the upper leaves with Verdone. With stronger more persistent weeds like polygonum, SBK may be used either painted on or sprayed on.

Annual Weeds

Every time a gardener hoes he brings annual weed seeds up to the surface where they germinate and grow. But the compost gardener does not hoe, he puts the compost on top of the ground 1 in. deep as a top dressing or mulch. It doesn't matter at what time of the year this is done. If the worms pull in a $\frac{1}{4}$-in. layer, then a top dressing is given to make up the loss. If, on the other hand, the humus content of the soil is high then the compost mulch may not have to be replaced or top dressed for 8 or 9 years. There are rose beds at Arkley that have not been hoed for 10 years, and the layer of brown compost all over the soil makes the surface look very attractive. The layer of powdery compost on top of the ground prevents annual weeds from growing – thus hoeing is not necessary.

THE FLOWER GARDEN

The compost gardener is a minimum work gardener, so in the flower garden he concentrates on roses, flowering shrubs, and dwarf herbaceous plants, which are sturdy and so do not need any staking or supporting.

It is important not to attempt to dig in or fork in the compost. The living creatures that provide the plant food naturally, like to live in the top 4 ins. of soil, so this should never be buried. The rose bushes should be planted in the normal way, firmly, and when the bed has been made level afterwards, the compost is applied as a top dressing. This will provide all the plant foods needed and will ensure that moisture is not drawn out of the soil by the action of the sun and wind. Further, the mulch prevents the spores of the black spot disease from blowing up on to the leaves. In addition it is seldom that mildew troubles the leaves, as the mulch prevents the leaves from suffering from dryness and this always discourages the mildew spores from entering and attacking.

In the case of the flowering shrub border, once again there is no digging or forking. Holes are made for the roots of the specimens. The planting must be done firmly as in the case of the roses, and again after

Erica ciliaris 'Globosa'

Erica vulgaris 'Purple Beauty'

levelling and firming, the compost is applied – or where there isn't enough compost, sedge peat is used. The shrubs grow extraordinarily quickly, and healthily, for the roots can come right up to the surface because no hoeing is done. This factor is very important.

In the case of the herbaceous border, the same rules hold good – the planting is done as in the case of the usual chemically-fed borders, except that more room and space is given to the plants as they grow larger more quickly. Further, a well-planned compost herbaceous border can stay put, so to speak, for 8 years or more. No digging up of the border and replanting it every 3 years as has invariably to be done in the case of the 'chemically-fed – hoeing-and-forking' garden. Once again, this can be proved, because readers can come to Arkley Manor and see borders that have been down for this period and beautiful borders too, with plants flowering from the spring until late autumn.

Other beds could be planted with various varieties of *Hemerocallis* or with different types of scented plants. A smother border is so called because it is planted up completely with smother plants like rose of sharon, periwinkles, the creeping ivy, the prostrate juniper, or Spanish brooms. Such a border needs to have nothing done to it year after year, and yet it looks quite attractive all the year round. The periwinkle bears its blue flowers and the rose of sharon and Spanish gorse, golden flowers.

THE HEATHER GARDEN

One of the types of gardens which fits in perfectly with compost growing is the heather garden. The hardy types prosper in an open situation, while if the soil is sandy, the Mediterranean region types should be grown, as they are more tolerant of drought than the other varieties. Heathers need little or no attention other than a clipping-over of the plants immediately after flowering. Those who have naturally limey soils should grow the varieties of *Erica carnea*.

Part of the author's heather garden, planted on undug land and mulched with compost. Heathers respond well to the rich humus content and moisture-holding properties of good compost.

The heathers may be planted in sloping banks or in beds. They should be planted 1–2 ft. apart according to the variety, because the plants spread quickly. Put in a group of, say, three plants to a variety, and see to it that there are species and varieties which flower during different months of the year. By careful planning, it is possible to have some part of the bed in flower every single month of the year. Buy little plants in pots and set the roots firmly but not deeply in the soil. Then cover the whole bed with powdery brown compost 1 in. deep, or use sedge peat instead. Planting can be done any time between October and March.

Species and varieties we have grown with great success at Arkley Manor compost-wise include:

SUITABLE ROSES FOR THE COMPOST GARDEN

Bush Hybrid Tea

Amazing Grace. A gorgeous deep silvery pink; sturdy but elegant and graceful – lasts well when cut.
Bettina. A rich old gold, distinctly veined with a deep orange hue. Free flowering and fragrant and vigorously healthy.
Blue Moon. Huge ice-blue blooms with delightful lemon perfume.
Crock O' Gold. Golden yellow – each bloom produced has the perfect classic formation of the old-fashioned high-centred rose.
Fragrant Cloud. Magnificent large coral red blooms produced freely. Foliage resistant to all rose diseases. Exquisitely fragrant.

Floribunda 'Elizabeth of Glamis'

Grandmere Jenny. More fully-coloured successor to the golden pink-tipped 'Peace'. Fragrance outstanding.
Madame L. Laperriere. Deep, rich crimson blooms, sweetly scented. Vigorous growth with healthy amber green foliage. Disease resistant.
Mischief. Coral salmon rose which blooms to perfection. Growth is excellent and the blooms last very well in rain or sun.
My Love. A superbly fragrant, dark red rose – the petals glow and remain unmarked by rain or sun. Vigorous.
Peace. Golden yellow, daintily edged with vivid pink. Large blooms show delicate shades of yellow, pure gold, cream and ivory. Erect petals have slightly ruffled edges.
Shot Silk. Bright warm colour between cherry pink and orange, flushed rose with yellow base. Fragrant. Shiny green foliage.
Super Star. Superb vermilion blooms, an entirely new shade. Sweet fragrance.
Uncle Walter. A rich red rose – excellent shape. Heavily veined foliage and stem hold erect each perfect bloom.
Wendy Cussons. Pure rose red, fragrant petals. Flowers are high-centred and perfectly shaped. Growth good and bushy.
Whisky Mac. Deep harvest gold, bronzed in bud and opening to a lovely rose. Glorious scent.

Floribunda Roses

Dearest. Soft salmon rose blooms perfect in form and produced in abundance. A fragrant variety.
Elizabeth of Glamis. Deep salmon flowers of perfect shape and wonderfully strong fragrance.
Golden Slippers. A golden floribunda with dainty miniature perfectly-formed hybrid tea type blooms. Bi-coloured blend of orange and golden yellow. Perfect for indoors.
Highland Fling. Vivid scarlet. Buds perfect in shape and petals deeply veined. Intriguingly fragrant. A gay variety.
Me Darling. Peach, pink and silver perfectly suffused to give a warm glow. Delicately perfumed.
Nan Anderson. Clean clear pink with a coral sheen. Low bushy growth. Disease resistant with shiny, dark green foliage.
Picasso. Crimson colour with a white banding and marking on the petals which varies throughout the season. Flowers semi-double.
Woburn Abbey. Vivid tangerine buds open-

Name	Description	Height	Flowering Months
Erica carnea			
Springwood Pink	Free flowering	6 ins	Feb–Apr
Springwood White	Masses of large white flowers	6 ins	Feb–Apr
Erica ciliaris	Large purplish-red bells	2 ft	July–Sept
globosa	Large pink flowers with greyish-green foliage	18 ins	July–Oct
Mrs C. H. Gill	Very free blooming, clear red	1 ft	July–Sept
Erica cinerea			
Ann Berry	Produces yellow foliage in abundance	1 ft	July–Oct
Apple Blossom	The white flowers have an edging of pale pink	1 ft	June–Oct
atro-sanguinea	Dark crimson and very dwarf	6 ins	July–Oct
Golden Drop	Its golden foliage turns to red in winter	4 ins	June–Oct
Hookstone White	Large white flowers covering the whole plant	9 ins	June–Oct
Pink Ice	A very pretty soft pink	8 ins	June–Sept
Purple Beauty	Bright purple, very attractive and new	1 ft	June–Oct
rosea Knaphill variety	Deep rose-pink flowers – produces freely	6 ins	June–Oct
Erica hybrida			
Cherry Stevens	Dark pink flowers – good in spring	1 ft	Dec–Apr
Gwavas	Yellow-tipped young shoots in the spring, flowers pink	1 ft	June–Oct
Watsonii	Large pink flowers on a good dwarf	6 ins	July–Oct
Erica mediterranea hibernica			
Brightness	Red flowers – a dwarf. The buds are bronzy	2 ft	Mar–Apr
rubra	A long red flowering type	6 ins	Jan–Apr
Erica tetralix			
Con Underwood	A very rich, deep crimson	9 ins	June–Sept
Ken Underwood	Large cerise blooms	1 ft	June–Sept
Mackiana	A bright pink – semi-prostrate	6 ins	July–Sept
Erica vagans			
George Underwood	Strong compact plants with long spikes of pink flowers	2 ft	July–Oct
Hookstone Rosea	A clear shade of rose-pink	18 ins	July–Oct
Erica vulgaris			
August Beauty	Free flowering – a beautiful white	1 ft	Aug–Sept
aurea	Foliage deep gold changing in winter to red	1 ft	Aug–Oct
coccinea	Deep crimson flowers, pale grey foliage	9 ins	July–Sept
Goldsworth Crimson	Throughout this plant odd orangey-yellow growths show	2 ft	Sept-Oct
Mrs Ronald Gray	Purple flowers on a prostrate heath	3 ins	Aug–Sept
Orange Queen	Yellow and orange foliage in summer turns to bronze in winter. Flowers purple	18 ins	Sept–Oct
Silver Queen	Mauve flowers on 'woolly' silver leaves	18 ins	Aug–Sept

ing to a warm soft golden yellow. Blooms very fragrant and long lasting.
Zambra. Glowing orange with pure yellow reverse. A most striking floribunda.

Grandiflora Roses
Diamant. Brilliant orange scarlet – a solid lasting colour. Perfect blooms carried in clusters, large and full. Vigorous and healthy.
Scarlet Queen Elizabeth. Brilliant orange scarlet. Perfect blooms. Vigorous and healthy.
Yellow Queen Elizabeth. An excellent yellow, borne in clusters.

Shrub Roses
Blanche de Coubert (a Rugosa). Beautiful, double snow-white flowers – June to autumn.
Blanche Moreau (a Moss rose). Pure white, well mossed, beautiful, healthy variety.
Cornelia (a Musk rose). An apricot-flushed pink rose.
Fabvier (a China rose). Dazzling crimson with a few white lines on petals. Vigorous, free flowering.
Lady Penzance (a Penzance Briar). Beautiful soft tint of copper.
Red Provence. Deep rose; large open flower.
Rosa alba (White Rose of York). White, single or semi-double with lovely stamens.
Rosa centifolia (Cabbage Rose). Fragrant – bears double rose pink blooms. Grows to 6 ft.
Rosa foetida (Austrian Briar). Yellow-scented flowers. Various colours, i.e. coppery red, yellow, cherry red shaded to golden centre.
Rosa pomifera (the Apple Rose). Carmine in bud – clear pink when full.

FLOWERING SHRUBS
The following is a list of flowering shrubs that have done particularly well under compost mulching conditions at Arkley Manor.

Name	English Name	Colour of Flowers	Flowering Month	Normal Height	Normal Spread	Evergreen or Deciduous
Berberis darwinii	Barberry	Orange	Apr	7 ft	7 ft	Evergreen
Camellia williamsii	Camellia	Pink	Mar	8 ft	8 ft	Evergreen
Ceanothus dentatus	Californian Lilac	Bright blue	May	10 ft	10 ft	Evergreen
Choisya ternata	Mexican orange	White	May	7 ft	6 ft	Evergreen
Deutzia elegantissima	Deutzia	Pink	May	4½ ft	6 ft	Deciduous
Forsythia Lynwood	Golden bells	Yellow	Mar	7 ft	7 ft	Deciduous
Kerria japonica	Batchelor's buttons	Yellow	May	8 ft	6 ft	Deciduous
Magnolia stellata	Star magnolia	White	Mar	7 ft	7 ft	Deciduous
Mahonia japonica	Berberis	Primrose	Jan	6 ft	7 ft	Evergreen
Pieris floribunda	Lily of the valley shrub	White	Mar	5 ft	6 ft	Evergreen
Ribes Scarlet	Flowering currant	Scarlet	Apr	8 ft	5 ft	Deciduous
Rosmarinus officinalis	Rosemary	Lavender	Apr	5 ft	5 ft	Evergreen
Viburnum bodnantense	Viburnum	Deep rose	Feb	10 ft	8 ft	Deciduous
Weigela rosea	Weigela	Pink to ruby	May	6 ft	6 ft	Deciduous

SUITABLE PERENNIALS FOR THE COMPOST MINIMUM WORK BORDER

Name	Description	Height
Acanthus longifolius	Free flowering and compact.	2½ ft
Achillea Coronation Gold	London succession of yellow plate heads.	3 ft
A. Moonshine	Silvery leaves, clear yellow heads.	18 ins
Aconitum bicolor	Open branching spikes, blue and white flowers.	3½ ft
Actaea spicata rubra	Small white flowers, red berries.	2 ft
Adonis Fukujukai	Ferny foliage – single golden yellow flowers.	9 ins
Ajuga pyramidalis	Striking plant with dense spikes of brilliant gentian blue.	9 ins
Alchemilla mollis	Attractive foliage, masses of tiny sulphur yellow flowers on loose sprays.	18 ins
Amsonia salicifolia	Small periwinkle blue flowers. Arching stems.	2 ft
Anchusa angustissima	Intensely blue, flowers for months.	12 ins
Anemone japonica Bressingham Glow	Semi-double, warm rose-red. Neat growing.	2 ft
Anthemis Mrs E. C. Buxton	Soft primrose yellow.	2½ ft
Aquilegia Biedermeier	Densely clustered heads in variable shades.	15 ins
Armeria Bee's Ruby	Heads little globes of glistening pink.	15 ins
A. caespitosa	Tiny tufts and pink heads.	3 ins
Aster acris	Clouds of small mauve blue flowers.	2½ ft
A. novae angliae Elma Potschke	Large flowers of glowing salmon pink.	3½ ft

Choisya ternata

Magnolia stellata

Continued on pages 50/51

Achillea 'Moonshine'

Dicentra spectabilis

Kniphofia, mixed

Solidago × hybrid 'Crown of Rays'

Name	Description	Height
Astilbe	Beautiful plants, at their best in rich moist soil.	
Bressingham Beauty	Spikes of rich pink, free flowering, long lasting.	2½–3 ft
Montgomery	Deep salmon red in dense spikes.	2 ft
Astrantia carniolica		
Roses	Neat growing and colourful.	2½ ft
Campanula carpatica		
Blue Moonlight	Light blue cups, upstanding.	9 ins
Campanula glomerata		
Joan Elliott	Violet bells, early flowering, good cutting.	15 ins
Centaurea cynaroides	Handsome deep pink tufts on strong stems.	3 ft
Centaurea dealbata		
John Coutts	Fine clear pink cornflowers, robust.	2 ft
Centranthus ruber		
coccineus	Deep colour form of valerian.	2½ ft
Chelone obliqua	Striking reddish pink flowers, dark foliage.	2 ft
Coreopsis lanceolata	Long lived and free flowering.	2½ ft
Crocosmia		
Bressingham Blaze	Intense orange flame red.	2½ ft
Delphinium		
Blue Bees	Clear light blue.	3–4 ft
Pink Sensation	Rose pink.	3 ft
Dicentra eximia		
Adrian Bloom	Crimson pendants followed by pretty foliage.	12 ins
Dictamnus fraxinella	Erect spikes of lilac flowers.	2½ ft
Erigeron adria	Rich lavender blue, erect.	2½ ft
Eryngium alpinum	Large blue bracts, green leaves.	2½ ft
Gaillardia		
Mandarin	Orange flame variety.	3 ft
Galega orientalis	Robust green bushes, deep blue flowers.	3 ft
Geranium armenum		
Bressingham Flair	Softer shade with decided flush of pink.	2½ ft
Geranium pratense		
Coerulea-plena	Double light blue.	2 ft
Geum borisii		
Fire Opal	Intense orange red sprays.	2 ft
Lionel Cox	Drooping sprays of rich yellow flowers.	12 ins
Helenium		
Butterpat	Pure yellow.	3 ft
Heliopsis		
Ballerina	Warm yellow flowers.	3 ft
Hemerocallis		
Black Magic	Deep ruby mahogany, yellow cup.	3 ft
Fandango	Ruffled rich orange.	3 ft
Pink Damask	Pink variety.	2½ ft
Heuchera		
Coral Cloud	Graceful sprays of coral crimson. Free flowering.	2½ ft
Oakington Jewel	Bronzy marbled foliage. Coral red flowers.	2 ft
Hosta crispula	Broad, cream wavy-edged leaves, mauvish flowers.	3 ft
H. Honeybells	Mauve flowers, green leaves, scented.	3 ft
H. Royal Standard	Perfumed white flowers, green leaves.	3 ft
Kniphofia caulescens	Massive evergreen glaucous rosettes. Stumpy red and yellow spikes.	3 ft
K. Bressingham Flame	Deep orange spikes, graceful and free.	2½ ft
Liatris callilepis	Striking lilac purple 'Gayfeather'. Fluffy spikes.	2½ ft
Lobelia		
Blue Peter	Hardy hybrid, good size and colour. Erect spikes.	2 ft
Monarda		
Cambridge Scarlet	A favourite red bergamot.	3 ft
Prairie Night	Rich violet purple heads.	3 ft
Oenothera cinaeus		
Fireworks	Purple-green foliage. Red buds and bright yellow flowers.	18 ins
Papaver orientale		
Goliath	Crimson scarlet flowers carried erectly.	3 ft
P. Mrs Perry	Salmon pink.	3 ft
Phlomis fruticosa	Grey-leaved bushes, whorled spikes of light yellow.	2 ft

Continued on page 51

Name	Description	Height
Phygelius capensis	Tubular scarlet flowers, branching stems.	3 ft
Polygonatum commutatum	Flowers quite large, shiny foliage.	3 ft
Potentilla		
Flamenco	Showers of large single intense red flowers.	18 ins
P. recta warrenii	Bright golden yellow, bushy habit.	2½ ft
Poterium obtusum	Pink bottle brush flowers on wiry stems.	2½ ft
Ranunculus acris		
Flore-pleno	Fully double yellow buttercup.	2 ft
Rudbeckia deamii	A free flowering 'Black-Eyed Susan'.	2½ ft
Salvia ambigens	Intense deep blue flowers on erect green growth.	3½ ft
Scabiosa caucasica		
Bressingham White	Strongest growing white variety.	2½ ft
Clive Greaves	Mid-blue flowers, reliable growth.	2½ ft
Sidalcea		
Loveliness	Shell pink with a compact habit.	2½ ft
Solidago		
Crown of Rays	Yellow horizontal spikes on dense bushes.	2 ft
Golden Shower	Deep yellow arching plumes.	2½ ft
Trifolium pannonicum	Large creamy-white clover heads, neat growth.	2 ft
Trollius		
Canary Bird	Large lemon yellow flowers.	2½ ft
Verbascum		
Golden Bush	Bright yellow erect – in flower for months.	2 ft
Pink Domino	Spikes of deep rose flowers.	3½ ft
Veronica variegata	Leaves prettily marked buff.	18 ins
Veronica longifolia		
Foerster's Blue	Rich blue, strong and free.	2 ft

THE FRUIT GARDEN

Here it is easy to produce first-class soft fruits and top fruits. The apples, pears and plums do particularly well when growing in a grass sward, providing the grass is cut regularly in the summer and allowed to lie on the turf for the worms to pull in. It is the same in the autumn. The leaves that fall must not be swept up, but left for the worms to pull into the ground. Twice a year, say in March and October, a fish manure or seaweed manure may be applied at 3 oz. per sq. yd., so as to make up for the loss of food that went into the apples and pears themselves.

There are various ways of growing apples and pears in grass, i.e. as bush trees, cordons or as pillar trees. I much prefer the pillar trees, for you can plant them as close as 8 ft. by 8 ft., and train the tree upright with short side branches. Allow it to grow up to say 7 ft. and then prune the leader quite hard and aim to keep the tree at that height. Thus the trees are easy to pick and to spray. It is better to grow dessert varieties as these can also be used for cooking.

In the case of pears, stick to 2 or 3 fertile varieties such as Conference, Emile D'Heyst, and Packham's Triumph, and buy trees that are guaranteed grafted on to a dwarfing quince stock. Always plant pears shallowly but firmly, so that the trees remain growing on the quince roots – and do not grow out roots from the variety grafted on the quince stock.

First-class apple varieties to grow on the compost system are: *Red Charles Ross* – a large common delicious variety which crops regularly. *Ashmead's Kernel* – a delicious russet; very good keeper; flesh juicy and aromatic. *Late Discovery* – flushed light red; flesh juicy and sweet; described by the young as 'chewy'; pick late August. *Crispin* – a heavy cropper; pick October; good-sized yellowy apples. *Spartan* – reddish mahogany apples; white, juicy, sweet; pick October, use November to January. *St Edmund's Pippin* – delicious; light brown russet with cream juicy flesh; pick mid-September.

Idared – pick end October, keep to March and April; bright red; heavy cropper; flesh white, juicy. *Merton Prolific* – moderate grower, round apple, mainly red; resistant to scab; season November to February. *Wagener* – an apple anyone can grow; seems pest and disease proof; use as a cooker December to April, or as a dessert April to July.

In the case of plums, have trees with say a 4-ft. stem, and then the branches can be allowed to develop naturally, and the trees won't be too tall for easy picking. The best varieties to grow in grass under the compost system are: *Victoria* – a delicious variety; fruits carmine with pale blue bloom; heavy cropper. *Early Laxton* – bears oval-shaped yellow fruits; is not a strong grower, and so is suitable for a small garden; it is pollinated by Victoria. *Giant Prune* – a large red plum, really a cooker but bottles well.

Soft Fruits
Soft fruits should be grown on the straw or hay mulch system. The raspberry rows will be 5 ft. apart with canes planted 2 ft. apart in the rows. Do not dig the area over but just make holes for the canes, and then tread the soil level before covering the ground with the straw or hay 1 ft. deep. Fish or seaweed manure should be applied at 3 oz. per sq. yd. in February and it will act as an activator *in situ*, allowing the worms to pull some of the mulch in.

The best raspberry varieties to grow under the compost system are: *Norfolk Giant* – large, well-shaped fruits of good quality, producing fruit into autumn. *Malling Exploit* – heavy cropper but will require protection from wind. *Malling Jewel* – resistant to disease; firm fruit with superb flavour; withstands bad weather. *Malling Promise* – an extremely heavy cropper. *Glen Clova* – very delicious, heavy cropping; fruits of good shape and size.

Strawberries do particularly well as they are plants which live naturally on the edge of woodlands and so receive a constant application of leaves from the trees. Thus, in nature, they are mulched and not disturbed. In the garden they should therefore be planted in undug but clear land. The strawberry is a surface rooter and prefers to have no cultivation done once it is in position. Plant carefully with a trowel so that the roots are not 'bunched up'. The rows should be 2 ft., and the plants 18 ins. apart. It is best to plant in August. Always plant maidens, i.e. plants that are only a few weeks old. This is important. You can only get strong healthy plants from one year old!

Once the strawberries have been planted, cover the whole area with powdery brown compost 1 in. deep, or if there isn't enough compost, use medium-grade sedge peat instead (note the word 'sedge'). Because strawberries are so subject to virus diseases, it is tremendously important to buy strains of varieties that have been certified under the Ministry of Agriculture's scheme.

The author's raspberry canes grow 9 ft. high and crop at 9 tons to the acre, without digging, forking, or hoeing.

Strawberries on compost-fed ground. No hoeing is needed, the compost being spread as a generous mulch.

Blackcurrant bushes laden with fruit – the typical reward of the compost gardener.

Always buy gooseberry bushes on a short leg or stem so that the branches are produced well off the ground. The leg or stem should be 8 ins. in length. Plant the roots shallowly but firmly. Have the bushes 5 ft. apart each way. After planting, cover the whole of the soil with straw or hay 1 ft. deep, or use sedge peat 1 in. deep.

The land where the planting is to take place must, of course, be cleared of perennial weeds first, as described under the heading 'Perennial Weeds' on p. 47.

Gooseberries are pruned by the thinning method. One or two branches are cut out in the centre of the bush to let in light and air, and branches tending to droop on to the soil are pruned back to an upright pointing bud. The pruning is usually left until February as the birds are apt to peck out the fruiting buds, and if the branches are left thickish, then the birds cannot get in among the twigs so easily.

We feel, at Arkley, that gooseberries are very fond of potash, and we apply wood ashes each season, i.e. early February at ½ lb. per sq. yd. – this is in addition to a seaweed manure at 3 oz. per sq. yd.

Good dessert varieties of gooseberries to grow on the compost system are:

Golden Drop. Medium-sized fruit of excellent quality, flavour and colour.

Howards Lancer. Superbly flavoured with yellowish-green berries; a late fruit.

Lancashire Lad. Very large fruit; turns red when it ripens in mid-season.

Leveller. Greenish-yellow fruits, oval in shape and with an excellent flavour; mid-season.

London. An extremely large gooseberry with dark green berries.

New Giant. Large fruit which turns yellow; Leveller flavour; vigorous in growth.

Whitesmith. Mid-season fruit; large oval white berries of excellent flavour.

THE VEGETABLE GARDEN

This is the only part of the garden where very light cultivations have to be done. The best tool to use for the purpose is a drag fork. Buy an ordinary digging fork and get the local ironmonger or blacksmith to bend the long tines to form an L. The prongs are bent at the half-way mark, thus forming a rake with long tines. Next remove the short handle and insert in the metal part a long rake handle. Now you have what is called a drag fork, and this is used to rake the compost into the top 1½ ins. of soil in the spring, so that the seed can be sown.

It is at this time that the fish manure or seaweed manure is applied at 3 oz. per sq. yd. Where peas and beans are to be grown, wood ash can be given in addition at 6 oz. per sq. yd. After raking the area over where seed sowing is to be done make a V-shaped drill with a corner of the draw hoe.

The depth of the V-shaped drill will depend on the size of the seed, but in compost growing it is never necessary to sow as deeply as when soil is dug and chemical

The best varieties to grow are: *Crusader* – an outstanding early, superb flavour, and clear red colour. *Templar* – a late variety of vigorous growth; well-shaped rich red fruit; heavy cropper. *Red Gauntlet* – mid-season; large fruit, scarlet; excellent under cloches. *Cambridge Favourite* (*Elite Clone*) – excellent flavour and appearance; rich red colour.

Blackcurrants produce outstandingly large fruits on the no-digging mulching system. At the Arkley Demonstration Gardens this fact is outstanding, and causes great interest each year. Bushes under this system may last for 30 years. The planting should be done in November with the rows 5 ft. apart and the bushes 4 ft. apart in the rows. Firmly plant 2-year-old bushes, which carry 4 shoots apiece, shallowly, on undug land, and cover the whole area with straw or hay 1 ft. deep. Free the land of perennial weeds before planting takes place.

After planting, the branches must be cut back to within 2 ins. of the base. In subsequent years, the pruning each winter is merely to cut out 2 or 3 of the older branches. Fish manure should be applied each February at 3 oz. per sq. yd. Under this system no hoeing is necessary. This is indeed minimum work gardening.

Good varieties for growing on these compost methods are: *Boskoop Giant* – very early, large fruits, thin skins. *Blacksmith* – mid-season; large fruit on long stems, the berries are big. *Mendip Cross* – early; large berries; delicious flavour. *Wellington XXX* – mid-season; likes moist soils; heavy cropper; berries fine flavour.

Gooseberries are not the most popular soft fruits, and when growing compostwise, it is a good thing to concentrate on the large dessert kinds that are juicy and sweet, and can be eaten like plums.

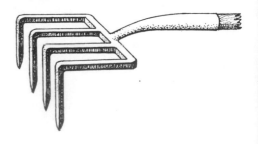

A handy drag fork is easily made.

fertilisers are added. So the small seeds go in about ½ in. deep and the bigger seeds, like peas and beans, about 2 ins. deep. After the seeds are in, the surface of the soil should be given a light raking. It is important to leave the soil level so that any rain that falls will be evenly distributed and will not end up in puddles!

It is well worthwhile buying the *best* seeds. May I recommend the following varieties of vegetables, as the result of compost-fed trials carried out at Arkley.

Broad Beans
Red Epicure. This is a quite extraordinary bean. It is long-podded with chestnut-red beans which turn straw colour after cooking. It is a vigorous grower.

Dwarf French Beans
Phoenix Claudia. A really stringless French bean. It is merely picked and cooked; delicious!
Processor. This is a stringless bean with rounded pods. Tolerates bad weather conditions. The quality and flavour are good.

Runner Beans
Streamline. This must be picked on the young side for flavour; a tender bean.

Beetroot
Boltardy. If this is sown early bolting will be prevented.
Spansbjerg Cylinder. This is a beet of a deep red colour throughout; cylindrical in shape with first-class table qualities.

Broccoli
Green Comet. A delicious, sprouting broccoli; good bud clusters; deep green heads.
Markanta. Most appetising snow-white heads; an April–May curding broccoli.

Brussels Sprouts
Aristocrat. First-class in flavour, and although medium-sized, these sprouts are very solid.

Sanda. A mid-season variety; grow and pick for the deep freeze.

Cabbage
Emerald Cross. First-class flavour, flat, solid-hearted; few useless outer leaves.
Fillgap. Practically all 'heart'; round and firm, and lasting well in winter.

Carrot
New Scarlet Intermediate. Flesh sweet and solid with hardly any core. A first-class quality carrot with uniform roots.

Cauliflower
Snow King. Solid ivory-white curded; delicious; ready for use 3 months after sowing.

Leek
Marble Pillar. Produces stems longer than any other kind. It is good to grow a large variety like this.

Lettuce
Little Gem or *Sugar Cos.* Small, crisp, tender cos, almost all 'heart', never bolts! Excellent flavour.
Wonderful. Crumpled, crisp, tender, icy-tasting leaves; solid, lovely firm hearts even in drought; lasts well.

Onion
Unwin's Reliance. Mildest flavoured of all the onions we have grown. It is a firm onion. Sow it in the autumn and thin the seedlings out to 6 ins. apart in spring. Use the thinnings as saladings.

Pea
Early Onward. Crops heavily and gives superb flavour. It is an 'early' and grows about 2 ft. tall.
Histon Kingside. A delicious and heavy main cropper! Grows 3½ ft. high.
Lord Chancellor. A robust main crop giving excellent flavour and growing to 3 ft. high.
Sugar Sweetgreen. Not only are the peas eaten but the pods as well – as with French

Runner bean 'Streamline'

beans. The flavour is good.

Potato
Craig's Royal. This is a second early, shallow-eyed, and the quality is good.
Foremost. Excellent variety for a heavy yield and good-quality potatoes. White-skinned oval tubers. Cooks extremely well. Delicious.
Home Guard. Having nice shallow eyes and being easy to peel this makes a good 'chip' potato; compost growing ensures its fine flavour.

Parsnip
Avonresister. Practically immune from parsnip canker. Uniform roots. Delicious when roasted in the same way as roast potatoes.

Tomato
Easicrop. Very fleshy; good for making into sandwiches; first-class in flavour, with firm texture.
Outdoor Girl. An early outdoor kind; heavy cropper.

Thinning
When growing carrots, beetroot, and the like, on the normal digging plus chemicals method, it is necessary to thin out the seedlings when they are 1–2 ins. high. In the compost garden, however, there is no need to thin out, providing the seeds are sown moderately thinly. All the roots tend to grow to a fair size, and thus it is easy to pull the roots when small, but big enough to eat, and to leave the others to grow bigger.

Planting Out
Members of the cabbage family (the brassicas) have their seed sown in rows 6 ins. apart, in a special narrow bed specially prepared for the purpose. Fine powdery compost is added at the rate of 2–3 bucketfuls to the sq. yd., so that the mulch of organic matter is about ½ in. deep all over the bed. This is then raked in lightly and following this, the bed is trodden down evenly. The plants from this bed, when they are 3 or 4 ins. high, can be planted out where they are to grow. The seed bed must be watered with the fine rose of a can, a day or so before planting out, if the weather is dry. It is important to plant out the seedlings when the leaves are turgid and firm.

Carrots and onions on compost-fed land. Inter-planting like this minimises the attacks of both carrot fly and onion fly.

Lettuces grow large and succulent on compost-fed land.

worry the keen amateur gardener. There are numerous predators which never do anyone or any plant any harm. I refer to ladybirds and their young, usually called niggers; the wasp-like hover flies; the 'black-kneed' capsids which love eating aphids; the beautiful lacewing flies; and, of course, the anthocorid bugs. There are also other parasites and beneficial insects which are less well known. But all of them are valuable and precious, and must not be killed.

It is undoubtedly important not to use such persistent sprays as DDT or BHC, or such systemic sprays as malathion, for these will exterminate the predators. What invariably happens when the predators have no natural food to live on is that they (a) exist by feeding on the larvae and eggs of their own species, or (b) they die of hunger – or both.

Don't believe those who say it is better to kill all creatures. It is always far better to work with nature than to fight against her.

There are, for instance, small, flattish red bugs (called the anthocorid bug), which look something like tiny capsid bugs. These bugs feed on the red spider and suck their eggs dry.

One of the most interesting parasites is the one that attacks the cabbage caterpillar (*Apanteles glomeratus*). This is the ichneumon fly, which actually lays its eggs in the young caterpillars themselves. The larvae which hatch out feed on the caterpillars and so kill them. They then form yellow cocoons; the gardener therefore, should never destroy caterpillars surrounded by such cocoons.

There are numbers of ground beetles and rove beetles which are most useful to the gardener. The devil's coach-horse beetle, for instance, devours hundreds of harmful insects in a year. It can be recognised by its funny habit of cocking its tail up into the air when disturbed.

Another mite is known as the red velvet mite. It is a bright velvety red, and is

If it is very hot and sunny at planting-out time, cover the plants with an upturned flower pot to give them shade during the day. The pots should be removed each evening so as to allow the morning and evening dews to reach the leaves. After a few days the pots may be removed altogether.

Distances
The distances of planting out will depend on the type of brassica grown. Brussels sprouts and the large kales need to be 3 ft. sq., the broccoli, cauliflowers, and savoys, should be 2 ft. sq., the cabbages may be as close as 18 ins. by 1 ft. When sowing seeds of onions, turnips, carrots, beetroot and the like, they should be in rows 18 ins. apart. Normal peas and beans should be sown in rows 2 ft. apart. Climbing runner beans are best grown at the end of the plot, and under compost mulching conditions it is usually possible to cut the plant down to soil level at the end of the season.

The Increasing Value of Compost
A gardener new to compost growing should realise that the effects of compost will be cumulative. After a few years, exciting things begin to happen. The cabbage white butterflies will not lay their eggs on the brassicas. There will be no bad attacks of black aphis on the beans. Carrot and onion fly maggots will not appear. It all sounds so wonderful and impossible, but yet it is the experience of many, and is due, it is believed, to the effect of the antibiotics in the compost plus, of course, the fact that the vegetables are far more healthy, and so are able to resist pests and diseases.

Weeds
In other parts of the garden annual weeds will not grow because the weed seeds are buried under the 1-in. layer of compost, or sedge peat, all over the soil. In the vegetable garden, however, the compost is raked in and so some annual weeds will grow, but it is surprising how these decrease year by

year as the composting scheme continues. So a little light hoeing will be necessary during the year, but it will be light and easy to carry out.

THE COMPOSTER'S ATTITUDE TO PESTS AND DISEASES
Whenever we spray or dust in order to kill an 'enemy' in the garden, we must always be thinking of the friends – creatures provided by nature to control the troubles that

Turning down the leaves of the onions in the compost vegetable garden. Note, from the author's hands, how 'clean' the composted soil is.

usually found walking about the branches of fruit trees in a rather 'stately' manner. It is also a useful insect in that it feeds on woolly aphids. Its Latin name is *Allothrombidium fuliginosum.*

Compost gardeners will be delighted to know that there is at least one slug which is a friend. Its Latin name is *Testacella.* It is pale yellow in colour. Its length when moving is about 3 ins., closing to about 1 in. It can be distinguished from the harmful species by the small flat shell on its tail end. It feeds on slugs and other ground creatures.

Centipedes are definitely beneficial and are distinguishable from millipedes because they have only one pair of legs to each body segment, compared with two pairs in each segment on millipedes. They are more rapid-moving than millipedes and have longer legs too.

Unfortunately there are many people who do not recognise predators and, furthermore, they have no idea what their eggs look like. Most people know ladybirds, but they do not recognise the little black alligator-like creatures called niggers. They are a little bit longer than the ladybirds themselves but are not as fat and wide. They are however, often covered with a few pinkish dots.

You have probably seen some wasp-like flies hovering in the air, especially in a pathway. As you walk down it the little creatures suddenly dart off to left or right. This is the hover fly. Don't kill it whatever you do. It feeds on aphids, greenflies, black flies, rose aphis, etc., and should be encouraged. It seems to love buckwheat, and multiplies if this is grown in the garden. Sow the dark brown seeds early in April, in rows 8 ins. apart, and the seeds 4 ins. apart in the rows. Have 4 rows 8 ft. long and you'll have a hover fly nursery in one corner of your garden.

Then you may notice on the leaf of a plant or tree a bright green body with golden eyes. This is the larva of the lovely lacewing fly which is one of your greatest friends. So please don't squash with your fingers any larvae, pupae or eggs just because you do not know what they are. They may well be friendly creatures, and you will be doing yourself harm.

I have known gardeners kill the little 'black-kneed' capsid bugs because they thought they were harmful capsids. The result of this killing was that they stopped the creatures from eating tens of thousands of red spider mites. Believe it or not, one of these special capsids can eat 4000 red spiders during one season!

Two safe sprays which can be made up at home are:

1 *Quassia* Put 1 oz. of quassia chips in a quart of water. Boil for 60 minutes. A yellow liquid will be formed. Decant this into a bottle and keep corked. Use the spray any time in the summer.
For greenfly, black fly, etc., 1–4 cupfuls of water.
For caterpillars 1–3 cupfuls of water.

A fine crop of 'Early Onward' peas.

Rows of carrots and autumn radishes in a compost garden.

Compost grown plants are generally almost immune from pests and diseases – but, if one has to spray, Derris or Pyrethrum should be used.

This will kill the pests but not the beneficial insects.

2 *Garlic* Buy a large garlic at the local greengrocer or delicatessen. Split up the whole thing into its 12 or 16 cloves. Now select 6 cloves and smash them up well on a wooden chopping board. Scrape off the juice and the smashed garlic cloves with a knife into a jug containing 1¼ pints of water. Add 3 large tablespoons of a good detergent liquid, and shake well. Cover the jug with an upturned saucer and leave for 72 hours. Then pass the liquid through a fine tea-strainer, and you will have a spray you can use for aphis on roses, black fly on broad beans, carrot fly on carrots, and so on. It can also be used to discourage pigeons.

Safe Insecticides that may be purchased ready to use:

Liquid derris and liquid pyrethrum can also be used with safety to control pests, and can usually be bought at a garden centre.

The Good Gardeners' Association supplies its members with a special Garlic Oil. This Association, known as The International Association of Organic Gardeners, welcomes membership from readers, who should write to Arkley Manor, Arkley, Herts.

LABOUR-SAVING GARDENING

Brian Walkden

There is a lot to be said for reducing time and effort spent on the garden. If we can do this, there will be more time left in which to enjoy our gardens and more time to unwind from the pressures of work. But how can we save time and effort in our gardening activities? Simply by the careful selection and use of labour-saving equipment. To a certain extent, some of the latest equipment will add expertise and give those 'green fingers' which every gardener would like to have! This is especially so when it comes to propagation equipment.

Such has been the tremendous development of garden accessories, that there is virtually mechanical aid for every 'department' of gardening. Let us take a look at some of these aids.

LAWN CARE

One of the biggest tasks is cutting the grass, and today there is a mower designed to suit every size of lawn and type of grass, whether it is coarse and long, or close and fine. The rotary mower is the best type for mowing tougher and longer grasses, whereas the cylinder mower is the one to use for that nice close cut on the better-quality grasses. The rotary mower does, in many cases, give the best of both worlds as it were, because the better types can give a good cut to the domestic lawn as well as tackling the rougher grasses.

In large areas of grass the ride-as-you-mow mower is ideal, because large areas of grass can be cut quickly and effortlessly. Some large cylinder mowers can have a seat attached – their turning circle round trees or flower beds is quite amazing. Many ride-on mowers take the form of miniature jeeps and are really fun to drive!

For considerable labour-saving, the hover or floating mower is a tremendous breakthrough in design. Light as a feather, this machine requires minimum effort to handle, and is especially useful for cutting grass banks. There are several lightweight mains electric mowers which are especially useful for the woman gardener.

Lawn edging can be quite demanding on time and effort, especially if the lawn is extensive. Push-along grass edgers with star-shaped cutting wheels make quick work of grass-edge cutting. For larger lawns there are mains electric edgers and battery operated designs, some of which are capable of cutting about 1 mile of edge on a full battery charge!

Lawn aeration can be a very tiring task, especially if the lawn is large. A push-along design with numerous 'teeth' or tines, will cover the area quickly and with minimum effort. There are special spiking attachments which can be fitted to power mowers,

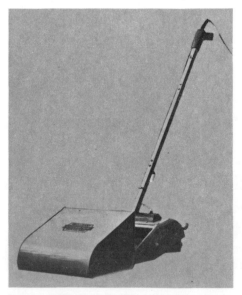

Motor mowers are basic labour-savers for everyone with more than the smallest of lawns. The sit-on kind can be good investment for really large areas.

For the smaller lawn the lightweight mains electric mower is useful particularly for the lady gardener.

Lawns need aerating and an aerator like this can save hours of back-breaking work with a fork.

The collection of fallen leaves is an easy task if a leaf sweeper is used.

A neat, electronically controlled mist propagation or watering system for the small greenhouse.

and these certainly minimise labour and effort in this important lawn management operation.

The autumn can be a problem time for the owner of a lawn, because falling leaves have to be cleared, and the work is one which has to be carried out frequently if the garden is to be kept neat and tidy. Mechanical leaf-sweepers are the answer, and their broad sweep of from about 1½–3 ft. or so, means that the work can be carried out quite quickly. Some designs are capable of removing lawn mowings, and are ideal where a rotary mower with no grass box is used. The leaf sweepers will also remove leaves from paths and drives.

A fertiliser distributor is a good investment, as this device applies lawn dressings quickly and accurately. Pushed up and down the lawn at walking pace, the distributor can be set to deliver at various rates per sq. yd.

WATERING

This can be a big time- and labour-consumer, because it is an operation which needs some diligence to maintain good growth. Watering under glass requires even more care and can become quite a problem, at holiday times!

For outdoor watering, several devices are available which can make life a lot easier. The most labour-saving design is one which can be set, or dialled, to water a certain area. This oscillating sprinkler moves its spray bar arm from full left to right; partial left to right; left only; right only; and a few degrees left and right from centre. Quite a versatile arrangement and one which is bound to suit most garden layouts.

Then there are the reciprocating-head types of sprinkler, which can be adjusted to turn full circle as they water, or to turn in a small segment for watering confined places.

One of the latest watering ideas is an underground system which has pop-up watering heads which, when in operation, stand proud of the ground and deliver water over quite a considerable area. When the water is turned off, the heads pop down just below ground.

For watering under glass there are several useful devices. Most are highly automated yet quite simple to install and set in motion. One of the latest systems is the capillary mat. This is a highly absorbent material which in one form, is capable of absorbing about a gallon of water per sq. yd. of material. Large areas of staging can be converted to this system. Automation is provided by a mains water tank with ball valve control and a water level control unit, which keeps a water trough constantly supplied with water. One end of the mat is inserted like a tongue into this trough to take up the water.

Special trays can also be used for automatic watering. These are filled with sand, which is kept moist via a feed pipe in the tray's base. Pot plants standing on the damp sand take up their own individual supplies of water, as do pot plants placed on the matting system. Several trays can easily be linked together.

Water can also be supplied via special drip nozzles attached at intervals to a water pipe. A nozzle is placed in a plant's pot, and the nozzle adjusted to apply a regulated amount of water in drip form. Plants in borders in the greenhouse, such as tomatoes, can be kept watered simply by arranging several of these drip feeds around the base of each plant.

In the raising of cuttings and many seeds, a misting technique can be adopted. This consists of one or more fine mist or spray heads fixed to the top of short stand-pipes. These pipes are placed at approximately 3-ft. intervals along the staging and above the cuttings or seed trays. A sensing device, placed near the plants, turns the water or mist on when it becomes dry and, after a short burst of water, switches the water off. The mist watering system requires the use of low-voltage mains electricity to operate the solenoid or water valve.

An oscillating type of garden sprinkler which can be set to water specific areas of garden or lawn.

An electrically heated propagator will provide high soil temperatures at very low running costs and with minimal attention from the busy gardener.

VENTILATION

In the greenhouse, this is a most important requirement, and it is possible to turn this into a labour-saving arrangement simply by attaching a non-electric ventilator opener to each greenhouse ventilation. When the internal temperature of the greenhouse rises above a certain figure (usually 65°F), then the opener begins to function.

Another method of keeping a good circulation of air, and reducing high temperatures, is by means of electric fan extractors, which can be set to cut in at a pre-fixed figure or temperature.

The frequency of watering under glass can be reduced if greenhouse blinds are fixed inside the greenhouse. There are green plastic spring-loaded types as well as a metal louvred type. Ideally, greenhouse blinds should be fixed on the *outside* of the greenhouse with a small space between the roof section and the blinds. This provides a much cooler atmosphere, and these blinds can be raised or lowered easily by means of pulleys and cord.

HEATING

A great deal of labour is saved where greenhouse heating is concerned, because automatic systems are available to the gardener. Electric heaters can be controlled by sensitive rod-type thermostats or built-in thermostats. These can be set to the desired temperature, and will switch the heater on and off to maintain a temperature very close to the set one. Natural gas heating is available, also propane or bottle gas, with thermostatic control. Electric propagators are labour-savers too, because they have automatic heating control which can look after itself.

CULTIVATING THE SOIL

This can be quite a laborious business without the use of mechanical aids. There are various types and capacities of cultivators available to suit soil conditions and size of plot. Many designs have a wide range of

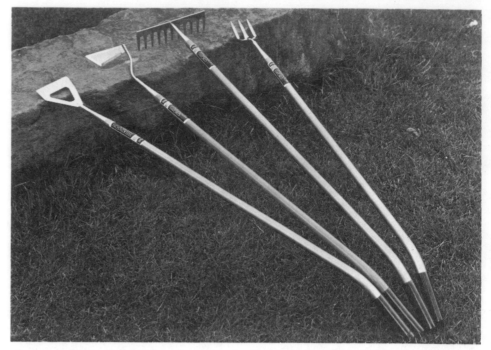

Good examples of well-designed stainless steel tools with lightweight shafts and comfortable handle grips. Stainless steel is worth the extra cost in ease of cleaning and length of life.

accessories available, which include items such as ploughs, rakes, grass-cutters, cultivating tines or 'teeth'. Soil can be prepared for sowing or planting very quickly, and with far less effort than is required for digging by hand! Engine capacities range from 2–3 h.p. to as much as 7 h.p. The more powerful types are better suited to the heavier soils, and where large areas of ground have to be cultivated. In the vegetable garden especially, the rows should be spaced to allow the free use of a cultivator between plants, as this will save a lot of time and effort.

Some hand tools are specially designed to relieve the user from a lot of hard toil. The stainless-steel finishes to working heads, such as spades, forks, and hoes, enable the blades or tines to slip through the soil more easily – especially the sticky clay soils. There is a range of tools which is designed to be pulled rather than pushed, and two-edged

hoes, angled cultivating tines, and soil-tillers, help to reduce effort.

Several hand tools will be appreciated by the elderly or infirm gardener, as they are lightweight with aluminium alloy shafts and comfortable moulded plastic grips. There are long-handled border forks, with three-pronged heads, which enable the user to reach to the back of wide borders without too much effort or stooping.

CARRYING THINGS

It is surprising just how much carrying is required around the garden – especially if a new or neglected garden is being tackled! Debris, soil, paving, cement, sand, etc. are some of the items which need some form of barrow to ease the load. A wheelbarrow can be an invaluable accessory, and several of the modern designs are so constructed that they are well balanced with most of the load or weight distributed over the wheels.

A powerful cultivator will easily cope with quite rough ground. They can be hired in most areas.

A tip-up wheelbarrow is useful, as debris can be raked or swept into its mouth.

A truck is a handy accessory, especially if a bag can be attached when required.

A mains electric hedge trimmer soon makes short work of hedge shaping or cutting. The hedge or bush has to be fairly thick and firm for the tool to operate efficiently.

The modern pressure sprayer is light, easy to clean, and very efficient.

Two-wheel designs are easy to manoeuvre, and ideal for the woman gardener. Some designs can be tipped forward so that debris can be easily brushed into the wheelbarrow. More attention is paid to tyre designs too, and the pneumatic and solid rubber tyres with wider treads ensure more comfortable use. There are one or two garden trucks available, and these are particularly useful for carrying bags of peat, fertilisers, cement bags, and paving stones. Special designs can be quickly adapted for use as a water hose reel carrier, or a refuse bag holder and transporter. The latter is very handy for taking around the garden when weeding or generally cleaning up.

SPRAYING
The fight against pests and diseases in the garden is made a lot easier by the introduction of the modern sprayers. Pre-pressurised types certainly take a lot of the effort out of routine spraying, and with a few priming pumps, a large capacity type can provide several minutes of useful, forceful spray.

Plastic tanks or bodies ensure non-corrosion, and they are much lighter than the metal types. There are capacities to suit all needs from the modest 1-pt. sprayer for indoor and greenhouse use, to the 2–3-gal. capacities for bigger requirements.

TRAINING
A lot of labour and time can be involved with the training of plants in the garden. A good training system will be a sound investment, especially where trailing and climbing plants are concerned. The use of plastic-coated wire or steel has much to commend it. It is virtually weatherproof and, unlike most timbers with the exception of cedar, does not rot, warp, or need replacing every few years.

It can be a neat and pleasant system to look at and is relatively quick to erect. There are several types available. Some consist of a square design, which is ideal for the train-ing and support of outdoor climbing plants such as wisteria, honeysuckle, roses, etc. Sections of smaller mesh material can be cut and wrapped round posts or pillars to provide adequate support for climbing plants.

Thinner material in the form of plastic mesh or net is excellent in the vegetable garden for bean supports, and in fine mesh net for the protection of vegetables and fruit against bird attacks. In fact, there are special fruit and vegetable cages available, with tubular metal framing and plastic or nylon netting for this type of labour-saving protection.

HEDGE AND TREE TRIMMING
This can be a very laborious business if there are extensive hedges in the garden. The battery and mains electric hedge trimmers will reduce work considerably and give a better finish also. Where there are long runs of hedges away from the house, a powerful battery-type trimmer will solve the problem of extensive mains electric cable needs.

In the case of trees and tall shrubs, it is often quite a difficult task pruning those out-of-reach branches! The long-arm pruners can solve a lot of these problems, especially if an extending type is used. These have lightweight alloy tubular handles, which can be clipped together to form various lengths to suit requirements. Many branches can be reached from ground level and if the gardener uses a pair of ladders as well, quite tall trees and shrubs can be pruned with minimum effort. Rather tough branches often have to be removed from shrubs, and specially designed pruners or loppers are available which will reduce effort. These have unique pivots in the blade junctions, which add more power and leverage as they are used.

PAVING
It might seem strange to include paving here, but it *can* be a real labour-saver in the

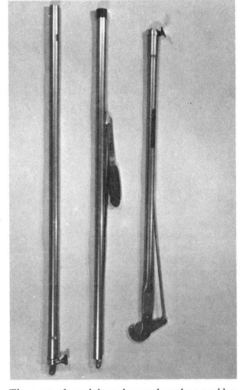

Those out-of-reach branches need not be a problem if a long-handled pruner of lightweight construction is used. The tubular sections are quickly assembled and considerable cutting pressure can be applied.

garden! Laid on a mortar foundation, it will suppress weeds and thus reduce time and effort spent on weeding. A terrace can be an attractive feature in a garden and where there is little time to spare for gardening activities or where, through old age or infirmity, garden work has to be dramatically reduced, paving in a garden can certainly cut down on time and labour.

CHEMICALS WISELY

Arthur Billitt

To the idyllically minded, it might seem ideal to leave nature to solve her own problems, but apart from the fact that her solution would not necessarily suit our needs, once we have cultivated the ground, and have turned it into what we call a garden, nature no longer rules in the area. The gardener imposes *his* judgement as to what plants shall be encouraged to flourish, which shall be eliminated, and what standard of perfection his harvest or mature plants will reach. This changes the plant population drastically and so alters the pest and disease situation.

Our concentrated human population demands concentrated crops, which attract concentrated pests and diseases. A knowledge of nature and the use of naturally occurring materials takes the gardener so far, and certainly incurs no dangers, but to achieve the high yields and quality in garden food-production, and the healthy high standard in ornamental subjects, which are the present-day aim, some use of chemicals is essential.

Chemicals, used to combat pests, diseases, and weeds, are the strangers in the garden – either complete outsiders or, in the case of those of organic origin, substances employed in a changed and more powerful form. Wise use of chemicals in the garden implies respect for the materials involved, knowledge of just when chemical help may be safely called upon, and willingness to draw the line before reaching the point beyond which more problems may be created than are solved.

It is of cardinal importance, however, to remember that the use of chemicals must be combined with good gardening practice, and must never replace it, for it is the correct combination of the two which is the basis of wisdom in the present context.

SAFETY

Most chemicals used as garden aids are potentially dangerous to man, animals, birds, etc., so we must look for relative safety, and positively beneficial effects, from the substances we choose to use. Never consider any product which does not have Ministry of Agriculture approval for home use. An official leaflet listing recommended compounds is obtainable from The Ministry of Agriculture, Fisheries, and Food (Publications), Tolcarne Drive, Pinner, Middlesex.

Whenever food crops are concerned, restrict chemical applications to the minimum. Remember that, if present, an injurious residue on a home-grown crop, especially at its most appetising, is more likely to affect the family over a period of time than when vegetables or fruit are bought here and there in the shops. The latter course can be a way of hedging one's bets, even allowing for the high level of chemical treatment undertaken in commercial growing. If danger lurks in your fruit and vegetable plot, the family may well eat

every bit. Safety where food crops are concerned, lies in a careful choice of sprays, and strict adherence to the manufacturers' directions relating to the timing of applications, and the delay period before harvesting and eating. For the plant's safety, manufacturers' warnings regarding sensitive subjects (listed on the wrappers) must be noted.

Storage

The safe storage of chemicals in the home must be ensured. The user may think that he will never forget what that tiny drop of so and so is, but his may not be the next hand on the bottle or packet. Correct and clear labelling, followed by placing well out of the reach of children and pets, is the only sure way to avoid accidents.

INSECTICIDES

Insect pests do some of the most noticeable and annoying damage in the garden. They spoil the face of ornamental plants and make food plants unpalatable. At worst they cause the deaths of plants by their various debilitating and destructive eating habits, and may also carry disease if they are allowed to move freely. Most insects are easily seen, therefore it is usually possible to act quickly against the harmful ones. A suitable spray or dust applied directly on to the insects, or their food as the case may be, will give a good kill or control. Systemic insecticides (e.g. malathion) are ideal for use against sucking insects such as aphids. The spray applied to the foliage goes into the plant system, and is carried round in the sap so that however well hidden the insect is, when it sucks away at the plant it is bound to receive a lethal dose.

Chewing insects, e.g. caterpillars, leaf miners, etc., have immense appetites. As they will chew everything in front of them, a stomach-poison type of insecticide applied to the plant surface, will be readily taken up.

For preference choose organically based insecticides, for they are the safest types. Derris for instance is relatively safe and effective against all aphids. Nevertheless, when dealing with insect pests, the ideal is to aim at a complete knock-out and for this reason malathion among other modern insecticides has come into general use.

Make up all sprays to the correct strength as directed. Whatever the method of application see that the whole of the insect colony or feeding area is covered, so that the insecticide can be 100% effective. The survivors of an inefficient insecticidal treatment can easily form the nucleus of a resistant strain of insects, in which case future counter measures will be more difficult, and chemicals which are more toxic from the human point of view may have to be employed.

Beneficial Insects

Not all insects are enemies of the gardener. The most obviously beneficial group are

those which feed on nectar or collect pollen. As they work pollen adheres to their legs and bodies and is transferred from flower to flower as they travel, making them excellent (often essential) pollinating agents. Their activities are of particular value to the fruit grower. To safeguard such insects try never to spray open flowers. If spraying has to be done at this stage, do it as late in the evening as possible, when the insects' working day is over.

Some insects prey on others. If the predator does no harm to the gardener's interests but the prey does, then we should be careful not to interfere with the natural course of events. This is one good reason for limiting chemical use to essentials only, and for making sure that spraying, dusting, etc., is kept on target and never indiscriminate. When available, a selective insecticide which kills the offender only, is advisable for the protection of bees, etc.

FUNGICIDES

Some of the worst plant diseases are caused by fungi. Once established on a host plant a fungus will produce countless spores. These minute, complete, viable structures which are shed during favourable weather conditions are capable of initiating new infections. They become airborne, alight on any appropriate plant surface, and cause a new infection. The control of fungal diseases depends on preventive action. Healthy subjects should be sprayed with a suitable fungicide when warmth and high humidity indicate ideal conditions for spore release. In this way you use the fungicide as an insurance policy against outbreaks of plant disease.

Since no fungicide is based on naturally-occurring substances, their wise use comes from a respect for the chemicals involved, and an appreciation of the fungal way of life, which indicates *action in advance* of spore release as the most successful control. Unless they are controlled, fungi will destroy the tissue in which they live. This can be seen in such diseases as apple scab and rose black spot.

Packs

Insecticides and fungicides are available as concentrates, to be mixed with water just prior to their use as liquid sprays, or as pre-packed aerosols suitable for small-scale applications. Alternatively they may be in dust form, ready to go into a large-sized duster, or contained in puffer packs which are handy for limited application.

SPRAYING EQUIPMENT

Bearing in mind the size of the area and number of plants you have to deal with, it is wise to buy the best equipment you can afford. If there is enough work to justify the outlay, a pneumatic sprayer is well worthwhile – the pressure is pumped up ahead of use, leaving both hands free to ensure a good, well-aimed job.

Black spot is a fungus disease of roses that is usually more unsightly than deadly. Control by spraying and burning affected foliage.

Powdery mildew is another fungus disease which attacks many plants. Control is by spraying with Benomyl or equivalent or copper and sulphur.

Chemical sprays cannot be efficiently applied with run down equipment, so clean the sprayer thoroughly after use and check on its working ability some days before it is required. Many an ideal spraying day has been missed for want of an un-jamming session, spare part, etc.

Application Technique

Avoid a ritual approach to the use of insecticides and fungicides. Going through the motions is useless unless the spray, dust, etc., gets to the right place, at the right time, and remains there without being rained or blown off. Study the pest or disease problem you are out to control, and then go into action when a vulnerable stage coincides with suitable weather conditions. Manufacturers give good advice on this all-important timing factor. When overall cover is essential, as for example the application of winter washes, use a coarse nozzle and spray until the run-off stage is reached. Always watch out for drift, especially when a fine nozzle is used. Other plants, neighbours' plants, sensitive young growth, food crops approaching harvest time, and fish ponds, must never be allowed to receive spray drift. Spraying or dusting on a windy day is not only a waste of good spray, it can be positively dangerous.

When potted greenhouse plants have to be sprayed or dusted, e.g. against white fly on fuchsias, take them outside so that the job is not done in an enclosed space. In the open it will be easier to achieve a good all-round cover, and excess inhalation of the chemical by the gardener will be avoided.

To sum up always follow the manufacturers' directions regarding safety precautions, mixing, and rate of application. Keep the application under control in respect of direction and area, and do the job on a dry, windless, frost-free day.

HERBICIDES

Herbicides are potentially very dangerous, therefore never relax safety precautions on any account where they are concerned. A label with the word 'WEEDKILLER' in large lettering, should be on all containers and equipment used for application. These containers, watering cans, etc., must not be used for any other purpose, otherwise valuable plants may be damaged or killed by mistake.

It is very important that weedkillers only go where they are wanted. Under garden conditions a watering can gives the easiest, controlled application, and with a dribble bar attachment it can be done quickly and evenly.

On the lawn, selective weedkillers are at their most efficient. For the maximum effect apply the lawn weedkiller during a period of rapid plant growth, and when there is little likelihood of rain. Sprays based on 2,4-D or MCPA, with CMPP added to eradicate clover can be recommended. Using small packs for the spot treatment of individual weeds in the lawn does not seem worth the expense, when almost less effort would bring them out by hand.

In cultivated ground both selective and total weedkillers may have a place, but do not let either be used to avoid essential cultivations. The selective weedkillers offer an attractive prospect of flower beds kept clean throughout the summer without the chore of weeding. As an illustration – if simazine is applied to the soil of established rose beds in the spring, annual weeds will be controlled for the whole of the season as long as the surface of the soil is not disturbed. The success of this scheme depends on the application of the correct dose rate, because simazine used to excess would become a total weedkiller, and only the roses would survive in the bed. Interplanting with, say, pansies, would be out of the question for they would be killed. This underlines the need for thinking ahead whenever weedkillers are to be applied to cultivated soil.

If the future planting of a sensitive subject or crop is contemplated, weed control should be done by cultivation, rather than by chemical means. Because of the mixed planting usual in ornamental parts of the

Spraying mildewed roses with Benomyl. The treatment should be regularly repeated.

Verticillium wilt, another fungus disease, can destroy tomato plants if left untreated.

Applying fruit setting spray to tomato blossoms can pay dividends in heavier cropping.

garden, selective weedkillers tend to be unsuitable. Where they do suit present needs there is still the question of residues remaining in the soil for quite long periods. How long they will persist depends on rainfall and soil type. The washing away of residues takes place more quickly on lighter sandy soils than on heavy clays, but as the weather factor is involved it is hard to calculate a safety margin.

Apart from residue trouble there is a risk of destroying those valuable soil bacteria which are so essential for the maintenance of high soil fertility. They process vegetable matter (humus), in such a way that vital plant foods are made readily available in the soil.

In the interests of human health, it is best if the home gardener does not use any chemical weedkillers near food crops.

Obviously *non-selective* weedkillers act drastically. They include that well-known weedkilling chemical, paraquat, which has a high toxicity to man, and must therefore be handled and stored with extreme care. Weedkillers based on this chemical are helpful when new ground has to be broken in. Paraquat will kill all plants with which it

comes in contact by causing their leaves to rot away. After a few weeks when the parts of weeds above ground are dead, they can be dug in easily for their bulk will have been reduced considerably. There are no residue problems with the use of paraquat, as the substance does not persist in the soil. This means that safe sowing or planting is possible straight away after digging. It must be borne in mind that the underground parts of the weeds, particularly those of nettles, thistles, docks, couch grass, etc., will *not* have been killed, so after a time plenty of new growths will appear, and from then onwards a period of weed control by cultivation is to be recommended.

Paths may be kept weed-free with a total weedkiller such as sodium chlorate, and here there is a real saving of time and effort. Care must be taken not to endanger trees whose roots go under the path. It is better to hand weed near large shrubs and trees because there is no second chance if the killer seeps down to the roots. When treating sloping paths watch for areas where run-off could reach plants in the border.

CHEMICAL SOIL STERILISATION
The seed composts we buy at the garden shop or centre contain loam, which has been steam sterilised to kill those soil fungi which might otherwise cause serious troubles, such as the 'damping off' of seedlings in their early growing stages. Steam sterilisation is used commercially to control soil-borne diseases in greenhouse soils – diseases such as verticillium wilt of tomatoes, which builds up after 3 or 4 years of continuous tomato growing in one soil. The same build-up of pests and diseases occurs for the gardener, but steam sterilisation is not practical in his case. Fortunately Dazomet provides a good chemical alternative, enabling the gardener to deal with some disease build-up problems himself. Dazomet is available in granular form. It is important to carry out the maker's directions carefully. Allow at least 6 weeks after the sterilising treatment before sowing or planting. To make sure that it is safe to sow or plant, sow a little cress seed to act as an indicator. Wait for the cress to succeed before going ahead. Household disinfectants may be used as sterilising agents, but they are only partial sterilisers with a less than 100% effectiveness.

ROOTING COMPOUNDS
To accelerate the rooting of hard- or soft-wooded cuttings, dip the base of the cutting first into water then into rooting powder (active ingredient indolyl-3-butyric acid). Make the basal cut just below a node, and keep the cutting in closed conditions until rooting has taken place.

CHEMICALS FOR FRUIT SETTING
Fruit-setting sprays based on beta-napthoxyacetic acid are available for use on several fruiting plants, but for the home gardener it is the tomato crop which provides worthwhile subjects on which these sprays may be used. Early in the season when the days are short, and light intensities are low, the bottom trusses of tomato plants tend to fail to set their fruit. This is due to the poor quality of the pollen that needs good light and warmth for maximum viability. There is a natural improvement later in the season. To overcome this 'dry set' problem on the first 2 or 3 trusses, spray each truss once with a tomato fruit-setting spray, when the flowers are fully open. If the first flowers have just died at the time of spraying it will still be effective. Use a hand

sprayer with a nozzle to give a fine spray. The fruit will be seedless but of good quality. Repeated applications to a truss are inclined to produce misshapen and hollow fruit.

WOOD PRESERVATIVES
Most timber is subject to decay if it is exposed to moisture and air together, which really means that wood anywhere out of doors, above or below ground, is vulnerable. Wood-destroying fungi are likely to get to work. As a common example wooden posts are always attacked just below ground level. Creosote is suitable for the treatment of posts and fences which are not used to support plants, but it must not be used for seed boxes, garden frames or greenhouses – in fact not for any wood which is likely to come close to valued plant life. In closed conditions the vapour given off by creosote or creosote-containing wood preservatives is toxic to plants. Time and exposure cannot be relied upon to decrease the risk where seedlings, etc., are concerned, so once it is creosoted, wood must be regarded indefinitely as a potential source of toxic vapour. When buying wood preservative for horticultural use, make quite sure that it is one clearly recommended for that purpose.

ATTACK THE COMMON PESTS
Without reference to specific crops or plants there are a few common pests which can be dealt with universally on sight by the wise use of chemicals.

Aphids
Aphids are a group of sucking insects whose members feed on our whole range of garden plants – fruit, vegetables, ornamentals, and even our hedging subjects. By their sap-sucking activities they weaken the plants and their presence either makes edible plants unacceptable for eating, or in the case of ornamentals, it mars the beauty of both flower and foliage. Aphids (green, white or black fly) should be attacked whenever they appear, but never more promptly than when they are seen on plants which are susceptible to virus diseases, such as tomatoes, strawberries, raspberries, dahlias, etc. The sucking aphis carries infected sap from an ailing host plant to a previously healthy one, and by its 'inject and suck' method of feeding, infects it with the virus concerned. As there are no remedies for virus diseases of plants, it is essential to use the preventive measure of eliminating all aphids if the spread of such disease is to be restricted. A liquid derris insecticide may be used safely against any aphids on sight, but action must be quick to forestall their ability to breed and build up colonies very rapidly. Newcomers must be watched for and dealt with throughout the season.

Caterpillars
Caterpillars are potential spoilers wherever they hatch out in the garden. Some are in the complete-pest class. They remove foliage to varying extents, eating so much at times that only the skeletons of leaves remain. No plant can live properly without an adequate leaf structure, nor can it look attractive when full of holes. On plants which suffer badly, as soon as any egg-laying by moth or butterfly begins, dust all the leaves of the prospective host plant with a derris insecticide dust, so that the caterpillars' first meals are fatal.

Slugs
Slugs occur everywhere but are more of a

problem on heavy land which has a wetter surface atmosphere than the lighter, sandy types. On all soils slugs will be more troublesome during the autumn and winter, when dampness prevails generally, especially on crops or plants with low-growing foliage which itself provides food and cover. It is impossible to get rid of slugs completely, but their numbers may be reduced by the use of slug baits. These are available in proprietary pellet form. They attract and poison the slugs, but as they are also harmful to pets and birds the recommended way of laying them is to cover a small heap with a tile or slate so that only slugs have access to it. Keep the pellets out of the reach of children.

ATTACK THE COMMON DISEASES
The following diseases affect a wide range of garden plants.

Botrytis
Botrytis is a fungus disease which shows up as a grey mould. The surrounding tissue breaks down and rots, so that ornamental plants are spoilt, and fruits (e.g. strawberries, tomatoes, etc.) become useless. The disease thrives and spreads in moist, cold conditions where there is little air movement, so when such conditions occur spray susceptible subjects with a fungicide based on benomyl. Repeat as directed. It is also important to try to change the conditions under which the plant is growing.

Mildew
Mildew adversely affects beauty, and cropping, in the garden. It is another fungus disease – this time one which shows up as a powdery deposit on leaves and stems (of varying degree according to the particular mildew involved). The incidence of mildew is related to climatic conditions. It is high in those seasons which have long periods of warm humidity, for this condition is ideal for maximum spore release by the fungi. Acting as soon as the mildew is seen, by spraying with the fungicide karathane (Dinocap), should give a good control.

Virus Diseases
By the time virus diseases are recognised, which is by the change and progressive deterioration of the plant they affect, it is too late to do anything. There are no remedies, chemical or otherwise, but the chemical control of aphids at all times is a good insurance against their introduction and spread. Affected plants should be dug up and burned to prevent further spread.

DETER THE BIRDS
Chemical bird deterrents used for the protection of fruit crops are safe and effective, but the spray materials used are easily washed off by rain, which means that a sudden heavy shower can leave fruit buds or blossom unprotected at a crucial time. In the small garden protection by the use of nylon netting seems to be a better method, unless the gardener is prepared to re-apply the deterrent spray after each rainfall.

CHEMICALS AND FOOD PRODUCTION IN THE GARDEN
If trees or plants are grown to provide an edible harvest for the family, that harvest should be as large and of as high a quality as possible. Firstly to reward the grower with quantity, and secondly, to make sure that its presentation in the kitchen will be welcome.

In the fruit and vegetable garden, plants of the same group are grown close together,

Apple scab is a fungus disease that renders the fruit unusable. Captan sprays are safest, as some varieties are susceptible to lime-sulphur sprays.

therefore pest and disease hazards are increased. On the other hand chemical applications to specific plants are easier to make, e.g. to crops grown in rows. In this situation it is obviously sensible to use some of the relatively safe chemical means of crop protection.

Protect Fruit Trees
The protection of fruit trees and bushes against pests and diseases is a year-round task. Success is dependent on the correct action being taken at vulnerable stages of pest and disease development. Simple spray programmes to deal with the individual problems of particular fruit crops, can easily be carried out as part of the garden routine. Winter washes may be regarded as the start of the spraying round. Tar oil, tar-petroleum, or DNOC in petroleum oil, applied during the dormant season (November is ideal), will kill insect eggs which are over-wintering on bare stems and branches. If they are undisturbed these eggs will hatch out in the spring, the pest will be on the move and, by then, will also have the protection of foliage. In the winter, branches, etc., are bare, so that a good overall cover is easy to achieve, while tender leaf and fruit buds, which would otherwise be damaged by this type of spray, are tightly closed and safe.

Top Fruit
Apples and pears require the carrying out of a routine spray programme if the fruit produced is to be at its best, but in both cases a simple minimum procedure may be suggested which is designed for use in the small garden, and which will be quite effective. The correct timing and thorough application of the sprays recommended is all-important.
Apples. Between November and February, when the weather conditions are favourable, apply a tar distillate winter wash to destroy the eggs of aphids, moths, etc. At bud-burst, spray with BHC and captan (mixed spray) for aphids, cater-

pillars, and the fungus disease – apple scab. Repeat this at the green-bud stage, i.e. just before the pink petals show through. At the pink-bud stage, spray with captan only, against scab. At petal-fall spray again with BHC and captan together, for codling moth and scab. The egg-laying of the codling moth is responsible for the maggots found in mature apples later on, if nothing is done at petal-fall. Apple scab causes dark roughened patches on the skin, which enlarge with the swelling fruit.

For really clean fruit repeat the captan spray at 14-day intervals until August. If red spider mite is troublesome, add Dinocap to all sprays from petal-fall onwards. If mildew is a problem in your district, add Dinocap to all sprays from bud-burst onwards.
Peaches, Nectarines, Apricots. Apply a winter wash in January. The worst disease of peaches and nectarines is peach leaf curl. This is a fungus disease which causes the leaves to be puckered and covered with red blisters. If the disease is not controlled the trees will deteriorate progressively, and eventually be ruined. To be effective, treatment must be carried out before the end of February. To make quite sure, spray with a copper fungicide in November and repeat in February.

Apricots are not affected by peach leaf curl but otherwise they should be treated as peaches and nectarines. Spray all three fruits with malathion as soon as any aphids are seen during the growing season.
Pears. Apply the winter wash as on apples. At bud-burst, spray with BHC and captan together, for aphids, caterpillars, and pear scab. Repeat at the white-bud stage. At petal-fall, spray with captan against scab and for a really clean crop that will remain unmarked by scab, repeat the captan spray at 14-day intervals until August.
Plums do not have many serious troubles, but they should be included when applying the winter wash in November and February. Spray with BHC if any aphids or caterpillars are seen during the growing season.

Applying liquid derris to cabbage to control caterpillars. Spray before caterpillars eat their way into the interior.

Applying BHC dust to young onion plants to protect them against onion fly.

Soft Fruit

Blackcurrants. Apply a winter wash in January. The biggest problem on blackcurrants is big bud mite. The mites feed and multiply inside the developing buds causing them to become swollen, with the result that many fail to open, and others produce inferior flower trusses. The well-tried treatment is lime sulphur, but care must be taken not to spray this at full strength on varieties which are susceptible to damage from lime sulphur.

To be on the safe side you can limit your blackcurrant growing to the variety Baldwin, which is not adversely affected by the use of lime sulphur. Apply the spray when the leaves are the size of a 10p piece, and repeat once or twice, leaving 14 days between treatments. American gooseberry mildew will affect blackcurrants. For this, spray with a fungicide based on benomyl immediately the first characteristic powdery mildew symptoms are seen, or else the trouble will spread rapidly. Spray aphids, capsid, and thrips, on sight with malathion. Other currants (red and white) have few problems but you should include them when you apply the winter wash. Use malathion to kill aphids.

Gooseberries should have a winter wash application in January. For American gooseberry mildew use benomyl as on blackcurrants. Gooseberry sawfly is the most common pest on this fruit. The black-spotted caterpillars of the sawfly are great eaters, and if nothing is done to prevent it they may carry on until the gooseberry bushes are devoid of green leaf. At the first appearance of the caterpillars spray with a liquid derris insecticide. Repeat 10 days later.

Raspberries are extremely susceptible to virus diseases so if you do nothing else, at least eliminate aphids by spraying them on sight with malathion. Other troubles include raspberry beetle, whose larvae may be found inside the ripe fruits at picking time. Control the beetle by spraying with a liquid derris insecticide at the full blossom stage, with a repeat after 10 days.

Strawberries. This is another fruit which is very susceptible to virus diseases, and after making sure that the stock planted is virus-free, the only way to see that it has a chance to remain so is to take the usual precautions against aphids. If these are allowed to build up, virus infection will almost certainly follow. Spray aphids on sight with malathion, which will also deal with another strawberry pest, the red spider mite. Botrytis, or grey mould, infects strawberry flowers, and in damp seasons especially, it will go on to affect the fruit, making it initially unpresentable and ultimately rotten and useless. To guarantee a quality crop, spray with benomyl at the early flowering stage, and repeat the application once or twice at 10-day intervals. Do not continue after flowering.

Chemicals in the Vegetable Garden

Remind yourself that everything in the vegetable plot is probably going to be eaten, and then restrict chemical treatments to cases where success is unlikely without some chemical help.

Brassicas. Many brassicas are grown for their leaves however tightly closed they may be (as in the hard-headed cabbage for example) when used in the kitchen. If leaf-eating caterpillars are allowed their freedom, there is no point in growing them at all. As soon as any cabbage white butterflies are seen, dust the brassica leaves with a derris insecticide dust ready to kill emerging caterpillars.

The cabbage root fly produces larvae which eat and destroy the root structures of brassicas. Affected plants collapse and die. To prevent this happening dust the roots with a BHC dust at planting time. If your garden soil is infected with clubroot, the use of a heaped teaspoonful of 4% calomel dust mixed with the soil in each planting hole when brassicas are transplanted, can make growing just possible, although there is no cure for clubroot in the soil, and the disease will persist for many years.

Broad Beans. Black fly is the aphis which spoils the broad bean crop. It is often the practice to pinch out the growing tip of the plant and so remove the point of infestation, but a sure way of control is to spray with malathion when the first black fly is seen.

Carrots will not succeed unless something is done about the carrot fly, whose maggots burrow and feed in the root. They are at their very worst just before lifting time, making the carrots difficult to accept as edible. Dust the drill at sowing time with a BHC dust, and when the seedlings emerge, apply a liquid BHC insecticide to the row using a watering can with a fine rose attachment.

Celery. The brown trails often seen on the leaves of celery are made by the larvae of the celery fly, which hatch from eggs laid on the foliage. As soon as the signs are seen, spray with a BHC insecticide.

Celery seed will almost certainly have been treated chemically by the seed firm to control the fungus disease known as leaf spot, but if rusty spots do appear on the leaves, a copper fungicide is the answer.

Lettuce is a quick-growing crop with a good hope of maturing before serious problems arise, so long as the seedling stage is passed satisfactorily. Greenfly can be a nuisance, and unpopular in the kitchen, so spray with malathion if necessary. Allow a week before eating. If root aphis is troublesome water the row with diluted malathion, and again let a week elapse before eating.

Onions grown from sets or transplants are not liable to be troubled by onion fly but those grown from seed sown in the open may suffer seriously from the activities of onion fly larvae. In the case of these directly sown onions, dust the drill with BHC dust at sowing time, and dust the seedlings in the row soon after they come through. This will ensure that emerging larvae from eggs laid by the visiting onion fly do not survive. Do not be tempted to pull onions from the row for use in salads, as the odour released would make doubly sure that onion flies were attracted to the bed.

Onion white rot causes rotting at ground level. The fungus responsible becomes established in the soil, and once this has happened the only real answer is to change the onion growing site. Meanwhile spray the infected row with benomyl to check the outbreak.

Big bud in blackcurrants is caused by the gall mite. Control by a lime-sulphur spray.

Applying a 4% calomel dust preparation to cabbage seedlings as they are planted out to combat the ravages of clubroot. The infection can linger in the soil for years.

Selective weedkiller is easily applied to lawns, though large areas really require a pressure sprayer.

Peas. Early and mid-season peas usually escape the attention of the pea moth, but late varieties attract it for egg-laying purposes at the flower stage. Later on maggots are found inside mature pods, which spoils the finished product. To avoid maggoty peas spray late varieties at flowering time with a liquid malathion insecticide. For mildew which is the particular hazard of a late pea crop, maturing in say October, spray with benomyl as soon as the signs appear.

Potatoes. Fungicides are advocated for the control of potato blight, but it is better for the gardener, when an attack occurs in September, to cut off the haulms and to prevent the infection reaching the tubers.

Tomatoes. Most tomato difficulties arise on the management side, especially in the greenhouse (e.g. the problem of tomato leaf mould), where temperature and ventilation are the great factors. On the insect side, white fly can be a serious pest on tomatoes, and its presence can ruin the hopes of a good crop. The greenhouse atmosphere just suits the white fly for breeding, so the first comers must be killed quickly before there are legions around to suck the life out of the tomato plants. Use a malathion aerosol. Repeat twice at 10–14-day intervals. If red spider mite is present use the same aerosol but repeat at 5–10-day intervals.

Chemicals in the Ornamental Garden

Dealing with the pests and diseases already mentioned as being those which occur most commonly, will go a long way, but the following plants are often grown in greater numbers than others, and their value as providers of cut flowers for the house makes it desirable for them to be as pest- and disease-free as possible.

Chrysanthemums suffer disfiguring damage to leaves and buds from various insects among them, aphids, capsid, and thrips. For these use a BHC liquid insecticide. Treat powdery mildew on sight with benomyl.

Dahlias are liable to virus diseases therefore the routine attack on aphids is important. In the case of dahlias, aphids will be killed together with caterpillars, capsid, and earwigs, if a routine BHC-dimethoate spray is applied every 14 days.

Roses. If roses are grown in clean air districts they are more likely to suffer from the fungus disease – rose black spot. In polluted areas the SO_2 (sulphur dioxide) content of the air helps to restrict the disease. For a good control, spray with captan beginning in February and repeating at fortnightly intervals. Caterpillars as well as aphids are a nuisance so to get both, spray with BHC-dimethoate every 14 days. As soon as rose mildew is seen spray with benomyl.

IN CONCLUSION

Many additions to the foregoing recommendations are carried out in the commercial field, and in that area they are often related primarily to economic factors – in which case savings of labour and money must be weighed against the unavoidable drawbacks of seeking a chemical answer to every problem. More sprays and powders can be added to the list for garden use but we are considering here a wise approach to the use of chemicals by the home gardener. He grows plants and cultivates his soil for

Aphids are a pest on strawberries as on other plants. Malathion is an effective control.

the happiness it affords him to do so, therefore the need has been to suggest chemical usage which is complementary to good active gardening, and which, at the same time, carries a minimum risk for his family and animals. The wise gardener has a unique opportunity for combining the best and safest of modern horticultural discoveries, with the natural zest for life that his garden plants are so anxious to express.

MAKING

A PATH, TERRACE, STEPS

Reginald Kaye

What do you do when the new house is finished and you are confronted with a new garden to make? Or perhaps the problem is how to make the best of an existing garden of no particular merit, surrounding an older house? Much will depend on your particular interests, whether to concentrate on growing flowers and roses, or to provide home-grown vegetables. And of course the size of the plot, its slope and orientation, and the immediate surroundings, must all be taken into consideration.

But irrespective of the final picture there are certain basic matters to plan, and the first of these is to make the best of the immediate surroundings of the house, for every type of building is enhanced by being framed within some kind of formalised layout, no matter how informal the rest of the garden may be.

PATHS

Access to entrances or to windows for cleaning, demands some kind of hard-wearing footpath. If possible, arrangements should be made with the builders not to supply the usual 3-ft. concrete paths right up to the house walls, thus making it impossible to grow wall shrubs and climbers, but to leave a 1-ft.-wide (or preferably more) planting space between the path and the house. If it is not too late, decide on the type of path you want, paved, gravel or anything other than concrete,* which to my mind is the least attractive kind of path in a garden.

The ways in which paths may be surfaced should be in harmony with the materials used for the house, especially for those paths in close proximity to the building. For instance where the house is of brick, paths may be surfaced with bricks, narrow-side up arranged in various patterns, such as herringbone, basket weave, and so on. To give a bit of variety, panels made with cobblestones on edge could be introduced. For very modern buildings, paving with random rectangular flags of reconstituted stone will look well. This may be had in various colours which may be chosen to blend with any other schemes. Gravel paths fit in with almost anything and can be had in various colours, granite chips, limestone chips, or flint gravel in warm browns. They are easy and quick to make, but need frequent raking, and yearly treatment to prevent weeds growing.

All paths, paved or otherwise, should be finished with a slight crown in order to shed excess rain. Principal paths should not be less than 5 ft. wide, so that two people can walk alongside one another, wider if there is enough room.

Whatever kind of path you choose, it should be given adequate foundation. This is done by excavating at least 9 ins. throughout the whole length, filling this with broken stones to a depth of 4 ins. and rolling or ramming it down firmly to 3 ins. On this solid base, a 3-in. layer of gravel should be scattered and rolled down to 2 ins. This will leave 4 ins. for a bedding of sand followed by the finishing material, brick, paving, york stone, etc.

In the case of a *grass path* a line of drain tiles, arranged with a slight fall, say 1 in. in 10 ft., should be laid along either side below the layer of broken stone. These should lead to a main drain or soakaway. Soil is necessary, so the gravel layer should be only 1 in. thick, topped up with about 4 ins. of good top-soil on which the turf may be laid. If, on the other hand, the paths are to be sown, a further 1 in. of loam lightened with sand should be added to bring the surface up to the required height. Until the grass is thoroughly established the edges of paths to be sown must be supported in some way,

Three of the many possible patterns for a brick path: (left to right) herring-bone; with cobble inserts; basket-weave.

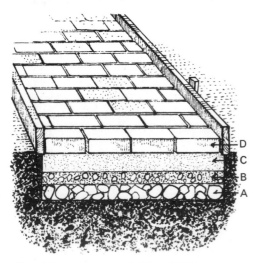

Foundation for a path: A, 4 ins. of broken stones, rolled to 3 ins.; B, 3 ins. of gravel rolled to 2 ins.; C, 4 ins. bedding of sand; D, surface, in this case brick.

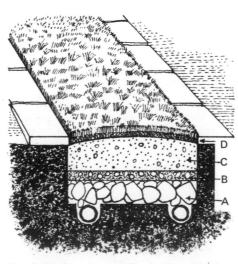

Foundation for a grass path: A, 4 ins. of broken stones, rolled to 3 ins., with drainage tiles below; B, 1 in. of gravel; C, 4 ins. of good top-soil; D, turf. Note the camber and edging slabs.

Coloured paving slabs of different sizes can be used effectively to set off tubs or urns on a patio or terrace.

Instructions for making concrete, and mortar, are given at the end of this chapter.

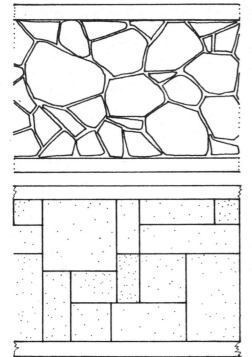

The effect to be aimed at with crazy paving (above) and reconstituted rectangular slabs (below).

A nice use of crazy paving and a dry wall. The plants growing in the wall must be planted as the wall is built. The in-filling of the crevices in the paving saves much tiresome weeding.

either with plastic edging strip or with lengths of timber, supported with pegs driven into the ground.

Grass paths look well when kept in perfect order, but need constant care, and are not suitable for regularly used access paths. A compromise here is to sink pieces of paving stone, squared or random-shaped, just below the grass level so as not to interfere with mowing, placing them an average pace apart.

Random-squared york *paving*, a hard sandstone, makes a most attractive path but it is very expensive nowadays. Old york stone slates sometimes may be had from old property being demolished, and these are ideal for crazy paving. If there are any sandstone quarries in your area it is sometimes possible to get off-cuts sawn from large blocks. These are fine, for the sharp edges can be trimmed with a sharp cold-chisel to fit.

When laying crazy paving use larger pieces a pace apart and fill in with smaller pieces, leaving $\frac{1}{2}$-in. gaps between the stones. These gaps are best filled in with concrete to prevent weeds growing, at least in the principal paths. Concrete can be tinted in various colours to match the stone and so avoid the sterile appearance of plain concrete.

With crazy paving, I like to keep the crevices between the stones more or less the same width, by trimming the stone with a cold chisel, after picking out stone near to the shape required. The bits chiselled off go towards the foundations of the path further along.

Crazy paving is usually sold by weight; one ton paving, average $1\frac{1}{2}$ ins. thick, covers from 10–11 sq. yds. Rectangular paving is sold by the square yard.

Reconstituted rectangular paving, which is of uniform thickness, is laid in the same way as bricks, but sandstone paving usually varies in thickness, even in the same slab, so that each piece must be levelled up individually.

I like to firm the sand under the slabs with a brick hammer. Firm the sand by tapping it tight under the slab, always keeping the straight-edge in play. It is not advisable to try to knock the slabs down to a level, this usually results in splitting them into bits.

Gravel is simply tipped on the path foundations and raked to a level, but some form of edging is advisable to contain the gravel or chippings in place. Suitable edgings can be made from reconstituted stone in various tints, bricks set either parallel to, or at right angles to the path, or narrow slips of paving stone. Avoid making edgings of brick set in dog-tooth fashion – this looks terrible. Hard edgings of all kinds should be set in concrete and cemented together to prevent movement.

If *bricks* are used for surfacing or edging paths, make sure that they are weather-resisting, for bricks made for interior use will shell badly with every frost and be useless after a year or two. The rough-surfaced 'rustic' brick is one of the best and the colour is pleasing.

When surfacing a path with brick, carefully rake the bedding material to the correct level (not forgetting the crown), roll it, and if necessary top up with more sand so that the bricks when set are just at the right height. The bricks should be cemented together with a very thin layer of concrete mortar, and constantly checked with a straight-edge to make sure that an even surface is being achieved. Use the straight-edge with a spirit-level across the path – allowing for a crown which need not be more than 1 in. above the sides in a 5-ft. path – and also along the length of the path both along the sides and along the crown. Paths immediately around a house should be quite level if at all possible. If the ground is sloping and there is room, the whole area adjacent to the house will look better if it is levelled to a convenient width, and finished off with terrace walls. Brick paving requires 48 bricks to the sq. yd., bricks being sold by numbers.

If the ground slopes greatly so that there is a considerable difference in levels in the two ends of the house it is still better to keep the paths level and take up the fall with steps placed in convenient places. Steps will be dealt with later.

The only largely used stone for paving other than sandstone is slate, natural-surfaced. The green slates make an attractive path, but are costly compared with sandstone. In the less formal parts of a garden, paths will still require careful construction and attention given to drainage, so that even in very wet weather it will be possible to get around the garden without wet feet.

Paths in the vegetable garden are best paved in some way, so that damage from frequent wheeling of laden barrows is avoided. Paths in woodland glades are sometimes made from sawdust, tan-bark, and similar substances. Such materials should be avoided as they encourage the appearance of the dreaded honey-fungus, which can cause havoc amongst valuable trees and shrubs. Similarly steps made from lengths of timber are suspect. Stone steps and gravel are durable and will afford a good walking surface, and if untrimmed stone slabs are used as steps, they will harmonise with the surroundings.

Some interesting effects can be obtained by introducing random panels of *cobblestone* paving amongst other materials, e.g. rectangular stone paving, or brick. A path made entirely of cobblestones can be attractive in the more rustic type of garden. To get variety in such a path it could be divided up into sections with the cobblestones in adjoining sections lined in opposing directions, or the stones could be set in lines radiating from a centre, as for instance at a junction between two paths. To lay such a path the foundations are the same as for any other path, made firm by rolling before the surface is started. A layer of sand for bedding is then raked smooth, some form of edging having been placed first. The cobblestones are then set in lines, narrow edge up, close together, until a good length of path has been laid. All the time keep checking to ensure that the top edges of the cobbles are level throughout the path. For this you will require the straight-edge and spirit-level, and a piece of boarding to press down the stones to an even surface. Then the path should be grouted with a 3 to 1 mixture of sand and cement, applied on the sloppy side and brushed between the cobblestones with

A pleasant patio that provides a sheltered spot for sitting. The owner is watering a cascade of small-leaved ivies.

A shady terrace with ample provision for decorative climbers – just the setting a passion-flower or Clematis montana would thrive in.

a stiff broom. A gentle sprinkling with water through a fine-rosed can will wash the stones, and settle the concrete down after which it should be left severely alone for 5 or 6 days to harden. Premature walking on such a surface would loosen the stones.

Additional variety in the surface may be had by including pieces of paving, which also might be used for edging, or panels of brick in symmetrical designs, where brick is used as an edge to the path.

TERRACES AND RETAINING WALLS

The restful effect of horizontal lines contrasting with the vertical lines of buildings, trees and foliage masses gives a sense of harmony to the immediate surrounds of a home, and also adds dignity to the house itself. Of course a lot depends on the space available, but if possible an area as wide as the house is high, up to the eaves, laid out in paths surrounding formally shaped flower beds, will give a satisfying proportion.

The part in front of the house might be in the form of a forecourt with a wide path leading to the main entrance, bordered with rectangular beds of roses, if the type of

house harmonises with such treatment. On the other side of the house the horizontal area might terminate in a low wall, or an evergreen hedge of yew, broken with a gap leading to the other parts of the garden.

If the ground is sloping away from the house, *here* is the place to build the first terrace wall, with steps leading down from the upper level. First of all this second area should be levelled, by removing the top-soil to one end and then, having decided on the width of the second level, put down a line the full length of the area, half-way across the width. Then the subsoil from the higher side is dug out and spread over the lower side until a level is achieved. Then the top-soil is wheeled back and spread evenly over the entire area.

Now a retaining wall must be built to support the level around the house, with one or more flights of steps arranged through it. The individual treatment and materials used should be related to the type of house. For instance it would be inappropriate to build balustraded walls of dressed stone to frame a rustic cottage or converted barn. In such a case walls of random walling stone would look best,

either built 'dry', or with mortar. A well-built dry wall will stand for many years, and will provide a home for lovely rock plants, aubrietia, phlox, rock rose and the like. Such a wall ideally is planted as the wall is built, each layer of stone being spread with a layer of good soil as the work proceeds. But to begin at the bottom good foundations are essential, so a foot or so should be dug out for these, at least a foot in front of the wall bottom so that the weight of the wall will press down on the centre of the foundation stones and be supported by the whole world below. If the front edges of the wall and foundation stones were flush, the weight of the wall would gradually depress the front edge of the foundations, causing the wall to belly out and finally collapse.

Foundations to walls may be made with largish stones, wide enough to take the bottom stones of the wall and project an equal distance in front of the wall so that the weight of the wall thrusts against the centre portion of the foundation stones. Or a layer of concrete may be used, at least 6 ins. thick on undisturbed subsoil, and also projecting in front of the wall face 9–12 ins., as well as supporting the whole width of the bottom wall stones.

When dry-walling always set the stones with their wider edges to the face, wedging them in the right position with chockstones tapped in behind. The front edges should bite into the layer below, with the soil filling any inequalities between the stones behind the face. You will need a tight line stretched along the length of the wall attached to stakes driven into the bank and just, and only just, touching the top edges of the layer being set. The line must be lifted up with each layer. In the case of dry-walling, the wall should be given a 'batter' of about 1 in. per foot rise, to give better stability and to withstand pressure from the bank behind. As a guide, posts should be firmly driven into the ground at either end of the wall, at the correct slant, and the line attached to these. Having laid the first layer of stones, the next layer must be laid so that the stones cover the joints between the lower stones. With random walling the stones will not be

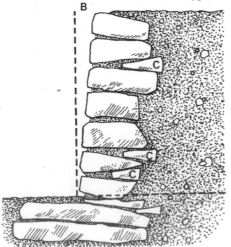

Construction details for a dry retaining wall. B: batter. C: chockstones.

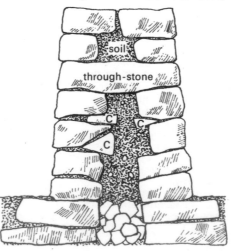

Construction details of a double-sided dry wall designed for planting.

of uniform thickness, and occasionally it will be necessary to level up with thin stones so that the courses are kept as near horizontal as possible. These stones should also be set with their thicker edges to the face, and wedged from behind. Never wedge up a stone on the face, such wedges always work out sooner or later and this allows the stone to sag and cause a weakness. Fill up behind each layer with good soil as the work proceeds and *hammer* the soil firm. If not made as firm as possible it will settle and cause trouble later. Save some good flattish stones for the final course, finishing them off by levelling up the soil behind, to the level of the top terrace. If built correctly you should be able to walk along the top of the wall without disturbing the stones.

If you wish to build an apparently dry wall with cement mortar, use a mix of 3 parts soft sand to 1 part cement amongst the foundations, and 6 parts sand to 1 part of cement higher up, keeping the mortar out of sight by applying it to the inner half of the stones. Here and there, particularly low down, leave unmortared gaps to allow water to drain through the wall, otherwise water will collect behind and expand in frosty weather, damaging the wall.

A mortared wall may be built vertical – without a batter – if desired, but for this you will need a builder's combined level and plumb to check the work.

If you wish to bring the wall above the upper terrace level, it should be built double-sided from the base to the required height and finished off with rectangular coping stone firmly set in concrete mortar. Sitting height above the top terrace is very convenient. The copings should project beyond the wall face 2 ins. or so.

The different types of stone used in the above type of walling usually will be some form of sandstone, or limestone. Some forms of york stone have a very smooth micaceous surface which acts as a lubricant causing the stones to slip over one another when pressure is applied by wet soil behind a wall. Such stones are best mortared.

Walls made with rustic brick look well when the dwelling is brick-built. These should always be built double thickness, though common brick may be used for the inner side against the soil. The two sides must be well bonded together and finished off with a coping to prevent rain soaking into the mortar and causing damage in frosty weather. Brick walls should always be built on concrete foundations, and drain tiles should be built through the wall at intervals to relieve the pressure of excess water.

When demolition work is being carried on in derelict property it often is possible to acquire good building stone very reasonably. It will be roughly dressed and have acquired a patina of age, so useful in garden stone. Also it will probably have lime mortar adhering to it. This should be knocked off and used to improve the soil for such plants as the dianthus which love it. Long walls often are improved by building in buttresses at regular intervals, and these will provide varying aspects for planting. They are simply made; their foundations should be set at right angles to the slope of the buttress, the stones being laid with their bases parallel to the foundations, their faces of course to the required slope. Each course should be bonded into the main wall where it meets.

Walls made from reconstituted stone would be in keeping with modern villas. A type known as 'Tudor' is cast in various sizes and tints which blend together to make an interesting finish. These walls also

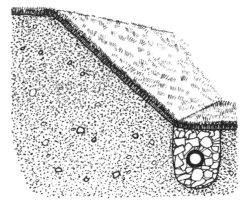

A cross-section to show how a drain can be placed at the foot of a sloping bank.

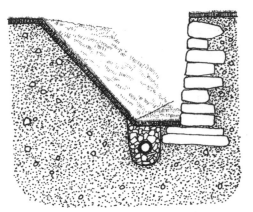

A 'ha-ha' boundary wall – a vertical wall, ditch, and drainage, showing the construction.

must be built double, the inner wall may be made with ordinary concrete blocks tied to the face wall by wire 'butterflies' set in the mortar. As with brick walls, copings must be used, cementing them on to the wall top with a projecting lip of $1\frac{1}{2}$ ins.

Grass banks are another way of separating terraces, which eliminates any sense of being shut in by walls. This consists simply of a slope from one level to the next covered with turf. It is easy and inexpensive to make, but a perfect nuisance to keep trim. The angle of slope should be such that a mower managed by one person can traverse the length without slipping down the bank. An angle of 30° with the horizontal is steep enough. Along the entire length at the bottom of the slope a drain should be made by digging out a trench about 1 ft. wide and deep, filling with broken stone in which drain tiles are buried to lead excess water away to a main drain or soakaway. The top is finished off with 2–3 ins. of earth and covered with turf, level with the terrace.

Then there is the 'Ha-Ha' fence which sometimes is used to give the impression that the garden is continuous with the fields beyond the garden boundary. This takes the form of a wall and trench. The garden lawn is laid right to the edge of the property on top of the wall, which is built in a trench from the bottom of which a turfed slope leads up to the field beyond. From a short distance the continuity of garden lawn and field seems unbroken.

A variation is to treat the wall top with pillars joined with chains, panels of wrought iron, or railings of metal or wood. But these elaborations really belong to the more pretentious layouts designed for the stockbroker belt and are not likely to be attempted by the 'do-it-yourself' gardener. No matter how you decide to lay out your garden, it should be a place of relaxation and peace, a place for re-creation in the literal sense after all the chores have been done, the borders weeded, the grass mown and any other tasks cleared out of the way.

STEPS

To provide access from one terrace to another it will be necessary to build steps, and this affords an opportunity to utilise all manner of variations in design. The simplest steps are built of stone slabs, which should be about $5\frac{1}{2}$ ins. thick, and 12 ins. or more wide so that by leaving a tread of 11 ins. there will be at least 1 in. for the next step to rest on. Steps should be filled behind with broken stone, well firmed. They may be recessed into the wall, in which case the ends of the steps should be built into the side

Steps leading to a terrace under construction. Note the effective use of warm, decorative coloured slabs instead of stone or brick. The terrace will eventually have raised island flower beds.

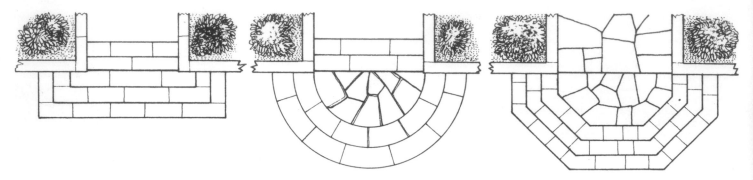

Plans of three types of step design: (from left to right) expanding rectangular steps with recessed upper steps; expanding circular steps with rectangular recessed upper steps; expanding octagonal steps without recessed upper steps.

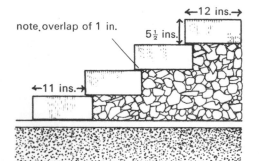

note overlap of 1 in.

←12 ins.→

5½ ins.

←11 ins.→

Construction details for simple steps using stone blocks.

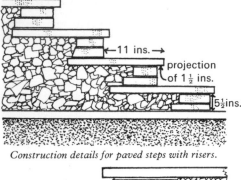

←11 ins.→

projection of 1½ ins.

5½ ins.

Construction details for paved steps with risers.

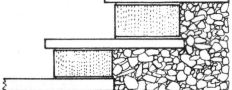

Construction details for brick steps with stone flag treads.

walls making sure that both are on sound footings made very firm. If for instance the wall should settle, even a small amount, the steps will be cocked up and some rebuilding incurred.

Or the steps might be half recessed, half extended beyond the terrace, each step expanded both sideways and forwards as it descends. In plan the extended section could be rectangular, semicircular, or octagonal according to taste. Steps required at the ends of a terrace might be in the form of a spiral sweep within wing-walls. In fact there are any number of combinations of form which could be used, making the steps one of the more interesting features of a garden. Of course flights of steps should be placed to meet the more important paths, and form part of an overall design for the garden. When the paths are paved, the steps should be made with risers of walling stone, cemented to the path, and filled in behind with broken stone. They should be finished to a height of 5½ ins. with paving slabs, which should project over the risers about 1½ ins. The risers for the next step are cemented to the first step leaving a tread of 11 ins., and flags cemented to these, and so on till the top is reached. When recessed, the risers and paving should be bonded into the wing-walls, all being built at the same time, and made very firm as each step is built.

Probably some cutting may be necessary to fit the paving accurately to get an even step. Sandstone paving is easy to trim with a cold-chisel – once you get the knack. First the flag should be marked where it is to be cut with a lining chisel or 'bolster'. This is a chisel with a thin wide blade 3–4 ins. in width. Then the mark is followed round with a ¾- or 1-in. chisel, using a walling hammer of sufficient weight, until a continuous groove has been cut. Then tap along the groove with the walling hammer, when the stone should part along the cut. Use a bed of soft sand on which to perform the chiselling, otherwise the stone may break where inequalities in the ground do not support it evenly. Slate paving is extremely difficult to cut cleanly, it tends to splinter badly so slate flags for steps are best ordered to be sawn to a straight edge. By the way, slate walling should always be built with the natural surface showing, never the sawn ends. It is extremely easy to split slate walling along the grain to get the right thickness for slate risers, but it is extremely difficult to trim against the grain. Limestone is also difficult to cut to a shape, and limestone paving cannot be had in even thicknesses unless sawn, a job for the expert. Reconstituted stone slabs are easy to trim by following the same method as for sandstone paving. Steps made in brick cannot be cemented on to the brick path to bring the steps to the correct height unless ¾-in.-thick tiles are used as risers. Bricks used in paving are set edge up and are 4½ ins. deep. It is better therefore to set bricks as risers in concrete below the paving level, so as to project above the path ¾ in., then the step is finished with a row of bricks laid edge up, narrow end as face. All cemented down and together of course.

An alternative is to make the lip of the step with a trimmed stone flag the width of

A fine pergola with a garden room above – an interesting way of clothing the wall of a house, but be careful that any raised bed does not interfere with the damp course.

Mesembryanthemum can provide a vivid splash of colour in sunny crevices.

the steps and 1 ft. or more wide, and 1 in. thick, cementing the brick risers to the stone, and allowing the stone to project over the riser the usual 1½ ins. Steps in gravel paths usually are made with stone flags set on risers of stone, or with solid stone slabs.

Pillars

Stone or brick pillars make an interesting decoration at the ends of a terrace wall, at breaks for steps or at the beginning of a flight of steps. They need not be more than sitting height above the terrace. Pillars must have a sound foundation all round, concrete or stone, on ground which has not been disturbed – i.e. right down to undisturbed subsoil, otherwise settling of the soil will cause the pillars to settle unevenly. They usually are from 18–24 ins. in width, square or circular, and when building should be checked constantly with a builder's plumb for verticals, particularly on the corners. They should be finished off with a squared or circular coping, on which, if desired, tubs of plants may be placed. It is not recommended to use the pillars themselves as plant receptacles, for the effect of frost on wet soil is to expand with great pressure, cracking the pillar walls – which should be mortared of course.

Design

In addition to the various suggestions of design mentioned earlier, terraces lend themselves to unlimited variations of treatment in the way of formally shaped beds surrounded by turf or paving, and perhaps edged with dwarf hedges of box, lavender, or other subjects which lend themselves to close clipping. Such beds may be designed round a central feature such as a formal pool, a sundial, or stone figure. The ends of the central path, if such there be, might terminate in an alcove with a seat of stone or timber, or some kind of garden ornament in keeping with the garden. The thing to do is to get the measurements of your garden down on paper, decide how to make the best use of the area and what special points of interest can be worked into that area to create a harmonious whole. Any special features in the surroundings, an interesting view for instance, might suggest orienting the principal paths to lead the eye towards it as a kind of vista. Each garden has some point of interest, however modest, which should be taken into account. There is a tremendous satisfaction to be had from having created your own garden and having done all the work yourself.

MAKING CONCRETE

The standard mix for concrete for surfacing paths is 4 parts clean ¾-in. gravel or stone chippings, 2 parts clean sharp sand, and 1 part fresh cement. The sand must be 'sharp', that is gritty with all the very fine particles washed out of it. The ingredients are thoroughly mixed dry, by turning over the heap at least four times until it appears a uniform colour. The centre of the heap is then pulled to the sides with a spade until there is a central hollow surrounded by a circular ring of mixture. Water is run into the hollow to half fill it and then the sides are gradually mixed into the centre and gently worked until the whole heap is a plastic mass, but not sloppy. The mixture is then laid gently on the path foundations, and worked level with the edge of a piece of board moved backwards and forwards until a smooth surface is obtained. Wet mixed concrete must be used immediately, before

Utilising a terrace to good effect. The slabs provide cool, moist root-runs. Plants should be chosen to provide contrasts in colour and shape and year-round interest.

A generous layer of stones can help eliminate weeds and provide an effective foil to the colour of flowers and foliage in surrounding beds.

it begins to set, to get the best results, and if convenient, enough should be mixed to surface an entire path in one operation. If a powered mixer is being used, the dry ingredients are shovelled into the bucket, mixed dry, then water added, and mixed again until homogeneous. It is then tipped out into a barrow and wheeled to the job. Important – tools used with concrete must be washed clean immediately after use.

For grouting, surfacing, or for use as mortar, a mix of 3 parts of fine sand to 1 part of cement should be dry mixed thoroughly.

Then add water and mix, to a consistency which will spread like butter. Use a cement trowel or float for applying it. Any bits of grit in the sand will create problems when trying to float a very smooth surface.

If large quantities of concrete are required, it can be obtained from a builder's supplier ready mixed by the cubic yard. A cubic yard will cover 36 sq. yds., 1 in. thick, or 18 sq. yds., 2 ins. thick. The latter is quite thick enough to lay on a broken stone support, which is brought up to a level 2 ins. below the finished level of the path.

A ROCK GARDEN

Reginald Kaye

Why make a rock garden? Well, why not? It can be good fun and very satisfying to create a well-planned and correctly built rock garden, both as an interpretation of nature and for providing an attractive background for rock plants in your own garden. Not that a rock garden is essential for growing the 'children of the hills', for the majority of these are quite happy in any well-drained soil in an open position. But a *well-constructed* rock garden can be a most attractive and fascinating addition to your garden, and one which you can be proud to show your friends.

Sadly however it is rare to find a really well-conceived and artistically carried out example of good craftsmanship with rock. That grand old man of the rock garden world, Reginald Farrer, used to classify some of the examples he came across as:

1) the 'dog's grave' in which flat slabs of stone were arranged at random over the site;
2) the 'Devil's lapful', in which it appeared as though a wagon-load of stone had been tipped in a heap and then more or less covered with soil;
3) the 'almond pudding' in which a mound of soil was covered with stones set up as erect spikes.

Although Farrer's words were written about sixty years ago, one can see many similar examples in recent work.

One of the secrets of success in correct building is to familiarise yourself with the ways in which rocks appear in undisturbed outcrops. There are many hillsides peppered with rocks which have fallen down from their original beds through the forces of nature, e.g. erosion, ice pressure, land tremors, and the like. Such rocks probably will have settled down cocked at all angles, even bottom-side up. Of course this chaos is natural but should not be copied in a small garden. You should look for groups of rock outcroppings with their beds parallel.

We are considering sedimentary rocks – limestones, sandstones, mudstones, etc., which were formed originally by eroded particles from older rocks being carried out to sea and deposited in layers on the sea floor. Ages of pressure, consolidation and impregnation with sea-water salts, hardened these deposits into rock, which at some remote era was heaved up above the sea by earth movements to form dry land again, and immediately was subjected once more to the effects of erosion. In this way the beautifully sculptured mountain limestones, the most popular of all rocks for rock garden construction, were formed. Very pleasing gardens however can be made from other weathered sedimentary rocks, in fact it is usually better to use local rock if such is available. You should avoid freshly quarried stone as this is almost always broken up, raw, and angular-looking, and extremely difficult to build into a pleasing scheme.

All undisturbed sedimentary rocks lie with their beds more or less parallel, though these beds may be tilted at some angle to the horizontal. This angle is termed the 'dip' and is constant for any group of outcrops within areas small enough to suggest a rock garden scheme. In larger areas, the dip may vary considerably from place to place. In my own village the dip of the limestone varies from 0°–90° within two miles of my home, but this is unusual. In many of the Yorkshire limestone scarps the beds run parallel for miles. The point is that in a garden, in the interests of unity and the creation of a restful scheme, the dip of the rocks – the stratification if you like – should be uniform throughout, variety being achieved by the other faces of the rocks.

All this sounds as though some tremendous job was being planned, but the principle applies just as much to miniature rock gardens created in old pig troughs, window-boxes, or even in seed trays. Furthermore an interest in how our landscapes are affected by their rock formations adds very greatly to our enjoyment of the countryside.

The non-sedimentary rocks such as the granites, the so-called volcanic and plutonic rocks, often weather into very attractive shapes, and can be built into fascinating rock gardens by balancing the rock masses in a harmonious design. Stratification problems hardly exist but in the interests of good gardening, and the provision of suitable planting areas, it is as well to avoid extremely dramatic faces. One sets the rocks with their more attractive sides showing, usually the largest side being chosen as a base.

The non-sedimentary rocks are not so easy to use, and the sedimentary types are thought to be more sympathetic to plant growth, though I do not think there is any firm basis for this belief. The only rock I know which is of definite assistance in the growing of rock plants is neither sedimentary nor plutonic but is a deposit from the soil-solution in limestone areas called 'Tufa'. This extremely expensive rock is very porous, and can be drilled to provide planting holes in the rock itself. Difficult high alpine plants, which can only be kept alive with great care under usual conditions, often thrive in such holes, rooting right into the rock itself. But the majority of rock garden plants do not need any such elaborations and do well enough in any well-drained gritty soil. The rock is merely a setting, though of course it is used to form raised beds, vertical planting crevices, shady corners, and cool root-runs for the plants. The rocks have a beauty in their own right, so much so, that a really well-built piece of rock architecture may actually suffer in

A natural outcrop of limestone 'pavement' in Westmorland. This is one kind of natural arrangement that the rockery builder should seek to imitate by placing his stones carefully.

appearance by the intrusion of too much vegetation. However the main reason for making the rock garden is to provide a congenial setting for the plants, so where should we site it?

SITING THE ROCK GARDEN

First and foremost the site must be in the open, away from trees, from which the drip and the shade may damage or actually kill many rock plants. An unseen hazard from nearby trees is invasion into the rock garden of their ever-extending root system, which will compete only too successfully for the available plant foods and moisture.

The great majority of rock plants need all the sunshine they can get. The few which require shade should have this provided by being planted on the north side of rocks and dwarf trees. Rock plants prefer a good soil provided it is well enough drained, and rain can get away quickly without causing waterlogging – a common cause of winter losses. If your particular garden is badly drained or has a very retentive soil it is advisable to provide a 'soakaway' when preparing the site to remove excess water.

A well-clothed small rockery in spring.

Construction details for a soakaway. Layers, from the bottom, are: subsoil dug over deeply, broken bricks or larger stones, small stones, fibrous material, top soil.

Ideally all the good top-soil should be moved to one side, the subsoil broken up and arranged into mounds for the bases of the planned outcrops. The lowest part should be dug deeply and the subsoil replaced with old bricks, stones, hard-core, etc., topped up with smaller stones and finally covered with rough fibrous material, reversed turves, or other means of preventing fine soil clogging the soakaway. Then the top-soil should be spread evenly over the area and allowed to settle for a period of 2 or 3 weeks, before introducing the stone. If the soil is heavy, or sticky when wet, it should be well mixed with humus in some form – compost, half-decayed leaves, fibrous peat with the dust removed, or spent hops. Also incorporate lots of gritty material, stone chippings, crushed brick, or very coarse sand. All this preparation may seem a lot of trouble but it need only be done once, and it is of the greatest assistance in providing a happy rooting medium for the plants. Of course if your soil is light, or gravelly, and quickly drained, your problem may be to *retain* moisture, but here again the incorporation of humus will help considerably.

If your garden is naturally sloping, it will only be necessary to diversify it by creating mounds and valleys and improving the soil as necessary.

No doubt at the beginning you will be most interested in having lots of freely growing plants, which will give a good display of colour at their various seasons throughout the year, and quickly clothe the garden. For these the above preparations are all that is required. Such plants are the mossy saxifrages, alyssum, aubrietia, the rock phloxes, bellflowers, rock pinks, rock roses and so forth, but as your interest grows you will probably want to buy some of the 'choicer' alpine plants, the kabschia saxifrages, rock primulas, soldanellas, and others of the rarer and less easy plants of the higher mountains.

There is a staggering wealth of plant material in this country, collected over the years from all the mountain ranges of the world by dedicated plantsmen such as George Forrest, Reginald Farrer, Kingdon Ward, and many others. The books about their travels make fascinating reading and whet the appetite to try some of their introductions in your own garden.

Scree Beds

The very high alpines are plants for the expert. It is impossible to reproduce ideal conditions for these in our gardens, because in their native fastnesses they do not have to put up with the extremes of British winters. They spend 4 or 5 months completely dormant under a cosy coverlet of snow which keeps them dry, and at a temperature very little above freezing point. When spring is well under way, the snow melts rapidly, growth starts up, flowers appear – sometimes before the snow has gone – and summer comes steadily. Seed is set and in early autumn the snow blanket returns until the following spring. Compare this with an average British winter where the temperature jumps up and down from week to week, from freezing hard to wet and warm, which starts growth only to be checked or frozen by the next cold spell. But we *can* manage many of the alpine plants which grow in the scree slopes. These are steep beds of small to medium stones mixed with gritty soil, kept moist by drainage from snow melting higher up. We can imitate these conditions in the garden by making scree beds, which consist of various proportions of stone chips to a compost of mixed loam, peat, and coarse sand. My average mixture is 4 parts of $\frac{1}{2}-\frac{3}{4}$-in. stone chips, 2 parts good loam, 1 part peat, and 1 part coarse sand, with

4 oz. bonemeal per barrowload (approx. 2 bushels of the mixture), all well mixed and passed through a $\frac{3}{4}$-in. sieve. This mixture takes the place of the ordinary soil and should not be less than 1 ft. deep. Some plants prefer a higher ratio of stone chips, up to 90%. This can easily be arranged in one or two selected spots. The type of stone chips does not matter, except it should match the kind of rock used as near as possible.

The surface of the scree beds should be diversified by small rock outcrops to provide varied slopes and levels.

Nearly all rock plants will thrive and over-winter better in scree beds, but such beds are essential for growing those plants which naturally prefer rock crevices and the rock debris below the crags. In very dry areas some form of irrigation system may be desirable, though an established scree will retain moisture amongst the stones better than will an average soil. One way to irrigate

One way to irrigate a scree bed.

is by sinking drainage tiles vertically every 3–4 ft. and filling these with water now and again in very dry weather. The tops can be masked with small flat stones, or one of the new perforated plastic irrigation tubes could be placed just below the surface out of sight. In normal weather however no artificial watering will be required, provided a good soaking is given to each new planting.

Setting the Rock

When the stone arrives it is a good plan to separate it into heaps of rocks of similar sizes, retaining the largest and boldest for the higher, more important outcrops and keeping the very best for some dominant feature. Such a feature should be placed off centre. A good position is about two-thirds from the front, one-third from one side of the area, with a secondary balancing feature about one-quarter from the other side. Start the outcropping with the smaller rocks, making sure that they are quite firm by

Setting the rock at an appropriate angle.

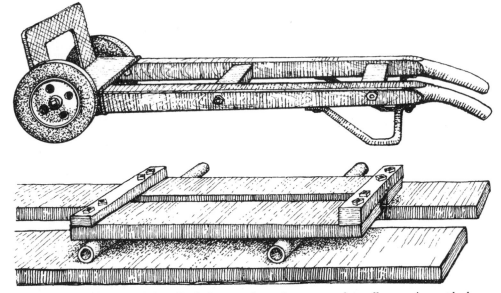

(Above) A 'sacktruck'. (Below) Really heavy rocks can be transported on rollers running on planks.

ramming soil underneath them all. A hammer shaft or similar tool is ideal for this work. One sometimes reads that rocks should be buried at least a third of their depth but this practice is quite unnecessary and a waste of good rock. Provided that the base of the rock is covered so that it appears to be part of imaginary depths of rock below the surface, this is all that is required. Fill in behind the outcrop with soil or scree mixture, tread firm, and start another layer of rocks making sure that the beds lie at the same angle to the horizontal throughout. Most of the rocks should fit closely to their neighbours so as to retain the soil, but here and there leave a 2-in. gap between the larger rocks to provide vertical planting places for such plants as the silver saxifrages, houseleeks, and forms of *Primula marginata* which will form in time a boss of foliage to mask the joints. Shady north-facing crevices should be provided for such plants as the Pyrenean ramondas and their cousins the haberleas and also for various forms of *Saxifraga cotyledon*, which do better in slight shade. Between the more massive outcrops introduce miniature valleys or scree shoots, keeping the outcrops 1 ft. or more apart for this purpose.

A useful tip when planning a rock garden is to arrange the main outcrops so that their tops lie touching an imaginary arc. This arc may be flatter or sharper according to the degree of dramatic effect desired.

This tip applies more particularly to rock gardens being built on a flat or gently slop-

ing site. Where there is a fairly steep bank to treat, you should still plan to have some dominating feature, diversifying the foreground with projecting outcrops to support such a feature.

Where the introduction of a pool is envisaged this might well be the dominating feature of the design, and the outcrops so disposed to suggest a reason for the position of the pool. The top-soil and subsoil dug out for the pool could be used to create mounds for the more dominant features of the rock, always keeping the top-soil separate for returning to the tops of the mounds.

The amount of rock required will vary and of course will depend on the area to be treated, but a rough guide is a minimum of 1 ton per 100 sq. ft.

The sizes of rock also should be specified when ordering. For the average modern plot it is unlikely that more than 200–300 sq. ft. will be needed. In such a case the rock sizes should vary from $\frac{1}{2}$-cwt. pieces to 2–3-cwt. blocks. For a larger area the larger rocks should not be less than 5 cwt. each, or even larger, if a really impressive feature is desired.

The problem of handling the larger rocks by the amateur rock-builder who is unaccustomed to such work, and without special equipment, may seem too much of a good thing, but with a little practice it is surprising what can be achieved.

I have been rebuilding my own rock garden, single-handed, with the aid of a 5-ft. crowbar, a spade, fork, pick, and

mattock – the last two to remove some 15-ft. sycamore and ash trees which had seeded into my garden. Some of the rocks were well over 2 tons each but by taking things steadily, and applying leverage at the right places I managed very well. Not bad for a septuagenarian with an artificial hip joint.

One of the most useful helps to move biggish rocks is a sack truck with pneumatic wheels. The usual iron wheels are useless, except on hard ground, as they bite into the ground and stop progress. With the handles upright, and someone to tip the rock against the truck, the handles can be used to lever up the rock into the travelling position, care being taken to balance the rock evenly.

The larger barrows with twin wheels fixed below the centre of gravity of the barrow can be used in the same way, by tipping the barrow to a vertical position, getting an assistant to tip the rock into the barrow, and then using the handles to bring up the barrow to the travelling position while the assistant stops the rock sliding out again. Always keep the fingers out of the way of possible traps when loading barrows in this way.

A double plank runway, carefully graded, will help a rapid and smooth delivery of the rock to its resting place.

Rocks too large for the above means of transport can be moved on sledges made from two lengths of plank joined by two cross-pieces, one bolted across either end, leaving a 2-in. gap between the planks. The rock is levered on to the sledge, and wedged into position so that the weight is evenly distributed. One end of the sledge is levered up to allow the introduction of two planks below it. A roller is then placed across the planks below the sledge, and the sledge levered along the planks from the other end, the lever being placed between the gap left between the sledge members. As the sledge is moved forward, additional rollers are placed so that movement becomes more or less continuous. Rollers may be 2-ft. lengths of 1–2-in. pipe, or lengths of broom handle. They should be kept at right angles to the plank-run as the sledge moves, by tapping into position as needed. If working single-handed, the larger rocks can be moved with a bar by rolling them over and over. To begin with the bar is used with a fulcrum in the form of a hard piece of stone and is inserted centrally below the edge of the rock. On levering up, the rock is chocked up at each

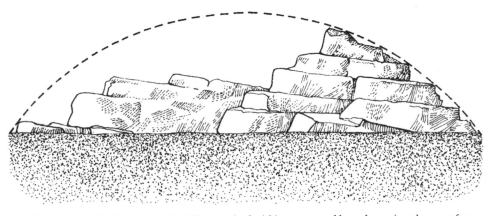

Ideally the 'outcrop' of the rockery should be contained within an arc roughly as shown, in order to conform to nature.

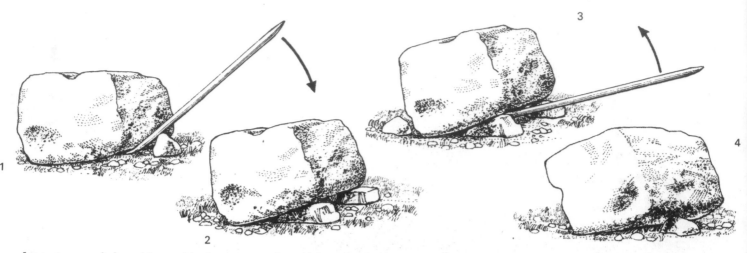

Large stones can be levered into position in easy stages. One edge is levered up (1) and stones or wedges are inserted (2). The stone can then be toppled over on top of a stone or brick placed so as to leave the front edge raised ready for a repeat (3 and 4).

corner. Possibly another lift will be required with a larger stone as fulcrum, and larger chocks inserted at the corners.

Then the bar is reversed and pushed as far as possible under the rock and then used to heave the stone over, first placing a stone, brick, or similar hard object, for the rock to roll on to and partly topple over. This makes it much easier to turn the rock over a second time – and so on.

It is surprising how much one can move in this way by applying leverage correctly without the need for using expensive lifting equipment, to say nothing of the sense of satisfaction you gain by having done the job with your own hands.

For still more ambitious schemes you would no doubt employ powered equipment for moving rock, but my purpose is to inspire the amateur rock-builder to 'have a go'.

Having built the rock garden to your satisfaction it is as well to let the work settle 3–4 weeks before starting to plant. In the meantime you can be planning the planting, and accumulating suitable plants for the various beds and crevices. If you have some spare ground elsewhere in the garden you could 'heel' in the plants in close rows until the time comes to put them in their permanent quarters. The best time to plant, if pot-grown plants are obtained, is any time between March and September. Avoid mid-October to early March when the ground will be too cold for effective root action. It is very important that plants should be well rooted in their new environment before cold frosty spells arrive. Frost can lift newly planted rock plants right out of the ground, and then the roots become frosted and dry out in the cold frosty air, unless carefully replanted at once. Do not plant in very wet weather, for the texture of the soil can be ruined for months by working it when saturated. In fact it may require another winter's frost to bring it into good condition again.

Ideally the soil should be just moist and crumbly enough to be easily broken up when lightly forked. To avoid trampling the soil, stand or walk on the rocks as much as possible. Kneel on the rocks when planting, or have short lengths of planks arranged for this purpose. Good soil is a precious asset, one which should be well cared for and treated with respect.

Paths

For easy access to the various parts of the rock garden, informal paths with stepping stones or rough steps, made from the same stone as the rock garden, will provide an unobtrusive means of reaching the beds without the necessity of treading on the soil.

I make my own paths from the many stones I dig out of my garden. Excavate 6 ins. or so where the paths are to go, fill up with stones, and top up with stone chippings. This stabilises the larger stones and provides a level surface for easy walking. Such paths need not be more than 18 ins. wide. The edges of such paths merge into the rock garden and can be masked with such creeping plants as the forms of *Thymus serpyllum, Acaena, Raoulia*. It will not matter if the paths are invaded somewhat by such plants, for they will stand up to occasional treading, and the thymes will give a bonus of delightful perfume when bruised. The tiny Corsican mint (*Mentha requienii*) gives off a very pungent peppermint odour when bruised, and can be used on paths of light sandy nature. Crazy-paving paths provide a good walking surface, but to my mind are not in keeping with the idea behind the rock garden, which is to create the illusion of a miniature mountain landscape as well as a background for plants.

However it is still more or less a free country and if you must have crazy paving make sure that the stones are set firmly. To achieve this, having excavated the areas for the paths about 6 ins. deep, fill in with 3–4 ins. broken stone, broken brick or other drainage material, cover this with smaller material to prevent the finer bedding medium washing down, and top up with fine sand or finely sifted ashes. Firm each stone as it is laid, by ramming the sand below it with a rammer until it is quite firm, before placing the next one. Use a straight-edge – a 3–4-ft. length of board with a straight edge – to check that the paving is even. If you are not prepared to do a lot of weeding, the interstices between the stones may be grouted with concrete.

The type of stone should match the rock used. In the case of a sandstone rock garden, random pieces of york paving will be excellent or old stone slates from demolished buildings, if available. Limestone paving is more difficult to obtain in thin pieces, so a greater depth of bedding material will be needed. Do not use broken concrete paving slabs in a rock garden.

PLANTING

Now we come to the fascinating job of planting the garden. This is where the rock garden really shows itself to be the most interesting part of a garden, for there can be something of interest to see throughout the year. When the herbaceous beds are still a stretch of bare soil, or the rose garden a collection of dead-looking sticks and manure, the early rock plants are starting to come into flower.

In February there are the kabschia saxifrages, which provide a succession of flowers into April. Also from February to March are *Hepatica triloba* (*Anemone hepatica*), the little Swiss anemone with vivid blue flowers, the forms of *Cyclamen coum* in crimson, pink, and white, and *Hacquetia dondia*, soft greenish yellow, followed in April by the many varieties of aubrietia, alyssum, arabis and mossy saxifrages. This takes us into May when an embarrassing wealth of fine plants clamour for a place, such as the early gentians, *verna* and *acaulis*, moss phloxes, the encrusted saxifrages followed in June and July by the myriad forms of rock pink, rock roses (*Helianthemum*), rock geraniums, bellflowers (*Campanula*), summer-flowering gentians, and a host of others.

Many of the rock pinks (*Dianthus*), bellflowers, and veronicas, will carry on until the early autumn gentians begin to flower late in August. Rock cyclamens, *Cyananthus*, and *Polygonum lowndesii* flower through September into October when the winter savories (*Satureia*) take over with *Gentiana sino-ornata* in deep blue and white, followed by *Saxifraga fortunei* lasting into November. November to February is a blank period for flowers but here the dwarf evergreen conifers in many shades of golden green, glaucous blue, and pure gold, take their place, and the forms of *Erica carnea* show buds for an early spring show. Many of the dwarf evergreen ferns enliven the winter scene especially when their fronds are outlined with hoar frost, creating entrancing pictures in the darkest part of the year.

To begin the planting programme the placing of some miniature trees brings a sense of scale to our rock garden. The slender columnar forms should be planted in the lower parts of the garden as a foil and contrast to the more dramatic heights above. The more prostrate forms give the impression of windswept heights if planted on the higher bluffs, and look more appropriate in such positions than the more erect varieties. When choosing varieties for the rock garden, unless it is one of great area, be very careful to choose really dwarf kinds. Many so-called dwarf conifers should be designated 'slow-growing conifers' for their ultimate height and overall spread may be 10 ft. or more, however attractive they may appear in their young stages.

Here then are a few suitable varieties which will not get out of hand:

Erect Columnar Varieties

Chamaecyparis lawsoniana 'Minima Aurea'. This is a slow-growing slender pyramid unlikely to exceed 3 ft. in height. Light golden in colour. The forms of Lawson's cypress should be planted well away from walls and buildings for the back draught and direct draughts from around houses can cause one side of the bushes to brown and die.

Juniperus communis 'Compressa'. The Noah's Ark juniper. This is the dwarfest-growing columnar conifer of them all. In very good conditions it may reach 3 ft. high, and 6–9 ins. through. Glaucous-green needles with bluish reverse, closely set, forming a dense slender pointed bushlet.

Said to be slightly tender but plants grown hard from the start seldom suffer from cold.

Juniperus communis 'Suecica Nana'. A freer-growing version of the last which may reach 5 ft. in time, not so dense, and occasionally producing stronger-growing branchlets, reversions to the type, which should be cut out when spotted.

Picea albertiana 'Conica'. Correctly *P. glauca* 'Albertiana Conica'. A perfect slender pyramid of emerald green, very fine needles, closely set, like a miniature church spire. Slow-growing. A 50-year-old plant in my garden is now 6 ft. high.

Thuya plicata 'Rogersii'. Broadly columnar, densely set rich coppery gold foliage. My oldest plant, over 20 years old, is about 2 ft. high. In its later years it may become more globular than columnar.

Prostrate Varieties

There is a much greater range of prostrate dwarf conifers from which to choose.

Juniperus communis 'Saxatilis'. Dense slow-growing with glaucous-green leaves and intense blue-white reverse. A shrub of character, seldom exceeding 6 ins. in height.

Juniperus horizontalis has many varieties, mostly too vigorous for the average garden. The variety 'Bar Harbour' in its best form is absolutely prostrate, pea green, with very fine needles closely adpressed, and not so rampant as the others, but there seem to be several clones in the trade so it is best to see your plant before purchasing it.

Juniperus procumbens 'Nana'. Forms a dense mat, glaucous green, and seldom gets out of hand.

Juniperus sabina tamariscifolia. I must confess to a weakness for this plant, it is such a lovely thing, even if it does require careful pruning to keep it within bounds. Left to its own devices it will extend to 20 ft. across but the glaucous overlapping sprays of foliage are a delight.

Picea abies pumila. Makes a low mound perhaps 9 ins. high and eventually 4–5 ft. across after many years. The horizontal branches bear pea-green leaves. *P.a.* 'Procumbens' is a stronger-growing variety, slightly coarser than the last.

Pinus pumila. Dwarf Siberian pine. Slow-growing prostrate pine, well worth its place on the higher slopes.

Sequoia sempervirens 'Prostrata'. A truly prostrate variety of the giant redwood, very slow growing, making a neat carpet.

Intermediate Varieties, Broad Pyramids, Bun-Shaped, Globular, and Decumbent Kinds

Of these there is a vast range available, the following are recommended as compact, slow-growing varieties:

Juniperus communis compressa

Chamaecyparis obtusa nana or false cypress

Abies balsamea nana, Abies balsamea hudsonia. Two similar low bun-shaped, never getting out of hand. Glossy green foliage.

Chamaecyparis lawsoniana gimbornei. Slow-growing broad pyramid, but may reach 6 ft. in time. *C. l. minima glauca.* Glaucous green, dense, broad pyramid. *C. l. pygmaea argentea* 'Backhouse's Silver'. Dense ovoid bush, tipped with creamy white variegation. Very slow-growing, I have a 30-year-old plant about 2 ft. high.

Chamaecyparis obtusa. There are several extremely dwarf varieties of this Japanese species especially suitable for growing in trough gardens. *C. o. caespitosa,* and *C. o. juniperoides compacta* and the rare *C. o. minima (tetragona minima)* never exceed 4–5 ins. high. I have a 60-year-old plant of the first mentioned about 1 ft. across and 4 ins. high. Really too small for competition in the open garden. *C. o. intermedia* reaches 1 ft. or so but needs some shelter. Probably the most useful forms for the amateur grower are *C. o. kosteri* with twisted branchlets, and *C. o.* 'Nana Gracilis' with lustrous fanned branchlets of deep glossy green. These will reach 6 ft. in time but are very slow-growing and extremely attractive.

Chamaecyparis pisifera provides many dwarf varieties, some of the dwarfest are, *C. p. nana,* a low bun-shape, and its golden variegated form *C. p. nana aureo-variegata* is equally desirable. *C. p. plumosa aurea compacta* makes a low golden green bun, *C. p. plumosa compressa* is even smaller. *C. p.* 'Boulevard' is an extremely beautiful glaucous form of fairly recent introduction, but I imagine it might get large in time.

Pinus pumila or dwarf Siberian pine

Thuya orientalis aurea nana or golden dwarf thuya

Cryptomeria japonica compressa and *C. j. vilmoriana* are two dense globular pygmies well worth a place.

Juniperus. On the whole the slow-growing junipers eventually get too large for the average garden, apart from the columnar varieties mentioned above. The new *J. squamata* 'Blue Star' may be an exception. The blue-grey cushions are vivid and dense.

Picea abies. The Norway spruce has provided a host of dwarf varieties of which the following can be relied upon to keep within bounds. *P. a. echinaeformis, P. a. gregoryana, P. a. humilis,* are all low bun-shaped bushlets, *P. a. remontii* forms a beehive-shape reaching about 4 ft. in time. *P. a. repens* starts life as a more or less prostrate bush but gradually mounds up to 1 ft. or so.

Picea glauca nana, usually listed as *P. mariana nana,* is invaluable. It forms a low mound of bluish-grey seldom exceeding 18 ins.

Pinus sylvestris beauvronensis is perhaps the most reliable dwarf pine, slow-growing and has great 'character'. Usually it remains a low dense bush, broader than high.

Thuja occidentalis caespitosa is a slow-growing mound wider than high. *T. occ. recurva nana,* deep lustrous green, has flattened branchlets curving downwards and seldom exceeds 18 ins.

Thuja orientalis aurea nana is a tight ovoid bushlet little over 1 ft. high, the bright golden flattened branchlets are disposed uprightly like the leaves of a book. *T. or. minima (minima glauca)* is a dense broadly ovoid bush, yellow-green in summer and becoming reddish-brown in winter.

Arenaria montana

Aubrietia 'Blue King'

Rock and Alpine Plants

Perhaps the best definition of rock plants is 'plants of such character and size that they appear "right" in a rock garden'. They may not be alpine at all. The true alpines are the jewels of the floral world, and generally are of tight compact growth and vivid flower. But there are some even from the high Alps which grow too large for the smaller garden, and these are omitted from this short review of desirable plants for the garden. Once one gets away from the alyssum, aubrietia, arabis syndrome, which results in a brilliant mass of colour for a month or so and a blank the rest of the year, there is always something fresh coming into flower from February to October. Of course there is a place for aubrietia and alyssum in moderation.

Acaena. New Zealand burr. Bronze mats, crimson-spined fruits.

Achillea. Finely cut foliage, silvery to grey-green. *A. lewisii*, lemon; *A. tomentosa*, yellow; *A. argentea*, white. Midsummer.

Aethionema 'Warley Rose'. Grey-green bushlet, deep pink 'candytuft' flowers. 4–5 ins. June–July.

Alyssum. The forms of *A. saxatile* give a brave show in spring, but get large. *A. s. compactum*, yellow; *A. s. citrinum*, lemon; *A.* 'Dudley Neville', biscuit, are good. Allow for 2-ft. spread. *A. montanum* is more prostrate, *A. serpyllifolium* ideal for a trough garden.

Androsace. Scree plants. *A. sarmentosa* and *A. sempervivoides* have umbels of warm pink in May–June, 3–4 ins. *A. lanuginosa*, trailing silver foliage, pale pink flowers.

Anemone hepatica (*Hepatica triloba*). Bright blue flowers in March, trifoliate leaves. 3 ins. Slight shade.

Antennaria dioica rosea. Silvery carpet, fluffy pink flowers in May. 3 in.

Aquilegia (columbine). Several dwarfs. *A. pyrenaica*, deep blue, 4 ins., June.

Arabis (white rock). Very rampant. *A. albida coccinea* has deep pink flowers.

Arenaria (sandwort). *A. balearica*, free-growing green film, white flowers on ½ in. stems. Good in paving. *A. montana grandiflora*, trailer with large white flowers. Plant to fall over rocks. Summer.

Armeria (thrift). The forms of *A. caespitosa*, 'Bevan's var.', 'Ardenholme', make

tiny tufts of fine foliage, heads of pink. 2 ins. June.

Aster. *A. alpinus* has large mauve, pink, or white daisies in June–July. 5 ins. *A. natalensis*, glossy foliage, bright blue flowers, 4 ins.

Astilbe. The miniature Japanese *A. simplicifolia*, bronze foliage, 5-in. spires of fluffy pink flowers in August is a must. The hybrid *A. s.* × 'Wm. Buchanan' is deeper pink.

Aubrietia. Mats of brilliant colour in spring. To keep the mats neat and healthy, clip back after flowering. Allow 18 ins. per plant. No trouble in well-drained soil in clean air, but resents polluted air. The named varieties are far better than any you may get from seed. Recommended are 'Bressingham Pink', double; 'Crimson Bedder'; 'Dawn', large double pink; 'Greencourt Purple', deep double purple; 'Gurgedyke', the deepest purple; 'Joan Allen', deep mauve double; 'Red Carpet', red.

Campanula (bellflower). These are legion and indispensable for June–August flowering. The many varieties of *C. carpatica* with upturned saucers from white to deep purple

Campanula 'Queen of Somerville'

Campanula cochlearifolia

Cyananthus integer

Dianthus neglectus

Dianthus × allwoodii 'Magic Charms', mixed pinks

are fine in the larger garden, they reach 9–12 ins. in flower, but keep to a fairly close clump of 12 ins. More prostrate but spreading are 'Birch Hybrid' and its parent *C. muralis*, bright purple; *pusilla* 'Fairies Thimbles', in blue and white, 3 ins.; 'Stella', very deep blue starry flowers. Avoid *C. poscharskyana* unless you want to cover a few yards. The forms of *C. garganica*, sky blue to deep blue starry flowers on compact cushions, 3 ins., are ideal.

Cheiranthus alpinus 'Moonlight'. Dwarf perennial wallflower, soft yellow, April–May. 9 ins.

Cyananthus lobatus. Prostrate. Large deep royal blue flowers, August.

Cyclamen. Plant on shady side of bush, whose roots draw away excess moisture and ripen corms. *C. hederaefolium (neapolitanum)*, pink or white, September–October. *C. coum*, purple or pink, March.

Dianthus (rock pink). Many good species and dozens of hybrids give colour June–August. Mostly lime-loving, but *D. neglectus* dislikes lime. All for well-drained sunny positions, making mats of fine glaucous foliage, rarely green. *D. alpinus* needs scree,

large cerise flowers, 2 ins.; *D. caesius* and varieties, pink or white, 3–4 ins. The soldiers – 'Bombardier', 'Fusilier', 'Grenadier'; 'Mars', shades of deep double red are tricky except in scree. *D.* 'Whitehills' is a fine-leaved miniature, clear pink flowers 2 ins. *D. deltoides*, the maiden pink, makes a spreading green mat and has good colour forms, 'Flashing Light', 'Steriker'. Allow at least 1 sq. ft. for this. 6-in. squares for the others will be ample.

Dryas (mountain avens). Makes prostrate mats of tiny 'oak' leaves, large white flowers. The native form is less invasive than the alpine species.

Erinus alpinus. Showy dwarf, red, purple or white flowers, 3 ins. Dislikes moving and best established from seed sown direct.

Gentiana. There are three main groups of gentians:

1) the spring-flowering species, *G. acaulis* forms, and *G. verna*;

2) the summer-flowering species *G. septemfida* and allied species;

3) the autumn-flowering species and hybrids typified by *G. sino-ornata*.

The great majority of the spring- and sum-

mer-flowering species are lime-loving or lime-tolerant, and all the autumn-flowering kinds are lime-haters. *G. acaulis* is a very easy plant to grow but sometimes does not flower freely. Frequent root disturbance by dividing and replanting every second year, in soil containing humus and general fertiliser, usually results in production of the glorious vivid blue flowers. *G. verna*, perhaps the most vivid blue of any flower, should be planted in good soil with some old cow manure worked in below the root level, and given some competition by association with such plants as *Antennarias*, thymes, or other small fry. Without some competition this gentian is short-lived, lasting 2 or 3 years and then fading away. I have kept plants growing and flowering over 10 years with competition. Any decent soil suits the summer flowers, they are all easy plants. *G. lagodechiana*, *G. septemfida* and *G. freyniana* all produce annual flowering stems from a perennial central rosette, a 9-in. circle for each plant. The autumn gentians start with *G. farreri* in August, followed with hybrids like *G. × caroli*, *G. × macauleyi*, and finishing with *G. sino-*

Erinus alpinus 'Mrs C. Boyle'

Gentiana acaulis, the typical gentian

Gentiana carolii, pretty but more difficult

Geranum napuligerum

Helianthemum alpestre

Lithospermum diffusum 'Grace Ward'

Phlox douglasii

Potentilla fragiformis

Primula 'Linda Pope'

Saxifraga moschata 'Dubarry'

Saxifraga × gaertner 'Iris Prichard'

ornata in October. Shades of sky to deep blue. Requirements, humus-rich, lime-free, always moist soil, and division and replanting every second year.

Geraniums. The varieties *G. farreri*, *G. lancastriense*, and *G. dalmaticum* are 'musts' with clear pink flowers in July–August and later. Allow 9-in. distance apart.

Helianthemum hybrids give a marvellous show from white, yellow, pink, red, orange to deepest crimson for 3 months from midsummer onwards, if prevented from seeding. At least 12 ins. apart, plant to fall over outcrops.

Lithospermum diffusum 'Heavenly Blue' requires lime-free soil, and will spread widely. The dwarfer *nimulus* is grand in a moist low-lying corner, flowers all summer. 'M. Whitecroft Scarlet', 4 ins., is a good one.

Phlox. The rock phloxes are indispensable in the garden, the various varieties of *P. douglasii* make compact mounds covered in late May and June with charming flowers, in white, various shades of pink to cerise. The varieties of *Phlox subulata*, equally free-flowering, make much looser cushions growing more freely and requiring much more room. Plant to fall over rocks. *P. s.* 'Betty', rich pink, and *P. s.* 'Temiskaming', brilliant magenta-purple are among the best.

Potentilla. Potentillas, too, are invaluable. *P. nitida rubra*, prostrate silvery mats, large dog-rose flowers and *P. eriocarpa*, cool yellow in August are the best. *P. tonguei*, yellow with reddish centre needs plenty of room.

Primula. Needs a book to itself. The true rock primulas are fascinating plants. Combinations of neat habit and glowing flowers they are a 'must'. For garden purposes the alpine auricula – not the florist kinds – the forms of *P. marginata* and P. × *pubescens* are the most useful, the many tiny species and their natural hybrids come later when you wish to extend your range. All the above are best treated as plants for vertical crevices when they will form cushions of foliage, welding the rocks together, and covered with lovely flowers with a heavenly fragrance in early summer. If planted on the flat they grow out of the ground on trunks and need to be constantly replanted deeper. The planting of vertical crevices needs some explanation. First fit a stone at the bottom of the crevice (which should be 1–2 ins. wide), fill level behind it with good gritty soil, and lay in the plant with its rosette flush with the rock. Cover with a thin layer of soil and wedge in another small stone, fill in, place another plant, and so on till you reach the top of the crevice, finishing off with another small stone, fitting as close as possible to the rocks. In time the primula roots will bind the soil and prevent it washing out. The woodland and marsh primulas, the candelabra types, may be too large for the smaller garden, but we cannot do without the many hybrids of *P. juliae*, itself a charmer. The hybrids, *P.* × *juliana* varieties are many and all provide a feast of colour in April. And we really cannot do without a few 'Drumstick' primulas, forms of *P. denticulata*, in white, pale and dark blue, and shades of pink and crimson. *P. rosea* especially in the form 'Micia de Geer' is a 'must' for a damp corner, vivid carmine flowers, 9 ins.

I think of all rock garden plants the primulas come first in my permanent loves. The only snag is vine weevil, whose grubs dote on primulas and their cousins the cyclamens, eating away the roots unseen until the damage is done. A routine dusting with BHC powder will prevent trouble.

Ramonda must be mentioned, with its cousins the *Haberleas*, just the job for shady crevices in rather peaty soil.

Saxifraga. You cannot go wrong with any of the saxifrage family, except that the kabschia group really demand scree treatment. The 'silveries' forms of *S. aizoon*, *S. cochlearis*, never forgetting the magnificent cultivar *S. longifolia* 'Tumbling Waters', are all crevice plants, to be treated like the *Primula marginata* varieties. Their arching plumes add grace to the garden in June.

But February–April is the time for the kabschia group, tight little hoary tuffets covered with lovely flowers. But they must have scree treatment, or they will dwindle away. The brief selection *S. apiculata*, primrose, *S. burseriana* forms, white or sulphur, *S.* 'Cranbourne', raspberry-pink, *S.* 'Faldonside', the best yellow, are 'musts'. The mossies, bright green mats with white, pink or red flowers ask only a cool root run, and spread widely.

They should be pulled apart and replanted every other year. *S.* 'Triumph' is the best unfading red. The engleria group is best until you are experienced, but the porphyrion group, forms of *S. oppositifolia* make prostrate thyme-like mats covered with bright purple flowers in March. The dwarf London pride, *S. primuloides* must be included, and for late October *S. fortunei* sends up its spires of irregular white flowers, 12 ins., over glossy bronzed foliage.

Sedums and **Sempervivums** are all colourful plants in foliage and flower, though they can be invasive. They do fine in town gardens. *Sedum cauticolum* brings colour in October, rich purple. *Sempervivum arachnoideum*, the cobweb houseleek is a 'must' for binding crevices.

Thymes. And now another jump, leaving out many desirables, to the thymes. These are indispensable carpeters, which give a mosaic of white, pink, and vivid purple flowers in the forms of *Thymus serpyllum*.

Veronica. These should be included because of their neat mats of pale to deepest blue flowers in late summer. *V. skellumi*, *V. rupestris*, and *V. selleri* are good ones.

Viola represented by *V. gracilis* 'Martin', deep purple, and *V. g. sulphurea* 'Moonlight' are neat colourful perennials. *V. cornuta* spreads too much for the smaller garden, *V. c.* 'Grovemount' is one of the best.

Wahlenbergia serpyllifolia. You cannot omit this for the scree. Quite prostrate and relatively huge deep blue/violet bells in midsummer.

So many omissions, but what a wealth of fine things to meet as you gain experience, and revel in the beauties of the high hills at your disposal.

Sedum cyaneum

Sempervivum arachnoideum tomentosum

Thymus serpyllum

Viola odorata, the sweet violet

Viola gracilis 'Moonlight'

Wahlenbergia serpyllifolia major

MAKING

A POOL OR STREAM

Reginald Kaye

I suppose that, sooner or later, every gardener thinks of introducing a pool of some kind into his garden in which to grow one or two waterlilies or other aquatic plants. There is no doubt that a sheet of water brings a new dimension into the garden. It is a magnet which draws one's steps towards it, a place of relaxation where one can rest awhile and gaze at the opulent beauty of waterlilies, the graceful movements of fish gliding amongst the water plants, or the reflections of cloud and sky, and thereby enjoy a feeling of serenity undisturbed by one's daily cares. Like all worthwhile garden operations a certain amount of hard work is entailed, but the rewards are great.

Nowadays there are all manner of materials which can be used to make a pool, mostly based on plastics which enable you to start, finish and furnish a pool within a few hours. It depends on what you want, how ambitious you are, and how much you wish to spend.

SITING

When you have decided to make a pool it is as well to spend a little time thinking over the various requirements you have to meet, before you rush out to dig holes in the garden. Possibly the most important problem is the correct siting of the pool. If water plants are to thrive and flower well they must get all the sunlight they can. The site must therefore be well away from anything which will shade the water, especially trees,

for they cause trouble in many ways apart from shading the pool. In autumn the fallen leaves collect in the water and their subsequent decomposition uses up all the available oxygen, creating conditions detrimental or even fatal to fish as well as inhibiting the growth of aquatic plants. Their ever-expanding roots will creep under the pool, exerting tremendous pressure which can rupture the fabric of rigidly constructed pools, be it fibre-glass or concrete. The drip from branches will harm the waterlily leaves, and deposits from aphids can cause fungal troubles to develop.

The next problem is the siting of the pool in relation to other features of the garden. Water has such a dominating effect that it becomes the focal point of any garden design. For instance it could provide the central feature of a formal terrace layout combined with formally shaped flower beds. It might be the terminal incident in a garden vista or at the junction of principal paths. Wherever the pool is sited it becomes the chief point of interest to which the surroundings form a frame.

Where the garden has a steep gradient the natural site would be towards the lower end of the slope, provided that it was open to the sun. If the pool is associated with a rock garden, it should be sited as the central point of interest supported by the disposition of the principal outcrops of rock as a background. If you want to combine a pool and stream there is no reason why the latter

should not appear from a shaded 'woodland' part of the garden, provided that the pool part is in full sun. The shaded end could then be devoted to plantings of shade-loving plants, and in fact such a scheme might well be the most delightful part of the garden. Picture groups of silver birch with an underplanting of graceful ferns, hostas, and primulas, from which soar spires of lilies with a winding stream coming out into the sunshine, with waterlilies glowing in a sunny pool framed with plantings of iris, ornamental grasses, reeds and marsh plants, such as the double caltha, with marginals like callas, pontederia and sagittaria.

Formal pools may be square, rectangular, circular, elliptical, or a combination of these shapes, such as a rectangular pool with semicircular ends. More elaborate shapes tend to lose dignity and appear 'fussy', though perhaps they might be considered, say, in a small patio garden on Moorish lines.

The informal pool is more likely to interest the gardener whose chief preoccupation is to provide a home for aquatic plants, for there is much more scope for planting a wide variety of subjects there than in a formal pool, where planting should be confined to one or more waterlilies and one or two contrasting upright-growing subjects such as irises and reeds.

CONSTRUCTION AND MATERIALS

Basically anything which will contain water can be utilised for growing aquatics. Years

An attractive small formal square pool with fountain, within the capability of most average handymen to construct.

A less formal pool for the small garden, also simple to construct and forming an effective focal point for one corner.

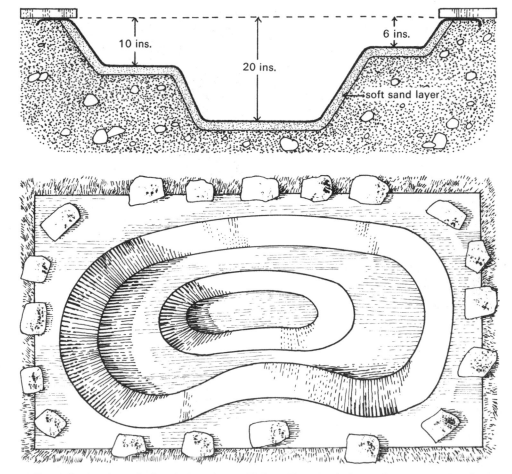

ago I put up for an award at the Chelsea Show a bulb-bowl about 10 ins. wide and 4 ins. deep, containing a miniature pink waterlily with 5 or 6 flowers out. Afterwards it continued to flower all summer on a sunny windowsill. In emergencies I have used packing cases lined with polythene, old baths, and on one occasion I remember borrowing a zinc bath from the family wash-house – but I prefer to draw a veil over that incident. By the way galvanised containers must be well weathered, and preferably painted with a non-poisonous plastic paint. Once I poisoned a pool, killing several 12-in. golden orfe by running in water over some new galvanised guttering.

Lining Material

The use of modern plastic membranes makes it possible to make a pool, fill, and plant it, in the course of a single day. Having decided on the site you simply dig out the hole, line it with soft sand or dampened newspaper to prevent any sharp stones damaging the liner, stretch the liner across the hole and after anchoring the edges with heavy stones, run in the water. The liner will stretch with the weight of water, sagging until it fits the hole closely. Then it is just a matter of placing the plants in containers on the pool bottom. There are several types of plastic liner on offer these days, of various strengths and durability, and with reason-able care some of these will last for several years. Polythene sheeting is the least dur-able, becoming fragile and brittle after a year or so, but it is very useful in an emergency. Polythene sheeting will not stretch very well so the pool should be lined with it, folding where necessary to fit the contours of the pool. It is wise to use double thickness.

Reinforced laminated vinyl plastic liners are perhaps the most useful. The strongest of all, Butalene, is used for lining large pools and reservoirs. This product has a labora-tory-tested life of 80 years, which is long enough for most folk. All the above liners are made up into rectangular sheets by the makers, by electrically welding sufficient lengths together to the required size. When ordering these vinyl liners the makers will require the overall length plus twice the depth and the overall breadth plus twice the depth. For polythene allow a further 2 ft. in both length and breadth for overlapping the sides as this material does not stretch.

Then there are all kinds of informal pools made of resin-bonded fibre-glass, semi-rigid and quite tough, but these are limited in size and will not accommodate very many plants, especially strongly-growing ones. The formally shaped fibre-glass liners are quite useful for incorporation in the smaller terrace designs where no great area is in-volved, but they are relatively expensive and if you are doing the work yourself without paid help the concrete pool might well cost less. The largest rectangular pool of this type I have seen for sale would accommo-date at most two of the smaller waterlilies and perhaps a score of marginals.

For their long-term development the stronger-growing waterlilies need deeper water than that usually recommended. Their foliage spread might well be 10 ft. in diameter while their roots need at least two or three bushels of good loam to keep them in character, though they will do well enough for a year or so in shallower water. So for the larger pools the only materials advised are laminated reinforced vinyl, Butalene, which can be made up to any size, or concrete, and the pools provided with depths varying from 2–4 ft. to accommodate the strongest lilies.

(Above) Section of a pool using vinyl membrane. (Below) Plan of a similar pool with rectangular plastic sheet anchored with stones prior to running in water.

A pool that could serve as the centre-piece for a town garden. Its semi-formal design can be adapted to suit most garden layouts.

Osmunda regalis gracilis, the royal fern.

Athyrium filix-femina, the lady fern.

Tools and Excavation

You will need a collection of tools when you are ready to start work on the pool. A good spade, a garden fork, a pick or mattock, a wheelbarrow and a light shovel are needed for the excavation, and a good spirit-level, a straight-edge, stakes and pegs to mark out the boundaries, and a line to link up the pegs or – what I use often – a long hosepipe which can be laid in pleasant curves between the pegs. A good straight-edge should be 8–10 ft. long of $\frac{3}{4}$–1-in. timber, and about 5 ins. wide. Test it by resting one end on the ground, on edge, and lifting the other end up to the eye. A glance along the edge will detect any departure from the straight. A faulty straight-edge is no use for checking levels. Having marked out the outline, dig out the cavity. If you are also making a rock garden the soil can be used for this, keeping the good top-soil for the tops of the mounds, which may be shaped with the subsoil.

The excavation should be made leaving a shelf varying in width around the perimeter, and 6–10 ins. below the planned water level. This will accommodate marginal plants and pygmy waterlilies. The central part should be dug out to a depth of at least 2 ft. to take the waterlilies.

Having removed the soil, establish a true level around the pool with the use of the straight-edge and spirit-level from an established reference point on the pool edge, or place a stake in the centre of the pool knocked in until the top is at the water level, and use the straight-edge from this to all points around the pool edge. By the way if there is a low spot it is better to bring down the whole edge to that level instead of filling up the low spot with loose soil, for made-up ground always settles, however beaten, and eventually will cause an overflow where water can get away.

The sides of the hole should be sloped outwards at such an angle that the soil stays in the position of rest. If you intend to make a concrete pool add at least 6 ins. to all depths to accommodate the concrete layer.

Plastic Pools

If you are using a plastic liner you will need plenty of heavy blocks to hold down the sheet while the water is run in. If you intend to pave around the pool, paving stones placed around the edges will be admirable for holding down the sheet. When the pool is full and the liner stretched, trim off surplus liner to within a foot or so of the pool edge, tucking the liner edges under the soil, and carefully lay the paving around the pool on a mixture of 6 parts soft sand to 1 part cement, leaving about $1\frac{1}{2}$ ins. of paving projecting over the pool edge. The joints between the paving stones should be grouted with 3 parts sand to 1 part cement, and left a week to harden before walking on it.

Pick a warm day when using plastic liners, leaving them stretched out on a lawn while the hole is being dug, for they are much more flexible when warmed up a little. Avoid a windy day if you value your sanity!

Fibre-glass Pools

In the case of fibre-glass pools dig out the hole as before, lining the cavity with soft sand to take care of any sharp stone in the subsoil, place the pool in position and fill up around the edges with either soft sand or soil which has been put through a $\frac{3}{8}$-in. mesh sieve to eliminate stones. Tamp down the filling with a wood rammer, fork-handle, or similar object, carefully checking levels the while. It is easy to cock up one end of a fibre-glass pool by too earnest ramming. Make sure that any shelves of the container are well supported and able to take the weight of water, which is considerable.

Concrete Pools

If you want a pool with vertical sides, as for instance in a fairly ambitious formal layout, it must be concrete, or built with stone or brick laid with concrete mortar and well concreted behind. Second-hand already-squared stone can be bought quite cheaply as a rule from a convenient demolition site. Stone or brick walls should always be built double with all the interstices well mortared with cement mortar. If the pool sides are to be raised above ground level, say to sitting height, of course the walls must be solidly built up from the level of the pool bottom, otherwise they will sink and get out of vertical. The tops of masonry or brick walls must be sealed with copings bedded in concrete to prevent weather getting into them.

If you wish to make the pool without the aid of shuttering, you will have to dig the sides out to leave them sloping outwards at 45° so that the concrete can be laid without slipping down. If the sides must be vertical you will need shuttering. If the pool is dug out of loose gravelly soil, which will not stand without support, external shuttering will be required as well. This can be expendable material left in position, such as old corrugated sheets, old hardboard, and the like.

The shuttering for the inside of the pool is made up of panels of 1-in. boards held together with battens nailed on one side only, the side towards the concrete being kept as smooth as possible, and treated with grease or old sump-oil to prevent the concrete sticking to it. It is advisable to use some form of reinforcement. Strong galvanised chain-link netting is good, or special steel reinforcement netting can be used. Old rusty material should be avoided, as rust reacts with cement, ultimately rendering the concrete weak.

First the pool bottom should be well rammed with broken stone to a hard level surface, then the concrete bottom laid. A depth of 3 ins. freshly-mixed concrete is laid evenly over the entire bottom, then the reinforcement laid, with the ends turned up to key into the sides when they are put in. Then another 3-in. layer of concrete is laid over the reinforcement and well worked in to make good contact with the lower layer, finishing all level. After 4 days the bottom will be hard enough to do the sides. Place any external shuttering first, wedging the bottoms of the sheets in the correct position with stones. The sheets should be cut if necessary so as to be the exact depth of the finished pool.

Then the panels should be erected on the long sides, held in position by shores across the pool bottom. The panels of course should be made to the correct length. Then the end panels are placed just inside the side panels, and shored in position. The tops of the panels may be held erect by battens lightly nailed across the pool, and to stakes rammed firm outside the pool, the nails being left 'proud' so that they can be withdrawn easily. The panels should not be nailed to each other. Reinforcement netting is then carefully placed half-way between the inner and outer shuttering, and concrete laid gently on either side of it, tamping it down gently with a stake, pick handle, or similar tool. Concrete should always be 'placed' and not thrown into position, as the aggregate will separate somewhat when thrown, rendering the concrete weak. Gradually bring the concrete up to the required level – allowing for any shelves for marginal plants.

The concrete should be made by thoroughly mixing clean 1-in. gravel 4 parts, clean sharp sand 2 parts, fresh, new cement 1 part. Or it may be got ready mixed from builders' suppliers. But the whole operation of the sides should be done in one operation, sufficient concrete being mixed for this purpose. You can estimate how much is required by multiplying the area of the sides and ends in feet, by the thickness of the walls, 6 ins. equals $\frac{1}{2}$ ft. So in a pool 10 ft. long by 5 ft. wide, and 3 ft. deep, you would require 30 plus 30 plus 15 plus 15 ft. $\times \frac{1}{2} =$ 45 cu. ft. plus 25 cu. ft. for the bottom. 70 cu. ft. is divided by 27 to get cu. yds., the unit in which you order the materials as mixed concrete.

It is very important that the sides be finished in one operation, if you knock off for the night half-way through, the joint next day will be a weakness, and of course mixed concrete begins to set after it has been mixed half an hour or so. After 3–4 days the concrete will be hard enough to remove the shuttering without damaging the work. (Separate mixes for bottom and sides of course.) If a drain is to be installed, a suitable length of pipe should be set in with the concrete near the floor of the pool. More details on draining further on. By the way never use cement which has been stored too long, or dirty aggregate, both cause weak concrete. A well-made concrete pool will remain good for many years, a badly made one is a perennial source of trouble. After the shuttering has been removed the whole of the pool interior should be rendered with a strong mix of 3 parts soft sand to 1 part cement, with a smooth trowel (sand with tiny pebbles in it makes it impossible to get a smooth finish). A waterproofing compound should be added to this mix. When half set, the new cement finish should be gently brushed with a wet soft brush, or with a damp rag, to make sure that a smooth surface without pinholes is obtained.

When hard, a brush over with a silicate solution will render the concrete iron hard, and help to seal in harmful chemicals.

After a preliminary soak the pool should be emptied, and refilled for a few days, emptied again, and the whole surface washed over with a dilute solution of acetic acid, and the pool filled once more. After a few days, empty and refill, and check the water in a few days with a pH outfit. If the water is practically neutral the concrete should not require further seasoning.

Draining

To empty a pool the simplest method is to start a syphon, if there is ground lower than the pool bottom within easy reach. You put one end of a hosepipe into the pool, take the other end to a point below the pool, and suck hard. All being well you will get a sudden rush of pool water, and you promptly lower the pipe end to as low a position as you can. Or, you can coil the pipe carefully into the pool, coil by coil, so that water fills the pipe without airlocks, secure one end so that it keeps in the pool bottom, stop the other end with a cork or the thumb, pressing firmly, and withdraw the pipe to the low point as before, and all should be well.

If there is no flow you have an airlock in the pipe and must start again.

If no lower ground is available it is best to use an electric pump. Place a submersible pump on the pond bottom with a hose attached to the output side and the other end led to a drain. Start the pump, and switch off as soon as the water falls to the suction input. With a non-submersible pump the suction side will require a hose fitted with a footvalve, which is placed vertically to the pond bottom. The pump will require priming after which it may be switched on and will empty the pool down to the valve. The surplus water is best mopped out – baling is a messy business. When emptying an established pool the pump or hose should be fitted with a strainer to prevent debris, snails, small fish, etc., getting into the pipe and perhaps blocking it. It is unusual and indeed difficult to fit a permanent drainage system to plastic-lined pools, but with concrete- or masonry-built pools a drain may be installed to drain the water through a stopcock into drain tiles which are led to a main drain or to a soak-away. The stopcock may be fitted either inside, by the side of the pool, or outside in a brick-built shaft for the use of a key. The top of the shaft can be masked under paving. The orifice into the pool must be provided with an adequate filter. If no main drain is near at hand, a soakaway must be made. This consists of a pit into which the drain is

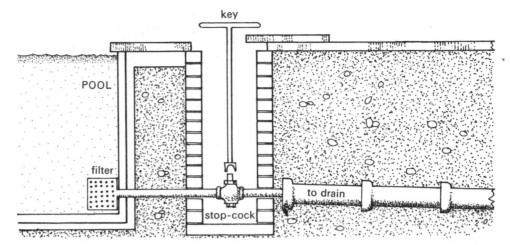

Cross-section to show shaft for controlling drainage stopcock.

led, the pit filled up with broken stone, bricks, etc., topped up with finer material to prevent soil blocking the stones. The soak-away should be placed reasonably near the pool. In loose gravelly soil a pit of 3 or 4 cu. ft. will be ample, but in heavy retentive soil a pit equal in volume to that of the pool is the ideal, though a smaller one will work more slowly. The pit must of course be below the level of the pool bottom.

Masking

The edges of the pool will require masking, and with a formal pool it is usual to do this with paving, cemented down to a hard base, and projecting slightly over the pool edges. In the case of a rock garden pool the masking is more of a problem. Paving may answer in part, but where the rock comes to the edge of the pool it is impossible to mask the edges satisfactorily by cementing rocks to the concrete edge, they cannot be got low enough. If part of the rock is supported by soil, frost will lever it loose in the first winter, and if the rock is set below the edge of the concrete, sooner or later frost will loosen it and start a permanent leak. The best way is to provide a shelf about 6 ins. below the surface on which masking rocks can be cemented securely, joining up to the rocks of the garden and so covering the concrete completely, giving the illusion of a completely natural rock-pool.

STREAMS

Frequently I am asked to advise on the use of natural water in a landscaping project. The answer is that if the water is to be used for growing aquatics as well as for display, forget it. In this country naturally running water is too cold to grow other than unsuitable native species which are used to low temperatures. Furthermore a natural stream is subject to floods which wash away any marginal planting. The only way to avoid this is to make an artificial watercourse to divert water above a determined level, controlling the flow with a sluice. If you wish to grow waterlilies and other aquatics to flower well, the only method is to construct a system whereby the water is pumped from the lower pool to the head of the stream, to circulate all the time. If the same water is used all the time the temperature will not drop appreciably.

Inasmuch as running water rises above its level when still, it is very difficult to mask the edges of a stream made with plastic liners, especially when falls are involved.

The makers of fibre-glass pools also make fibre-glass stream sections and waterfall pieces, made to simulate stone, but these are only for use in quite small installations, and

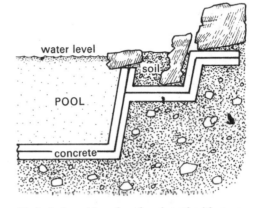

Method of masking edge of rock pool with stones cemented on a submerged shelf

(Above) Iris pseudacorus or yellow flag
(Below) Iris kaempferi

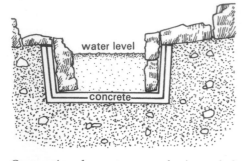

Cross-section of concrete stream showing method of masking with stones cemented within trough.

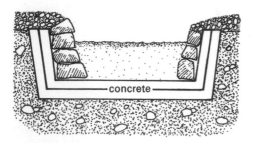

Method of masking stream edges with gravel.

The pool shown on page 82, this time at the onset of autumn. The net prevents leaves from falling into it and avoids irksome cleaning the following spring.

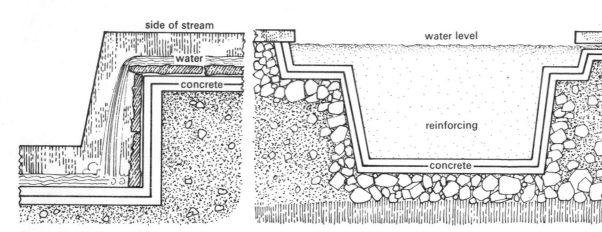

Cross-section of arrangement of concrete stream bed for a waterfall.

Cross-section of concrete pool with balancing tank.

for more ambitious schemes I prefer to use concrete. Over the years I have made many artificial streams and I have evolved a method which I find most satisfactory for making a very naturalistic stream garden. This is to construct a suitably winding waterway in concrete, about twice as wide as the finished stream is to appear, with sides high enough to take any required flow without loss of water. The edges are masked from within the trough by means of cementing suitable stones to the sides of the trough, or slopes of gravel, pockets of wet soil for bog plants enclosed by stones cemented to the trough, and so on. Of course a sound job must be made of the concrete trough, as any trouble with leaks is difficult to trace after the masking is finished. Depending on the flow required the trough sides should be built accordingly. For instance with a flow of 1000 gals. an hour 2 ft. wide, the stream will rise 4 or more ins. when running, depending on the amount of obstruction placed in its way, so troughs with sides at least 6 ins. higher than the 'still' level will be necessary.

It will be obvious that a considerable body of water, depending on the length of the stream, will be drawn from the lowest pool before all the stream and falls are running fully, and this will result in exposing a considerable area of pool-side while the stream is running. To obviate this difficulty

I recommend the forming of a 'balancing' tank into which the lowest pool overflows, the suction pipe of the pump drawing water from this tank instead of the pool. In this way the pool remains full. Such a tank must be quite full before the pump is started and should be of such a size that all systems are running fully before the tank is emptied, and plenty of water left to cover the pump suction pipe.

The required capacity for such a tank is found by careful measurement of the water system, pools and stream, in square feet, multiplied by the rise of water, say 4 ins. ($\frac{1}{3}$ ft.). A pool and stream 50 ft. long with average width 3 ft., say, would need 50 cu. ft. of water to start all stream and falls flowing fully. To this should be added the volume required to keep the pump under water, say another 4 cu. ft. You would require a balancing tank 6 ft. deep and 3 ft. sq. as a minimum. By the way it should be emphasised that all concrete should be laid on a firm undisturbed subsoil or on hard foundations built up from such a subsoil. Concrete laid on made-up soil will crack sooner or later through the soil settling and leaving the concrete inadequately supported.

PUMPS
Pumps are available today in all manner of sizes to provide the amount of flow desired.

Of the two main types the submersible pumps are placed within the pool itself, the non-submersible pumps must be housed in a suitable well-drained, well-aerated, weatherproof container masked from view, but readily accessible. The suction side of the latter types must be as near water level as possible, and in no case more than 5 ft. above the water. The actual flow from a pump is governed by the 'head', that is the height to which the water is lifted before flowing back, and it is reduced proportionally to the height of the head. Flow is also affected by pipe friction, so the outlet pipe should be of as wide a bore as possible, laid in a sweeping curve to the head without sharp bends, and having if possible no joints in between. Alkathene piping is recommended as the most useful for garden work. The pump makers will supply all information about their pump's performance. It cannot be stressed too much that all electric appliances associated with water, must be beyond criticism, and installed by a qualified electrician in such a way that all leads are protected from possible damage.

FOUNTAINS
The use of fountains should be confined to the more formal types of pool. Here again there is a multiplicity of models producing from a single jet to a complicated water display with patterns changing periodically.

Sagittaria sagittifolia, common arrow-head

A somewhat larger pool, with fountain, showing the splendid effect that can be obtained when the time and effort are available.

It is a matter of choice for the individual, and, the area available. Nothing looks nicer than a small patio pool with a modest fountain playing on a hot day – when we have one. However, I do not consider fountains in keeping with informal pools, and if the primary object is to grow waterlilies well, a fountain can prove actually injurious. Although using the same water over and over again, the effect of evaporation on the millions of tiny droplets in a good display is to reduce the water temperature appreciably, and so retard the growth of aquatics whose success is directly affected by temperature. The cooling effect of streams and small falls is not appreciable.

PLANTING

So far as the successful cultivation of aquatics depends on water temperature and day length, the best time to plant is from mid-May to mid-June. After Midsummer Day the conditions gradually become less favourable. Waterlilies in particular should not be moved after the end of July, unless they are able to be removed complete with container, for any root damage may not heal in time to withstand the coming cold weather. Moving waterlilies between August and the following March usually is fatal – as I have proved many a time, after taking chances.

Marginals are not so particular, but still often fail if moved too late or too early. The best soil is plain fibrous loam from stacked turf, but any good garden soil will serve provided that it does not contain peat, leaf-mould, or traces of manure. The rotting of organic matter below water uses up oxygen and poisons fish and eventually plant life. A matured pool correctly balanced is a valuable asset, easily upset by unwise interference. Autumn leaves should be prevented from fouling the water by covering the pool with a nylon net at leaf-fall, and removing the leaves to the compost heap. Any in the water should be removed. The majority of marginals are quite happy in the plastic containers supplied for them, but those made for waterlilies do not hold enough soil to keep them growing freely after one season, unless this is supplemented by one of the slow-action fertiliser packets developed for this purpose.

I prefer to provide planting squares about

A fine stand of Iris sibirica flourishing by the water's edge. There are also several white forms (I.s. alba and 'Snow Queen').

A good specimen of one of the most spectacular of water plants, Nymphaea or water-lily.

3 ft. diameter, 9 ins. deep made with three courses of brick laid without mortar, filled up with good loam, with a little bone meal mixed in the lowest layers. Newly planted waterlilies should not be placed in the full depth they finally require, until they are making growth freely. At first they should be given about 9 ins. of water over the container, and the latter gradually moved into deeper water as the plants grow. Or the container could be stood on an upturned flower pot or bricks to keep it near the surface, until growth is active. If put to the correct depth before they are established, newly planted waterlilies may not have the strength to reach the surface.

Here are a few varieties you may like to grow.

FOR 10 INS. OF WATER: *Nymphaea pygmaea*, white; *N. p. helvola*, sulphur; *N. p. rubra*, wine-red.

FOR 18 INS. (above the plants): *N. ellisiana*, wine-red; *N. froebelii*, wine-red; *N.* 'James Brydon', purple-red; 'Rose Ayrey', rich pink.

FOR 24 INS.: *N.* 'Attraction', red; *N.* 'Escarboucle', bright red; *N.* 'Gonnere', very double white; *N. marliacea* 'Chromatella', yellow; *N.* 'Wm. Falconer', deepest garnet-red.

MARGINALS: *Acorus calamus variegatus*; *Butomus umbellatus*, pink; *Calla palustris*, white; *Caltha palustris plena*, double yellow; *Iris laevigata* and *I. kaempferi* in many hybrids; *Pontederia*, blue; *Sagittaria* species, white; *Scirpus zebrinus* (Zebra Rush); *Typha minima*; *Villarsia* (*Limnanthemum*) *peltatum*, yellow.

WITH STREAMS, damp soil: *Astilbe* in variety, *Hosta* in variety, various species of *Iris*, *Ligularia*, *Lythrum*, *Mimulus*, *Primula*, *Rodgersia*, *Spiraea*, many hardy ferns such as *Onoclea*, *Osmunda* and *Struthiopteris*, and of course many more.

OXYGENATORS, so-called, produce oxygen freely in sunshine, when growing freely, but absorb it at night, and of course do not do anything during the winter. *Elodea* (*Anacharis*), *Hottonia*, *Myriophyllum*, are all good oxygenators, but their chief value is in using up excess nitrogen, helping to keep the water clear, and as a refuge for young fish from their larger relatives. The most important source of oxygen is from the atmosphere, so the number of fish you can keep is directly proportional to the surface area of the pool. Allow 3 sq. ins. of surface to each 1 in. of fish (excluding fins).

FISH are important, apart from beauty, they keep down insect larvae, and in an established pool will find enough to live on in the water. Over-enthusiastic feeding can cause trouble, for food not taken immediately will ferment and foul the water. A mature pool should keep itself clear, newly planted pools frequently develop a crop of green algae; this is harmless and usually disappears when the plants are growing freely. It is wise to leave the pool to clear itself, frequent change of water prevents reaching a stabilised 'balanced' pool and encourages new crops of algae. Have patience!

Lythrum virgatum 'Dropmore Purple'
Filipendula purpurea or Spiraea palmata
Mimulus cardinalis, a form of musk

MAKING

A LAWN

Brian Walkden

A lawn is one of the most important features in a garden, providing a perfect foil for the colourful borders which frame it. The lawn is a place on which to relax, and enjoy the rewards of routine garden work. It can even be an area where one can enjoy suitable garden games such as tennis, bowls, or croquet!

WHICH IS IT TO BE – SEED OR TURF?

Although it is possible to make a lawn from an existing neglected site, first by regular mowing with a rotary-type mower to get the rough grass down, followed by a building up of the hollows with frequent top-dressings of compost, or reducing high spots by cutting open the turf area and removing some of the soil underneath, a really satisfactory, quality lawn, is seldom achieved. It is by far the best policy to start from scratch and make a thorough job of the whole scheme.

In the initial stages, however, one question must be answered. That is, whether the lawn is to be made with seed or turf. Most lawns today are made from grass seed. It is a cheaper method and one which ensures the best type of lawn, depending, of course, on the quality and blend of grass seed which is sown. There is much more flexibility also with the use of seed. Where there is a problem of shade, damp, poor soil, or even types of soil, there is usually a mixture of grass seed suited for that particular situation.

More care and attention to detail is needed in preparing the soil for a lawn made from seed, for a finer surface is necessary, and careful application rates are required. The covering of the seed needs care also.

Perhaps the main advantage which will appeal to the gardener is the fact that, in most cases, a *quality* lawn can be established, and a 'velvet green' area is not such a dream, if attention to detail and a good soil is provided. For a good quality lawn, the finer types of grasses are required, and these usually include such intriguing names as the bents and fescues. The cheaper grass mixtures include a proportion of the coarser grasses such as perennial rye grass.

Usually, lawn grass seed is available in the local garden shop or garden centre in special packs, several of which have such useful information as the area of ground the pack will cover, e.g. 8 sq. yds., 25 sq. yds. and 50 sq. yds. Selection is further simplified by the seed merchants offering just a few standard mixtures which will cater for most popular requirements. Usually there are three such mixtures. First is a blend which will produce a top quality lawn of fine dwarf grasses with a rich green colour. This mixture is ideal for the 'showpiece' lawn at the front of the house! It will not withstand much hard wear, however, and is more for admiring than anything else. The second mixture, or blend, will give a more hard-wearing lawn, which is still very pleasing to

look at with fine dwarf grasses and still of good colour. For the really tough treatment, the third mixture is suitable, with its tougher leafy grasses subtly mixed with some of the finer grasses. This sort of blend produces a lawn which is capable of recovering quite quickly after heavy usage – even by the children!

All these blends are able to withstand periods of dry weather quite well without losing much colour. Another interesting point is that, once established, their rate of growth is reduced and less mowing is required.

A lawn made from turf is a more expensive proposition, as the turves will cost in the region of £5 per 100 turves. Each turf is 3 ft. long by 1 ft. wide, although some other sizes may be sold such as 18 ins. by 1 ft. The quality of turf is difficult to rely upon as so much will depend on the source and the supplier, and you can receive some rubbish if you are not very careful! A well-established turf supplier will offer the best quality local turves which will be cut accurately. An even depth of cut also is a good buying point, and generally the turves are between 1 in. and 1½ ins. thick. A reliable supplier will have treated his cutting fields with selective weedkiller, so that the turf received will not contain too many weeds.

It is as well to try to obtain turf from as local a source as possible, so that the soil it has been growing in is similar to your own. Remember too that you will need a suitable area for off-loading the turves, and five hundred turves can take up a lot of room. It will be necessary to get them on to the site if there is no immediate or easy access for the delivery lorry, and the tedious and fatiguing business of wheeling the heavy turves to the lawn site must be considered also! Turves cannot be kept stacked for more than 2 days or so, or they will start to yellow.

A lawn from turf has the advantage that it is quickly established, and can be used reasonably within a week or so of laying. Seed, on the other hand, takes longer to get well-established, although many of the modern blends are extremely rapid in getting established.

SITING A LAWN

Grass is a remarkably tough plant! Although it will grow in a wide range of soils and situations, it is sensible to site your new lawn in the best possible area where it will receive plenty of light, good drainage, and the best soil you can provide. All this adds up to quality growth, and a lawn which will be a pleasure to look at and use.

Of course, the lawn is usually one of the biggest features in a garden, and should be so sited that it gives the maximum pleasure and appearance from the windows of the house. In the larger garden, two separate lawns can be incorporated in the design, one perhaps being made to withstand very hard usage from children, and the other

lawn, a more ornamental affair, with choicer grass seed mixtures which will be more suited for less rigorous use.

The size and shape of a lawn should be carefully considered also. It is easier and quicker to cut a square or rectangular lawn area with no island beds. A lawn with an irregular contour is more attractive perhaps, but needs that extra effort and time in negotiating those curves! Manoeuvring a mower between beds and narrow strips of grass can also prove irksome.

Site Preparation

This is the most important stage in lawn making, whether from seed or turf. Good drainage and a level site (where physically possible) are two of the most important requirements. Once the area has been marked out with pegs and line, cultivation of the soil commences. The area should be dug over to the full depth of the spade or fork, and as work proceeds, all the perennial weeds such as docks, dandelions, etc., *must* be carefully removed with as much root intact as possible.

Where the site is large, it is a good plan to divide the area into narrow strips – about 8 ft. wide, and dig down each one in turn. It's surprising how quickly the ground can be dealt with in this way. If the soil is poor or light, it is essential that some rotted manure or composted vegetable waste is incorporated as digging proceeds. One of the concentrated and prepared manures can be used if manure or compost is not available. Light soils tend to dry out badly, but the inclusion of plenty of organic matter in the form of old manure, horticultural peat, etc., will make the soil more retentive of moisture and will also encourage good root systems.

An application of bonemeal can be given at 3–4 oz. per sq. yd. On heavy soils, drainage may be impaired unless the bottom of the digging trench is opened up with the fork. In extreme cases it will pay to include some small rubble in the base, and to mix in some sharp sand or *well-weathered* gritty cinders. Under no circumstances should poorer subsoil be brought and left on the surface of the soil during digging operations. If there is only a thin layer of reasonable soil on the site, it would be an excellent idea to buy some good loam and spread this over the lawn site after it has been dug over.

Levelling

The lawn site should be as level as possible to facilitate mowing. Bad scalping, or missed patches of grass, will result if there are 'lumps and bumps'! During levelling operations, care must be taken to keep the good or top-soil at the top, and not to bury it or bring poorer, unfertile soil to the surface.

To level the site, a master peg should be driven into the ground to the desired overall level. This should be at a level which will produce the minimum of work and movement of soil from one high site to a low one. This 'mean' level is important, especially where large uneven sites are being dealt with.

Further level pegs are then driven into the area, spacing these to the length of the long board being used. This board or strong plank can be about 6–8 ft. long, and is placed on top of two pegs, and a level made with a spirit-level placed midway along the top edge of the plank.

Pegs are tapped carefully into the ground until a true level is indicated on the spirit-level. Work proceeds in this way, peg by peg, until the lawn site has been levelled. Soil is then raked to the tops of the pegs over all the site. It may be necessary, where the area is very uneven, to take off high spots and deposit this soil in a barrow to the lower areas.

As soil is levelled, it should be carefully trodden down (not on heavy soils though), and allowed to settle for about 3 weeks before final preparations are carried out.

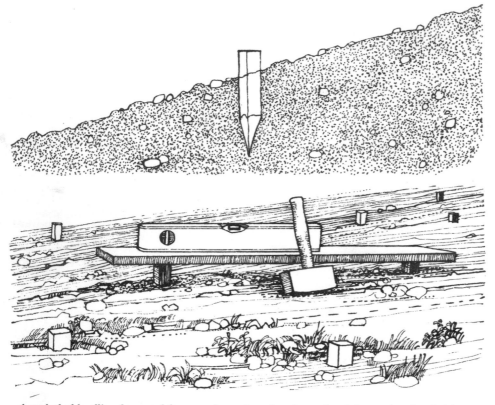

A method of levelling the ground for a new lawn. A peg broad enough to balance a board on is driven in to the required level and further pegs are driven in to the same level, using a board and spirit-level to check the accuracy. The board and spirit-level should be used in all directions over the whole surface.

An idea to help you level the soil for the lawn with a saving in time and energy. The rake should be used before and after to get the surface to a fine tilth.

This is especially important on lighter soils.

Basic cultivation work is best carried out in the late autumn, so that the soil can be overwintered and subjected to the frosts. It will be found that the heavier soils break down better after a period of freezing.

Where a lawn is to be made from seed, it is very important that the surface is broken down to a fine tilth, for this facilitates the more accurate broadcasting and covering of the tiny seeds. Lighter soils are easier to prepare as they break down or crumble readily, but for the heavier soils the work must be carried out in easy progressive stages.

First, the large lumps should be broken down with the back of the fork. Then a finer surface is achieved by raking and cross-raking. Work *with* the weather. A nice bright period will ensure that the soil is in good condition for this important breaking-down operation.

A reasonably fine surface should be prepared for turf lawns, but the soil particles need not be broken down so finely. As the work proceeds for either of the lawn-making systems, pick out the stones when they appear.

Sowing Grass Seed

There are two main seed-sowing periods – mid-August to mid-September, and April. The autumn sowing depends very much on weather and soil conditions, and many gardeners may well find that the month of April is preferable.

A day or two before seed is sown, a dressing of a general or balanced fertiliser should be raked in thoroughly at 2 oz. per sq. yd. Several lawn base dressings are available for this purpose. Rates should be according to the manufacturers' instructions.

Grass seed is generally sown at between 1 oz. and 2 oz. per sq. yd., but the suppliers' rates must be observed. The heavier rates will give a quicker coverage. Seed *must* be sown as evenly as possible and to facilitate this, the area can be divided up by garden lines into 3-ft.-wide strips, and these in turn, as work proceeds down each strip, can be sub-divided into 1-yard-wide areas. As a strip is sown, the seed should be covered by lightly raking the surface, first one way and then at right angles to this. Very small areas can be covered by some finely sifted soil, which has been prepared and placed to one side for this purpose.

Another method of sowing quickly and accurately is by the use of a distributor, which is pushed up and down the site at walking pace. The same machine can also be used for fertiliser applications, so it is a good investment, especially in large gardens.

Many grass seed mixtures are pre-treated with a bird deterrent preparation which does reduce seed losses after sowing. Where this is not used, some form of bird scarer is advisable!

Dryness or prolonged periods of dry weather can produce germination problems and patchy growth of the new grass, unless a sprinkler is at the ready for such occasions. Germination takes from 7–14 days according to seed type, soil conditions, and of course, weather conditions. The first cut of the grass can take place when it has attained a height of about 2 ins. The mower's blades should be set high for the first few cuts, and then gradually lowered for subsequent mowings.

Laying Turf

Once the site has been prepared (as for grass seed) the laying can commence. Avoid working in wet weather for the turves will

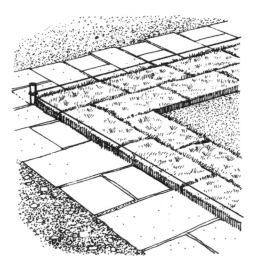

Laying turf. Notice how the joints are staggered – this is important.

A well-kept lawn in a fine setting. Grass and flowers set each other off to perfection. The arrangement of the borders provides a good model to follow.

be very heavy to handle and may well break, and the soil surface will become badly compacted.

A start is made across one side of the plot, laying whole turves down by the side of a garden line to keep a nice straight edge. The next row is laid close up to the first, but 'bonding' the turves like bricks in a wall – that is to say, no joint in one row is opposite that in the previous row.

Do *not* use bits and pieces of turf on the edges of the plot, as these will fall out before they have had time to root into the soil beneath them. Some gardeners like to use whole turves along the edges like a picture-frame and then fill in the centre with turves. This certainly ensures that no 'bits and pieces' are used!

Make sure that all turves butt up hard to each other as the work proceeds, and a gentle firming into place with the back of a spade or by a wooden rammer should be given. Fill in the joints with a trickle of fine soil to help them to bond together. This can be a mixture of peat, sand, and good loam. Afterwards, lightly work in with a brush or with the back of the rake. Working from a wide plank will reduce compression of the soil as the turves are laid.

If the weather is dry after laying has been completed, the grass should be given frequent waterings with a sprinkler. The newly-laid turf should not be walked on for about a week to give it time to settle in. About 10–14 days after laying, a *light* rolling can be applied and mowing can commence with the blades set high.

CARE OF THE LAWN

Types of Lawn Mower

Once the lawn is established it will be necessary to keep it neat and trim by mowing. Selection of the best type of mower for the particular lawn is most important, and, in these days, one is rather spoilt for choice!

It should be appreciated that there are two principal types of mower – the cylinder and the rotary. The former will provide the closest and finest cut, whereas the latter, although it gives a pleasant finish, will not cut as close as the cylinder machine. One does have, with the rotary cutter, the best of two worlds as it were, because most are capable of dealing with tough, coarse, and longer grass, whereas the cylinder can only cope efficiently with the domestic, shorter grass.

The more cutting blades a cylinder mower has, and the quicker they rotate, the finer the cut. The majority of popular-priced mowers have 5 blades, which give a satisfactory cut, but it's surprising the difference that 6 blades make to the finish of the lawn!

The size of mower depends on the area of grass to be cut. For the average domestic lawn, a cutting width of 12–14 ins. is usually adequate, but for larger areas, a machine with a 17-, 18-, 20- or 24-in. cut is desirable. For quite large lawns, the ride-on mower, with a 30-in. or more cut, is ideal.

Weight and size are important considerations where the woman gardener is concerned. There are several lightweight mains electric designs available, which are a delight to handle. They are also very handy where there are beds, trees, etc. to negotiate in the smaller garden!

Grass collection is a consideration, and the majority of mowers have this facility, including the rotaries. Most gardeners like to see the banded effect on a freshly mown lawn, and many of the rotary mowers now have a roller which produces this banding too.

The type of power – petrol, battery, or mains electric – is another selection point which needs serious deliberation. Instant starting is always available so far as electricity and a topped-up battery is concerned, but there could be a problem with a petrol machine, especially if it is not maintained well, or stored in a damp place.

A battery mower is limited to its cutting capacity according to the state of charge of its battery, and for large areas of grass, the battery mower is not a practical proposition. A small 12-in. battery mower can cut approximately 450–500 sq. yds. of lawn area on a full charge. Mains cable also limits the use on a large lawn, but the safety factor is much higher these days with double insulation. Even so, great care is required to maintain safety, i.e. cable in good condition and correct plugs and fittings used. Where there are several obstacles to negotiate, such as beds, shrubs, etc., an electric mower is not handy owing to the difficulty of keeping the cable 'in order'!

A front-mounted grass box on cylinder mowers poses the problem of cutting close up to walls, fences, flower beds, etc. The latest design is a mains electric cylinder mower with a rear-mounted grass collection box, which enables the user to cut really close up to walls, borders, etc.

In some situations there is a particularly tough grass-cutting problem, and for this need, there are specially designed rough cutters. Most are of a rotary cut design, but there are one or two which cut with a cylinder blade.

Cutting height adjustment is an important design feature, and some models have individual settings for each wheel. Others have a single lever which sets the height of two or more wheels in one operation. The former system is useful where the ground is uneven, or where there is a slope.

Summing up – there is really no such thing as *the* best mower. The answer is that there is the best or most suitable mower for *your* individual purpose or grass-cutting problem! Do try, if possible, to have a demonstration of *several* different machines before you make a final choice.

Feeding and Weeding

Although regular cutting will keep a lawn neat and trim, it is important to practise a routine of feeding and weeding so that good, healthy growth is stimulated, and competi-

Three stages in levelling a defective lawn, in this case one with a hollow. First the desired level is found by some such method as that shown (top), then the turf is carefully cut, and rolled back in strips, avoiding breakages (middle). The hollow can then be levelled with good top soil (foot). The soil is firmed, watered, and the turf replaced. High spot in the lawn can be rectified in similar fashion.

tion from weeds kept to the absolute minimum. A well-groomed lawn is a thing of beauty and is the perfect setting for the colourful plants which surround it.

Lawn care these days is less time-consuming than it used to be, and the effort required is reduced to the minimum. There are two reasons for this – the development of lawn fertilisers and weedkillers, and the design of equipment with which to apply these.

In many cases there are combined feed and weed control products, so that one application does two jobs for you! Examples of these products are I.C.I.'s Lawn Plus, and Gesal Lawn Food and Weed Control.

Sometimes particularly tough, persistent weeds establish themselves, and it is a good idea to wage an individual 'war' on these. Mouse-ear chickweed and pearlwort are two good examples, but these can be dealt with successfully with a weedkiller which is based on 2,4-D, dichlorprop and mecoprop (Lornox Plus or Supertox).

Unfortunately, there are several other difficult weeds which, unless treated thoroughly, can take over and spoil the appearance of a lawn. The blue-flowered speedwell can be controlled by applications of a preparation such as lawn sand, Actrilawn or Murphy Moss and Speedwell Killer. The woodrush is a very difficult weed which can only be successfully dealt with by digging out the affected areas, and then either re-sowing or re-turfing. As it grows well in an acid soil, the raising of the alkalinity in the autumn with a lime dressing will help to reduce its growth.

One of the most common problems is that of moss. This can be reduced by better aeration of the lawn, and by the use of special moss-killers. These include such products as Mosstox, Mosskill, lawn sand, or Velvas G. When the moss has been killed you will be left with black patches. Rake these off thoroughly. It's surprising also, how much living moss you can remove by frequent scarifying, or raking, during the autumn and spring months. Application time for moss control products is usually in the spring.

Do follow manufacturers' instructions carefully and accurately, and do not let it fall into nearby borders. Special applicator bars can be fitted to the watering can, and there are mechanical applicators or distributors, which can be pushed along at walking pace. These ensure accuracy with safety, and certainly reduce time and effort considerably.

Specially balanced lawn feeds are available to promote a good grass coverage of quality. Usually there are two main feed application periods – autumn and spring. The former dressing is prepared to encourage a good root formation, and the spring dressing encourages the rapid growth of leaf.

Do not apply feeds in dry weather, as grass can be scorched. If necessary, water a little time beforehand. If you apply dressings by hand, it will pay you to mark off the lawn into square-yard areas, to ensure accurate distribution.

A little time spent on your lawn will pay dividends and should enable you to achieve, with a good quality grass, that lovely velvet green sward which is the envy of every gardener!

Patching and Re-turfing

Renovating a lawn may be necessary in cases of damage, excessive wear, or alteration of the layout of the lawn. Patching is quite a simple way of dealing with small areas. The old turf should be cut out cleanly with either a spade or with an edging iron, using a piece of board to keep a neat, straight edge.

After the turf has been removed, the area should be carefully forked over at least 6 ins. deep, and a little moist peat or composted waste material incorporated. Where damage has been caused by soil contamination, the area should be dug out to a depth of about 12 ins., and replaced by new loam.

Try to cut out the area to suit the size of the new turf which is to be laid. Usually a piece of turf is 1 ft. wide and 3 ft. in length. Of course, it is quite an easy matter to cut the turf to fit accurately. Make sure that the soil in the area to be patched has been firmed well to prevent sinking later on. Butt the turves up to the existing grass area, and fill in all joints with some sifted soil.

Areas of lawn can be 'repaired' if seed is used instead of turf. The area should be prepared in the same way, and particular attention should be paid to making the surface nice and fine, to facilitate accurate seed coverage. Also make sure that the soil surface is brought to the level of the existing ground.

Sometimes it is necessary to deal with the problem of a lawn where there are areas of unevenness. A high area or mound can be tackled by cutting the turf of the area to be levelled in the form of a cross. Carefully peel back, or cut back the turf, and then remove the excess soil to bring it to the level of the surrounding turf. Replace the peeled-back turf, firm it, and fill in the joints or cut areas with some sifted loam.

The grass is dealt with in a similar fashion where there is a hollow area. This time, however, more soil is added to bring it up to the level of the surrounding lawn. Sometimes a slight depression can be gradually built up with dressings of peat and soil. This should be brushed or worked well into the grass at each application. A depth of about ½ in. is usually the maximum which should be applied each time.

Edging

A lawn is really only as neat as its edges, and these must be kept trimmed regularly. On a small- to medium-size lawn the long-handled edging shears are ideal for this work. For larger areas it is well worth considering the use of the real time- and labour-savers – the mechanical edgers. The simplest type is one which is pushed along the edge and a cutting blade revolves to trim off the grass. More sophisticated machines include a battery-powered edger which, on a full charge, can cut nearly one mile of edges!

Another type of mechanical lawn edger is powered by mains electricity, and there are versions with a cutting head which can be rotated to provide horizontal, as well as vertical cutting, along the lawn edges. The problem of cutting grass against a wall or other obstacle can be solved by the use of the latest cutting idea, which is a mains electric-powered edger which cuts by means of a short length of 'fishing-line' type of cord. As the cord wears down, further cord can be pulled out from a reel to the required length. This type of edger can cut where no other machine can, because there are no metal cutting blades which would get damaged if they struck a wall, or other obstacle.

The one-handed grass shear is a most handy tool for getting into the awkward places where the grass grows. They are so useful for cutting round flower bowls, ornaments, along a path edge, and especially round stepping stones set in a lawn.

A simple rectangular lawn can be an effective centre-piece in a small garden.

A less formal lawn – but still easily cared for – set off by a show of spring bulbs.

Watering

One of the important lawn care routine tasks is the watering of the lawn, especially during periods of drought. There are several different types of sprinkler available, and the selection will depend on the area of lawn which has to be watered. For the smaller lawns there are the simple, yet very efficient types, which are inserted in the grass by a thin spike. A simple orifice in the sprinkler top distributes water over an approximate area of 300–400 sq. ft. depending, of course, on the water pressure. One of the newest designs of 'spike' sprinkler has three separate heads which are screwed into the top of the head. A circle, half-circle, and a quarter-circle pattern can be produced.

Small, rotating arm sprinklers are very efficient, and some of these have adjustable jets, so that either a fine or coarse spray can be set. Many designs have a base which is in the form of a sled, so that the sprinkler can be pulled, by its hose pipe, to another watering position. Areas from about 900–1100 sq. ft. can be watered with these designs.

For larger watering capacities, the oscillating sprinklers are the ones to select. Areas up to about 2500 sq. ft. can be watered with the sprinkler set to water a full sweep left to right, left to right only, and, in some cases, just slightly left and right.

Another watering system is a sprinkler hose which is available in 25- and 50-ft. lengths. This hose has numerous tiny holes, which produce an exceptionally fine mist of water to fall gently on to the lawn. This hose is easily connected to the ½-in. water supply hose.

PATHS ACROSS A LAWN

Sometimes it is convenient to have a path across a lawn. This provides a clean and dryer access to other parts of the garden. There are several ways in which this can be done. Points to bear in mind are that the path should be constructed as attractively as possible, and the surface of the path *must* be kept just below lawn level, so that the mower can run over it while cutting.

There are several types of paving material which can be used. These include paving slabs of various size, with coloured and textured surfaces. There are even circular slabs which can be set into the lawn to make a fascinating stepping-stone path! The same effect can be achieved with ordinary paving slabs, if they are spaced about a stride apart in the lawn.

With slabs, a continuous path can be constructed, and a gentle sweep or curve here and there along its route will enhance its appearance. In an established lawn, the paving can be set down in the desired position, and then the turf cut out around the edges of the paving. In this way, after the turf has been removed and the soil excavated beneath to the required depth, a very accurate, neat fit can be achieved.

It is most important to make sure that the foundations for the path are well consolidated, and it is a good plan to place each piece of paving in a mortar bed. This mortar can be mixed up from 5 parts sand to 1 part cement. A stiff mix is desirable. As the work proceeds, make frequent checks for level with a spirit-level, or use a long piece of board across the surface of the lawn, and keep each slab slightly below this level. This method is excellent where a lawn slopes.

Of course, a solid concrete path can be constructed, but although this provides a durable, simple path, it is rather uninteresting, and there is a lot to recommend the *investment* in the more expensive slabs.

A path in a lawn can take several routes. This is purely a matter of personal taste and requirements. It is rather a nice idea, though, to make the path as practical as possible. A good example of this is to take the path along the edge of the flower border. This provides a pleasant walk and an area from which the gardener can attend to the border in comfort.

A path can link together several features in the garden along its route, and there is no reason why, in the larger lawn areas, a path cannot have one or more branches to different parts of the garden.

Loose materials, such as gravel, are not advisable for a path set in a lawn. The stones tend to be picked up on the feet, and are easily distributed on to the grass where they could damage the mower's blades.

A COLD FRAME

Roy Genders

A cold frame is one of the most helpful objects in the garden and can be kept in constant use the whole year round. In it, protected from frost and cold winds, may be grown early crops such as lettuce and other salad crops. It may be used for raising early seedlings, either over a hot bed made in the frame, or from sowings made in boxes or pans in February or early March, when the plants will begin to crop or flower at least a month before those from an outdoor sowing. Or, the seed of flowers or vegetables may be sown in a frame in September, and the young plants kept there until time for planting out in early spring. Early cauliflowers and Brussels sprouts, sweet peas and antirrhinums grow better from an autumn sowing, and will grow away rapidly when planted out on or about April 1st, after first hardening off. Not only will the crops be earlier, but, where the plants have had a long growing season they will also be of better quality.

When frames have been cleared of autumn-sown plants, they may be used for early strawberries in pots which can be lifted into the frame early in April. They will begin to bear fruit before the end of May. The frame may also be used for growing frame cucumbers, bush tomatoes or marrows raised over a hot bed, and which will remain in the frame until the end of summer, when the autumn-fruiting strawberries may be lifted into the frame in their pots. Dwarf beans may be sown between the cucumbers, and they will have finished cropping before the cucumbers (or marrows) have filled the frame with their trailing stems. Or again, early cauliflowers can be sown or winter lettuces can be planted. In this way, there will not be a day throughout the year when the frame is empty.

Winter mushrooms may be grown in a frame providing the light is excluded by covering with sacks, held down by wires. If the beds are made up in early September they will begin to crop about mid-October, and will continue to do so until prevented by the lower temperatures of winter. But as soon as the temperature rises in March, they will start to crop again. The frames can then be cleared in May to make way for tomatoes and cucumbers. The permutations are endless but as long as the frames are in regular use, they will be paying for their outlay.

Constructing a Frame

A frame can be made in many ways but it is not advisable to have the frame lights (glass panels) larger than 3 ft. × 4 ft. Years ago, lights were usually made 6 ft. × 4 ft. and were far too heavy to lift, and a woman could not easily manage them. The lights are made of wood and are either divided into three sections, each filled with small panes of glass, or they are of a single sheet of glass, when they are said to be of the Dutch-light type. As an alternative to glass, transparent polythene sheeting may be used.

This is tacked on to both sides of the light and is long-lasting and warm until it breaks. It is cheaper to replace, so that you must balance its possibly shorter life against the lower cost.

The frame itself may be made of two 9-in. boards fastened together, and held in place by strong wooden pegs driven well into the ground. The boards are cut to the size of the light(s) and they may be moved from one part of the garden to another, perhaps to cover a bed of early strawberries. If rhubarb is to be forced, then the frame should be at least three 9-in. boards high, fastened together, for rhubarb grows about 2 ft. tall. The roots are often planted in a hot bed made by removing 6 ins. of soil from the

frame and replacing it over the hot bed. When forcing the roots can be planted close together.

There are also frames made from aluminium, galvanised against rust. These are light to handle and may easily be moved about the garden. They are made 4 ft. long and 2 ft. 6 ins. wide, 18 ins. at the back and 14 ins. at the front. This enables rain and snow to drain quickly away whilst the lights, which should slope to the south, attract the maximum of sunlight. The frame is opened by sliding the light forward. The span roof light is made by placing two frames back to back. Each is a separate compartment and can be used for different plants.

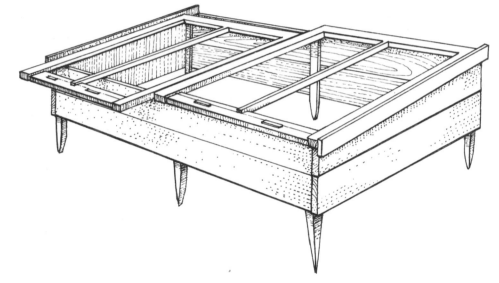

The construction of a simple wooden frame. Note how the vertical supports also serve as pegs to anchor the frame.

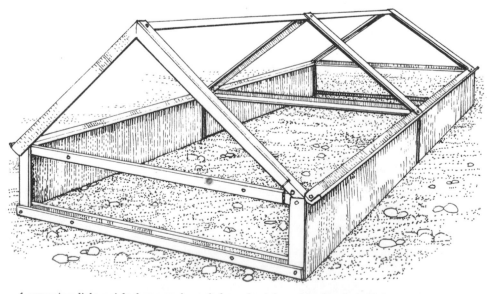

A convenient light-weight frame can be made from aluminium, either bought in kit form or from a D.I.Y. shop.

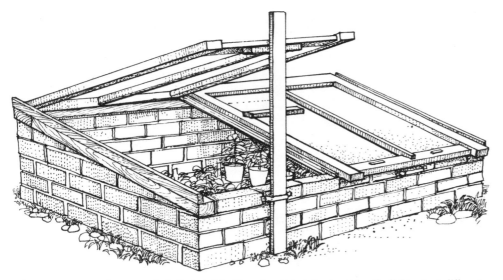

A more permanent frame can be built in brick. Note the support for propping the lights up at different heights.

A cold frame is ideal for hardening off bedding plants prior to planting out.

The Expandite frame, almost 3 ft. sq., is of similar construction, and is fitted with 3 sliding lights each of a single pane of glass. This frame, too, can be moved about the garden and may be placed directly over a hot bed on top of the soil.

A relatively heavy but simple frame may be made from old railway sleepers, placed one above another for the two longer sides, and with half sleepers at the back and front. Sleepers are 5 ins. deep, so two would be of a suitable height for most plants.

A more permanent frame can be made from old bricks or breeze blocks cemented together to the dimensions of the lights. The frame should be made sufficiently large to take 2 or even 3 lights, for this will make it more economical and much more can be done with 2 lights than with one. Plants may be in the seedling stage under one light and may be reaching maturity beneath another.

Materials are expensive, and if boards (or sleepers) are used for the frame, they must be treated with creosote or some other wood preservative before fixing in position. Allow at least 3–4 weeks to elapse after treatment before planting, so that the fumes have time to escape.

The wooden lights will need painting white or green after giving them an undercoat, whilst the glass will be fixed into position and held secure with putty. The lights should be given a coat of paint every other year to preserve them. It is also necessary to keep the glass constantly wiped clean, both on the inside and outside, for dirty glass prevents the maximum amount of sunlight from penetrating. If the glass becomes broken or is made loose, replace and apply fresh putty.

Hardening off Plants

A cold frame is a useful means of hardening-off plants which have been raised in a warm greenhouse or over a hot bed. This will be towards the end of April when half-hardy plants such as tomatoes, marrows, and cucumbers, will be ready to harden off. At this time the weather becomes warmer each day but the nights are cold, so at first keep the lights on by day and night. Then on all suitable days, admit a little air either by lifting the light at the side by means of a brick or block of wood, or pull the light forward or push it back 6 ins., but remember to close it in late afternoon. A few days later, admit more air by day, and after about 2 weeks, remove the light altogether by day and raise it at one side by night. In another

few days, remove the light both by day and night unless the weather is unduly cold. In this way, the plants will be gradually hardened and there will be little check to their growth when planted out.

Making a Hot Bed

A hot bed should be made up early in January or early February, by composting straw with an activator, and adding to it some poultry or pig manure, lawn mowings and pea and bean haulm, or some fresh farmyard manure. Composting is necessary to enable the bed to generate sufficient heat. It is prepared in the same way as compost for a mushroom bed, first shaking out the straw and making it quite damp, then adding the activator and whatever manure is available; it may be possible to obtain some horse manure from a riding stable. Build up the heap layer by layer, adding the activator so that it is evenly distributed throughout. Allow the heap to stand for a week, then turn again, repeating this once more and adding more water if too dry. In 3 weeks, the compost will be rich brown with a healthy aroma and will be generating considerable heat.

It may now be made into the hot bed, either by placing it in a deep frame to a depth of 12 ins. and treading or beating it down so that it will retain its heat for as long

as possible, or 6 ins. of soil may be removed first and the compost used to replace it, again treading it well down. If the seed is to be sown directly over the hot bed (and not in containers), replace the soil to a depth of 3–4 ins. Those plants which resent root disturbance, e.g. cucumbers and marrows, are sown in small pots, and these are pressed into the top-soil. After germination, the plants are moved to larger pots and grown on in the same way, moving them to another frame in early May in which they will fruit.

Vegetables in a Frame

The use of a hot bed made in a frame, or one covered by a frame and light, will greatly extend the growing season of vegetables. It is usual to make up the hot bed late in January or early February when a number of vegetables and flowers can be raised. These include tomatoes, marrows, cucumbers, sweet corn, celery and celeriac, aubergines and peppers, all of which require a long season of growth to produce heavy crops, and in this way at least 2 months will be gained. In addition, dwarf and runner beans, early cauliflowers, onions, and cardoons, will all crop earlier if sown in 3 ins. of soil over a hot bed (or in boxes) and planted out after hardening. Vegetables to raise over a hot bed are:

Vegetable	When to sow	To plant out	Maturing
Asparagus Pea	Early Apr	Mid-May	June–Aug
Aubergine	Jan	Early May (under cloches) Mid-June (in open)	July–Aug
Bean, dwarf	Feb	Early Apr (under cloches)	June–July
Bean, runner	Early Mar	Early May (under cloches)	Aug–Oct
Cardoon	Mar	Early May	Oct–Nov
Cauliflower, early	Mar	Early Apr	June–July
Celeriac	Early Mar	Early May	Oct onwards
Celery	Feb	Early Apr	Sept–Nov
Cucumber, frame	Early Mar	Early May (in frame)	July–Aug
Marrow	Feb	Apr (under cloches)	July–Aug
Onion	Feb	Early Apr	Oct
Tomato (for indoors and outside)	Mar	End May	July–Oct

Cucumber 'Baton Vert', an impressive example of cold frame produce.

Melons in a cold frame. Note the protection placed beneath each developing fruit.

In addition, radishes, turnips, and carrots may be sown in 3 ins. of soil over a hot bed in January, when the first thinnings will be ready to use by early March, and those plants remaining will be grown on to mature by early April. The frames can then be cleared to make way for boxes of seedlings to be hardened off, or for cucumber, marrow, and tomato plants, which will be grown on to maturity in the frame. When sowing over a hot bed, sow broadcast but if pelleted seed is used, these can be more evenly spaced out. Be sure to sow early-maturing varieties suitable for semi-forcing.

When growing cucumbers to fruit in a frame, 3 should be planted beneath 2 lights; 12 bush-type tomatoes such as Pixie, Sleaford Abundance, and Histon Cropper; and 4 bush and 3 trailing marrows. To give them more room, the lights may be removed entirely at the end of July when the plants will grow over the sides.

If dwarf beans are to be cropped in a frame, either in pots or directly into the soil, sow 6–8 ins. apart, but if they are going to be planted out in May under cloches or in the open, sow only 1 in. apart. Of runner beans, Hammond's Dwarf may be grown on to crop in a frame and the same remarks apply, though the seeds are set 10 ins. apart if the plants are to crop there. Cauliflowers raised over a hot bed are planted 12 ins. apart in a frame. Early Snowball is of compact habit and makes a firm head when grown under glass.

All plants grown in a frame will need care in their raising. They should be watered as little as possible. A hot bed will provide the humidity needed. Sweet pea, cauliflower, and Brussels sprout plants from autumn-sown seed in a frame, should be given almost no water during winter or they will tend to damp off. After sowing, water with Cheshunt compound (1 oz. dissolved in 2 gals. of water) to prevent the young plants being attacked by black leg. To prevent mildew, plants such as chrysanthemums, dahlias, geraniums, pansies, and violas, wintered in a frame, should be dusted with flowers of sulphur once a month. Green sulphur is best if it can be obtained. This is better than watering with a fungicide for it does not involve wetting the plants. Pot plants in frames should always be watered around the side of the pot.

For the same reason, ventilate freely whenever the days are mild and sunny, but guard against cold winds, for nothing will cause the plants more harm. On some days it may be necessary to admit only sufficient fresh air to clear the glass of condensation, lifting the light at the front (or back) by about 1 in. When the weather is unduly cold, cover the lights with plenty of sacking or hessian. Alternatively put on straw to a depth of 6 ins. with sacking or hessian on top of it to keep it in place. This, in turn, is held down by strong wires stretched across the lights. Under these conditions do not water the plants at all.

Straw may also be used to cover the soil where melons and marrows are growing in a frame. This will prevent evaporation of moisture and will keep the fruit from coming into contact with the soil and so prevent them from decaying. The straw should be in place before the plants make too much growth and before the first fruits are set.

Plants growing in a frame during spring and summer will need a daily syringe whenever the weather is warm and sunny, and copious amounts of water should be given, for at this time there is constant evaporation. As the plants make growth they will use up large amounts of water so on mild, showery days, the lights may be removed altogether.

Not all vegetables need a hot bed in a frame in order to crop well. Some need no warmth whatsoever apart from that generated by the sun through the glass, and which is retained by keeping the frame closed. Early cauliflowers, raised outdoors from a late July sowing may be planted 12 ins. apart in a frame in November, and will have formed large heads by early May. Lettuce, too, can be sown at the same time. One of the best for frame culture, forming a compact heart in the short daylight hours, is Amanda. The older variety, Continuity, also does well in a frame, and although the outer leaves have a reddish tinge, it is one of the best-flavoured of all lettuces. Plant lettuce 8 ins. apart in a frame and admit fresh air on suitable days.

Mustard and cress, radishes, and spring onions may be sown in October and again in December to provide a succession of salad crops. Sowings too, may also be made of endive, a crop which is a pleasant alternative to lettuce in salads, and for winter use sow Batavian Green. When the frames are cleared early in spring, a sowing of dwarf bean, The Prince, can be made and it will begin to crop early in June, a month or more before those from the first outdoor sowings are ready. Sow 6 ins. apart.

Early sowings of all kinds of vegetable seeds over a hot bed have been mentioned, but early varieties may also be raised where there is no hot bed. Sow directly into the frame, in a compost made friable by incorporating some peat and coarse sand. Sow broadcast early in March and press a cane into the soil to leave a mark to separate each variety. For cauliflowers, sow Delta or Snow King; cabbage, Greyhound or Primata; Brussels sprouts, Peer Gynt; and lettuce, All the Year Round. About mid-April, after hardening, plant out in prepared ground. They will crop at least a month before those sown in the open.

Rooting Cuttings

There are more uses for a frame than the growing of vegetables which could occupy the frame all the year if so required. Cuttings of every description can be rooted, and if inserted at the correct time need no artificial heat to root. Cuttings are one way of perpetuating named varieties; root division is another. If the frames have been cleared of the half-hardy plants in June, they can be used at once for rooting pansy and viola cuttings. But first bring the soil into suitable condition. For this purpose it should be made up of equal parts, by bulk, of loam (preferably sterilised), peat, and coarse sand, to a depth of 4 ins. Give it a dusting with superphosphate to stimulate root action, and leave the surface smooth and level. Cuttings of pansies, violas, miniature roses, sun roses, carnations, and pinks may be taken at this time. The cuttings are taken when about 2–3 ins. long, and only from unflowered shoots. They are removed with thumb and forefinger just below a node or leaf joint. Excess leaf is removed by a gentle upwards tug so as not to damage the stem. To encourage quick rooting, the ends of the stems may be treated with hormone powder.

Plant the cuttings 2 ins. apart with a dibber, and press them firmly in. When planting is complete, dust with sulphur and water in. Then place the light over them and whiten the glass to prevent scorching. The cuttings will have formed the first roots as soon as they are seen to be making new growth. They will then need more water and ventilation. Whenever they have formed a mass of roots, they are lifted and planted out. This will be towards the end of summer.

Cuttings can be taken of the following flowering plants to root in a frame:

When to take and root cuttings		When to plant out
Calceolaria	July–Aug	Grow on under glass
Carnations	July	Sept–Oct
Chrysanthemum	Sept–Mar	Apr–May
Dahlias	Apr–May	July–Aug (Lift Nov and winter under glass)
Delphinium (named)	May–June	Aug–Sept
Geranium	June–July	Grow on under glass
Helianthemum (Sun Rose)	June–Aug	Sept–Oct
Lupin (named)	Apr–May	July–Aug
Pansy	June–July	Sept
Pinks	June–July	Aug–Sept
Viola	June–July	Sept

Well-rooted viola cuttings, with some of the root-ball removed to show the ideal root development. Normally the root-ball is carefully preserved.

Chrysanthemum shoot ("offset") is carefully removed from the parent plant ("stool") in spring. Note that the offset already has its own roots.

After they have finished flowering, early and Korean chrysanthemums are propagated, either by root division, or by lifting the roots and packing them close together in one part of a frame. Pack soil around them and dust with sulphur before watering in. Cuttings will form from the old stems early in the New Year. They are completely hardy and can be removed with a knife just below the soil, and rooted in the frame for planting out in May. They will flower in the autumn. Later cuttings may be removed with roots attached and planted straight into the open ground in April. Plants will often have several rooted cuttings attached when lifted in the autumn, and these are detached, planted in a frame over winter, and planted out in April.

The dwarf pompon chrysanthemums are ideal for 4-in. size pots, planting one in each, or 3 in a larger pot. They grow less than 12 ins. tall and begin to bloom in early September, remaining colourful for at least 10 weeks. By growing early and later varieties you can have a succession of blooms until Christmas. The plants are grown on from cuttings as described, or by detaching rooted offsets. The pots are stood outside from early June, and go back in the frame early in September, to be taken indoors when showing bloom. One of the best is Denise, with its poms of bright yellow, whilst Fairie is soft shell-pink.

Many other herbaceous plants may be grown from cuttings, which is a quick way of increasing the stock. Erigerons, penstemon, gaillardias, phlox, perennial asters, aubrietia, and sweet rocket, all respond to this method of propagation. Most cuttings will be ready to take in May, before the shoots have grown more than 3 ins. tall. Sever them with a sharp knife and plant firmly in the frames 2–3 ins. apart. They will root in about 6 weeks, and can be planted in beds outside until moved to their flowering quarters in November or spring.

A large number of flowering shrubs may also be increased in this way, but here the cuttings will be mostly hard-wooded and should have the end dipped in hormone powder before planting. Cuttings of the conifers, especially juniper and species, and varieties of chamaecyparis, root readily if first treated with a suitable hormone. Plant 4 ins. apart.

Of shrubs, the artemesias, ceanothus, cotoneasters, daphnes, deutzia, the ericas (heathers), escallonias, forsythia, fuchsia, hydrangea, hypericum, lavender, olearia, viburnum, and weigelia, root readily, but will take twice as long as herbaceous plants. Plant cuttings of unflowered shoots during June and July, and leave them in the frame until the following spring when they are planted out.

Whilst geraniums are better wintered in a warm greenhouse or garden room, begonias may be started into growth in a frame. Early in April, the tubers, after wintering in boxes of sand in a frost-free room, are planted with their round part downwards, by pressing them into boxes containing 3 ins. of loam and peat. Plant them 2 ins. apart, water in, and keep the frame closed. They will soon begin to sprout at the top, and at the end of May are removed from the boxes with soil attached and bedded out.

Rex begonias, with their handsome leaf markings, are grown in pots in the home, but may be increased by leaf cuttings in a cold frame. The method is to make several cuts across the prominent veins at the back of the leaves. The leaves are then placed flat, on boxes of compost, and held down by small pebbles. Cover with a sheet of glass to

Dahlia cuttings cut from a parent tuber and rooted in a cold frame for potting on and planting out in late May.

encourage humidity and place in a frame. They will root at the cuts, and the tiny plants are detached and grown on in small pots.

Dahlias may be propagated in a cold frame. Store over winter in a frost-free room, then early in April, plant the roots close together in a frame or in boxes 6 ins. deep. Pack soil around the tubers leaving the crowns exposed. It is from here that the cuttings appear. Remove them with a knife, along with a small piece of tuber, and insert in boxes of sand and peat. They will root in about 4 weeks. They are then moved to small pots, and grown on for 3 more weeks before being planted out in June.

Pot-grown tubers, produced by nurserymen in this way and sold in spring, may be potted into 5-in. pots and placed in a cold frame. If kept comfortably moist, they will have made substantial growth by early June when they are planted out.

Flowers
Certain plants bloom earlier and better if seed is sown late in summer, and the plants are given biennial treatment. Sweet peas, spring and summer stocks, antirrhinums, and sweet williams, respond to this treatment. Seed is sown in boxes (or pots for sweet peas) in late July or early August in a frame, and there they remain until ready for transplanting to other boxes in September. They are grown on in the frame until ready to go out after hardening, in April. They will come into bloom early in June, at least a month before spring-sown plants.

Those less hardy plants, which will not safely winter in a cold frame, will give a good display if sown in boxes of J.I. compost over

a mild hot bed in February. Keep the compost comfortably moist and the seedlings will be ready to transplant in April. The plants are grown on under glass until planted out late in May, after hardening. The following are half-hardy plants which should be raised in gentle heat:

Ageratum	Lobelia
Alyssum	Matricaria
Antirrhinum (Plants from an autumn sowing are better)	Mesembryanthemum Molucella Nemesia Nicotiana
Aster	Petunia
Carnation, chabaud (If sown early will bloom same year)	*Phlox drummondii* *Salvia splendens* Statice
Dahlias (from seed)	Venidium
Delphinium chinensis	Verbena
Gazania splendens	Zinnia

There are a number of hardy annuals, such as salpiglossis and calendulas, which bloom earlier, if sown first in a cold frame. Sow them in early March and they will have formed sturdy plants to set out late in April. They will bloom a month earlier than those sown outdoors in April. Those annuals which do not take kindly to transplanting should not be sown in a frame.

Many different annuals can be sown in 5-in. pots in March, and grown on to flower in a frame, when they are taken indoors and placed in a sunny window. Pots of night-scented stock will be appreciated in the evening when they will fill a large room with their perfume. Others which enhance a room are the annual candytuft, Fairy Mixture; double dwarf cornflower; godetia, Blue Peter, which is really lavender-coloured and grows only 8 ins. tall; *Limnanthes douglasii*, the yellow flowers having white-tipped petals; *Nemophila insignis* (Baby Blue Eyes); and the hybrid Peter Pan zinnias, natives of Mexico, which are better grown under glass in the British climate where their brilliant colours show to advantage. Sow a few seeds evenly about the surface, water with care, and take indoors throughout summer as they come into bloom.

Another two annuals suitable for pot culture, are Carnation Juliet, which makes a bushy plant only 10 ins. high and covers itself for weeks in bright red flowers which are fully double, and Matricaria, Golden Ball, growing 12 ins. tall and bearing masses of tiny puff balls. These two plants are really perennial, but by sowing in a frame they can be treated as half-hardy annuals, for they come quickly into bloom. They may also be used for bedding.

The dwarf hybrid French and African marigolds are extremely rich when in bloom and make admirable pot plants. 'Mr Moonlight', of African type, grows only 9 ins. tall and bears clear yellow flowers like large carnations. Of the French type, 'Seven Star Red' bears fully double blooms of orange-red, and 'Yellow Nugget' is lemon yellow. The plants grow bushy and only 8 ins. tall.

Annual asters make delightful pot plants for late summer display but are equally lovely in the garden. The Pinocchio strain in mixed colours, bears compact mounds of bloom only 9 ins. tall. 'Daisy Mae' is another to charm, growing only 8 ins. tall and bearing single flowers of a unique shade of cerise pink.

Dwarf petunias raised over a hot bed

Gazanias make good cold frame subjects.

make impressive pot plants, and none is more striking than Razzle Dazzle, bearing large single blooms in shades of red, pink, purple, and blue, alternately striped with white. The double multiflora strain, with blooms like carnations, is also fine.

These annuals can be grown in a cold frame as pot plants:

Annuals	Height	Colour
Aster, Daisy Mae	8 ins	Cerise-pink
Aster, Pinocchio strain	9 ins	All colours
Aster, Thousand Wonders	6 ins	Rose-pink
Carnation, Juliet	10 ins	Red
Cockscomb, Chanticleer	6 ins	Red, yellow
Cornflower, Jubilee Gem	10 ins	Blue
Dianthus, Merry Go Round	6 ins	White, red centre
Dianthus, Scarlet Charm	6 ins	Scarlet
Felicia bergeriana	6 ins	Blue, yellow eye
Marigold, African Mr Moonlight	9 ins	Yellow
Marigold, French Big Shot	10 ins	Gold and red
Marigold, French Seven Star Red	10 ins	Mahogany red
Marigold, French Yellow Nugget	8 ins	Lemon
Matricaria, Golden Ball	10 ins	Yellow
Morning Glory, Early Tots	6 ins	Blue, edged white
Myosotis, Marine	6 ins	Mid-blue
Nolana, Lavender Gown	8 ins	Lavender, white centre
Stock, Night-scented	10 ins	Pink, mauve, white
Stock, 10 week double	12 ins	All colours
Vinca, Little Bright Eye	9 ins	White, red eye
Zinnia, Thumbelina	6 ins	All shades

Winter Flowering Plants

A number of winter-flowering pot plants may be raised in a cold frame and, grown well, no plants are more rewarding. Primulas, cineraria, calceolaria, impatiens, celosia, and schizanthus, present few difficulties. Saintpaulia, streptocarpus, and gloxinia, are more exacting, and must be raised in a temperature of 70°F. Even so, they can be raised over a hot bed made up in April. Sow in boxes or pans and cover with glass to increase humidity, before placing them in a frame. Remove the glass when the seed has germinated, and grow on the plants until ready to transplant. Continue to grow on until October, when they must be taken indoors, or to a greenhouse with a winter temperature of 60°F, when they will come into bloom.

Other indoor plants are raised in the same way but a hot bed is not necessary for quick germination. Sow in April or May, and do not cover the seed which is very small. To prevent the seed from being washed to one side of the container, water by immersing the base of the container for several minutes in a tank holding no more than 1 in. of water. A sheet of glass or plastic bag over the container will encourage germination.

Once the seeds have germinated, grow on as cool as possible, for these plants are almost hardy. Transplant to boxes when large enough to handle, and again to individual pots about July 1st. From early June the frame must be whitened. The plants will begin to flower from the end of July, the primulas remaining in bloom indoors for several years.

House plants to raise in a cold frame are:

House Plant	Sowing time	In bloom
Calceolaria	May, June	Mar–May
Celosia	Mar, Apr	Aug–Oct
Cineraria	May, June	Dec–Mar
Coleus	Apr–June	Mar–May (foliage)
Geranium	Apr	Aug onwards
Impatiens	May, June	Sept onwards
Primula malacoides	Apr–June	Dec onwards
Primula obconica	Apr–June	Dec onwards
Primula sinensis	Apr–June	Dec onwards
Schizanthus	Mar–May	Aug–Dec
Solanum	Apr	Dec onwards (berries)
Thunbergia	Apr	Aug–Dec

In addition, polyanthuses and primroses make admirable pot plants for springtime. Seed is sown in boxes or pans in early April in a cold frame, and if kept moist, the seedlings will be ready to transplant to other boxes or outdoor beds early in July. Here they are grown on until March, when they are bedded out and will come into bloom almost at once. Alternatively several may be planted out in 5-in. pots and placed in a frame to come into bloom early in April, when they are moved to the home. They bloom for a month, and second-year plants will make an even finer display. If grown in good soil and divided in alternate years, they will last indefinitely. The Pacific Giants and Hansen's hybrids are the best strains for pot culture, the flower heads being almost as large as cinerarias and with the same intense colourings.

Alpines in a Frame

Many alpine plants can be raised in a cold frame. Germination will be more certain if the seeds are sown in boxes in January, covered with a sheet of glass and left in the open to become frozen. Then if transferred to a frame early in March, they will germinate quickly.

Alpine plants may be grown on entirely in a frame after planting in small pots or other permanent containers. Here they come into bloom earlier than in the open, and the flowers are clean and undamaged by the elements. As most alpines withstand many degrees of frost, as much fresh air as possible must be admitted by raising the lights at the sides, except when there is a strong wind about, which may cause damage to the blooms. In spring and summer, the lights are removed altogether, except for show auriculas, which, when in bloom, though hardy, must be kept in a frame. This is to protect the paste-like centre of the blooms from rain, which will cause the paste to run over the ground colour. The lights are removed after flowering.

When alpines are grown in a frame, place the pots on a shingle base and also cover the potting compost with shingle. This will prevent soil from splashing on to the bloom. The plants may be taken indoors when reaching their best, so that they may be enjoyed in the home. They are most attractive when placed on earthenware saucers in a window, but they will bloom longer if away from sunlight. Some of the most beautiful alpines, so often damaged by rain when at their best, may only be appreciated to the full when grown in a frame. Amongst these are *Onosma echioides*, *Alyssum wolfenianum*, *Androsace sarmentosa* and the Lewisia hybrids.

Those alpines having woolly or silvered foliage are seen to their best advantage under glass. *Leptospermum scoparium* and *Pulsatilla vernalis* come to mind. These plants and those requiring scree conditions, i.e. a gritty well-drained soil with the minimum of moisture on their leaves, especially in winter, will grow better in the alpine house or cold frame. They include *Ramonda pyrenaica*, *Raoulia australis*, *Asperula suberosa*, and the encrusted (aizoon) saxifrages. Many of the scree plants are extremely small and will certainly be appreciated when seen close to, which is only possible when they are grown in pots or pans.

Shrubs from Seed

There are many flowering shrubs that grow well from seed if first exposed to the elements. The seed is then sown in pots or pans, which are placed in a deep box and covered with a sheet of glass before being placed in a frame. *Cotoneaster horizontalis* and *C. simonsii* come true from seed, and quickly make sizeable plants. *Hypericum calycinum* (Rose of Sharon) and the brooms, such as White Beauty and the coloured hybrids, are easily raised from seed but as they resent root disturbance, are best grown singly in small pots, sowing one seed to each. The tree lupins, too, should be treated in the same way, and are one of the most rewarding of shrubs to raise from seed, growing 4 ft. tall, and the same across, by the end of their first summer from an April sowing in a frame. Most other shrubs are kept in the pots for 12 months before planting out in April.

These shrubs may be raised from seed:

Shrub	Height	In bloom or fruit
Berberis darwinii (e)	5 ft	Apr–June
Berberis thunbergii	3 ft	May–June
Buddleia davidii	6 ft	Aug–Sept
Buddleia fallowiana	7 ft	July–Aug
Cistus laurifolius (e)	3–4 ft	June–Aug
Cotoneaster horizontalis	Trailer	Sept–Feb (red berries)
Cotoneaster simonsii	5 ft	Sept–Feb (red berries)
Cytisus albus (white)	4 ft	Apr–May
Cytisus scorparius (Yellow broom)	6 ft	May–June
Daphne laureola (e)	3 ft	Mar–Apr
Gaultheria shallon	1 ft	Aug–Dec (purple berries)
Genista aetnensis	15 ft	July–Aug
Hypericum calycinum	1–2 ft	July–Aug
Hypericum patulum forrestii	2 ft	July–Aug
Lupinus arboreus (e)	3–4 ft	June–Aug
Pyracantha lalandei (e)	10 ft	Oct–Mar (red berries)
Rosmarinus officinalis (e)	5 ft	July–Aug
Ruta graveolens (e)	1 ft	July–Aug
Ulex europeus	5 ft	Mar–June
Viburnum opulus	8 ft	June–July
Viburnum tinus	4–5 ft	Aug–Dec (blue berries)

(e) denotes evergreen

Perennial	Height	Colour	In bloom
Agrostemma coronaria	2 ft	Rose-red	July–Aug
Alyssum saxatile	1 ft	Yellow	Apr–July
Anchusa italica	4 ft	Blue	July–Aug
Anthemis sancti-johanni	2 ft	Yellow	June–Aug
Aquilegia, Dragonfly	20 ins	All colours	Apr–June
Armeria formosa	18 ins	Red, pink	June–Aug
Armeria maritima	6 ins	Red, pink	May–June
Aubrietia	Trailing	All shades	Mar–June
Campanula glomerata	20 ins	Purple	June–July
Campanula lactiflora	4 ft	Blue	June–Aug
Carnation, Raoul Martin	15 ins	All colours	June–Aug
Coreopsis, Golden Star	20 ins	Yellow	July–Sept
Delphinium	5 ft	Shades of blue	July–Aug
Doronicum	20 ins	Yellow	Mar–May
Erigeron	2 ft	Pink, purple	June–Aug
Gaillardia	2 ft	Mahogany, yellow	June–Sept
Helenium	3 ft	Red, gold	Aug–Nov
Heliopsis	3 ft	Yellow	July–Sept
Hollyhock, Chater's Double	6 ft	Rose, crimson	July–Sept
Lathyrus latifolius	Climbing	Rose, white	July–Sept
Linum perenne	2 ft	Blue	June–Sept
Lupin, Russell strain	3–4 ft	All shades	June–Aug
Lychnis chalcedonica	3 ft	Scarlet	July–Aug
Matricaria, Ball's White	20 ins	White	July–Sept
Myosotis (Forget-me-not)	9 ins	Blue	Apr–June
Oenothera missouriensis	12 ins	Yellow	June–Aug
Papaver nudicaule (Iceland Poppy)	2 ft	Yellow, red, white	June–Sept
Polyanthus	12 ins	All colours	Apr–July
Primula, Asiatic	2–4 ft	Yellow, pink	May–Aug
Primula denticulata	15 ins	Lavender, red	Mar–May
Salvia haematodes	3 ft	Purple	July–Sept
Saponaria ocymoides	Trailing	Rose-pink	June–Aug
Sidalcea	4 ft	Rose, pink	July–Sept
Sweet Rocket	2 ft	Purple, white	May–July
Valerian	2 ft	Crimson, white	June–Aug

A good use of a light-weight frame as a seed-bed for bringing on early vegetables.

comes true from seed and *A. formosa*, a large-flowered species, grows 18 ins. tall and remains in bloom all summer.

Aquilegia, the columbine, germinates as readily as mustard and cress, so do several of the campanulas, such as *Campanula glomerata*.. (clustered bell-flower) and *C. lactiflora*, with its tall spire-like stems clothed in bells of lavender and blue. The Raoul Martin carnations are the equal of the finest border carnations, and grow readily from seed, and even the perpetual-flowering greenhouse carnations can be produced in this way. The digitalis (foxglove), gaillardia, erigeron, helenium (at its best in autumn), delphiniums, *Lychnis chalcedonica* with its heads of geranium-red, rudbeckia, and sidalcea, all grow quickly from seed. From an April sowing in boxes or pans in a frame, they will have grown large enough to be planted in the border by the autumn. A complete herbaceous border may be obtained in this way for only £1 worth of seed in small packets.

The seedlings may be transplanted to other boxes and grown on in the frame, or they may be set out in beds to grow on through the summer.

The border perennials in Table on left are easily grown from seed.

Bulbs in a Frame

Most bulbs and corms may be grown in a cold frame, either in pots or boxes to bloom in the home, or in the frames as flowers for cutting. As so many bulbs come into bloom when the winter and early spring weather is all against their being at their best in the open, given the protection of a frame, they will take on a beauty rarely seen from unprotected plants.

It is possible to have bulbs in bloom in a cold frame all year round, and none respond better to frame culture than the crocus species. Beginning with the scented *C. longiflorus*, which bears its graceful violet tubes in November, and *C. asturicus*, there follows *C. laevigatus* at Christmastime, its white flowers feathered with royal purple, and *C. imperati*, bearing mauve flowers shaded with buff during the dull days of January. It is followed by *C.*

Perennials from Seed

Besides annuals, and those indoor plants which are raised in a cold frame, a number of hardy perennials can be raised in a similar way. This is an inexpensive way of hardy plant production. Modern seed strains make it possible to raise plants which are almost as near to type as can be obtained by vegetative propagation, and the seed of many is as easy to germinate as annuals. The polyanthus and primrose, so useful as pot plants and so easy to manage, have been mentioned. There are others.

Alyssum saxatile, the familiar Gold Dust of early spring, presents no problems and many dozens of plants may be raised from a small packet of seed. Arabis and aubrietia (Rock Cress), also spring flowering, are just as easy. *Armeria maritima*, the thrift, and a most valuable front of the border plant, also

Sowing sweet peas for germination in a cold frame. Note the spacing. The seeds are then covered to their own depth with an even layer of compost.

A cold frame can give valuable protection to species tulips and early hyacinths.

chrysanthus and its many varieties, and then the large-flowered Dutch hybrids. They are planted 4 to a 3-in. pot or 6 to a pan. As they come into bloom, take them indoors and place in a sunny window to enjoy through out winter.

Snowdrops always do well in pots in frames. In September plant 6 bulbs to a small pot and keep in the plunge bed for several weeks, while they are forming roots; then move to a frame in November. They will come into bloom early in the New Year.

Pots of the winter aconite (*Eranthis hyemalis*) are colourful at this time, like golden sovereigns in a ruff of emerald green. Plant 6–8 to a pan and treat in the same way as snowdrops.

The tiny but so colourful scillas are much to be desired in late winter and spring. *S. tubergeniana* is the first to bloom in the New Year and is followed by *S. sibirica* which, in the same way, bears several flowering spikes from each bulb. The tiny bell-shaped flowers open like a star, and are of porcelain blue striped with darker blue. *S. verna* is quite as lovely and is a native plant. Plant 6–8 bulbs to a pot and keep in the darkness of a plunge bed before they go in the frame.

Other delightful bulb plants for frame culture are *Fritillaria citrina*, its dainty bells of golden-yellow providing colour in early spring, and *Erythronium dens-canis* (dog's-tooth violet) with beautiful mottled foliage and violet-like flowers of purple or pink.

The tulip species are at their finest under glass and they too, may be planted for succession. One of the first to bloom in February, is *Tulipa aucheriana*, with pale green leaves which lie prostrate on the soil, its pink flowers, held on a 3-in. stem, opening star-like. The *T. kaufmanniana* hybrids are open at the same time, and are amongst the most brilliant of all flowers. 'Cesar Franck' has golden blooms, shaded scarlet on the exterior whilst 'Orange Boy' is clearest orange. Even lovelier is 'Coral Satin' which is coral pink with a satin sheen. They are held on 6-in. stems and 4 or 5 are planted to a pot. *T. tarda* (syn: *T. dasystemon*) is also admirable in the alpine house or frame. Its

glossy leaves lie flat, and its golden blooms resemble waterlilies with their pointed petals. It blooms in March.

T. greigii and its hybrids should not be neglected, for the foliage is as handsome as the blooms, being mottled with yellow, red, or purple, above which the flowers sit on 6-in. stems. 'Plaisir' bears flowers of vermilion and gold, whilst 'Red Riding Hood' is oriental red.

Many of the dainty bulbous irises are at their best under glass. Like the others mentioned, they do not need any degree of forcing to bring them early into bloom. *Iris danfordiae* bears its golden irises on 4-in. stems before the end of January, whilst *I. histrioides* bears its pale blue and ultra-marine blooms at the same time. Equally lovely is *I. reticulata* (J. S. Dijt), bearing scented blooms of reddish-purple, and 'Cantab', bright Cambridge blue on 5-in. stems. In addition, they are deliciously scented and remain in bloom for many weeks.

The tall Dutch irises are often planted by nurserymen in cold frames, to supply the florists with cut blooms at Easter when flowers are scarce. The bulbs are planted only 2 ins. apart in November, just pressing them into the surface. Leave off the light until early January when the bulbs will be rooted and begin to make growth. They bloom in early April on 2-ft. stems, so a deep frame is required.

There are other cut flowers to grow from bulbs or corms in a frame. Dwarf single early tulips may be planted in boxes, with the bulbs touching each other and covered with 3–4 ins. of soil. Plant in October and early in December. When rooted, shake off the top-soil and move the boxes to a frame. They will begin to bloom in February and may then be removed from the boxes and planted in pots or bowls to have indoors. Those early single and double tulips with longer stems may be grown in the same way. They will bloom in March and may be cut and removed from the frame before it is needed for hardening vegetable plants and annuals.

Daffodils, too, are grown in the same way, the cut flower varieties such as 'Carlton'

and 'Dutch Master' being ready at the same time, fully a month before those growing outdoors. This is the best way to grow the dainty miniature narcissi, in pots or pans of friable loam under glass. They may be removed to a sunny window when in bloom, but after flowering, place in the open with the pots on their side, and withhold water whilst the foliage is dying down. Do not remove the bulbs from the pots, they bloom better when not disturbed. Top up with fresh compost and replace in the frame in December.

Narcissus triandrus (Angel's Tears daffodil) is lovely, its white drooping flowers, like large tear drops, appearing in clusters of 3–9 on 6-in. stems. *N. cyclamineus* is equally attractive with its long elegant trumpet and swept-back perianth petals. The dainty 'Beryl' has a cup of deep orange and 'February Gold' a bright yellow trumpet frilled at the edge. The tiny, sweet-scented jonquils are equally handsome.

There are other bulbs and corms to grow in a frame and which do better than when outdoors. Some are natives of S. Africa and require a longer season to come into bloom than the average British summer. Others, such as the Crocus of the Andes (*Tecophilaea cyanocrocus*), require protection from winter rains if they are to bloom well. The corms require a dry cold winter, followed by a hot dry summer, and a frame provides these conditions. Plant 5 or 6 to a pot or pan in October and 2 ins. deep. They will come into bloom early in February, the flowers borne on 6-in. stems. They open star-like and are of rich gentian blue.

Another plant of S. America, the tigridia does better in a frame. *Tigridia pavonia* grows 18 ins. tall, whilst the blooms, measuring 6 ins. across, are most brilliant with a yellow central cup and violet segments, shading to scarlet at the tips. Plant the corms in November when they will bloom in June, and remain colourful for 2 months.

The freesia, native of S. Africa, also does well in a frame. Plant 5-cm.-size corms in pots or boxes in August, and place a light over them. Admit fresh air by raising the light at the side, but give very little water. As they grow, insert twigs or small canes about them to prevent them falling over, and give a little more water in spring as the days become warmer. They will bloom in April and May. Afterwards, place outside to ripen and grow on as before.

Freesias, ixias, and the closely related tritonia and sparaxis, may also be raised from seed sown either in boxes or directly into a frame, in April. The seeds germinate as readily as cress, and freesias may be grown on to flower without the need to transplant. The S. African corm-bearing plants should not be placed in a plunge bed.

A frame is an ideal place to raise lilies from seed and to grow on gladioli cormlets. These are detached from the base of the old corm when lifted in October and are kept in boxes of sand over winter. In April, they are planted 1 in. apart in boxes of compost, and placed in a frame to grow on until autumn when they are lifted from the boxes. When the foliage has died down, store over winter away from frost.

The early-flowering gladiolus species are grown on in a frame, the corms being planted in early October in 5-in. pots and kept in the frame until they come into bloom in April. They grow 2 ft. tall and require a deep frame.

The closely related *Acidanthera tubergenii* always does better in a frame than outdoors. It blooms in October, but in a cold, wet autumn may not bloom at all. Here again, the frame must be 2 ft. deep (3 × 9-in. boards fixed together). The corms are planted 2 ins. deep in April or May, in pots or boxes, and as soon as showing bloom, they are taken indoors where they will scent a large room with their perfume. The plants should be supported by canes placed at the side of the pot, and around which green twine is fastened.

Another lovely pot plant for indoors is the achimene. It is easily grown in a frame by planting the rhizomes or tubers in early April or May. Plant 5 to a large pot or pan, keep well watered and the frame closed. When growth begins, whiten the glass, and to keep the plants free from red spider, syringe the foliage daily. If small sticks are placed around the rim of the pot they will lift up the foliage, and the flowers will be seen to advantage, besides giving the plants a pleasing cascade effect. The Michelssen hybrids, in shades of violet, pink and red,

A temporary cold frame makes an excellent "plunge bed". Pots with bulbs are stood on a layer of sand to ensure drainage and peat is packed between them and over them.

are most colourful. They will bloom in July.

The cyclamen is another beautiful plant which may be started in a frame. Plant one corm level with the surface of the compost to a 5-in. pot in May and grow on through summer, spraying the foliage daily and shading from the sun. By early autumn, the plants will be filled with buds just above the corm, and half hidden by the handsome fleshy leaves. In a slightly warm room they will come into bloom and remain colourful throughout the winter.

Eucomis bicolor is a handsome plant for pot culture. The conical tunicated bulbs are planted in early April, one to a 5-in. pot, in a compost made up of loam, decayed manure, and coarse sand, in equal parts. The strap-like leaves grow to 2 ft. in length, whilst the flowers are borne in July on a 15-in. stem. They are greenish white and so densely clustered together that it is known as the pineapple flower.

These bulbs and corms are suitable for frame culture:

Bulb or corm	When to plant	Colour	In bloom
Achimenes	Apr–May	Pink, purple	July–Sept
Acidanthera tubergenii	Apr	White	Aug–Sept
Crocus asturicus	Aug	Purple	Oct–Nov
Crocus chrysanthus	Oct	Purple, yellow	Feb–Mar
Crocus, Dutch hybrids	Oct	Purple, white, yellow	Mar–Apr
Crocus imperati	Oct	Mauve	Jan–Feb
Crocus longiflorus	Aug	Violet	Nov–Dec
Cyclamen	Apr	Pink, red	Oct–Feb
Eranthis hyemale	Oct	Yellow	Jan–Feb
Erythronium dens-canis	Oct	Yellow, pink	Mar–Apr
Eucomis bicolor	Apr	Greenish white	July–Aug
Freesia	Aug	All shades	Apr–May
Fritillaria citrina	Oct	Yellow	Apr
Galanthus elwesii	Oct	White, green	Jan–Mar
Galanthus nivalis	Oct	White, green	Jan–Mar
Iris danfordiae	Oct	Yellow	Feb–Mar
Iris histrioides	Oct	Blue	Feb–Mar
Iris reticulata	Oct	Purple, blue	Feb–Mar
Narcissus cyclamineus	Oct	Yellow	Feb
Narcissus minimus	Oct	Yellow	Mar
Narcissus triandrus	Oct	Yellow	Mar
Narcissus watieri	Oct	Yellow	Feb–Mar
Scilla sibirica	Oct	Blue	Mar–Apr
Scilla tubergeniana	Oct	Blue	Jan–Feb
Scilla verna	Oct	Blue	Mar–Apr
Tecophilaea cyanocrocus	Oct	Blue	Feb–Mar
Tigridia pavonia	Nov	Yellow and purple	June–July
Tulipa aucheriana	Nov	Pink	Feb–Mar
Tulipa greigii	Nov	Red, pink, yellow	Feb–Mar
Tulipa kaufmanniana	Nov	Red, pink, yellow	Feb–Mar
Tulipa pulchella	Nov	Purple and green	Mar–Apr
Tulipa saxatilis	Nov	Pink	Apr
Tulipa tarda	Nov	Yellow	Mar–Apr

MAKING
A FLOWER BED & BORDER

Roy Genders

Flower beds and borders are an essential part of the pleasure garden if full enjoyment is to be obtained from it. Such beds are basically of two types. There is the herbaceous border containing perennials such as campanula, aquilegia, lupins, violas, etc. Being tolerant of frost these are hardy in most parts of Britain, and if planted in well-prepared ground will be almost as permanent as roses or other shrubs. Some plants, and the paeony is an example, will bloom freely for 50 years or more if given an occasional top dressing and will require no attention apart from staking the large handsome blooms if the garden is at all exposed. It is said that the herbaceous border and permanent flower bed can find no place in the modern garden as they demand too much labour, but exactly the opposite is the case. Modern border plants with their sturdy compact habit require the minimum of staking, and may be left down for at least 5 years before they are lifted, divided, and used to fill spaces in other parts of the border, or to make a permanent bed elsewhere. They are amongst the most economical of plants for they will last almost indefinitely for an outlay of a few pence each.

The second type of traditional border is the annual or bedded-out border in which more tender plants can be bedded out to give a massed colourful display through the summer months. In many cases seed may be sown in the border and left to flower *in situ*. The important point about such a border is that tender subjects such as petunias, geraniums, lobelias, etc., may bring great splashes of colour to a garden throughout the frost-free part of the year, but when the frost comes then the annuals die, and the geraniums, etc., are taken into the cold greenhouse or frames where they will spend the greater part of the winter before being propagated for next summer.

Such traditional herbaceous borders are possibly the most characteristic and splendid feature of great British gardens; but the enormous growth in the number of smaller gardens has encouraged the emergence of a third kind – the mixed border. This, as its name suggests, is a judicious mixture of herbaceous plants, annuals, and biennials. It is borders and beds of this description that we shall be describing in this section.

A well-designed border or bed will provide colour all the year round, and at all times the garden will be a place of interest. There will also be flowers to cut for indoor decoration. The long flowering period of many new varieties and their freedom of blooming ensures that where used for permanent or mixed beds, they will regain some of the popularity their less colourful relations enjoyed in the past, when the well-tended border was truly admired.

SITING A BORDER
With the wide range of garden plants now available, there are some which are suitable for all types of beds and borders. A border may be made along one side of a suburban garden, possibly where an interwoven fence divides one garden from another. Such a fence is an ideal background for the border, which should be made 5–6 ft. wide to keep it in proportion to the rest of the garden. Where there is a large garden or where there is ground available at both sides of a detached house the border may be made rather larger, say 8 ft. wide, allowing the owner to grow larger and taller subjects. With increasing space, variety can be introduced by varying the shape of the border, for example a curved border may be made, with an alcove, small summer house, or other focal point in one corner surrounded by the plants. If edged with a path of crazy paving stones or flagstones, with a well-kept lawn on the opposite side of the path, it can present a picture of beauty throughout the year. See plan A.

Alternatively the border may be made with an undulating sweep to present a pleasing vista from the house and the more informal this kind of border is, the more interesting it will be.

Where the garden is small, possibly rectangular in shape, as is the usual suburban garden, a border may be made down one side and then taken across, perhaps to divide the flower garden from the vegetable patch, with a trellis placed at the back of the border where it is taken across the width of the garden. See plan B.

Over the trellis, climbing roses and clematis can be grown. Perhaps at the back of the border several groups of evergreens can be planted, especially those of columnar habit like the Irish juniper, and they will remain green all winter while in no way interfering with other plants. In fact, the deep green of such species can provide a striking contrast to the brilliant reds and yellows of flowers, such as *Lychnis chalcedonica* and *Achillea eupatorium*, planted in front of them.

At all times the borders or beds should be seen in the context of the house itself and of the ground levels around it. For example one school of thought advocates the use of curved borders in a rectangular garden to break up the formality, others say it is best to accept the rectangular situation and use it as a guide to the type of garden you construct.

Island beds are beautiful things if carefully planted with well-chosen subjects, but can be completely out of place in a small garden where they will either make the garden too 'bitty' or will have to be so restricted in size that they lose their point.

Where possible the borders or beds should either contrast or blend with the other elements of the garden, such as the lawn or maybe a small patio or terrace. It is best always to sit in the house and look out of the windows considering what you would like to see and noting it down on paper. Then take a walk around the boundary of the garden trying to envisage the house in the setting of the garden. You will thus have two sets of ideas and the good gardener blends these to produce shapes, textures, contrasts, and blends of colour, which will make the house pleasing to live in, good to look at, and the garden a place in which to relax and enjoy life.

Where possible you should avoid shade but even if this is impossible there are many plants (see Table 6) which can be grown even under relatively dim conditions.

Plan A

Plan B

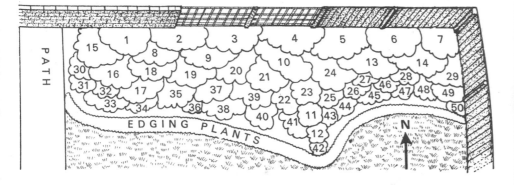

A possible plan for a small border: 30 ft. × 6 ft. Even a small border should be at least 6 ft. wide at its narrowest to allow sculpturing of plant heights and densities. Notice how in this lay-out the taller plants are at one point brought out from the back in a sweep towards the front to break the line of the border and stop the eye taking it all in at a glance. One has to walk up to and past numbers 11 and 12 to see what is behind them. 1 Michaelmas Daisy; 2 Delphinium; 3 Verbascum; 4 Heliopsis; 5 Thalictrum; 6 Delphinium; 7 Spiraea aruncus; 8 Sidalcea; 9 Eryngium; 10 Michaelmas Daisy; 11 Anchusa; 12 Achillea; 13 Echinops 'Blue Bell'; 14 Rudbeckia; 15 Phlox; 16 Paeony; 17 Lupin; 18 Campanula persicifolia; 19 Pyrethrum; 20 Sedum spectabile; 21 Dahlia; 22 Erigeron; 23 Aconitum; 24 Lupin; 25 Doronicum; 26 Monarda; 27 Gaillardia; 28 Potentilla; 29 Shasta Daisy Chrysanthemum maximum; 30 Anemone 'Queen Charlotte'; 31 Geum; 32 Iris; 33 Papaver; 34 Scabiosa; 35 Veronica; 36 Campanula glomerata; 37 Geranium 'Johnson's Blue'; 38 Tradescantia; 39 Aster amellus; 40 Centaurea; 41 Scabiosa; 42 Iris; 43 Incarvillea; 44 Erigeron, Gaiety; 45 Pyrethrum, Jas Kelway; 46 Aster amellus; 47 Gaillardia; 48 Chrysanthemum; 49 Hemerocallis; 50 Polemonium. Edging plants can be chosen from the smaller perennials and, of course, from the many colourful annuals available.

Hosta aurea marginata

Aquilegia pyrenaica

PLANNING A BORDER

If you want to do the job properly then you need *two* plans, one for the general disposition and shape of borders and beds in the garden, and the other of the planting scheme for each border. In this section it is the second plan which we will consider.

First take the measurement of the border and make a scale diagram on paper (if you can get graph or squared paper it is a very simple job). You must then consider the size of the border, the colours you want, and the variation in foliage throughout the season, and from these considerations a preliminary list of plants will emerge. Always bear in mind the fact that within almost any plant species you can find a wide range of varieties from the dwarf and cushioned to the tall and maybe spreading. You can therefore spend happy hours going over catalogues and mentally trying out different ideas. In your planning remember that three plants of the more compact species, in a triangle, will occupy about 2 sq.ft. but the more vigorous back-of-the-border plants may *each* occupy about 3 sq.ft., so it is possible to calculate exactly the number of plants required to fill the border, and these should be ordered in good time. If you are planting in the autumn or early winter, it is unwise to include blue-flowered species such as scabious, anchusa, or cynoglossum. These are best planted in March so spaces should be left which can be filled at that time.

Formal planting must be avoided and there must be no straight lines. It is also advisable to break up what might be an all too flat appearance, by planting at the centre several plants which will be rather taller than the rest. Even the front of the border will be improved and given a more informal look if there is an occasional group of plants growing several inches taller than the others. A better effect is produced if you arrange *several* features in the border so that parts of the area can be looked on as little islands or oases of smaller species snuggled down and protected by the taller plants, and the areas left for annuals and bedding out can

be discreetly scattered at appropriate places or used as a mass to make immediate impact.

Flowering times must also be noted, and the plants set out in such a way that the whole border will be colourful over as long a period as possible, rather than just one section of it with the rest of the border devoid of bloom for long periods. Therefore plant a group of May- and June-flowering plants such as aquilegia next to those which bloom from July until September, e.g. eryngium, and at the back of them set out michaelmas daisies and chrysanthemums, repeating this idea throughout the border, with taller varieties to the back and the more compact to the front. There are many variations in the height of most hardy plants, so a wide choice is available. See Tables 7–10.

A word about foliage. This should be given careful thought, for some plants have leafy stems and should be planted close to those with sparse foliage to give balance to the border. Some plants have especially handsome foliage, e.g. *Polemonium coeruleum*, the Jacob's Ladder of cottage gardens so called because of its ladder-like leaves. It is worth planting for its leaves alone, whilst Physostegia makes a thicket of leafy stems and *Incarvillea delavayi* has large dark green pinnate leaves. The foliage of several of the Bergenias have leaves which take on interesting shades of purple and bronze in winter. The pinks have evergreen silvery leaves, and *Anaphalis triplinervis* has leaves covered with silvery hairs, whilst a few clumps of *Stachys lanata* with its woolly grey leaves should be planted to the front of every border. *Sedum spectabile* 'Meteor' which in late summer bears large flat heads of rosy crimson frequently visited by butterflies, has grey sea-green succulent leaves that enhance the beauty of the flowers.

When planting, it is advisable to set out those of graceful feathery habit such as *Gypsophila paniculata*, with its billowing clouds of snow-white blooms, and 'Flamingo', soft pink, near plants of more formal upright habit so as to remove any appearance of stiffness from the border. The foliage of lupins, after the dead flower spikes

Paeonia lactiflora hybrid

Pelargonium 'Maxim Kovaleski'

are removed before they seed, is so light and informal that the plants should be in close proximity to the phlox with their stiff upright habit and rather sparse foliage, though a clump in bloom is one of the sights of the late summer border.

It is also important to plant near to each other, colours which do not clash. Near 2 or 3 plants of *Oenothera* 'Yellow River', which bears its golden chalices from June until August, plant *Cynoglossum nervosum*, which bears sprays of royal blue at the same time; and with *Monarda* 'Cambridge Scarlet' plant 'Snow Maiden' as a complete contrast. Close to *Kniphofia* 'Gold Else' with its spikes of soft yellow, plant one of the sea hollies with its holly-like foliage and cone-shaped flowers of steely-blue. *Eryngium planum* 'Blue Dwarf' is most effective.

Pink flowering plants should be near those bearing blue or purple flowers and the orange, bronze, and red shades be near those of yellow colouring. Blue and purple michaelmas daisies are at their loveliest near yellow chrysanthemums and both bloom together. Plant the spire-like *Campanula persicifolia* 'Percy Piper' with its lavender-blue flowers near the July-flowering *Helenium* 'Coppelia' with its orange-coloured blooms, and to the front of the border, *Erigeron* 'Darkest of All' with the hardy *Geranium endressii* 'Wargrave' with its informal habit and flowers of salmon-pink.

Do not be afraid to use white flowers, for they will give a cool appearance to the border at the height of summer and will be in marked contrast to the more blatant colours which are so prominent at the high noon of the year.

In a mixed border space should always be left for annuals and bedding out, and it is better to leave too much than too little. Another cardinal sin is to overcrowd the plants forgetting that they will increase in size, and height. Leave plenty of space, for it is easy to fill in, but expensive and wasteful to have to tear out.

PREPARING A BORDER

Where preparing a border (or permanent bed), it is necessary to double dig the ground, removing all perennial weeds as the work is being done, and adding drainage materials such as mortar or crushed bricks from an old building, or clearings from ditches. If the soil is heavy, add some peat or decayed manure where obtainable. Shoddy, or used hops, or material from the compost heap may be used, but the excessive use of plant foods is not necessary and, indeed, will cause the plants to make leaf at the expense of bloom. What they require is a friable loam in good heart, for a badly-drained soil from which winter rain cannot readily drain away will cause the roots to decay and the plants to die back after a year or so. On the other hand, the soil must be able to retain moisture in summer, otherwise the plants will never reach full stature, so some humus must be added when the border is dug over.

The best time to do the work is early autumn, so that planting can be done in November (to allow the plants to become established before the frosts), or at any time during winter when the ground is not too wet and does not contain frost. Planting can be done until early March, but autumn planting is best, especially in the drier parts of Britain, for the plants can grow away in spring without check and will give a good display in their first year.

After preparing the soil, it is advisable to mark out with sand or lime or with a slow

release fertiliser where the various groups of plants are to go, remembering that 2 or 3 plants of a variety will provide a more conspicuous splash of colour than will odd plants dotted here and there about the border. Delphiniums, kniphofias, and lupins are the exception for they make dense bushy growth, and so are planted singly.

At the risk of repetition, when making out a mixed border always leave ample space for annuals or bedding plants such as salvias, begonias, geraniums, etc., and there is always pleasure to be obtained by including bulbs in mixed borders. With bulbous subjects you can tap a wide range of heights ranging from tiny erythronium, muscaria, scilla, snowdrops, and species of crocus, up to large gladiolus, lilies, fritillaria, etc.

SOWING, PLANTING, AND MAINTAINING THE BORDER

If the border is marked out beforehand and a drawing made of the groupings, permanent planting can be quite an easy job, but do not work the border when wet. Wait until the soil is friable and the plants can then be well trodden in. Plant with a blunt-ended trowel and place the roots well down, spreading them out before covering with soil. Tread them in and insert a label showing the name. Visitors to the garden will appreciate being able to see the names without having to ask. Remember that most of the plants will make large clumps, so do not set too close.

Many plants can be raised from seed sown in the open ground. It is certainly a cheaper and satisfying way of completing the bed or border. One must differentiate, however, between seeds of annuals, which are sown where they are to grow, and the seeds of biennials and perennials which may be sown in a seed bed, and the seedlings transplanted to other quarters when large enough to handle. In either case the soil must be brought to a fine tilth just prior to sowing, for this encourages better root growth.

If the soil is at all heavy it is worthwhile preparing a seed bed for perennials and biennials such as wallflowers, sweet williams, etc. in the autumn. Allocate a tiny area of the garden for this purpose. Clear it of weeds and dig it deeply, leaving the earth clods to lie ruggedly and unevenly on the surface. In this way the winter frosts can penetrate, and it breaks down to a fine tilth in the spring. Level with a rake, and sow in straight drills, following the instructions on the seed packet. When transplanting to their permanent stations, select only the strongest and healthiest-looking seedlings.

Seeds of annuals can be sown broadcast in the areas where they are to flower. Thin to correct distance apart (as per seed packet) and again leave the healthiest-looking specimens and throw the rest on the compost heap.

There is an old adage which runs 'Sow dry, plant wet'. This is a very good guide for the soil should be dry or at worst drying when you sow, and it should be moist when you transplant from the seed bed in spring.

In many cases, it is necessary to sow seed under glass if one intends to use half-hardy annuals. A tray (wooden or plastic) has a layer of crocks in the bottom and is filled with a good compost well moistened and firmed. Seeds should be sown thinly and lightly covered with a layer of sand or fine soil. Often the box is covered with a sheet of glass or stiff plastic until germination occurs. When the seedlings are at the stage of having cotyledons, the first pair of true leaves, they should be lifted on the point of a

wooden label, pricked out and transplanted into rows in other boxes in a fairly rich compost. The soil should be kept moist and the young plants given maximum light to ensure sturdy growth.

In April or May they should be hardened off, if possible in a cold frame, and in May or June when the risk of frost is past they can be transplanted to their final positions in the bed.

Taller-growing plants may need staking, but as this tends to give the border a more formal appearance too much staking should be avoided. Paeonies, and those plants bearing large heavy flower heads or spikes, especially delphiniums, will require staking, otherwise the stems will break in a high wind or when the flowers, usually at their best, are heavy with rain. The way to support delphiniums is to place three 6-ft. canes around the plant, and to loop green garden twine around the stems and the canes as the plant makes growth. Front-of-the-border plants of spreading habit may be supported by inserting a few twiggy sticks amongst the foliage. This will lift the flower stems from the ground if there is a tendency for them to flop over.

Keep the hoe moving between the plants to suppress weeds and to aerate the soil, and after two or three years, give the plants a top dressing in winter with any form of humus material and a little decayed manure where obtainable.

In the case of wide borders or beds, or if there is a real chance of flowers being cut for floral decoration, then a few judiciously placed flat paving stones can be very useful. Do not make them obvious and if possible mask them with larger plants, but a firm, dry base from which one can hoe, stake, tie up, cut, or fertilise the plants, will be found a most useful asset.

When all flowering has ended, which will be about the year end, cut back the dead

The simplest method of staking effectively. The string tying the paeony in should be invisible.

foliage of perennial plants to within 3–4 ins. of soil level and burn it. Remove the canes and when the weather permits, fork between the plants.

All annuals and biennials which have flowered should be taken up and put on the compost heap. The ground where they grew can be lightly forked over in readiness for next season. It is often about this time of year that one plants bulbous subjects which help to brighten many parts of a mixed border in early spring.

A well-made border requires little maintenance. Obviously in a perennial border only a few things need attention.

1) Careful hoeing to keep it weed free and a light forking in the back end are the main operations. A light scattering of slow release fertiliser in spring will keep it going all the growing season, and the rest of the work is cutting away dead shoots in the winter and maybe dividing or removing the more strongly-growing subjects. Humus should be added as a mulch in late spring.

2) The mixed border needs all the above treatments but in addition it requires soil preparation and humus incorporation in the areas where the bedding out will be done. Weeding becomes more vital as areas of the mixed bed will be full of plants for some part of each year. Further you will be sowing seed or transplanting small plants so that competition from weeds could be a very important factor in reducing your success.

THE USE OF BULBS IN BEDDING

The use of bulbous plants in bedding is a long-established practice. Nowhere is this more evident than in the traditional spring-flowering bed, for by their very structure many bulbs are pre-set to flower in the spring when there is very little other colour to brighten a rather grey scene.

A bulb is fundamentally a perennial which flowers before it develops its food-supplying leaves. After flowering is finished the leaves continue to manufacture food which is passed down to the base of the plant where it is stored to be used the following year. At the same time as this storage is going on, a small embryo flower is being formed which will be dormant all winter surrounded by the stored food supply.

When conditions are right in the spring the flower will develop and the plant bloom, using up the stored food in the process. It is necessary therefore for a new supply of food to be stored if the bulb is going to flower next year, and this is the reason why plants such as snowdrops, crocus, tulips, daffodils, gladioli, etc., must be allowed to retain their food-supplying leaves even if their beauty as a garden bloom has gone.

Technically not all the objects we call 'bulbs' are indeed bulbs. Some of them, e.g. crocus, are 'corms', others such as iris may be rhizomes or tubers, but these are purely botanical concepts and since the method of growing is similar in all cases I propose just to call them all 'bulbs'.

Generalised Treatment

There are two basic techniques for growing bulbs in beds. The first is where the bulbs are planted in the autumn and are then left as permanent plants to appear year after year. The second, which demands a little more work but leads to much greater variety of effect, is where the bulbs are planted in the autumn, allowed to flower in spring, and then lifted to allow for summer bedding,

Iris 'Christmas Angel'

Muscari botryoides, or grape hyacinth

A hybrid lily, 'Pepper'

Lilium candidum or madonna lily

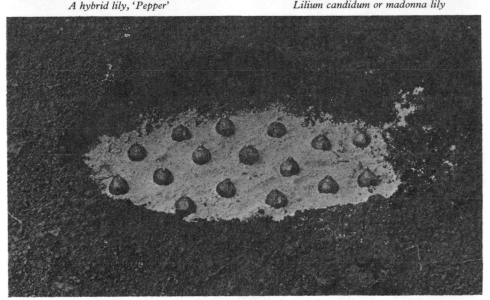

A satisfactory method of planting bulbs, in this case Scilla. The bulbs are placed on sharp sand to ensure good drainage and grouped to provide an effective show.

and transplanted to a nursery bed where the foliage can do its work and plump up the bulb with stored food for next year.

No matter what type of bedding you want, the preparation of the soil is the same and really follows the rules of good cultivation. Bulbs cannot do well and will often rot away in a soil which is wet and is badly drained. This is specially noticeable in clay soils and if the soil is of this type then as much humus as possible should be worked in during double digging. The humus can be compost, peat, shoddy, seaweed, or even farmyard manure. Lime is useful and at about 4 oz. per sq. yd. will help to sweeten the soil, but if you are putting the bulb in a mixed

bed or border you must be sure that it does not contain azaleas, rhododendrons, or any other lime hater.

Planting bulbs is a simple matter. First of all work out the area to be planted, and within it lay the bulbs on the surface. Then make a hole for each bulb. Small bulbs such as crocus should be about 2–4 ins. deep, and large ones such as gladiolus may be put 6 ins. down and the hole filled with sand.

An alternative method is to dig a hole of the appropriate depth and size and then place the bulbs on a layer of sand in the bottom of the hole and then simply fill the hole with the soil dug out, firm it down and make it level. This latter is probably a better

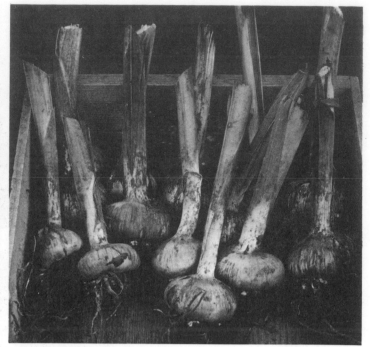

Lifting gladioli for drying and storage. If the ground is wanted before the leaves have died back the corms, complete with roots and leaves, can be heeled *into a trench or a box of sand to die back. They can then be stored as shown. Store in a cool, dry, frost-proof place.*

way for it ensures that the base of the bulb is in contact with the soil and they are not suspended half-way down a hole.

Usually bulbous subjects require no feeding, but after the flowers have faded liquid feeding can be given, or a slow release fertiliser used in permanent beds. When the time comes, the seed heads should be removed to allow all the food manufactured in the leaves to go towards next year's bulbs.

Bulbs in Spring Bedding
In most cases the bulbs should be interplanted between more permanent subjects which means of course that the heights must match, for it is a waste of money and time to have dwarf bulbs hidden by taller subjects. Colours should be used either as contrasts or as matching. Thus winter pansies or violets which are yellow, white, or pale blue, may be interplanted with *Tulipa eichleri* which is a deep vivid red. The tulips can be left for several years and will bloom from March until May.

Hardy pinks retain their silvery foliage all year and spread fairly rapidly. If at the time of planting, *Crocus susianus* or *Iris reticulata* are used in small groups of say 3 or 5, the spring flowers will grow through the foliage of the pinks and create a very pleasing effect.

Along with primroses, a good contrast is *Tulipa praestans* 'Fusilier' with its deep red flowers, or 'Red Riding Hood' which would stand over the primroses about 9 ins. high, bearing globes of dark red.

Tulips can be bedded by themselves and *Tulipa greigii* and *T. kaufmanniana* will give beautiful flowers and leaves which carpet the beds, thus discouraging weeds. Similarly, hyacinths look well on their own. The Siberian Squill, *Scilla sibirica*, with its deep blue flowers, can be bedded with bellis double daisies.

There are so many other happy spring combinations that if your interest is aroused, a good book on bulbs should be consulted.

Bulbs in Summer Bedding
In late spring and summer, many bulbs can be used with telling effect in all kinds of borders. In the dead time between late spring and early summer, in the more frost-free parts of the country, colour can be provided by sparaxis, ixia, streptanthera, and best of all lachenalia.

Gladiolus is usually grown in small groups in a mixed bed or for cut flowers. The fact that they are tall and brightly coloured will add variation to a flat bed, and if used along with dahlias you can have the latter in July and early August by which time the gladioli will be coming into their full pomp. In an exactly parallel fashion lilies can be used, and if both are planted in April using say *L. regale* and *Gladiolus carinatus*, then the lily will cover the period June–July and the gladiolus July–August.

Gladiolus 'Blackpool'

TABLE 1 Bulbs for Bedding

Species & Variety	Height in ins.	Colour	Planting Time	Depth in ins.	In Bloom
Acidanthera tubergenii	30	white	Apr	4	Sept
Anemone blanda	6	blue	Sept	1	Feb–Apr
Anemone St Brigid	8–12	various	All year	1	Feb–July
Chionodoxa species	3–6	blues	Sept	1–3	Mar
*Crocus a) autumn	3–6	varied	June–July	3	Sept–Dec
b) spring	3–4	varied	Sept–Oct	3	Jan–Apr
Eranthis tubergenii	3–5	yellow	Oct	2	Feb–Mar
Galanthus elwesii	6	white	Sept	4	Mar–Apr
Galanthus nivalis	4	white	Sept	4	Jan–May
Gladiolus species	24–48	varied	Apr	4	July–Sept
Hyacinthus orientalis	10–12	white, pink, blue	Oct	3–6	Apr–May
Iris germanica (rhizomatous)	24–36	purple	July	1	May–June
Iris reticulata (bulbous)	6	blue-purple	Sept	3	Feb–Apr
Ixia maculata	12	yellow, blue	Oct	4	June
*Lilium candidum	36–48	white	Sept	1	June–July
Lilium tigrinum	48–60	orange	Sept	6	Aug–Sept
Narcissus species	6–24	white-yellow	June–July	2	Feb–Apr
Scilla autumnalis	9	lilac-pink	Mar	3	Aug–Sept
Scilla sibirica	6–8	blue	Oct	3	Mar
Sparaxis tricolor	15	orange	Sept	4	May
*Tulipa species	3–24	yellow, red, etc.	Oct	6	Apr–May

*There are so many species and varieties that a specialist catalogue should be consulted.

ISLAND BEDS

The size of an island bed will depend upon the area of lawn. The bed may be circular, oval or kidney shaped, and at the centre (or thereabouts), taller-growing plants (3–4 ft.) can be used. Around these, on either side, use plants growing 2–3 ft. high, with those of more compact habit at the edge of the bed. Planting should be done so as to give colour over as long a period as possible. Choose plants of neat, compact habit so that there will be the minimum of staking and tying. If the bed is made no more than 6 ft. at the widest part, it is possible to hoe and do most of the staking without treading the soil excessively.

The mixed island bed is especially valuable, since by the simple fact that it is possible to walk around an island bed, a large number of different facets can be constructed so that the bed from one side or end can look totally different from the other. This variation is most easily done using annuals or bedding-out plants. Thus one end of an island bed could feature a mass of bright red salvias or begonias, while the other could show the multicoloured gaiety of petunias. One side could feature celosia and pansies and the other cornflowers, sweet williams and dianthus. The edge could be carpeted with dwarf nasturtiums, nemophila, lobelia, and mesembryanthemum, and the level broken up by the hummock of *Portulaca grandiflora*.

The appearance is enhanced if pinks, or *Stachys lanata* 'Silver Carpet' with its silvery woolly leaves, are planted around the edge, for these plants are evergreen and are as handsome in winter as in summer; or plant *Nepeta mussinii*, which has attractive grey-green foliage in summer and autumn but which dies down in winter. For all that, it makes a delightful informal edging to an island bed.

Where the garden blends into the distant vista of the surrounding country, as at Port Lympne in Kent, which overlooks the Romney Marsh, a border may be seen at its best, for it provides a natural link between the formal flower beds of geraniums and calceolarias of the parterre, and the distant landscape. Here, the border was made on either side of the lawn so that when seen from the house, it converged in the distance, with the landscape as a back-cloth.

Much the same use may be made of a narrow strip of ground almost anywhere, and rather than split up a narrow garden into numerous small beds, which contribute little to its aesthetic value, make two good-sized borders, or perhaps two island beds, on each side of a lawn, with ornamental trees in the background beneath which flowering bulbs are planted in generous groups.

THE SHADED BORDER

For those who wish to make a border in a shaded part of the garden, deprived of the midday sun possibly by the shade cast by the house itself, there are a number of plants which grow better under such conditions than in full sun, and seem to enjoy the coolness and the moist soil about their roots. For a selection of suitable plants see Table 6.

PERMANENT BEDS

One of the most important features of permanent beds is the opportunity they give for interplanting many very attractive combinations of colour and size. If rightly chosen there will be flowers all the year round or at worst there will be foliage of many shades of green, yellow and red.

For example hardy border plants may be used for permanent small bedding display, interplanting with spring-flowering bulbs or with dwarf pompon chrysanthemums for autumn colour. It is not necessary to lift any of the plants, merely cut them back towards the year end after flowering. Long-flowering perennials should be used with polyanthus to bloom from March until June, and *Anchusa* 'Little John' will continue the display until the end of August when *Chrysanthemum* 'Jente Wells' comes into bloom, by which time it will have made a neat bushy plant 15 ins. tall, and will be covered with deep yellow poms of the size of a 10p. piece until November. As an alternative chrysanthemum choice, plant 'Denise', also yellow and even more compact, or 'Fairie' with its flowers of soft strawberry pink. These plants are inexpensive to obtain and may be left down for several years, lifting only when necessary to increase the stock. Polyanthus and anchusa are increased by division, the chrysanthemums by offsets, pulled away from around the main stems which are then discarded. This work is best done early in spring.

When making up the bed, set out the plants 15 ins. apart so that each variety is well spaced about the bed. If the bed is edged with winter-flowering pansies, which in well-prepared soil will bloom for several years, they will be colourful almost the whole year.

It is only rarely that perennial plants are used for bedding, but a splendid plant for this purpose is *Brunnera macrophylla* used as ground cover for yellow cottage tulips. It makes plenty of grey-green foliage early in spring, and from mid-April until the end of June, bears billowing masses of bright blue forget-me-not flowers on 18-in. stems, which will hide the bare stems of the tulips. Plant 18 ins. apart with the tulips between, and in this case both may be planted together in late autumn for brunnera is completely hardy, and in two years will have spread to cover the soil entirely. No harm will be done if the plants are disturbed when planting the tulips. Along with it plant *Doronicum* 'Spring Beauty', which makes a shapely little plant 15 ins. high and bears double bright yellow flowers. Include in the same bed a few plants of *Cynoglossum nervosum*, which will continue the display from June until the end of August, bearing clustered sprays of bright royal blue on 20-in. stems. Then follow with the pompon chrysanthemums and dwarf michaelmas daisies, such as 'Jenny' with its mounds of double violet daisies, or 'Chatterbox', rich rosy-pink, which will continue the display until almost the year end, thus providing a permanent bed of colour from April to Christmas.

Nor should the allwoodii pinks be neglected for permanent bedding, for they bloom from June until the end of summer,

Scilla sibirica or squill

To divide a plant like polyanthus, grip the roots low down and carefully pull and tease apart. These young plants can now be planted out into their permanent position in the border.

Propagating a michaelmas daisy by detaching an offset with its own roots. Usually the parent plant need not be lifted unless it needs dividing.

A dahlia tuber like this can be carefully divided with a sharp knife. March is the best time. Insert the young shoots in sandy soil in gentle heat. They should be ready for planting out in May.

and their silvery-green foliage lends colour to the garden throughout the year. Especially long-flowering is 'Doris' with its double blooms of salmon pink, which tone beautifully with the silver foliage, and 'Susan', its pale mauve blooms zoned with rich madder-purple. Both flower on 9-in. stems, and if the dead blossoms are regularly removed, the plants will bloom throughout summer and into autumn.

Two more perennials which are amongst the easiest to grow and are an ideal complement to one another are erigeron and heuchera, both of which bloom from May until the early autumn when the dwarf michaelmas daisies and chrysanthemums take over. *Erigeron* 'Darkest of All', its pretty violet flowers having a striking golden eye, provides just the right contrast to *Heuchera* 'Scintillation' with its dainty sprays of vivid carmine-pink. Or plant 'Red Spangles' which is deeper red. Each of these plants blooms on 15-in. stems, and if cut, will remain fresh in water for several days.

Another striking plant used for permanent bedding is *Hosta fortunei aurea*, its broad-ribbed leaves being margined with gold as they begin to unfold early in spring, giving early tulips protection from cold winds. Plant the hostas 18 ins. apart and use bulbs or other plants between them.

SOME FAVOURITE SUMMER BEDDING PLANTS

Dahlias

Where possible, space should be found in a sunny border or island bed for that most colourful of autumn flowers, the dahlia, which, in the milder parts of Britain and in a well-drained soil may be left in the soil over winter, cutting back the stems to several inches above soil level with the rest of the border. Elsewhere, the tuberous roots should be lifted when the border is tidied late in November. The roots are placed in boxes of peat and stored in a frost-free room during winter. In January if you have a frame, or in April if not, they should be planted in boxes of peat and soil, just covering the tubers and placed in a greenhouse or frame to start them into new growth. Alternatively they can be planted in deep boxes, covered with a sheet of clean glass and placed in a sunny position outdoors. They are planted outside when the shoots are about 4 ins. tall, and when frosts have ended. The plants must be staked, as they make succulent growth and attain heights of 3–5 ft. in the border. They will bloom from late in July until well into November if the weather is mild, and no plants give as much colour at this time of year.

There are dahlias of all types, those with thin fluted petals being known as 'cactus' dahlias, whilst those with broad overlapping petals are the 'decoratives'. There are large, small, and miniature varieties. The large bear flowers as big as a dinner plate. Decoratives and cactus are the types most widely planted in borders. Those with small ball-shaped flowers, the pompons which grow 3 ft. tall, and the single Coltness type growing 18 ins. tall, are used for bedding. There are also a number of modern decorative and cactus dahlias which grow only 18 ins. tall, and these too are admirable bedding plants. They should be planted into a friable loam containing some peat or leaf mould and a little hop manure, and spaced 18 ins. apart for the bedding varieties, 3 ft. for the border types. Bedding dahlias do not require staking. Table 2 lists some of the best dahlias from the many hundreds of outstanding varieties available.

TABLE 2 Dahlias for Bedding and Borders

Varieties for Bedding	Type	Height in ins.	Colour
Border Princess	S–D	20	salmon
Coltness Gem	S	16	scarlet
Downham	S–C	18	yellow
Irene van der Zwet	S	15	yellow
Margaret Geerlings	S	16	vermilion
Murillo	S	15	pink
Park Beauty	S–D	16	orange
Park Princess	M–C	20	deep pink
Yellow Cheer	S–D	20	yellow

Varieties for Borders	Type	Height in ft.	Colour
Ann Weidner	P	3	white, tipped pink
Bacchus	M–C	4	blood red
Beauty of Crofton	Min–C	3½	apricot
Belle Epoque	M–C	3½	pink
Bowland	Min–D	3½	salmon
Caroussel	M–C	3½	purple
Chinese Lantern	S–D	4	orange & gold
Dedham	S–D	3½	cream & lilac
Exotica	M–C	4	white, tipped lilac
Gerrie Hoek	S–D	4	deep pink
Golden Festival	M–C	4	golden orange
Hamari Bride	S–C	3	ivory white
Hamari Fiesta	S–D	4	yellow & red
Hit Parade	M–C	4	scarlet
Lampe	P	3½	rose-pink
Lavengro	L–D	5	terracotta
Majuba	L–D	4	cardinal red
Newby	Min–D	3	peach
Princess Beatrix	M–D	4	gold, tipped white
Twiggy	S–D	3½	pink & yellow

L–D = large decorative
S–D = small decorative
Min–D = miniature decorative
P = pompon

L–C = large cactus
S–C = small cactus
Min–C = miniature cactus
S = single

Dahlia 'Wootton Monarch'

Dahlia 'Edinburgh'

Begonia 'Sam Philips'

A display of begonias

Begonias

The tuberous-rooted begonias are admirable plants for summer bedding doing especially well in a dull wet summer. The large carnation-flowered begonias, obtainable in all colours except blue, produce large double blooms almost the equal of named greenhouse varieties, and are easy to cultivate. Ordinary soil containing some peat and a little decayed manure, or some used hops, is all they require to give a continuous display from early June until the frosts. Start the tubers in boxes of peat towards the end of April by just pressing them in 1 in. apart with the round side downwards – and placing in a frame or cover with glass. They will soon begin to sprout at the top, which should not be covered. Keep them moist and plant out 12 ins. apart in early June, when they will have formed 2 or 3 leaves, and they will begin to flower at the month end.

The multiflora begonias are equally rewarding when planted 9 ins. apart in small beds, and bear masses of bloom from late June until early November. The tubers are started in the same way, and after flowering, should be lifted and placed in a frost-free airy room. There the foliage will die back and should be removed before placing the tubers in boxes of peat, where they will stay until the following spring.

Amongst the best of the multifloras are 'Mrs Helen Harms' which bears double blooms of coppery-yellow; 'Switzerland' scarlet; and 'Mrs Richard Galle' salmon orange. The dark green foliage is often tinted with bronze or purple.

Geraniums and other Plants

Though the multiflora begonias were used in France for parterre bedding throughout the 19th century, it was the geranium which took pride of place for bedding in gardens of Victorian Britain, for its flamboyance ideally matched the times. It is, however, more difficult to maintain through winter, for it requires a few degrees of heat to keep it free from mildew, whereas begonia tubers can be kept secure in boxes of peat. For all that, there is no plant to equal the geranium for tubs and bedding. It blooms from June until the frosts, and the brilliance of its foliage matches the rich reds and pinks of its flowers. In milder parts, they may be left in the beds and cut back in early summer to give them a tidier appearance before they begin to grow again.

Geraniums like a dry soil, preferably well limed, and so enjoy some lime rubble in their diet and a little decayed manure. At the end of summer, nurserymen take cuttings when the plants are lifted, and these root easily in gentle heat around the side of earthenware pots. They are then potted singly into 3-in. pots and are usually planted out 15 ins. apart in May, with the soil ball intact. Anyone interested in bedding geraniums should certainly master the simple art of propagating from cuttings.

Amongst the best of the zonal pelargoniums (to give the geranium its correct name) for bedding, are 'Paul Crampel', striking with its huge flowers of pillar box red; 'Gustav Emich' which has enjoyed a new popularity since it was used to fill the beds outside Buckingham Palace, its semi-double

Antirrhinum

Aster 'Carpet Ball' mixed

Aster 'Pepite White'

blooms of orange-scarlet producing an impressive sight; 'Mrs E. Hill' with its flowers of a delightful shade of salmon-pink; 'Banbury Cross', brick red with a white centre; and 'Marechal McMahon' which bears only small scarlet flowers, but has the most colourful foliage with zones of light and dark green, bronze, and gold.

Several of the decorative foliage geraniums will lend distinction to a bed if planted amongst those bearing brilliantly coloured flowers. Besides 'Marechal McMahon', 'Caroline Schmidt' has a pale green leaf edged with silver, and 'Lass o' Gowrie' has a golden leaf marked with crimson. For edging a bed of 'Paul Crampel', there is no more striking plant than the dwarf variety, 'Golden Harry Hieover' which has tiny leaves zoned with bronze and gold. It grows only 6 ins. tall and makes a rounded bushy plant. The colour scheme is even more effective if alternately planted with 'Black Vesuvius' which has leaves of darkest bronze.

With geraniums, the Victorians used white marguerites, scarlet salvias, the purple heliotrope, and calceolarias in yellow and bronze, all propagated from cuttings in the gentle heat of a greenhouse or conservatory, to be planted out from small pots in May and June. As an edging to the beds, dark blue *Lobelia* 'Mrs Clibran', or white alyssum, were used as they still are. The plants can be raised in heat, from seed sown in January. Or the new dwarf French marigold in shades of yellow, crimson, and orange, and growing no more than 6 ins. tall is a suitable alternative, which will bloom until the frosts. The closely related *Tagetes*, 'Golden Ring', orange, and 'Lulu' yellow will be colourful alternatives.

Pansies and Violas

Nor must the humble pansy and viola be forgotten, either for edging or to provide ground cover for beds of antirrhinums or gladioli with their tall, upright habit. Violas require a soil containing plenty of humus and they always do better in the north than in the south for they like a cool climate. Most have been in constant use for bedding for a century or more, and many excellent modern strains are readily raised from seed sown in the open ground in April. The named varieties are to be especially recommended amongst which 'Maggie Mott', mauve; 'Pickering Blue', 'Moseley Cream' and 'David Wheeldon', golden-yellow, are outstanding.

TABLE 3 Plants for Summer Bedding

Species & Variety	Height in ins.	Colour	In bloom
Ageratum, Blue mink, Blazer	4–9	blue, mauve	June–Sept
Alyssum, Carpet of Snow (HHA)	2	white	June–Sept
Alyssum, Rosie O'Day (HHA)	2	mauve	June–Sept
Amaranthus, Shoojoy	24	foliage	June–Sept
Antirrhinum, Little Darling	6–12	yellows	June–Sept
Antirrhinum, Rocket, Mme Butterfly	24–36	yellow, pinks	July–Sept
Antirrhinum, Sweetheart (HB)	12	rose-pink	July–Oct
Aster, Pirette (HHA)	14	red/white	July–Oct
Aster, Thousand Wonders Rose	12	rosy-pink	July–Oct
Begonia Multiflora (HHP)	9	various	June–Oct
Calceolaria, Bronze Beauty (HHP)	10	bronze	June–Oct
Calceolaria, Golden Gem (HHP)	10	yellow	June–Oct
Carnation, Juliet (HP)	10	scarlet	June–Sept
Celosia, Cockscomb	36	yellow, red	June–Oct
Celosia, Dwarf Red Plume (HHA)	12	dark red	July–Oct
Cleome, Pink Queen	36–42	pink	July–Sept
Cornflower, Jubilee Gem (HA)	12	blue	June–Sept
Cornflower, Snowball (HA)	12	white	June–Sept
Dahlia, Redskin (P)	16	various	July–Nov
Dianthus, Scarlet Charm (HA)	6	scarlet	June–Sept
Gaillardia, Lollipops	12–24	yellow, red	July–Sept
Gazania hybrida	9	white, yellow, red	June–Sept
Heliotrope, Marine (HHP)	15	mauve	June–Oct
Kochia trichophila	24–36	red foliage	Aug–Oct
Lobelia cardinalis (HHP)	36	scarlet	July–Oct
Lobelia, Crystal Palace (HHA)	2	sky blue	May–Oct
Lobelia, Mrs Clibran (HHA)	2	dark blue	May–Oct
Marigold, Golden Frills	6	chestnut	June–Sept
Marigold, Yellow Nugget (HHA)	8	yellow	July–Oct
Matthiola, 10-week stock	12–18	white, pinks	July–Sept
Mesembryanthemum criniflorum	4–6	very varied	June–Sept
Nemesia strumosa grandiflora (HHA)	12	various	June–Aug
Nicotiana, Crimson Rock (HHA)	12	crimson	July–Sept
Nicotiana, Dwarf White (HHA)	12	white	July–Sept
Pelargonium, Banbury Cross (HHP)	15	brick red	June–Oct
Pelargonium, Gustav Emich (HHP)	15	orange-scarlet	June–Oct
Pelargonium, Paul Crampel (HHP)	9	various	June–Oct
Petunia, El Toro (HHA)	9	dark red	June–Oct
Petunia, Razzle Dazzle (HHA)	9	red/white	June–Oct
Phlox drummondii, Cecily (HHA)	8	various	July–Oct
Portulaca grandiflora	6	yellow, red, purple	June–Sept
Salvia, Harbinger (HHP)	9	scarlet	June–Oct
Schizanthus pinnatus	24	varied	July–Sept
Tagetes erecta	18–36	yellows, reds	June–Oct
Tagetes, Golden Gem (HA)	6	yellow	June–Sept
Verbena, Sparkle (HHA)	9	various	July–Oct
Viola, Maggie Mott (HP)	4	mauve	May–Nov
Viola, Moseley Cream (HP)	4	cream	May–Nov
Viola, Pickering Blue (HP)	4	blue	May–Nov
Zinnia elegans	6–30	reds, yellows, etc.	June–Sept

HA = hardy annual
HHA = half hardy annual
HB = hardy biennial

P = perennial
HP = hardy perennial
HHP = half hardy perennial

A typical strong-growing campanula

Clarkia pulchella

A fine selection of delphinium

FLOWERS FROM SEED (HARDY & HALF HARDY ANNUALS)

Annuals & Half Hardy Annuals

Hardy annuals are the same types of plant as our ordinary wild flowers. Like our weeds they can germinate, grow, flower, seed, all in one year, although we do not often let them seed. There are so many new varieties that in a short section only a few of my personal favourites can be chosen, but they can all be sown in drifts directly into their allocated spot.

The taller types include godetia which reaches a height of 2 ft. and has beautiful double flowers in pastel shades of pink and red. Larkspurs have a range of blues and pinks, and the mallow, *Lavatera trimestris*, is soft pink and white. For tall massed colour the corn poppies and sweet scabious, *Scabiosa atropurpurea*, are very impressive.

In the middle range of sizes are the aurantiaca hybrids of dimorphotheca, the Star of the Veldt, in yellow, pink or white, Californian poppies, love-in-a-mist, with its lovely delicate blue flowers, mignonette, marigolds and a host of others.

For the front of the border or bed there are dwarf nasturtiums, *Lobularia maritima*, candytuft, *Nemophila insignis*, called baby blue eyes, *Phacelia campanularia*, and of course the delicate blues of the many varieties of forget-me-not. If some of the bright colours are shown between silver foliage plants such as *Stachys lanata*, or *Cineraria maritima*, the effect is much enhanced.

When discussing annuals one must never forget the sweet pea, truly called the queen of annuals. This beautiful plant is very rarely at its best in a bed and deserves to be seen grown by an expert in isolated rows, where the delicacy of colour and richness of scent are there for all to enjoy.

Sow in March and provided it has a trellis or some frame to climb up it will thrive. Of course if you want to grow exhibition sweet peas start them in heat the previous October. The soil should be well dug with much organic matter, and 4 oz. of bone meal to the sq. yd. A sprinkling of lime helps, especially in an acid soil and during the growing season sulphate of potash at about ½ oz. per sq. yd. The other essential is water. The plants should never be allowed to go short, hence have plenty of organic material in the soil.

As a cut flower it is supreme, especially when colours are mixed, and is the pride and joy of many a cottage and house garden.

Half hardy annuals are usually started under glass and put out when the risk of frost is past. They are not usually very tall, but zinnia, cosmos (white, orange and red), and nicotiana with its lovely fragrance may reach 2½ ft.

It is in the middle height range that they come into their own, for here are the asters with their varied colours of white, pink and blue, *Celosia plumosa* and *C. cristata*, lovely plumed plant species 1–2 ft. high, with splendid yellow or scarlet plumes. Gaillardia is in the middle size range as are many phloxes, salvias and stocks. A selection from Table 4 will produce a riot of colour during the summer and many cut flowers for the house.

The front of the border can be catered for by using dwarf varieties of many of the above plus mesembryanthemum, ageratum, portulaca, and many more.

TABLE 4 Hardy Annuals for Sowing in situ

Species	Height in ins.	Colour	When to sow	In bloom
Adonis aestivalis	12	crimson, yellow	Apr–May	June
Alyssum maritimum vars.	30	white, pink, purple	Apr–May	June–Sept
Anchusa capensis vars.	15	blue	Apr–Sept	June–Sept
Asperula orientalis	12	blue, fragrant	Apr	June–Aug
Bartonia aurea (Mentzelia)	15–18	yellow, fragrant	Apr–May	June–July
Calendula officinalis	18–24	yellows	Mar–May	June–Aug
Centaurea cyanus	12–30	blues, rose, white	Mar–Apr	June–Sept
*Chrysanthemum carinatum**	18–24	very varied	Apr	June–July
Clarkia elegans	24	salmon, pink, purple	Mar–Apr	June–Aug
Convolvulus tricolor	12–18	blue, yellow, pink	Mar–Apr	June–July
Coreopsis tinctoria	9–18	yellows, reds, brown	Apr	June–July
*Delphinium ajacis**	30–36	blues, pinks, white, etc.	Mar–Apr–Sept	June–July
*Dimorphotheca aurantiaca**	12	golden, salmon, white	Apr	June–Sept
Echium plantagineum	12	blue, pinks, white, etc.	Mar–Apr	July–Sept
Eschscholzia californica	6–9	rose, yellow, orange	Mar–Apr–Sept	June–Aug
*Godetia grandiflora**	6–24	pinks, reds, white, etc.	Mar–Apr–Sept	June–July
Gypsophila elegans	15–18	white, pink	Mar–Apr–Sept	May–Sept
Helianthus annuus vars.	36–96	gold, yellows	Apr	June–Sept
*Iberis umbellata**	9–12	varied	Mar–Apr–Sept	May–Sept
*Lathyrus odoratus**	climber	very varied	Feb–Mar	June–Sept
Lavatera trimestris	36	rose, white	Mar–Apr	June–Aug
Linaria maroccana vars.	9	yellows, red, white	Mar–Apr	May–Sept
Linum grandiflorum	18	carmine, scarlet	Mar–Apr	June–Aug
Nemophila insignis	6	blue	Mar–Apr	May–July
Nicandra physaloides	36	pale blue	Apr	June–Aug
Nigella damascena vars.	18	blue, white, rose pink	Mar–Apr	May–Sept
Papaver rhoeas	24	red, yellow, etc.	Apr	June–Sept
Phacelia campanularia	6–8	blue	Mar–Apr	May–Oct
Saponaria, Vaccaria segetalis	24	pink	Apr–May	July–Aug
Scabiosa atropurpurea	36	blues, pinks, rose	Apr	July–Sept
Tagetes signata pumila	5–7	yellows, crimson	May	July–Sept
Tropaeolum majus	6–84	varied	Apr–May	July–Oct
Tropaeolum peregrinum	climber	yellow	Mar–May	July–Sept

*Hybrid   vars. = varieties

Sweet William or Dianthus barbatus

Border carnation (Dianthus hybrid)

Eryngium oliverianum

Eschscholzia californica

Linum perenne, a blue flax

Russell lupins

Nemesia 'Carnival' mixed

Nepeta mussinii

There are many other plants suitable for bedding that can be readily raised from seed. One is the dwarf dahlia Redskin, a strain originating in the USA. The plants grow 16 ins. tall and remain neat and compact throughout the summer. From a sowing made in gentle heat, or over a mild frame hot bed, early in the year, they will begin to bloom in June and continue until the frosts. The plants have bronzy-green foliage and bear double blooms in all the dahlia colours. The Rigoletto strain is even more compact, growing only 10 ins. tall, the double blooms having the same colour range.

Another favourite for bedding is the carnation 'Juliet' which makes a bushy plant 10 ins. tall, covered throughout summer with fully double scarlet flowers, the size of a 10p. piece.

The antirrhinum, though perennial, is usually treated as a biennial, seed being sown in a frame in June. The seedlings are transplanted when large enough to handle, and the plants grown on in the frame over winter to be bedded out in May. Modern varieties have transformed the antirrhinum as a bedding plant, several strains being suitable for the smallest beds. The Sweetheart strain grows less than 12 ins. tall and bears compact spikes with rosy-pink penstemon-like flowers, whilst 'Delice' bears flowers of rich creamy-apricot.

Modern petunias, half hardy annuals which are raised in gentle heat by sowing early in the year, make admirable bedding plants and none is more striking than 'Razzle Dazzle', the petals having alternating stripes of scarlet and white. Also single-flowered is 'El Toro', the colour being a hot crimson red. The double Multiflora strain bears flowers like carnations, and in all the familiar petunia colours.

Celosia, or feathered cockscomb, should be given the same treatment, and is planted out in June 10 ins. apart. The dwarf Red Plume and Golden Plume strains, growing only 12 ins. tall, are admirable for bedding, either planted separately or together.

Asters, too, are invaluable for summer bedding, for many make compact mounds which are smothered in small flowers for weeks on end. The variety 'Thousand Wonders Rose' grows less than 12 ins. tall and bears fully double flowers of deep rose-pink from July until October. The pompon aster 'Pirette' grows slightly taller, its tiny double blooms being scarlet with a large contrasting white centre. The Pepite strain grows 10 ins. tall, the plants being covered in tiny single flowers in shades of mauve, white, pink and red.

The introduction of the dwarf cornflower 'Jubilee Gem' in 1934 gave this lovely old flower a new lease of life in that for the first time it made an ideal bedding plant, making a rounded bush 12 ins. tall with grey-green foliage, and bearing masses of cornflower-blue flowers during the whole of the summer. There is now a white counterpart, 'Snowball' which has the same excellent bedding habit. For a striking display, use both colours together and interplant with Dianthus 'Scarlet Charm' which is also an annual and makes a spreading mound 6 ins. tall, smothered in scarlet flowers all through summer. The variety, 'Merry-go-Round', is equally effective, the single flowers being white with a scarlet centre. The cornflowers and the dianthus are completely hardy and may be planted out early in May.

The new strains of Nicotiana, the tobacco plants, make an effective bedding display and outstanding is 'Crimson Rock' which makes a bushy plant of emerald green, above which the crimson flowers are

Two fine borders

A delphinium border

borne in profusion on 12-in. stems. Plant with them 'Dwarf White Bedder' which grows to the same height. They require half-hardy treatment, likewise *Nemesia* of which the *strumosa grandiflora* bears the largest flowers in the widest colour range, and is one of the earliest to bloom of all summer bedding plants.

SOME FAVOURITE SPRING BEDDING PLANTS
The garden should be as colourful in spring as it is in summer, for besides the wide variety of bulbs suitable for this purpose, there are other plants which bloom at the same time and can be grown with them, either to provide ground cover or in beds by themselves.

Wallflowers are perhaps the most widely planted of spring- and early summer-flowering plants. They are really perennial but are so easily raised from seed that they are usually treated as biennials. Sow seed in April to bloom from March–June the following year. For small beds 'Orange Bedder' and 'Scarlet Bedder' grow less than 12 ins. tall and bloom with freedom. For the larger bed, 'Scarlet Emperor', 'Fire King' and 'Cloth of Gold' make bushy plants 18 ins. tall. *Cheiranthus allionii*, the Siberian wallflower, comes rather later into bloom and bears its orange flowers on 12-in. stems. 'Golden Bedder' bears bright yellow flowers.

Also biennial is the sweet william, which is also suitable for early summer flowering, especially the dwarf double strain which grows only 10 ins. tall and bears 70% double blooms in scarlet, pink, and auricula-eyed varieties.

Stocks with their rich perfume are universal favourites, the Trisomic 7-week strain producing almost 100% double flowers (if weaker seedlings are discarded) in shades of crimson, pink, flesh, and mauve, and at a height of only 12 ins. The double 'Early Cascade' is also good, bearing its flowers in large thick spikes on 15-in. stems.

To provide an edging for the beds, or ground cover for tulips and other spring-flowering plants, there are no lovelier plants than the Juliae primroses. 'Wanda' with its claret-purple flowers is well known, but there are others of equal beauty including 'E. R. Janes', salmon-pink; 'Perle von Bottrop', glowing purple and 'Lady Greer', like a tiny yellow polyanthus. For the same purpose are the double daisies, *Bellis perennis* of which 'Haubner's Fairy Carpet' in crimson and rose is outstanding. It makes a tiny compact plant 3 ins. tall, the large double daisies having attractive quilled petals. Even more dwarf is the Double Pomponette strain, the convex flowers also having quilled petals and of crimson, pink, and salmon colouring. They are suitable for troughs and window-boxes, as well as for an edging to spring-flowering plants.

TABLE 5 Plants for Spring Bedding (see also Bulbs)

Species & Variety	Height in ins.	Colour	In bloom
Bellis perennis	3–9	white, rose, crimson	Apr–June
Cheiranthus × allionii	12	yellow, orange	May–June
Cheiranthus cheiri	9–18	yellow, red, orange	Apr–June
Dianthus barbatus	12–18	crimson, pink, white	May–July
Erysimum arkansanum	9	yellow	May–June
Matthiola incana (7-week strain)	12–18	crimson, mauve, pink	May–July
Myosotis alpestris	6–12	blue, red	
Myosotis scorpioides	5–12	blue	Apr–Sept
Primula auricula	6–9	red, purple, pink	May–June
Primula denticulata	12	blue, white, red	Apr–May
Primula polyanthus	6–8	white, yellow, blue, red	Apr–June
Primula vulgaris	6–8	yellow, white, pinks	Apr–May
Viola hybrida (pansy)	4–6	many colours	Apr–Oct

TABLE 6 Plants for the Shaded Border

Species & Variety	Height in ins.	Colour	In bloom
Aconitum wilsonii, Barker's Variety	60	purple	Aug–Sept
Anemone japonica alba	36	white	Aug–Oct
Anemone vitifolia	48	pink	July–Sept
Astilbe, Ostrich Plume	36	pink	July–Aug
Astrantia major	24	greenish-purple	July–Sept
Astrantia major alba	24	white	July–Sept
Bergenia, Abendglut	18	carmine	Mar–May
Bergenia, Morgen Rote	15	rose-pink	Mar–Sept
Brunnera macrophylla	18	blue	Apr–June
Cimicifuga cordifolia	48	cream	July–Aug
Dicentra spectabilis	24	pink	July–Aug
Digitalis ambigua	36	honey	July–Aug
Doronicum plantagineum	36	yellow	Apr–June
Epimedium elegans	15	yellow	Apr–June
Euphorbia robbiae	18	green	May–June
Helleborus corsicus	20	green	Mar–May
Hosta glauca robusta	36	grey-mauve	July–Aug
Ligularia veitchiana	60	yellow	July–Aug
Lysimachia punctata	36	yellow	June–July
Monarda, Croftway Pink	36	pink	June–Aug
Paeony, in variety	24	red, white	May–June
Polygonatum multiflorum	24	white	May–June
Primula denticulata	10	purple	Apr–May
Ranunculus acris plenus	24	golden	May–June
Solidago, Loddon Gold	36	yellow	Sept–Oct
Spiraea aruncus	60	cream	July–Aug
Spiraea magnifica	60	pink	July–Aug
Thalictrum aquilegifolium	48	rose-purple	June–July

Phlox 'Beauty' mixed

Primula vulgaris or primrose

Primula malacoides

African marigold (Tagetes erecta, F1 Hybrid)

Echeveria and French marigold make unusual but effective companions at the edge of the border.

THE HEIGHT OF PLANTS

To enable you to choose plants for the border which are of the correct height and colour to suit your purpose, here are four lists of plants each arranged in alphabetical order and grouped according to height. They range from 8 ins. to 6 ft. and are of almost every colour imaginable.

TABLE 7 Plants to Edge Front of All Borders

Species & Variety	Height in ins.	Colour	In bloom
Aster, Jenny	12	violet	Aug–Oct
Aster, Little Red Boy	15	crimson	Aug–Oct
Aster, Rose Bonnet	12	pink	Aug–Oct
Auricula, Old Irish Blue	8	dark blue	Apr–June
Bergenia delavayi	12	pink	Mar–May
Betonica grandiflora	12	purple	July–Aug
Campanula, Pouffe	12	blue	July–Aug
Coreopsis, Goldfink	10	yellow	July–Sept
Dianthus allwoodii, Helen	15	salmon	June–Aug
Dianthus, Earl of Essex	12	pink	June–July
Dianthus (Pinks), Mrs Sinkins	12	white	June–July
Dicentra, Adrian Bloom	12	crimson	Apr–June
Doronicum, Goldzwerg	12	yellow	Mar–May
Geum borisii	12	orange	May–June
Hemerocallis, Orangeman	15	orange	May–June
Heuchera, Red Spangles	15	scarlet	May–July
Hosta fortunei aurea	15	lilac	June–July
Lychnis viscaria plena	15	carmine	June–July
Nepeta mussinii	12	mauve	June–Aug
Polyanthus	10	all colours	Jan–June
Polygonum, Darjeeling Red	12	rose-red	Aug–Sept
Primula denticulata	10	mauve	Mar–May
Prunella, Pink Loveliness	12	pink	July–Aug
Prunella, Webbiana	12	violet	July–Aug
Salvia, Nainacht	15	violet	May–Aug
Sedum, Ruby Glow	15	ruby-red	Aug–Nov
Stachys, Silver Carpet	12	silver foliage	Evergreen
Stokesia cyanea	12	mid blue	Aug–Sept
Tiarella, Bridget Bloom	15	shell-pink	May–Aug
Tiarella cordifolia	12	white	June–July

TABLE 8 Back Row Plants for a Narrow Border

Species & Variety	Height in ft.	Colour	In bloom
Achillea, Moonshine	2–3	pale yellow	July–Sept
Aconitum, Bressingham Spire	3	violet-blue	July–Sept
Anchusa, Loddon Royalist	2–3	deep blue	June–July
Anemone, Max Vogel	2–3	deep pink	Aug–Oct
Aquilegia longissima	2–3	pale yellow	May–June
Aster, Crimson Brocade	3	crimson	Aug–Oct
Aster, Ernest Ballard	3	rose-red	Sept–Nov
Aster, Royal Velvet	3	violet-blue	Aug–Oct
Astilbe, Prof. Wellen	2–3	white	July–Aug
Campanula persicifolia, Percy Piper	3	lilac-blue	July–Aug
Chrysanthemum maximum, T. Killin	3	white	July–Sept
Echinops, Veitch's Blue	2–3	steel-blue	July–Aug
Eryngium, Donard Blue	2–3	grey-blue	July–Sept
Euphorbia griffithii	2–3	red	Apr–June
Fritillaria imperialis (bulb)	3	orange, yellow	Apr–June
Helenium, Moerheim Beauty	3	bronze	July–Sept
Kniphofia, Maid of Orleans	3	white	July–Sept
Liatris callilepsis	3	purple-pink	July–Sept
Lupin, Mrs Micklethwaite	3	pink/yellow	June–July
Lychnis chalcedonica	3	scarlet	July–Aug
Monarda, Cambridge Scarlet	3	scarlet	June–Aug
Monarda, Snow Maiden	3	white	June–Aug
Paeony, Kelway's Glorious	2–3	white	June–July
Phlox, Brigadier	2–3	orange-red	July–Sept
Phlox, Look Again	2–3	glowing purple	July–Sept
Ranunculus acris plenus	2–3	yellow	Apr–June
Salvia haematoides	3	lavender	June–July
Solidago, Lesden	2–3	pale yellow	July–Sept
Trollius, Prichard's Giant	2–3	deep gold	May–July

TABLE 9 Back Row Plants for Wide Border

Species & Variety	Height in ft.	Colour	In bloom
Achillea, Gold Plate	4	gold	July–Sept
Aconitum, Barker's Variety	5	purple	Aug–Sept
Anchusa, Morning Glory	4–5	deep blue	June–July
Aster, Harrington's Pink	4–5	deep pink	July–Sept
Astilbe tacquetii	4–5	heather	July–Aug
Bocconia, Coral Plume	5–6	coral	Aug–Sept
Chrysanthemum maximum, Horace Read	5	white	July–Sept
Delphinium, in variety	5–7	purple, blue	June–July
Dierama pulcherrimum	5–6	claret	July–Aug
Echinops, Blue Ball	5	soft blue	July–Aug
Eryngium giganteum	4–5	sea-green	July–Aug
Helenium, Spatrot	4–5	bronze	Aug–Sept
Heliopsis, Ballerina	5	golden-orange	July–Sept
Kniphofia, Samuel's Sensation	5	orange-red	Aug–Oct
Ligularia clivorum, Othello	5	orange	July–Aug
Lupin, Venus	4	orange	June–July
Lupin, Wheatsheaf	4	yellow	June–July
Rudbeckia, Golden Glow	6	orange	July–Sept
Salvia uliginosa	5	blue	Aug–Sept
Sidalcea, Rev. P. Roberts	4–5	pink	July–Aug
Solidago, Golden Wings	4–5	yellow	Sept–Nov
Spiraea aruncus	6	cream	July–Aug
Thalictrum, Hewitt's Double	6	purple-pink	July–Aug
Verbascum, Boadicea	6	coppery-buff	July–Aug

TABLE 10 Plants for Middle of Small Border and Front Centre of Wide Border

Species & Variety	Height in ins.	Colour	In bloom
Aconitum, Blue Sceptre	24	blue & white	July–Aug
Anchusa, Little John	18	deep blue	June–Aug
Anemone, Queen Charlotte	20	pink	Aug–Sept
Armeria formosana	18	pink & carmine	May–Oct
Aster amellus, Brilliant	20	rose-pink	Aug–Sept
Aster amellus, Chequers	24	purple	July–Aug
Aster amellus, Napsbury	18	purple	July–Aug
Aster amellus, Royal Ruby	24	ruby-red	Aug–Oct
Astilbe, Finale	24	pink	July–Aug
Brunnera macrophylla	24	blue	Apr–June
Campanula glomerata	18	purple	June–July
Centaurea, John Coutts	24	pink	May–Aug
Chrysanthemum, Paul Boissier	24	copper-red	Oct–Dec
Chrysanthemum rubellum, Mary Stoker	24	buff-yellow	Oct–Dec
Coreopsis verticillata	24	yellow	July–Sept
Cynoglossum nervosum	24	blue	June–Aug
Dicentra, Bountiful	18	rose-pink	May–Sept
Doronicum, Spring Beauty	18	yellow	Apr–May
Erigeron, Darkest of All	24	violet	June–Sept
Erigeron, Gaiety	24	pink	June–Sept
Gaillardia	24	crimson, gold	June–Sept
Geranium, Johnson's Blue	18	violet-blue	June–Aug
Geum, Lady Strathedon	20	yellow	June–Aug
Geum, Mrs Bradshaw	20	red	June–Aug
Helleborus corsicus	20	green	Mar–May
Helleborus niger	10	white	Jan–Apr
Hemerocallis, Pink Lady	20	pink	June–Aug
Hemerocallis, Radiant	18	apricot	June–Aug
Hemerocallis, Tejas	20	crimson	June–Aug
Incarvillea delavayi	16	rose-mauve	June–July
Iris, Jane Phillips	24	clear blue	June–July
Iris, Limelight	24	yellowish green	June–July
Iris, Pink Cameo	24	pink	June–July
Kniphofia, Gold Else	24	yellow	June–Aug
Oenothera, Yellow River	18	yellow	June–Aug
Papaver, Mrs Perry	24	salmon-pink	June–Aug
Papaver, Stormtorch	24	orange	June–Aug
Physostegia, Summer Snow	20	white	Aug–Sept
Physostegia, Vivid	20	lilac-rose	Aug–Sept
Polemonium coeruleum	18	blue	June–July
Potentilla, Melton	18	flame	June–Sept
Poterium obtusum	24	pink	July–Aug
Pyrethrum, Evenglow	20	salmon	May–July
Pyrethrum, Jas. Kelway	20	crimson	May–July
Scabiosa, Clive Greaves	20	pale blue	June–Oct
Sedum spectabile	24	pink	Aug–Oct
Tradescantia, Isis	18	blue	June–Oct
Tradescantia, Purewell Giant	24	pink	June–Oct
Veronica, Royal Blue	18	deep blue	June–July

A fine bunch of mixed sweet peas

A convenient method of growing sweet peas

Garden thyme (Thymus vulgaris)

Viola 'Blue Bonnet' and 'Sunny Gold'

GARDEN SHRUBS

J. A. Hingston

I love shrubs. I love trees, too, but shrubs are nearer my own size and don't overwhelm me. They are always there – not ephemeral like petunias, nor unseen most of the year like scillas, and their beauty grows with their stature.

In the mind's eye they are always beautiful. The dormant winter stem may or may not have special charm, but it is seen as burgeoning into leaf and flower, and the spent flower into ripening fruit. The withering leaf has charming colours, and in the final resort, the plant that dies of old age or ill-health has its own apt message – *memento mori*.

A shrub standing alone with irregular shape but perfect poise is statuesque, a quality sought in Loudon's gardenesque style before this degenerated into fussy lawns and flower beds. A shrub's special beauty may be its large, shapely, and textured leaves; or its flowers so prolific as to hide every leaf; or winter flowers, scarcely seen but overpoweringly fragrant; or fruit, abundant and colourful – and if the wild birds assume it is for them, accept repayment in spring song.

Shrubs are useful too. Nothing is better to hide a fence or a hut or a view which you would rather not see. They also carpet the ground and smother weeds, break a buffeting wind, or frame a tranquil lawn.

PLANNING THE SCENE

A garden is an atmosphere for living in and for looking at, and the pleasure of gardening is to create one's own chosen environment. The picture 'for looking at' from a particular vantage point is usually of spaces framed by shrubs and trees, with places for floral colour, and a clearly identified focal point. In most gardens there are two main vantage points, the front garden gate, where one pauses to sense a welcome home, and the main window from which one admires the pleasing garden scene. Subsidiary vantage points, strung along the route one meanders, are the places where one pauses to imbibe a different view.

So with feet on the ground and head in the clouds, stand at the vantage point and create in the mind's eye a picture of background and borders which you would like to see. How long have you got, what is the time scale? The things you would like, will they thrive? Those are the fundamental questions to be considered in turn. For posterity the main framework would be trees, but if we plant for a decade or two it should be shrubs. Small when planted, but taking shape in 2 or 3 years, they are never static, and mature with the seasons like their owner.

Almost certainly there will be a dilemma in choosing the plants which will flourish and appear happy, as against those one might have preferred. In the classical phrase, consult the genius of the place. A subtle concept, but a good starting point, is to look over the fence to find out what flourishes in this soil and climate. The first requirement is to be certain whether one is in rhododendron and heather country, or in viburnum, clematis, and helianthemum country. On acid soil with high rainfall it may be the former, and on chalk soil with low rainfall probably the latter. Only a few people are favoured with the happy medium of soil and climate where everything flourishes.

The shrub border, whether a back-drop or feature, should first be sketched on paper. Mark any features to be retained such as existing trees and plants, walls and paths. Remember evergreens, or evergolds, are decorative throughout the year, and tend to be more expensive to buy, but too many dark greens seem gloomy: summer deciduous growth is needed to lighten the picture. The border must have variety, but may well be dominated by a particular genus which can be relied upon to thrive in that place, e.g. buddleia, rhododendron, or magnolia, as the case may be. Apart from the limitations of soil and climate, the plants are of your own choice for your own pleasure. You can shun hydrangeas or rhododendrons if you dislike them, but it could be said that hydrangeas at Folkestone and rhododendrons at Ascot are so intrinsic to the *genius loci* that it would be difficult to avoid them entirely.

Plant in groups – perhaps 3 or 5 of a kind together. Have adjoining groups of contrasting habit, or with foliage of different shape or texture. Rather close spacing makes for a mature effect within a year or two – say 2 ft. apart for hebe, 4 ft. for weigela and 6 ft. for buddleia. In a large border this may seem extravagant, but it is certainly effective, and the careful gardener removes elsewhere some plants as they fill their spaces, and before they suppress their neighbours.

PREPARATION AND PLANTING

A shrub border is intended to remain several years, and adequate preparation can only be done at the outset. The needs are simple. Cultivate two spits deep for the sake of free passage of plant roots and water; incorporate manure because you desire abundant growth; remove the roots of perennial weeds or they will become very troublesome later.

At planting time work only when the soil is amenable; make holes large enough for the outspread roots; firm the soil around and over the roots; if subsequently wind loosens the plant, firm the soil again and perhaps offer a stake. During the first spring and summer give water if the soil becomes dry.

CONTINUING CARE

The shrub border should appear a happy community of plants, united to overpower invading weeds, but careful to allow each other space to develop their charms. That is the perfect state, but in reality some weeds will invade, calling for careful use of the

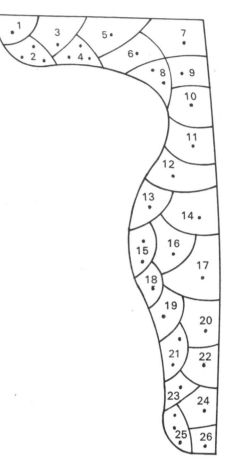

A possible plan for a shrubbery (30 ft. × 15 ft.) to frame a small garden. The front of the shrubbery can be planted with things like heathers and bulbs – crocus, dwarf daffodils, scillas, grape hyacinth, and so on. Roses are best in a bed of their own.

KEY TO NUMBERS

1 *Fatsia japonica*
2 *Vinca minor*
3 *Berberis × rubrostilla*
4 *Hebe pagei*
5 *Choisya ternata*
6 *Fuchsia riccartonii*
7 *Aralia chinensis*
8 *Cotoneaster dammeri*
9 *Elaeagnus pungens 'Maculata'*
10 *Spiraea × arguta*
11 *Escallonia edinensis*
12 *Olearia macrodonta*
13 *Cotoneaster conspicua decora*
14 *Buddleia alternifolia*
15 *Viburnum davidii*
16 *Yucca gloriosa*
17 *Rhus cotinus*
18 *Ceratostigma willmottianum*
19 *Juniperus tamariscifolia*
20 *Griselinia littoralis*
21 *Euonymus fortunei variegatus*
22 *Clerodendron trichotomum*
23 *Cytisus × praecox*
24 *Cornus spaethii*
25 *Erica carnea*
26 *Poncirus trifoliata*

hoe. Disturb the shrub roots as little as possible, and remove perennial weeds with a garden fork occasionally. After two years the shrubs should have largely covered the soil and inhibited seedling growth. By this time their own roots should be so secure, that herbicide applications may be considered on the remaining open spaces. After very carefully reading the instructions and avoiding shrubs known to be susceptible to damage, you may find the need for such surface soil-acting herbicides as simazine or 'Caseron G'.

Mulching with peat or leaf mould does nothing but good at any time, and every few years a generous spring dressing of fertiliser is well worthwhile.

But the gardener's determination to get a quart into a pint pot, to have all the world's vegetation in his little plot, leads to the necessity of containing the exuberance he has encouraged. To transplant and re-use the overcrowded, to cull the unwanted, and to prune the excess with subtle discretion, are the tasks required to keep the shrub border young and beautiful.

Whole books are written on pruning, but one can identify some basic principles: winter pruning stimulates new growth, summer pruning discourages growth; flowering shrubs generally can be pruned after flowering; evergreen shrubs are best pruned lightly in April; flowering hedges are trimmed after flowering, other hedges once a year in August, providing one wisely avoids too rampant privet and lonicera.

There is an intriguing paradox in the old saying that the best shrub pruner is a generous woman. We would all agree that the removal of the spent flowering sprays of forsythia encourages the plant to make vigorous new shoots. Imagine the sprays being cut off in full bloom – will that not stimulate the new growth we desire at an even earlier time?

HEDGES

A hedge will do almost anything you ask. Hide the view if it is tall and evergreen; frame the view if it is tailored to size; obstruct intruders if it is dense or spiny; welcome strangers if it is low and colourful; define a formal garden if it is precise and architectural; or express nature's exuberance if it is a billowing mass of flower.

When the purpose is decided there are two questions to be asked: How high shall it be? and, Do you enjoy clipping? Trimming hedges, like mowing lawns, is to some people a soothing and satisfying pastime, to others a burdensome chore. Compulsive clippers love lonicera and privet. Cut them twice a week the summer through and they will always look neat, and spread pride and joy. Anti-clippers will choose beech and hornbeam, perhaps yew and holly, although these grow slowly, because their green growth is pleasing and they are controlled by one annual trim in late summer.

If you are impatient for a visual screen in the shortest possible time think first of Leyland cypress. If there is ample space, and you have no prejudice against its large shiny leaves, consider cherry laurel. There are many slower-growing evergreens which have a rightful place such as evergreen oak, Portugal laurel, laurustinus, rhododendron, Japanese euonymus, pyracantha, golden privet, and box.

A flowering hedge is a beautiful feature in its own right. Almost any flowering shrub can be planted in straight lines to make an informal boundary, division, or backdrop, if its personality, stature, and season of beauty meet your needs. Prune it in the way

Planting a clematis. (1) Dig a generous hole 18 ins. square and two spits deep. Fill the bottom with limestone chips or old mortar rubble (clematis are lime lovers in the wild). Spread the roots carefully and fill with a good soil or compost (2) Plant the stake (essential) at the same time, not afterwards. The vulnerable stem should be protected (3) and a trellis provided for support for the plant in flower (4).

Clematis is one of the most beautiful of climbing plants. It can be obtained in a variety of colours, two of which are shown above. The popular 'Nellie Moser' is on the left.

Azalea 'Unique'

Azalea 'Satan Red' and 'Princess Pink'

Berberis × stenophylla

Rhus cotinus

When these techniques are mastered you will no doubt wish to investigate the many variations appropriate to rare and difficult subjects.

The quicker and easier way of course is to buy the shrubs from your garden centre, or nurseryman.

GROUND COVER

Some say the best ground cover is a lawn, but to look fresh it has to be mown twice a week. Concrete paving demands less care, but it becomes discoloured and moss-covered. A carpet of periwinkle or of horizontal juniper or cotoneaster may have the perfect qualities. It covers the ground with verdure, suppressing weeds, allowing occasional pedestrians to pass, and requires only an annual trim to maintain its tidiness. The popularity of this kind of ground cover is well deserved, because it is beautiful and economical when properly managed. The initial cost of plants may be formidable, but nurserymen offer sensible rates for large quantities raised in their clever polythene rolls.

PLANTS FOR WALLS

There is a school of thought which advocates a soil border at the foot of every wall so that pyracantha and Japanese quince can furnish it; or self-clinging vines can climb over it; and if wires are fixed to the wall, twining clematis and wisteria can add floral beauty to mere brickwork and masonry. This maybe is asking too much, but there are certainly times and places for such embellishment of house and garden.

FIRST THOUGHTS FOR PARTICULAR PLACES

Peaty and Acid Soils

Calluna	Hamamelis
Camellia	Kalmia
Corylopsis	Pachysandra
Cytisus	Pernettya
Daboecia	Pieris
Desfontainea	Rhododendron
Enkianthus	Styrax
Erica	Tricuspidaria
Fothergilla	Zenobia
Halesia	

Chalk and Alkaline Soils

Choisya	Mahonia
Cistus	Potentilla
Daphne	Rosa
Forsythia	Rubus
Fuchsia	Spartium
Hebe	Syringa
Helianthemum	Weigela
Laurus	Yucca

Sunny Banks

Artemisia	Hypericum
Berberis	Phlomis
Cistus	Rosmarinus
Colutea	Santolina
Cotoneaster	Ulex
Cytisus	Vinca

Ground Cover

Calluna	Hedera
Chaenomeles	Helianthemum
Cotoneaster	Hypericum
Erica	Mahonia
Euonymus	Pachysandra
Hebe	Vinca

Moist Ground

Arundinaria	Sambucus
Cornus	Symphoricarpus
Hippophae	Viburnum
Leycesteria	

appropriate to contain its spread, and keep it young and beautiful. The most familiar subjects are berberis, escallonia, cotoneaster, forsythia, fuchsia, lavender and rose.

Decorative effects of a different kind can be obtained by mixing plants with contrasting foliage. Popular is the tapestry effect of alternating green-leaved myrobalan with purple-leaved plum.

The rules for preparing the ground are straightforward. Dig deeply, removing perennial weeds; incorporate manure to the full depth – it may be years before you offer more plant food, and you will expect the plants to thrive nevertheless. Plant with a garden line, usually in a single row, but a staggered row will give a quicker effect. Space the plants from 1–3 ft. apart according to the species, and tread firm. Remove competing weeds punctiliously for the first year or two.

First Steps in Propagation

Shrubs shouldn't be expected to live as long as trees, or even as long as men. Successors are needed, hence the great nursery industry, and hence also the pleasurable task of raising young plants to replace the old. The basic method is to raise plants from seed, and for wild species, as opposed to garden varieties, it is the natural way.

Many garden plants are far removed from their wild ancestors and will not pass on their special attributes to their seedlings. Vegetative propagation may mean borrowing another's roots, as grafting a rhododendron hybrid on a 'ponticum' seedling, or budding a rose on a briar. Deft-fingered enthusiasts can master the art and find great pleasure therein.

But most shrubs are happier on their own roots than on borrowed ones, and the propagator's task is to persuade a shoot cut from its parent to make roots and take on an independent life. Nurserymen have well-proven techniques for every variety of plant – cold frames for semi-ripe cuttings, sand beds for hardwood cuttings, and a propagating house with intermittent mist for soft cuttings of almost anything.

Gardeners may well start by adopting the first method, and a vast number of shrubs can be persuaded to comply. Cut from the plant in July a leafy shoot 3–4 ins. long. Remove the lower leaves and dip the cutting in a hormone rooting powder. In a corner of the garden prepare a 6-in. depth of compost, peat, sand, and garden soil, in equal parts. Push the cutting in and firm the compost round it. Then the secret is to invert a 2-lb. jam jar over the cuttings. This gives them a moist, draught-free environment, with minimum loss of water. Only a small intake of water is required via the cut stem, the leaves remain turgid and continue to photosynthesise, and the plant has no worries. It can put all its energy into the task of emitting roots. When this is achieved the new plant has its own identity. Remove the covering jar after a month or so, leaving the plant where it is until the autumn or the following spring. Grow it on to a larger size in a nursery bed before it takes its rightful place in the garden.

Hardwood cuttings of deciduous shrubs are taken in autumn when the leaves have fallen. Six inches is an average length. Inserting them in sand stimulates the healing of the cut stem with a callus, and promotes root initials, which grow into real roots in the spring. As with semi-ripe cuttings, a little encouragement is given by dipping the newly made cutting in a hormone rooting powder.

Cotoneaster horizontalis

Cytisus praecox (Warminster broom)

Shade

Aucuba	Pachysandra
Camellia	Pernettya
Choisya	Rhododendron
Fatsia	Rubus
Garrya	Skimmia
Gaultheria	Symphoricarpus
Hypericum	Viburnum
Mahonia	Vinca

Seaside

Atriplex	Hebe
Berberis	Hippophae
Buddleia	Olearia
Colutea	Santolina
Elaeagnus	Senecio
Escallonia	Spartium
Fuchsia	Ulex
Griselinia	Yucca

Climbers and Twiners

Actinidia	Parthenocissus
Akebia	Polygonum
Clematis	Schizophragma
Hydrangea	Vitis
petiolaris	Wisteria

For a Favoured Climate

Abelia	Hibiscus
Abutilon	Leptospermum
Carpenteria	Pittosporum
Desfontainea	Punica
Eucryphia	Tricuspidaria
Fabiana	Vitis
Fremontia	

200 OF THE BEST SHRUBS

Abelia × grandiflora (5 ft.) really deserves a climate kinder than ours. It is a delicately aristocratic cousin of the weigela, with smaller pinkish bell-shaped flowers.

Abutilon megapotamicum (6 ft.) bears clustered pendent flowers with bright red calices, yellow petals, and purple stamens. It is an exotic gem for Cornwall or whereever that climate may be simulated. So is *A. vitifolium* (15–30 ft.) with its greyish leaves and mauve mallow-like flowers.

Actinidia kolomikta (10–20 ft.) a twiner for wires fixed to a wall – a joker with harlequin leaves streaked white and pink.

Akebia quinata (30–40 ft.) is another twiner to embellish a structure or a tree-stump and produces in May chocolate-coloured pendent flowers which look delicious enough to eat!

Amelanchier canadensis (20–30 ft.), the 'Snowy Mespilus' would grow into a tree, but it can be contained by pruning hard when its abundant white flowers have faded

in April. You will enjoy too its rich autumn foliage and purplish winter twigs.

Aralia chinensis (up to 45 ft.) has majestic pinnate leaves up to 5 ft. long, and in winter vicious-looking spiny Hercules' clubs. Suckers emerge from the roots all around until you might have an armoured palisade.

Artemisia abrotanum (3–4 ft.), the 'Southernwood' of old fashioned gardens has aromatic feathery leaves and yellow flowers of less appeal. It is sensible to keep it compact by trimming in April. *A. arborescens* (1½–3½ ft.) is more highly esteemed.

Arundinaria nitida is the first choice among bamboos if you have room for a woody grass 10 ft. tall. Of more modest size but still evocative of tropical romance is *A. angustifolia* (2–6 ft.).

Atriplex halimus (4–8 ft.), the 'Tree Purslane' of south Europe has a loose shapeless habit but smooth silvery leaves of unusual texture. Its chief merit is its persistence in the face of strong ocean gales.

Aucuba japonica (6–12 ft.) in golden or variegated forms may be despised for symbolising the Victorian shrubbery, but its toughness and brightness cannot be denied. Under trees, in smoky towns, on dry banks, you may well need its humble aid.

Azara microphylla (12–30 ft.), with tiny evergreen leaves has a graceful charm. When established (not earlier please) it is an excellent source, throughout the year, of the foliage needed by flower arrangers.

Berberis. In this alphabetical sequence, the first of the major shrub genera. All are spiny and unkind to children, and their small leaves on interweaving shoots may suggest monotony. But their yellow or orange flowers in spring, their yellow, red, or purple berries, the rich autumn tints of the deciduous kinds, and shapely shiny leaves of the evergreens, are qualities to be widely admired. Of the slow-growing evergreens consider *B. darwinii* (8–10 ft.) or *B. verruculosa* (3–5 ft.). For faster growing *B. × stenophylla* (up to 8 ft.) is the first choice for a flowering hedge. For a spiny impenetrable barrier consider the evergreen *B. gagnepainii* (4–5 ft.) or *B. julianiae* (10 ft.). For colourful fruit and autumn leaves, think of *Berberis × rubrostilla* (4 ft.) and *B. thunbergii* (4 ft.).

Buddleia. Another prince among genera of plants, bold of stature, colourful, and quite dependable. The least princely may be *B. globosa* (10–15 ft.) of vigorous loose habit, but with flowers of tangerine orange colour and shape in June. *Buddleia alternifolia* (up to 20 ft.) also flowers in June and it is a gem, described by Farrer who dis-

covered it in China as 'a gracious small-leaved weeping willow when it is not in flower, and a sheer waterfall of soft purple when it is'. The ubiquitous plumes of August belong to *B. davidii* (up to 15 ft.), in its many coloured varieties shading from white to blue and deep purple.

Calluna vulgaris (3–24 ins.) makes the moors of Britain purple in August. Its garden varieties, some with golden foliage, some with double flowers, in all shades of pink and purple, are quite essential in every peaty garden. The grouse moor practice of burning every 5 years reminds one that old plants become decrepit. In the garden they are kept vigorous by trimming with shears after flowering.

Camellia japonica (up to 20 ft.) is joy to some gardeners, despair to others. Given a lime-free soil, enough sunshine to ripen the wood, and shelter from the coldest winter winds, there is promise of pink and red flowers as large and beautiful as the rose in early spring. The foil is shiny evergreen foliage, but too often wind or hail spoil the blooms. A good display compensates for the poor years, but it brings an extra chore when the fading blooms look so untidy that they need to be picked from the plant. Beside the japonica varieties, enthusiasts will want the vigorous free-flowering hybrids 'Donation' and 'J. C. Williams'.

Carpenteria californica (6–8 ft.). This very aristocratic cousin of the common *Philadelphus* presents a challenge you will, sooner or later, resolve to accept.

Caryopteris × clandonensis (up to 5 ft.), the so-called 'Blue Spiraea' with greyish foliage, and a haze of violet-blue flowers in early autumn, is a charming front-of-border plant.

Ceanothus has a confusing range of hybrids and varieties, but for practical purposes one can say the evergreen kinds thrive on a sheltering wall and flower in May, and the deciduous kinds flower in August. Of the evergreens 'Russellianus' has small notched leaves and fluffy flower heads of rich blue. The deciduous 'Gloire de Versailles' with powdery blue flowers is the best known of its type.

Ceratostigma willmottianum (2–4 ft.) is a dwarf blue flower of the summer. We extend it the courtesy title of shrub, but because of its indecision we cut the stems to ground level in spring as though it were a mere herbaceous perennial.

Chaenomeles, the Japanese quince, has many names including simply japonica, and many varieties. Traditionally trained on a wall, its shoots are shortened in October, to produce a wealth of scarlet flowers in March

Desfontainea spinosa

Elaeagnus pungens

Genista hispanica or Spanish gorse

before the leaves appear. 'Knaphill Scarlet' is the most widely acclaimed variety.

Chimonanthus praecox (up to 8 ft.) needs a sheltered site to protect the delicately scented December flowers, which earn its name of 'Winter Sweet'.

Choisya ternata (6–10 ft.) is remarkably hardy for a plant from Mexico. It is remarkably beautiful too with its light evergreen trifoliate leaves, and fragrant 'orangeblossom' flowers in April. What more could one ask of a plant?

Cistus, with the charm of a wild rose wide open on a sunny stony bank, earns the name 'Rock Rose'. Compact evergreen shrubs thriving in mild districts, but *Cistus × cyprius* (6–8 ft.) and 'Silver Pink' have been grown in most parts of Britain. *C. ladanifer* (3–5 ft.) with large crinkled petals and chocolate-coloured blotches is particularly fine, and *C × purpureus* (3–4 ft.) is its companion for favoured climates.

Clematis, the queen of climbers. You must have a spring flowerer, a summer flowerer, and in sheltered places, a winter-flowering evergreen. They are scandent or twining things which will neatly enhance a porch, or a doorway, if there are wires in the right places, or more spontaneously will climb posts or old trees or just flop over a bank. Of the innumerable varieties, one's first choices might be *Clematis montana rubens* (20–30 ft.) for May, *C. jackmanii* 'Superba' (10 ft.) for July, and *C. armandii* (12–20 ft.) for favoured places in March.

Clerodendron trichotomum (10–20 ft.) deserves a sheltered spot to display its handsome leaves and, in late summer, white starry flowers with maroon calices, followed by bright blue berries. A distinctive unusual plant.

Colutea arborescens is an easily grown large shrub (up to 12 ft.), with yellow peashaped flowers and (special novelty) inflated pods which give it the name 'Bladder Senna'.

Corokia cotoneaster (up to 8 ft.) is a slow-growing quaint little angular plant which always creates interest.

Cornus, or cornel, the everyday 'Dogwood', is esteemed for its coloured stems in winter. As the wit said, it is called dogwood because of its bark. *Cornus alba* 'Westonbirt' (up to 10 ft.) might be first choice, and if it is cut to ground level in spring, a thicket of summer shoots should ripen to display brilliant red stems next winter. Other kinds of cornel have floral beauty, *C. nuttallii* (15–25 ft.) has large white bracts surrounding the flower clusters, and they are decorative throughout the summer.

Coronilla emerus (5–7 ft.) is an undemanding shrub with yellow pea-like flowers. *C. glauca* (5–9 ft.) is rather more attractive.

Corylopsis spicata (up to 6 ft.) demands peaty soil and gives in return, charming, fragrant, catkin-like flowers in late winter.

Corylus. The hazel of the woods has two notable garden kinds – *purpurea* for its coloured leaves, and *contorta* which requires only the description 'Harry Lauder's walking stick'.

Cotinus coggygria (6–10 ft.), the 'Smoke Bush' formerly called *Rhus cotinus* makes a long-lasting spectacle. Try 'Atropurpurea' with its billowy masses of wispy inflorescences.

Cotoneasters are accommodating and beautiful, with flowers and berries suggesting a refined hawthorn. A vast genus, but five kinds must be noted. *C. horizontalis,* with herring-bone branches is indispensable, and all it asks is a wall to lean against. *C. dammeri* is the perfect prostrate ground cover. *C. conspicuus* 'Decorus' is indeed the most conspicuous and decorative of shrubs. *C.* 'Cornubia' reaches tree-like dimensions, and *C. simonsii* (up to 9 ft.), although less beautiful, is a hardy hedging plant.

Cytisus, the broom. The native kind grows on dry, acid hillside, and was traditionally used for the besom readily made from a bundle of twigs. *C.* × *kewensis* is dwarf (18 ins.), *C.* × *praecox* (3–5 ft.) flowers in May, and the colourful hybrids of *C. scoparius* (up to 8 ft.) flower the summer through. In a different category is *C. battandieri* (12–15 ft.), with larger silvery foliage and great heads of fragrant yellow blooms in June.

Daboecia cantabrica (1–3 ft.), the 'Irish Heath' is a bell heather writ large, and it adds variety to the heather garden.

Daphne cneorum is a gem for the rock garden, and *D. mezereum* (up to 5 ft.) is the charming purple flower of midwinter; of the summer kinds, *D.* × *burkwoodii* (3 ft.) might be first choice. All have richly scented flowers, and although quite adaptable, seem most at home on limestone.

Desfontainea spinosa (up to 10 ft.), an aristocrat resembling, in foliage, a light green holly, but bearing in late summer spectacular tubular flowers of scarlet tipped with gold. Difficult but well worth cosseting with shelter, shade, and peaty soil.

Deutzia discolor × *elegantissima* (4–6 ft.) is one of the best among the many kinds, with white or pink flowers in June. Compact, reliable, and beautiful.

Elaeagnus pungens 'Maculata' (up to 15 ft.) is the most highly prized among green and gold evergreen shrubs. It grows slowly so give it a few years' start before cutting shoots for winter flower arranging.

Embothrium lanceolatum, the 'Chilean Firebush', evergreen and spectacular in June when covered in scarlet honeysuckle-like flowers. Not easy to please, but peat, protection, and patience, sometimes have their reward.

Enkianthus campanulatus, with refined pendent bell-shaped flowers on a plant a few feet high is a joy in woodland or heather garden.

Erica and its relatives of the heather tribe deserve a garden to themselves wherever the soil is acid and the aspect sunny. Every colour from white to purple can be seen in every month of the year. *Erica carnea* (up to 12 ins.), which tolerates even a calcareous soil, in numerous varieties, flowers through the winter. *Erica* × *darleyensis* (2 ft.), *mediterranea* (4–10 ft.) and *arborea* (up to 20 ft.) flower in spring. The varieties of *E. cinerea* (9–24 ins.) and *tetralix* (12–20 ins.) support the allied genus of *Calluna* in summer and autumn. Although not quite so tough, enthusiasts will desire to add the Dorset and the Cornish heaths, *E. ciliaris* (12 ins.) and *E. vagans* (1–3 ft.).

Escallonias come into their own in seaside gardens. Charming pink to red flowers in summer, and foliage most of the winter. They tend to flourish less well in colder parts. 'Edinensis' is a delightful hybrid, and the vigorous evergreen *E. macrantha* (6–10 ft.) makes a fine hedge.

Eucryphia × *nymansensis* is the first choice in this genus of small evergreen trees. White flowers with many stamens in August.

Euonymus. The deciduous spindle berry of our native limestone woods has beautiful red fruit which opens to reveal orange-red seeds. Exotic kinds do the same. The evergreen kinds seem less exciting, but *E. japonica* makes an effective hedge, and *E. fortunei* (or *radicans*) is the unsurpassable ground cover.

Exochorda racemosa (10–12 ft.) may be just another white flowering shrub in May, but its clear white racemes are truly beautiful.

Fabiana imbricata is a small-stature plant (3–6 ft.) vaguely like a heath, with white tubular flowers.

Fatsia japonica (8–15 ft.) with large smooth palmate evergreen leaves thrives in shade, and always suggests tropical luxuriance.

Forsythia × *intermedia* is the never-failing golden welcome to spring, seen in every garden in March. *Forsythia suspensa* (10 ft. or more) has a more scandent habit and can be trained effectively on a wall.

Fothergilla monticola (6–8 ft.) is a pleasant modest plant for lime-free soil, notable for its autumn tints and white flower tufts in April.

Fremontia californica (15–30 ft.). If one can find a sheltering sunny wall, and coax the yellow flowers to open in summer, the reward is the most beautiful of plants.

Fuchsia magellanica (6–12 ft.), thriving in maritime air makes one of the greatest features of the Isle of Man. It grows elsewhere of course, as a specimen or as a flowering hedge.

Garrya elliptica (6–12 ft.) is a novelty of winter when the male plant's flowers open in January – long drooping catkins, set off by grey-green foliage.

Genista hispanica (1–3½ ft.) is the 'Spanish Gorse' – a spiny cushion obscured by golden-yellow flowers in May and June. At the other extreme *Genista aetnensis* has tall slender stems to a height of perhaps 15 ft., colourful in July.

Griselinia littoralis (20 ft.), an evergreen for coastal gardens, has remarkably clean-looking golden-green leaves.

Halesia carolina bears snowdrop-like flowers in May. Where suited by a lime-free soil it grows into a small tree.

Hamamelis mollis (10 ft. or more), the 'Witch Hazel' opens its curiously twisted petals of bright yellow in midwinter. It demands a peaty soil and grows slowly, but it is a prince among plants.

Hebe. This large genus of evergreen shrubby veronicas, is said to be not very hardy, but some are found in most British localities. Certainly *Hebe speciosa* (up to 5 ft.) flowers best by the sea, but *H. brachysiphon* (6–7 ft.) is widely grown; and *H. pinquifolia* 'Pagei' (1–3 ft.) is the best evergreen flowering ground cover.

Hedera helix (can climb to 100 ft.), the ivy is the ubiquitous self-clinging climber, unloved by many, but its variegated kinds are useful for covering fences and sheds, although not dwelling houses.

Helianthemum, the dwarf 'Sun Roses' of multifarious colours are indeed shrubs, but of only rock garden dimensions.

Hibiscus syriacus (6 ft.), a hardy member of a tropical genus, giving its best blue or pink mallow flowers in mild and sunny places only.

Hippophae rhamnoides (40 ft. or smaller), the 'Sea Buckthorn', with silvery leaves; both male and female plants are needed to obtain the decorative orange berries.

Hoheria lyallii in a sheltered sunny corner may be covered in July with white flowers with prominent golden stamens suggesting the most aristocratic cherry blossom.

Hydrangea macrophylla (2–10 ft.). The 'mopheads' provide generous masses of pink and blue in late summer. Attractively obese, they respond to rich food, moisture, and sunshine. In an acid soil some varieties produce blue flowers. The 'lace-

Witch hazel (Hamamelis mollis)

Hydrangea macrophylla or common hydrangea

Hypericum patulum or St John's Wort

Hypericum calycinum or Rose of Sharon

Magnolia soulangeana, one of the most popular for the small garden

Virginia creeper or Parthenocissus quinquefolia

Pieris formosa

Philadelphus (mock orange) 'Beauclerk'

caps' are varieties with frilled petal-like bracts, and they are especially charming. *Hydrangea petiolaris* is entirely different – a climber (60–80 ft.) clinging to a wall by aerial rootlets. It needs coaxing, but where happy, it will clothe a shaded wall with summer foliage and white June flowers.

Hypericum (1 ft.) with rich golden petals surrounding masses of stamens is a maid of all work. *H. calycinum* (1 ft.) is the 'Rose of Sharon' thriving in shade or sun, under trees, or on banks, an evergreen ground cover with bright summer flowers. More highly esteemed is *H. patulum* ($1\frac{1}{2}$–3 ft.), the rounded shrub with perfectly formed large waxy flowers.

Indigofera potaninii (4–6 ft.) also flowers through the late summer, but otherwise is the exact opposite of the last two genera mentioned. It has lax twiggy growth and small pink pea flowers, and thrives almost everywhere with a distinct charm.

Jasminum nudiflorum (wall height 12 ft.) is indispensable with its starry yellow flowers on bare green stems throughout the winter, trained on a wall or flopping over a bank. *J. officinale* (about 20 ft.) is its summer counterpart, with white, fragrant flowers.

Juniperus, the conifer which has strayed into this list on account of its ground-hugging neatness or its evergreen feathery foil. The catalogue names of the junipers are multisyllabled in the extreme, but these are worth mastering: *J. sabina tamariscifolia* is the neatest slow-growing dwarf; *J. communis* 'Horpibrookii' covers the ground more quickly; *J. squamata* 'Meyeri' adds a sculptural dimension to any group of small plants.

Kalmia latifolia, most choice of the small Ericaceae. Needs an acid soil and has masses of pink flowers in June. Their unique shape in bud has been likened to pink sugar icing.

Kerria japonica (4–6 ft.), in the double yellow form, is a commonly seen suckering shrub to which the writer has taken an irrational dislike.

Kolkwitzia amabilis (5–6 ft.), summer flowering, pink and beautiful. In appearance midway between *weigela* and *abelia*.

Laurus nobilis, the bay tree (30–60 ft.), the classical laurel, is not hardy everywhere, but is worth growing for its aromatic evergreen leaves and evocation of antiquity.

Lavandula spica (3–4 ft.), the old English lavender has many varieties. 'Hidcote' is the favourite compact one, and 'Grappenhall' the more robust. They become leggy with age, and although they are commonly trimmed, it is sensible to replace them periodically with young plants.

Leptospermum, the delicate pink myrtle from the antipodes suggests, in the mildest parts of Britain, the appearance of a refined *Escallonia*.

Leycesteria formosa (4–8 ft.) has green suckering stems, and its unique pendent inflorescences are decorative from July onwards. Reddish bracts set off the flowers and later the berries.

Lonicera can be climbing honeysuckle, fragrant shrub, or a dwarf evergreen hedge. There are several varieties of the common honeysuckle, and 'Halliana' is an evergreen kind. *L. fragrantissima* (6–8 ft.) is a winter-flowering shrub, fragrant and charming. *L. nitida* (6–10 ft.) makes the small neat hedge which is neither very hardy, nor long lived, and often disappoints.

Lupinus arboreus (5–6 ft.), the yellow tree lupin is fast growing and reliable on the sea coast, although not long lived.

Magnolia, the most refined of all the elite. Very adaptable, tolerating all soils, and widely grown, is *M. × soulangeana*, with bold erect flowers in shades of purple before the leaves unfold. *M. stellata* (10 ft.) is more compact, and has masses of pure white flowers in early spring. *M. grandiflora* (up to 30 ft.) is its opposite – tall with large evergreen leaves, white flowers in August, seen at its best on the sunny wall of a house. Most other magnolias like an acid peaty soil and *M. denudata* (25–40 ft.) is the finest of all; the white flowers are – it sounds mundane – like an inverted electric light bulb. *M. sinensis* (up to 20 ft.) and *M. wilsonii* (up to 25 ft.) have wide-open white pendent flowers in summer.

Mahonia aquifolium is the utilitarian evergreen ground cover, but its elegant relative *M. japonica* (6 ft.) is highly esteemed for its pinnate glossy leaves and large racemes of fragrant yellow flowers in midwinter.

Nandina domestica (6–8 ft.) is a curiosity – related to the berberis, but growing like a bamboo.

Olearia haastii (4–8 ft.) is the very hardy and useful, but undistinguished, daisy bush. *O. oleifolia* (5–10 ft.) is more refined, and *O. macrodonta* (up to 20 ft.) with grey-green holly-like leaves is distinctly handsome. All have white daisy flowers.

Osmanthus delavayi (6–10 ft.), a slow-growing evergreen with white fragrant flowers in April. More of a novelty is *O. heterophylla* (10–20 ft.), with spiny leaves often mistaken for holly, and there are variegated kinds.

Osmarea × 'Burkwoodii' (8–10 ft.) is a hybrid between *Osmanthus* and *Phillyrea* – an evergreen of distinct charm.

Osmaronia cerasiformis (5 ft.), a modest thicket-forming shrub covered with rather charming white flowers in early spring.

Pachysandra terminalis, a dwarf evergreen shrublet (about 12 ins.). It is highly esteemed as a pleasing ground cover under trees, but it flourishes only in moist acid soil.

Paeonia suffruticosa (up to 6 ft.) is the Moutan tree paeony of which there are many garden varieties, single and double, white, pink and red.

Parrotia persica is slow growing and eventually makes a small tree (30–40 ft.). Spectacular autumn foliage and curious midwinter flowers.

Parthenocissus tricuspidata 'Veitchii' is the excessively clumsy name for the invaluable climber known for generations as *Ampelopsis veitchii*; self-clinging with neat three-lobed leaves turning to brilliant colour before they fall. *P. quinquefolia* is the 'Virginia Creeper' useful for covering walls, but not to be trusted on dwelling houses where it will block gutters and loosen tiles. *P. henryana* is a smaller better-behaved species.

Pernettya mucronata (1–3 ft.), evergreen, ericaceous, and peat-loving, is small and neat and extremely decorative with its variously-coloured berries.

Philadelphus, the 'Mock Orange' with distinctive scented white flowers, is elegant and indispensable. *P. lemoinei* 'Erectus' (5–7 ft.) is the best of the small-flowered kinds, 'Belle Etoile' is one of the many large-flowered vigorous kinds, and 'Virginal' has double flowers.

Phillyrea angustifolia (up to 10 ft.) may seem undistinguished but it has held its place in gardens for centuries as a small-leaved evergreen shrub with tiny fragrant flowers.

Phlomis fruticosa (2–4 ft.) is a short-lived shrub, with grey aromatic leaves and whorls of bright yellow flowers in summer. It is native to the Mediterranean area, and commonly called 'Jerusalem Sage'.

Phygelius capensis, the 'Cape Figwort' is sometimes uncertain whether to be shrubby or herbaceous. In front of a sunny wall it may reach 3 or 4 ft. and display its scarlet 'hunting horn' flowers to advantage.

Pieris. Another genus of ericaceous peat-loving evergreens. Their spring flowers resemble lily of the valley. *P. floribunda* (4–6 ft.) and *P. japonica* (up to 10 ft.) are both popular, and *P. formosa forrestii* (6–11 ft.) has remarkably decorative unfolding leaves of bright red when spring growth begins.

Piptanthus laburnifolius is a lax fast-growing plant with laburnum-like flowers in May, followed by large long seed pods.

Pittosporum tenuifolium (up to 30 ft.) thrives in Cornwall, and its bright green undulating leaves set on black stems are useful to florists. An evergreen of great character, when it can be persuaded to grow in mild districts, especially by the sea.

Polygonum baldschuanicum, 'Russian Vine', the irrepressible rampant twiner, covers in next to no time the unsightly shed. Festoons of small white flowers in late summer.

Poncirus trifoliata (up to 15 ft.), 'Japanese Bitter Orange' grows, given time, into a great curiosity. Trifoliate leaves, vicious spines, sweetly scented flowers like orange blossom in spring, and in autumn tiny orange fruits. Its other names are *Aegle sepiaria* and *Citrus sinensis*.

Potentilla fruticosa. An indispensable small shrub which flowers continuously the summer through. It is native in some limestone areas of England, and its many garden forms have white, yellow, or orange-coloured flowers, and grow from 1–4 ft. high.

Punica granatum (15–30 ft.), the 'Pomegranate' presents a challenge. Cosseted against a sunny wall, it may produce spectacular scarlet tubular flowers, and even a fruit, occasionally.

Pyracantha coccinea 'Lalandei' (up to 20 ft.) is the most popular 'Firethorn'. It will stand freely like hawthorn, but is traditionally trained on a wall where its berries make a fiery spectacle.

Rhododendron. This great genus is a contender for the title of queen of plants. It includes the giant species of the Himalayas and the heather-like carpets of the Alps, deciduous azaleas and evergreen trees. Their inflorescences range from great trusses of fragrant flowers to tiny saucers in every colour from white to yellow, pink, red, mauve and almost blue. The first rule of garden making is, that if the soil is calcareous or the climate dry, rhododendrons should be ruthlessly banned, and planning should start with roses and viburnums. But conversely if the soil is acid or neutral, and the climate moist and mild, rhododendrons must inevitably take pride of place. These notes apply to such a garden.

One of the intellectual pleasures of the rhododendron lover is to master the botanical divisions, the species in their series, their genetical evolution, their geographical distribution, and no indulgence could be more rewarding to its disciples. It stands with philately or breeding horses. For the present exercise let us take a mere sample of the most obviously decorative kinds.

Deciduous Azaleas, reaching say 5 ft. in height, make the most colourful spectacle of May in gardens large or small wherever the soil is peaty and moist. First choice might be from the Knap Hill hybrids.

The traditional Hardy Hybrid Rhododendrons are for the larger garden, and when

Rhododendron 'Frome' (an azalea)

Rhododendron damaris 'Logan'

Rhododendron 'Blue Diamond'

Schizophragma integrifolia, akin to the hydrangea

Viburnum tomentosum 'Mariesii'

Weigela 'Eva Rathke'

Wisteria sinensis

not in flower have undeniably monotonous evergreen foliage. Nevertheless 'Pink Pearl' and red 'Britannia' are among the great plants of all time.

Modern hybrids have greater variety of foliage, form, and flower character, and it is every gardener's ambition to produce enormous lax trusses of creamy pink flowers on the delicate *R. loderi* 'King George'.

Low growing evergreens. Perhaps the most famous are 'Praecox' with mauve flowers in February or March, and 'Blue Tit' for April or May.

Species. Everyone who has fallen under the spell of this great genus will want some of the wild species, and from many hundreds of beautiful kinds I would covet most *falconeri* for its foliage, *thompsonii* for its blood red flowers, and *williamsianum* for its compactness and bell-shaped pink flowers.

Rhus typhina (20 ft.), the 'Stag's Horn Sumach' has large distinctive pinnate leaves in summer, and in winter, angular furry branches suggestive of a deer's antlers in velvet.

Ribes sanguineum (6–9 ft.), the ubiquitous 'Flowering Currant' grows quickly into a background plant. Choose a deep red variety; its hanging sprays and fragrance are attractive.

Romneya coulteri (6–8 ft.), the 'Californian Tree Poppy' has large white poppy flowers in late summer. Commonly, the stems die to the ground each winter, but new shoots arise from the rootstock, behaving like a herbaceous perennial.

Rosa. The rose in its multifarious kinds fully justifies, and has, a section to itself, but every shrub collection must contain some of the species of the modern hybrid shrub roses: no other genus can replace their beauty and charm. A starting point could be *R. hugonis* (6–9 ft.), and *R. moyesii* (6–12 ft.), and the next additions 'Nevada' and 'Complicata'.

Rosmarinus officinalis (up to 7 ft.), the rosemary makes an attractive informal hedge, evergreen and fragrant.

Rubus 'Tridel' has the most decorative flowers of all the brambles, and *R. cockburnianus* (8–10 ft.) is the most unusual with its seemingly whitewashed stems in winter.

Sambucus canadensis 'Aurea' (up to 12 ft.) is a fast-growing elder, decidedly coarse, but sometimes useful to fill a space. There is another red-berried elder, with deeply-cut golden leaves, namely *S. racemosa* 'Plumosa Aurea' (8–10 ft.), and this is more pleasing.

Santolina chamaecyparissus (1½–2½ ft.), the dwarf 'Lavender Cotton', silvery-grey all the year, will make a dwarf hedge or a pleasing foil to almost any other plant.

Schizophragma integrifolia (30–40 ft.), a self-clinging climber, a superior relative of *Hydrangea petiolaris*.

Senecio greyi (up to 8 ft.), deservedly the most popular of compact evergreen shrubs, with yellow daisy flowers from July to September. *S. monroi* is smaller (2–6 ft.), and has undulate leaves.

Skimmia japonica (3–6 ft.), small dark evergreen, an adaptable plant, with fragrant white flowers in April, followed by bright red berries seldom eaten by birds. Male and female flowers are borne on different plants, so both are needed for a fruitful display.

Solanum crispum (12–14 ft.) is a scrambling plant, not very hardy, deserving the shelter of a wall if it is to display its blue and yellow potato-like flowers.

Spartium junceum (up to 10 ft.), the 'Spanish Broom' is larger and bolder and later flowering than the common broom. A great plant for the seaside.

Spiraea × arguta (4–8 ft.), a dense-growing shrub which when covered in tiny white flowers deserves its title 'Foam of May'. *S. japonica* (3–5 ft.) is less refined, with flattened pink heads of flower in summer, but the variety 'Anthony Waterer' dwarf, with bright red flowers, is indispensable.

Staphylea colchica (8–12 ft.), trifoliate leaves, panicles of creamy white flowers, and bladder-like seed capsules.

Sranvaesia davidiana (up to 30 ft.) is a vigorous evergreen with hawthorn-like flowers and fruit.

Styrax japonica (10–25 ft.), a choice subject for a lime-free soil. It grows into a small tree and has white pendent bell-shaped flowers in June, hence the apt name of 'Snowbell'.

Symphoricarpus albus (up to 10 ft.) is the too common 'Snowberry', but its relative *S. orbiculatus* is smaller (2–6 ft.) and neater with pink berries and small ovate leaves.

Syringa, the ever-popular lilac, in time becomes a tree, and a great spectacle in early June. 'Madame Lemoine' is the best-known white, 'Massena' is deep purple, and 'Madame Charles Souchet' is the traditional soft lilac colour. Enthusiasts will also want to master the more graceful race known as *Syringa × Prestoniae* in its many varieties.

Tamarix. The very distinctive 'Tamarisk' with wiry stems and masses of tiny pink flowers, is particularly associated with the seaside, but it thrives in most sunny places. *T. tetrandra* (10–15 ft.) flowers in May, and *T. pentandra* (10–15 ft.) in late summer.

Tricuspidaria lanceolata (10–30 ft.) is an aristocrat for peaty soil in a mild climate, and its pendent red lantern flowers set off by dark evergreen leaves make it a unique spectacle in May.

Ulex europaeus 'Plenus' (2–4 ft.) is the common gorse, enriched with semi-double flowers, superb in the right place, perhaps the heather garden.

Viburnum carlesii (4–8 ft.) is an adaptable medium-sized shrub, loved for its strongly scented pink-white flowers in spring. *V. davidii* (3–5 ft.) is a neat evergreen low-growing shrub with distinctive turquoise blue fruits. *V. opulus* 'Sterile' (8–12 ft.) has its flowers massed into snowballs. *V. plicatum* 'Mariesii' (6–10 ft.) has horizontal branches arranged in tiers, and white flowers on the upper side suggest laden snow.

Vinca major and *Vinca minor* (1–2 ft.), the greater and lesser 'Periwinkle', are invaluable evergreens for carpeting shady places, and producing bright blue flowers.

Vitis, the ornamental vines which support themselves with twining tendrils on arbours and trellises. *V. coignetiae* (climbs up to 90 ft.) has the largest leaves and is most spectacular, becoming scarlet in autumn. *Vitis vinifera* (50–60 ft.) is the grape vine, and *Vitis* 'Brandt' is the most highly esteemed hardy fruiting kind.

Weigela is an invaluable early summer flower. The garden hybrids make shrubs of medium size with open tubular flowers, and they flourish in most situations. 'Abel Carriere' is a favourite pink, and 'Eva Rathke' the unsurpassed red.

Wisteria sinensis (climbs to 100 ft.), with its wonderful racemes of mauve fragrant flowers in May, before the leaves unfold, is the most beautiful of all climbing plants. The south-facing wall of a house is its traditional home, given some wires on which to twine. To keep it within bounds shorten straying shoots in August.

Yucca gloriosa (1½–2 ft.), the exotic-looking 'Adam's Needle' adds extra quality to any situation. A stout stem bears a rosette of stiff evergreen leaves from which emerges an erect panicle of pendent white lily-like flowers.

Zenobia pulverulenta (4–6 ft.) is a worthy name to conclude this select list. Lily-of-the-valley flowers, larger than the related *Pieris*, are extremely beautiful in early summer.

A ROSE BED

J.C.Shortland

Do you want a festival of flower and fragrance for many months of the year, year after year? Then plant roses. Make a rose bed. Not without good reason has the rose been called 'The Queen of all flowers', for what other plant is so versatile? So many types and varieties are available that whatever the requirement, the rose can fulfil it – together with the additional bonuses of scent and a wide range of colours. So, let us make our rose bed.

PREPARATION

The rose requires a cool, moist root run, but will not tolerate waterlogging, so the first essential is to ensure adequate drainage for our new bed. A good way of checking this is to dig a hole in the proposed site, the size of a 3-gal. pail, or bucket. Then procure a 3-gal. pail or bucket and fill it with water. Next empty the water into the hole. If, twenty-four hours later, that water has drained away, then drainage is adequate and you can begin work. If, on the other hand, water still remains in the hole then steps must be taken to provide drainage. One method is to import more soil, thereby raising the bed so as to enable water to drain away, but the disadvantage in this method is that it tends to create a 'plum pudding' effect, spoiling the appearance. The only other solution is to lay land drain-pipes, a tedious and very expensive alternative.

The next requirement for our site must be position. Never plant roses under a tree, for, quite understandably the plants will struggle to reach more light and air, and will become thin and straggly in the process. Never plant in full shade; a sunny site is preferable, but shade for half the day is permissible. It could in fact be an advantage, as the richest colours will be retained longer, and there will be less risk of burning and scorching, as there would be in full sun.

Digging the site will depend largely on the type of soil to be dug. Clay soil though basically more fertile than sandy soil, requires very hard work put into the job of improving it. Autumn is the ideal time for preparing such soil, and the method employed is known as 'ridging', as shown in diagram. The soil is thrown or drawn into steep ridges so as to expose the maximum surface to the winter frosts, rains, ice, winds and thaw. The effect of these conditions will be to flocculate the clay, and together with the liberal application of gypsum (calcium sulphate), say 1 lb. per sq. yd., will greatly improve the texture.

Mark the plot into three 1-ft.-wide strips, each of which is dug separately lengthways, i.e. starting at one end and working backwards down the length of the strip with narrow trenches. When digging, the centre spadeful is always turned forward, but the left and right-hand spadefuls are turned inwards to lie on top of the centre one and thereby form a ridge as shown in the illustration.

Now, whereas on a clay soil the main object must be to improve the tilth and drainage, on a sandy soil just the opposite applies. Here every effort must be made to make the soil retentive of moisture, and moisture-retaining ingredients of every type must be added. The type of digging employed here is known as bastard or half trenching, midway between trenching and digging, and simply means turning over the soil one spade deep, and forking the spit (spade's depth) immediately below, without actually altering its position. Incorporate into this second 'spit' animal manures, peat, hay, straw, leaf-mould, spent hops, wool shoddy, old matting or clothing, newspapers, ANYTHING that will break down in the earth to make humus. All these materials should be forked in, as should animal manures to a clay soil, in springtime. Remember when digging your new bed that first a trench should be opened across one end of the plot, 10 ins. deep and about the same in width. The soil removed is then barrowed to the other end. Then a further narrow strip is turned over into the trench, the process being repeated backwards across the plot until the far end is reached, when the barrowed soil is used to fill in the last trench. Care must be taken to turn each sod right over so that weeds or grass are completely covered.

As already stated, autumn is the best time for preparation of the new bed, but if for any reason this work has to be delayed, then a minimum of 6 weeks is needed between preparation and planting, in order to allow the soil to settle naturally. After digging, bonemeal can be applied to the surface at the rate of 2–4 oz. per sq. yd.

Types of Roses

Hybrid Tea. This type of rose is suitable for growing in formal beds and bears double well-shaped flowers. These blooms are borne singly or in small groups.

Floribunda. Although in general, the flower form is inferior to that of the hybrid tea, the effect is very much better, as this type bears its flowers in large clusters, or trusses, with many blooms opening at the same time so providing a mass of colour over a longer flowering period, from June to the frosts of winter.

Floribunda – Hybrid Tea type. Here one can enjoy the beauty of perfect blooms as produced by the hybrid tea, but with the benefit of them in clusters flowering together. If disbudded to one bud on a stem these will give moderate sized decorative hybrid tea type flowers.

The Floribunda Dwarfs are small, dense, low-growing plants, vigorous and bushy, between the 'miniatures' and the floribundas. About 15 ins. in height, they are very suitable for edging.

The Miniature China Roses are very dwarf recurrent-flowering bushes from 6–12 ins. or so in height with tiny flowers usually perfectly formed. They also are ideal for edging, and look exquisite in small beds on their own. Another superb way to use them is by random planting in rockeries.

The Shrub Roses are species from the wild roses or their near hybrids, including more highly bred types of similar flowering habit to the floribundas, but which normally grow too tall for formal beds. They are more suitable for planting as individual specimen bushes, or in the shrub border, and as hedges. Some of them have a prefix to indicate which group they most closely resemble, e.g. Floribunda shrub; Hybrid Musk shrub; Alba shrub; Bourbon shrub. Within this group are found some of the most beautiful, fragrant and disease-resistant roses in existence, and any garden, regardless of size, should contain at least one or two varieties to enhance the landscaping.

The Ramblers are of vigorous lax growth, bearing small flowers in clusters. They have many uses from covering arches and pergolas, or for shrouding stumps, steep banks, and as ground cover generally, to their suitability as weeping standards. As such they need no supporting framework and will fall naturally down to the ground. Their one disadvantage is that they are summer-flowering only.

The Climbers are of stiffer, very vigorous growth and with larger flowers. They include the climbing hybrid tea varieties and many others with flowers and foliage resembling those of hybrid tea type. The more vigorous of these are eminently suitable for growing on walls, whereas the varieties of

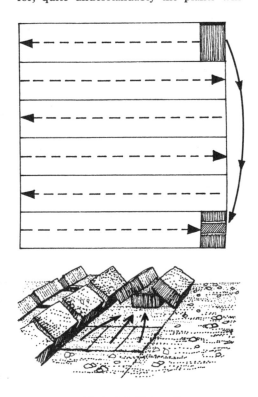

Method of ridging soil

moderate vigour make ideal pillar roses. Don't expect too much from climbers in their first year; they do take some time to become properly established, but once they are, then there is no better contributor to the beauty of the garden.

Standard Roses carry their heads on stems approximately 3½ ft. high. They are available as hybrid tea, floribunda, rambler (weeping standard), or shrub, and will give height to your rose bed. Bordering paths, they will give roses at eye and nose level, thereby eliminating the necessity for stooping to savour their rich fragrance. A list of recommended varieties covering all the foregoing types will be found at the end of this chapter.

Selection and Ordering

As each new rose catalogue finds its way through the letter-box, the recipient can be forgiven for becoming increasingly confused by the ever-growing list of new varieties contained therein. With colour processing becoming more natural each year, and the descriptions more enticing, it is so easy to fall into the trap of over-enthusiasm by placing orders indiscriminately, in the whole-hearted belief that each new variety described was just made for your particular requirement. Reader beware! Before your imagination runs riot look further into the matter.

All the new award-winning varieties can be seen growing at the Royal National Rose Society's Display Gardens at Chiswell Green Lane, St Albans, Hertfordshire, where the grounds are open to the public every day between mid-June and the end of September at the following times: Monday to Saturday 9 a.m. to 5 p.m., Sunday 2 p.m. to 6 p.m. Members of the Royal National Rose Society (and every rose-lover should be a member) are allowed to visit the gardens before and after the dates mentioned Monday to Friday only.

People living in the provinces are advised to visit the displays of rose varieties that have received awards at St Albans which are provided at Roath Park, Cardiff; Saughton Park, Edinburgh; Pollok Park, Glasgow; Harlow Car, Harrogate; Heigham Park, Norwich; The Arboretum, Nottingham; Botanic Gardens, Southport; Vivary Park, Taunton; Borough Park, Redcar, Teesside. All these gardens are open daily. The wise thing to do of course is to visit the gardens nearest to you, so that you can see how varieties in which you are interested will grow in conditions similar to your own. It is also advisable to make several visits before making up your mind, so that you can observe their behaviour in varying weather conditions, and their resistance, or proneness, to disease. It is far better to learn of these things beforehand, rather than pay dearly for the experience. There is often a tremendous difference between the blooms glowing at you from the glossy pages of a catalogue, and the live blooms of that same variety after a few hours of heavy rain.

When, after considerable observation and deliberation, you have finally decided upon your choice, place your order with a reputable grower as soon as possible. Apart from ensuring you get your bushes early, this will also enable him to plan his output.

Arrival of Bushes

Although the planting of roses may be undertaken when conditions are favourable any time between the last week in October and the end of March, the best time is before the end of November, when, under normal weather circumstances, the soil is

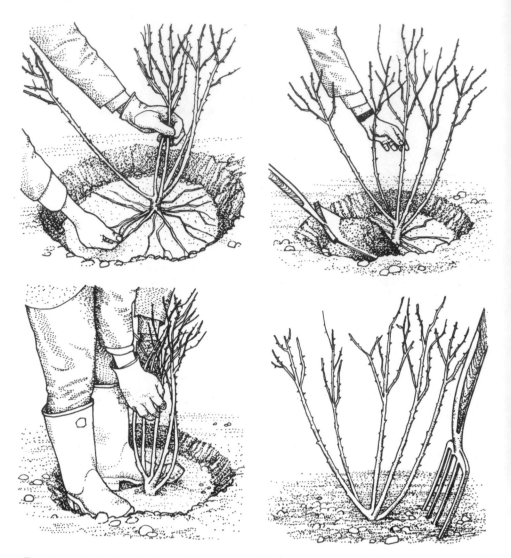

Four stages in planting a bush rose. The roots should be spread out over a little mound so that the old soil mark on the stem is level with the surface. The surface should be carefully firmed so that the bush sits neither in a hollow nor on a hillock.

warm enough to produce new root systems before winter sets in. Never attempt to plant in waterlogged or frozen soil, so should your roses arrive when adverse conditions prevail, leave the package containing the bushes unopened in a cool but frost-proof shed, garage or cellar, where they will take no harm for up to ten days. It is a good idea when anticipating the arrival of roses to cover the planting site with tarpaulin sheets or other protective material, in order to exclude frost or rain and thereby ensure that the soil is kept in its crumbly and friable condition, so essential when planting at this time of year.

If unfavourable conditions extend for longer than ten days then it will become necessary to remove the bushes from their package, and heel them in. This means digging a shallow trench and spreading the plants against one side of it. Cover the roots and lower stems with frost-free soil, and firm with the foot. Hence the expression 'heeling-in'. The bushes will then be adequately protected until the weather improves, even if this is many weeks ahead.

Planting

If your bushes arrive from the nursery in favourable weather, then all you have to do is unpack them, place the roots in water overnight, and plant them the following day. Have some moist peat and bonemeal well mixed and ready for use as a planting mixture. You must half fill a 3-gal. bucket

with moist peat, then add two double handfuls of bonemeal, i.e. approximately 1 lb. Mix thoroughly with gloved hands (always wear gloves when handling bonemeal because of the risk of anthrax), then complete the filling of the bucket with more moist peat and a similar amount of bonemeal. By using the soil you excavate from the holes you will now have sufficient planting mixture for 6 bushes.

Be sure to keep the roots of your plant moist at all times. Therefore having removed them from the bucket of water, place a wet sack over the roots to protect them from the drying action of wind and sun, and having removed one bush for planting, immediately replace the wet sack over the rest, repeating this process until all are planted.

All foliage should have been removed by the nurseryman before the bushes were packed, but if this has not been done, then cut off the leaves at the base of the leafstalk. This will prevent the loss of any moisture through the leaves and the consequent shrivelling of the stems.

The place where the union of the cultivated variety with the rootstock takes place, is known as the graft union, and sometimes the nursery may forget to cut away the dead stump of the rootstock, which will protrude above the union with the scion, so this must now be done with sharp pruners. Unripe or soft wood should also be cut back, as these are the shoots which have begun to grow late in the season, and would almost surely be killed by winter frosts. While you have your pruners handy, shorten the roots to about 9–10 ins. This, together with the friable nature of your planting mixture, will ensure the quick reproduction of fibrous roots, so essential for newly-planted bushes to become established.

Now open up a hole in the prepared site, wide enough to accommodate the roots, without having to tuck the ends in, and deep enough so that the union of scion and stock will be level with the surrounding soil when planting is completed. Thoroughly mix into the soil in the bottom of the hole, two handfuls of the moist peat and bonemeal mixture, and draw the soil into a low mound. Rest the crown of the bush on this and spread the roots round it, taking care that the roots do not cross one another. Cover the roots with the planting mixture and replace the excavated soil gradually, lightly shaking the bush up and down, so as to see there is no possibility of an air pocket being left. Place the heels of your feet together and shuffle around the perimeter of the hole. This will keep the crown up to the required level. Never firm the soil by placing the foot close up to the stem, as this will result in the hair roots being torn off. When all the remainder of the soil has been replaced, tread lightly, from perimeter towards centre, and then finish off the job by lightly pricking over the soil with a fork, no deeper than 2 ins.

Planting should never be attempted if the soil is any more than just moist. If however the operation is interrupted by heavy rain on no account must heavy firming-in be undertaken. It is far better to wait for better conditions and then to tread in again when the soil is drier. Firm contact between roots and soil is essential, but consolidation to the extent of complete expulsion of air would be disastrous. If for any reason spring planting is to be undertaken, then once the risk of severe frosts has receded, the bushes should have their stems pruned in the hand, i.e. before planting, thereby eliminating the need for further bending and stooping afterwards.

When planting standard roses the stake should be inserted first, and much thought should be given to the choice of stake, for in subsequent years when the head is heavy with foliage, flower, and rain, a very large surface is exposed to high winds so that the stake must be strong enough to allow for all contingencies. A 1½-in.-diameter galvanised steel tube is recommended for this purpose, as there is no risk of it rotting off at ground level when the standard is at its best, and the strain on the stake is at its greatest.

Although standards will vary in height, under no circumstances should some be planted deeper than others, in an attempt to level up their heads. A good guide to depth can be derived from the soil mark which will be seen on the tree when it arrives from the nursery. Care should be taken to see that the standard is tied securely to its stake in three places – 4 ins. above the ground, half way up the stem, and finally at the top of the stem. The best 'ties' are made from vinyl plastic electricians' tape, wound in figure-of-eight fashion around stake and stem. This method ensures the standard is held securely, and at the same time allows for the expansion of the tree as it grows. It is advisable to plant standards not less than 3 ft. apart.

When planting climbing roses it must be borne in mind that if planted on a house side, or against a fence or wall, much of the rain will, due to the protection of the fence or wall, miss the ground directly below, so be sure to plant the climber some 18 ins. away from fence or wall, and to slope its stems inwards. Don't worry if your climber is only 2–3 ft. tall when it arrives from the nursery, as this length is plenty for the roots to support until it becomes established. Climbers generally are slower to establish than other types of roses and are seldom at their best during the first three years after planting so be prepared to wait for the pleasure they give. They will more than repay your patience.

Planting distances for the different types of roses are as follows:

CLIMBING ROSES . . . . 8 feet
HYBRID TEA AND FLORIBUNDAS (low-growing varieties) . . . . 1½ feet
HYBRID TEA AND FLORIBUNDAS (vigorous varieties) . . . . 2 feet
HYBRID TEA AND FLORIBUNDAS (very vigorous varieties) . . . . 2½ feet
LOW SHRUBS . . . . 3 feet
WEEPING STANDARDS . . . . 6 feet
RAMBLING ROSES . . . . 10 feet
MINIATURE ROSES . . . . 1 foot

BUSH ROSES must not be planted less than 18 ins. from edge of bed, as, when in full bloom they would be in danger from the passing mower, barrow, etc., and might damage the clothing of passers-by.

CONTAINER-GROWN ROSES may be planted at any time of the year when the soil is not waterlogged, frosted, or covered by snow. When suitable conditions prevail, and when the subject has arrived from garden centre or nursery, water well into the container, and leave overnight. This will ensure that when the container is removed the next day the soil will remain in a block instead of crumbling away from the roots. Take out a hole 3 ins. deeper and wider than the container, and then with a planting mixture previously described, i.e. moist peat and bonemeal, cover the base of the hole 3 ins. deep. Next, with a sharp knife, slit down the sides of the container, taking care not to sever the roots, and with caution peel it away from the rootball, and place gently into the hole. Carefully fill in with the planting mixture, and if the soil is heavy add some sand, to help the roots to spread more quickly. Firm with clenched knuckles, add more mixture, firm again, and water well in. If the weather is dry and sunny at the time of planting, then water regularly until well established. Correct planting procedure is of vital importance, as it will ensure that the roses get off to a good start in their new quarters, where they will provide so much pleasure in the years to come.

If, when moving house, an old rose bed is inherited, with gaps needing filling, do not attempt to plant replacements in the old soil. After ten years or so in the same soil, rose roots exude a poison which causes 'rose soil sickness', and new bushes planted in such soil will never flourish. The fact that the remainder of the roses in that bed are thriving, is due entirely to their roots being many yards away from 'base' in a constant quest for healthy soil. Excavate an area some 18 ins. square by 12 ins. deep, and barrow that soil away to some other part of the garden that has not grown roses before, where it will grow anything else perfectly. Replace the soil in the barrow with soil from where the old soil has been dumped. Fork well-rotted animal manures, or other compost into the bottom spit of the excavation before filling with new soil. When consolidated, proceed as for normal planting, already described, and very soon the old bed with its new additions will be a joy to behold.

Hybrid Tea Peer Gynt

Floribunda Molly McGredy

Climber Golden Shower

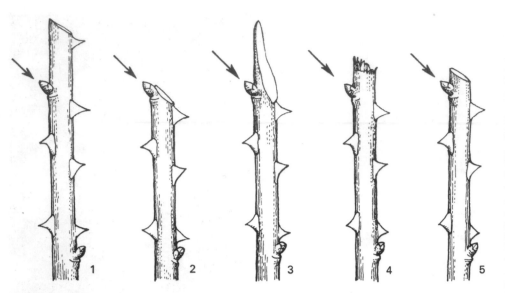

Prune by making a sloping cut parallel to and a little above an outward-facing bud. The first four examples (from left to right) are wrong: too far above the bud; too close to the bud; too long a cut; too jagged. The last example is correct.

Pruning

If a new rose bush were to be planted and then left unpruned for a few years, it would become a tangled mass of shoots and stems, the oldest of which would be losing their vigour, becoming shrivelled and diseased before dying back and breaking off as a result of the effect of gales and strong winds. As the old stems died, new ones would grow from the base of the plant, but they too would eventually succumb.

Nature's way of pruning is a slow process therefore, and by knowing the reasons for pruning we can speed up the job considerably. A rose bush will only give its best if properly pruned, and when undertaking this simple annual routine it helps to remember the three 'D's' – dead, diseased, and damaged. All wood coming under these headings must be removed completely, as must any under pencil thickness. Pruning is done for health reasons. If the centre of the bush becomes overcrowded with unwanted stems, it forms the ideal place where disease can establish and spread because there is no circulation of air. The first object in pruning therefore must be to provide an

open-centred, or cup-shaped bush, where new growth can take place under conditions of perfect hygiene. The second reason is to shape and maintain annual growth to blend in with the rest of the plants in the same bed, or to train specimen bushes to conform to their particular location or requirement. The third reason, in short, is to put a new top on old roots each year, thereby retaining vigour. All parts of the plant can then enjoy maximum light and air with the result that bigger and better roses can be produced.

Having provided an open centre, the remainder of the stems when grown on a light hungry soil, should be lightly pruned. This consists of cutting back the shoots to the first or second eye below the footstalk of the flower to an inward or outward direction, depending on the habit of the variety. An upright grower will be pruned to an outward-facing bud, whereas a variety that tends to spread or sprawl will be cut to an inward-facing bud, in order to encourage vertical growth.

Moderate pruning means cutting back the shoots to half their length, again to an eye pointing in the right direction.

Hard pruning means cutting back to 3 or 4 eyes from the ground, or 4–5 ins. in other words. This method is favoured by many exhibitors, for on rich, heavy soils, hard pruning gives excellent results. The general rule is, the lighter the soil, the lighter the pruning.

The time for pruning is the subject for much debate as some favour autumn pruning whilst others prefer spring for the job. The foolproof time is when the bushes are just finishing their dormancy. When the sap begins to rise, the little eyes, the growth buds, will start to gleam red. This is the sign to watch for. It is no use at all pruning to a calendar date from year to year, as quite obviously weather conditions vary considerably one year from the next, and whereas this year if the winter is mild, pruning may be best started in early February, next winter may be very severe, and it may be late March at the earliest before pruning could commence. Never prune in periods of severe frost.

So to the actual pruning, which, like amputation, is a surgical operation. The instruments used must be clinically clean and razor sharp. Never use blunt secateurs as all this will do is to crush the stems, destroying the cells. Die-back spores will then enter, and if not cut out completely, will start a fungal infection which may travel down the stem, ultimately killing the bush. Therefore, if this browning of the stem is encountered, it is essential to prune below it into healthy green wood. Not one speck of brown centre must be retained. If the pith in the centre of the wood shows even the minutest trace of brown then cut down to the next healthy bud, no matter how near the base that might be. Then a $\frac{1}{4}$ in. above the bud, make the pruning cut, sloping slightly, just sufficient to carry raindrops away from the bud rather than into it, for they would rest on the bud and with overnight frost would freeze and kill it. The correct angle of cut should be as in diagram. When pruning always wear a strong but supple pair of gloves, in order to prevent lacerations of the skin and flesh by the very sharp thorns.

With a *first-year bush*, cut all shoots back to an outward-pointing bud, or eye, to approximately 6 ins. from the ground. In *second*, and *subsequent years*, proceed as pre-

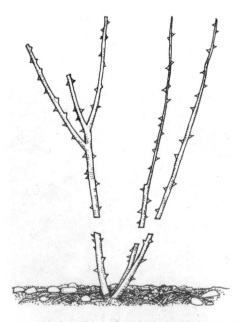

A newly-planted hybrid tea bush should be pruned hard to encourage strong growth from low down and restrict growth in the first year.

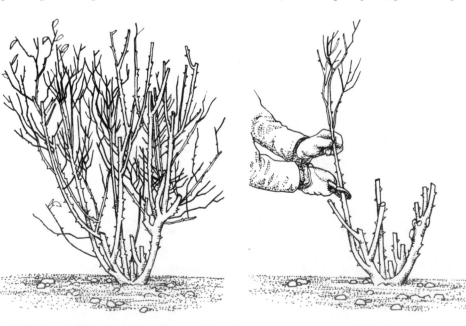

Pruning an established hybrid tea. Cut out all spindly and weak growth, all tangled shoots, and branches that grow in towards the centre. The centre should be left airy and fairly open. In general prune back strong shoots to two or three buds above last year's cut.

viously mentioned, i.e. remove all dead, diseased, and damaged wood, all unripe growth, all growth pointing into the centre of the bush, and all thin, spindly shoots. Regardless of variety and type, after the first year's pruning, always cut one stem back to one eye from the base, as this will encourage new basal growth to form annually, eliminating the retention of hard, decadent, non-productive stems. The modern shrubs and repeat-flowering climbers are best treated by removing frost-damaged tips in early spring, and cutting out any stems which have suffered damage. With this type too, always remove one stem to within one eye from the base annually. Miniature roses can have all growth removed one inch from the ground.

Climbing roses depend more on training and tying-in than on pruning and here the success of the plant depends on regular attention, on training new growth horizontally, or when grown as pillar roses, spirally, so that the rising sap is arrested, thereby encouraging the plants to flower low down on the plant as well as higher up. Established climbers can be made to do this by untying the stems in spring, and laying them on the ground for a few days so that rising sap will induce new growths. The problem then is how many growths to retain? Every 18 ins. or so is ideal, so that there is no possibility of bare stems spoiling the beauty of the plant.

Standard roses are treated in exactly the same way as bush roses, both as first-year bushes, and in their pruning for second and subsequent years. Dead-heading is a form of summer pruning, and when the blooms fade on their stems in the garden, cut them back to only the first or second eye below the flower, again in the direction in which you want new growth to shoot, because the more stem and leaves removed, the more the plant is robbed of its energy. Furthermore the eyes at the top of the stem are always more mature than those lower down, so by removing excessive lengths the flowering interval between the two crops is increased.

In order to prevent damage by wind rock, caused by the gales and strong winds of autumn and winter, it is best to reduce the growth in late autumn. If this is not done the bushes are blown about so badly that

Ways of using roses to good effect. Top: a colourful floribunda garden. Centre: a bower of roses makes a pleasant corner from which to enjoy a summer evening. Right: Nevada, one of the best long-flowering shrub roses, makes an effective hedge. Above: Hugonis, a vigorous climber, has pale yellow single flowers and rather decorative foliage.

Hybrid Tea National Trust

Hybrid Tea Wendy Cussons

Climber Pink Perpetue

Hybrid Tea Pascali

Hybrid Tea King's Ransom

holes may form round the base. Water collects in these holes and when it freezes may kill the roots. Tall-growing varieties should be cut back by half, and medium and low growers by a third. Remember always to use clean, sharp secateurs.

Feeding

All the food that is taken out of the soil by growing roses must be returned to it somehow or other. Leaves of other trees fall and enrich the earth for their future sustenance, but not so with roses, where flowers, stems and leaves, are removed and not returned. Even the weeds are kept down and cannot therefore provide humus. Stable manure contains all the nutrients roses require, but if this, or farmyard manure, is unobtainable then garden compost must be used in conjunction with chemical fertilisers. Many excellent proprietary brands of compound rose food are on the market, and these contain the correct proportion of major, intermediate, and trace elements, which the rose must have to stimulate leaf, stem, and root growth, to ripen new wood, and to obtain top quality blooms.

Those people who prefer to mix their own fertilisers will find the following recipe excellent: 7 lb. dried blood, 7 lb. superphosphate of lime, 7 lb. sulphate of potash, 1 lb. sulphate of magnesium and $\frac{1}{4}$ lb. ferrous sulphate. Mix all the ingredients thoroughly, then apply one handful (about 2 oz.) per bush. Do this first in March, immediately before the mulch is applied. Store the mixture in an air-tight tin in a dry place, and label the tin. Use again in June. This quantity is enough for approximately 80 bushes twice a year. A word of warning about all chemicals – follow the manufacturers' instructions to the letter, *never* exceed recommended amounts.

Mulching

Mulching means the covering of the rose bed, after the completion of pruning and feeding, with such materials (in order of preference) as strawy animal manures, peat, spent hops, or lawn mowings, providing the lawn has not been treated with weedkiller. Mulches should be applied to a depth of 4 ins. They keep the soil moist and cool during the summer months, so that the roots can spread and feed.

Pests & Diseases

As soon as the leaves begin to open in April and May keep a sharp look-out for the insects that, unless destroyed, will spoil the roses. Nowadays there are many different sprayers available to the gardener and one should select the size that will adequately deal with the quantity of bushes grown. Sizes range from half-pint hand sprayers through to 4-gal. knapsack units which strap to the back of the operator, and can spray up to two hundred trees at one filling. These sprayers can be used for the application of either systemic insecticides, which will effectively control insects such as aphids (greenfly), caterpillars, chafer grubs, thrips (thunder flies), capsid bugs, leaf-hoppers and frog-hoppers, or systemic fungicides which will effectively control the three main diseases that attack the rose, namely black spot, mildew, and rust. Your local garden centre or nurseryman will advise on which preparation to buy, as there is constant research being carried out on more effective treatment so that it is advisable to consult these people from season to season in order to keep oneself informed.

Regardless of which control is used, be sure to follow the manufacturer's instructions to the letter, both as to rate of application, and also as to times of treatment. The systemics are by far the most effective to use, as they give a longer period of control due to the fact that they are taken up via the roots and leaves into the system, so that any sucking pest will be destroyed up to a full month after spraying. The big disadvantage with systemics is the danger they pose to nature's predators – the ladybirds and bluetits – as the same poison that kills the pest will also kill the predator. The alternative is to use pyrethrum which is harmless to birds.

The common deficiency diseases are relatively easy to diagnose. By looking at the leaves it is possible to see from their colour what is causing the trouble, e.g.:
Nitrogen shortage. Leaves are small and pale green, sometimes with red spots on them. There is early leaf fall, and stems are stunted and weak.
Phosphate shortage is the reason for small and dark green leaves, with purplish tints underneath. There is early leaf fall and weak stunted stems.

Potash shortage is diagnosed when the leaves have brown brittle edges, and when the flowers are small. This is a common fault on sandy soil. The cure for all three problems is to apply a compound rose fertiliser at the rate recommended by the manufacturer.

Leaves which are pale at the centre with dead areas close to the midrib, denote a shortage of magnesium, and the remedy is to apply a rose fertiliser containing magnesium. Iron shortage causes leaves with large yellow areas, the younger leaves being the worst affected. Avoid overliming in this case and apply a compound rose fertiliser. Leaves with yellow bands between the veins means a shortage of manganese so avoid overliming the ground. When leaves become abnormally dark green and misshapen, there is a shortage of the trace element boron, so simply apply a compound fertiliser containing it. Oxygen shortage causes the veins and midribs of the leaves to yellow first, then large areas turn yellow also. This is a sign of waterlogged roots. There is no cure, the bush must be transplanted to a better site.

So there it is. By following the foregoing instructions your rose bed will give many years of pleasure to all who behold it – an annual festival of flower and fragrance.

Floribunda Lilli Marlene

RECOMMENDED VARIETIES TO GROW
(F) denotes fragrant varieties

Hybrid Tea

Alec's Red	2' 6" (F)	National Trust (red)	3' 6"
Alexander (vermilion)	4' 0"	Pascali (white)	2' 6"
City of Bath (deep pink)	2' 6" (F)	Peace (light yellow)	3' 6"
City of Gloucester (yellow)	2' 6"	Perfecta (cream shaded red)	2' 6" (F)
Elizabeth Harkness (cream)	2' 6" (F)	Pink Favourite	3' 6"
Ernest H. Morse (red)	2' 6" (F)	Prima Ballerina (deep pink)	3' 6" (F)
Fragrant Cloud (turkey red)	2' 6" (F)	Super Star (light vermilion)	3' 6" (F)
Grandpa Dickson (yellow)	2' 6"	Tenerife (coral/peach)	2' 6"
King's Ransom (yellow)	3' 6" (F)	Wendy Cussons (cerise)	2' 6" (F)
Mullard Jubilee (cerise)	3' 6" (F)	Whisky Mac (bronze/orange)	2' 6" (F)

Floribunda

Allgold (golden)	2' 0" (F)	Evelyn Fison (red)	2' 6"
Anne Cocker (vermilion)	4' 0"	Lilli Marlene (scarlet)	2' 0"
Anna Wheatcroft (vermilion)	2' 0"	Michelle (pink)	2' 0" (F)
Arthur Bell (yellow)	4' 0" (F)	News (purple)	2' 6"
City of Belfast (red)	2' 0"	Orange Sensation (orange)	2' 0" (F)
City of Leeds (salmon)	3' 0"	Picasso (carmine/silver)	2' 0"
Dearest (salmon)	4' 0" (F)	Pineapple Poll (orange/red)	2' 0" (F)
Dorothy Wheatcroft (red)	4' 0"	Queen Elizabeth (pink)	5' 0"
Elizabeth of Glamis (pink)	2' 6" (F)	Rob Roy (crimson)	2' 6"
Escapade (magenta)	2' 6" (F)	Southampton (apricot/orange)	3' 6"

Repeat Flowering Climbers

Casino (yellow)	(F)	Joseph's Coat (yellow, orange, red)	
Compassion (salmon/orange)	(F)	Marigold (golden)	(F)
Danse du Feu (scarlet)		New Dawn (pink)	(F)
Golden Showers (golden)	(F)	Pink Perpetue (pink)	
Handel (cream/pink)		Zephirine Drouhin (carmine)	(F)

Shrub Roses – Repeat Flowering

Ballerina (pink/white)	4' 0" (F)	Fred Loads (vermilion/orange)	5' 6" (F)
Bonn (orange)	6' 0"	Heidelberg (red)	5' 0"
Chinatown (yellow)	6' 0" (F)	Kassel (scarlet)	6' 0"
Cornelia (pink/yellow)	5' 0" (F)	Nevada (cream)	6' 0"
Elmshorn (crimson)	5' 0"	Penelope (creamy salmon)	5' 0" (F)

Miniature Roses
(6 to 9 inches in height)

Baby Masquerade (yellow/red)	New Penny (salmon)	
Cinderella (white)	Pour Toi (white)	
Coralin (coral)	Rosina (yellow)	
Easter Morning (ivory)	Starina (orange)	
Little Buckaroo (red)	Yellow Doll (yellow)	(F)

Floribunda Nan Anderson

Floribunda Arthur Bell

GROWING

GARDEN TREES

Peter Hemsley

Because trees are the largest woody plants, they are the most important structural components of the garden. A tree is such a grand object in itself, with so many dynamic visual attributes; beautiful shape and tracery, colourful foliage, spectacular flower displays, attractive fruits and stems. When these features are thoughtfully combined with the splendour of other garden plants, beautiful compositions can be created.

Apart from their visual contribution to a garden, trees can be very functional objects. A tree canopy filters out the wind to give shelter, thus creating a more favourable microclimate for outdoor living, and for the growing of less wind-hardy plants. The mass of foliage makes an excellent screen to give privacy and seclusion, or to obscure an unsightly view. The same canopy will also help to reduce levels of traffic noise, and in summer, the cool shade of a tree is most refreshing. How can a garden be complete without them?

PRE-PLANTING CONSIDERATIONS

When to Plant
The normal planting season is between the months of October and April. I prefer to have trees planted before Christmas, because root activity is minimal during this period, and also in my experience there is always a surfeit of other jobs to get on with in early spring. The exception to this rule is for conifers, which can either be planted during September or alternatively during April. Container-grown trees can be planted throughout the year, although ideally, they are best planted during the normal growing season. Avoid planting in frozen ground or in soil that is very wet and sticky.

Where to Plant
Before planting, some thought should be given to the actual position a tree will occupy in the garden. The two main considerations are firstly, visual or functional requirements, and secondly, any factors which are likely to interfere or impede future growth and development of the tree. In the first instance, trees need to be positioned to show off their visual qualities to best effect. Some, like holly, weeping cherry, and weeping elm, with boughs furnished to the ground, look well when grown in open situations such as lawns. Birch, Tibetan cherry, and snake bark maples, which have attractive stems, should be planted beside pathways, or in positions where the beauty of their bark can be admired and not obscured by the thicket of a border. Others, with attractive foliage or flower, can be integrated into borders to give a greater dimension in height.

Apart from the tree looking right there are other important considerations when deciding where to plant. Trees should not be planted too close to buildings, or where they can interfere with services like telephone or electric cables. This is where some foresight is needed if problems in later years are to be avoided. Visualise the young tree as a mature specimen and see if it has adequate room for development. Trees which have to be lopped to allow more light into the house can look unsightly, and detract from the appearance of the garden, when their real purpose is to enhance the scene. The root spread is also important.

Vigorous moisture-loving trees like weeping willow can be a nuisance when their roots block up drains, so always consider what is underground as well as what can be seen. Spare a thought for the neighbours when siting your trees, for boundary trees adjoining neighbouring property can be a source of friction when they begin to develop and overshadow. These problems can be avoided by a little considerate forethought in deciding where to plant.

Choosing the Right Species
One of the most difficult questions to resolve is what species to choose. There are only about 35 trees regarded as being truly native to Britain, but the plant collectors, breeders, and nurserymen, who have so enriched our gardens over the years, have provided us with an enormous number of new species and variants from which to choose. A few generalities, however, will help you to make the right choice for your own particular situation.

Firstly, the visual requirement. All the intricate visual qualities of a tree need careful analysis so that the desired effect can be achieved – the colour and texture of leaves, the tracery and form, the beauty of flower and fruit. These I have endeavoured to describe in more detail for each individual plant in the alphabetical list. At this planning stage we need to know something of a tree's growth rate and ultimate dimensions, so that we choose trees that are in scale with our house and garden. For example, a blue atlas cedar may be just right in terms of colour and shape, but in a small garden, 50 years after planting, it may well have to be reluctantly felled on account of its overbearing size. In comparison, a slower-growing, narrow-crowned blue spruce would have been a better choice.

Secondly, the functional requirement needs brief consideration. If, for example, shelter is needed, wind-hardy subjects should be chosen. Where backgrounds or visual screens are needed, evergreens are preferable, so that the desired effect is there throughout the year. Thirdly, and perhaps most importantly, we have to decide whether or not the tree will grow well in the locality and especially on the chosen planting site. Here three things are important – soil, climate, and atmosphere. Changes in soil type bring about natural divisions in plant communities, and therefore in gardens we have to select those species that grow best in the soil we have. For small garden plants it is possible to create an artificial soil, e.g. peat beds for acid-loving plants, but this is not practical for trees. Climate is another limiting factor, and this of course varies considerably in the British Isles. In the south and west coast regions, sub-tropical trees can be grown, whilst at the other extreme we have areas where only subarctic plants will thrive. The degree of exposure and microclimate of your garden will to some extent affect the choice of trees

A group of conifers pleasantly contrasted in size, shape, and colour.

to grow. Finally, the atmosphere affects tree growth: many conifers will not grow well in a smoke-polluted town atmosphere, although the situation is much improved since the introduction of the Clean Air Act. Salt-laden winds in coastal regions likewise affect many trees.

Do not despair, however, as nature has been generous in providing trees for almost any situation. They are after all the natural green mantle of Mother Earth and few gardens in Britain need be devoid of trees. In the alphabetical list, I have endeavoured to note the limitations of specific trees, but many are tolerant of a wide variety of soils and conditions.

Buying a Tree

Having decided on what trees to grow in the garden, the next step is to go out and purchase them, unless of course you have chosen to raise your own. Many trees are purchased through catalogues, and there is nothing wrong with this method, providing you tell the nurseryman exactly what you require in terms of species, type, and size of tree. Undoubtedly the best way is to visit your local tree nurseryman or garden centre, and choose the tree for yourself. In either case, know what you are looking for in a good specimen. What size of tree will best meet your needs? Trees may be purchased from one-year-old seedlings right up to the semi-mature specimen of 20–30 years old. A few large trees – if you can afford them – are excellent on a bare site to give some immediate effect, and provide a structure to the garden.

In most cases, however, we are thinking in terms of young feathered or standard trees, and possibly rootballed or containerised conifers. These are the sizes I would generally recommend, as small trees suffer very little check to growth after transplanting, and grow away more rapidly. To examine a tree, start with the roots. Look for a well-balanced, fibrous root system; one-sided root systems often result in unstable trees. If buying containerised trees, avoid those with constricted root systems; these also produce unstable trees and are very slow to establish.

Next we come to the stem or trunk. This needs to be sufficiently strong and sturdy to support the head of the tree. Check that it has not been constricted at any point so as to form a weakness. Finally the head; most trees should have a good leading shoot with a nicely balanced framework of branches radiating from it. (Though this is not the case with all trees; for example, ornamental crab apples, and some forms of flowering cherry have a branched head.) Choosing a tree is basically a question of using your common sense and good judgement. If you are in any doubt, your nurseryman will usually offer friendly advice.

After purchase, trees should be planted as soon as possible, and at no time should they be left lying around with their roots exposed. When a consignment of trees arrives in a package, open it as soon as possible, and after checking the contents, 'heel' the trees into a temporary trench until they can be planted.

PLANTING PROCEDURE

Preparation

Too often trees are planted in ground which has received the minimum preparation; of those that survive, growth during the early years is usually very poor indeed. In gardens it is desirable that trees establish themselves quickly, so that we can enjoy the re-sults of our labours at the earliest opportunity. To this end thorough ground preparation is the first step.

Apart from the exception of swamp cypress, there are few trees that will grow really well in waterlogged soil. The first task therefore is to ensure that the site is adequately drained. Ideally, this would be done as part of the overall garden construction, but alternatively the area of the tree pit may be drained into a soakaway dug close by and filled with coarse rubble or weathered clinker.

My maxim is to prepare an area of ground at least 5 ft. in diameter. All soil should be dug out one full spade depth, and the sub-soil dug or forked over. Surface vegetation or bulky organic manure, e.g. well-rotted compost, farmyard manure, or peat (especially for conifers), can be incorporated into the lower spade depth. If the subsoil (or lower spade depth) is of poor quality, dig it out and replace it with good-quality top-soil. Where staking is needed, this is the stage to insert a single stake firmly into the bottom of the prepared planting pit.

Planting

The tree can now be placed ready for planting. Just before doing this, however, examine the roots, and trim cleanly any damaged ones with secateurs or a sharp knife. Large pruning wounds should be painted with a wound sealant. Set the tree at the correct depth (using the soil mark on the trunk as a guide) by digging deeper or by adding soil as necessary to adjust the root level. If necessary use a long stick across the top of the planking as a guide. Deep planting should be avoided and I would suggest that the upper roots should only require a 4-in. covering of soil. Backfilling should be done in easy stages, using friable soil. Shake the tree lightly, so that the soil falls amongst the roots filling up voids and air pockets. Firm gently as backfilling proceeds, taking care not to damage the roots or break up the rootball on balled trees. If the soil is dry when planting out of the normal season, thoroughly water the area before adding the final layer of soil. Secure the tree to its stake, using suitable ties such as proprietary plastic buckles or rubber straps. If twine is used, wrap some hessian around the trunk to prevent injury. Two ties should be sufficient for normal standard trees, one placed at the top of the stake giving support to the head of the tree, and the second midway down. Remember to leave sufficient space in the tie to allow for one year's increase in the girth of the stem, otherwise constriction can occur and retard a tree's development.

After planting, prune back any damaged branches either to the trunk or to a suitably placed lateral branch or bud. Although little other pruning should be needed, any double leaders can be reduced to a single main stem. Likewise, if the branch framework is irregular, a little light pruning to restore the balance will assist the tree to form a satisfactory crown.

All plants respond to feeding and trees are no exception. After planting broadcast 4–6 oz. of a general fertiliser containing the three main plant foods (nitrogen, phosphate, and potash) over the prepared area. John Innes base, 'Fison's Plus', or 'Growmore' will suffice.

In many gardens protection for newly planted trees is not required, but if you live in the country, rabbits can be a nuisance, and even in town gardens that 'ginger tom cat from next door' can damage and disfigure stems if he decides to choose your new tree as a scratching post. Where such damage is likely to occur, either a plastic tree guard around the trunk, or a small fence of wire netting should be erected.

ESTABLISHMENT

Correct selection, thorough preparation, and careful planting, are the first steps to success with garden trees, but equally important (and yet so often neglected) is the aftercare or what I call the establishment phase. This is the period of approximately 5 or 6 years during which time the tree recovers from its planting check and begins to grow away vigorously.

Watering

Like humans most plants can survive only for short periods without water. Lifting and transplanting impairs the efficiency of water uptake, but at the same time water loss continues unabated. This is especially true of conifers and evergreen trees. It follows therefore that on no account should the soil around the tree be allowed to dry out. Remember that the roots go well down into the soil, therefore water thoroughly to ensure that all this depth of soil is wetted. On small trees in leaf, water loss can be reduced by spraying the foliage with an anti-desiccant spray such as 'Clarital' or S.600. This puts a thin plastic film over the leaf surface and reduces physical water loss through the leaf pores. To ensure a good effective covering, two sprays can be given.

Feeding

Feed the trees for at least the first 5 years after planting with a $1\frac{1}{2}$–1–1 nitrogen, phosphate, potash fertiliser. Scatter approximately $\frac{1}{2}$ lb. per tree around the root area. Late winter or early spring are the best times for application, so that the nutrients are available as root activity increases. The value of such feeding is to be seen in the increased vigour and shoot extension, and in the healthy appearance of the leaves.

There is plenty of evidence to indicate that tree bases should be kept free from competing vegetation during the first few years, whether this be grass or other ground cover planting, e.g. small shrubs. Bare soil can either be mulched with bulky organic material like well-rotted farmyard manure, or occasionally lightly forked over to aerate the soil to keep the site looking tidy.

Attention to Stakes and Ties

Each year the stem will increase in girth, and it follows that ties should be regularly adjusted so that the stem is in no way constricted. After 2 years, the root system should be firmly anchored, and providing that the stem is strong enough to support the head of a tree the stake can be removed. I am a great believer in dispensing with the stake at the earliest opportunity, so that the trunk begins to lay down tissues to support the tree against wind stresses, as young trees in the wild do. They grow up unaided with straight sturdy trunks.

Training

Most trees will develop into satisfactory specimens with the minimum of attention, but some guidance may occasionally be necessary. First the tree needs a sound structural framework. The majority of trees develop a central trunk and it is important to keep a single leading shoot, removing any double or competing shoots which develop. Trees with *opposite* buds such as maple (*Acer*) and ash (*Fraxinus*) are prone to this if the terminal bud is damaged. This results in a weak, narrow crotch, which is liable to split as the tree grows older. The maxim for

A dangerously split crotch in an 8-year-old elm tree.

this type of pruning should be prune with secateurs and not the saw, in other words do it early before any structural weakness occurs. There are occasions where a single leader is not required. Multi-stemmed trees make architecturally satisfying features in many garden situations. In these cases several basal stems or sucker shoots are allowed to develop. Some small garden trees, like ornamental Japanese cherries and flowering crab apples, naturally develop a branching head, and it is wrong to impose the centre leader habit on them.

Weeping trees require special attention during their formative years; the central shoot should be tied up to a cane until it has become stout enough to support itself. If this is not done a rather low sprawling specimen will result. Some weeping trees are grafted on to tall standard stocks and further upward training is not always needed.

THE CARE OF EXISTING TREES

Existing mature trees in a garden are an invaluable asset, and we should recognise that they represent many years of growth. With this in mind we should respect the tree's growing requirements and use all our gardening skill to keep the tree attractive and in good health. Let me emphasise at the beginning that working safely in large trees, and carrying out pruning and tree repair work, is a highly skilled task, and should not be undertaken without the proper training or the right equipment. For large jobs seek the advice of a tree consultant.

Pruning

This is the operation of cutting out branches to regulate and guide future growth of the tree and also to keep it in good health by the removal of dead, dying, diseased, or damaged branches.

Formative pruning. Following on from nursery training and the establishment phase of young trees, occasional pruning is desirable to assist the continued development of a satisfactory crown that is structurally sound. On centre leader trees, double leaders or branches competing for dominance need to be removed or suppressed, to avoid the development of weak forks. Ideally a crown should have reasonably balanced growth; on exposed sites growth is often heavy on the leeward side of a tree.

Such imbalance can be rectified by cutting back main branches to suitable lateral or side branches on the leeward side, and doing little or no pruning on the windward side. This operation may need repeating several times during subsequent years until the tree has formed a larger branch framework. As a tree increases in size, it may be desirable to prune off some of the lower branches, for example, to give more headroom for mowing a lawn, or to raise the crown to allow more light into underplanted areas.

Crown thinning. This is aimed to reduce the density of foliage, thus admitting more light and air into the crown, and reducing wind resistance. On trees close to buildings this technique, in conjunction with crown lifting, is an excellent way of letting more light in without destroying the overall beauty of a tree. On large trees it is a job only for the qualified tree surgeon. On small trees like Malus and Crataegus, which often develop dense congested crowns, the procedure I would advise is firstly to prune out all the obvious wood, i.e. diseased or damaged branches, weak, suppressed, and crossing branches. Having done this reduce the number of remaining sound branches until the crown is sufficiently thinned out to meet your requirements. Bear in mind however that once you have cut a branch off it cannot be replaced; therefore carefully think ahead before cutting out too many branches. Also bear in mind that the normal response to hard pruning is vigorous re-growth; thus it may often be necessary to repeat such crown thinning in subsequent years.

Crown cleaning. To keep a tree in good health, and to avoid accidents and damage from falling dead branches, periodic crown cleaning is advisable. At the risk of boring the reader may I again stress the need for a qualified tree surgeon for large trees. The procedure is simply to prune out dead, dying, and diseased branches or branch stubs back to live wood. It can be quite surprising to see the amount of dead wood that accumulates in trees. Occasional crown cleaning will not only improve the appearance and make the tree safer, but, by arresting dieback of branches into the trunk, it keeps a tree much healthier and by doing so extends its life.

Timing of pruning operations. Pruning can be done throughout the year in most cases, but the following are exceptions;

birch, hornbeam, sycamore, and other maples, should not be pruned between January and early June because of excessive bleeding. Walnuts, on the other hand, bleed heavily when dormant and are best pruned when in full leaf. Prunus are best pruned after flowering in May and June. Conifers which require pruning are best done in late spring after growth has commenced. Dead wood can be seen more clearly when deciduous trees are in full leaf, therefore crown cleaning can be a job for the summer.

Pruning tools. Pruning is made much easier if you have the right tools for the job. Various saws are available, but whatever your choice, ensure that it is sharp. A hand saw for cutting green wood should have no more than five points to each inch, otherwise it makes too fine a cut and jams. Tubular framed saws or bow saws cut through green logs easily, and the type with a tapered bow is preferable for getting in amongst branches and narrow angled crotches. When these saws get blunt a new blade can be inserted in seconds. A Grecian saw has a pointed curved blade, which is ideal for very narrow crotches when thinning out small branches; remember these only cut when the blade moves downwards so put the effort into the 'pull' stroke. Some pruning saws have a double-edged blade, one side with coarse teeth, the other with fine teeth. These are difficult to use in some situations, as there is a tendency to accidentally cut into the upper branches as well as the one being cut off, so I prefer single-sided blades. Small chain saws may be used but these need careful and sensible handling. Ensure that the instruction book is carefully studied beforehand if you are a beginner. Practise on a few spare logs before you start on a tree to get the feel of the saw. Ensure that the chain is correctly tensioned and kept well lubricated during operation. I would advise beginners not to use chain saws in the crown of a tree – leave this work to the qualified tree surgeon. Loppers, secateurs, and pruning knives, may be useful tools for small branches when formative pruning is undertaken.

Making cuts. Pruning may involve complete removal of a branch back to the main trunk, or partial removal back to a lateral branch. Final cuts should always be into live wood so that the wound can heal. The best procedure for cutting off a branch is firstly to reduce the weight by cutting it off in manageable lengths. An undercut, about one-third of the branch diameter, is made to prevent tear back. A second cut is made 1–2 ins. away from this undercut on the side farthest from the trunk. Thus as this cut reaches the depth of the first cut, the fibres tear back to it and the branch comes off cleanly. When cutting large branches or near-vertical branches, the first cut can be taken out as a wedge, so that the branch can fall and break cleanly as the second cut is made. The final cut is made as flush to the main stem as is practical to avoid leaving stubs that can rot back. On branches which have a large shoulder, try to minimise the area of the final wound by making a compromise on the cutting angle – remember the smaller the wound the quicker it will heal. As soon as possible after making the final cut, paint the wound with a sealant to keep it waterproof and to prevent the entry of fungal spores. 'Stockholm Tar' and 'Arbrex 805' are two examples of materials which are suitable. Give two applications to ensure a watertight seal. This should be inspected each year and repainted as necessary until wound occlusion is reached. Occlusion occurs when the callus tissue,

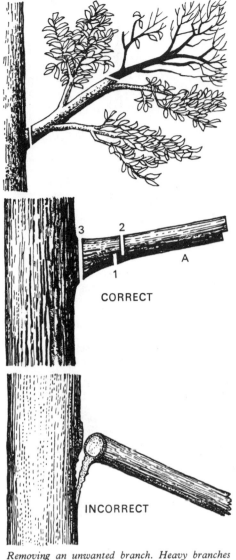

CORRECT

INCORRECT

Removing an unwanted branch. Heavy branches should be removed in manageable sections (A), to avoid 'tear back' (bottom).

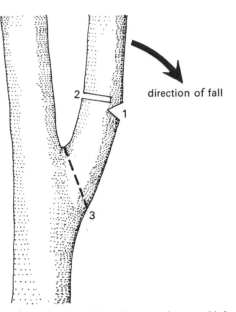

direction of fall

Pruning a vertical branch. 1: wedge one-third through branch. 2: second cut. 3: final cut.

A beech tree damaged by lightning

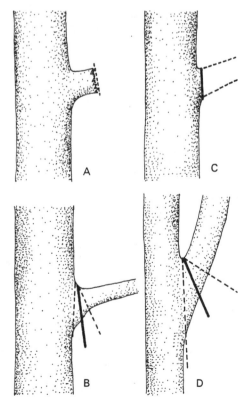

A: stub leads to decay. B: the middle angle is correct. C: a correct cut. D: the middle angle is correct.

growing from the outer ring of tissue just beneath the bark, completely covers the heartwood of the wound.

Tree Repair

Neglected wounds on trees eventually decay, and gradually cavities begin to develop in the heartwood. A tree, however, continues to grow vigorously as all the life-sustaining transport of water and nutrients goes on unimpaired in the outer sapwood. Outwardly therefore a tree can look perfectly healthy, but inwardly its main structural strength (the heartwood) is being eaten away. Eventually the tree is weakened to the point where structural failure occurs, and either large branches fall off, or the trunk snaps. Such damage is frequently seen after gales. It follows from this that wounds should always be dealt with before decay occurs. Pruning wounds I have already mentioned, but likewise, other bark wounds on the trunk should be trimmed cleanly by paring the wound with a knife back to live bark. The area is then painted with two coats of fungicidal sealant. All wounds should be inspected each year and repainted as necessary.

Structural weakness is not always visible to the layman, and it follows that large trees close to buildings or roads should be periodically inspected by a qualified tree surgeon or consultant. If your trees have already developed cavities do not be alarmed as the decay may only be superficial. These

will need inspection to determine the possibility of repairing them. Small cavities can be cleaned out of all debris and decaying wood and then painted with wound sealant. Ideally a cavity should be left open so that there is free circulation of air, thus creating conditions least conducive to fungal activity. Such open cavities also need to drain freely.

Weak forks can be secured by the installation of a cable brace about two-thirds of the distance above the crotch. Flexible steel cables are secured to eye bolts or screw eyes which are fitted into the branches so as to avoid constriction. Cavity repair and cable bracing are highly skilled jobs which need to be done correctly if they are to be successful; I would strongly advocate that these are jobs which should only be undertaken by a qualified tree surgeon.

Basal Protection

People often tend to forget that a large part of a tree is underground; and any damage to the roots affects the health and vigour of that tree. Damage often occurs without realisation. Compost heaps, for example, and surplus garden soil heaped over the root area on large trees, can cause suffocation of the root system, leading to dieback in the crown. The building of garages and extensions can sometimes cut roots or cause compaction and suffocation. Occasionally I find trees in gardens badly injured by fires which have been lit beneath them. Sometimes damage is not immediately apparent, but when large

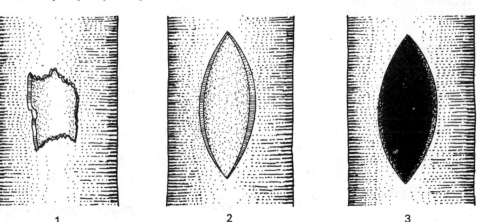

Bark repair. 1: jagged wound. 2: the wound tidied and cleaned. 3: painted with wound sealant.

flakes of bark peel away as a result of heat scorch, the deed is realised. No special guidelines are needed here except to say, always bear in mind a tree's growth requirement and consider the needs of the roots and trunk.

Pests and Diseases

Trees, like other living things, are not free from the ravages of pests and disease organisms, as is borne out by the recent scourge of Dutch elm disease. There are many pests and diseases of trees, but fortunately most occur as localised outbreaks and many are not sufficiently serious to warrant control measures. Control is usually only practicable on young trees, as specialised equipment is needed to apply chemicals to large specimens. Before undertaking any control it is vital to diagnose the cause of the problem correctly, which may not always be a pest or disease organism. To ascertain this refer to a specialist book or, better still, consult a qualified tree man.

RAISING YOUR OWN TREES

It is always rewarding to observe the growth and development of plants that you have raised with your own hands and therefore I shall briefly explain how this may be done in the case of trees.

Propagation by Seeds

The easy way of propagating many trees is by seed, but firstly it must be realised that many garden variants, such as forms with a particular different growth habit or foliage variation, will not always come true to the parental type. In these cases vegetative propagation methods have to be used, e.g. cuttings or grafting. If you decide on sowing, the first requirement is viable seed. This may be purchased in small quantities from ornamental plant seedsmen, or it may be obtained from garden society seed lists. A third possibility is to collect your own seed, either from the trees of gardening friends, or from trees growing wild in the countryside.

Springtime between March and May is the most favourable time for sowing. A 5-in. half pot, of the type used for growing pot chrysanthemums, makes an ideal container for small batches of seed. This is filled with John Innes seed compost, levelled, and gently firmed. Space the seed evenly, but not too thickly, on the prepared surface, and finally carefully cover the seed. Compost may be used for covering the seed, but I prefer to use grit, which has a particle size of about $\frac{1}{8}$ in. Depth of cover is fairly critical as deep sowing can be detrimental. For small seeds like birch, $\frac{1}{8}$ in. deep is adequate. For larger seeds, e.g. oak, $\frac{1}{4}$ in. is preferable. Large seeds like chestnuts can be lightly pressed into the compost until they are completely buried beneath the surface, before covering. The name of the tree and its sowing date, can be written either on to a label, or on to the side of plastic containers with a waterproof, fibre tip pen, for identification purposes after germination. An open frame, sheltered, is ideal for germinating most tree seeds. The only requirement is a cover of wire netting as a protection against birds, and you must ensure that the pans are never allowed to dry out. Many trees succeed when the seeds are sown directly into the open ground. To do this, prepare a slightly raised seed bed in weed-free ground, and sow in late April. The seed can be drilled or broadcast on the bed, lightly pressed into the soil surface with a flat board, and covered with $\frac{1}{4}$ in. of grit. The beds should be watered during dry periods, and kept free of weeds. Because of complex physiological processes within some seeds, germination may be delayed for up to 2 years, consequently after sowing a little, or even a great deal of, patience may be called for.

In the autumn or spring following germination, seedlings are pricked off into either an open frame, or some sheltered part of your garden for growing on. A few examples of trees that can be raised from seed include birch, oak, chestnut, maple, sorbus, laburnum, beach, ash, pine, spruce, cypress, and cedar.

Propagation by Cuttings

One of the remarkable things about plants is their ability to regenerate from detached stems, and in some cases, roots. Because only vegetative parts are involved, the resultant plant is genetically identical with its parent. This means that cultivars and forms propagated from cuttings will develop

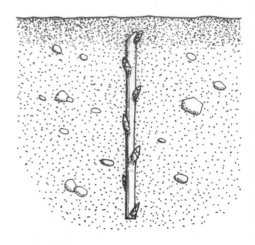

A hardwood cutting, 7–9 ins. long with all buds intact, slanting cut at top, straight cut at bottom.

identical parental characteristics; thus cuttings from a golden form of Lawson's cypress will produce plants with the same golden leaves.

Stem cuttings are most commonly used, and these may be of three types, namely hardwood, softwood, or semi-ripe wood cuttings. Hardwood cuttings are taken from fully ripened shoots produced during the previous growing season. The best time is in autumn, soon after leaf fall, but they may be taken at any time during the dormant period up until a few weeks before the next season's bud break. Choose healthy but not over-vigorous shoots, which can be cut into lengths of 7–9 ins. Make a clean cut below a bud at the base, with a slanting cut above a bud at the top of the cutting. After preparation, the freshly cut basal end of the cuttings can be dipped into a hormone rooting powder, which will not only increase the number of cuttings rooted, but also the number of roots which form on each cutting. Cuttings can be given one of two treatments. They can either be lined out into the garden direct, or alternatively, they may be plunged into moist sand and stored over winter ready for lining out in springtime. In the north I prefer the latter method as it seems to give better results. Hardwood cuttings of trees are inserted vertically by making a slit trench with a spade into previously prepared ground. Ideally, the cuttings should be inserted full depth with the top bud just $\frac{1}{2}$ in. below soil level. Cuttings need to be spaced about 8 ins. apart, with 18 ins. between rows, to allow sufficient room for their development during one growing season. This method is excellent for most species of poplar and willow and also the London plane.

Semi-ripe shoots may also be used successfully without the need for sophisticated propagation facilities. These are taken between July and September when the current season's extension shoots are becoming woody at the base. This is often indicated by a colour change from green to brown. Lateral shoots root better than terminal shoots, and these may be gently pulled off with a 'heel'. Take care, however, not to cause unnecessary damage or disfigure the parent tree when collecting cuttings. If you are collecting evergreens, for example conifers, remember to prevent them from drying out between collection and insertion by placing them into a moistened polythene bag. (An essential item for any gardener to carry, with a knife, when visiting gardening friends!) Cuttings, usually about 4–6 ins. long, are trimmed cleanly at the base or at the 'heel' with a sharp knife. Conifer cut-

A seed-bed before preparation, with oak seed sown in drills, sown broadcast, and finally covered.

tings benefit from a light wounding. This involves the paring off of a thin sliver of bark about ¾ in. long to expose the cambium cells just beneath the bark. Like hardwood cuttings, they can be dipped into a hormone rooting powder before insertion. Small batches of cuttings can be placed around the edge of a plant pot filled with a suitable rooting medium. Equal volumes of peat and sharp sand is a good general purpose mixture, but for conifers my preference is for 60% peat, 20% fine sand, and 20% ⅛-in. grit. Success depends largely on the environment in which the cutting is kept, and on its aftercare. For evergreen cuttings a humid environment is required to prevent desiccation. Few of us have the ideal facility of a mist unit, but we have the ingenuity to provide an environment that will suffice. A cool garden frame with shaded lights, or alternatively, a small white polythene cloche or tunnel can be made. On a small scale a Ward propagator is excellent. Whatever facility is used, remember to water the cuttings thoroughly at insertion time, and to look at them periodically to ensure that they are not drying out. An occasional watering with captan minimises losses caused by fungal rots. Examples of trees propagated by semi-ripe wood cut-

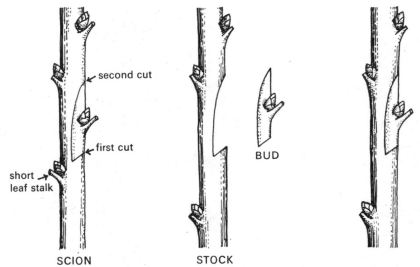

Chip budding, showing bud removed from scion and inserted in stock ready for tying.

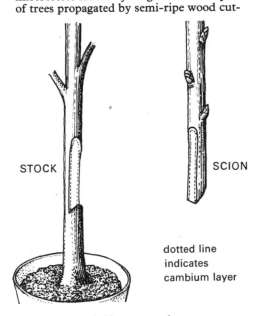

A side veneer graft

tings include Chamaecyparis, × Cupressocyparis, and Thuja.

Propagation by softwood cuttings does not have a wide application for beginners, and is of limited use for trees. It requires a mist propagation unit for success. Briefly it involves the removal of soft, succulent lateral shoots during June and July. These are trimmed cleanly, inserted into containers, and placed in either a humid environment or preferably into a mist unit. Examples of trees propagated include dawn redwood (*Metasequoia*), birches, and white poplar.

Several trees are capable of regeneration from chopped-up root pieces, and trees which send up suckers will usually respond to this method. Fleshy root pieces are required, and these have to be carefully exposed and identified as coming from the parent tree. The alternative is to trim off one or two roots from young lifted trees. Roots should normally only be detached during the dormant period and midwinter is the best time. To be sure that the cuttings are correctly inserted, it is normal to make a straight cut at the top of the cutting with a slanting cut at the bottom. Root cuttings of trees should be at least 4 ins. long, as the energy for regeneration comes from the stored food reserves, hence shorter cuttings tend to fail or produce weak plants. Chances of success are increased if cuttings are rolled

in captan powder. Prepared cuttings can be inserted into pots, deep boxes, or frames. They are pushed vertically into soil, or John Innes compost, until the cutting is ¼ in. below the soil surface. Cuttings in containers are best over-wintered in a frame, to produce young plants ready for growing on a year later. Stag's Horn Sumach (*Rhus typhina*) is an example of a garden tree which can be propagated quite successfully by this method.

Propagation by Grafting
This is an exciting and challenging way of propagating trees, and it is the only way of increasing many aberrant and unusual forms. Successful grafting requires a great deal of skill, but nothing is lost by trying.

A graft consists of two parts, the stock which forms the roots, and the scion which forms the head of the tree. Rootstocks are usually young seedling trees which may be pot grown for indoor grafting, or lined out into the garden for outdoor grafting or bud grafting (budding). Occasionally grafts are placed 7 ft. up the stem of a 2- or 3-year-old tree, e.g., to make a standard weeping elm, but normally grafting is done very low down on the rootstock.

There are five main points for successful grafting. First the stock and scion must be compatible. This means that the two tissues must be able to unite and grow together

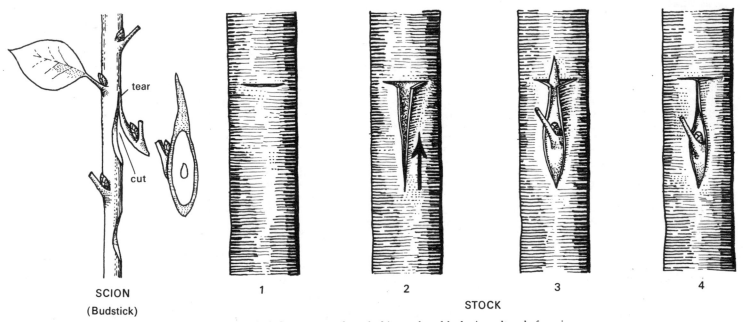

T-budding, showing bud, first cut, second cut, bud inserted, and bud trimmed ready for tying.

The brilliant autumn foliage of Acer platanoides

A fine specimen of Aesculus × carnea var. briotii, the red horse chestnut

successfully. To achieve this choose a root-stock that is very closely related to the scion. For example, weeping beech (*Fagus sylvatica* 'pendula'), would be grafted on to common beech (*Fagus sylvatica*). Likewise golden-leaved false acacia (*Robinia pseudoacacia* 'Frisia') would be grafted on to common false acacia (*Robinia pseudoacacia*).

Secondly, the operation of grafting must be done at the correct time of year, when the rootstocks are in the right physiological condition. Indoor grafting on to potted stocks can be done from mid-January to early March. Outdoor grafting is best done in March, as rootstocks come into growth and budding in July and August.

Thirdly, the cambium cells (the layer of tissue just beneath the bark) of stock and scion must be in close, intimate contact. This is achieved by skilful carpentry in joining the two parts together by cutting with a sharp, straight-bladed grafting knife. Fairly simple grafts for beginners to try are the side veneer, T budding, and chip budding. Side veneer grafting is used for conifers and for indoor grafting of orna-mental trees on to potted stocks, e.g. beech and birch. T or chip budding is used out-doors for forms of maple, sorbus, crataegus, malus, and prunus.

Fourthly, after grafting, the stock plants and the graft union should be prevented from drying out. The union can be sealed with polythene tape, or a dressing of water-proof tree wound sealant, beeswax, or petroleum jelly. This is put on after the two parts have been secured together. Indoor grafts need not be sealed, providing they are placed in the humid environment of a closed propagation case.

Finally, after union has taken place, and the scion begins to grow, the plants must still be given proper care and attention. For example the rootstock above the union has to be cut off, to allow only the scion to grow. Any constricting ties used to secure the graft should be cut. Grafts on to potted stocks should not be allowed to become pot bound, in case a constricted root system develops.

AN ALPHABETICAL LIST OF TREES FOR GARDENS

Broadleaved Trees

Acer capillipes. This delightful small Japanese tree growing up to 30 ft. in height,
is one of the group of snake-barked maples which are characterised by the striated pat-tern of bark. It is a hardy tree and grows well in most soils, but has a preference for rich moist soils. In springtime the young growths are reddish in colour and in autumn the leaves take on similar attractive tints.

Acer cappadocicum. A small- to medium-sized maple from Asia Minor eventually growing up to about 50 ft. in favoured local-ities. It reminds me of a miniature Norway maple, as the smooth palmate leaves turn bright yellow in autumn. For this effect to be extended, planting in a sheltered corner is advised. There are two notable cultivars (probably more often seen in gardens than the type), namely *rubrum* in which the young leaves are red, and *aureum* with bright yellow leaves in spring, which turn light green during the summer. All forms grow well on chalk soils.

Acer davidii. This is one of the best snake-bark maples from China. It forms a small tree 35–45 ft. in height when full grown, and like many other maples it has spectacular autumn colours.

Acer griseum. Commonly known as the paper-bark maple on account of the bark, which peels off in thin flakes to reveal new reddish-brown bark. It makes an excellent tree for small gardens as it only grows about 30–40 ft. in height. In autumn the leaves turn reddish-brown and for best effect it needs some shelter.

Acer × lobelii. The attraction of this maple is the erect branching habit which gives a narrow upright oval shape to the crown. It is quick-growing eventually reach-ing up to 60 ft.

Acer negundo. This North American tree, commonly referred to as box elder, has leaves more like an ash tree, and often makes a rather untidy specimen unless it is regu-larly trained during its early development. Two cultivars worthy of use in the garden are firstly *auratum*, which in my opinion is one of the outstanding golden-leaved trees. The second is *variegatum*, a form with white leaf margins. Both forms make small trees eventually growing up to 35 ft. They are all suited to chalky soils.

Acer platanoides. The Norway maple has long been one of my favourite trees. It is a hardy, vigorous species eventually growing up to 80 ft. in height. Aesthetically it is a pleasing tree with smooth green leaves, a tidy oval crown, and attractive autumn tints,
which on some trees are yellow and on others orange and reddish. Clusters of greenish flowers are borne in springtime, just before the leaves unfurl. It seems to grow well in a wide range of soils and conditions. A num-ber of cultivars are suitable for use in gar-dens. *Schwedleri*, 'Crimson King', 'Golds-worth Purple' and 'Faasen's Black' have leaves varying in intensity from greenish-purple to very dark purple. *Drummondii* has a white leaf margin, and 'Cleveland' is a form with a narrow oval crown.

Acer pseudoplatanus. Sycamore is gener-ally a rather dull tree for gardens and often it can be a weed. Nevertheless in exposed areas and on difficult sites it is a useful pioneer species for providing shelter or nurse to assist the establishment of other trees. There are several cultivars more suited to gardens. *Corstorphinense* and *worleei* have yellow leaves during spring. *Brilliantissimum* is quite spectacular with its gaudy, coral-pinkish leaves. This cultivar is slow-growing and makes a compact tree, ideal for the small garden.

Acer rubrum. Red or Canadian maple is notable for its fiery autumn colours in its native eastern North America. For British gardens two cultivars must be mentioned. The first, *schlesingeri*, is an American clone, selected for its outstanding and reliable autumn colours. The second is 'Scanlon', which has a narrow columnar crown making it suitable for planting in small gardens or confined areas, where room for crown de-velopment is restricted.

Acer saccharinum. Silver maple derives its name from the whitish, silvery under-sides of its cut, palmate leaves. These give the tree a fine texture, and in autumn some trees colour exceptionally well. It is a fairly fast-growing species eventually reaching up to 70 ft. with a spreading crown. A dis-advantage is the rather brittle wood and fragile branches which makes it unsuitable for exposed gardens.

Aesculus × carnea. This is a hybrid be-tween horse chestnut and American red chestnut. It does not make such a large tree as the horse chestnut, and is usually about 30 ft. with a dome-shaped crown and pendu-lous branches. Reddish-pink flowers cover the tree during May, making a delightful picture for any garden. The cultivar *briotii* is even better, being a more compact form with larger, redder flowers.

Aesculus hippocastanum. Common

horse chestnut is our largest flowering tree, which is really too large and overbearing for small gardens. It grows over 80 ft. in height and has wide spreading heavy branches. Leaves are large and distinct, giving a coarse textural effect which is especially dramatic as the leaves unfurl in spring. The 'candles' are alight during May, and these give rise to 'conkers' in October (unless the sterile double-flowered cultivar *baumannii* is planted). Horse chestnut grows well in most lowland situations, and is widespread throughout our towns and cities. In some autumns, leaves turn red, orange, and russet brown.

Alnus glutinosa. Common alder is not such a spectacular tree for gardens, but it is an excellent subject for wet soils, growing extremely well beside streams and ponds. Likewise on poor impoverished soils this tree does remarkably well. I think it looks best when grown as a multi-stemmed tree. Usually it has an upright oval crown and grows 50–65 ft. in height. For additional interest two cultivars for gardens are *aurea*, which has bright golden leaves, and *imperialis*, which has deeply cut fern-like leaves, giving a feathery appearance to the tree.

Betula pendula. Silver birch is one of our native trees that is quite outstanding for gardens. Visually it has much to offer and provides interest at any season of the year. Springtime brings forth a flush of bright green leaves, in summer the graceful habit of pendent branchlets, yellow and russet tints remind us that autumn has arrived, and even in winter there is the delightful tracery and colourful stems to admire. Generally it grows 50–60 ft. in height, and because of its small leaves and graceful lines it never seems oppressive in small gardens. Silver birch is also a useful pioneer plant for growing on poor soils and in exposed areas. Small copses or woodlands of birch are ideal for the growing of rhododendrons which benefit from the dappled shade. Several cultivars are additionally interesting for gardens. *Dalecarlica* is a cut-leaved form with long pendent branchlets. *Youngii* is the weeping cultivar which should have its leader trained upwards for a few years, otherwise it grows into a low sprawling tree. In complete contrast is *fastigiata*, which has a habit like a miniature Lombardy poplar.

Betula ermanii. This species is notable for its creamy-white bark and yellow autumn foliage. It is a fairly quick-growing tree eventually reaching up to 65 ft., and is certainly a most beautiful tree for gardens.

Betula jacquemontii. A Himalayan tree growing up to about 50 ft. Some forms of this tree have brilliant creamy-white stems which make other species look inferior.

Carpinus betulus. Common hornbeam is a native tree growing especially well on chalky and clay soils. It develops a neat, usually rounded crown 50–60 ft. tall. The cultivar *fastigiata* has a narrow columnar crown and is more suitable for small gardens. Hornbeam looks best in autumn, when the leaves turn bright yellow and the fruits hang in great profusion like small yellow Chinese lanterns. It also responds to clipping and can be used for hedging.

Cercidiphyllum japonicum. Providing you have a reasonably fertile soil, preferably one rich in humus, and a fairly sheltered garden, this delightful Japanese tree can be grown. It has distinct broad, heart-shaped leaves which turn a variety of colours in the autumn. These may be hues of green, yellow, orange, pink and red. It often grows as a large shrub but it will form a tree if trained as such when young.

The common alder, Alnus glutinosa var. imperialis

Graceful trunks of silver birch, Betula pendula

Cercis siliquastrum, the Judas tree, less common but well worthwhile

Laburnum × vossii, a summer shower of gold

Magnolia kobus grows to some 30 ft

Cercis siliquastrum. This has similar-shaped leaves to the previously mentioned tree, but in this case it is the bright pink pea-like flowers which attract attention. These are borne in clusters along the older branches in springtime. It does not grow too well in the north of England, but reasonable specimens can develop if a sheltered, sunny position is chosen. Normally it is a small tree up to 30 ft.

Crataegus monogyna. Hawthorn is a small round-headed tree 20–30 ft. in height. Commonly known as 'May Blossom', but in the north it is usually early June when it is smothered in clusters of white fragrant flowers. In October it becomes festooned with scarlet berries which are rapidly devoured by birds. It is not the best of garden trees, but they can develop into trees of character with gnarled old stems.

Crataegus oxyacanthoides. 'Paul's New Double Scarlet'. This is the tree with double red 'May Blossom'. It grows easily in most lowland situations and is common in towns. It is sometimes weak-rooted and needs support until well established. Thinning helps to reduce wind resistance.

Eucalyptus gunnii. For those looking for something out of the ordinary this 'Cider Gum' may suffice. It is the hardiest of the Eucalypts, which generally favour the south and western areas of Britain, where severe winters are less likely. It is an evergreen tree with blue-green, spatula-like leaves. Somehow it never seems to stop growing and will establish itself fairly quickly. Like other species it has unusual patterned bark.

Eucalyptus niphophylla. This is another fairly hardy species, quick-growing, and with an eye-catching bark and foliage.

Fagus sylvatica. A visit to a native beech-wood brings out the true magnificence of this tree. Fresh bright green leaves in spring, russet leaves in autumn, and silvery vertical trunks in winter. It is a tall, spreading tree, with a dense canopy and heavy limbs which can overwhelm a small garden. The dark-leaved copper forms close to buildings, cast an even darker shade and can be somewhat depressing. There is an upright form called 'Dawyck' which has a habit like a Lombardy poplar. In my opinion they are fine trees providing you have a large enough garden to accommodate them. They are native to chalk downland, but judging by their wide distribution in Britain, they thrive on a wide range of soils.

Fraxinus angustifolia lentiscifolia. This is a striking, graceful variety of the fine-leaved ash. It produces a delightful textural effect, because of the pendulous leaves. It grows into quite a large tree, over 70 ft., therefore is only suitable for larger gardens.

Fraxinus excelsior. Common ash is rather a dull tree for gardens, but it grows remarkably well on heavy clay and chalky soils. Likewise it succeeds in towns and especially in areas with smoke-polluted atmospheres. More interesting cultivars are *pendula* with strong, downswept branches. *Jaspidea* is known as the golden ash, because of its yellowish leaves which colour brighter yellow in autumn. Young stems are also golden coloured.

Fraxinus ornus. Manna ash is normally a medium-sized tree up to 60 ft. with a round spreading or domed crown. It is also known as the flowering ash, on account of its large panicles of creamy-white flowers which are borne in late May.

Ilex aquifolium. Holly is a useful evergreen tree for providing backgrounds and shelter. Equally they have a singular beauty when grown as lawn specimens. They usually grow up to 35–40 ft. in height, with a broad columnar shape. They also respond to clipping and can be trained as features in a formal garden. Most hollies are shade tolerant and can be used for underplanting. Hollies, with few exceptions, are unisexual trees. This means that both male and female need to be planted if berries are desired. To determine whether a tree is male or female the centres of the white flowers which open in May and June need to be examined. Male trees have a small cluster of anthers whilst the female only has a single style, which after fertilisation develops into the berry. The thick glossy leaves withstand atmospheric pollution and salt spray. There are many cultivars of the common holly. 'Silver Queen' and 'Handsworth New Silver' have white variegated leaves. 'Golden Milkboy' and 'Golden Queen' have yellow variegated leaves. The cultivar *pyramidalis* has a distinct conical shape and bears a heavy crop of large red berries. A bisexual variety for the small garden is *altaclarensis* 'J. C. van Tol'.

× Laburnocytisus adamii. For those who like novelties in the garden this is a tree to include. It occurred as a result of grafting purple broom on to common laburnum. The graft was damaged, and the resultant growth was a shoot with a core of purple broom surrounded by laburnum tissue. This produces a tree in which some parts are purple broom and others are common laburnum and some are intermediary having purplish-pink laburnum flowers. It makes a small tree 20–30 ft. in height.

Laburnum anagyroides. Common laburnum is most spectacular when in flower during late May and June. Visually it is an ideal tree for small gardens as it only grows 20–30 ft. in height. Laburnums grow well on most soils and are especially at home on chalk. The only drawback is that the seeds contain a poisonous alkaloid, and each year there are distressing reports of children becoming seriously ill or dying as a result of eating these. The golden-leaved cultivar *aureum* is quite dazzling in the springtime.

Laburnum 'Vossii'. This hybrid is even more impressive when in flower as the pendulous racemes are much longer. The flowers are also sweetly scented. Fortunately it produces less seeds as many seem to be sterile. Nevertheless, it would be wiser to gather seed pods from the tree if young children are likely to play in the garden. Laburnum trees are not long-lived, but when planted to form an archway or trained over a pergola so that the racemes droop down the centre they really live up to their name of 'The Golden Rain Tree'.

Liquidambar styraciflua. The sweet gum from the eastern USA has small maple-like leaves which can be relied upon to turn brilliant reddish and crimson colours in the autumn. It is fairly slow-growing eventually reaching about 35 ft. Ideally it requires acid soil and a sheltered situation.

Liriodendron tulipfera. Tulip tree also originates from North America. It has distinct leaves which colour yellow in autumn. The 'tulip'-shaped flowers are a greenish yellow, and rather inconspicuous. It is slow to establish in the north of England, but given shelter when young it soon begins to grow quickly. Eventually it grows into a large tree, and even in Yorkshire there are trees over 65 ft. tall. Deep, rich soils are preferred, but it will grow on chalk soils. For small gardens there is an upright cultivar *fastigiatum*, which develops into a narrow, columnar tree.

Magnolia kobus. All magnolias grow best in deep, rich soils, and in sheltered situations. This hardy tree species eventually grows up to about 27 ft. and is noted for its pure white flowers borne in late April. Like most magnolias it requires 10–15 years' growth before regular flower crops can be expected. Nevertheless, if you have patience, it makes a wonderful picture when in full bloom.

Malus floribunda. The ornamental crab apples bring their own cheer to a garden in springtime. This Japanese tree is appropriately named, as its branches are literally smothered with an abundance of rosy pink flowers in late April and early May. It has a dense roundish crown and grows to about 20 ft. in height. Flowering crab apples grow well in a wide range of soils and conditions, and tolerate the atmosphere of industrial towns. They are however susceptible to the disease fire blight, and are unsuitable for areas in the south of England where outbreaks are prevalent.

Malus pumila 'Golden Hornet'. This is a cultivar that has spectacular fruits which are a rich golden yellow in colour and produced in great profusion along the branchlets.

Malus pumila 'John Downie'. The blush-pink to white flowers of spring have developed into clusters of miniature red and yellow fruits by autumn. The overall effect is to make this one of the best and most spectacular fruited crab apples. The fruits are also edible and suitable for preserves.

Malus × purpurea. This hybrid has purplish-crimson flowers followed by small scarlet crab apples in autumn. Leaves are also tinged with purple. *Lemoinei* and 'Profusion' are two similar cultivars belonging to this group of outstanding easily grown small flowering trees.

Malus tschonoski. Don't be put off by this difficult name, as it is an excellent tree for gardens. It grows fairly quickly and has a tidy, broadly pyramidal habit, suitable for small gardens. Whilst it is not so floriferous as other crabs it has beautiful autumn colours. Eventually it grows up to 50 ft.

Populus nigra italica. The Lombardy poplar is a fast-growing tree with its familiar upright habit. It is often planted as a quick-growing screen, but in small gardens and near buildings it can become a nuisance, because of its root encroachment into drains and under foundations. They eventually grow over 90 ft. in height.

Prunus 'Amanogowa'. Unbecomingly this is often referred to as the Lombardy poplar cherry on account of the erect-growing branches. It forms a narrow columnar tree, bedecked with double, pale pink flowers in May. It is the ideal tree for small courtyard gardens where space is limited. It is not a long-lived subject and eventually reaches about 20 ft. in height.

Prunus avium. Our native wild cherry will grow into a larger tree than many of the Japanese cultivars. The flowers are not long lived and for gardens the double-flowered form *plena* is more suitable.

Prunus cerasifera pissardii. For a small, purple-leaved garden tree there is no finer choice than this. White flowers are borne in early spring, but the dark purple leaves add colour to the garden throughout the summer and then turn reddish in autumn. It forms a round compact crown and grows about 25 ft. in height.

Prunus dulcis. The almond tree is one of the earliest cherries to flower. It is quite charming when bearing its bright pink blossoms, but they often look unattractive in summer when the leaves are attacked with the leaf-blistering fungus disease called peach leaf curl.

Prunus 'Kanzan'. This outstanding garden tree is extensively planted by local authorities, and as such is often much maligned. It is an easy tree to grow and can be relied upon to produce a wonderful show of double pink blossoms every May. The tree develops like an inverted cone but the branches become more spreading with age. It grows in a wide variety of soils and situations, and is unquestionably one of the best garden trees.

Prunus 'Kiku-shidare sakura'. In contrast to 'Amanogowa' this is the best weeping cherry, with strong pendulous branches covered in double pink blossom. It is fairly easy to grow and tolerates a wide variety of soils and conditions.

Prunus serrula. Tibetan cherry is noted not for a spectacular show of flowers but rather for its delightful bark. This is thin and peeling, to reveal a glossy brown stem that is often described as resembling polished mahogany. The attraction occurs on young trees and increases as they age.

Prunus subhirtella autumnalis. This is an ideal subject to provide that bit of winter cheer in a garden. It begins flowering in November, and whilst it is never as spectacular as other flowering cherries, the display continues intermittently until March. A few sprigs cut and arranged with other winter-flowering shrubs is most pleasurable at Christmas time.

Prunus 'Tai-Haku'. One of my favourite flowering trees is this 'Great White Cherry' of Japan. It has large single white blossoms and coppery leaves. Set against a blue sky in May it really is a sight to behold.

Pyrus salicifolia. Often referred to as weeping grey-leaved pear which describes its colour and pendulous habit; this is one of the best grey-leaved trees for small gardens, and looks well contrasted with the purple-leaved plum. Usually the crown is dense and congested, but occasional thinning will keep the specimen tidy and more open. It will grow to about 25 ft. if a leader is trained upwards on young trees.

Quercus robur. Common or English oak, occasionally finds its way into gardens from acorns planted by children. Oaks are long-lived trees and can become quite large with dimensions greater than 80 ft. tall and often almost as broad. Oaks do not transplant well as large standard trees, and seedlings are preferable. They need to be kept well watered until fully recovered from their transplanting check. I have a certain fondness for our native oaks, but for gardens there are other species which are visually more exciting.

Quercus rubra. Red oak is an American species with large, handsome leaves, which turn reddish and russet-brown colours in autumn. It makes a large tree over 65 ft. tall with a widespreading crown and a tidy branching habit. In springtime it has conspicuous bright, yellow-green, young leaves. This feature is even more spectacular in the cultivar *aurea*, which has bright yellow leaves during May and June, but this is rather a rare tree and may be difficult to obtain.

Quercus coccinea. The scarlet oak is another American species which has scarlet red leaves, and is one of the most impressive trees for autumn colour. It prefers the south of England but there are good specimens in sheltered northern localities.

Rhus typhina. Commonly known as the 'Stag's Horn Sumach'. This tree has large, handsome pinnate leaves like those of an ash tree. These colour bright orange and red in autumn. This architectural foliage is very striking, and the tree lends itself to a foliage border as it only grows between 15–20 ft. high. The cut-leaved cultivar *laciniata* is even more impressive with its fern-like leaves. It will sucker fairly freely if roots are damaged when digging around its base. This is an easy subject and grows well in most localities.

Robinia pseudoacacia. False acacia is an American tree with an open crown, which eventually grows over 65 ft. in height. The pinnate leaves give the tree a distinct, rather delicate texture. In June it bears clusters of white, pea-like flowers. It grows well in adverse conditions tolerating poor dry soils

Malus × purpurea

Malus 'Golden Hornet'

Prunus serrulata 'Kanzan'

Stem of Prunus serrula

Sorbus aria var. chrysophylla

143

Cupressus macrocarpa 'Goldcrest'

Picea pungens or Colorado spruce

Pinus sylvestris or Scots pine

and smoke-polluted atmospheres. The cultivar *frisia* has become a sought-after plant for gardens on account of its bright yellow leaves. Another cultivar *bessoniana* makes a smaller, compact round crown, and is more suitable for small gardens than the type.

Salix alba. A fast-growing tree for moist soils but too vigorous for small gardens as it grows over 65 ft. It has rather attractive silvery-grey leaves.

Salix alba chermesina. This willow has bright orange-red stems, and the plant can be cut back annually to keep it as a multi-stemmed shrub to take advantage of this feature.

Salix alba tristis. This weeping willow is a graceful tree, with long pendulous branchlets which reveal attractive golden bark in winter. It is a beautiful tree for the waterside, and like other willows, it thrives best in moist ground. Frequently it is planted in gardens and close to buildings where it has insufficient room for proper development. A leader should be trained, otherwise it develops a sprawling, congested crown.

Salix matsudana tortuosa. Known as the 'Corkscrew Willow' on account of its unusual twisted branches and leaves. It grows fairly quickly despite its aberration.

Sorbus aria. A native chalkland tree that has much to offer in gardens, especially its cultivars. Visually it starts off the year with greyish-coloured leaves which turn to green by the time the white flowers show in May. By September the flowers have developed into clusters of large orange-red berries which attract birds to the garden. Usually it forms a small dome-shaped tree 20–30 ft. in height. Whilst it prefers chalk or lime soils, it will grow satisfactorily in acid soils. In addition it has good tolerance to polluted town atmospheres and seaside exposure. Notable cultivars include *chrysophylla*, which has yellowish leaves and especially good yellow autumn colour. *Decaisneana*, sometimes listed as *majestica*, has larger leaves and fruits. *Lutescens* has greyish leaves because of a covering of small woolly hairs.

Sorbus aucuparia. This is another splendid tree for small gardens growing 25–35 ft. high with a small oblong crown. Commonly known as the rowan tree or mountain ash. The latter is an appropriate description, as

it grows at elevations of 3000 ft. in Britain and has small ash-like leaves. It grows well on chalk and acid soils, and tolerates polluted town atmospheres. In May, plate-like groups of creamy-white flowers are borne, followed by heavy clusters of scarlet berries in late summer and early autumn. These must be a delicacy to the palate of blackbirds judging by their antics when feeding. The leaves also turn yellow and golden colours in October. Several cultivars are also useful; *fastigiata* has very upright branches and makes an attractive small, narrow, columnar tree. *Xanthocarpa* has yellow fruits.

Sorbus 'Embley'. More widely known as *Sorbus discolor*, this is a small tree up to 35 ft. It is similar in appearance to the rowan tree, except that it does not bear heavy clusters of fruit. This is compensated however by the richness of its orange and fiery scarlet autumn colours.

Sorbus intermedia. The Swedish whitebeam is a very reliable tree for difficult places. It makes a neat dome-shaped crown 35–40 ft. in height when full grown. It does well in exposed situations and in coastal regions, likewise in polluted town atmospheres.

Sorbus vilmorinii. A delightful small sorbus from China growing up to 20 ft. in height. It has miniature, rather delicate ash-shaped leaves, and rosy-pink bead-like fruits which turn white as they get older. It prefers a sheltered site, and makes an excellent courtyard or small garden tree.

Tilia petiolaris. Weeping silver lime is a tree that grows over 65 ft., and therefore is only suitable for the larger garden where it has room to develop. The branchlets are pendent giving it a neat, yet graceful outline. Some of the leaves expose their silvery undersides, hence its common name. In autumn, leaves turn rich yellow. It is not fastidious about soil and it grows well in fairly open situations and towns with polluted atmospheres. Unlike some lime trees this species does not become heavily infested with aphids.

Ulmus glabra. The tragedy of Dutch elm disease has temporarily curtailed the planting of elms in the southern part of Britain, but in areas not affected one can but hope that trees will survive. Wych elm is a large

dome-shaped tree more suited to the rural scene, but some cultivars may find a place in your garden. *Camperdownii* is a distinct weeping form, with very pendulous branches and large handsome leaves. *Pendula* has more spreading branches, but both remain fairly small trees, growing to about 25 ft. *Macrophylla aurea* is a splendid large-leaved golden variant.

Ulmus × sarniensis. Guernsey, Jersey, or Wheatley elm makes a fine conical tree which has light branches, making it suitable for medium-sized gardens. It grows over 65 ft. in height. Unfortunately it is not immune to the ravages of Dutch elm disease. Being a late-leafing tree it is excellent for coastal planting, and for tolerating smoke-polluted atmospheres.

CONIFEROUS TREES

Abies concolor. This is a most impressive tree as a young conifer, with long, blue-green, upswept needles. When open-grown it develops a neat conical crown with branches sweeping to the ground. Like other silver firs it does not do well in towns. Eventually it grows to over 65 ft. in height.

Abies koreana. The Korean silver fir is a slower-growing species eventually reaching 25–30 ft. The main attraction is the purple cone. These are borne in abundance on quite young trees and sit upright on the branches.

Abies procera. Noble fir is really a forest tree, but in the wetter parts of Britain this is an attractive conifer that grows quickly. It eventually reaches over 100 ft., therefore you need a large garden before considering this tree. It bears large pale-green cones which sit upright on the upper branches like rows of baby owls.

Araucaria araucana. Monkey puzzle was such a favourite with Victorian gardeners, but seems very much out of favour at the present time. It is a difficult tree to position in the garden, and often it is planted where there is insufficient room for its development. After a slow start it eventually grows between 65–85 ft. It is quite hardy and tolerates a wide range of soils, but prefers the wetter areas of Britain.

Calocedrus decurrens. One of my favourite conifers is this one, known commonly as the incense cedar. It is quite unlike a cedar, however, and forms a narrow column of bright green foliage which eventually grows over 65 ft. As it is rarely seen in parks I suspect that it does not grow well in own atmospheres. The strong vertical lines of this subject look splendid when several are carefully arranged to form a group.

Cedrus atlantica. The atlas cedar needs a large garden to reach its true grandeur. It is a tall spreading tree over 85 ft. tall and 65 ft. across. The same can be said of the blue-leaved cultivar *glauca*. This eventually grows into a magnificent tree, and people can be forgiven for planting it in medium-sized gardens to obtain 60–80 years of its beauty. Cedars grow satisfactorily in chalky or acid soils, and surprisingly they tolerate smoky town atmospheres reasonably well.

Cedrus deodara. Deodar has a more graceful appearance than the atlas cedar with its flat branching habit and drooping leaders. It is a beautiful tree for a lawn where it will remain furnished to the ground. Like the atlas cedar it will eventually grow into a large tree, so give it plenty of room to develop.

Chamaecyparis lawsoniana. This is undoubtedly the most ubiquitous garden conifer. It seems to grow everywhere in town and country gardens in a great diversity of soils and situations. The common Lawson's cypress makes a fine, narrow, conical tree 60–85 ft. tall. It is an ideal tree for making a tall screen or for providing backgrounds. There are over 200 named cultivars that vary in colour, texture, and shape, from the type. Many are dwarf forms suitable for the miniature landscape of a rock garden. Those which develop into notable garden trees include *glauca*, which is a blue-leaved form; 'Triomf van Boskoop' also has blue-grey foliage, and is a tall-growing conical tree with a more open habit. 'Spek' is a Dutch selection that is one of the really outstanding blue forms. A magnificent cultivar with rich golden-yellow foliage is *stewartii*, whilst *lutea* has brighter yellow leaves; *intertexta* is a really handsome form with flattened, fan-like sprays of foliage giving a very distinct texture. Another distinct medium-sized tree with a spire-like habit is *wisselii*, its branches are covered in short fern-like sprays of dark green, blueish foliage; *potenii* has bright green, feathery foliage and a neat columnar shape.

Chamaecyparis nootkatensis. Nootka cypress is a beautiful species forming a broadly conic crown with graceful pendant sprays of foliage. It grows over 85 ft. in height and is fairly quick growing, especially in the wetter areas of western Britain. It is tolerant of a wide range of soils and conditions. The cultivar *pendula* is even more graceful, with long pendulous shoots. Normally it grows less quickly than the type.

Cupressus macrocarpa. Commonly called Monterey cypress. This is another fast-growing tall tree reaching over 85 ft. in height. It is especially suited to coastal exposure along the south and south-west coasts of Britain. It is, however, subject to frost injury in northern inland areas. It does not transplant very easily and should be planted out when 2 or 3 years old. 'Goldcrest' is a bright, yellow-leaved cultivar which grows into a medium-sized garden tree.

× Cupressocyparis leylandii. This is a hybrid between Nootka cypress and Monterey cypress. It is a fast-growing narrow columnar tree eventually growing up to 100 ft. Its rapid growth is one of its main attributes, as it is excellent for forming a quick screen to give privacy or shelter to a garden. If required it can be clipped to form a hedge. It makes a fine specimen tree, but on account of its rapid growth make sure there is sufficient room for development; very tall trees can look hopelessly out of scale in small suburban gardens.

Ginkgo biloba. This tree is a botanical oddity being neither a hardwood nor a conifer. It has distinct roundish, lobed leaves which colour yellow in autumn. From a distance the leaves resemble maidenhair fern hence its common name of 'Maidenhair Tree'. It is a hardy subject of moderate vigour, which grows over 70 ft. in the south of England. Surprisingly it tolerates polluted town atmospheres. The cultivar *fastigiata* has a very narrow crown suited to small gardens.

Larix kaempferi. Japanese larch is really a forest tree, but its quick growth makes it suitable for forming screens, or acting as protection and nurse for other developing trees. It is also a very beautiful tree, with bright green needles in spring, which turn yellow in autumn. European larch may also be used, but this species is more susceptible to several diseases.

Metasequoia glyptostroboides. The dawn redwood was only known from fossil records until 1941, when a tree was seen in the remote Shui-sha valley of Hupeh province in China. In 1944 a specimen was collected and described, but it was not until 1946 that this remarkable discovery was realised. In 1948 an Arnold Arboretum expedition collected seed and distributed this throughout the world where it has since become one of the most popular garden conifers. It is a highly ornamental, fast-growing deciduous tree, which has reached between 50–60 ft. since its introduction in 1948. It thrives best in moist soil and prefers some shelter. Like the closely related *Taxodium* it has attractive autumn colour.

Picea abies. Norway spruce or Christmas tree is not one of my favourite conifers, but they are frequently seen in gardens as a result of post-Christmas plantings. They are a large, relatively unattractive tree for gardens once they have lost their lower branches.

Picea breweriana. I shall never forget my first impression of this graceful conifer, it really is a gem for gardens, providing you have the space and conditions for it to grow. They prefer a rich, moist soil, but not one which is waterlogged, and preferably a soil which is slightly acid. It is not a tree for chalky soil nor one for polluted town atmospheres. This impressive tree has long drooping branchlets which hang vertically, rather like dark green curtains draped along the branches. It is usually a medium-sized tree about 35 ft., although some specimens have reached 50 ft.

Picea omorika. Serbian spruce from Yugoslavia has a narrow conical crown, with downswept branches which curve upwards at the tips giving it a rather distinct outline. It is an outstanding tree for polluted town atmospheres. Growth is satisfactory on both chalky soils and deep acid soils, and in favoured localities it will reach 60–85 ft. in height.

Picea pungens 'Glauca'. Blue spruce is a beautiful garden tree with intense blue-grey foliage; forming a medium-sized conical tree eventually growing to about 65 ft. It makes a fine subject for lawns where its branches can sweep to the ground. Once established it grows with moderate vigour.

Pinus cembra. Arolla pine is fairly slow-growing, and forms a narrow column of dark green, bushy needles. Eventually it will reach 55 ft. in height. This is a much-neglected garden conifer and one that is not difficult to grow.

Pinus parviflora. This Japanese white pine is said to be the dwarf pine on the famous 'Willow Tree' pattern. It is a tree very reminiscent of Japanese gardens, with its low-growing spreading habit, and short curly needles. Cones are borne profusely along the branches of quite young trees adding to its attraction. Rarely does it grow over 35 ft. in height, making it one of the best pines for smaller gardens.

Pinus sylvestris. Scots pine is one of our three native conifers that is really a highly ornamental tree. When young, they form conical trees with blue-green needles. At this stage they are ideal for screens or shelter planting. Older trees become flat-topped, with a few spreading branches which have a distinct orange-red bark. Whilst having a preference for deep acid soils, Scots pine will grow satisfactorily on chalky soils. Normally they grow up to about 85 ft. I prefer to see them planted in groves; a group of mature Scots pines makes an attractive setting for underplanted rhododendrons.

Taxodium distichum. This originates from the famous Everglades region of Florida, whence it derives its common name of swamp cypress. This remarkable tree can grow with its roots in water and obtain life-sustaining oxygen from special air-breathing roots called pneumatophores. It follows therefore that it prefers moist ground, but good specimens can grow in quite dry conditions. Swamp cypress is a deciduous tree turning to attractive russet tints in the autumn. It usually has a fairly narrow conical habit and will grow to about 65 ft.

Taxus baccata. Common yew is a rather dark sombre tree, reminiscent of churchyards and not really a favourite subject for gardens. It is native to chalkland, but obviously by its wide distribution in Britain it grows well in a wide range of soils and conditions. Being poisonous to stock, it should not be planted adjacent to agricultural land where it is likely to be browsed by animals. When clipped it makes a first-class hedge, and is an ideal subject for formal gardens. In contrast the cultivar *aurea* is a bright golden tree, sprawling out rather like a large shrub. *Fastigiata* is the familiar Irish yew with upright pinnacles of foliage. There is also an attractive golden-leaved variant of this.

Thuja plicata. This is quite a useful screening plant for gardens. Known as the Western red cedar, it makes a broad conical tree when open-grown as a lawn specimen. Growth can be fairly rapid once established, and it will often exceed 80 ft. Being tolerant of shade it can be planted to increase the density of a shelter screen when the lower canopy has become thin. It prefers chalky soil, but will grow quite well on a wide range.

Tsuga mertensiana. Mountain hemlock is a much-neglected garden conifer. It is a beautiful medium-sized conical tree with blue-grey foliage and outward-sweeping branches. In good localities it will grow over 50 ft. in height. They prefer moist, but freely drained soils, which are slightly on the acid side.

MAKING

A FLOWER ARRANGER'S GARDEN

Eileen Poole

The need of any flower arranger is to be able to go out into the garden at any time of year and cut material for the house in the quantity and variety necessary to satisfy the creative demands of the moment.

That this needs careful planning, tight organisation, and skill in selection, goes without saying. But there is one rule which to my mind dominates everything.

This is that it is far more important to grow a wide range of shrubs and plants for foliage, form, and shape, than it is to concentrate on flowers. After all, if your arrangement has a well-organised, attractively shaped and presented background of plant material, a bunch of flowers can always be found to complete it, even if they have to be bought.

Try to buy foliage or plant material at any time of year and you will see my point.

The basis of any good arrangement which gives interest, is the shape, form, texture, colour, and sculptural qualities of the plant material used in it.

You will already be thinking of the long time needed to get suitable shrubs and foliage plants established well enough to allow hard cutting to satisfy your demands, and this is one of the problems. From my own experience I would say that patience

An attractive triangular arrangement of spidery chrysanthemums, with thistles, ornamental kale leaves, and berries to give contrast. The base is polystyrene sheeting on cake pillars.

and restraint are as important as good cultivation in the first year, with most subjects, and for several years with a few. However, if your preliminary cultivation is well done and you allow this settling-in time, your shrubs and other plants should burst into luxurious growth with the right feeding and watering programme.

Ground preparation has already been described, but every arranger should use on the foliage parts of the garden a fertiliser with a high nitrogen content, like dried blood or nitro-chalk, or even large doses of sulphate of ammonia. With plenty of water and feeding like this, you will get the maximum extension growth. In fact the harder you cut the more they will grow.

Whatever the size of your garden, room to accommodate all the shrubs and trees you wish to have will be a problem, so this hard cutting back helps to keep them within your area limit too. Then, when they really get too big, you must be ruthless and grub them, starting all over again. One or two taken out and replaced each year is the way. If you are limited to one tree it should be the copper beech, for cut liberally, with the top regularly taken out and thick stems removed before they become trunks, it can be controlled.

Difficult places in the garden can be used for some of the coarser but vitally useful subjects. For example laurel will thrive almost anywhere, so will the golden privet. Ivy can establish itself in the dust-dry spots, and hang to old and ugly walls, yet give good foliage and beautiful seed heads.

I have not assumed that you will have a small greenhouse, but if you do, it opens the door to a galaxy of foliage all the year round, ranging from the aspidistra, through *Begonia rex* to cacti and succulents, many of whose lovely rosettes of leaves can transform the most humble outdoor material into an exotic scheme. So if you are investing in one, cram it full of subjects which can be cut all the year without too much trouble, and leave the chrysanthemums and other space-taking flowers to the professionals, from whom you can buy half a dozen carnations or whatever at any time of year.

You should have evergreens outside in the garden. I have already mentioned the laurel which also cuts and glycerines into a rich brown texture for winter. Laurustinus has a big variegated leaf. I would put *Choisya ternata* high on any list with its massed rosettes of small shiny dark green leaves, its solid round bush being covered with white blossom in spring.

The holly-leaved barberry (*Mahonia aquifolium*) is a fast rampant grower, which can be cut to death and will still thrust back with its prolific yellow-wooded stems and deep green foliage that turns bronze and crimson in autumn. On acid soil, magnolia and camellia are fine, but are such slow growers.

Although it is advised only for warm areas we have established for 14 years two small

trees of *Eucalyptus*, var. Dalrympleana, providing endless stems throughout the year with attractive bark and grey-blue rounded foliage. Plant out of the north and east wind, and cut back hard to get plenty of young leafy wood. *E. gunnii* is another suitable variety.

Space saving but useful evergreens are *Elaeagnus pungens aureo-variegata* with its attractively green and yellow striped leaves, and *Euonymus fortunei*, a small semi-prostrate shrub with gold green and pink leaves. Others will be found in the tables.

Next in importance is a good range of herbaceous foliage plants to give the widest possible variation in size, shape, texture, and line. And do not stick only to those usually recognised as being for foliage use only. Many plants grown normally for their flowers give lovely leaves as well, from the small early *greigii* tulips to ornamental maize and peonies. These are a matter of personal preference but some are listed here.

Leaves should be chosen which will play not only a part in the arrangement design itself, but will also act as essential screeners of the 'works' or 'mechanics' used to build the arrangement. Where, for example, would the line arrangement in a shallow container be without them?

Most important here I place items like hostas. Grow the biggest range possible, selecting with care to include the white and yellow wavy-edged types as well as the huge *fortunei*. Their lilac-coloured flowers are useful in summer too. Especially important is their ability to produce sufficient leaves to disguise the heaviest raids with flower scissors. Bergenia is next in importance, for besides being a lovely spring-flowering garden plant, its huge leathery leaves are glossy green in summer and burnished red and copper in autumn and winter. They are the best-tempered arrangement material I know, lasting a month or more in water.

These two subjects will grow well in paved areas, as well as in the open ground where most of the other 'leaves' are happy in the conventional herbaceous border or island beds of various shapes. Place, where they are easily accessible during all seasons, the grey *Ballotta* with its tiered rosettes of leaves, the pinkish-tinged *Tellima*, furry grey-green *Verbascum*, the erect and spiky *Acanthus* and the tall *Bocconia* with silver burnished leaves and interesting coppery plumes.

All these will stand regular cutting, but to obtain the masses of foliage that the normal arranger requires, the ground in which they are grown must be really well cared for. Deeply moved soil with plenty of humus incorporated, watered well and regularly with a high nitrogen fertiliser for rapid growth, will ensure that the plants respond all season through with thrusting growth. A word of warning, though. The balance between nitrogen and potash in the fertiliser must be kept, for with too much of the former, the leaves in their lush growth will

Two more types of arrangement. Left : A diagonal arrangement of pom-pom dahlias and decorative clematis seed-heads. The shallow container stands on a polished wood base. Right : A dried arrangement of corn, nicandra, poppy and nigella seed-heads, dried hydrangea heads, and Chinese lanterns.

lose some of the colour for which you are growing them. Therefore after the boost with straight nitrogen, such as dried blood, early in the year, a fertiliser containing potash should be used.

Other foliage plants can be grown as screeners (the ivy 'Glacier' for example), and of course the clematis with its startling blooms, attractive leaves, and seed heads in autumn.

The colour grey is vital, especially as most of the standby plants in this colour will thrive in dry poor soil, or garden hot spots where nothing else takes off. Most are low-growing or mat-forming, some are shrubby, purely herbaceous, but all in my list can be hacked to pieces and recover in the space of a week or two with never a sign at any time of the onslaught.

Starting with the bigger *Senecio greyii*, whose yellow flowers make it a dual purpose plant, through *Cineraria maritima* with its furry texture and incredible growth rate, down to the matted ground cover of *Chrysanthemum poterifolium*, all can provide material for twelve months without fail, as well as highlighting their place in the garden for the same period.

But enough of all the background materials. The focus of most arrangements must be flowers, and here the arranger is torn in two. Some of the most striking blooms are not cut-and-come-again types, as for example lilies and gladioli. Yet their usefulness should mean their inclusion in the arranger's garden.

Since many of the more spectacular blooms used in arranging are treated as annual plants or crops, we must have two distinctly different approaches to flowers in the garden.

For the plants which are perennial – and among these I include all the bulbs in spite of having to dig them up and replant every year or so – there is a place in the garden proper. The roses, delphiniums, gloriosas, rudbeckias and border chrysanthemums, the shasta daisies and achillea, along with all those other welcome cutting flowers, have their place in the herbaceous border, rose bed, or shrubbery, either for ground cover, interest points, or pot plants.

The remainder, treated as annuals, need to be grown purely for the scissors, where their unsightliness after cutting will not

matter. They can, of course, be dotted about among the border plants but I find this inhibits growth and makes servicing them difficult.

Therefore I have a strip alongside the vegetable garden, 1 yd. wide and 30 ft. long, beside a concrete path in which all these are produced. At either end I have permanent metal posts between which I set my sweet peas for a 15-ft. row. These I treat specially, growing on single stems, nipping out all the side shoots as they occur, and tying them in to canes. In this way they produce giant flower spikes with 4 and 5 blooms on 12-in. stems in profusion.

The remaining 15 ft. takes my dahlias, which need the permanent support. They are set too close together really, but with generous feeding and constant cutting they flood me with blooms – pom-poms, decoratives, cactus, and the rest – from July to November. Behind the sweet peas, too close for comfort, I have six early and six October-flowering chrysanthemums, to disbud for large heads, as a change from the spray types in the border. A line of gladioli and Dutch iris completes this second row with, in both cases, the bulbs being set so close that they touch each other, which gives both mass production and support.

The remainder of the ground takes annuals raised from seed; green love-lies-bleeding, green zinnias, green tobacco plants, freesia corms, three sweet william plants, three pyrethrums and then a small space for trials of new things every year.

This plot kept well watered and fertilised and constantly tended is my snipping ground, producing flowers for cutting over the longest possible period. Its output is surprising, keeping not only my own home regularly supplied but helping me with church flowers, for social events, friends' weddings, and so on.

It is a highly individual plot, and I have described it in some detail because I am sure that the principle can be applied and adapted to suit any taste or requirement. The path alongside is a prime point. On it I can stand my cutting bucket and plunge all the flowers deeply from the moment of taking, even in the pouring rain. The other point is the denseness of planting which suppresses all weed growth, the few which do intrude being easily pulled up.

Roses are a special subject in themselves and have elsewhere been dealt with in great detail. The arranger requires three things from them: first, good blooms which will stand several days in water after cutting, and this means lots of petals; second, good and interesting foliage; third, striking hips (heps) which in winter are top value. This really means finding room for one or two shrub roses in addition to hybrid teas and floribundas, and any good catalogue will help here. My choice would be 'Roserai de l'Hay' and 'Blanc Double de Coubert' and one of the moss species.

Seed heads, berries, and fruit, are a main ingredient of winter arrangements and the list of plants has been drawn up to provide plenty of interest here. Most of the shrub berries can be cut during their season and will stand for long periods. Subjects like *Iris foetidissima* which reveals bright orange seed as the pods containing them split, require little assistance to stay beautiful.

For the rest, drying is needed, and I grow only those which will give results by simply hanging them upside down in a warm atmosphere (above the domestic boiler is perfect). Here the annuals like helichrysum and acroclinium, the perennials like golden rod and achillea take on their preserved nature for winter use along with the tassels of the love-lies-bleeding, and bells of Ireland. There are more difficult techniques using silica gel in air-tight containers for preserving flowers in their natural colours but these are outside the needs of the general arranger. When these are added to the wild-gathered giant hog weed, dock, and other items, a massive collection can be built and stored along with the glycerined leaves of shrubs and trees.

With a greenhouse, foliage and flowers, like geraniums, can be kept going all year but even in the average house there is room for a few plants to give luxuriantly. A warm north-facing windowsill will accommodate several pots of *Begonia rex* and aspidistra which can be cut regularly.

There now follows five tables which have been specially designed to give the maximum help to the flower arranger. Table 1, for example, groups subjects by colour, and in addition to saying when available, gives the cutting height and the length of time that one can expect each to last. The

Hosta, Alchemilla, and Sedums growing together

Euphorbia 'Chariacus'

Mixed chrysanthemums

Dahlia 'Redskin', mixed

second table deals with trees and shrubs and indicates how each item can be used by the flower arranger.

The next two tables list, with descriptive notes, plants which provide attractive foliage and those which can be preserved by drying. The last table is one for quick reference. Plants referred to already in the previous tables are here listed in alphabetical order under the *month* when the flower arranger will find them of most use.

Cultural notes for a number of the plants listed will be found on p. 244. Regarding the times for blooming and duration of cut life, there can be quite considerable variation according to the geographical situation, and the weather in any one season. Therefore they should be taken only as a guide.

FLOWERS FOR CUTTING AND ARRANGING GROUPED UNDER COLOUR
GREEN

Name	Cut height	Time	Cut life	Remarks
Alchemilla (*A. mollis*)	2 ft	June–Aug	1 week +	Sulphur green
Bells of Ireland	2 ft	June–Aug	1 month	Very difficult to germinate; can take weeks
Euphorbia (*E. wulfenii & epithymoides*)	1–2 ft	Mar–May	2–3 weeks	Invaluable for colour and foliage; rampant growth
Helleborus (*H. foetidus & corsicus*)	1–1½ ft	Mar–May	1–2 weeks	Fine when there is little else
Kniphofia	1–2 ft	Aug–Sept	1 week	For those unusual exotic designs
Love-lies-bleeding	1½ ft	June–Aug	1 month	Huge greeny white tassels which remain intact
Zinnia	1 ft	June–Aug	1 week	Envy, is the variety

MIXED COLOURS

Name	Cut height	Time	Cut life	Remarks
Alstroemeria	2 ft	June–Aug	5–10 days	The new hybrids
Anemone (corm)	6 ins	Mar–May	1 week	Long drink needed
Antirrhinum	6–24 ins	June–Aug	1 week +	Usefulness depends on variety
Aquilegia	2 ft	June–Aug	5–10 days	Newer hybrids
Aster	18 ins	Aug	5–10 days	In variety
Candytuft	6–12 ins	June–Aug	1 week	In variety
Carnations	18–24 ins	year round	1 week or more	Wide range of uses. Can be dyed to suit as well
Chrysanthemum (florist types)	4 ft	Sept–Nov or year round	2–3 weeks	Range from huge japs to small sprays
Dahlias	1–4 ft	June–Nov	1–2 weeks	Many different varieties
Gladiolus	3 ft	June–Nov	2 weeks	Remove blooms as they fade
Primula	2 ins–3 ft	Mar–Aug	1 week	Huge family, many types
Ranunculus	12 ins	May–Aug	1 week	Get good mixture
Roses	12 ins	May–Nov	5 days	In variety; get good cutting types from catalogues
Stocks	18 ins	Mar–Aug	1 week	In variety
Sweet peas	12 ins	June–Aug	1 week	In variety; long season
Sweet william	12 ins	May–July	2 weeks	In variety; long season

WHITE				
Name	**Cut height**	**Time**	**Cut life**	**Remarks**
Anemone (*A. japonica*)	to 3 ft	Sept–Nov	1 week	Useful for added height
Aquilegia	2 ft	June–July	1 week	Newer hybrids only
Aster	18 ins	Aug	5–10 days	In variety
Canterbury bells	3 ft	June–Aug	1 week +	In variety
Carnation	2 ft	year round	1 week	Wide range of uses
Chrysanthemum (florist types)	4 ft	Sept–Nov or year round	2–3 weeks	Range from huge japs to small sprays
Chrysanthemum (*C. maximum*)	3 ft	Sept–Nov	1–2 weeks	Several useful varieties
Daffodil	1 ft	Mar–May	5–7 days	In variety
Dahlia	1–4 ft	June–Nov	1–2 weeks	Many different varieties
Galtonia	to 2 ft	June–Aug	1 week	Summer snowdrop – dangling bells for special uses
Gladiolus	to 3 ft	June–Nov	2 weeks or more	Great standby for pedestals; remove blooms up stem as they fade
Helleborus (*H. niger* and *orientalis*)	2–12 ins	Dec–May	1–15 days	Gorgeous; temperamental indoors
Hyacinth	6 ins	Dec–May	7–10 days	For special uses
Iris (bulb)	6–8 ins	May	1–2 weeks	Arrange with the leaves
Iris (bearded)	2½ ft	June–Aug	1–2 weeks	Remove blooms as they fade
Lily (madonna)	5 ft	June–Aug	1 week +	Full sun; don't move
Paeony (*P. lactiflora*)	18 ins	June	3–7 days	Care needed with heavy flower heads
Phlox	to 3 ft	June–Aug	1 week	
Primulas	2 ins–3 ft	Mar–Aug	1 week	Huge family, many types
Pyrethrum	2 ft	May–June	1 week +	Under-rated; useful
Solomon's Seal	to 3 ft	May–June	1 week	Unusual interest
Stocks	18 ins	Mar–Aug	1–2 weeks	In variety by season
Sweet pea	to 12 ins	Mar–Aug	up to 1 week	In variety; long season
Tulips	to 18 ins	Mar–May	1 week	In variety
Zinnia	to 18 ins	June–Aug	1 week +	In variety

A typical decorative type dahlia

Bearded iris 'Cliffs of Dover'

Lilium candidum or madonna lily

Hyacinth 'L'Innocence'

Primula japonica

Paeonia lactiflora, the so-called Chinese paeony

Campanula latifolia

Flowers of delphinium 'Melissa Hope'

Scabious 'Clive Greaves'

BLUE AND MAUVE				
Name	Cut height	Time	Cut life	Remarks
Acanthus	3 ft	June–July	1–3 weeks	Unusual; fine spikes
Aconitum	3 ft	July–Aug	up to 1 week	Large erect flower spike substitute for delphinium
Allium	to 12 ins	June–Aug	1–2 weeks	Effective for modern arrangements
Anemone (*A. pulsatilla*)	6 ins	Mar–May	up to 1 week	Good long drink up to neck
Anemone (corm)	6 ins	Mar–May	1 week	Good long drink up to neck
Asters	18 ins	June–Aug	5–10 days	In variety
Campanula and Canterbury Bells	to 3 ft	June–Aug	1 week +	Many varieties; small to huge bells, cup and saucer
Clary	to 1 ft	June–Aug	to 2 weeks	Brilliant bracts
Clematis	stem 4 ins	June–Aug	to 1 week	Fine for placement and spot effects
Cobaea (*C. scandens*)	6 ins	June–Aug	to 1 week	Rampant climber, bell flowers of great interest and use
Cornflower	8 ins	June–Aug	to 1 week	Brilliant colour
Dahlias	1–4 ft	June–Nov	1–2 weeks	Many different varieties
Delphinium	to 5 ft	June–Aug	to 2 weeks	Plunge in water on cutting
Echinops	3 ft	June–Aug	to 3 weeks	Globe thistle; round head, downy leaves
Eryngium	2–3 ft	June–Aug	to 3 weeks	Dries naturally when in an arrangement
Gladiolus	to 3 ft	June–Nov	2 weeks	Great standby in variety
Iris (bulb)	6–8 ins	Mar–May	1–2 weeks	
Iris (bearded)	2½ ft	June–Aug	1–2 weeks	Remove blooms as they fade
Liatris	2 ft	Sept	1 week +	Flowers in 15 in. spikes
Lily (*L. martagon*)	3–6 ft	July	1 week +	Lovely true lily flowers
Lupins	to 2 ft	June–Aug	up to 1 week +	Invert and fill hollow stem with water before using
Meconopsis	3 ft	June–Aug	to 1 week	Singe stem before using
Michaelmas daisy	to 2 ft	Sept–Nov	1–2 weeks	
Phlox	3 ft	June–Aug	1 week	Round heads for mass effect
Primulas	2 ins–3 ft	Mar–Aug	1 week	Huge family, many types
Scabious	2–3 ft	June–Oct	to 1 week	
Stocks	18 ins	Mar–Aug	1–2 weeks	In variety by season
Sweet peas	to 12 ins	June–Aug	1 week	In variety; long season
Verbascum	5 ft	June–Aug	1 week +	Violet flowers; hairy leaves
Veronica	18 ins	June–Aug	1 week	Wide variety; lovely shades

PINKS TO REDS				
Name	**Cut height**	**Time**	**Cut life**	**Remarks**
Allium	to 12 ins	June–Aug	1–2 weeks	
Antirrhinum	6–24 ins	June–Aug	1 week +	Usefulness depends on variety
Aquilegia	2 ft	June–Aug	5–10 days	Newer hybrids only
Asters	18 ins	June–Aug	5–10 days	In variety
Astilbe	to 12 ins	June–Aug	1 week +	Wide range of shades
Candytuft	to 1 ft	June–Aug	1 week	Good for small arrangements
Chrysanthemum (florist types)	4 ft	Sept–Nov or year round	2–3 weeks	Range from huge japs to small sprays
Clarkia	1–3 ft	June–Aug	3–5 days	For points in large arrangements
Dahlia	1–4 ft	June–Nov	1–2 weeks	Many different varieties
Dianthus	6 ins–1 ft	June–Aug	1 week	Flower heads for infilling
Dicentra	2 ft	Apr–May	1 week +	Arching sprays
Eremurus	to 8 ft	June	1–2 weeks	Unusual flowers; spikes to 3 ft. long
Geranium (pelargonium)	stem only	June–Aug or year round	1–2 weeks	Splashes of red at any time from greenhouse
Gladiolus	to 3 ft	June–Nov	2 weeks	Remove blooms from stem as they fade; in variety
Helichrysum	3–4 ft	June–Aug	ever-lasting	Dry too for winter
Lilies	2–6 ft	June–Nov	1–2 weeks	For opulence; wide range of varieties and types
Nerine	2 ft	Oct	1 week	Dainty, lily-like
Paeony	18 ins	June	3–7 days	Care needed with heavy flower heads
Penstemon	2 ft	June–Aug	1 week +	Range of types and varieties
Phlox	to 3 ft	June–Aug	1 week	
Polygonum (knotweed)	1–4 ft	June–Aug	2 weeks +	Easy to grow
Primulas	2 ins–3 ft	Mar–Aug	1 week	Huge family, many types
Pyrethrum	2 ft	May–June	1 week +	Under-rated; useful
Red hot poker	3–7 ft	Aug–Sept	1 week	Exotic; useful for modern or abstract designs
Salpiglossis	18 ins	June–Aug	1 week	Exotic, multicoloured
Salvia	1 ft	June–Aug	1 week	Fantastic colour
Sidalcea	2½ ft	June–Aug	2–5 days	Useful for large short-life arrangements
Stocks	18 ins	Mar–Aug	1–2 weeks	In variety by season
Sweet peas	to 12 ins	June–Aug	1 week	In variety; long season
Tulips	to 18 ins	Mar–May	1–2 weeks	In variety

Aster callistephus 'Ostrich Plume'

Phlox paniculata or garden phlox

Salpiglossis

Chrysanthemum 'Golden Julie Anne'

Kniphofia uvaria or red-hot poker

Narcissus triandrus alba 'Angels' Tears'

YELLOW TO ORANGE				
Name	**Cut height**	**Time**	**Cut life**	**Remarks**
Achillea	3–4 ft	June–Aug	1 month	Large heads for autumn pedestals to stand a long time
Alstroemeria	2 ft	June–Aug	5–10 days	Difficult to establish but rampant when it is
Chrysanthemum (florist types)	to 4 ft	Sept–Nov or year round	2–3 weeks	Range from huge japs to small sprays
Crocosmia (includes montbretia)	18 ins	Aug	5–10 days	Use improved forms only
Daffodils	to 1 ft	Mar–May	5–7 days	In variety
Dahlias	1–4 ft	June–Nov	1–2 weeks	Many different varieties
Doronicum	1–2 ft	Mar–May	7–10 days	Very useful; grow like weeds
Fritillaria (Crown Imperial)	to 2 ft	Mar–May	1 week +	Sensational
Iris (bulb)	6–8 ins	Mar–May	1–2 weeks	Arrange with foliage attached
Iris (bearded)	2½ ft	June	1–2 weeks	Remove blooms as they fade
Kniphofia	3–7 ft	Aug–Sept	1 week	Useful for modern or abstract designs
Lilies	2–6 ft	June–Nov	1–2 weeks	For opulence; wide range of varieties and types
Lupin	2 ft	June–Aug	up to 1 week	Invert and fill hollow stem with water before using
Narcissus	1 ft	Mar–May	7–10 days	Many types and varieties
Physalis	2½–3 ft	Sept–Nov	1 month	Orange lanterns; lasts almost permanently and dries
Primulas	2 ins–3 ft	Mar–Aug	1 week +	Huge family, many types
Rudbeckia (inc. gloriosa daisies)	2½ ft	June–Nov	1–2 weeks	Rampant grower; huge blooms
Solidago (golden rod)	3–4 ft	Sept–Nov	2–3 weeks	Be ruthless chopping back, or will take over garden
Trollius	18 ins	May–June	1 week +	Large double buttercups
Verbascum	5 ft	June–Aug	1 week +	Large hairy leaves and stems
Zinnia	18 ins	June–Aug	1 week +	In variety

Zinnia 'Sprite' mixed

Narcissus pseudonarcissus, the large trumpeted garden daffodil

SHRUBS AND TREES

Name	Tree or shrub	Reason for use	Time
Acer (Japanese maple)	tree	Colourful finely cut leaf	Mar–Aug
Azalea	shrub	Delicate colourful bloom heads	Mar–May
Beech (copper)	tree	Invaluable copper foliage	all year
Berberis (*B. darwinii*)	shrub	All year foliage, bronze in autumn and winter; yellow flowers spring; autumn berries	all year
Berberis (*B. stenophylla*)	shrub	Long sprays, yellow flowers	Mar–May
Broom	shrub	Long stems can be curved for line arrangements	all year
Buddleia	shrub	Long arching spikes of purple and lilac blooms	June–Aug
Ceanothus	shrub	Heads of fluffy blue bloom	June–Aug
Chaenomeles	tree	Gorgeous red, orange bloom	Mar–May
Choisya (Mexican orange blossom)	shrub	Glossy green, useful leaf heads of scented white 'orange blossom'	all year
Conifers	trees & dwarf trees	Huge family of evergreen cone-bearing trees in all shapes and sizes. Vital for cutting	year round
Cornus	tree	All varieties have attractive leaves and stems	June–Aug
Cotoneaster	trees & shrubs	Large family from fishbone horizontalis to large cornubia; all have flowers and berries. Most last well	most of year
Elaeagnus	shrub	Bright yellow and green variegated leaves	Dec–Feb
Erica	shrubs	Large family suited to all soils and seasons; for cutting sprays of bells	all year
Escallonia	shrub	For crimson flower spikes and glossy foliage; lasts well in water	all year
Euonymus	shrub	Var. fortunei has greyish green, margined white leaf, most others large fruit or seeds	Dec–Feb
Forsythia	shrub	Lynwood var. forces well indoors in winter and cuts for spring flower backing	Mar–May
Garrya (*G. eliptica*)	shrub	Long pale silver-green catkins. Lasts well cut	Dec–Feb
Hamamelis (witch hazel)	shrub	Fragrant feathery blooms in winter; only grow if you can wait years for establishment	Dec–Feb
Hebe (veronica)	shrub	Pointed sprays, blue bloom	June–Aug
Hedera (ivy)	climber	Useful leaves; heads of black berries	Sept–Feb
Hydrangea	shrub	Large heads of colourful bloom. Lasts very well	June–Nov
Jasmine	climber	Sprays of yellow stars	Dec–Feb
Laurel	shrub	Dark green foliage	all year
Lilac	tree	Huge pointed bloom heads	Mar–May
Magnolia	tree	Exotic blooms; glossy evergreen foliage; needs acid soil	Mar–May
Philadelphus	shrub	Scented white flowers. Lasts well in water	June–Aug
Pieris	shrub	Green rosettes of leaves, red when new; evergreen; white bell flowers spring. Lime free soil. Lasts well	Mar–May
Privet (golden & silver)	shrub	Large branches of gold or silver foliage for backgrounds	all year
Pyracantha (firethorn)	shrub	Masses of scarlet berries	Sept–Nov
Rhododendron	shrub	Large blooms, glossy green and many other leaf forms. Evergreen	Mar–May

Berberis thunbergii erecta

Ceanothus hybrid

Forsythia × intermedia

Hebe ochraceae

Continued on page 154

Rhododendron fastuosum

Viburnum tomentosum

Begonia rex 'Colour Vision'

Bergenia cordifolia

SHRUBS AND TREES (cont'd)

Rhus (smoke tree)	shrub	Copper form has lovely leaves and wispy smokey flowers	June–Aug
Ribes (flowering currant)	shrub	Branches of small pink blooms will force indoors	Mar–May
Roses (hybrid tea floribunda & shrub)	shrubs	Select and plant according to taste and needs; they cover most flower forms; leaf and fruit uses	June–Aug
Senecio (*S. greyii*)	shrub	Silver foliage; small yellow flowers in summer	all year
Skimmia	shrub	Brilliant red berries, glossy foliage	Sept–Nov
Sorbus (includes mountain ash and whitebeams)	trees	Mountain ash has clusters of berries in autumn; whitebeams have white-surfaced leaves which turn grey green	Mar–Nov
Spiraea	shrub	Useful spikes for outlines	Mar–Aug
Viburnum	shrub	Large family; fragrans is winter bloomer	all year
Willow (*Salix tortuosa*)	tree	This contorted willow has fantastically shaped branches suitable for modern abstract designs	all year
Winter cherry (*Prunus subhirtella autumnalis*)	tree	Sprays of white flowers during winter	Dec–Feb
Wisteria	climber	Long racemes of fragrant blue bloom	Mar–May

FOLIAGE

Name	Description	Time
Acanthus	Large mauve spikes	June to Aug and then dried
Alchemilla (*A. mollis*)	Round leaves and long feathery flower sprays complement showy flowers	May–June
Artemisia	Silvery grey, finely cut leaves; profuse growth	June–Aug
Aspidistra	Large strap leaves plain green and variegated	From greenhouse pot or indoors; year round
Atriplex (mountain spinach)	Large burgundy-coloured leaves on tough stems; grows anywhere anyhow	June–Aug
Ballotta	Rosettes of grey-green leaves	June–Nov
Begonia (*B. rex*)	One of the most useful, coming in many shapes, colours, and sizes of leaf.	From greenhouse or indoors in pots all year. Immerse under water for 1 day before arranging
Bergenia	Huge round shiny green leaves in summer, burnished copper in autumn	year round
Bocconia	Large silvery grey leaves for use singly or on stem	Aug–Sept
Crambe	Huge heavily lobed leaves	June–Aug
Euphorbia	Most varieties have large rosettes of leaves	Mar–Aug
Hosta	Many different varieties of varying leaf shapes and colours	May–Aug
Ivy	Variegated forms like Glacier	all year
Paeony	Leaves good in summer and blood red in autumn	June–Nov
Stachys (*S. lanata*)	Lambs ears. White woolly leaves and stems	all year
Tellima	Mats of round hairy leaves which are splashed red in winter	June–Feb
Verbascum	Several sorts; downy grey leaves or green	June–Aug
Zea (ornamental maize)	Striped strap leaves, very effective	June–Aug

Name	Cut height	Season	Comments
MATERIAL FOR PRESERVING			
Achillea	3–4 ft	June–Aug	Hang upside down out of sun to dry. Bright gold heads
Acroclinium	6–12 ins	June–Aug	Flowers easily from seed; blooms dry well with papery texture. Delicate pastel shades
Amaranthus (love-lies-bleeding)	1 ft	June–Aug	Hang upside down to dry
Anaphalis	to 1 ft	June–Aug	Hang upside down to dry
Artemisia	1 ft	June–Aug	Hang upside down out of sun to dry. Bright gold heads
Beech	as needed	June–Aug	Preserve in glycerine (2 g. to 1 water) by standing in jar until leaves look glossy
Bells of Ireland	2 ft	June–Aug	Hang upside down to dry shell-like flower sheaths until they become cream, or glycerine method
Eryngium	2–3 ft	June–Aug	Hang upside down to dry
Eucalyptus	as needed	June–Aug	Will dry, but better preserved with glycerine mixture
Helichrysum	18 ins	June–Aug	Cut before fully open and hang upside down out of sun in cool
Honesty (lunaria)	18 ins	Sept–Nov	Cut and hang when seed pods form and remove sheath for silver discs to show
Hydrangea	1 ft	Sept–Nov	Cut heads and stand in 1 in. of water when green; leave until petals go papery
Laurel	2 ft	June–Aug	Treat in glycerine until brown
Physalis	18 ins–2 ft	Sept–Nov	Hang upside down to dry out red lanterns
Solidago	3 ft	Sept–Nov	Hang upside down
Statice (sea lavendar)	1 ft	June–Aug	Hang upside down

A wide range of flowers, leaves, branches and seed-heads can be dried for winter use. This is merely a selection of the easiest and most useful.

Hydrangea macrophylla

A fine show of rose hips on Rosa coriifolia

Aralia elegantissima, grown for its elegant foliage both on the plant and in arrangements

Osmunda regalis, the royal fern, a decorative plant with notable autumn colour

MONTH WHEN AVAILABLE FOR FLOWER ARRANGING			
fl = FLOWER sh = SHRUB t = TREE fol = FOLIAGE			

January	February	March	April
Aspidistra (fol)	Aspidistra (fol)	Aspidistra (fol)	Anemone (fl)
Begonia rex (fol)	*Begonia rex* (fol)	*Begonia rex* (fol)	Aspidistra (fol)
Berberis darwinii (fol, sh)	*Berberis darwinii* (fol)	*Berberis darwinii* (fol)	*Begonia rex* (fol)
Bergenia (fol)	Bergenia (fol)	Bergenia (fol)	Bergenia (fol, fl)
Broom (sh)	Broom (sh)	Broom (sh)	Broom (sh)
Choisya ternata (sh)	*Choisya ternata* (sh)	*Choisya ternata* (sh)	*Choisya ternata* (sh)
Chrysanthemum (fl)	Conifers (t)	Conifers (t)	Conifers (t)
Conifers (t)	Elaeagnus (sh)	Daffodil (fl)	Daffodil (fl)
Elaeagnus (sh)	*Euonymus fortunei* (sh)	Elaeagnus (sh)	Doronicum (fl)
Euonymus fortunei (sh)	*Garrya eliptica* (sh)	*Euonymus fortunei* (sh)	Elaeagnus (sh)
Garrya eliptica (sh)	*Hamamelis mollis* (fl)	Forsythia (sh)	*Euonymus fortunei* (sh)
Hamamelis mollis (fl)	Hedera (ivy) (sh)	*Garrya eliptica* (sh)	*Euphorbia epithymoides* (fl)
Hedera (ivy) (sh)	Hellebores (fl)	*Hamamelis mollis* (fl)	Forsythia (sh)
Hellebores (fl)	*Jasmine nudiflorum* (sh)	Hedera (ivy) (sh)	Fritillaria (fl)
Jasmine nudiflorum (sh)	Laurel (sh)	Hellebores (fl)	*Garrya eliptica* (sh)
Laurel (sh)	Privet (sh)	*Jasmine nudiflorum* (sh)	*Hamamelis mollis* (fl)
Privet (sh)	*Prunus autumnalis* (t)	Laurel (sh)	Hedera (ivy) (sh)
Prunus autumnalis (t)	*Senecio greyii* (sh)	Primulas (fl)	Hellebores (fl)
Senecio greyii (sh)	Tellima (fol)	Privet (sh)	Hyacinth (fl)
Tellima (fol)	*Viburnum fragrans* (sh)	*Prunus autumnalis* (t)	*Jasmine nudiflorum* (sh)
Viburnum fragrans (sh, fl)	Willow, contorta (t)	Ribes (flowering currant) (sh)	Laurel (sh)
Willow, contorta (t)		*Senecio greyii* (sh)	Pieris (sh)
		Tulips, early (fl)	Primulas (fl)
			Privet (sh)
			Prunus autumnalis (t)
			Ribes (flowering currant) (sh)
			Senecio greyii (sh)
			Stachys lanata (fol)
			Stocks, brompton (fl)
			Tulips (fl)

May	June	July	August
Anemone (fl)	Acanthus (fl, fol)	Acanthus (fl, fol)	Acanthus (fl, fol)
Azalea (sh, fl)	Acer (t, fol)	Acer (t, fol)	Achillea (fl)
Beech, copper (t)	Achillea (fl)	Achillea (fl)	Aconitum (fl)
Berberis stenophylla (sh)	Alchemilla (fol, fl)	Aconitum (fl)	Acroclinium (fl)
Chaenomeles (t)	Allium (fl)	Alchemilla (fl)	Alchemilla (fol)
Choisya (sh)	Antirrhinum (fl)	Allium (fl)	Allium (fl)
Conifers (t)	Aquilegia (fl)	Alstroemeria (fl)	Amaranthus (fl)
Daffodils, late (fl)	Astilbe (fl)	Antirrhinum (fl)	Antirrhinum (fl)
Dicentra spectabilis (fl)	Azalea (sh, fl)	Aquilegia (fl)	Aquilegia (fl)
Erica (fl)	Broom (sh)	Artemisia (fol)	Artemisia (fol)
Escallonia (sh)	Campanula (fl)	Aster (fl)	Aster (fl)
Euphorbia (sh, fl)	Candytuft (fl)	Astilbe (fl)	Atriplex (fol)
Hedera (ivy) (fol)	Ceanothus (sh, fl)	Atriplex (fol)	Ballotta (fol)
Iris (bulb) (fl)	Clarkia (fl)	Buddleia (sh, fl)	Bocconia (fol)
Iris, bearded (fl)	Clary (fl, fol)	Candytuft (fl)	Buddleia (fl, sh)
Laurel (sh, fol)	Clematis (fl)	Canterbury Bell (fl)	Ceanothus (fl, sh)
Lilac (fl)	Conifers (fol, t)	Ceanothus (sh, fl)	Chrysanthemum (fl)
Magnolia (t, fl)	Cotoneaster (sh, fol)	Clarkia (fl)	Crambe (fol)
Polygonatum (fl, fol)	Delphinium (fl)	Clary (fl)	Crocosmia (fl)
Primulas (fl)	Dianthus (fl)	Conifers (t)	Dahlias (fl)
Privet (sh)	Echinops (fol)	Dahlias (fl)	Gladiolus (fl)
Pyrethrum (fl)	Eremurus (fl)	Delphinium (fl)	Honesty (fl, fol)
Ranunculus (fl)	Eryngium (fol)	Dianthus (fl)	Hosta (fol)
Rhododendron (fl, fol)	Escallonia (sh)	Echinops (fol)	Hydrangea (fl, fol)
Roses (fl, sh)	Gladiolus (fl)	Eryngium (fol)	Kniphofia (fl)
Senecio greyii (fol)	Hebe (veronica) (sh)	Galtonia (fl)	Lilies (fl)
Sorbus (t, fol)	Helichrysum (fl)	Gladiolus (fl)	Love-lies-bleeding (fl)
Spiraea (fl)	Iris, bearded (fl)	Hebe (veronica) (fl)	Michaelmas daisy (fl)
Stachys lanata (fol)	Liatris (fl)	Helichrysum (fl)	Penstemon (fl)
Stocks (fl)	Lilies (fl)	Honesty (fol)	Phlox (fl)

Continued on page 157

May (cont'd)	June (cont'd)	July (cont'd)	August (cont'd)
Trollius (fl)	Lupin (fl)	Hosta (fol)	Polygonum (fl)
Tulips (fl)	Molucella (fl, fol)	Hydrangea (fl)	Roses (fl)
Viburnum (sh, fl)	Paeony (fl)	Liatris (fl)	Rudbeckia (fl)
Wisteria (sh)	Penstemon (fl)	Lilies (fl)	Solidago (fl)
	Polygonum (fl)	Love-lies-bleeding (fl)	Stocks (fl)
	Primulas (fl)	Lupin (fl)	Sweet peas (fl)
	Pyrethrum (fl)	Meconopsis (fl)	Verbascum (fol)
	Ranunculus (fl)	Penstemon (fl)	Zea (maize) (fol)
	Rhododendron (fl, sh)	Philadelphus (fl, sh)	Zinnia (fl)
	Rhus continus (fol, sh)	Phlox (fl)	
	Roses (fl)	Physalis (fl)	
	Salpiglossis (fl)	Polygonum (fl)	
	Salvia (fl)	Primulas (fl)	
	Scabious (fl)	Ranunculus (fl)	
	Sidalcea (fl)	Rudbeckia (fl)	
	Spiraea (sh, fl)	*Rhus cotinus* (sh)	
	Sweet peas (fl)	Roses (fl)	
		Sidalcea (fl)	
		Solidago (fl)	
		Spiraea (fl, sh)	
		Stocks (fl)	
		Sweet peas (fl)	
		Verbascum (fl, fol)	
		Zinnia (fl)	

September	October	November	December
Ballotta (fol)	Ballotta (fol)	Azalea (fol, sh)	*Berberis darwinii* (fl, sh, fol)
Bocconia (fol)	Bergenia (fol)	*Berberis darwinii* (sh)	Bergenia (fol)
Chrysanthemum (fl)	Bocconia (fol)	Broom (sh)	Broom (sh)
Cimicifuga (fol)	Chrysanthemum (fl)	*Choisya ternata* (sh)	*Choisya ternata* (sh)
Crocosmia (fl)	Crocosmia (fl)	Chrysanthemum (fl)	Conifers (t)
Dahlias (fl)	Dahlias (fl)	Conifers (t)	Chrysanthemum (fl)
Gladiolus (fl)	Erica (fl)	Elaeagnus (sh)	Elaeagnus (fol, sh)
Hosta (fol)	Gladiolus (fl)	Euonymus (sh)	Euonymus (fol, sh)
Hydrangea (fl, fol)	Hedera (ivy) (fol)	*Garrya eliptica* (sh)	*Garrya eliptica* (sh, fol)
Kniphofia (fl)	Hydrangea (fl, fol)	Hedera (ivy) (fol)	Hamamelis (t)
Lilies (fl)	Lilies (fl)	Laurel (sh)	Hedera (ivy) (fol)
Michaelmas daisy (fl)	Michaelmas daisy (fl)	*Prunus autumnalis* (fl, t)	Hellebores (fl)
Physalis (fl)	Nerine (fl)	Pyracantha (sh)	Jasmine (fl)
Polygonum (fl)	Physalis (fl)	*Senecio greyii* (sh)	Laurel (fol, sh)
Roses (fl)	*Prunus autumnalis* (fl, t)	*Stachys lanata* (fol)	Privet (fol, sh)
Rudbeckia (fl)	Pyracantha (sh)	Tellima (fol)	*Prunus autumnalis* (fl, sh)
Skimmia (sh)	Roses (fl)	*Viburnum fragrans* (fl, sh)	*Senecio greyii* (fol, sh)
Solidago (fl)	Rudbeckia (fl)	Willow, contorta (t)	*Viburnum fragrans* (fl, sh)
Sorbus (t)	Skimmia (sh)		Willow, contorta (t)
Stachys lanata (fol)	Solidago (fl)		
Statice (fl)	Sorbus (t)		
Stocks (fl)	Statice (fl)		
Sweet peas (fl)	Stocks (fl)		
Tellima (fol)	Willow, contorta (t)		
Verbascum (fol)			
Willow, contorta (t)			
Zea (maize) (fol)			
Zinnia (fl)			

GROWING

YOUR OWN VEGETABLES

Roy Genders

There is nothing so rewarding as growing your own vegetables. Not only is there a big saving on the household budget but the vegetables come to the table fresh from the garden, full of flavour and packed with health-giving vitamins and mineral salts. And they are also available whenever required. In addition, varieties which are rarely seen in the shops may be grown, adding to the interest of one's diet.

Today, with increasing interest in vegetable growing, many new varieties have been developed which will ripen in the shortness of an English season. Sweet corn is one. It reached popularity during World War II, but the older strains would scarcely ripen in the average British summer. Now, however, in those parts which can expect above average sunshine, sweet corn can be a satisfying crop.

New introductions now prolong the season, making it possible with careful planning, to enjoy fresh vegetables all the year round. Nor is there any long wait before a crop is ready to use, as rapid maturity is one of the more important qualities of modern varieties. Dwarf bean, Limelight, will reach maturity at least 2 weeks earlier than the older varieties, and with the cabbage, Velocity, if sown early spring in rows and thinned to 9 ins. apart, no transplanting will be necessary (apart from the thinnings), and the young well-hearted cabbage will be ready to cut 12 weeks from sowing. Carrot, Little Finger, is another vegetable to mature rapidly and the same may be said for Little Ball beetroot.

The introduction of Golden Self-blanching celery now makes it possible to grow celery without the need for earthing up, and from an early sowing in a frame, the plants will have formed large hearts before winter.

Then there are the First Cross (F1) introductions which possess the enormous cropping qualities of hybrid varieties. Brussels sprout, Peer Gynt, for early picking, and Fasolt to stand through winter, will bear as many as a hundred firm sprouts on each plant if grown well. One may pick sprouts throughout autumn and winter, and feed a large family from a dozen plants of each variety.

To grow vegetables well, an open sunny situation and a well-nourished soil are required. They will not grow in the shade of tall trees, and they will not heart well in a poor, dry soil. Instead, they will quickly run to seed. If the vegetable garden has a gentle slope to the south or west, this will ensure early crops, for the plants will catch the maximum amount of sunlight and the soil will begin to warm up early in the year. A garden with a gentle slope will be usually well drained in winter so that the land may be worked at all times, except when frozen.

If the area is exposed to strong winds, plant a hedge of the quick-growing *Cupressus leylandii* on the side of the prevailing wind, or erect fencing panels, against which black-berries can be grown. Cement the posts into the ground. In a wind-swept area, it is preferable to grow broccoli, kale, and Brussels sprouts, of compact habit. Always plant and stake runner beans end-on to the prevailing wind, so that it will pass between the rows.

Dwarf, compact plants enable more to be planted in a given area, or in a small garden, and they will come more quickly to maturity. These dwarf varieties will provide an all-year supply, and are most suitable for the small garden. See Table C on p. 162.

PLANNING THE VEGETABLE GARDEN

In planning the vegetable garden, you may consider having at one end a place for the taller plants, such as globe artichokes, sweet corn, and tomatoes. Full sun is necessary for them to ripen, and as they must be staked correctly they will not interfere with greens and root crops. In front of them could come a row of cold frames in which to raise early crops, and for sowing seed of those which require a long season to mature, e.g. leeks and celery. The frames will be in constant use, to raise and harden plants, and for the summer culture of the more tender crops.

Along the side of the garden protected from the winds could be a row of runner beans, and in a more shaded part beds of mint, rhubarb, seakale, and chicory. Here, too, may be grown the tall Nine-star perennial broccoli, one of the most valuable of vegetables bearing multitudes of small white cauliflower heads for at least 3 years. Asparagus, a permanent crop, will be planted in a sunny bed to itself.

The main bedding area should be divided into four sections so as to give a 4-course rotation of crops. Moving the crops each year prevents the soil becoming 'sick' of any crop, with diminishing yields. Rotation also decreases the chance of the ground becoming infested with pests and diseases peculiar to one crop. Potatoes should follow green crops; greens should follow the legumes (peas and beans); and they in turn will follow the roots and so on, with a move each year.

Besides maintaining healthy crops, this

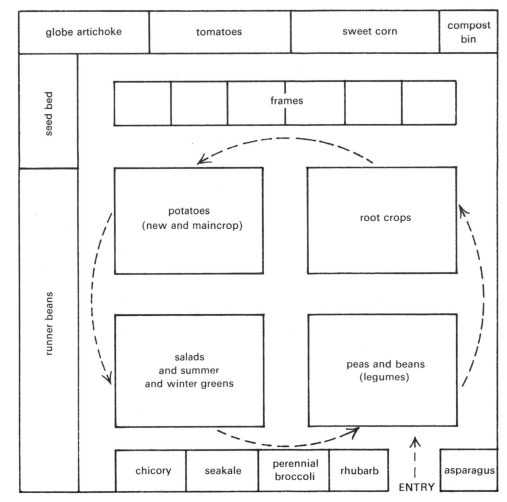

A typical layout for a small vegetable plot

A convenient size and design of compost bin for the average garden. The slotted planks are simple to build up as material is added and to remove as the compost is used.

enables the plants to obtain the maximum value from the fertilisers used. For example, greens take large quantities of nitrogen from the soil as they make a profusion of leaf, while the leguminous crops put this nitrogen back into the soil through the ability of the root nodules to 'fix' the nitrogen. Therefore greens should follow peas and beans. The growing of potatoes helps to clean the ground. They also require plenty of manure or compost and this adds humus to the soil. Humus is necessary for bacterial action, and to make the soil retentive of moisture in summer. A starved soil will not grow good vegetables.

PREPARING THE SOIL

First the land should be thoroughly cleaned and broken down. This is achieved by double digging or trenching. Land that is badly drained should have some grit or crushed brick incorporated into the lower spit when trenching. Mortar from an old building site may be used; anything that will assist excess moisture to drain away. If water remains about the plant's roots it will prevent healthy growth. It also makes the land sour. November is the best time for digging. If the soil is left in a rough condition over winter, it will be broken down to a fine tilth by the elements. Beginning at the top of the plot, soil to a depth of at least 12 ins. (2 spits or 2 spades' depth) is removed and taken to the bottom of the plot. This is used to fill in the last trench. Into the bottom of the first trench is put material from the compost heap.

After the compost is placed in the trench (farmyard manure is even better if you can obtain it), fill the trench with the soil removed from the next trench, and so on, until the whole area is dug.

If the land is a little sour, then lime applied at this time will rectify this condition. Heavy land should be treated with caustic (unhydrated) lime, which, in contact with moisture in the soil, sets up a violent reaction, breaking up the soil particles so that when plants are growing, air may penetrate to the roots, enabling bacteria in the soil to begin working.

FERTILISERS AND MANURES

Your County Agricultural Officer if asked will carry out a soil test to determine whether the land needs lime, and in what

quantity. Or, one can do it oneself, by using the simple and inexpensive BDH soil indicator set, which contains a bottle of indicator solution, barium sulphate, some distilled water, several glass test tubes, and a colour chart. A small amount of soil is placed in a test tube and a small quantity of barium sulphate added. Then almost fill to the top with distilled water, and add 2 or 3 drops of the indicator. Shake up the contents and allow it to settle. Then compare the colour of the liquid with that on the chart, to find the pH value. pH stands for the hydrogen ion concentration of moisture in the soil, and its acidity or alkalinity varies accordingly. The scale extends from 0 (extreme acidity) to 14 (extreme alkalinity), with neutrality at No. 7. Deep purple denotes the highest degree of acidity, and deep green the highest degree of alkalinity. To correct an acid soil, give 7 lb. of hydrated lime to each ˙100 sq. ft. of garden area for every unit of pH value below 7 (shown on the chart), to bring the soil to neutrality. It is rarely that a soil shows excessive alkalinity.

Lime also has the ability to release various plant foods stored in the soil and well-manured ground will not release its plant foods without it. Thus to add manure to soil which lacks lime is wasteful and uneconomic.

Other forms of humus are decayed leaves, clearings from ditches, peat, and straw which has been composted by an activator. Peat and leaf mould, however, contain little or no plant food, and where used to provide humus, they must be augmented by fertilisers of either an organic or inorganic nature. Poultry manure which has been stored dry, and fish meal, contain all the main plant foods. For those who live near the sea, chopped up seaweed contains nitrogen and potash. For those living in the north, wool or cotton shoddy is rich in slow-acting nitrogen, and used hops from a brewery contain both nitrogen and phosphates. Dried blood is rich in nitrogen and bone meal in phosphates. In addition, these organic fertilisers provide the soil with humus. Organics deficient in any plant food, can be augmented by the use of inorganic fertilisers such as nitrate of soda, nitro-chalk, and potassium nitrate, each of which has a high nitrogen content, and potassium

nitrate and sulphate of potash which are rich in potash.

The 'greens' require nitrogen to make healthy leaves, while all plants require potash to bring out the flavour, and to build 'hard' tissue to withstand the winter. Phosphates are necessary to promote vigorous root action. In a cold spring, cabbages will come into vigorous growth if the ground is given a light dressing with a nitrogenous fertiliser. Nitrates, however, should not be overdone for they will encourage the plants to form leaf at the expense of 'heart'. Cauliflowers need potash to make a large solid head; an excess of nitrogen will cause them to make too much leaf. Brussels sprouts need nitrogen in quantity, but also require potash to form solid sprouts. Fish meal, guano, and poultry manure, are rich in potash but wood ash contains only a small amount. If the land is in good heart, rake in 1 oz. per sq. yd. of sulphate of potash at planting time.

A good water supply is essential for vegetables, and growing crops will benefit from an occasional watering with dilute liquid manure, either in the proprietary form or made by half filling a sack with some form of animal manure and suspending it in a tank or barrel filled with several gallons of water. Leave it for a few days to allow all the goodness to be washed out of the manure, then remove the sack and use the manure water as required. It may be necessary to dilute the manure water still further before using.

RAISING THE PLANTS

Almost all vegetable crops may be raised by sowing seed directly into the open ground. Cauliflowers, sprouts, cabbage, savoy, leeks, onions, broccoli, and kale, are sown mostly in spring, in drills made 1 in. deep and 8 ins. apart to allow for hoeing and weeding. The plants are moved when about 3 ins. tall, and planted where they are to grow to maturity. They should be sown as early in spring as the condition of the soil allows but not before the frost has gone and not when the soil is sticky. A seedbed should be made at one corner where the soil is brought to a fine tilth, some peat or leaf mould being incorporated into the top 3 ins. before sowing, and 1 oz. per sq. yd. of superphosphate of lime raked in, which will help the plants to

TABLE A

Fertiliser	Action	Nitrogen Content	Phosphatic Content	Potash Content
Basic slag	slow	15%		
Bone meal	slow	5%	20%	
Dried blood	medium	10%		
Farmyard manure	slow	0.5%	0.25%	0.5%
Fish meal	quick	10%	8%	7%
Guano	quick	15%	10%	7%
Hoof and horn meal	slow	14%	10%	
Kainit	slow			13%
Nitrate of soda	quick	16%		
Nitro-chalk	quick	16%		
Potassium nitrate	quick	14%		40%
Poultry manure	medium	3%	2%	6%
Rape meal	slow	5%	2%	1%
Seaweed	slow	5%		1.5%
Shoddy (wool)	slow	12%		
Spent hops	slow	4%	2%	
Sulphate of ammonia	quick	20%		
Sulphate of potash	medium			50%
Superphosphate	medium		15%	

form a mass of healthy roots. If seed is sown towards the end of March, the young plants will be ready to move by the end of April, before they become too tall and leggy, and at a time when gentle rain will enable them to re-establish themselves quickly. Always plant greens firmly, and before doing so dip the roots in calomel solution.

Root crops are sown directly into the ground where they are to mature. Sow thinly, for they will later need thinning to enable those left in the rows to grow to a good size. Thinnings are not transplanted.

Always use fresh seed, obtained from a reliable seedsman, who is bound by a Government order to guarantee reliable a certain standard of germination and quality. Most vegetable seeds are now obtainable in pelleted form, in which the seeds are first dried to a low moisture level, and then given a coating. This increases their size almost a hundred-fold. After sowing the coating breaks down rapidly, giving quicker germination than with ordinary seeds. Pelleted seed may also be sown singly, giving them the right spacing so that there is no waste, and no time is spent in thinning and transplanting. With all seeds, but especially pelleted seed, germination will be retarded unless the soil is kept moist after sowing.

Early crops may be enjoyed where a frame is available or by sowing under cloches. This may take place in March, when the early-maturing varieties are sown. There will thus be a saving of about 3 weeks to the time when the crops are ready for harvesting. Early peas, too, may be started under cloches.

An inexpensive tunnel cloche may be made from polythene sheeting supported by steel hoops and holding wires. They may be of any length up to about 36 ft. and are used for peas, dwarf beans, early carrots, and lettuce. Dobies cloches are box-sectioned cellular structures, similar to double glazing. They are made of translucent plastic, which is unaffected by frost, and helps to prevent plant scorch in bright sunlight. They are ideal for raising seedlings, and for starting off peas and beans. The barn type of cloche is 15 ins. wide, and will cover three rows of seedlings. Cloches should be in position at least 10 days before sowing time so that the soil can begin to warm. When removing the cloches, begin by doing so for a few hours on warm days, and then throughout the day, before finally leaving them off altogether. In this way the plants will be gradually hardened.

Marrows, sweet corn, frame cucumbers, also indoor and outdoor tomatoes, are raised in heat, for they need a night temperature of 60°F. A heated greenhouse or frame hot bed is therefore necessary, so that the seedlings are ready to transplant into a cold frame for growing on, or moved there for hardening about the first of May, before planting out a month later. But artificial heat is not essential, for marrows, outdoor cucumbers, and tomato plants, may be purchased from specialist growers, hardened off, at the right time for planting.

Where growing to maturity under cloches, the seedlings need thinning before they grow too large, and at all times they need careful watering, though in wet weather sufficient moisture will trickle under the cloches to keep the plants growing. Crops which are not protected also require watering during dry weather to keep them growing, and the soil between the rows should be regularly hoed to let air reach the roots, and to kill annual weeds.

Plants are best watered in the evening when the sun is going down, by giving them

TABLE B

	Variety	Sowing Time Under cloches	Maturing
VEGETABLES TO MATURE EARLY			
Bean, broad	Aquadulce	Sept	Apr–May
Bean, dwarf	Earligreen	Apr	July
Beetroot	Avon Early	Apr	June
Brussels sprout	Early Dwarf	Mar	Aug–Sept
Carrot	Amsterdam Forcing	Feb	Apr–May
Carrot	Little Finger	Feb	May
Cauliflower	Early Snowball	Mar	June–July
Cress	Extra Double Curled	All year	All year
Lettuce	All Year Round	Feb	May–June
Lettuce	May King	Feb	May–June
Pea	Feltham Early	Feb	June
Pea	Kelvedon Wonder	Feb	June
Pea	Meteor	Feb	June
Radish	Cherry Belle	Mar	Apr–May
Turnip	Early Milan	Mar	May–June

Dwarf French beans; part of a row showing the mulch of lawn mowings.

a thorough soaking so that moisture will reach down to the roots. To give only a light watering during the day, causes the plants' roots to turn upwards to the surface in their search for the water.

All plants, however, benefit from a daily syringing with clean water in dry weather, and this also helps the flowers to set in the case of beans and tomatoes.

HARVESTING THE CROPS

Never allow vegetables to grow too large and coarse. Peas should be removed as soon as they have filled the pod (check by pressing them). Beans should be rich green (not yellow), and should snap readily. Beetroot and turnips should be no larger than a tennis ball, when they will be sweet and succulent. Cauliflower heads should be removed when firm and snow-white, long before they begin to go to seed; marrows and cucumbers should be picked quite small when they will be tender and full of flavour, and others will be encouraged to take their place on the plants. Quality and flavour are lost if vegetables are allowed to remain on the plants too long.

Those who do not have a freezer can preserve many vegetables by simple methods. Some can be left in the ground through winter and will be improved by frost. Leeks, Brussels sprouts, sprouting broccoli and large heading broccoli, cabbage and savoys, also celery, celeriac, parsnip, and

Typical rewards of good gardening: (from top to bottom) artichoke 'Grande Beurre'; dwarf bean 'Remus'; cauliflower 'Snow King'; lettuce 'Little Gem'.

swedes, come into this category, and may be lifted as required through winter (except when hard frost prevents it). Potatoes, carrots, and turnips, deteriorate if frosted, and should be lifted during October and November. They may be stored in a cellar, shed, or outhouse, in deep boxes covered with straw or bracken to exclude frost and light. Potatoes will turn green if the tubers are exposed to light for any length of time, and will be harmful to eat.

The root and tuberous rooted crops are lifted when the soil is fairly dry and friable, so that it may easily be shaken from them. Lift with care, using a garden fork, so as not to damage the tubers. The correct way to lift roots is to hold the top leaves with one hand and to lift with the other. Shake off surplus soil, spread them out on sheets, and leave for several hours to allow them to dry off as much as possible. Then cut away, or with beetroot screw off, the leaves before placing the roots in boxes on layers of dry peat. Store, away from hot pipes and any other form of heat, in a dry, airy, frost-free room, and they will keep throughout winter and will be available when wanted.

Dwarf and runner beans, if salted, remain in good condition for at least a year. Remove them when young and tender, top and tail them, and slice them into a large glass or earthenware jar to a depth of 3 ins. Then give them a generous covering of salt before adding another layer and so on until the jar is full.

When required for use, remove a number of beans, wash free of salt, and allow to soak in cold water for an hour before use.

Haricot or butter beans are harvested at the end of summer and can be left to grow quite large. Remove the beans on a dry day, spread them out on paper and leave them in a dry, airy room for several weeks to complete their drying. Then remove the seeds from the pods and store the seeds in a wooden container which does not attract moisture. They keep for months.

Winter squashes, or marrows, are hard skinned and will keep for the entire winter, but, unlike summer marrows, they must remain on the plants until fully matured in autumn. Handle them with care, for they will decay if bruised. Place on a layer of cotton wool on a shelf in a dry room, in a temperature of 45°–50°F and they will keep in perfect condition.

Onions and shallots are also lifted in autumn on a dry day. Allow them to remain on the ground for several hours to dry off, then shake away the soil and tie the necks together, so that they can be strung up in an airy room to dry. They will keep all winter if correctly dried and protected from frost.

If hard frost is likely, celery may be lifted, and will store for several weeks if the roots are left on and the plants placed in a cellar or shed. Brussels sprouts keep well for a month or more in an ordinary refrigerator, provided they are put in immediately they have been gathered.

Mushrooms will keep for a few weeks, if dried in a slightly warmed oven before placing in wooden boxes. Do not peel them. They will also keep well if bottled, but for this method small button mushrooms should be used. After trimming the stems, place them in a saucepan, cover with water, add the juice of a lemon and 1 oz. of salt to every 3–4 lb. of mushrooms, and bring to the boil for 4 mins. Place in screw-top jars, cover with liquid, and boil for 1½ hours in a saucepan of water.

TABLE C

DWARF COMPACT VARIETIES SUITABLE FOR THE SMALL GARDEN			
	Variety	Sowing Time	To Mature
Bean, broad	The Midget	Oct	May–June
Bean, dwarf	Cordon (8 ins)	Apr	July–Aug
Bean, runner	Hammond's Dwarf (1 ft)	June	Aug–Sept
Beet	Little Ball	Apr–May	Aug–Oct
Borecole (Kale)	Dwarf Green Curled	May	Nov–Feb
Brussels sprout	Early Dwarf (1½ ft)	Apr	Oct–Dec
Brussels sprout	Prince Askold (1½ ft)	Apr	Dec–Mar
Cabbage, summer	Babyhead	Mar–Apr	Aug–Oct
Cabbage, winter	Christmas Drumhead	June	Dec–Mar
Carrot	Little Finger	Mar–May	July–Sept
Cauliflower, summer	Early Snowball	Mar–Apr	July–Aug
Cauliflower, winter	April Purity	Apr–May	Feb–Apr
Celery	Golden Self-blanching	Apr	Sept–Nov
Lettuce	All Year Round	Mar–Sept	All Year
Lettuce	Tom Thumb	Mar–May	June–Sept
Lettuce (Cos)	Little Gem (Sugar Cos)	Mar–Apr	June–Aug
Marrow (bush)	Gold Nugget	Apr	July–Sept
Marrow (trailing)	Little Gem	Apr	July–Sept
Onion	All-Rounder (Sturon)	Sets in April	Sept–Oct
Parsnip	Intermediate	Apr	Sept–Dec
Pea (early)	Little Marvel (1 ft)	Mar–Apr	July
Pea (2nd early)	Lincoln (1½ ft)	Mar–Apr	Aug
Pea (maincrop)	Rentpayer (2 ft)	Apr–May	Sept
Savoy	Dwarf Green Curled	Apr–May	Nov–Feb
Sweet corn	Golden Bantam	Plant June	Aug–Oct
Tomato	Sleaford Abundance (1 ft)	Plant June	Aug–Oct
Turnip	Golden Ball	Apr	Aug–Dec

THE VEGETABLE GROWER'S CALENDAR

Vegetable	When to Plant or Sow	Thinning or Planting Distances Apart	When to Harvest
Artichoke, Chinese	Apr	9 ins	Oct–Dec
Artichoke, Globe	Apr	3 ft	July–Aug
Artichoke, Jerusalem	Mar	12 ins	Oct–Jan
*Aubergine	Jan	18 ins	July–Oct
Bean, broad	Oct & Mar	6–8 ins	May–June
Bean, dwarf	May	9 ins	July–Aug
Bean, pole	May	9 ins	July–Sept
Bean, runner	May	9 ins	Aug–Oct
Beetroot	Apr–May	4–6 ins	July–Oct
Borecole	Apr	2 ft	Sept–Mar
Broccoli, large-heading	Apr–May	3 ft	Oct–May
Broccoli, sprouting	Apr	3 ft	Oct–July
Brussels sprouts	Aug & Apr	3–4 ft	Sept–Mar
Cabbage, Chinese (Pe-tsai)	July	8 ins	Aug–Sept
Cabbage, red	Sept	2 ft	Sept–Mar
Cabbage, spring	July	18 ins	Apr–June
Cabbage, winter	Apr–May	2 ft	Sept–Mar
Calabrese	Apr	3 ft	Aug–Dec
Cardoon	May	18 ins	Nov–Mar
Carrot, early	Early Apr	3 ins	May–June
Carrot, maincrop	Apr–May	4 ins	Sept–Mar
Cauliflower, summer	Aug & Apr	18 ins	July–Sept
Cauliflower, winter	(See Broccoli, large-heading)		Oct–Jan
Celeriac	Mar	12 ins	Oct–Mar
Celery, self-blanching	Feb	9 ins	Sept–Mar
Chicory	June	10 ins	Oct–Dec
*Cucumber, frame	Mar–Apr	3 ft	July–Sept
Cucumber, indoors	Jan	2 ft	July–Oct
Cucumber, ridge	Apr	3 ft	Aug–Oct
Endive	July	10 ins	Aug–Sept
Garlic	Oct & Mar	6 ins	Aug–Sept
Good King Henry	Apr	12 ins	Apr–June
Hamburg Parsley	Mar	9 ins	Sept–Apr
Kohl Rabi	Mar–June	8 ins	July–Mar
Leek	Mar	6 ins	Sept–Mar
Lettuce, spring & summer	Mar–June	9–15 ins	Apr–Sept
Lettuce, winter	Aug	8 ins	Oct–Mar
Marrow	Apr	4–6 ft	July–Oct
Mustard & Cress	All year	—	All year
Onion, bulbs (sets)	Apr	4 ins	Oct–Nov
Onion, spring or green	July & Mar	1 in	All year
Parsley	Apr	6 ins	All year
Parsnip	Mar	10 ins	Nov–Dec
Pea, early	Aug & Mar	2 ins	May–June
Pea, maincrop	Apr, May	2 ins	July–Oct
Potato	Mar–Apr	2 ft	July–Nov
Radish	All year	2 ins	All year
Rhubarb	Apr	3 ft	May–Oct
Salsify	Apr	8 ins	Nov–Mar
Savoy	Apr	2–3 ft	Oct–Mar
Shallot	Mar	9 ins	Sept–Oct
Spinach, summer	Apr–June	9 ins	June–Sept
Spinach, winter	Aug	9 ins	Mar–May
Spinach, perpetual	Apr & July	15 ins	All year
Swede	Apr	9 ins	Oct–Mar
Sweet Corn	Feb	15 ins	Aug–Oct
Sweet Potato	Apr	15 ins	Oct–Nov
Swiss Chard	Apr & July	12 ins	Aug & spring
*Tomato	Jan	18 ins	June–Nov
Turnip	Feb & Apr	6 ins	June–Nov

* Sow under glass in heat

Artichoke, Chinese (*Stachys tubifera*)

The French know it as Crosnes. First introduced to European gardens about a century ago. At one time a popular food. The tubers are difficult to clean and so are rarely used today.

CULTURE

Plant tubers in April, in drills 4 ins. deep and 18 ins. apart. Allow 9 ins. between the tubers. The soil should be deeply dug, working in plenty of humus. An open, sunny situation is required. In a dry season, the plants will need plenty of water. Lift tubers at the end of October when the foliage, which grows about 2 ft. tall, begins to die back. Store in boxes of peat in a cool place, or the tubers will shrivel. In gardens rarely troubled by severe frost, the tubers may be left in the ground until required, where they will keep firm and sweet.

Artichoke, Globe (*Cynara scolymus*)

Introduced into Britain from N. Africa by the Romans. It is a perennial, related to the cardoon, and its flower heads with their thick, overlapping scales is the part eaten.

CULTURE

A sunny position, sheltered from cold winds, is necessary. Plant in a rich, deeply worked soil for sweet and tender heads. Decayed manure, old mushroom bed compost, and humus in any form suits it well. Or you may dig in some chopped seaweed, together with 2 oz. of kainit, and 2 oz. of superphosphate per sq. yd. The plants should remain productive for 5 years or more. Use the suckers or shoots which form around the crown of the old plant, to increase the stock. Detach these with a sharp knife when about 6 ins. tall and with a few roots. Plant well into the ground, treading the soil firmly after planting. Early April is the best time. Allow 3 ft. between each for they grow 4–5 ft. tall. To produce succulent and tender heads, keep the plants well supplied with water, and give them a mulch of peat and a little decayed manure in May.

The main heads will grow large if the laterals are removed when about golf ball size. They are delicious fried whole in butter. Remove main heads in July and August when 4 ins. in diameter. Afterwards, cut back the stem to 15 ins. above soil level, and water with dilute liquid manure when the new shoots come. When 2 ft. tall, tie them together and earth up, to blanch the stems. They will be ready to cut in October. Cut into 6-in. lengths, remove outer skin and simmer until tender.

VARIETIES

There are two forms Green Globe and Purple Globe. Of the green, the best variety is Vert de Laon, which has almost spineless heads and is prolific from its second year. Most have spines at the end of the overlapping scales which must be removed before cooking.

PESTS & DISEASES

Cockchafer. The grubs of the common cockchafer beetle are fat and greyish-white. Occasionally they feed on the roots and cause the plants to die back. To prevent, treat the ground with Gammexane or malathion before planting.

Leaf Spot. May be troublesome in a wet summer. Grey spots appear on the leaves causing them to turn brown at the edge. A heavy infection may cause the plant to die back. To give control spray with Bordeaux mixture at half strength as soon as spots are seen.

Artichoke, Jerusalem (*Helianthus tuberosus*)

Native of N. America and closely related to the sunflower. Its knobbly skins make it difficult to clean, hence its loss of popularity, but the tubers are nourishing and delicious sliced, after boiling, and fried in butter.

CULTURE

Requires a light soil containing some humus and, just before planting, a dressing of 2 oz. per sq. yd. of superphosphate and 1 oz. of sulphate of potash.

The tubers should be of walnut size. Plant in trenches 3–4 ins. wide and 6 ins. deep, early March in the south, and end of March in the north. Allow 12 ins. between each, and 2 ft. between the rows for the plants grow tall. Water copiously during dry weather. When the foliage has grown 2 ft. or more, earth up the plants to increase the yield. Support the foliage by fastening to wires extended along the rows.

Lift in October, when the tops begin to die down. Dry the tubers for several hours in the sun or wind then store in boxes of sand or peat. In the south, however, the roots may be left in the ground and used when required from early October onwards.

PESTS & DISEASES

This vegetable is troubled by none.

VARIETY

The silver-skinned type is best, being of a mild, delicate flavour. Boil in their skins, which are then removed before baking or frying. They are delicious baked and served with white sauce.

Asparagus (*Asparagus officinalis*)

For the epicure, but is rarely grown because it takes several years for a bed to become fully productive.

CULTURE

Purchase 2-year crowns (roots) from a specialist grower, or, raise from seed; but this will take 2 more years to become productive. Seed is sown early in April in drills, in soil brought to a fine tilth. Use fresh seed only, as old seed takes too long to germinate. The seed is large so plant singly 1 in. apart and 1 in. deep, allowing 8 ins. between the rows for hoeing. Even fresh seed will take a month to germinate. Keep the soil moist. Leave the seedlings in the rows for 12 months, then lift and plant into permanent beds.

Dig 3 trenches, 8–9 ins. wide and deep, with 2 ft. between each. Put in some decayed manure or seaweed and cover with several inches of finely screened loam. Plant the crowns about 20 ins. apart on small mounds of soil so that they are only 2 ins. below the surface. Spread the roots out as evenly as possible. Pack fine soil and peat about the crowns and fill in the trench. Add to the topsoil 1 oz. of superphosphate and sulphate of potash per yd. By mid-May, shoots will be seen, but no cutting is done for another 2 years. They will make plenty of fern-like foliage which is left to die back in autumn. Limited cutting is done in the third year and more the next year but always allow some shoots to grow into fern each year to maintain its vigour, but do not let them go to seed.

Cutting begins in May and continues for a month only. No more sticks are then removed. Cut when the sticks are 6 ins. above ground, and use a sharp saw-edged knife. They are cut about 2 ins. below ground. Handle with care for the succulent tips are easily broken. 20–24 crowns will produce, at one cutting, sufficient for 3 or 4 people. Tie the sticks together before cooking, and stand them upright in a deep pan in 2–3 ins. of water. In this way, the tips are not broken.

For an early crop, give a mulch of decayed manure, surround the bed with 12-in. boards, and cover with frame lights. If kept moist, the first sticks will be ready to cut one month before uncovered plants.

After cutting is finished, dress the beds with salt at a rate of 2 oz. per sq. yd. A well-cultivated bed will remain productive for about 20 years.

PESTS & DISEASES

Asparagus beetle. The grubs feed on the foliage in summer with resultant loss of vigour to the plants. As routine, spray with derris solution or dust with derris powder in July and August.

Rust. The only troublesome disease, it appears as rusty-brown spots on the foliage early in summer. Control by spraying at fortnightly intervals with Bordeaux mixture made by dissolving 1 lb. of quicklime and 1 lb. of copper sulphate into 12 gals. of water.

VARIETIES

The old American, Conover's Colossal is still unsurpassed for earliness and quality. Excellent, too, is Mary Washington, highly resistant to rust, and excellent for freezing. The shoots are dark green with tight tip scales.

Aubergine (*Solanum melongena*)

Known also as the egg plant from shape of fruit. It is a native of southern USA but crops well in Britain with minimum of artificial heat.

Aubergine (egg plant) in an 8″ whalehide pot.

CULTURE

Sow in January in a temperature of 60°F, using John Innes sowing compost, and just covering the seed. To hasten germination, place a sheet of glass over the pan or box and keep compost moist. When the seedlings are large enough to handle, move to small pots, and 3 weeks later to larger pots containing J.I. potting compost. A temperature of 50°–52°F is necessary at this time. When the plants are established, nip out the growing point to encourage bushy growth. Artificial heat is no longer needed, but the plants will require plenty of moisture and ample ventilation. Grow on in a cold greenhouse in large pots, containing plenty of decayed manure, or outside in a frame, or beneath barn-type cloches, in a rich soil in full sunlight. Plant out at the end of May. A daily syringing with clean water during hot weather helps the fruit to set, and as they begin to colour, give the plants a weekly application of dilute manure water. This increases the size and improves the flavour.

Each plant will yield 10–30 fruits during a season which, when ripe, will weigh about 1 lb. each. Remove before they become too large, and when the skin has a brilliant gloss. Under glass, plants in pots from a January sowing in heat, begin to fruit after 70–80 days, and will continue through summer. During hot weather, give the plants plenty of water or the skins will split.

PESTS & DISEASES
See Tomato.

VARIETIES
Early Beauty is reliable. It comes into bloom quicker than any others, and maintains a heavy crop of medium-sized fruit of darkest purple through the summer.
Long Tom. An F1 hybrid, bearing almost black fruit of cucumber shape, about 6 ins. long, and will produce up to 50 in a season if grown well.

Bean, Broad (*Vicia faba*)

Rich in protein and nourishment. Introduced into Britain by the Romans to sustain the legionaries on their long marches. Not all enjoy their 'earthy' flavour, but are appetising if steamed and served with parsley sauce.

CULTURE
Grows well in soil that has been limed and manured for a previous crop. A sowing in October will crop in May. A second sowing in March will mature in June. Sow the seeds singly 6 ins. apart and 2 ins. deep in double rows 9 ins. between. Use a trowel rather than a dibber. If the soil is heavy, sow on a layer of sand.

Keep the weeds down and the soil broken up by periodic hoeing between the rows. When 12 ins. tall support them with twine taken along the row and looped around each plant. Tie the twine to stakes which are 3 ft. above the ground. Most varieties reach this height and may need a further supporting. Early sown plants may be covered with barn cloches to start with. The long-pod varieties are the hardiest and suitable for autumn sowing, but the Windsor types have the best flavour and should be sown in spring.

The beans are ready to gather when the seeds can be seen bulging through the pods. After cropping cut the stalks at soil level and leave the roots in the ground for they have valuable nitrogen content.

PESTS & DISEASES
Black Fly. A troublesome pest which rarely affects autumn-sown beans. The flies collect on the leaves at the top of the plant, thereby reducing the crop. If the top shoot is removed when the plants have made maximum growth it will discourage the fly and make for earlier maturity. Control by spraying with derris solution during April and May.
Slugs. They attack the succulent growths of autumn seeds whether under cloches or not. To prevent this, water the ground with Slugit after sowing, and again in early spring.

VARIETIES
Imperial Green. A Windsor for spring sowing, each pod bearing 7–8 seeds of brilliant green, and of delicious flavour.
Longfellow. For autumn or spring, it is a tremendous cropper, the long straight pods bearing 8–9 beans.
Promotion. For autumn sowing, the pods are 9–10 ins. long, each with 5–6 beans. They are white and of excellent flavour.
The Midget. It grows only 15–18 ins. tall with each plant producing 3–4 stems which are best supported by short twigs. Plant in a single row, spacing the seeds 18 ins. apart. Each stem bears clusters of pods 6 ins. long which resemble pea pods.

Bean, Dwarf (*Phaseolus vulgaris*)

Also known as the French bean. They are quick to mature, and seldom need staking. They can be grown in boxes, in large pots on a verandah, or even between autumn-maturing greens.

Dwarf bean 'The Prince'

CULTURE
Dwarf beans are not fully hardy. For a crop to mature in June, sow the seeds in a soil containing plenty of humus early in April, and cover with cloches until end of May. Make the first sowings of unprotected plants about May 1st, and at monthly intervals until late July. There will then be beans to pick from June until October.

The soil should be well limed and in good 'heart'. Particularly good is hop manure or old mushroom bed compost. For a quick-maturing variety sow either The Prince or Earligreen, which crop 7–10 days before all others. Sow the beans 2 ins. deep and 9 ins. apart in rows 12 ins. apart. If growing under cloches, make a double row 8 ins. apart, and space the beans to 10 ins. Beans transplant well so plant a dozen or more extra seeds, which can be used to fill any failures in the rows.

Plants can also be raised in pans or boxes in a sunny window, sowing early in May and transplanting to open ground about June 1st.

After the seed has germinated, keep hoeing between the rows. Tread in any plant that has been loosened by wind. In dry weather, water copiously. This helps the flowers to set and prevents the beans growing hard and stringy.

They begin to crop in 8–9 weeks after the seed is sown, and continue for a similar period. Gather when 5–6 ins. long, before the beans show through the pod, and whilst deep green. Cut with scissors so as not to disturb the roots. The beans grow quickly, so look over the plants daily.

Dwarf beans are easily grown under glass, but require a temperature of 60°–65°F. Sow 5 or 6 seeds in a 10-in. pot filled with a mixture of loam and decayed manure, plus a little sand for drainage. If sown in January, the plants will begin to crop in April. Support them with a few twigs inserted round the side of the pot. Water occasionally with dilute liquid manure to increase the crop and improve the quality.

PESTS & DISEASES
Anthracnose. Beans become affected by brown sunken spots which attack first the pods, then the seeds. It is prevalent in a wet season. Spray with half-strength Bordeaux mixture, and repeat 14 days later.
Black Fly. May trouble dwarf beans growing near broad beans which are attacked. The cure is the same – dust with derris powder.
Halo Blight. Causes plants to turn yellow and die. It differs from anthracnose in that the pale brown spots have a transparent halo around them. Treatment is the same.

VARIETIES
Cordon. New maincrop bean with oval pods 6–7 ins. long, held well above the soil. Succulent, stringless, and highly resistant to disease.
Earligreen. First to mature. Makes a compact plant and bears heavy crops of slim dark green beans of excellent flavour.
Kinghorn Wax. A yellow Waxford bean. The round pencil-thin pods should be cooked whole.
Masterpiece. An old but most reliable maincrop bean, bearing heavily. The long green pods are crisp when sliced, and of delicious flavour.
Royalty. A purple-podded variety. Does well in all soils. Outstanding flavour. The beans turn deep green when cooked.
Tendergreen. Early variety. The pods are round and stringless when sliced. Bears heavily in all weathers.

Bean, Pole (*Phaseolus vulgaris*)

Climbing form of the French bean. The beans, smaller than the runners, are of exceptional flavour. They may be grown against a trellis or up netting.

CULTURE
Sow late in April, in well-manured soil. When the plants are 6 ins. tall, pinch out the growing point. This encourages side shoots to form and greatly increases the crop.

Plants may also be raised under glass in boxes or pots early in May, planting out at the month's end. Or they may be sown early in March, and grown on in a temperature of 60°F to crop in May. Sow one seed to a 6-in. pot containing loam, decayed manure, and a little sand or grit. Grow them against 4-ft. canes, or against the glass, and tie them as they make growth to wires stretched across the roof. Stop when 6 ins. tall to encourage side growths, and again when at the top of the canes or roof. Ventilate freely in sunny weather, and spray often to prevent red spider.

VARIETIES
Blue Coco. Introduced by Bunyards 50 years ago. Has remained one of the aristocrats of vegetables. It is early, and crops for at least 10 weeks. The purple-blue beans surpass all others for flavour.
Blue Lake. Has purple pods, which turn deep green when cooked, with fine flavour. The pods may also hang until the white seeds have grown large, when they may be dried and used through winter as haricot beans.
Kentucky Wonder. Excellent for freezing. The dark green pods grow 9 ins. long, and are tender, stringless, and full of flavour.

Bean, Runner (*Phaseolus coccineus*)

A red-flowered bean, at its best during late summer and autumn. Of climbing habit it is grown against a trellis, or over netting fastened to a wall, also up canes or laths, which are fixed in the ground at intervals of 9 ins. and held in place by strong galvanised wire fastened to posts at the end of rows.

CULTURE
The ground should be trenched in winter. Remove soil to the width of a spade, and 18 ins. deep, and place in the trench decayed manure and unwanted leaves of winter greens, so that by the end of winter, the trench is filled. Tread it to consolidate, then top up with soil to which has been added 1 oz. of superphosphate and ½ oz. sulphate of potash per yd. of trench. The laths or poles can now be put in place.

Another method is to make the trench in the form of a circle, 3 ft. in diameter. Fix 8 poles in tent fashion, placing them 15 ins. apart. Secure by tying them together at the centre of the circle, 6 ft. above soil level.

Sow one seed, 3 ins. deep, at the base of

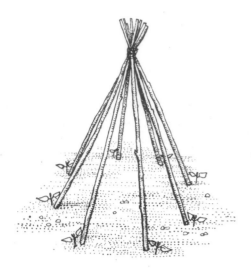

A method of growing runner beans on 8-ft poles tied like a wigwam.

each pole. Do not sow before early May in the south, mid-May in the north for runner beans are easily damaged by frost. Extra seeds can be sown in a small bed for loss replacement.

Soon after germinating, the plants start to climb up the supports. In dry weather keep them well watered. The foliage should also be syringed with clean water after the first flowers appear. This keeps away the red spider, and helps the flowers to set. The first beans will be ready mid-August, about 14–15 weeks after sowing. Picking continues into November. Always remove the beans before they grow too large and coarse. The pods should be slim and snap cleanly when the ends are pressed together. When the plants have reached the top of the poles, pinch out the growing points, to concentrate their energy on crop production.

PESTS & DISEASES
Runner beans are one of the most trouble-free of all crops. To prevent slugs from damaging the stems treat the ground with Slugit.
Rust. Now rare, thanks to the resistant varieties that have been raised. Should it occur, the leaves will be covered in dark brown pustules. There is no cure and infected plants should be destroyed.
VARIETIES
Hammond's Dwarf. Dwarf form of the long-established Prizewinner, making a bushy plant 15 ins. tall. Sow and grow like dwarf beans, spacing the seed 18 ins. apart. Rows should also be 18 ins. apart. No staking necessary. Does well under cloches when seed is planted in April.
Long as Your Arm. A heavy and reliable cropper with beans up to 18 ins. long. They remain crisp and tender, even if not removed immediately they are ready.
Yardstick. The exhibitor's favourite. It is early and bears a profusion of straight beans up to 20 ins. long.

Beetroot (*Beta vulgaris*)
A maritime plant, introduced into Britain during Tudor times. Has been a popular vegetable ever since, either for boiling and serving with white sauce, or to use in salads. It will keep well for many months if pickled in malt vinegar. The tops may be screwed off, and used like spinach.
CULTURE
Likes a sandy soil which has been manured for a previous crop. Before sowing, rake in 1 oz. per sq. yd of common salt and the same amount of superphosphate and sulphate of potash mixed together. Sow end of April in

the south, early May in the north. Frost damage may occur if sown too early. Sow in drills 1 in. deep and allow 15 ins. between each drill. When large enough to handle, thin out seedlings to 4 ins. apart. In dry weather, water copiously to avoid the roots growing tough and 'woody' and the plants running prematurely to seed.

Keep hoeing between rows, and when they reach golf ball size, remove alternate plants to allow the others room to develop. Those removed may be boiled and used in salads, or pickled. At this stage, the plants will benefit from another dressing of salt given, as previously mentioned, during showery weather. Make a second sowing in June to provide more roots for winter storing.

Lift them in October, before the frosts come, taking care not to bruise the skins, or they will bleed, and when cooked will be pink instead of red. Screw off the tops rather than cut them for this also prevents bleeding. Place the roots in boxes of peat or sand in a frost-free place, and use as required.
PESTS & DISEASES
Phoma lingam. A seed-borne disease causing the young plants to turn brown and decay. Seedsmen now packet seed which has been soaked in thiram which prevents an outbreak.

Beet is rarely troubled by pests.
VARIETIES
Avon Early. The best for sowing early, or under cloches. Does not readily run to seed (bolt). Produces evenly-sized roots which retain their deep red colour after cooking.
Boltardy. A globe-shaped beet which does not easily bolt in hot weather, for which reason it should be grown in the south.
Burpee's Golden. An entirely new colour break. Delicious cooked and served with sauce, or sliced into salads. It does not 'bleed'. The flesh has a mild sweet flavour, and is ready to use within 60 days of sowing.
Detroit Globe. A round beet introduced in the 1930s and unsurpassed. The flesh is crisp, sweet, and tender, and free from any paler 'rings' when cooked.

Borecole (*Brassica oleracea*)
Name comes from the Dutch Boerenkool, 'peasant's cabbage', for in Europe it has been grown in cottage gardens since earliest times. Grows well however severe the winter weather. The curly kales, by which name they are known in Britain, improve with frost. It is one of the most valuable of winter greens.
CULTURE
A friable soil containing humus, and not lacking lime, is needed. Rake in at planting time a 1 oz. per sq. yd. dressing of super-

Kale 'Dwarf Green Curled'

phosphate and sulphate of potash in mixture.

Sow in shallow drills early in April, setting out the plants towards the end of May, 2 ft. apart. Plant firmly, and tread around the plants whenever loosened by winds. To encourage a bushy habit, trim the tap root before planting, or transplant the seedlings when large enough to handle, to beds of specially prepared soil, and move to their permanent quarters after 3–4 weeks.

From early autumn remove the curled leaves, and to bring out the delicate flavour, simmer (rather than boil) in a little butter.
PESTS & DISEASES
Troubles rarely affect this crop, but for cabbage caterpillars, dust with derris powder from early June until September, and to avoid club root, treat the roots with calomel before planting.
VARIETIES
Dwarf Green Curled. The best for a small garden, or one exposed to strong winds. Height 15 ins., with handsome parsley-like leaves.
Frosty. Outstanding. Extremely hardy. Height 15 ins., with finely curled leaves held well above the soil.

Broccoli, large-heading (*Brassica oleracea*) The most widely grown form, also known as winter cauliflower. It is hardier than the summer varieties. But even so, it must be grown well from the start, to withstand a severe winter.
CULTURE
Plants take 12 months to mature so the seed is sown in shallow drills early in April (to cut in April), and in May (to cut in May). Sow thinly (so that the plants do not grow thin and leggy) in a frame, or under cloches. Transplant the seedlings to permanent quarters when large enough to handle. Like cauliflowers, the plants frequently damp off if the soil is not treated at sowing time with Cheshunt compound.

The plants need a well-manured soil, and to counteract any tendency to soft growth, rake in at planting time 1 oz. per sq. yd. of sulphate of potash. Prior to planting, give a 2 oz. per sq. yd. dressing of hoof and horn meal.

Space 3 ft. apart and plant firmly to ensure compact curds. Tread round the plants if made loose by winds. Water copiously in dry weather otherwise the heads will quickly run to seed. During severe weather, bend the outer leaves over the curds to protect them from browning. This also keeps them clean.
PESTS & DISEASES
Cabbage Caterpillar. The grub of the cabbage white butterfly, causes such havoc amongst brassica crops. The eggs are laid on the leaves, and in a few days, creamy-white grubs hatch out and begin to devour the leaves, later penetrating into the heads. For this reason the heads should always be inserted in salt water before cooking. To control, dust the plants with derris from June until September.
Club Root, or finger and toe disease. The roots become swollen and knobbly, and growth is stunted. It is caused by a slime fungus in the soil but is rarely present in well-limed land. As a precaution, dust the roots with calomel or dip into calomel solution before planting. Give infected ground a rest from brassicas for at least a year.
Cabbage Root Fly. All Brassicas can be affected, also turnips. Fly lays eggs near the stem. The emerging larvae enter the soil and begin to eat the roots. The flow of water to leaves is impeded and wilting follows. If unchecked the plant will die. To control,

White sprouting mini-cauliflower

Savoy cabbage 'Ice Queen'

dust around the base of the stem with either 4% calomel dust, or a good insecticide such as malathion or BHC. Repeat two or three times during the growing season if necessary.

VARIETIES

Matchless. Forms a large tight curd of purest white, during May and June.

Royal Oak. Makes neat, compact plant, maturing in June and July.

Snow's Winter White. First of the winter varieties. From a March sowing, the large compact heads will be ready in February and March.

St George. Curds grow tight and uniform in size and are ready in March and April.

Broccoli, Sprouting (*Brassica oleracea*)
A most valuable vegetable. It is hardy and rarely fails to crop well. At its best from early New Year onwards.

CULTURE

Plants grow up to 4 ft. in a well-manured soil. Plant them where they are protected from winds, and they will yield shoots (like tiny cauliflowers) over a long period. Work in plenty of humus, decayed manure, shoddy, or garden compost, and at planting time give a 1 oz. per sq. yd. dressing of sulphate of potash.

Sow in drills in April, and move the young plants to permanent quarters, 3 ft. apart, before they grow too large. Firm planting and treading in after gales is necessary.

Cut the shoots regularly before they go to seed. A dozen plants will yield sufficient at one time to serve 4 people. If the shoots are left on the plants too long, their cropping powers are reduced. Plants will benefit from a mulch given in November.

PESTS & DISEASES

Sprouting broccoli suffers little in this respect, but dip the roots in calomel solution before planting, and dust with derris from June to September, to guard against cabbage white caterpillars.

VARIETIES

Early Purple Sprouting. From an early spring sowing, there will be purple shoots to cut from New Year onwards. Late Purple Sprouting takes over in May, and will continue through the summer.

Nine Star Perennial. A most valuable vegetable. If some decayed manure, bone meal, or dried blood is dug into the soil each autumn, it will remain productive for several years, yielding a continuous supply of white curds, like small cauliflowers, which form around a large main head. Plants will be stimulated into new growth in the spring if ground is given a ½ oz. per sq. yd. dressing of nitrate of soda.

Brussels Sprouts (*Brassica oleracea*)
An important winter vegetable. By planting 3 or 4 varieties, sprouts can be obtained from October until April. A single plant can yield up to 100 sprouts. Any surplus may be frozen, to use when severe weather makes picking difficult, though frost will not harm them.

CULTURE

To have firm sprouts, plant firmly. Good culture is necessary for they occupy the ground for at least 12 months, and yield for six. Dig in plenty of humus in any form, and provide organic fertilisers which release their nitrogen steadily over a long period. Prepare the ground in plenty of time. Prior to planting, fork in 4 oz. per sq. yd. of hoof and horn meal and 2 oz. of superphosphate and sulphate of potash mixed together. This helps to form plenty of tight, crisp sprouts.

Sow in August for an early autumn crop the following year, and in April to provide a crop early next year, which will continue until summer. You can never have too many sprouts, and they like a long season to mature.

Plant out 3 ft. apart and tread in firmly if the soil is friable, or if the plants are loosened by strong winds. Keep hoeing between plants, and water copiously in dry weather. They will benefit from a mulch of strawy manure in late summer, or from an occasional watering with liquid manure.

When the sprouts are 1 in. in diameter, gently remove from the stem, taking several from each plant. This allows the others more room to develop. At the same time remove any dead leaves.

PESTS & DISEASES

Downy Mildew. It attacks all brassicas, but especially Brussels sprouts, covering them with a grey mould. To control, spray the plants with Bordeaux mixture once a month from the time the seedlings appear.

VARIETIES

Avon Cross. An F1 hybrid. Forms firm sprouts of even size in 12 months from a September sowing. Unpicked sprouts will retain their quality for some weeks.

Fasolt. Perhaps the best late sprout ever raised. Height 2 ft., with stems covered in medium-sized sprouts of brilliant green, which are at their best in January to March.

Jade Cross. A hybrid. Follows Avon Cross. The sprouts continue to increase in size all winter, whilst retaining their firmness and texture. They are packed in tight rows around the plants which grow 2 ft. tall.

Peer Gynt. A hybrid, outstanding in every way. Height 18–20 ins. The emerald green sprouts, tightly packed around the stem, are ready by early November.

Prince Askold. All modern varieties freeze well, including this one. Height less than 18 ins. At its best in December when the dark green sprouts are crisp and tender.

Cabbage (*Brassica oleracea*)
A most worthy vegetable, providing 'greens' throughout the year if a number of varieties are grown for succession, as the following table shows:

Variety	Sowing Time	When Ready
January King (S)	Apr–May	Dec–Jan
Christmas Drumhead	Apr	Nov–Dec
Ormskirk Late (S)	Apr	Feb–Mar
Ice Queen (S)	Apr	Dec–Mar
Flower of Spring	July	May–June
Springtide	July	Mar–May
Wheeler's Imperial	July	May–June
Babyhead	Mar–Apr	Aug–Oct
Golden Acre	Mar	Aug–Oct
Greyhound	Mar	Sept–Nov
Rozanda	Mar	Oct–Dec

* (S) denotes Savoy

CULTURE

Spring cabbages, those with pointed heads, are especially useful. They are sweet and tender and come at a time when few other vegetables are about. To have plants large enough to survive a hard winter, and yet not too forward to bolt in a warm, dry autumn, sow the seed early July in the north and late July in the south.

Sow in drills 1 in. deep and 8 ins. apart. Move the seedlings when 3 ins. tall to where they are to crop. The soil need not be so rich as for sprouts and cauliflowers, but dig in whatever humus is available, and give a 2 oz. per sq. yd. dressing of basic slag at planting time. Plant spring cabbage 18 ins. apart, for they do not grow as large as the round-headed autumn and winter varieties, which should be spaced 2 ft. apart.

For spring cabbages to make quick growth in spring, rake into the soil around the plants in March or early April, preferably on a showery day, ½ oz. per sq. yd. of nitrate of soda.

After cutting the heads in early summer, leave the plants in the ground, and where the cut was made, 2 or 3 small cabbages will form which will be ready in about 2 months. These are sweet and tender, especially if steamed and not boiled.

PESTS & DISEASES

For cabbage white caterpillar, club root, and cabbage root fly, see under Broccoli, large-heading.

Dark Leaf Spot. A fungus disease appearing as dark brown spots on all parts of the plant, spoiling the appearance and retarding growth. Spray with Bordeaux mixture every 3 weeks.

VARIETIES

Babyhead. Makes a small round head for autumn use. Ideal in the smallest garden.

Christmas Drumhead. At its best in midwinter, when the large round heads will provide food for several meals.

Flower of Spring. Of exceptional hardiness, the medium-sized heads are firm and pointed, with outstanding flavour.

Golden Acre. For autumn use. Forms a compact round head, and appears to sit on the ground.

Chinese cabbage 'Sampan'

Cardoon plants tied for blanching

Carrot 'Chantenay Red Cored'

Greyhound. May be sown at any time to mature 6 months later. Its large pointed heads have fewer outer leaves.

Primo. Makes a small ball-head. Matures 5–6 months from sowing.

Rozanda. Best for October–November cutting. Makes a medium-sized flat head, blue-green, with a white centre when cut.

Winter Keeper, or *Winter White.* The solid pale green heads are ready in November, but if at the year's end the cabbages are pulled up with stem and roots, they will remain fresh in a cool room for at least 3 months.

Cabbage, Chinese (*Brassica pekinensis*)

Also known as Pe-Tsai. Eastern in origin, it is a valuable dual-purpose vegetable with greater heat resistance than ordinary cabbage. May be used raw in a salad in autumn, in place of lettuce, or steamed like cabbage, and served with meats.

CULTURE
Treat like endive, sowing early in July in well-manured ground. Will quickly run to seed if the soil is lacking in humus. Old mushroom bed compost is ideal. Sow seed broadcast and rake in. Thin the seedlings, when large enough to handle, to 8 ins. apart. Like endive, they will not transplant. Keep ground well watered in dry weather, and use as soon as the heads have hearted.

PESTS & DISEASES
Free from both.

VARIETY
Tropical Pride. Ready to cut within 60 days of sowing, when the globular heads will weigh 3 lb. or more. When cut open, the head will reveal a mass of creamy-yellow leaves packed tightly together.

Cabbage, Red (*Brassica oleracea*)

Valuable for pickling, but requires a long season for it to grow well.

CULTURE
Sow seed early in September in rows, where the plants remain over winter. Early in spring, set out 2 ft. apart, into well-manured ground which does not lack lime. At planting time, rake in a 2 oz. per sq. yd. dressing of superphosphate and sulphate of potash in mixture. Water copiously in dry weather.

PESTS & DISEASES
Plants are rarely troubled by either, but for cabbage white caterpillar and club root, see under Broccoli, large-heading.

VARIETY
Dobies Early Blood Red. Forms a medium-sized, compact head, earlier than any other. Turns brilliant red after pickling, and retains its crispness over many months.

Calabrese (*Brassica oleracea*)

Another name for the green-sprouting broccoli. The calabrese has an excellent flavour, not unlike asparagus, and like all the broccolis, is useful for the freezer.

CULTURE
It is not so hardy as the other sprouting broccolis, and is at its best in autumn and late winter.

Sow in drills in April, with a second sowing in early June. Set out the plants 3 ft. apart. Make firm, and tread in the plants after strong winds. They require a soil rich in humus, so dig in some used hops, shoddy, or old mushroom compost.

PESTS & DISEASES
They suffer little in this respect, but take precautions against cabbage white caterpillars, and dip the roots in calomel solution before planting.

VARIETIES
Express Corona. A hybrid, reaching maturity 8 weeks after planting. When the large central head is removed, side shoots will form, which allows cutting to continue until Christmas.

Green Comet. An F1 hybrid. It matures early, and the large green head is ready to cut by end of July.

Cardoon (*Cynara scolymus*)

Closely related to the globe artichoke. It has handsome, silvery, fern-like leaves, and was introduced from the Mediterranean regions.

CULTURE
Whereas the globe artichoke is usually propagated from offsets, the cardoon is raised from seed sown in a frame early in February. Set out the young plants early May, 18 ins. apart, in ground that was trenched during winter. Seed may be sown directly into the trench and covered with cloches. Later, thin the seedlings to 18 ins. During dry weather keep the plants well watered. At the end of September tie the foliage together in loops, and earth up the plants, using the soil removed from the trench. As much of the stem as possible should be blanched. This is made easier if some straw is placed around the stems before earthing up. By early November the stems should be ready to use as required. Remove the outer leaves and cook the hearts as for celery.

PESTS & DISEASES
Cardoons are troubled by none.

VARIETY
Ivory White. Of Spanish origin, it is hardier and better than the French variety. When well blanched, the inner leaves are crisp and tender.

Carrot (*Daucus carota*)

A native plant. By raising an early crop over a mild hot bed, or in a frame, it is possible to enjoy home-grown carrots all the year round.

CULTURE
Make the hot bed, place over it 2 ins. of finely screened soil, and sow early February. Replace frame, and keep the young plants when they appear, comfortably moist. As the weather warms in spring, admit fresh air, and by early May the carrots will be ready to pull. Amsterdam Forcing, Little Finger, or Sweetheart, are suitable for early crops.

In the open, choose a quick-maturing variety, such as Chantenay, or Early Gem. Sow early April in drills ¾ in. deep and 9 ins. apart. Fresh manure must not be used, for this will cause the roots to fork. The soil should be friable and manured for a previous crop. A 1 oz. per sq. yd. dressing of sulphate of potash will prevent the roots splitting. Sow thinly for the roots need room to develop. They will be ready to pull by mid-June. Use at finger thickness.

For the maincrop, sow later in April, and in May. Allow 12 ins. between the rows. Keep hoeing between rows, and water well in times of drought, otherwise the roots will be hard and pithy when cooked. When finger thick, thin to 2 ins. apart. Use the thinnings to grate into salads, to steam in butter, or to serve with white sauce.

Carrots do not improve with frost, and should be lifted before the end of November. Cut off the tops, and store the roots in boxes of peat or sand.

PESTS & DISEASES
Carrot Fly. The most troublesome pest. The flies lay their eggs in the soil, and the yellow larvae burrow into the carrots. To control, either dress the seed before sowing with Dieldrex 'B' (1/16th oz. to an oz. of seed), or dust the soil with Lindex at sowing time.

Flea Beetle. May attack the foliage and cause yellowing. Treat soil with Lindex to prevent an outbreak.

Downy Mildew. May attack the leaves as dark brown spots in a wet summer, causing them to turn yellow, shrivel, and die. To control, spray the plants with a copper fungicide.

VARIETIES
Chantenay. Stump-rooted and of excellent flavour. It matures quickly and keeps well. May be sown for an early or late crop.

Early Nantes. Cylindrical stump-rooted carrot which forces well. Flavour and quality are outstanding.

Goldinhart. A fine carrot growing 6 ins. long and 2 ins. across the shoulder. The orange flesh continues to the centre, there being almost no core.

Little Finger. A long slender carrot for forcing and early sowing. Roots are crisp and tender and without core.

Scarlet Perfection. Long tapering scarlet roots, free of core and of excellent flavour. They retain their quality through winter.

Cauliflower (*Brassica oleracea*)

Grown in Britain at an early date, though its heads were no larger than a tennis ball. Modern varieties bear heads of purest white up to 9 ins. across, and weigh several pounds.

CULTURE

Plants require a really rich soil, containing plenty of moisture-holding humus, otherwise the heads will run to seed, so dig in shoddy, hop manure, or old mushroom compost. There must be plenty of food available for them to form large solid heads. To assist with this, rake in at planting time, 2 oz. per sq. yd. of sulphate of potash.

For an early crop, sow seed late in August, in a frame or under cloches, and transplant the seedlings under glass to 3 ins. apart. Keep them there until early April then harden off and plant out 18 ins. apart. They will form heads by early June. The plants may also be grown on in the frame or under cloches, planting them 12 ins. apart when transplanted. Plant firmly. Give plenty of air on suitable days, but water sparingly. When sowing, remember to dust the drills with calomel to guard against cabbage root fly and club root.

For a July crop, sow in drills 1 in. deep in April, and plant out in May. For cauliflowers in August and September, sow in May and June. Sow little, and often, so that there will be heads to cut over the summer and autumn. Those that cannot be used should be put in the freezer. If no freezer available, lift the heads with their roots, and hang head down in a cool room, where they will keep fresh for several weeks.

PESTS & DISEASES

Black Leg. Attacks the seedlings at the roots and then the stems, causing them to heel over. There is no cure, but prevention is by watering after sowing (and when transplanting) with Cheshunt compound, 1 oz. to 2 gals. of water.

Cabbage White Caterpillar. A troublesome cauliflower pest. The butterfly lays eggs in the heads, and the grubs devour both heads and leaves. Dust with derris at intervals of 10 days throughout summer.

VARIETIES

Early Snowball. Best for under glass, or early crops outdoors. Heads are tight and of medium size.

Snow King. Of vigorous habit. Makes a large tight head for late summer cutting.

South Pacific. Extremely hardy. Is best for October–November cutting.

Unwin's Snocap. Follows Early Snowball. Large pure white heads, even in size.

Celeriac (*Apium graveolens* var: *rapaceum*)

Form of celery, but makes a bulbous root instead of stalks. Has same flavour, and should be grown where celery proves difficult.

CULTURE

Like celery, it requires a long season of growth. Sow seed early March, either over a hot bed covered with a frame, or in a greenhouse (60°F). Transplant seedlings to boxes and harden in a cold frame. Plant out at end of May. Soil must contain plenty of humus and decayed manure. Plant in rows

15 ins. apart, allowing 12 ins. between the plants. Do not bury the bulbous root; sit it on top of the soil and water in. Keep the plants well watered in dry weather, and they will continue to swell and not grow woody. From end of July, give dilute manure water once every ten days. This will improve both texture and flavour. As the roots swell, pull away the soil, and remove any lateral shoots with a sharp knife.

The turnip-like roots will be ready at the end of October. Leave in the ground until required.

PEST & DISEASES

They will be troubled by none.

VARIETY

Marble Ball. It has superseded the old Giant Prague. Has many times more edible flesh, which cooks white and possesses excellent flavour.

Celery (*Apium graveolens*)

It is the self-blanching type that is now most widely grown by amateurs for it is more easily managed.

CULTURE

Requires a long season to develop. Sow seed in February over a mild hot bed, or in a greenhouse or frame. The seedlings will be ready to transplant early in April. After hardening, set out the plants at the end of May. This type does not require trenching, but likes a soil with plenty of humus. Old mushroom bed compost or used hops are suitable, but use anything that retains moisture. Plant 9 ins. apart and make firm. They will benefit from a mulch of decayed strawy manure in July.

The roots should be ready by mid-September, and although earthing up is not necessary, the stems will be more succulent if pieces of cardboard are tied round the plants 3–4 weeks before being used. Fasten cardboard round the whole length of stem but exclude foliage. The stems are self-folding, and will blanch themselves at the centre, but if light is excluded from the outer stems, these too will be white and succulent.

PESTS & DISEASES

Celery Fly. Eggs are laid on foliage during the summer. The larvae attack leaves and stems, causing blisters. The maggots are killed by bruising the blisters, but to prevent, spray the plants with quassia solution in midsummer.

Leaf Spot. A troublesome celery disease. Brown spots appear on the leaves, then the stems, causing them to die back. Sow seed that has been treated for leaf spot, and spray with Bordeaux mixture early in summer as an additional precaution.

VARIETIES

Golden Self-blanching. The outer sticks are golden-yellow, the heart pure white. Height 15 ins. Matures early autumn, when it is crisp and nutty eaten raw.

Greenstick. Also American Green. It grows less than 15 ins. tall and makes a large heart. Sticks are greenish-white and of delicious flavour.

Chicory (*Cichorium intybus*)

A native plant, also known as succory. One of the easiest to manage yet is so little grown. At its best when forced and blanched.

CULTURE

Sow seed about June 1st in a well-nourished soil. If sown earlier, the plants may run to seed. Sow in rows 15 ins. apart and thin plants to 10 ins. Keep them growing by watering when the soil is dry. In November the foliage dies down, and the roots are ready to force.

Do this in cellar or garage, preferably where there is slight warmth, to bring on the shoots in about 4 weeks. One method is to half fill (about 6 ins. deep) an orange box with composted, strawy manure (as used to grow mushrooms), and over this place 3 ins. of loam into which the roots are planted closely together. Water in, and place a sack over the top of the box to exclude light. The shoots will have about 6 ins. in which to grow, and after about 4 weeks should be ready to cut. They may be grown in this way beneath the kitchen sink. Cut the shoots just before they are required for cooking, removing outer leaves before doing so.

PESTS & DISEASES

Troubled by none.

VARIETY

Giant Whitloof. The best form – heads are large, and as fat as one's wrist when ready to cut. They are pure white, and are sweet and succulent after simmering for an hour. Or use raw, grated into a winter salad.

Cucumber (*Cucumis sativus*)

Modern hybrid varieties have now brought this vegetable new popularity. It may be grown in a greenhouse, or frame, or in the open, for which purpose grow the ridge varieties.

CULTURE

For an early crop, they need more heat than tomatoes, and to have them ready by midsummer, sow seed in January in small pots containing J.I. seed compost, in a temperature of 70°F. Plant the seed 1 in. deep on its side. In 3 weeks, the seedlings will be ready to move to larger pots containing a mixture of turf loam and decayed manure. By the end of March move to still larger pots, in

Cauliflower 'Autumn Giant'

Celeriac

which they will crop. Place at the back of the greenhouse roof, and train the main stem up canes fastened to wires stretched across the roof. The laterals are 'stopped' at the second leaf. Maintain a moist atmosphere by frequent syringing and damping down, but air must only be admitted on warm days. Top dress with decayed manure in early June. From then onwards, feed once a week with dilute manure water.

For a heated greenhouse, Pepimex or Femina, F1 hybrids are reliable, or the older Telegraph, which bears heavy crops of evenly-sized deep green cucumbers.

For a frame, sow seed over a hot bed at the end of March. As the plants resent root disturbance, sow where they are to grow, after covering the hot bed with 4–5 ins. of soil. A frame 5 ft. × 4 ft. takes 3 plants, so plant 2 seeds near each other in three places. Retain the stronger in each group. Keep the frame closed almost throughout the life of the plants, and cover with sacking at night when frost is about. Spray the plants often, to maintain a humid atmosphere, and to keep down red spider.

Train the shoots about the frame, pegging them down. Stop the laterals at the second leaf, and train the sub-laterals about the frame. It is advisable to whiten the glass on the inside to prevent sun-scorch. Hand pollination of the flowers is not necessary with cucumbers. It is important to remove the fruits before they grow too large, or they will lose flavour as well as taking too much out of the plant. If fruits are removed when 6–7 ins. long, the plants will crop until early autumn.

For frames, Femina bears nearly all female flowers and is most prolific; Topnotch, also a hybrid, has thin skin and mild flavour; and Tasty Green. All are disease resistant and vigorous.

Ridge cucumbers may be grown in the open, like marrows. Plant on ridges of soil and compost, or between the ridges if garden is exposed. Sow seed in small pots over a hot bed in April, and after hardening, set out the plants early June. For 10 days after planting out, it is an advantage if cloches (on their sides) are placed around the plants. When 12 ins. high, stop the plants to encourage lateral shoots, which carry the crop. Mulch with decayed manure early August and keep the soil moist at all times.

The best varieties are Hampshire Giant, growing to 12 ins. long, with skin pale green, and flesh sweet and juicy; and Burpee Hybrid, with smooth dark green skin, and the flesh crisp and white.

PESTS & DISEASES

Leaf Blotch. Small pale green spots appear on the leaf surfaces. Later, the spots turn grey, then brown before falling away to leave holes. It will later attack the fruits. To control, remove infected leaves and spray with liver of sulphur solution.

Mildew. Also attacks marrows. Forms a white powder on the underside of the leaves, causing the foliage to turn brown and die. Routine spraying with weak Bordeaux mixture will prevent, or control, an outbreak.

Endive (*Cichorium endivia*)

A native of the near east. Has been grown for salads since earliest times. May have been introduced into Britain by the Romans.

CULTURE

It is best to sow where it is to mature, for it runs to seed if transplanted. Sow in shallow drills 12 ins. apart, and thin the seedlings to 10 ins. Endives like plenty of humus in the soil to retain summer moisture, so dig in peat, hop manure, decayed leaves, or garden compost. Do not sow before July 1st for

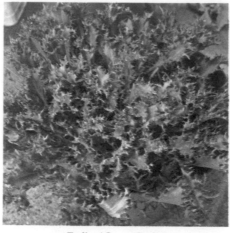
Endive 'Green Curled'

plants grow better in the cooler days of early autumn. For this reason, choose a northerly aspect. Keep well watered in dry weather.

Blanching is important. Draw in the leaves, by tying rafia round the top as soon as the plants reach maturity. After 3 weeks, the heads will be a creamy-white, sweet, and tender. By covering with cloches early December it is possible to have endive until Christmas.

PESTS & DISEASES

This vegetable is troubled by none.

VARIETIES

Batavian Broad Leaf. Forms a large heart of crinkled leaves, and is crisp and tender.

Giant Fringed Oyster. The head will reach 15 ins. across, filled with dark green laciniated leaves, which blanch to golden yellow.

Garlic (*Allium sativum*)

Native of the east, and rich in alkaline salts and blood-purifying sulphur compounds. It is said that the legions of ancient Rome obtained sustenance by chewing garlic as they marched across Europe.

CULTURE

Requires a light warm soil which has been manured for a previous crop. Plant the cloves (as the offsets are called) early October in the south, early March in the north, in drills 2 ins. deep and 6 ins. apart. Allow 12 ins. between rows, and leave the soil loose.

October-planted cloves will be ready to lift the following August, and March-planted cloves in October, when the foliage turns yellow. Dry the bulbs in an open shed, and string them up in a dry, frost-free room. Use as required.

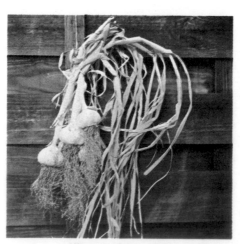
Allium sativum or garlic

Good King Henry, an alternative to spinach.

Good King Henry (*Chenopodium bonus-henricus*)

A native perennial plant known as mercury or wild spinach. Grows 2 ft. tall, with arrow-shaped leaves which are cooked like spinach. Cut the young shoots when 6 ins. long in May and June. Simmer, and serve like kale, or with melted butter like asparagus.

CULTURE

Sow seed in April in drills 1 in. deep. Set out the young plants 12 ins. apart, in a rich, deeply dug soil. They will be ready to use the following year. Alternate plants may be lifted and divided in March when they are grown large. Give the plants a mulch of decayed compost each year. In April, when growth begins, earth up the shoots to make them more tender.

PESTS & DISEASES

This plant suffers from none.

Hamburg Parsley (*Petroselinum crispum tuberosum*)

The turnip-rooted parsley is much appreciated on the Continent, but has not found favour in Britain.

CULTURE

Roots grow at least 6 ins. long, and are 2 ins. at the neck. They are parsley flavoured when grated raw into salads, but taste more like celeriac when boiled and served with white sauce. Plants require a long growing season. Sow seed mid-March, in shallow drills 15 ins. apart, and thin seedlings to 9 ins. when large enough to handle. They transplant well. Make a second sowing in July to mature in the spring. They are perfectly hardy, and stand the winter well. Keep plants well watered in dry weather. Roots are ready to use in early November but may be left in the ground until required. When lifting, insert the fork well down so as not to break them.

PESTS & DISEASES

This crop is troubled by none.

VARIETIES

Only the type.

Kohl-Rabi (*Brassica oleracea*)

Resembles a swede, but is really a cabbage which forms a large globe on the stem almost at soil level. It grows quickly, the globes being ready to use within 12 weeks

Hamburg parsley, used like parsnips

Kohlrabi 'Purple Vienna'

of sowing, when they will be 3–4 ins. across.

CULTURE

Likes a light sandy soil, enriched with some humus. Old mushroom compost is ideal. Make first sowing in early April, in shallow drills 15 ins. apart. Thin to 8 ins. Further sowings can be made each month until July. Those from later sowings can be left for winter and spring use. Sow early March over a mild hot bed to obtain a crop early in June. To use, trim off roots and stem below, and the leaves above, and boil or steam. Do not allow them to grow too large or the flavour will be lost.

PESTS & DISEASES

This crop is troubled by none.

VARIETIES

Early Purple Vienna. Forms a globe like a Bramley apple in size and shape, and has a purple skin. The white flesh is sweet and tender. Sow this to stand over winter.

Early White Vienna. Not as hardy, but quicker to mature. Use it for early sowings. Has a smooth pale green skin, and a creamy-white flesh of especially mild flavour.

Leek (*Allium ampeloprasum*)

Native of S. Europe, it must have reached Britain early in history, as Saxon writings speak of it as a valuable food.

CULTURE

To grow leeks well, they should be planted in ground that has been trenched. Make the trench 10 ins. deep, and at the bottom place some garden compost or any other kind of humus. Then into the soil which is to cover it, add ½ oz. of superphosphate and ½ oz. sulphate of potash per yard of trench. One suggestion is to place on both sides of the trench, the soil removed from it. One side is used to cover the humus and the other side for blanching.

Sow seed in shallow drills in a frame, or under cloches, early in March, for leeks require a long season. Move the plants to the trench early June. To plant, make a hole with a pencil or dibber 5 ins. deep and drop in the plant. Do not cover in with soil but water them in. Make a double row 6 ins. apart, and allow 6 ins. between each plant:

Plant so that the wide leaf, the blade, lies along the row and not across it. Water well in dry weather. In August, give an occasional watering with dried blood, or liquid manure. They grow until late November when the first 'sticks' may be used. Leeks are so hardy they may be left in the ground all winter, and lifted as required.

PESTS & DISEASES

Eelworm. Attacks most bulbous plants causing leaves to turn yellow. If observed, treat the soil the following year with Jeyes Fluid (2 tablespoons to 1 gal. of water), about a month before planting. To guard against seed-borne eelworm, seedsmen now fumigate with methyl bromide before packeting.

White Tip. Attacks the leaf tips, then spreads down the plant causing it to decay. When noticed, spray with weak Burgundy mixture.

VARIETIES

Catalina. The long slender sticks mature before other varieties, and are of mildest flavour.

Marble Pillar. Produces the longest stick of all, blanching pure white, and cooking sweet and tender.

Musselburgh. First of the named leeks, and still outstanding. Extremely hardy, with thick stems blanching to 15 ins.

Lettuce (*Lactuca sativa*)

Indispensable for summer and winter salads, and to use in sandwiches. Can provide and all-year supply.

CULTURE

Requires a well-limed and well-nourished soil, containing humus. Dig in old mushroom compost, used hops, or garden compost, and at planting time, rake in 1 oz. per sq. yd. of sulphate of potash. This encourages the plants, especially winter lettuce, to grow 'hard', and survive adverse weather.

For *early* lettuce, sow under glass late in August and transplant 8 ins. apart in a frame in early October. They will be ready in March. If grown over a mild hot bed, the plants will mature by Christmas. Water sparingly during winter, and then only the soil around them. Dust the plants with flowers of sulphur to prevent mildew.

Trocadero and Suzan are excellent for frame culture. Frame lettuces require plenty of fresh air when the weather is mild.

Arctic King and Sutton's Imperial are good for outdoors, either under cloches or unprotected. Both form large heads with few outer leaves, and are hardy enough to withstand 10° of frost.

Sow seed mid-August, and set out the plants 10 ins. apart in September. They will be ready by the New Year. For spring and early summer, sow Spring Market in a frame, or under cloches, in early March to plant out early April. They will be ready in May and June. Follow with sowings of All the Year Round and Constant Heart in April, and at monthly intervals through the summer.

Lettuces require ample moisture in summer to form solid hearts, otherwise they will be tough, and will go to seed in hot weather. Planting distances will depend upon variety. For Avon Crispy plant 8 ins. apart; for Webb's Wonderful 12–14 ins. apart.

PESTS & DISEASES

Botrytis. Appears on the leaves as a grey mould, especially attacking plants under glass. Ample ventilation will help to keep it down, and dusting with equal parts lime and sulphur, or orthocide captan, will prevent an outbreak. The same treatment is also suggested for downy mildew.

Millipede. The most troublesome pest, black in colour, which attacks the roots, causing the plants to wilt. Control by treating the soil before sowing with malathion (1 oz. per sq. yd.).

VARIETIES (for summer)

Avon Crispy. Highly resistant to downy mildew. Forms a solid heart and stands well in hot weather.

Buttercrunch. A cross between a cos and cabbage lettuce. Outer leaves are olive green, the heart yellow. It never becomes bitter.

Histon Crispie. A self-folding cos lettuce. The leaves grow upright and crinkled, which makes for crisp eating. With older cos varieties, it was necessary to tie the outer leaves to blanch and heart, but not with this one.

Salad Bowl. Interesting American variety of endive type, forming a fern-like rosette of crinkled leaves.

Webb's Wonderful. The best ever raised. Forms a huge ball-like head of crisp, crinkled leaves, which do not wilt in the warmest weather.

Marrows and Squashes (*Cucurbita* species)

These are most useful summer and winter vegetables. The summer marrows and squashes are derivatives of *C. pepo*, and the winter keepers, of *C. maxima*. They require full sun and shelter from cold winds. They also resent root disturbance and must be pot grown from the start.

CULTURE

Raise plants in small pots of J.I. sowing compost in a temperature of 65°F, or over a hot bed in a frame. Just press in the large seeds, pointed end upwards about April 1st. Keep compost moist and the plants growing. By early May, move to a cold frame, and grow on in larger pots of compost containing some decayed manure. They will now need more water, and on warm days fresh air. By the month's end, leave off the lights by day. Plant out early June.

Marrows require a deep bed made up of as much humus as possible, preferably decayed manure. For each marrow allow an area of 4 sq. ft. for the bush type; 6 sq. ft. for trailers. If growing under cloches, make the bed fit the cloches. Plants can be grown on in the hot bed over which they were raised, after covering it with 4 ins. of soil. Keep frame light on until late June, but planting may be done early in May.

Under glass, syringe daily, and from early June, give plants copious amounts of water. When they have grown to 18 ins., nip out the growing points to encourage side shoots. The first flowers should be hand pollinated by dusting them with a camel-hair brush.

Marrows will form early July, ready to remove 10–12 days later. Allow them to

Mushroom cultivation: (1) the compost should be rammed down firmly; (2) inserting the spawn in the compost; (3) a flush develops very quickly at temperature 56°–58°F; (4) by the seventh day growth is rapid, and the mushrooms have reached maturity.

grow to a reasonable size only. If too large they become tough and lose flavour. When removing, take care not to damage the plants.

PESTS & DISEASES

See under Cucumber.

VARIETIES

Butternut. Of trailing habit, it grows to 12 ins. long and as thick as one's forearm. Flesh is firm and full of flavour. It keeps well into winter.

Gold Nugget. A bush variety growing as large as a grapefruit, and golden in colour. Each plant bears 7–8 fruits. They are delicious if cut into halves and chilled. They can also be stored through winter.

Rotherside Orange. Richly flavoured. Bears fruits of grapefruit size and similar colouring. A trailer, the fruits should be chilled after cooking. Cut into halves and serve with cream and sugar, or ginger.

Sutton's Superlative. A bush variety. Fruits grow large, but are at their best when small. The skin is dark green, the flesh rich orange and russet.

Courgettes. Have long been appreciated on the Continent as one of the most delicious vegetables. The true French is a variety which looks like small green sausages. Remove when 4 ins. long, and fry in butter either whole or sliced like a carrot.

The golden courgette is similar in size, but is of a deep golden colour with a skin so tender that it may be sliced, uncooked, into salads.

Mushroom (*Psalliota campestris*)

This popular food is so easily digested that invalids find it nourishing. It is not necessary to have a special mushroom house, or heated building. Mushrooms can be grown in boxes stacked along the sides of a garage, outhouse, or cellar, or in a cupboard, or even under the kitchen sink.

CULTURE

Make up the boxes in April (boxes or buckets of compost already prepared, may be obtained from seedsmen) and they will begin to crop at the end of May, and continue until late July. Have more boxes ready then to crop early October. Mushrooms will not grow in a temperature below 40°–50°F, but should the compost become frozen solid, no harm will be done. Cropping begins again when the temperature rises to 50°F. Unless there is warmth in winter, the amateur should have boxes cropping during the summer and autumn only.

The compost can be prepared from a bale of wheat straw, obtainable from a farmer. Shake out in the corner of a yard or shed, and soak with water. Use part of it to make the base of a heap, and sprinkle over it Adco 'M', or other mushroom compost-maker. Add another layer of straw, more activator, and so on, until the heap is made as high as possible, to retain the heat. If dry poultry manure, or fresh horse manure from a riding stable, is added in stages, this will make a better compost.

After a week, the heap will have heated and be ready for turning. Shake it well out, and add more water if it is dry or has not heated. Make the heap again and leave for another week. Then turn it again, and after another week it will be ready to fill the boxes. Fish boxes, which are 6 ins. deep, are best. Press the compost well down with a brick, or piece of wood, to within 1 in. of the top, and stack them up in this way:

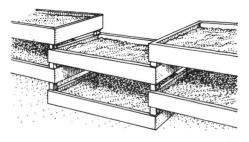

In an unheated room, the heat of the compost will soon fall and the boxes can be spawned almost at once. Obtain a carton(s) of Pure Culture Spawn, well in advance, but make sure it has not been in stock too long. Break it into pieces the size of a walnut, and press them into the compost, just below the surface, 4 ins. apart. A carton will spawn 40 sq. ft. Re-firm the compost, and leave until the spawn can be seen 'running' as white threads. Then cover with fresh pasture loam to a depth of 1 in. Commercial growers use a mixture of peat and chalk, or sterilised soil, to prevent disease. Mush-

Onion 'Giant Fen Globe'

Parsley 'Green Velvet' in a 12" pot

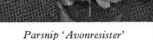

Parsnip 'Avonresister'

room flies may be troublesome in summer so dust the boxes with Black Arrow powder.

Keep the surface moist, but no more. Mushrooms will appear in 3 weeks, and be ready to pick in a further 5 days. Twist them out, do not pull, and fill in the hole. The boxes should remain in production for 2–3 months.

Mustard (*Sinapis alba*) & Cress (*Lepidium sativum*)

So valuable is it for salads, sandwiches, and garnishing, it should be grown throughout the year.

CULTURE

Make first sowing early in January in a slightly warmed greenhouse, or in the kitchen window. Sow thickly on 1 in. of soil or on pieces of damp velvet. Keep moist, and when 2 ins. high, cut stems just above soil level. Hold a bunch in one hand and cut with the other.

In a temperature of 45°F, the cress will be ready to cut within 3 weeks of sowing, and the mustard 4–5 days later. To have them ready together, sow the mustard 4–5 days earlier.

Sow more in a cold frame in March, and again in autumn. Make outside sowings in a seed bed from April until September.

PESTS & DISEASES

This crop is troubled by none.

VARIETY

Moss Curled. The best cress, making plenty of 'top' of deepest green and with mildest flavour.

Onion (*Allium cepa*)

A native of the near east. To obtain large, long-keeping bulbs in Britain, the onion is best grown from sets raised from seed in Holland. Or, as for spring onions, sow in July in drills 1 in. deep in well-nourished soil and transplant to 4 ins. apart in spring. They will reach tennis ball size by October.

Spring onions will be ready for use in salads early June. If another sowing is made in March, these will be ready in late summer. White Liston is the best variety for spring onions. Dust the rows with calomel before sowing.

Plant onion sets in April, by pressing the bulbs into the surface of a well-prepared

bed. Onions may be grown in the same ground year after year without deterioration in quality. Before planting, rake in 4 oz. per sq. yd. basic slag, and 2 oz. sulphate of potash, then tread or roll the bed. Allow 6 ins. of space between the bulbs. Stuttgarter Riesen or Dobie's All Rounder are best. There are about 300 sets to a lb. Sets are not troubled by onion fly and they rarely bolt in dry weather if the soil contains humus.

About the end of August, bend over the necks of the bulbs to stop them growing. Leave them to ripen for a month and lift in early October, preferably when dry. Spread them out in an airy room to dry off, then string up in nets in a frost-free room, and use over the winter.

PESTS & DISEASES

Downy Mildew. Attacks first the foliage, as a coating of white fungus, then the bulbs, causing decay. Control by spraying the plants with sulphide of potassium, 1 oz. to 2 gals. of water.

Onion Fly. By far the most troublesome. It lays its eggs in the soil in May, when the maggots begin to tunnel into the bulbs. Dust rows with calomel before sowing to give control. If transplanting, dip the roots into calomel solution.

VARIETIES

Ailsa Craig. Best for keeping; it makes a large solid bulb of rich golden yellow.

Autumn Queen. Crops especially well if sown in August. Large flattish bulbs having light brown skin and cream-coloured flesh. An excellent keeper.

Reliance. A flat onion of good keeping qualities, and of mild flavour. Grows best from an autumn sowing.

Showmaster. Large round bulb with straw-coloured skin. Flavour is good and it keeps well.

Parsley (*Petroselinum crispum*)

First seen in England about 1600. Said to be one of the most health-giving of all foods, rich in vitamins and mineral salts.

CULTURE

Germination is slow. Always use fresh seed. Sow in a rich humus-laden soil, in drills ½ in. deep. Thin where there is overcrowding. It will be ready to gather in July from an

April sowing and will remain green through winter. Can last for more than one year if plants are given an occasional watering with liquid manure.

VARIETIES

Champion Moss Curled. Of compact habit, the emerald green leaves are tightly curled and borne in profusion.

Cluseed Winter Green. Makes an abundance of thick dark green leaves held well above the ground.

Parsnip (*Pastinaca sativa*)

A native plant requiring a deeply worked soil, and long growing season. Exhibitors can grow parsnips 3 ft. long, but only at the expense of their flavour.

CULTURE

The soil should be dug up to 3 ft. deep, and be friable and free from stones.

For ordinary use, sow in ground already manured for a previous crop in March, in drills 15 ins. apart. Thin first to 5 ins. apart, then to 10 ins. Use fresh seed, as old seed may not germinate. Keep roots well watered in dry weather. An occasional feed with dilute manure water certainly improves the quality.

Lift the roots mid-November, taking care not to damage the ends. After removing the foliage, store in boxes of peat or sand. They can also be left in the ground, for frost will not harm them.

PESTS & DISEASES

Canker. This disease may occur if fresh manure is used, or if the soil lacks lime. It attacks first the crown causing it to turn brown, then large brown scabs cover the root. There is no cure, so lift and destroy those attacked, and do not grow parsnips in the same ground for at least 2 years.

Carrot Fly. This pest may also attack parsnips. For control, see Carrot.

VARIETIES

Avonresister. Widely grown on land which has caused cankering. Roots are carrot size and of good texture. Thin to 4 ins., and many more can be grown.

Dobies Intermediate. Comes half-way in growth between the other two varieties. Matures early and is of excellent flavour.

Hollow Crown. Hollow at the crown, it has long tapering roots with a clear bright skin.

Pea (*Pisum sativum*)

Man's staple food since earliest times. There are round-seeded and wrinkled varieties. The latter, known as marrow fat peas, are the sweeter. They are not suitable for autumn sowing. Use round peas for this purpose.

CULTURE

With careful planning, it is possible to enjoy peas all the year, from May–October fresh from the garden, and in winter from the freezer.

Make the first sowings in September, planting the early round-seeded varieties such as Feltham First, Meteor, and Kelvedon Wonder. In March, sow Little Marvel and Histon Mini, followed in April by Greenshaft and Early Onward (second earlies), and with Onward and Histon Maincrop for later picking. Plant the quick-maturing Meteor and Histon Mini in June to mature early autumn. Cover peas from an autumn or early spring sowing with cloches, which are removed at the end of April.

Peas like a rich friable soil, well limed. Sewage manure is particularly valuable, also hop manure. To ensure early maturing and well-filled pods, rake in 2 oz. of super-phosphate and sulphate of potash in mixture at planting time.

Sow peas singly in a trench 2 ins. deep, spacing them 2 ins. apart. In this way ½ pt. of seed (peas are sold by the pint) will sow a 10-yd. row which should yield up to 30 lb. Allow 2 ft. between the rows for those growing less than 3 ft. tall, and 3–4 ft. for those which grow taller. Achievement and Alderman will grow to 5 ft.

Peas require careful staking. When 6 ins. high, place small twigs about the plants for the tendrils to cling to. Later use sticks which will support the plants to the height to which they grow. If difficult to obtain, place canes around the rows, and surround the peas with plastic netting, also across the top. The plants will twine about it and keep themselves erect.

Pick peas as soon as they are seen to have filled the pod. They lose quality if left too long. After cropping, cut away the haulm at ground level but leave the roots. Cauliflowers and maincrop cabbages can follow early peas.

PESTS & DISEASES

Fusarium Wilt. A fungus which attacks the roots, causing the foliage to turn yellow. No cure is known but if experienced, plant only resistant varieties, such as Recette (maincrop) and Vitalis (early).

Leaf Spot. Attacks leaves and stems, forming small brown spots, causing the pods to fall before they are filled. Spray with weak Bordeaux mixture when noticed.

Mexican chilli pepper

Pea Moth. Moths are most troublesome in early summer, laying their eggs on the flowers. Later, the grubs eat into the pods. To prevent, treat soil with malathion before planting, or spray with Sybol when flowers first appear.

For a list of varieties see Table below.

Sugar Peas are grown in the same way, but are cooked in the pods (after topping and tailing). Pick before the peas begin to swell. Make two sowings to give a succession, one in April, the other in early June. De Grace is the best variety. Grows 3 ft. tall and bears heavy crops of juicy pods.

Pepper (*Capsicum annum*)

Bears fruits, like large rectangular tomatoes, which add piquancy to salads and curries. Can be grown outdoors in the milder parts. For salads, slice thinly.

CULTURE

Sow seed in a temperature of 65°F in February and prick out to Root-o-Pots by mid-March. Grow on in a temperature of 58°F, and harden in a frame before planting out early June. Into the soil work some decayed manure, and allow 18 ins. between plants. They may be grown entirely under glass in large pots, like tomatoes, but take care that the plants are not exposed to draughts. In warmer weather, a daily syringe will prevent an attack by the red spider, whilst a weekly application of dilute manure water will enhance the quality of the fruits, which are green but turn red when ripe.

PESTS & DISEASES

Fruit Spot. Spots appear on the fruits as brownish-red depressions. Control by spraying plants with dilute Bordeaux mixture.

Grey Mould. Attacks the stems, leaves, and

Potato 'Majestic'

then the fruits, as grey spots covered in mould. As a precaution, spray before flowering with Shirlan AG.

VARIETIES

Canape. An F1 hybrid, early to mature and hardier than most. Grows 30 ins. tall with dark green leaves, and crops heavily. The 3-lobed fruits are about 3 ins. square with flesh sweet and juicy.

Early Bountiful. Also a hybrid with the vigour of Canape, and making a much-branched plant 20 ins. high. The fruit is 3–4 ins. long, with thick fleshy walls.

Fordhook. A heavy cropper. The 4-lobed fruits are almost 3 ins. square, have a thin skin, and flesh which is sweet and juicy.

Potato (*Solanum tuberosum*)

Native of S. America, and introduced into Europe late 16th century, when it quickly became the staple diet. It is valuable for cleaning rough ground, and should be included in any rotation of cropping.

CULTURE

Potatoes are gross feeders. Prepare the ground over winter by taking out V-shaped drills 9 ins. deep and lining them with humus materials, such as garden compost. Make the drills in a north to south direction, 2 ft. apart to allow room for earthing up. Just before planting, give 2 oz. per yard of super-phosphate and sulphate of potash in mixture. Space the tubers 15 ins. apart.

Plant only top-quality certified seed potatoes. After planting, cover the tubers with 6 ins. of soil. If the soil is heavy, plant on top of the soil thrown up when making the V-drills. Between the drills make another V-drill 6–8 ins. deep and treat as previously explained. There is an old adage which says, 'Plant early potatoes late and late potatoes early for best results' so plant earlies at the end of March, to be ready in June, and the lates (or maincrop) early April, for maturing in October.

Tubers can be started into growth by placing them wide end upwards in seed trays, in a frame, about March 1st. Plant out when the shoots are about 1 in. high, having rubbed off all but the 2 strongest shoots.

As soon as the haulm (the foliage) is 6–8 ins. high, earth up to prevent the plant from being broken by the wind. Further earthing should be done at monthly intervals until the end of summer.

When the haulm begins to die down, lift the tubers with a fork, taking care not to damage them. Begin well away from the haulm and work towards it. Remove soil from the potatoes. Maincrop potatoes can be stored in sacks in a dark, frost-free room, or in a home-made clamp, covering

Varieties	Type	Height	When to sow
Histon Mini (R)	Early	15 ins	Sept & Mar
Feltham First (R)	Early	18–20 ins	Sept & Mar
Kelvedon Viscount (R)	Early	2 ft	Sept & Mar
Early Bird (W)	Early	18 ins	Mar, Apr
Early Onward (W)	2nd Early	2 ft	Mar, Apr
Kelvedon Monarch (W)	2nd Early	2–3 ft	Mar
Green Shaft (W)	2nd Early	2–3 ft	Mar
Lincoln (W)	2nd Early	18 ins	Apr, May
Alderman (W)	Maincrop	5 ft	Mar
Onward (W)	Maincrop	3 ft	Apr, May
Recette (W)	Maincrop	2–3 ft	Apr
Little Marvel (W)	Late	18 ins	June

(R) = Round seeded   (W) = Wrinkled.

them with straw and peat to exclude frost and light.

New potatoes are lifted as required. They retain their flavour better if cooked as soon as possible after lifting.

PESTS & DISEASES

Blight. A prevalent disease attacking the foliage as brown spots which spreads to stems and tubers. As a precaution, spray the haulm with Bordeaux mixture early July, and a month later.

Colorado Beetle. Rare, but so destructive that it is a 'notifiable' pest. Measures $\frac{1}{2}$ in. long, and has black and orange striped wings. The orange grubs quickly destroy a crop. As a precaution, treat the soil with malathion before planting.

Eelworm. Treat soil with Jeyes Fluid, as for leeks.

Wart Disease. A 'notifiable' disease. On infected land grow only wart-resistant varieties such as Arran Pilot, Home Guard, Majestic, Desiree. Attacks the stems and tubers which appear to be covered in cauliflower-like structures. There is no cure.

VARIETIES

Arran Pilot. Probably the best early. Immune to wart. It crops heavily, and the white kidney-shaped tubers are of excellent flavour.

Desiree. Heavy cropper. The oval tubers are deep red, and cook to rich golden-yellow with the flavour of a Golden Wonder.

Dunbar Rover. A second early, immune to wart, and crops well in a light soil. The oval tubers are pure white.

Eclipse. May be classed as a later early. It bears heavily, and the white kidney-shaped tubers cook well.

Majestic. A reliable old favourite for maincrop. Immune to wart and bears heavily in all soils. The round tubers cook well.

Pentland Crown. For maincrop. Immune, and crops heavily. The round tubers have a creamy-white skin covered in russet markings.

Radish (*Raphanus sativus*)
Introduced in Saxon times. Its bright scarlet colour and hot, nutty, sweet and mild flavour add interest to salads.

CULTURE

Radishes may be grown almost the whole year. Sow over a mild hot bed in February to mature in April. Sow again under cloches, or in a frame, towards the end of March to pull in May. Outdoor sowings follow on from April until July.

Sow broadcast, or in drills $\frac{3}{4}$ in. deep and 8 ins. apart. Radishes require a rich soil for rapid growth, but no fresh manure. In a poor, dry soil they grow hard and bitter. Pull long radishes when of little finger-thickness, and round varieties when the size of a cherry.

Sow China Rose and Winter Black varieties in July and they will be ready for early November. Roots can be stored in boxes of sand for winter use.

PESTS & DISEASES

Club Root. Attacks radishes in the same way as brassicas so dust rows with calomel before sowing.

Radish Fly. Lays eggs in the soil and the larvae attack the roots. Dust the soil with Lindex before sowing. (Lindex must not come into contact with potatoes.)

VARIETIES

French Breakfast. The market grower's favourite. An intermediate variety, the red roots are tipped with white.

Inca. Forms a root like a large red cherry, and is crisp and white inside.

Saxa. Ideal for early forcing. Has a round scarlet root with crisp white flesh.

Sparkler. Ready 3 weeks after sowing, the scarlet globes are tipped with white and are sweet and nutty.

Rhubarb (*Rheum rhaponticum*)
Often classed as a fruit, but always grown in the vegetable garden. Its earliness and ease of culture contributes to its popularity.

CULTURE

Except for November and December it may be pulled all the year. For really early rhubarb, lift established plants early December, and after several nights' frosting, plant in deep boxes half filled with manure and soil. Place under the greenhouse bench or in garage, shed or cellar, and cover with sacking to exclude light. Keep the soil moist, and pale pink sticks will be ready to pull by early February; or several weeks earlier if in a heated greenhouse.

To have sticks in April, give established plants outdoors a forkful of strawy manure in February before covering the roots with a deep box or large inverted plant pots. Uncovered roots begin to bear sticks in May until October.

Rhubarb is readily grown from seed. Sow in shallow drills in early April and transplant to 20 ins. apart in July. The following year one or two sticks only should be pulled from each plant but the next year, several roots may be selected for gentle forcing outdoors. Those selected for forcing should not be pulled during the previous summer, nor the summer after, to allow them time to recover. A dozen plants will give a continuous supply year after year.

Stock may further be increased by division during winter and replanting into well-manured ground. Rhubarb requires a soil containing plenty of humus, preferably rotted manure.

PESTS & DISEASES

This plant suffers from none.

VARIETIES

Early Superb. The earliest to mature and forces well. The large red sticks are of excellent flavour.

Holstein Red. A strong grower, producing an abundance of thick crimson-red sticks.

Royal Albert. Also known as Prince Albert. It bears long crimson sticks over an extended period.

Stott's Monarch. A vigorous grower, it matures green and when cooked has a unique pine flavour.

Timperley Early. Forces well. The deep red sticks are even in size.

Salsify (*Tragopogon porrifolius*)
Native of Europe but not Britain. Known as the 'vegetable oyster' because of its unique flavour.

CULTURE

Requires a soil containing plenty of humus, but not fresh manure, or the roots may 'fork'. Sow seed early in April in drills $\frac{3}{4}$ in. deep and 9 ins. apart. Thin plants to 8 ins. Water copiously in dry weather. In August water once a week with dilute liquid manure.

Roots will be ready to use about mid-November. Either lift and store in boxes of sand, or leave in the ground and use as required. Scrape the roots clean just before cooking, then place in a bowl of water to which a few drops of lemon juice are added. This preserves their whiteness after cooking. Do not peel or they will 'bleed' and lose flavour.

PESTS & DISEASES

This crop is troubled by none.

VARIETY

Sandwich Island Mammoth is the best form. Roots grow 9 ins. long and are about 1 in. in diameter, tapering slightly. When cooked, the flesh is white with the delicious taste of oysters.

Savoy (*Brassica oleracea*)
The hardiest and largest form of the cabbage. Has crinkled leaves which are untroubled by frost. When cooked, it is more pleasant to eat than most winter cabbages.

CULTURE

Requires a long season of growth. Sow seed in drills early April and move plants to their permanent quarters early May. They like a well-nourished and well-limed soil containing plenty of humus. If lacking lime, rake in at planting time, 4 oz. per sq. yd. of nitro-chalk. Allow 2–3 ft. for each plant, and keep hoeing around them. The first will be ready to cut in November and others in the New Year.

PESTS & DISEASES

They suffer little in this respect but to guard against club root, dust the roots with calomel before planting.

VARIETIES

Asmer Shortie. The best for a small garden. It makes a neat round head of crinkled leaves and is ready in November.

Radish 'French Breakfast'

Salsify

Seakale

Seakale beet

Ice Queen. A magnificent hardy variety. Leaves are darkest green, and hearts ice-white when cut. Ready at Christmas.

January King. The enormous heads weigh 4–5 lb. and are at their best during December and January.

Ormskirk Late. For long the best variety to stand the winter. Improved by frost, and can be used from February–April.

Ostara. Best for autumn and early winter. Medium-sized heads.

Seakale (*Crambe maritima*)

A native maritime plant of easy culture. Delicious to eat, but takes 2 years to produce roots suitable for forcing.

CULTURE

Enjoys a deeply worked soil containing plenty of humus. Also requires salt in the form of kainit. Rake in 2 oz. per sq. yd. as the bed is prepared.

Sow seed in April in drills 1 in. deep and 12 ins. apart. Thin plants to 6 ins., and leave until the following April. Transplant into a prepared bed 9 ins. apart and grow on for another year. These two years may be saved by purchasing 2-year thongs (as the roots are called) from nurserymen in March. They come in bundles, each thong of pencil thickness. Cut level at the top, slanting at the bottom.

Make a 5-ft.-wide bed, slightly raised above surrounding ground. Work in plenty of decayed compost, then plant the thongs with the level end about 1 in. below soil level. Space 15 ins. apart each way. Keep them growing by watering in dry weather and by mid-October the foliage will begin to die down. The roots are lifted early November. Remove the side shoots, which will be grown on next year, and store in boxes of sand.

The main shoots can now be forced. They need darkness, so a cellar or garage is ideal, or, make a 'pit' against an outside wall with corrugated sheeting on three sides. In it, place composted straw or manure to a depth of 8 ins., and cover with 6 ins. soil. Plant the thongs into this 4 ins. apart, with crowns level with the top of the soil. Water in and cover with straw and sacking to exclude light. The shoots will be ready when 6–7 ins. long (in 4–6 weeks' time).

Cut at soil level, and cook by steaming until tender. To over-cook causes them to become tough and lacking in flavour. Fresh shoots are delicious served in short pieces (or shredded) in a salad. The roots are then destroyed and the process begins again in March.

PESTS & DISEASES

This crop is troubled by none.

VARIETY

Lily White is the best, producing long, tender shoots of pleasant flavour.

Shallot (*Allium ascalonicum*)

Believed to have been brought from the east by Richard I, whence it became a valuable part of the winter diet.

CULTURE

Shallots require a rich soil containing plenty of humus. Before planting, work in 2 oz. per sq. yd. of sulphate of potash. Bring the surface to a fine tilth and either tread or roll the bed. Plant, before the end of March, by pressing the shallots into the surface 9 ins. apart. Keep well watered in dry weather.

Towards end of August, bend over the necks to encourage bulbs to ripen. In early October lift the clumps of small bulbs and dry in an airy room. Pickle within a month of drying to retain flavour, or use raw for flavouring, or boil as a vegetable.

Shallots are rarely raised from seed, which can take a year to reach the size of 'sets'. This is left to the specialist growers in Holland.

PESTS & DISEASES

See under Onion, but onion fly and downy mildew rarely attack sets of either onion or shallot.

VARIETY

Long Keeping Yellow. The standard variety, deep yellow when peeled. They retain their firmness for 12 months.

Spinach (*Spinacea oleracea*)

Rich in iron and mineral salts.

CULTURE

Make several sowings from April 1st to late July. To prevent plants going to seed in hot weather, select a northerly position and dig plenty of humus into the soil. To produce an abundance of leaf, rake in around the plants when they are 3–4 ins. tall (and on a rainy day), a ½ oz. per sq. yd. dressing of nitrate of soda.

Sow seed 1 in. deep in drills 15 ins. apart, thinning to 9 ins. The first leaves are ready to pick in about 8 weeks. If the plants do run to seed, dig them in, for they make valuable green manure. To have spinach at its best simmer in its own moisture and serve with melted butter.

For a winter crop sow Long-Standing Prickly early August. Do not pull too many leaves, but rather use it in spring before the summer spinach is ready.

PESTS & DISEASES

Downy Mildew. Pale yellow spots form on the upper surface of the leaves. The spots are grey on the underside. To control, dust with flowers of sulphur.

VARIETIES

Bloomsdale Long-standing. Best for winter use. Hardy, and of good flavour. The leaves are formed in rosette fashion.

Cleanleaf. A summer spinach, bearing masses of dark green leaves, rounded at the ends and held above the soil on long stalks.

Superb. Highly resistant to downy mildew. Produces an abundance of good-quality emerald green leaves of excellent mild flavour.

Tampala. An American summer variety, ready to pick within 8 weeks of sowing. Retains its deep green colour and flavour after freezing.

Spinach Beet (*Beta vulgaris*)

Known as perpetual spinach. Valuable for dry soils where ordinary spinach runs quickly to seed. May be picked all year.

CULTURE

Sow in April in drills 1 in. deep and 18 ins. apart. Thin to 15 ins. The more humus and plant food dug into the soil, the more leaf produced. If another sowing is made in July, it will be most productive in spring when the leaves from the earlier sowing are finished. Use the leaves before they become coarse. Cook as for spinach.

Swede (*Brassica napus* var: *naprobrassica*)

Called rutabaga in America. Hardier than turnips, and thought by many to have a better flavour. Roots may be left in the ground over winter to use as required.

CULTURE

Sow seed in April or early May, ¾ in. deep in drills, 18 ins. apart. Swedes require a friable soil, manured for a previous crop, and plenty of water in dry weather. When the seedlings are large enough to handle, thin to 9 ins. apart. Swedes grow to 6 ins. or more in diameter but are all the sweeter if used when they reach tennis ball size, or from early September.

PESTS & DISEASES

See Turnip.

VARIETIES

Chignecto. A purple top variety of excellent flavour. Can be grown where club root has proved troublesome.

Purple-top Yellow. Deep yellow flesh, sweet, and of good flavour.

Sweet corn (*Zea mays*)

Also maize, or corn-on-the-cob. First achieved popularity in Britain with the arrival of American Forces in World War II, but there was then no variety which would ripen its cobs in the average British summer. The hybridist has now changed this and it has become a more reliable crop.

Sweet corn 'Kelvedon Glory'

Sweet potato

Rhubarb chard

CULTURE
Requires a long season to develop. Sow seed in a temperature of 60°F in February, or over a mild hot bed early March. Sow one seed to a small pot or Jiffy pot of John Innes compost which should be plunged into the top of the hot bed. If cloches are available, set the plants out mid-May, or early June if unprotected, after hardening. Protect the plants from cold winds by placing cloches on their sides, around the plants, or place boards round them.

Plants require an open situation and a rich soil. Shoddy, strawy manure or used hops are suitable.

Pollination is important. Male flowers are produced at the top of the inflorescence, whilst the females develop from the leaf joints lower down the stem. The silky tassels catch the pollen grains as they fall. Plants pollinate each other, so plant in blocks of 4 rows, 15 ins. apart.

Water heavily in dry weather, and stake each plant as it grows 6 ft. tall.

Harvest the cobs when seeds are firm and juicy, but not hard. Remove the husks and if not used at once, place the cobs in a plastic bag in a cool room or in the refrigerator. To prepare, boil for 20 mins. and serve with white sauce or melted butter.

PESTS & DISEASES
Damping Off. To guard against pre-emergence damping off, ask your seedsman to treat the seeds with orthocide, containing 65% captan.

VARIETIES
First of All. An F1 hybrid of great vigour, producing fine-quality medium-sized cobs which are the earliest to mature.
Golden Cross. A hybrid of great uniformity of cob. Has 12–14 rows of golden kernels which are sweet and juicy after cooking.
North Star. Early to mature, forming large well-filled cobs of excellent flavour.
White Midget. The most dwarf form, growing only 3 ft. tall, and bearing 6-in.-long cobs of white, delicately flavoured kernels.

Sweet Potato (*Ipomoea batatas*)
The first 'potato' used in England, and though in no way connected, it was a valuable part of the diet until the introduction of the common potato.

CULTURE
The dahlia-like tuberous roots require a long warm summer to grow large. Best grown in the south. They require a friable soil, enriched with decayed manure. Plant in April 6 ins. deep on the flat, and 15 ins. apart, and keep well watered in dry weather. A once-weekly watering with liquid manure will increase the tuber size.

Lift in October as the foliage dies down and before the frosts. Store in boxes of sand or peat in a frost-free room.

PESTS & DISEASES
This plant is troubled by none.

VARIETY
Fir Apple Pink. Tubers are of deep pink and cook to deep yellow. They are waxy when eaten, whereas ordinary potatoes are floury.

Swiss Chard (*Beta cicla*)
The white is known as seakale beet, the red-stemmed as rhubarb beet. The long stems become soft with simmering. Serve with white sauce. Cook the green tops like spinach.

CULTURE
Requires a soil with a high humus content to retain moisture. It is a maritime plant so before sowing, rake in 1 oz. per sq. yd. of salt. Sow seed in April 1 in. deep, in drills 18 ins. apart. Thin the plants to 12 ins. apart. Water well in dry weather. Should be ready to use in early autumn. If another sowing is made late in July, the leaves and mid-ribs will be ready to use in spring and early summer, but it is advisable to cover with cloches in winter. If the outer leaves and stems are gathered first, this will enable the inner ones to mature.

Pull the stems (as for rhubarb), for cutting them causes bleeding, when both colour and flavour are lost in cooking.

PESTS & DISEASES
It is troubled by none.

VARIETY
Ruby Chard. The rich crimson stems and crinkled leaves look like rhubarb. Grows 15 ins. tall, and one of the most ornamental of vegetables. Often used in flower arrangement.

Tomato (*Lycopersicum esculentum*)
Called the love apple. Reached Europe early 16th century, when it was grown for ornamental purposes. Since then it has been used as a food of some importance.

CULTURE
Modern varieties crop as heavily outdoors as under glass. Sow in February in a temperature of 60°F. Transplant the seedlings, when they have formed their first pair of leaves, to individual pots containing John Innes potting compost. Maintain a temperature of 58°F, but give fresh air whenever the weather is warm. By mid-April, the plants will be ready to move to 10-in. pots, or deep boxes placed on the greenhouse bench near the glass, or, if a Dutch-type greenhouse, on the ground. Allow 15 ins. between plants and give them a rich compost, containing plenty of decayed manure and fresh loam in

equal parts. Plants may also be set out in the open, in which case make a trench and half fill with composted straw. This provides aeration for the roots. Add some poultry manure to supply the much-needed potash. Then fill up trench with fresh pasture loam.

By early May, artificial heat will not be necessary. Ventilate freely except on cold windy days. Support the plants with canes, or twine suspended from strong wires stretching across the roof. Twist the twine round the stems as they grow. Remove all side shoots and confine the plant to a single main stem. Plants raised in heat will have a long growing season but may be stopped when 6 ft. high, after forming 7–8 trusses, each weighing about 2 lb. Plants respond to a mulch of strawy manure given in July. Heavier crops will set if the flowers are pollinated by hand, touching each with a camel-hair brush. Do this throughout the summer when the flowers are dry – it takes only a few minutes daily.

Towards the end of summer, partially defoliate the plants so that their total energy may be put to swelling and ripening the top trusses.

Soil must be kept moist at all times. If it becomes dry, the tomato skins will split at the next watering. Towards the end of summer, give a weekly application of dilute manure water.

For an early crop outdoors, sow seed over a hot bed made in a frame, early April. Transplant seedlings to small pots and place over the hot bed which will still retain some heat.

By mid-May, begin to harden by moving them to another frame, removing the light by day. In early June, plant out in ground prepared as described for greenhouse culture. Tomatoes are heavy feeders, so add to the trench whatever humus is available – shoddy, chopped seaweed, garden compost to which some poultry manure is added, or farmyard manure. Alternatively work in just before planting 2 oz. per yd. of hoof and horn meal, and 1 oz. sulphate of potash.

Some varieties of outdoor tomato grow bushy, and do not need staking; others do need staking for they form their trusses from one main stem. Side shoots on these must be removed. Keep the soil watered in dry weather or the buds will drop, but do not splash soil on to the plants for this may result in botrytis and buckeye rot. Bush varieties form much of their fruit at soil level, so spread clean straw or bracken around the plants when the first fruit begins to set, or spread pieces of black polythene over the soil, which is removed when the plants are mulched in July.

Tomato 'Moneymaker'. Its heavy cropping properties make it a popular choice.

Turnip 'Purple Top White Globe'

ins. tall and 2 ft. across. Bears large trusses of well-shaped fruits, which ripen quickly and evenly.

Turnip (*Brassica rapa*)

May have been introduced by the Huguenot refugees in the 16th century. It is more popular in Europe than in Britain.

CULTURE

For an early crop sow Early White Milan over a hot bed, or in a frame, in February. Sow thinly and space 5 ins. apart. Keep the soil moist and admit fresh air as the weather becomes warmer. By early May, the roots will be of tennis ball size and ready to use.

Outdoors, make a sowing of Early Snowball early in April, to mature in July. Another sowing can be made in May, to provide the winter crop. Sow in drills $\frac{3}{4}$ in. deep and 12 ins. apart. Thin to 6 ins. Turnips require a well-nourished soil, preferably manured for a previous crop, with plenty of humus.

The main crop will be ready in November. Remove the tops and place the roots in boxes of peat or shavings. Keep in a cool place.

PESTS & DISEASES

Club Root. Attacks all brassicas and swede and turnip, but well-limed land will rarely support the disease. Dust soil (in the drills) with calomel before seed is sown, for additional protection.

Turnip Fly. Lays its eggs on young foliage. The grubs devour foliage and later, the roots. Dust plants with derris in May, and again a month later.

VARIETIES

Early Snowball. A white globe-shaped turnip with sweet and tender flesh.

Early White Milan. The earliest to mature. The flattened roots are white with purple shading. Excellent flavour.

Golden Ball. Best for late sowing. Resembles a swede in its hardiness and its yellow flesh, which is sweet and rich in flavour.

Bush tomatoes may be grown in frames, or under cloches, which can be removed when plants have set their first trusses. Tomatoes in the open will not need hand pollination.

PESTS & DISEASES

Blight. A fungus causing grey spots to form on the fruits. It occurs mostly in a cold, wet summer. Spray or dust the foliage with Bordeaux mixture to give control.

Botrytis. Causes the fruit to fall. It is prevalent where greenhouse plants are grown in excessive humidity (poor ventilation), or in a wet summer. It spreads from plant to plant if close together. Spray with Shirlan AG at the first signs, or as a precaution.

Leaf Spot. Also known as cladosporium. Appears first as brown spots on the underside of the leaves, later covers the whole plant. It takes several forms, but there are a number of hybrids resistant to all. If caught in time, spraying with a copper-oil preparation will give control.

White Fly. Attacks mostly greenhouse and frame-grown plants. Resembles a tiny white moth, whose larvae cause great damage. To control, spray on derris every 3 weeks.

VARIETIES

Dobies Peach. Similar to Moneymaker. The peach-coloured fruit has low acid content and a most distinctive flavour.

Histon Cropper. Of compact habit. Makes little foliage so the sun ripens its fruit more quickly. For outdoor planting, it bears a heavy crop of medium-sized fruit with a unique 'tart' flavour.

Moneymaker. Possibly the best. Crops well under glass and in the open, where it should be planted against a sunny wall supported by canes. If outdoors, stop at 5 trusses, which ripen well even in a poor summer.

Pixie. A bush tomato growing to 2 ft. In a good season outdoors will ripen 20 or more trusses of well-flavoured, medium-size fruits.

Red Ensign. A hybrid, resistant to all forms of cladosporium. A tremendous cropper which sets its first truss better than any. Excellent flavour and firm flesh.

Sleaford Abundance. A hybrid growing 20

YOUR OWN FRUIT

Leslie Jones

All gardeners at some stage or other have a desire to produce good fruit for the family, and of course in these days of rising prices a fresh impetus has been given to the production of food from the garden, some of which will be used fresh, and the remainder frozen. A deep freeze has obviously increased the value of any fruit crop for it enables the surplus to be carefully used and stored, and has created a new interest and encouragement in fruit growing. Gardens have decreased in size, so that the quantity of fruit grown in each individual garden will be less than in the past, but the ways in which the crop can be utilised have increased, and although few gardens can accommodate apples, pears, plums, gages, peaches, cherries, and apricots, plus the range of soft fruit, sufficient space can usually be found for one or two trees or bushes selected for their usefulness to the household.

Fruit can be grown throughout the British Isles, and by the careful choice of cultivars, and good management, crops of fine home-grown fruit can be produced. It goes without saying that some areas are more suitable for fruit growing than others, and the counties where the largest proportion of apples are grown are in the southern part of the country. This observation indicates that climatic conditions play a part in fruit production. Soil is also important when fruit is to be grown on a large scale. In the garden the condition of the soil can certainly be improved so that some fruit can be successfully grown almost anywhere.

SOILS

There is no doubt that if one could choose the soil for one's garden one would select a deep loam capable of retaining moisture throughout the year, but at the same time allowing surplus water to pass through into the drainage system. However, few of us are fortunate enough to have gardens with this type of soil, and those that have can consider it a blessing. Retentive, and heavy soils can be lightened by working in sand, compost, peat or farmyard manure, and on the worst type of heavy soils sharper grit or sand will also help to improve the texture. Soils which are extremely light, and dry out readily, can be enriched with compost which improves their water-holding capacity, and fruit can be grown without suffering from shortage of moisture during the drier part of the season.

These light soils however have other advantages. They are easily worked in the spring, warm up quickly, and do not become compacted during picking, pruning, and other operations. Most of these soils are slightly acid, but this is not a disadvantage, as sufficient calcium is usually present to supply the needs of the plants. Where stone fruits are grown, such as plums, cherries, or peaches, lime may have to be added annually to maintain a satisfactory level. Over-liming should be avoided

as it causes far more problems in fruit growing than the slight acidity which it is being used to correct.

DRAINAGE

The movement of water in the soil is of paramount importance where fruit is grown, and it is necessary to find out something about the water table, and the drainage of the site. Information can be obtained in the autumn, by digging a few holes 18–24 ins. deep, seeing how soon they fill with water, and how long it takes to drain away. If the water level remains constant during the winter this will give some indication of what depth of soil remains well drained during this period. A constantly high water table is not a good sign, for although fruit will grow on wet land, the trees are short-lived and succumb to diseases such as canker and collar-rot. Where only a few trees are being planted the planting sites can be raised 12–15 ins. above the general soil level. Drainage can be helped by digging a sump 4 ft. square and some 4–6 ft. deep at the lowest point in the garden, and filling it with material such as brick rubble, or reject gravel. This will then serve to drain much of the surplus water away from the growing areas, and ensure that the trees are not sitting in water throughout the winter period.

FROST RISK

Spring frosts are most dangerous, for they occur when the trees and bushes are in flower and setting the fruit. Frosts in late May and early June will often kill off quite large fruit and disfigure many others. Most spring frosts are radiation frosts, and occur on still clear nights when much heat is being lost from the ground to the atmosphere, and a layer of air near to the ground level is cooled to below freezing point. There are many nights when the temperature at ground level itself drops below freezing without doing any damage, but when the layer of very cold air reaches a height of 4 ft. or more, then damage occurs.

Radiation frost is most serious in valleys, hollows, or in gardens surrounded by walls and hedges, where air movement is reduced to a minimum and a blanket of cold air can be formed and remain static for a long period. When attempting to grow fruit in areas subject to late frosts, the choice of appropriate cultivars may assist in reducing the damage. Late-flowering apples such as Crawley Beauty, Edward VII, and Royal Jubilee, will stand a better chance of producing a crop than the early-flowering ones.

Protection from Frost

To give any protection at all is often considered impossible, and frost damage is often accepted as inevitable by a person growing one or two fruit trees. Of course it is impossible to protect large standard and bush trees, but the informed gardener is not likely to grow this type of tree in the small garden. Cordons, espaliers and fan-

trained trees, whether against a wall or on a free-standing framework, can be given protection by hanging hessian or even strong wrapping paper during nights when frosts are forecast. This protecting material must be lowered or raised during the day to enable the blossoms to develop and the pollinating insects to do their work. On east-facing walls, do not remove the protection too early in the sunny mornings, as a sudden rise in temperature can do much damage in a short time if the sunlight is particularly strong.

SHELTER

Although shelter has to be provided for commercial orchards where they are in open country, this is seldom necessary when considering growing fruit trees within the small garden. It is seldom that fruit trees in this situation have to withstand the full force of autumn gales, which can play havoc with the fruit plantation. But bush trees and cordons grown in the small garden must be firmly staked, and the structure on which cordons are grown must be properly erected, if damage from gales is to be avoided.

THE APPLE

The apple is the most popular of the hardy fruits, and almost without exception every garden contains one or more trees. In some gardens far too many are planted for the space available. Often the wrong type of tree is chosen, and more often than not, incorrect management afterwards leads to disappointment. The apple tree, of which so much is expected, is used as a convenient structure to hang nuts on for feeding birds in the winter, or to support one end of the tennis practice net during the summer.

Fruit has to be grown, just as the prize dahlia or marrow, and so it needs attention. The more you understand how the tree grows and produces its fruit, the better able you will be to encourage and assist in the development of a tree capable of producing an annual crop of fruit of first-class quality. Incorrect management leads to a badly shaped tree with overcrowded crossing branches, little or no fruit, and in extreme cases, just a mass of vigorous shoots.

Firstly, you must therefore decide what form of tree you are going to plant. The fruit nurseryman will supply several forms of tree, and the choice is left to you to select the one that will serve your purpose best.

Space available for growing apples is an important factor in the small garden. The trees can be had in different forms as follows:

The Standard Tree. This consists of a root system, and a single upright stem at least 6 ft. in height, at the top of which will be a number of primary branches or shoots up to the length of 2 ft. This type of tree is vigorous and will ultimately grow to a mature specimen of 20–25 ft. in height, with branches spreading to approximately the same width. It must be allowed to develop

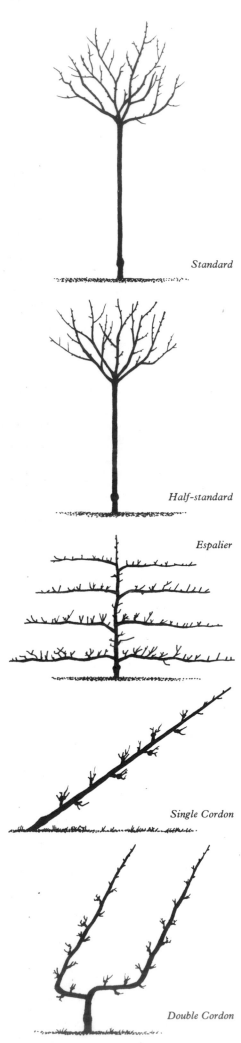

Standard

Half-standard

Espalier

Single Cordon

Double Cordon

Bush

Dwarf Pyramid

to this stature if satisfactory crops are to be gathered, and any attempt to confine it by pruning will lead to disaster.

It is quite unsuitable for a small garden, but ideal for the larger garden as a specimen tree growing in a lawn to provide flower, fruit, and welcome shade, during the summer months. This is an example of using a fruit tree in a dual role. Standard fruit trees are never planted by the commercial grower these days, because of the difficulty of picking, pruning, and spraying. If more than one standard is planted the distance between trees must not be less than 25 ft.

Half Standard. The only difference between this tree and the standard is the length of the stem. In this tree the stem is approximately 4½ ft., its ultimate size will be much smaller, and the tree is usually less vigorous. It is a useful form of tree for the larger garden, especially when a number of trees are planted in an area of grass. The spacing should be 15–18 ft. between trees. Individual specimens can be planted in the smaller garden but as the branches are rather low it is not possible to walk under them and they tend to occupy too much space. This form of tree should be planted in preference to the standard, because the tree is much easier to manage, and the quality of fruit generally better.

The Bush Tree. This form of tree is generally purchased and planted, because it is assumed that it will only develop into a small tree when mature, but this is not correct. The size to which the tree will ultimately grow depends on several factors, other than the form of training.

The characteristics of a bush apple tree are that the stem length is usually 3 ft. or less, and the primary branches are selected to form an 'open-centred tree' so no central trunk exists above the 3-ft. stem. Bush trees at maturity will range from 10–20 ft. high and there is equal variation in the spread of branches. So it follows that just to purchase a bush-trained apple tree does not ensure that the tree will adopt a small compact form. The planting distances between bush trees range from 12–18 ft. according to the vigour of the tree. However, over the years, in an attempt to increase the efficiency of fruit production and orchard management, a number of modified forms of bush trees have been developed.

The *dwarf pyramid* is one. The description of this tree growing up to 8 ft. in height and of neat pyramidal shape, appeals to anyone thinking of planting a number of apples. The planting distance of 4 ft. between trees also allows a greater variety of apples to be grown.

The training and management of this form of tree unfortunately needs a high degree of skill to maintain the pyramidal form, control excessive growth, and pro-

duce a satisfactory crop. Most of these plantings have to undergo a further modification to maintain cropping after 6–8 years. This involves removing alternate trees and reverting to a traditional bush-type tree. So, for the gardener wishing to grow apples as bush trees, I would suggest planting the traditional open centred form.

Espaliers. The espalier was widely planted in old gardens as a useful informal hedge between sections of the flower and vegetable beds, or to clothe the walls surrounding the gardens, and can be used in exactly the same way today. It is better to purchase this type of tree partly trained, for it is not easy to get pairs of horizontal branches established and growing at an equal rate. A well-grown espalier will have a total span at maturity of 15–20 ft., and some old trees of vigorous cultivars span up to 40 ft., so should not be planted too close together as the growth potential of this type of tree can be under-estimated when purchasing.

A well-grown espalier will have 3–4 tiers of branches established at the time of sale, each pair of branches being approximately 1 ft. apart, and this training must be continued until sufficient tiers have been developed to cover the area allotted to it.

Apples are seldom trained as *fans* nowadays, but they can be, and some dessert cultivars can be grown to perfection trained as fans on a south or west wall. However, unless one particularly wants fan-trained trees, other forms can produce the quality of fruit with far less work.

Maiden Trees. This is the smallest and youngest form in which apple trees can be purchased. It is from a maiden tree that all the forms described above are developed by pruning and training, and much of this work is best left to the fruit nurserymen who have the skill and the expertise.

Cordon. The last form of tree to be described is the *cordon* which can take a number of forms, namely the single, double, or treble cordon, depending on the number of stems allowed to develop. The single cordon can be grown vertically or obliquely, and this form of tree is simple, for it consists of only one stem with the small fruiting branches along its length.

For the purpose of growing cordons you can either purchase maiden trees consisting of just one year's growth, probably 2½–4 ft. in length, nothing more, or, if you prefer it, you can purchase trees which have been developed as cordons over a period of 2 or 3 years by the nurserymen. I see no advantage in buying this type of tree, as the disturbance and replanting tends to set the tree back for at least one or two seasons, so I would prefer to plant maidens when establishing single-stem cordons.

The advantages of the single cordon are that it takes up little space, produces high-quality fruit, is easily managed, and can be protected from frost and bird damage with little extra cost. If there is a disadvantage it is that few cooking apples are satisfactorily grown in this form, and a framework and wires have to be erected on which to train the trees. If planted against a wall or in the open ground on a framework, as a vertical or oblique cordon, the spacing should be $2\frac{1}{4}$–3 ft. between trees according to the soil, the greater distance on the lighter poorer soils. Cordons use a strip of land as little as $2\frac{1}{2}$ ft. wide, so for economy of space together with the opportunity to have a wide selection of cultivars, the single cordon is the ideal form of apple tree for the small or large garden where first-class fruit is the main consideration.

Root Stocks, Vigour and its Control

Having discussed the forms of apple tree available to the would-be grower, and given a brief outline of the size of the tree into which each form may develop, it is quite obvious that certain questions arise:

1) How does one know the eventual size of any particular tree?

2) If it does grow too easily is there anything that can be done to control it?

To deal with the first question we have to turn to the production of the apple tree. All apple trees are produced by budding or grafting on to a classified root stock. These root stocks are produced in large numbers by vegetative means so that each one is an exact replica of the parent stock. Any cultivar budded or grafted on to the stock, will produce a tree of similar growth habit and vigour, so that if we budded 50 James Grieve on to a particular root stock all would develop into trees of similar size and vigour. There would be some variation if each were planted in different gardens in various parts of the country, the variation being caused by differing soil conditions, varying climatic conditions, the amount of fertiliser and manures applied, and the pruning techniques used, but the influence of the root stock would remain paramount.

The root stocks in general use today have been selected and raised during years of research by establishments such as East Malling, Kent, John Innes at Merton, and Long Ashton, Bristol. The research work at East Malling, for example, started 50 years ago. Root stocks are now classified into four main groups:

Dwarfing stocks. Malling 9 and Malling 26.

Semi Dwarfing. Malling 7 and Malling Merton 106.

Vigorous. Malling 2 and Malling Merton 104, 109, 111.

Very vigorous. Malling 25

Standard. You will see that to produce the large standard tree with its 6 ft.-stem and 30 ft. spread and height, a very vigorous root system is required, so that the nurseryman producing such trees would use the root stock Malling 25. This is the advantage of using classified stocks.

Half Standards. These are usually budded on a less vigorous stock such as Malling Merton 104 or Malling Merton 109, and sometimes on Malling 7, where a small half standard is required.

Bush Trees. These are budded on to a variety of fruit stocks. The trees for the commercial orchard are usually worked on Malling 2 and Malling Merton 106 and sometimes Malling 7. For the garden, however, it would be far more suitable to purchase trees worked on Malling 9 or Malling 26. Both these dwarfing stocks produce a smaller and more compact tree.

Apples grown as cordons give good crops in little space

Espaliers. These are usually worked on a more vigorous stock, such as Malling 2 or Malling Merton 106 or 109, to maintain the growth necessary to build up the framework in a reasonable time.

Cordons. Where maximum control of vigour is required these are worked on Malling 9 and Malling 26. However, on poorer soils it is often advisable to have trees worked on a more vigorous stock to compensate for the poor soil conditions. Malling 9 must have a fertile soil if it is to produce a reliable compact tree cropping regularly.

So having chosen the *form* of tree, you must now ensure that it has been worked on the correct root stock to produce the *size* of tree to fit the area allocated to it. Fruit trees in my opinion should always have the root stock marked clearly on the label, especially in garden centres, where this vital information otherwise is usually unavailable.

The use of the correct root stock is the first positive step towards controlling the vigour of the tree, but even in the best-managed fruit plots problems of excessive vigour do arise. In the smaller garden the problem is usually caused by the trees being worked on too vigorous a root stock. The second cause is incorrect pruning, followed, in the better-cared-for garden, by the amount of fertiliser applied. Because of the confined space, the fruit tree, with its spreading root system, may get more than its fair share of this food. Another cause, and one which is far more common than it ought to be, is deep planting, whereby the union between the cultivar and the root stock is buried below soil level. This allows the cultivar to develop a separate root system, thus nullifying the restricting effect of the classified root stock.

The correct approach to pruning vigorous specimens will be discussed later. The application of fertiliser to the garden can be modified to avoid the area where most apple roots are situated, or can be counterbalanced by a dressing of sulphate of potash in the spring of each year.

Where this treatment has no effect we can resort to bark ringing. This operation can be carried out in May, and entails removing a complete ring of bark from around the main stem, $\frac{3}{8}$ in. wide. Cover with adhesive tape as soon as the operation has been completed to keep out dirt, which might otherwise become embedded in the open wound.

This operation tends to check the downward flow of sap, and encourages the build-up of fruit buds. If bark ringing leads to the carrying of a good crop 2 years later, this will bring the excessive growth problem under control.

Root Pruning

A pruning operation, which was carried out regularly in gardens where fruit was intensively grown, is 'root pruning'. This operation is undertaken every 4 or 5 years on wall-grown trees, and despite the fact that this is looked on as a laborious task, it usually has the desired effect.

If young fruit trees planted 4–6 years previously, are growing very strongly, but show no signs of producing a crop, it is a good sound practice to dig a trench right round the tree 18 ins. wide, approximately $2\frac{1}{2}$–3 ft. away from the trunk, to expose the roots. The stronger roots should be severed carefully with clean cuts, and treated with a pruning paint. The tree should be lifted, and any strong roots growing in the downwards direction removed. Having completed this the tree is now ready for replanting. First, carefully respread the roots in an even manner, and refill with the soil that has been excavated. Work the soil thoroughly between the roots, and firm, as the work proceeds. When completed, firm the soil, and then lightly fork it over to leave an even surface. If the tree is free standing it is essential to restake it firmly to prevent movement in windy weather, as this reduces the speed of recovery. The root area can be dressed with well-rotted dung or garden compost, to prevent the severest frosts reaching down to the roots during the winter months.

Crop Failure

From experience I find that the most regular question asked is: Why do my fruit trees fail to crop? Or, I have an apple tree that never carries a crop, but the flowers are lovely so am I satisfied with this? There are several reasons for the failure of a fruit tree to crop properly. The four main reasons are: (1) spring frosts which can completely destroy bud, flower bud, and the young fruitlets, (2) damage of the buds by birds, (3) damage before and during flowering by insect pests, and (4) the absence of effective pollination, due to the lack of pollinating insects, or insufficient good pollen.

Losses from all factors occur each year to some degree, but it is only when one or more factors reach a high level that failure takes place.

Spring frosts. To protect from frost is difficult for the amateur except when the trees are grown as cordons, or wall-trained specimens. The nets used for protecting the fruit against birds, can be hung double thickness to form a curtain in front of the flowering trees on a wall; this will give protection against most frosts experienced at blossom time. Cordons need to be protected on both sides of the row when grown in the open, the nets are suspended from T pieces of wood, or, metal placed on the supporting posts; while small bush trees can be protected by supporting the nets on a few canes placed around the tree.

Bird damage is widespread, and in the urban areas seems to get worse each year. Protection by spraying with bird repellent is not wholly effective, and despite all sorts of ideas on the subject, and the variety of materials, cottoning appears to be still the most effective method of control. It is easily applied to bush trees by first of all taking a 6-ft. length of 2 × 1 timber, and nailing four reels of second-grade cotton to the lath at 9-in. intervals from one end. Now take the ends of the cotton from each reel, tie together, and hook on to the tree. Then lift up the lath, pass it over the tree, and attach the unwinding cotton to the tips of the branches, until you feel you have netted the tree sufficiently. Cut the cotton and move on to the next tree. Cotton is to be preferred, for nylon is too strong and lasts into the next season, and can be a bit of a nuisance if too persistent.

Damage from insect pests. Damage from insect pests can be dealt with by spraying with insecticide when the leaf buds burst, and again at the pink bud stage of the flowers, and again at petal fall. These sprays will prevent damage to the flower at a critical time when the process of pollination and fertilisation is taking place.

Pollination. This leaves the last important factor. The failure of pollinating insects to transfer the pollen, or, a lack of suitable pollen. The failure to get an even distribution of pollen is caused by dull, cold, wet

and windy weather conditions, when the pollinating insects cannot operate effectively, or only visit the trees in small numbers. Under these conditions the pollen may also be in an unsuitable condition for transfer.

The absence of suitable pollen is of course due to the planting of unsuitable cultivars together, or planting cultivars which do not produce fertile pollen, in isolation.

Apples can be divided into two main groups:

1) *Diploids.* Most of the apple cultivars belong to this group and to some extent are self-fertile, and would set a crop of fruit if planted in isolation, but will produce a much better crop if planted in close proximity to other apples. Cultivars of this group must flower during the same period to be effective.

2) The second group are *triploids*, which produce pollen incapable of setting fruit, either with the particular tree or with any other trees. Such well-known varieties as Bramley seedling, Blenheim orange, and Warner's King, belong to this group, and must always be planted with at least two diploid cultivars, for diploids are the producers of good pollen and therefore all-important when planting trees.

The following list gives the main cultivars and the flowering season, which will assist in making a correct selection:

Diploid Apple Cultivars

EARLY FLOWERING

Egremont Russet	St Edmund's
George Cave	Russet
Lord Lambourne	Rev. W. Wilks
Merton Charm	

MID SEASON FLOWERING

Arthur Turner	Laxton's Superb
Charles Ross	Merton Worcester
Cox's Orange Pippin	Sunset
Discovery	Tydeman's Early
Ellison's Orange	Worcester
Emneth Early	Tydeman's Late
Epicure	Orange
Fortune	Worcester
Grenadier	Pearmain
James Grieve	

LATE FLOWERING

Ashmead's Kernel	Lord Derby
Crawley Beauty	Newton Wonder
Edward VII	Winston

The following are triploids and because these seldom produce fertile pollen, they must always be planted within close proximity of a good pollinator.

Blenheim Orange	Lane's Prince
Bramley Seedling	Albert
Crispin	Ribston Pippin

Apple 'Cox's Orange Pippin'

Ordering

Having decided which variety of apple tree you are going to plant, and in what form, and on what root stock, you then prepare an order for your nurseryman. Order early in June or July (this is not too soon), and ask for a November delivery. They may not come at the exact time you ask, for the lifting season begins in November and will finish in March, but the sooner you get on to the nurseryman's list the sooner your order will be lifted and supplied.

On arrival, unpack the trees and heel in. This means digging a trench wide enough to accommodate the roots, with sufficient room to lay the trees out singly. Cover the roots with soil, shaking it down between the roots by lifting the trees up and down slightly, and firm this soil around the roots. The trees can remain here until you plant them in permanent positions.

Preparation for Planting

If you look ahead, the planting area, whether in the open or against a wall, can be prepared well in advance. Late August or September is an ideal time, for the weather is usually good and the soil in a workable condition. Clear the site of weeds such as couch, ground elder, convolvulus, dandelions, and docks, for these will compete with the young trees, and may cause damage to those grown on weak stock such as No. 9.

Prepare a station at least 3 ft. in diameter in the open, and 3 ft. × 2 ft. against a wall or trellis. Remove the top spit of soil, and place to one side, for this is the best soil. Take out the second spit. This is usually poorer soil, and therefore is best spread on the surrounding area, the hole being refilled with surface soil from the surrounding area, at the same time working in a bucket of well-rotted manure, peat, or good garden compost. Having prepared the station, dig the planting hole of ample size to take the roots, put some loose soil back to form a mound in the centre and act as a seating on which to rest the tree.

Planting

Now inspect the roots, trimming off any damaged portions, and remove any evidence of suckers from the root stock. Place this tree on the prepared mound of soil, checking the planting depth, for this is important. The previous soil line on the stem will be a guide, but make quite sure that the graft union is well above the finished soil level, as failure to observe this rule will lead to much trouble later on if scion rooting occurs. Having adjusted the mound of soil to put the tree at its correct level, then cover the lowest layer of roots with a prepared soil. After the soil has been backfilled, shake the tree slightly up and down to work the soil between the roots, then firm by treading, add more soil, keeping the layers in the correct position and firming each successive layer. Continue until the hole is filled to the original level, or maybe a little higher for some sinkage will take place. Give the tree a final firm by treading, then fork over the surface to leave an even finish.

Staking

Stakes are not always needed, but if you are using a No. 9 stock it would be good policy to stake each tree. Use a round stake at least 2 ins. in diameter at the top and driven into the ground no less than 2½ ft. It is often best to drive in the stake before you plant the tree, for you can then check the tree against the stake before planting and so ensure that the top of the stake is 4 ins. below the lowest branch.

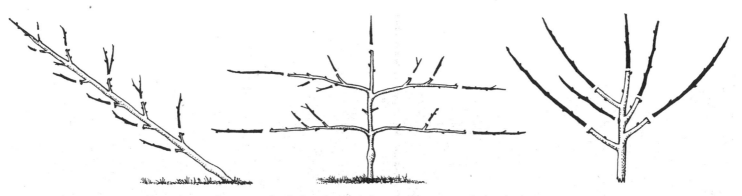

Formative pruning – to get a well-shaped tree – is done on the young tree during the dormant season.

Tying

This is best done by purchasing ready-made tree ties made of plastic, with a buckle which allows for adjustment. One tie is enough for the small bush tree, but half standards and standards would need two to keep the main stem straight for the first 4 or 5 years. Ties must be inspected regularly, for when the tree starts to grow rapidly the bark may be cut and permanent injury occur. Staking and tying are important on the heavier soils to prevent the tree from rocking, for this movement tends to puddle the heavy-type soil around the base of the stem, and it becomes impervious to water, which if retained around the stem during the winter months can cause severe damage to the bark during periods of frost, leading to the death of the tree.

Pruning

It is essential to understand the growth pattern of the apple tree before attempting to prune or manage it. Growth involves a three-year cycle. In the first year the tree produces wood in the form of a shoot. If left unattended in the next year, a number of the buds present on the shoot will grow into fruit buds. The following year these would produce fruit, so it takes three years to produce a fruit crop. The spur which carried the fruit will continue to do so for a number of years to come.

The tree will grow larger each year and produce more shoots, which form more fruit buds, and carry an increasing number of apples. If the tree always produced the same amount of growth, and annually formed fruit buds, then management would be quite simple, but like all living things there are variations from year to year. One year the tree may produce a good deal of young wood, and in another very little; some seasons the crop will be heavy, and the following season may be very poor. The term 'pruning' is used to describe the process which regulates these variations in growth and fruit production, so that we de-

velop a tree which will crop regularly throughout its useful life span.

In the management of a tree there are three phases of pruning; the first is concerned with building the framework of branches (the shape of the ultimate tree depends on this phase). The rigid single stem of the cordon and the open-centred bush, or the permanently dwarfed pyramid tree, have their basic framework laid down during this phase, and it involves hard pruning. The second stage is the encouragement of fruit bud formation and crop production. This type of pruning can be described as light. The third stage is concerned with keeping the tree balanced, in a state of healthy growth, and cropping regularly, and this will involve hard to light pruning according to the circumstances.

Pruning young trees. The formative pruning, during the first 3–5 years after planting, is carried out during the dormant season, i.e. after the leaves have fallen.

Bush trees. The newly planted bush tree will consist of 2–5 young shoots on the top of a 3-ft. stem. The pruning will consist of selecting shoots to form the permanent branch work. Four or 5 will be sufficient, but very often there are only two good shoots on some trees. One should retain these and cut out all other shoots. Then cut back the two selected shoots, removing at least two-thirds of the length of shoot, and cut to an outward-facing bud. This hard pruning will result in vigorous growth the next year, and more shoots will be produced from which to select branches to form a balanced head.

Espalier. The leading shoot which forms the central stem should be cut back to a strong bud 12–14 ins. above the last pair of horizontal branches. This will encourage the formation of at least three shoots, the uppermost one to continue the central stem, and two shoots immediately below to form the next pair of branches. The horizontal branches which are already formed, will have leading growths of young wood; it is necessary to prune these, removing at least

one-third of the shoot cutting back to a strong bud. This will encourage new vigorous growth the following year, so enabling the length of the branches to be increased annually until the allotted space is filled.

Cordons. The leading shoots of cordons should be left unpruned, but all side shoots should be cut back to 2 or 3 buds.

This formative type of pruning continues until the framework of the tree is well formed, and may take from 3–5 years. In the case of the espalier it continues until the appropriate number of branches have been produced and elongated to fill the allotted space. The leaders on the cordons will be allowed to grow unpruned until the ultimate height has been reached then the leader will be removed completely.

Pruning for fruit production. Once the formation pruning has achieved the object of establishing the form of the particular tree, then the pruner is concerned with two factors, the development of the tree, and the production of fruit. Pruning must now be modified, as hard pruning produces wood, while lighter pruning will encourage fruit, so a balance has to be achieved.

The first general rule is to reduce the amount of winter pruning. The leaders on the bush trees should be tipped, removing only one-third of the growth or less, the lateral side shoots should be left unpruned, or just have the tip removed. But if you leave all laterals in the tree it will soon become overcrowded, so about one-third of the laterals should be removed altogether.

The laterals left unpruned, or just tipped, will form fruit buds, and will crop in the next year, and once the cropping cycle has been established pruning follows a similar pattern each year.

Whether the pruning is hard or light, depends on the vigour of the tree. For poor growth prune harder, for vigorous growth prune lighter, or not at all, and be content with removing those laterals which produce overcrowding, or cross with existing branches.

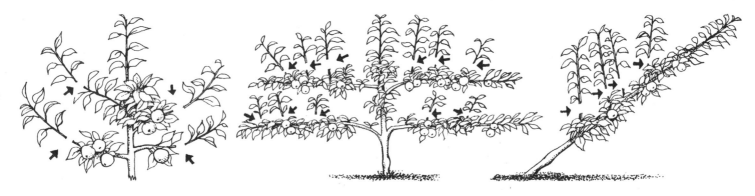

Pruning for fruit, especially on espaliers and cordons, is carried out in late July or early August.

Apple 'Ellison's Orange' grown as an espalier

Apple 'Winston' grown as a fan

Espaliers and cordons, having passed through the formative stage, should be pruned during the summer months of late July or early August. This consists of cutting back all the new growth with the exception of the leaders to 4–5 leaves. The removal of this percentage of the foliage reduces root activity, slows down growth, and encourages fruit bud formation. If one chooses, this type of pruning can be practised on small bush trees, and it works well, enabling the one or two trees in the small garden to be kept small and compact.

Branch Bending or Festooning

Trees newly planted on good soil will often produce new wood far in excess of that required to continue the formation of the tree, and the pruner is faced with either leaving too much wood or cutting it out, and increasing the problem the following year. Festooning, or branch bending, can be used with good results, and is an alternative method of dealing with surplus young wood. The branches are bent over to form an arch, with the tip secured to a suitable branch below, or tied down to a peg situated in the soil below the canopy, leaving other branches to grow upwards to form the tree. The branches can be tied down with string or taped down with adhesive tape. The tied-down shoot will form fruit buds along its whole length during the first season, and will crop the following year, producing a rope of apples along the whole length of the branch. The carrying of this crop will tend to reduce the vigour of the remainder of the tree, and so assist the pruner in the following years. These festoon branches can be removed when the remainder of the tree has settled down to bear normal crops.

June Drop and Thinning

To ensure the balance between growth and cropping, one is often obliged to thin the fruit, a task which amateurs find difficult, as a heavy crop set may make one feel that the tree should carry it to maturity.

Of course some fruit is lost every year during the 'June drop', a natural thinning process, but it may be necessary to carry out some thinning to improve the size of the re-

maining fruit, to get a uniform sample, and to maintain regular cropping by the tree.

Fruits of culinary cultivars like Emneth Early, should be thinned to 8 ins. apart to get large fruits. Miller's Seedling, a dessert cultivar, needs thinning to obtain dessert-sized fruit. When thinning, the centre or king fruit of each truss should be removed as it is often abnormal, and of poor shape and keeping quality. When thinning hold the stalk of the fruit between the first two fingers and push it gently but firmly with the thumb.

Gathering

Different cultivars of apples ripen in different months. Early-maturing types are not all ready at the same time, and may have to be picked over more than once. When picked they cannot be kept long, and it is better to use direct from the tree. Later-maturing cultivars develop more slowly, and those noted for good colour should be left on the tree as long as possible.

The fruit is ready for gathering when the apple comes away from the tree when it is gently lifted in the palm of the hand; tugging and tearing is not necessary, and is harmful to the tree and future cropping.

Fruit should only be gathered when the weather is dry, and ought not to be left lying about in full sun after picking, but taken into a cool place, and laid out in a single layer on shelves, or the floor. The fruit should be left in this position for up to ten days or a fortnight before finally storing in a permanent position. Late-keeping apples can be wrapped individually in wax paper, or placed in small plastic bags (for the amateur, the latter method is much to be commended, and fruit keeps remarkably well for long periods). It goes without saying that only perfect specimens should be given this treatment, those with blemishes should be set aside for immediate use.

Cultivars recommended for growing in the private garden in the various forms suggested are listed below.

The list could be extended of course, and fruit enthusiasts may wish to try other cultivars which become available from time to time. One is always tempted to try these

newcomers. If you have the space this is to be encouraged, but where the garden is small, it is better to be safe than sorry by planting cultivars which have stood the test of time.

The following is a brief description of a few apples suitable for garden planting.

Dessert

Ashmead's Kernel. December–March. An old russet, recommended for late keeping. Very good flavour.

Blenheim Orange. December–February. Famous old dessert apple, best grown as a half standard.

Charles Ross. Also culinary. September–October. A dual purpose apple, fruit large, good flavour, does well on chalk soils.

Cox's Orange Pippin. The best-flavoured dessert apple. Does not succeed in colder localities. Needs good management.

Discovery. August. Highly-coloured early dessert. Fruit is white-fleshed, crisp and juicy, makes compact tree.

Egremont Russet. October–December. A very useful apple for the small garden, producing russet apples. Crops regularly, resistant to scab and of compact growth.

Ellison's Orange. September–October. Crops regularly. Easy to grow. Has some resistance to frost, juicy, with a flavour resembling aniseed. Looks like Cox but has a much longer stalk.

Epicure. Early September. An early dessert variety of excellent flavour, shows some resistance to frost. Must be eaten as soon as ripe.

Fortune. Mid-September. A very sweet apple which crops regularly. Medium size, yellow with a red flush.

George Cave. August–September. A yellow apple, bright red on sunny side. Flesh white, juicy, but slightly acid flavour.

James Grieve. September. An apple of delicious flavour, easy to grow. Crops well. Is a satisfactory apple for the north of England. The best September apple and can be used as an early cooker.

Laxton's Superb. November–March. Good flavour producing regular crops, but often develops biennial bearing so needs careful management.

Lord Lambourne. November–March. Excellent flavour, easy to grow, forms a compact tree and comes between James Grieve and Cox's Orange Pippin.

Merton Charm. A red crisp well-flavoured apple, which in fact comes in roughly the same season as James Grieve and is worth a trial.

Merton Worcester. September–October. Fruit of good size, crisp and good flavour. Considered by many to be superior to Worcester Pearmain.

Ribston Pippin. November–December. An old apple of excellent flavour, considered by some to be superior to Cox. A regular cropper, and easily-managed tree.

St Edmund's Russet. September–October. This is considered to be the best early russet. The fruit is rather small, covered with a golden russet. The flesh is very juicy and fine flavoured, and makes an excellent tree for the small garden.

Sunset. November–December. This fruit has a Cox type of flavour and will often succeed where Cox is difficult to grow. Makes a compact tree and produces regular crops.

Tydeman's Early Worcester. August–September. Bright red fruits, flesh firm and juicy, ripens before Worcester Pearmain. Inclined to carry its fruit on the tips of short shoots.

Winston. January–April. A small juicy fruit which will keep firm until the end of the season. The skin is thick and some dislike this characteristic.

Worcester Pearmain. September–October. A first-class apple which crops regularly. Must be picked when fully ripe to get the best flavour. One of the most useful dessert apples.

Culinary

Arthur Turner. July–October. Fruits are large enough to pick in July, will stay on tree until September. Flavour good, regular cropper. One of the best early cooking apples.

Bramley Seedling. October–March. The best of all cooking apples. Very regular cropper and hardy. Can only be grown as a dwarf bush in the small garden.

Crawley Beauty. October–April. Very late-flowering therefore suitable for gardens liable to spring frosts.

Edward VII. December–April. A regular cropper with excellent quality. Can be successfully grown as a trained tree.

Emneth Early. Medium-sized light green in colour, good flavour, soft white flesh. Heavy cropper but does not keep. Needs the fruit thinned to reach a reasonable size.

Grenadier. August–September. Very reliable. Early cooking apple, compact in growth. A good tree for the small garden.

Lane's Prince Albert. November–February. Of compact growth and regular cropping. Suitable for the small garden. Can be grown as a trained tree.

Newton Wonder. This makes a large tree and should only be planted as half or standard form. Makes a good specimen. Excellent cropper and keeper, and does well in all areas.

Rev. W. Wilkes. October–November. Good cropper, but does not keep well, and should be used soon after picking. A dwarf habit, hardy, useful for the small garden.

THE APRICOT

This is one of the most delicious stone fruits we cultivate. It can be grown successfully in a sunny position on south, south-west, and west walls as a fan-trained tree, and no other form should be attempted.

Soil and Site

It can be successfully grown on all but light sandy soils, but it must have good drainage and adequate lime is essential. Prepare the soil to a depth of not less than 2 ft., ensuring that the drainage is good. If the soil is poor, add 2–4 oz. of fine bone meal and 2 oz. of sulphate of potash per sq. yd. It will also be helpful to work in a quantity of well-rotted farmyard manure, or garden compost, to improve the moisture-holding capacity of the lighter soils.

Planting

Trained trees are best planted as early as possible in the autumn, allowing 12–15-ft. span for each tree. Plant the tree firmly, making quite sure that the bud union is well above soil level and at least 9 ins. away from

Apple 'Charles Ross'

Bending an apple tree twig to tie it back on itself to induce forming of fruit-buds.

Apple 'Lord Lambourne'

the wall. This will mean that the tree will lean backwards towards the support.

Training

The young fan-trained tree will usually consist of between 5–7 primary branches when purchased, and training should begin immediately, for neglect is difficult to correct. The wall should have tightly stretched supporting wires 10–12 ins. apart, with straining bolts at least at one end so that they can be tightened at any time. Fix canes of 3–4 ft. in length radiating out from the position of the stem to the wires at an angle of about 45 degrees. If the tree has 5 primary branches, then four canes will be needed, two on each side.

First cut out the centre growth, and tie each of the other growths to a cane leaving the centre of the tree open. If the central growth is left in, it will be impossible to form a well-shaped fan. Prune the four branches, now trained to the canes, back to a strong bud leaving only about 6 ins. of growth. This drastic treatment is necessary if strong shoots are to be produced to form the bow framework.

When growth starts in the spring, tie the leader of each shoot to the cane as it develops, and encourage by training at least one or two strong laterals from each shoot to give you 8 or 9 primary branches in the second year. All unwanted shoots are pinched back to 4–5 leaves in July. This will then give you 4–6 branches on each side of the central space. When training in the second year, untie the branches and respace them to cover a wider area, still keeping the central space bare. You will gradually fill this space by respacing the branches over a period of 4–6 years, but when the operation is completed you will have no central stem.

Pruning

The apricot like most stone fruit dislikes being cut about, so no winter pruning is ever practised. When growth starts, and the shoots are about 1 in. long, inspect the tree closely and remove any which are likely to develop into misplaced, unwanted branches, and so avoid any cutting out later on. The shoots needed for extension of branches are tied in regularly, and all laterals are pinched back to 5 leaves in July, and cut back again to 3 or 4 buds in September.

Fruit Thinning

The flowers are carried on spurs which develop from the pinched laterals, and as all cultivars are self-fertile there are no pollination problems. Once the fruit has set and reached the size of a hazel nut, thinning should take place. The first stage should be to thin out where the clusters of fruitlets have set, the second and final thinning is carried out after the fruit has developed the stone and started to swell again. During the stoning period the fruits will appear to stand still, but after a fortnight to three weeks will begin to swell rapidly. It is then that the final thinning is carried out leaving the fruits from 6–8 ins. apart.

Picking

The fruit should be allowed to reach maturity on the tree, so that the full flavour is produced. Test for ripeness by placing the palm of the hand under the fruit, holding gently, then exert pressure on the branch carrying the fruit with the fingers – if ripe, the fruit leaves the branch. The habit of testing with thumb and finger will only damage the fruit weeks or days before it is ripe, and you will end up eating bruised

fruit with the inevitable loss of flavour.

The best cultivars are Early Moorpark, Hemskerke and Farming Dale.

CHERRIES

There are two main types of cherries, sweet and sour cherries. The former group contains scores of delicious dessert cultivars, while the latter are preserving types, and are most widely planted in gardens today although this has not always been so.

Soil and Aspect

The sweet cherry prefers a deep well-drained soil with a supply of lime, but I have seen sweet cherries trained as wall trees producing good crops on a wide range of soils, provided there was adequate drainage. Neither is it essential to have a wall, for the cherry can be successfully grown trained on a structure of upright posts, with a series of strained galvanised wires to form a support for the fan-shaped tree. The cherry flowers early, and should be protected from east winds at flowering time, so that some shelter is necessary for trees grown in the open. South or west walls offer the best positions in the garden.

The morello, or sour cherry, succeeds in any garden soil, and is popular as a fan-trained tree for the north wall, where it grows well and produces good crops.

Forms of Tree

The sweet cherry can be grown as a standard, but it produces a very large tree. To meet the need of the garden owner a bush form is offered, but it still has the same growth potential and usually gets too large for the space allotted to it after 10 or 12 years. As a fan-trained tree it is manageable, because of the restricted form. Management can be more detailed, and a greater control over the growth can be exercised. I would recommend this form of tree for garden planting.

There is at present no dwarfing root stock for cherries in general use, but some dwarfing stocks are at present being tested, and when released will bring the sweet cherry back into the collections of hardy fruits for the owner of the small garden.

Site Preparation

Again the planting site must be well prepared, and drainage attended to. The soil should be improved, and as lime is essential, a dressing of ground chalk should be applied to the surface after preparation, to be washed in by the rain and worked in when the planting takes place.

Planting

Autumn is to be preferred. Planting can be carried out throughout the dormant season, but if left until late spring much more care is needed to get the tree established before the dry summer period arrives.

Regular watering will have to be carried out to keep the growth moving.

Training

To deal with the sweet cherry first, the bush tree requires formative pruning to ensure a balanced branch of framework. Pruning needs to be carried out in September so that the healing of the wounds can take place before the winter. Crossing, or damaged branches, can be removed at any time during the growing season. The aim of the formative pruning should be to produce a well-balanced open-centred tree with well-spaced branch work. The training of the fans on walls and structures will be as described for

the apricot, but because the sweet cherry is more vigorous, fewer branches will be required to complete the fan, and the allotted area will be covered in less time.

The sour cherry is different, for it fruits on different wood, and although the formative pruning of the bush and the fan are the same, the treatment of the laterals is different. The training of the sweet cherry involves developing a framework of branches from which the laterals arise, and these are pinched to encourage the formation of fruit spurs.

The morello fruits on young wood of the previous year. While the leaders are used in the same way for branch extension the laterals are also kept and allowed to grow unpinched for these carry next year's crop. So while some part of the branch framework of the morello is permanent, a major part must be replaced each year by new growth.

Pruning

The established tree of a sweet cherry is treated like an apricot, the leaders being allowed to extend their growth and increase the overall size of the tree until the allotted space is filled. Then the leaders are tied down and left unpruned for a year, while the laterals are pinched to 6 leaves during the summer and reduced to 3–4 buds in September. In standard or bush trees this pinching is not possible, so control of tree size and any control of vigour is lost.

The pruning of the established morello or sour cherry is very different, the laterals of the previous year are left unpruned, and these shoots carry the flower and fruit. After the fruit has been gathered, a proportion of the old fruiting wood is cut out to encourage the young growth to develop further and ripen, for it is these shoots which carry next year's crop. On bush and half standards some pruning is necessary each year, consisting of cutting out unwanted and surplus branches and some wood that has fruited. The morello is a real lax grower so pruning is also needed to keep both a good shape, and sufficient strength in the branch system to carry the crop.

Wall-trained trees involve much more work than the sweet cherry, for the old fruiting wood has to be cut out, and the new laterals tied in to keep a balanced crop production. This work must be carried out immediately after cropping, for delaying until the leaves have fallen only leads to an attack of fungus diseases, and some branches will be killed during the winter.

Picking

Sweet cherries, being one of the first tree fruits to ripen, have endless volunteers to pick them; but a word of caution. Untold damage can be done by excited pickers competing with each other for the largest portion. Careful picking is a 'must' for the fruiting spurs are fragile and brittle, and damage is easily inflicted. The fruit is picked with the stalk intact and the fruit itself is not handled. Morellos are often cut off with scissors, for the trees have to be picked over several times to remove the ripe fruit. Any attempt to pull the ripe fruit off will mean the removal of several unripe ones as well.

Protection

First-class ripe cherries can never be produced in any area without the birds having prior knowledge, and nothing short of netting the whole tree and pegging down the net, will prevent the removal of the whole crop before you notice that the first fruit is ripening! When you plant a cherry

Succulent Morello cherries

tree, buy a net at the same time to cover it, for it is the only way to enjoy the fruits of your own labour.

Pollination
As all sweet cherries are self-sterile they should never be planted in isolation, but the problem is further complicated by the fact that just to choose two cherries will not necessarily solve the problem. Sweet cherries are divided into several distinct groups, each group being incompatible within itself, so cherries must always be purchased from a source where the pollination grouping is known and the suitable pollinator can be purchased.

It is also essential to have two cherries whose flowering periods overlap to ensure an adequate supply of pollen. The following are a few of the cultivars of sweet cherries which can be grown as fan-trained trees.

Sweet Cherries
Bigarreau Napoleon   Merton Bigarreau
Early Rivers   Merton Bounty
Frogmore Early
Waterloo

Sour Cherries
Morello

FIGS
The fig is perfectly hardy and has been grown in Britain, possibly since Roman times. It was grown in old gardens, and with the introduction of glass houses was extensively grown under glass both in the soil and in pots.

Fresh figs are not appreciated by all who try them for the first time, but this is often due to the fact that the fruit is not in prime condition.

However, if the space is available, the fig is not difficult to cultivate, but requires a site fully exposed to the sun all day. Success depends ultimately on well-ripened wood demanding maximum sunlight.

Soil and Site
Soil conditions are not important for the site can always be prepared, but there is a need to restrict the root space. The area required

is only 4 ft. × 4 ft. and 3 ft. deep, and in the past a brick wall using cement was built below soil level so that the roots could not escape. When preparing a site today it is far easier to use precast concrete pipe sections, 3 ft. in diameter and 3 ft. long, sinking them 2½ ft. into the ground. The base of the prepared area is covered with 6–12 ins. of brick rubble or gravel, this is then covered with a 6-in. thickness of fresh turves placed grass downwards. The remainder should be filled with a mixture of good medium fibrous loam with a small amount of sharp grit added. No manure is needed, but add 8 oz. of coarse bone meal and 1 lb. of charcoal. These supply a small amount of nitrogen and superphosphates; while the charcoal distributed evenly through the compost will help to keep it clean and sweet.

Tree Form
The fig can be grown either as a bush or as a fan, and is purchased as a quite small pot-grown specimen. Where wall space is available in a sunny position the fan-trained tree is to be preferred, and rapid growth will be made in the first few years even in the confined root run.

Planting
Pot-grown specimens can be planted any time during the year, but early autumn or early spring is usually best. Plant firmly and water in. The fig must be watered liberally every week during the summer, and it is essential to see that it does not dry out in the winter months.

Training and Pruning
The fan-trained tree is not developed from a single stem, as with the apricot and cherry, but by a number of stems arising from ground level or just below. To induce this type of growth, cut hard back at planting time to get the desired number of shoots. The aim is to have a number of stems trained out to form a fan with 12 ins. between each stem. The leaders are allowed to grow to form the extension growths, while the laterals are allowed to grow and are then tied in to the available space and the tips removed at 6–8 leaves. Sub-laterals will then develop, and these should be stopped at 5 leaves. This stopping has to be carefully timed if the maximum two crops per year are to be produced. If the shoots are stopped too early, the fruit which develops in the leaf axils will be killed in the winter. Between the end of August and mid-September is about the correct time, although this may vary with the locality.

The young figs, approximately the size of a pea, can be seen on the dormant wood after the leaves have fallen, and they remain there in a dormant state throughout the winter. If these come through undamaged they will produce the first crop in July.

When growth starts in the spring a close watch must be kept to ensure the shoots do not become overcrowded. The removal of surplus shoots when about 1 in. long is the first part of this operation. About two-thirds of the laterals which are left to develop should be stopped at 6 leaves to induce the formation of figs, giving a second crop of fruit in late September. It will also have a number of sub-laterals which will form the embryo figs to be carried through the winter.

The pruning and training while the young fig is growing rapidly during the first year or two must be kept up to date. Later on as growth slows down it is easier to cope with.

The secret of producing crops is to limit the growth, so that each shoot is exposed to

the sun, and air, and can be fully ripened before the winter sets in.

Root Pruning
If you have an established fig that is growing too vigorously and producing little or no fruit with an unrestricted root system, then root pruning is one way to induce fruiting and control the growth. Root pruning is best carried out in the late autumn, and involves digging a trench 4 ft. away from the tree and at least 18 ins. deep, severing all roots that are found. To deepen the trench to 2½ ft. will enable you to insert sheet metal, concrete blocks, or even pour in concrete, to form a barrier against any future root development.

Protection against Frost
Warm growing weather extending into the late autumn often causes the fruit to grow larger than one would wish, and in these conditions the crop can be saved by covering the tree with netting, or hessian, during the cold spells of weather.

Picking
The fruit must be fully ripe and this condition must be reached on the tree. If it is not ripened on the tree, it is never fit to eat – perfect flavour depends on absolute ripeness.

When reaching this peak condition, the fruit shows a tendency to split from the stem downwards, with the stem area soft to the touch, and the whole fruit should give under the slightest pressure. When picking support the weight of the fruit in the hand while lifting, and it will come cleanly away from the tree.

The number of cultivars available is limited, but experience has shown that the following are the most reliable for outdoor culture:
1) Brown Turkey
2) Brunswick
3) White Versailles
The last one is only suitable for growing outside in mild areas.

PEACHES AND NECTARINES
Peaches and nectarines are widely grown, for few can resist the idea of plucking luscious fruit from one's own tree, and it is possible to produce rewarding crops in most parts of the country. In the southern counties the trees can be free standing, trained as small bushes, but in other parts it is wise to select a wall site, for one is then fairly certain of getting an annual crop.

Soils
The peach and nectarine will grow in almost any soil, but drainage is important and must be good, or improved before planting. As with other stone fruits, lime is essential. Two to 4 oz. chalk in alternate years will ensure an ample supply (this may not be necessary where the natural soil is chalky). In these circumstances it should be used with caution as an excess will cause more problems than a deficiency.

Although peaches do well on thin poor soils if fed regularly, I would always advise preparing the site before planting with good loam and ample grit to keep it open. When preparing the compost for the planting site include a coarse bone meal 3–4 oz. per sq. yd., and a small quantity of charcoal. The whole prepared site must be firmed, or allowed to settle before planting.

Root Stocks
Peaches and nectarines are budded on to

(Above) Peaches grown under glass with the promise of a fine crop. (Right) Peaches can also be grown against a wall in the open if the flowers are protected in spring from wind and frosts.

selected root stocks, and of these St Julien A is the best for medium-sized trees, or those trained as fans on a wall, while the Brompton stock will produce large trees and could be useful on the poorer soils.

Planting

Bush trees should be planted 15 ft. apart, and wall trees require 15–20 ft. per tree. For training the tree, supporting wires will be required and these should be fixed on the wall or fence 9 ins. apart, with a space of at least 3 ins. between the wire framework and the wall. The wall tree must be planted 6–9 ins. away from the wall, which allows space for the stem to expand. The hole dug for the tree must be large enough to contain the roots, and the soil is then backfilled keeping the roots in the correct layers. Firm planting is essential, and if drought occurs during the summer after planting, the ground must be kept well watered and mulched with manure to conserve the moisture.

Pruning and Training

This is very important, and many trees are ruined because the fundamental details of training are not understood. This training is closely associated with pruning, and the two must be considered together.

The fan-trained tree supplied by the nurseryman usually consists of 5–7 primary branches produced from the growth of previous years. Although it has been the tradition to produce trees of this form it does present difficulties when it comes to training, for only 2 primary branches are retained.

In the spring, after planting, and just as the buds begin to move, the best primary branch on each side of the stem is selected and retained, and the remainder cut out. The chosen two are reduced by about half their length by cutting back to a strong bud. Each of these pruned branches will produce several young shoots when growth begins, and the selection and the care of these is very important.

The leading shoot of each branch is retained and the remaining shoots, two growing from the upper side of the branch and one growing from the lower side, are also retained. These shoots must be evenly spaced and all other young shoots are removed, directing all the energy to those that have been retained.

At the end of the first season the tree will consist of 8 strong shoots which will form

the first part of the framework. In the following spring reduce the length of the shoots by half, allowing a leader and two lateral shoots to develop from selected positions, removing all others, and ending the season with approximately 24 shoots.

Having started by forming the two basic branches at the bottom of the fan on either side of the stem, and developing the growth as described, the fan-shaped frame is built up from each side towards the centre. The process will take from 3–5 years according to the vigour of the cultivar and the space which has to be covered.

Pollination

The peach and nectarine flower early, the flowers being carried on the previous year's growth. To ensure a good set of fruit, assistance must be given to ensure even and effective pollination, and this can be achieved by brushing lightly over the flowers about midday with a wad of cotton wool tied to a cane, or better still a rabbit's tail attached to the top of a cane, which will act as a very suitable instrument for transferring the pollen.

Disbudding

The flowering period is soon over, and the shoots begin to develop rapidly. When these are about 1 in. long disbudding begins. It consists of retaining the leading shoot, one or two at the base of the lateral, and one or two in a central position. All these should be well placed to produce replacement shoots. All shoots growing out of the back of the lateral, or breast shoots which grow forward, must be removed. Disbudding should be spread over a fortnight or so, and not completed at one time.

The developing shoots are allowed to grow until mid-June, when they are tied loosely into the allotted space.

Fruit Thinning

Thinning of the fruit is always required on peaches and nectarines, for over-cropping will do a good deal of damage to the tree, and the resulting fruit will be small and of poor quality. The thinning is carried out in two stages.
1) When the fruitlets are the size of peas and
2) a few weeks later when the size is about that of a walnut. The first operation consists of thinning clusters to a single fruit and removing any badly placed fruits, i.e. those at

the back of the shoot, or at points where laterals are required. The second and final thinning is to reduce the fruit to one per lateral, if possible, and finish with an average of one fruit per square foot of wall occupied by the tree.

Management

As the fruit reaches full size and begins to show colour on the otherwise green skin, the young side shoots should be tied back into place so exposing the fruit to the maximum amount of sunlight. At the same time pinch out the tip of any laterals or leaders where further growth is not required.

Throughout the period from final thinning to gathering, make sure the tree is never short of water, for this affects the quality, and keep a sharp look-out for pests such as greenfly in the early part of the season and attacks of red spider mite from mid-June onwards.

Gathering

When fruit is ripening there is always a desire to test by feeling each one with thumb and finger. This practice causes so much damage by bruising that many fruits are ruined before ripe.

The technique of testing whether peaches and nectarines are ready is to place the palm of the hand lightly over the fruit and rock from side to side gently – if the fruit is ripe it will part from the branch. The tree should be checked over at least every other day. If this is not possible a thick layer of straw can be placed below the tree so that any falling fruits are not too badly damaged.

After the crop has been gathered pruning can be carried out, and at this point the decision is made whether to keep all the young shoots and how much of the old fruiting wood should be removed. How much is eventually retained will depend on how much space has to be filled and whether further extension growth is required to build up new branches. On older trees, branch replacement is often called for, and a decision can usually be made as to which portions have to be removed. It is as well if this major type of pruning can be carried out at this time of the season, for the wounds will tend to heal much more quickly and the chance of disease developing is much less.

Pests

Peach Aphids. Like all greenfly these can be controlled by winter washes, or insecticides applied in the spring as growth starts. Spray as soon as the pest is seen.
Red Spider. Syringing the tree with clean water daily will keep this pest at bay, but the amateur can seldom spare the time to do this, so a spray containing derris will control the pest and is safe. It must be applied at regular intervals from mid-June onwards if the control is to be effective.

Diseases

Peach Leaf curl. This is the most common disease and disfigures most of the foliage in some years. The leaves fall around midsummer, and although the tree seldom dies, the disease does weaken the tree if allowed to go unchecked. This disease is quite easy to control if a copper based fungicide is applied in mid-February, at the time when the buds begin to swell, but before any signs of opening are visible.

The best cultivars of peaches and nectarines are as follows:

Peaches

Amsden June. Medium size, good flavour, ripens in July.

Duke of York. Very good flavour, succeeds as a bush or fan. Ripens in July.
Peregrine. One of the best flavoured peaches, must have a wall position except in southern counties, ripens in August.
Rochester. The most reliable as a bush, good-sized fruit of fair quality, ripens in August.

Nectarines
John Rivers. Good flavour, excellent as a fan-trained tree. Fruit ripens in mid-July.
Elruge. Very hardy, excellent quality and ripens in August.
Lord Napier. The best all round nectarine, the fruit is of good size and quality, ripening in August.

PEARS
Second to apples in popularity the pear is planted widely in small gardens, and if properly managed produces good crops. Few gardeners really get the luscious fruits they should, for pears are difficult to bring to peak condition, and once reached this lasts only a few days before deterioration sets in. Knowledge of the cultivar, the period of ripening, and the best time at which they should be picked (for the storage life is more important than with any other fruit) is absolutely essential if the best results are to be obtained.

Soil
Pears are more particular than apples regarding soil conditions, they succeed best on deep, warm, moisture-holding soils. Light soils and cold, wet clays are unsuitable, but as with other fruit if trouble is taken to prepare the site then pears will succeed. Improved drainage, good loam soil, the addition of burnt earth and mortar rubble to heavier soils will enable the trees to establish themselves and to give good results over a number of years.

On light gravelly soils, mulching, to conserve moisture, is a must, and in dry seasons applications of water will be necessary to maintain size and quality of the fruit.

Form of Tree
The pear is budded on to quince root stocks and at the moment quince 'A' is used exclusively. The more dwarfing quince 'C' will be available again when the problem of virus disease has been overcome, but the trees worked on quince 'A' are quite suitable for planting in the average garden.

Bush Trees
These are the most popular and are treated in exactly the same way as bush apples. Cordons are often used when growing the choicest pears on walls and they can be trained as single, double, or even triple cordons.

Pears trained as fans are popular and they do well in this form being far easier to train and manage than, say, plums or cherries. Espalier trained trees crop well, and present no difficulties in management or training.

For gardens in the Midlands and northern areas, dessert pears do best if given a wall site, or at least a sheltered position, for they flower earlier than the apple and are susceptible to frost damage both to the flower and to the embryo fruit.

Planting
Bush trees should be planted 15 ft. apart, or about the same distance from neighbouring trees and shrubs if only one is being planted in the garden. Single cordons on walls or trellis, either upright or oblique, need 2–2½ ft. between trees, while more space must be allowed if you plant trees which are to be trained as double or triple upright cordons.

The actual planting is identical to apples. Ensure the site is well prepared by taking out a hole large enough to accommodate the roots, and allow space to spread these out and keep them in the correct sequence as you backfill the soil, always remembering to firm gently as the various layers are replaced. Firm planting and adequate staking as for apples.

Manuring
Once established the pear will need feeding to maintain healthy growth, and once fruiting spurs have formed nitrogen will be required to ensure satisfactory growth. While the need for potash is less pronounced than with apples, frequent supplies are needed and ½–1 oz. of sulphate of potash per sq. yd. should be applied any time during the winter, with 1 oz. of sulphate of ammonia and 1½ oz. of superphosphate per sq. yd. in early February, to maintain a satisfactory rate of growth, and supply sufficient nutrients to enable the tree to produce good quality fruit.

A dressing of compost or farmyard manure can be applied as a mulch in the spring to conserve moisture, and this can later be forked in during the winter. The rates of application of fertiliser to established trees will be governed by the rate of growth. Trees making less than 9 ins. of annual growth on the leaders would require dressings of nitrogenous fertiliser such as sulphate of ammonia or nitro-chalk at 3–4 oz. per sq. yd. While trees making adequate growth would receive 1 oz. per sq. yd., if the trees were too vigorous no fertiliser would be applied.

On very vigorous-growing trees sulphate of potash at 3 oz. per sq. yd. will help to check the growth, and encourage the formation of fruiting buds. Where sufficient wood is being produced annually and the crop is good 1 oz. of sulphate of ammonia and ¾ oz. of sulphate of potash per sq. yd. each year will keep the balance.

Pruning
The pruning described for apples will be quite adequate for pears, but pears will develop spurs more readily than some apples, and spur pruning may be necessary to prevent too many of them developing.

Summer pruning is essential on all trained trees on walls and trellis, and can be practised on bush trees as well, for the pear responds well to this type of pruning.

Older trees can be divided into two groups – those which grow vigorously and produce far too many shoots but little or no fruit, and those which produce no annual growth, and although plenty of fruit is produced it is all hard and of poor quality. For the former, root pruning, followed by late spring or summer pruning, usually checks the very vigorous growth and induces the formation of fruit buds. Where less drastic treatment is called for, bark ringing carried out in May will be sufficient to check the flow of sap and promote more fruit buds. The group producing little or no growth must have the spur system drastically thinned, and this often means removing two-thirds of the spurs on neglected trees. In the summer following this type of treatment, no summer pruning should be carried out, but left until the dormant season. This must be coupled with a dressing of nitrogenous fertiliser such as sulphate of ammonia, or nitro-chalk, applied at 2–3 oz. per sq. yd. in the spring.

Pollination
Pears flower earlier than apples so weather conditions often deter pollinating insects. Some pears are extremely light croppers for this reason. Others although described as self-fertile will produce much better crops when grown with other cultivars (Conference being an exception). As a general rule pears are best planted in twos, unless there are plenty in adjoining gardens, and it is very important to choose two which will flower at the same time.

EARLY FLOWERING CULTIVAR
Louise Bonne of Jersey
MID SEASON CULTIVARS
Conference   William's Bon
Durondeau   Chrétien
Packham's Triumph
LATE FLOWERING CULTIVARS
Beurré Hardy   Glou Morceau
Doyenné du Comice

While the above cultivars flower at a slightly different time it is usual for the flowering periods to overlap so pollination is effective in all but an odd season.

As with apples there are some triploid pears such as Jargonelle and Catillac, which should not be planted in isolation.

Pears Suitable for the Garden
Beurré Hardy. Dessert. Mid-October. One of the hardiest pears – should be picked a little before it parts readily from the tree. Flesh very tender and good flavour.
Beurré Superfin. Dessert. Ready October, medium-sized golden yellow fruit patched with russet. Does well on a west wall. Excellent flavour. Fruit should be picked early and eaten whilst still firm.
Conference. Dessert. October–November, the easiest pear to grow. Very hardy and prolific, excellent flavour.
Doyenne du Comice. Dessert. November–December. The best of all the late autumn pears. Ready for picking in October and will keep until mid-November. Must be planted with a good pollinator.
Durondeau. Dessert. October–November. Large brown russet fruit flushed red. Good flavour. Hardy and prolific in all forms of tree.
Glou Morceau. Dessert. December–January. A large oval egg-shaped fruit, pea green until it approaches ripeness. Flavour first class. One of the finest winter pears.
Gorham. Dessert. Mid to late September. Pale yellow colour practically covered with a brownish golden russet. Flesh white with rich musky flavour. Good cropper.
Jargonelle. A medium-sized greenish yellow fruit. Fine flavour, hardy, and good bearer especially in colder districts. Best grown as a trained tree on north or west wall.
Josephine de Malines. Dessert. December–January. Fruit sweet and perfumed. Very reliable. Fertility good, ripens successfully in store.
Louise Bonne of Jersey. Dessert. October. Reliable cropper of good quality. Flesh white, melting sweet and delicious.
Packham's Triumph. Dessert. November. A pear of good quality, ripens earlier than Doyenne du Comice. Makes a very small tree, useful for the small garden.
William's Bon Chrétien. Dessert. September. The best September pear. Easy to grow, susceptible to scab, but a good cropper. Should be picked while green and ripened in store.

Pests
The pests attacking pears include aphids which are controlled with tar oil winter washes and insecticides in spring. This

A bush pear in bloom

Blossom on a Conference pear tree

Pear 'Doyenné de Comice'

spraying will also control capsid buds. But there are two pests of pears which must be mentioned – the pear slug worm and pear midge.

The pear slug worm is a black slug-like creature which is really the larva of a saw-fly and not related to the garden slug. It appears in June and early July and feeds on the surface tissue of the leaf. The leaf then shows brown patches which on inspection will be seen to be skeletonised. If the attack goes unchecked it gets progressively worse each year. Derris or malathion will control this pest.

Pear Midge. The first sign of this pest noticed by the amateur is the falling of the attacked fruitlets in June and July. The small fly lays eggs in the opening flowers. These hatch in a few days and go into the centre of the forming fruitlet, causing the fruit to develop abnormally and ultimately to fall from the tree in June and July.

The maggots leave the fallen fruit but go into the soil and spin cocoons over the winter. This period of hibernation and life in the soil may last for two years.

They then hatch into midges which emerge in the spring to attack the opening flowers. The best method of control for the gardener is to water the soil under the tree (as far out as the branch spread) with a tar oil wash when the flowers begin to open. A systemic insecticide is also effective and does not damage grass.

PLUMS, GAGES AND DAMSONS

For the small-garden owner the plum tree has declined in popularity, chiefly because no dwarfing stock comparable to that of apples has been made available, and the management of plums and gages appears to be more difficult for many amateurs to grasp.

The use of the St Julien A root stock has given new hope that the plum and the gage may well be a worthwhile proposition for the small-garden holder. This stock has some influence on the size of the tree. Cultivars budded on it have responded to summer pruning, and small trained pyramid-shaped trees can now be developed which crop regularly, providing the buds are protected from the ravages of birds from early winter onwards.

Soils

Plums are nitrogen lovers and do best when well supplied but of course it helps to produce vigorous trees. Plums are also tolerant of a wide range of soil conditions. They succeed on good rich soils, on stiff loams over chalk; they also appear to do well on light

soils in some areas, if not too well drained.

Trees grown on high ground, or in sheltered spots on low ground, are liable to frost damage, for all flower early in the season and require some shelter, but free air movement will tend to reduce this danger.

Form of Tree

Standard trees are usually planted in plum-growing areas, but these produce large trees and therefore are unsuitable for the small garden. The half standard is a much more useful form of tree for the garden, and if properly managed can be kept in a healthy condition producing worthwhile crops for many years. Dwarf pyramid trees are a new development, arising from work carried out at East Malling with trees worked on St Julien A root stocks.

This form of tree has a central stem up to 9 ft. high, clothed from the base with a neat branch system developed by summer pruning. The fan-trained tree has been used for many years, and although the area of wall or trellis required is large, up to 24 ft. × 10 ft., the use of the more dwarfing St Julien root stock will reduce the area required. The space needed is based on the vigour of the individual cultivar and any attempt to restrict the specimen by hard pruning will lead to the production of more unfruitful wood and increase susceptibility to disease; so it is important to allow ample space for each tree to develop.

Planting

The planting of plums, gages, and damsons is the same as for any other tree, namely a well-prepared site, careful distribution of the roots, gentle firming of the soil as it is back-filled, remembering not to tie up trained trees to walls or trellis before the soil has had time to settle.

Firm staking of standard and half standard trees at planting time is required to prevent wind damage. Like peach and nectarine, the wall-trained trees will need greater care through the first and second seasons, to ensure that they grow away quickly and produce the wood required to form the branch system.

Pruning

Plums should be pruned as little as possible in the winter. Pruning back old shoots should be carried out in the late spring, while the removal of the larger branches should be delayed until the summer. The wall-trained specimens are dealt with as for peaches until the branch work has been pulled up. The encouragement of fruiting wood differs from the peach, for plums fruit

on the short laterals and these are encouraged by summer pruning, which consists of pinching all laterals when 6 or 8 leaves have been produced, if not required for extension of the branch work system.

After the crop has been gathered, the extension shoots are tied into place, and any dead shoots are removed, while pinched laterals which are not required are cut back to form short spurs.

Root Pruning

Without exception this operation is carried out on wall-trained specimens to induce fruiting and to control vigour, and is usually necessary 3–4 years after planting.

In the small garden the root pruning of half standards will prove worthwhile 4–6 years after planting, and the operation can be carried out over 2 years, pruning the roots on one side one year and completing the circle the following winter. October and November are the best months of the year for carrying out root pruning.

Manuring

If available, dressings of farmyard manure are ideal for plums, but if not, apply sulphate of ammonia at 1 oz. per sq. yd. in the spring to ensure adequate growth in the early years of training. Potash deficiency is seldom seen in plums but sulphate of potash at 1 oz. per sq. yd. applied every second year any time during the winter will ensure an adequate supply.

Thinning of Fruit

In some seasons the crop set is so heavy that thinning is necessary, firstly to ensure fruit size is maintained, and secondly to prevent damage to the branch system, especially on standard and half standard trees. The fruit should be thinned to 3 ins. apart, and the clusters of fruit reduced to 3 or 4. Even after this has been done it is sometimes necessary to support branches to prevent splitting. This should always be done early in the season before the fruit has become too heavy.

Picking

Like most stone fruits plums and gages reach the peak of condition if allowed to remain on the tree until fully ripe, when it is much better to cut the fruit off with scissors rather than pull them off, and risk damaging the wood and reducing the crop in future seasons.

Protection

This falls into three categories:
1) Protection of the buds during the win-

ter and early spring to prevent damage by birds. This can best be done by using ordinary cotton and stretching it from branch to branch over the extremities of the shoots to deter the birds from coming and attacking the flower buds.

2) Protection of wall trees is justified to prevent frost damage on the flowers, and ordinary fruit nets hung double thickness will prevent damage from spring frosts.

3) The nets used will be required later to protect the ripening fruit from bird damage; wasps can also be a nuisance but they are usually secondary, exploiting the damage caused by the tits and sparrows testing for the ripest fruit.

Pollination

Plums and gages can be divided as other fruits into three groups; some are self-fertile, others partially self-fertile, while others are self-sterile. The flowering period also differs; some flower early while others are mid-season and the remainder are late flowering.

When only one plum tree is being planted select a self-fertile cultivar, unless other plums are growing in the neighbouring gardens. Partially self-fertile and self-sterile cultivars should never be planted in isolation.

The following cultivars are grouped to assist selection:

Self Fertile
EARLY FLOWERING
Denniston's Superb   Early Transparent
  Gage   Gage
Ariel
MID SEASON FLOWERING
Reine Claude de   Victoria
  Bavay
LATE FLOWERING
Czar   Marjorie's
Laxton's Gage   Seedling
Oullin's Golden Gage

Partially Self Fertile
EARLY FLOWERING
Cambridge Gage   Early Rivers

Self Sterile
EARLY FLOWERING
Coe's Golden Drop   Jefferson's Gage
MID SEASON FLOWERING
Bryanston's Gage   Transparent Gage
LATE FLOWERING
Kirk's Blue

Pests

The chief pests of plums are the various species of greenfly which attack the trees throughout the growing season.

Leaf-curling aphids. These attack the trees from leaf burst onwards leaving the tree about midsummer and returning in the autumn.

Mealy plum aphids. This species is far less harmful than the former, but causes much concern around midsummer due to the large quantities of waxy secretion which fall from the leaves and the fruit. All aphids can be controlled with sprays of winter tar oil wash, which destroy the eggs, while attacks developing from early spring onwards can be dealt with by spraying with an insecticide based on malathion or rogor.

Red Spider Mite. This pest does cause damage in some areas, especially on wall-trained trees during a very dry season. Spray the trees with rogor at regular intervals throughout the summer.

Diseases

Silver leaf. All plums and gages are susceptible to this disease, and if the trees become affected, the branches showing the leaden grey or silver appearance of the leaves are usually obvious by July and must be removed. It is necessary to cut back until the purple stain in the centre of the branch, which accompanies the leaf discolouration, can no longer be seen.

Brown rots. These are particularly troublesome, attacking the fruit and causing them to become mummified, but the most serious aspect of this disease is the destruction of the fruiting spurs, which if allowed to go unchecked will reduce the cropping capacity to an uneconomic level. Collecting and destroying rotting fruits is a step in the right direction, but the most effective control is to spray the tree with a copper fungicide just prior to the flower buds opening in spring.

List of Cultivars

Ariel. Dessert. Mid to late September. Medium-sized oval yellow-green fruit with pink flush. Golden flesh. Trees crop regularly.

Bryanston's Gage. A medium-sized roundish greengage-like plum. Very sweet flavour. Ready mid-September. Hardy.

Cambridge Green Gage. Dessert. August. An excellent greengage. Crops more prolifically than any other greengage. Delicious flavour.

Coe's Golden Drop. Dessert. October. A valuable late pale yellow plum of good flavour. Best grown as a wall tree.

Czar. Cooking. Mid-August. The easiest plum to grow. Very hardy and frost resistant. This is one of the best cooking plums.

Denniston's Superb Gage. Dessert. Mid-August. Very hardy and can be relied upon to crop regularly. Medium sized, apricot yellow with crimson spots. Delicious flavour, one of the best early plums.

Early Rivers. Cooking. July–August. Very popular variety of early plum. It cooks well and the tree produces crops regularly.

Jefferson's Gage. Dessert. Early September. A large oval golden yellow fruit with a rich gage flavour. Can be relied upon to crop well in any form of tree.

Kirk's Blue. Dessert. Mid-September. One of the finest dessert plums, very rich with exquisite flavour. Not a heavy cropper, best grown as a wall tree.

Marjorie's Seedling. Dessert or cooking. October. A first-class plum which hangs longer than any other variety, thus prolonging the plum season. Good grower and cropper. Blooms late.

Oullin's Golden Gage. Cooking or dessert. August. A large golden fruit of fair flavour. Very valuable for cooking and bottling.

Victoria. Cooking or dessert. Early September. A heavy cropper of excellent flavour. One of the most popular plums planted. Rather susceptible to disease.

Plum 'Severn Cross' grown as a fan

Plum 'Czar' is a good cropper

GROWING

YOUR OWN SOFT FRUIT

Leslie Jones

There is nothing to compare with the flavour of soft fruit freshly picked from the garden, and with prices escalating in the shops, room should always be found even in the smallest garden for a few plants of the more popular fruits. A single blackcurrant bush should produce 6–7 lb. of fruit whilst a row of raspberry canes will yield 1 lb. of delicious berries per ft.

STARTING WITH SOFT FRUIT
Many gardeners, particularly beginners, make a mistake when starting to grow soft fruit by accepting offers of plants from well-meaning neighbours and friends. Strawberries, raspberries, and blackcurrants, are very susceptible to virus, which may not appear obvious in the early stages, but will quickly reduce the crop to an uneconomic level. Any young plants propagated from infected parents will also be affected, so it is essential to start with healthy plants obtained from a reliable source, and friends are not usually plant pathologists!

The Ministry of Agriculture run a certification scheme which covers strawberries, blackcurrants, raspberries and loganberries. The nurseryman's plants are inspected, and if they are found to be true to name and free from virus disease, he is allowed to sell them as certified stock, or as plants from certified stock if it is propagation material that has been inspected.

The importance of planting certified stock cannot be too strongly emphasised. These, and clean healthy plants of redcurrant and gooseberry which are not included, are readily available from specialist nurseries throughout the country.

Choice of Site
There are two factors which can seriously affect the cropping of soft fruit: spring frosts and wind. Currants, gooseberries and strawberries flower very early in the year, and frost at flowering time damages the blossoms and prevents them setting fruit. Spring frosts are always more likely in low-lying areas, since cold air is denser than warm, and on a clear still night tends to flow downhill and build up at the lowest point. If a frost is forecast those unfortunate enough to have a garden in a frost pocket should give their plants some protection by covering them with old cloth or even newspaper. It is generally realised that a clean moist soil will give off more heat on a cold night than one which is dry and covered in weeds or moss.

This small amount of warmth is often enough to protect the plants against frost, and it is therefore advisable to keep the soil clean and well watered while flowering. Avoid mulching with straw or manure until after the danger of frost has passed.

Fortunately, raspberries and blackberries flower late enough to avoid frost damage, and in a really low-lying garden it is best to concentrate on these plants rather than those which flower early.

Apart from the physical damage to the plants, the main problem with wind is that it discourages the pollinating insects from visiting the plants, resulting in a poor crop of fruit. If the site to be planted tends to be windy a hedge or fence to give some protection will prove to be a good investment.

Soil
The ideal soil for soft fruit is a deep loam, which encourages free rooting and provides a good supply of water during the summer without becoming waterlogged during the winter. Raspberries in particular do not like having their feet in water. Good crops, however, can be grown in heavy soil providing the drainage is adequate. In light land the addition of organic matter and watering during the summer will help to swell the fruit. Soft fruit grows best in a slightly acid soil with a pH of 6·5 and unless the soil is very acid, i.e. below pH 6, the addition of lime will be unnecessary.

Protection against Birds
Birds can cause considerable damage to soft fruit both in the winter when they will attack the dormant buds particularly of redcurrants and gooseberries, and during the summer when they will eat the ripening fruit. Odd bushes can be protected by throwing an old net curtain over them, and a few strawberries can be put in jam jars to ripen. Bird-repellent sprays are useful to protect buds during the winter, but the only really successful method of eliminating attack by birds is to use netting. Plastic netting of ¾-in. mesh is the most widely used, and with a few posts or even canes can soon be made into a temporary structure.

Many gardeners group their fruit together, and enclose them in a permanent structure, or fruit cage, but this is rather expensive. Permanent sides are built of angle iron posts and ¾-in. wire or plastic netting. The sides should be 7–8 ft. high to allow easy access. It is a mistake however to fit a permanent netting roof as this tends to deter pollinating insects from entering. It is much better to keep the roof open except at times when damage is likely to occur.

Preparation for Planting
Most soft fruits other than strawberries are likely to be in the same position for up to 15 years, and it is therefore very important that the soil is well prepared before planting. Any problem with soil drainage should be corrected at this stage, and perennial weeds such as couch grass or bindweed eradicated. The ideal preparation for the soil is double digging, incorporating manure or compost, since this will increase the rooting area and improve the drainage. Double digging should be carried out well in advance of planting to allow the land to settle.

Irrigation
An adequate supply of water is essential to swell the fruit and to produce new growth,

particularly during dry periods in early summer. A good watering should apply about the equivalent of 1 in. of rain which means approximately 5 gals. per sq. yd. either with a can or with a sprinkler.

Chemical Weed Control
There are two main chemicals used at present to control annual weeds in soft fruit, paraquat and simazine. Paraquat is a contact herbicide, which kills only the green part of plants, and becomes inactive with contact with the soil. It can therefore be used safely providing it is kept off the leaves. It is widely used for spraying around the base of redcurrants, gooseberries, etc., and between rows of strawberries.

Simazine on the other hand is a residual soil-acting herbicide, which if applied to clean soil in early spring will prevent annual weeds germinating for 6 months. It has been used commercially for many years, but it must be applied at the right time and at a rate suitable for the soil type. A gardener contemplating trying it should seek expert advice, or test it on a small area by using rate recommended for roses and shrubs.

STRAWBERRIES
The strawberry, unlike other soft fruit, is a herbaceous perennial requiring little space to produce a worthwhile crop. If the runners are planted early enough they are capable of producing a crop within 12 months.

An established healthy plant should yield between ½ and ¾ lb. of ungraded fruit. By nature strawberries are adaptable and could be easily placed in the vegetable garden rotation instead of being part of an area devoted to fruit. There are various types of strawberries available, but the most widely grown are the summer-fruiting cultivars which produce a main crop in the open from late June to August, depending upon the cultivar and the district.

Summer Fruiting Cultivar
Cambridge Favourite. Widely grown. Useful for forcing under cloches or polythene tunnels. Fruit large, good shape, medium flavour, second early.
Cambridge Prizewinner. Gives a good start to the season, rather sharp taste, but the berries are well coloured.
Cambridge Rival. Good flavour, sweet tasting, dark coloured. Fruits in the early part of the season.
Cambridge Vigour. Widely grown, good-flavoured fruits. As a young plant it fruits early in the season, but as the bed matures it fruits later.
Gorella. Large dark red fruits, heavy cropper, second early.
Red Gauntlet. Vigorous grower, heavy cropper, medium flavour, a mid-season cultivar.
Royal Sovereign. Light cropper but probably the best-flavoured strawberry. Rather susceptible to disease, early season.

Firming the soil round a strawberry plant after planting.

Strawberry propagation – pinning a cadet plant (a 'stolon') to the ground to induce rooting.

Strawberry propagation – trimming off an unwanted stolon from the pinned down cadet.

Talisman. Variable cropper, requiring good soil conditions to do well. Good quality and flavour, mid to late season.

Soil Preparation

Strawberries do best on a soil which contains a good supply of organic matter. Dressings of bulky organic matter should be incorporated into the soil in the initial cultivation, at least to the depth of the spade. Where the subsoil is hard, or the soil is slow to drain, double digging can only be of benefit in the long term.

On soils where no organic matter is incorporated, a general fertiliser such as 'National Growmore' is applied at 2 oz. per sq. yd. Distribute this over the planting area a few days prior to planting, mixing it into the surface of the soil as the final firming and levelling takes place.

Planting

Obtain runners from a reliable source, preferably certified stock, and no delay in planting should occur, once the plants are received. The young strawberry runners are best planted into moist soil, which may mean that the soil has to be watered the day prior to the planting. A small crop can be expected the following summer from runners which are planted from July to early September. Planting after early September or in the early spring, means that these plants should have their blossoms taken off as soon as they appear, enabling the plant to build up a strong crown for fruiting the following year.

Several planting systems are advocated; the most usual is to have the rows $2\frac{1}{2}$ ft. apart with the runners spaced at 15–18 ins. A trowel is used to plant the runner with its central crown positioned with its base just at soil level. Spread out the roots in the hole, fill in with moist soil, firming the soil around the roots. In order to establish the runners quickly, especially during dry weather, the soil in the immediate vicinity of the crown should be given a thorough soaking.

After Care

A well-maintained strawberry bed is capable of producing fruit for 4–5 years. During this time a number of tasks will have to be done to maintain a healthy plant capable of producing satisfactory crops.

De-runnering. Unless a matted row system is to be adopted, all runners which develop subsequently are removed. These runners are cut away from the parent plant as soon as they develop, while they are still soft and green. In the matted row system a number of runners are allowed to develop down the row giving a solid strip of plants of varying ages 15–18 ins. apart. The remainder of the space between the rows is kept free of weeds and runners. Heavier cropping can be expected in an average season from the matted row system, but in a wet season, fruits are lost due to overcrowding, and to poor air circulation which causes rotting.

Irrigation. The best time to apply water, to have a significant effect on yield, is after petal fall and before the first fruits start to turn colour. Watering at any other stage is not necessary unless the plants are suffering from obvious water shortage.

Weed control. Assuming all perennial weeds were eradicated before planting the runners, keeping the bed free of annual weeds should present no real problem. It is important not to allow annual weeds to become established because they compete for light, air, and moisture. Choose a dry day and tackle the weeds as early in their life as

A strawberry bed, showing the mulch of straw and protective Netlon netting.

A fine crop of strawberry 'Gento', showing the generous straw mulch.

possible, then they are quickly killed. The use of a dutch hoe is preferable to the draw hoe, as it is important not to draw the soil away from the crown of the plant during the hoeing process, as this tends to expose the roots near the crown.

Manuring. Providing a good supply of organic matter is present in the soil at the time of planting, all that is required is an annual dressing of ½–1 oz. per sq. yd. of sulphate of potash. Otherwise a general fertiliser such as 'National Growmore' at 2 oz. per sq. yd. needs to be applied. The fertiliser is distributed around the plants in late winter, working it into the surface of the soil with a hoe.

Strawing down. Before placing the straw in position get rid of any weeds. The purpose of strawing is to keep the ripe fruit clear of the soil. Strawing down is left as late as possible because it can increase the risk of frost damage. The straw (preferably barley) is spread thinly under the fruiting trusses just as they are being weighed down by the developing fruit. At this time of year straw also helps to conserve moisture and reduces weed growth.

Picking

This should be carried out regularly, preferably daily. To prevent bruising, the fruit is picked with a small amount of stalk attached. Ideally, the fruit should be dry when it is removed from the plant. Any damaged or diseased fruits are also removed, and disposed of by burning or burying.

Post-picking treatment. After picking, the next phase in the growth cycle of the strawberry plant is for it to make new roots and foliage, and to initiate flower buds for next year's crop. The strawberry bed at this stage looks rather untidy and is ready for a thorough cleaning up. All old foliage is removed without delay taking care to cut off the leaves approximately 4 ins. above the crown. The dead foliage and straw is then raked from amongst the plants and burned, thus getting rid of a large number of disease spores and insect pests. Loosen the soil around the plants with a hoe to aerate the surface, and before long the plants will

begin to make new foliage. In a few weeks the whole bed will take on a new look.

Pests

Aphids (Greenfly). Several different species feed on the foliage of the strawberry. The majority are found on the underside of the foliage, and as a result of their feeding the leaves are curled and distorted. It is important to appreciate that it is the aphids which spread a number of virus diseases, and a sharp watch should be kept for their presence during the growing season. Control measures should be taken as soon as they are detected. Amongst the most effective chemicals are the systemic insecticides, and are most useful between flowering and picking; however, it is important to read the instructions carefully, and note the period of time which should be allowed between spraying of the crop, and the picking of fruit. It is usually from 7–14 days. Other pests which occur occasionally include caterpillars, red spider mites, mice, slugs, and snails.

Diseases

Botrytis. If the weather is damp and humid this disease can cause considerable loss. The fruit turns soft, develops grey brown mould, and rots away. Good cultivation will help to keep the disease down to the minimum. Plants should not be overcrowded, for this hampers good air circulation. Systematically remove any infected fruits and dispose of them as picking progresses.

When chemical sprays are necessary to control diseases, benomyl has proved to be successful. Apply when the blooms are opening and repeat two or three times if necessary at 14-day intervals. Other materials such as captan and thiram can be used as described, but should not be used on the fruit if this is to be used for bottling because of the possibility of tainting.

Powdery mildew. A white powdery covering on the leaf is a sure sign that the plants are infected with the disease, often prominent in dry seasons. In severe attacks it spreads to the fruit and disfigures them, but if benomyl is used to control botrytis this will also take care of the mildew.

VIRUS DISEASES. A number of different virus diseases attack strawberry plants, and all have a gradual depressing effect on vigour and cropping. Some cultivars are more sensitive than others. Any plants that have depressed or stunted growth should be immediately removed and burnt. There are no sure control measures, but a number of steps can be taken of a precautionary nature which will assist in reducing infection. Always try to obtain certified runners when planting new beds, carry out a system of rotation and keep aphids under control.

RASPBERRIES

Raspberries are among the most expensive fruits to buy during the summer and so should be fitted in to the fruit growing programme. Providing sound fruit is used they are excellent for freezing as well as jam-making and bottling. The raspberry naturally flowers late in the spring and as a result is less likely to suffer from damage by frost. Canes, if treated correctly, produce a small crop in the second summer after planting, assuming they are in good health, and it is generally estimated that for each 1-ft. row, 1 lb. of fruit will be picked.

Siting the canes so that they receive protection from the wind is worth considering otherwise damage can occur, for in summer when the canes are in full foliage and carry a crop they are inclined to be top heavy.

Summer Fruiting Cultivars

Glen Clova. This is a new variety raised in Scotland. Medium-sized firm fruits and producing a heavy crop. Early season with fruits ripening over a long period.

Lloyd George. The best-flavoured raspberry, and where strong healthy growth can be maintained, is an excellent early cultivar. However it is susceptible to virus diseases, which often lead to rapid deterioration in vigour and cropping.

Malling Enterprise. This cultivar produces large round firm fruits of good flavour, but is sometimes reluctant to produce new canes. Mid-season.

Malling Exploit. Large crumbly fruits

ripening early. Canes very vigorous and freely produced.

Malling Jewel. This cultivar flowers late, and is less likely to suffer from frost damage. The fruit is of good quality and flavour. Ripening mid-season.

Malling Orion. This is a newly introduced cultivar producing semi-erect canes. The fruit is medium to large of moderate flavour. Mid-season.

Malling Promise. This is a well-tried and valuable cultivar producing fruit of medium size and slightly acid – a first-class preserving fruit. The canes can be damaged in very cold districts.

Soil Preparation

Good drainage is of paramount importance, and anything that can be done to improve this aspect during initial cultivation can only be beneficial subsequently. A generous dressing of organic matter prior to planting should be incorporated into the soil in a trench 2 ft. wide. For November planting the soil should be roughly prepared in September; this is especially important on heavier soils which take longer to settle naturally. On these heavier soils it may be worthwhile slightly raising the soil above the surrounding level, so giving the canes a better chance of becoming established while the soil is still warm.

Planting

It is most important to plant healthy canes, ideally obtaining them from a nurseryman who is offering certified stock. The best time to plant is late October or early November, but planting can be continued through the winter until March if weather and soil conditions are suitable. Plant with a spade taking out a hole large enough to spread out the roots and keep enough to cover them with 3 ins. of soil. Firm well to anchor the roots in the soil. Space the canes 18 ins. apart in the row, and if more than one row is planted a space of 6 ft. is left between rows.

After planting cut back the canes to 18 ins., and before growth commences in the spring, prune them back to within 9 ins. of ground level. This final cutting is made above a bud and is intended to stimulate the growth of new canes from below soil level. Under no circumstances must the canes be left unpruned in order to pick a few fruits in the first year.

Supports

Support is necessary for the fruiting canes each year. Posts of either timber or metal are erected 15 ft. apart. They should be at least 8 ft. long, and when put into position 2 ft. is driven into the ground with 6 ft. above ground level. Three wires are secured to the supporting posts at intervals of 1½ ft. and 5 ft. from ground level. Galvanised wire of 18- or 20-in. gauge is suitable.

Mulching and Manuring

Farmyard manure or garden compost can be applied as a mulch to the soil at the end of April, it will help to keep the roots cool and moist. Dry soil must be well watered before applying any mulching material. Care should be exercised when applying the mulch to avoid the soft growth of the new canes coming through the soil. If mulching material is not available extra nutrients must be applied, and a general fertiliser containing nitrogen and potash such as 'National Growmore' is satisfactory. Spread evenly, in late winter, over the whole area of soil into which the roots are, at the rate of 2 oz. per sq. yd.

Tying in new raspberry canes. Note how they are gently splayed outwards for added air and light.

Pruning

Only a minimum amount of pruning is required at the end of the first growing season following planting. This will consist of thinning out weak canes.

In established fruit, systematic pruning will be required each year. This can be done any time after fruit picking has finished, but should be completed by the end of the year. The tying material is cut away from the supporting wires prior to pruning, leaving all the growths free. Remove all the old fruiting canes, and any new canes which are particularly weak, by cutting back to as near the base as possible. Leave 5 or 6 of the strongest canes in the original clump, so that when they are spaced out and tied in, there is a new cane every 3–4 ins. Dig out any suckers which appear away from the main crop.

Tying in

The material used for tying must be durable and last for one growing season. Thin polypropylene string is suitable, for apart from giving support, tying helps to secure equal spacing to all canes along the row. A method of ensuring this should be adopted to pre-

vent the canes slipping along the wire in windy conditions. Traditionally, individual ties were given to each cane, but now a method of continuous stringing is gaining in popularity. For this method the loose end of the ball of string is fixed to the end of the row around the post, then hold the first cane in position passing the ball of string past the cane over the wire across the back of the cane and under the wire. Move on to the next cane, twisting the ball of string a couple of times around the supporting wire, and then repeating the operation, keeping the string taut at all times.

Tipping

This operation is carried out at the end of February, just before growth commences. Tied-in canes should have their tips removed about 6 ins. above the top wire, cutting above a sound bud to induce fruiting laterals to develop from the lower buds.

As an alternative to tipping the terminal portion of the cane is looped over and secured to the top wire. This improves cropping under certain conditions, and it may be worthwhile where growth has been

Raspberry 'Glen Clova'

exceptionally good and more than 18 ins. is above the top wire.

Weed Control

Where mulching has not been possible weeds will have to be controlled by shallow cultivation. Annual weeds can be readily controlled by hoeing, but care must be exercised to make sure that the surface roots of the raspberry are not damaged. A careful application of weedkillers, such as paraquat, can be used with advantage, as this eliminates root disturbance, and kills off the weeds. It is important to keep the paraquat off the foliage of the raspberry otherwise that too will be killed.

Irrigation

For the well-being of the raspberry, adequate supplies of moisture are necessary during the growing season. Not only is the fruit size improved, but also the quality of the cane produced for the following season's crop. To improve the fruit size the best time to apply the extra water is after the young fruit has begun to develop, but before it starts to turn colour.

Picking

The fruit ripens quickly, and canes should be inspected at least every second day, but if the weather is hot, daily picking is recommended. The fruit is picked by gently removing the fleshy part of the fruit, leaving the white core still attached to the cane. Pick when it is dry if possible, as the fruit does not deteriorate so rapidly as when it is picked in a moist state.

Pests

Aphids. These feed on the underside of the leaves, distorting them, and generally reducing the vigour of the plant. It is aphids which are responsible for the spread of certain of the raspberry virus diseases, and because of this it is important to control them. To reduce the number of over-wintering eggs spray the canes in midwinter with tar oil. In the spring before the flowers open use an insecticide such as malathion to prevent the build up of aphids on the plants. There are many other aphid killers available but

whichever one is used the manufacturer's instructions should be strictly followed.
Raspberry Beetle. The adult beetle lays its eggs in the centre of the flower. The eggs hatch as the fruit begins to swell and the young grubs feed on them, eventually tunnelling into the centre of the ripening fruit. It is generally at picking time that the presence of these grubs is first detected. The grub can be controlled by spraying or dusting with derris at 80% petal fall and 10–15 days later.

Virus Diseases

A number of different virus diseases affect raspberries and all have a gradual weakening effect on the canes resulting in a decline in cropping. It is wise to keep an eye open during the growing season for any canes which are not looking healthy.

One of the most widespread viruses is Raspberry Mosaic. The foliage develops an irregular yellow spotty or mottled appearance and over a period of time this can lead to general distortion of the leaf. The canes then become stunted and cropping declines as a result. When the virus symptoms are first recognised the infected canes should be lifted and burned without delay. Do not be tempted to replant in a vacant space even with healthy canes as a number of virus diseases are transmitted via the soil. Always replant a new fruiting plantation as far away from the established one as possible.

Autumn Fruiting

General cultivations are similar to those for summer-fruiting cultivars, except in the system of pruning. Whereas the summer-fruiting types fruit on the previous year's growth – autumn-fruiting types fruit on the current season's growth. Annual pruning is therefore carried out in late February when all canes are cut down to ground level. When new canes are being tied in, all thin and overcrowded shoots should be removed and the remainder tied to the wires. The cultivar September has been especially raised for fruiting in the autumn, but the summer-fruiting Lloyd George can be used and treated as above.

BLACKBERRIES AND LOGANBERRIES

The demand for each of these fruits is likely to be limited, and one or two of each should be ample for the average family. They are suitable for the less favoured positions and can be grown on a north-facing wall or fence, although the sunnier the position the better the quality and weight of the crop.

The flowers are not likely to be harmed by frost due to their late flowering, although it is not uncommon for some shoots of the loganberry to be killed in a severe winter.

Cultivars

Blackberry – Bedford Giant. A vigorous grower producing good-quality, shiny fruits, from the end of July onwards.
Blackberry – Himalaya. Very vigorous, constantly producing heavy crops of large berries ripening from August onwards.
Blackberry – Oregon Thornless. One of the more vigorous of the thornless types, cropping well from late August until the end of October.
Loganberry – Clone L.Y.59. Vigorous grower, heavy cropper, producing dark red fruits from mid-July onwards. Excellent for cooking and preserving.
Thornless Loganberry. Less vigorous than above, but given good conditions produces a worthwhile crop.

Soil Preparation

Although they are more tolerant of a much wider range of soil conditions than many other soft fruits, thorough preparation of the site is vital to maintain cropping over a number of years. Dig the soil deeply incorporating well-rotted farmyard manure to improve the structure.

Planting

This can be done at any time from the end of October to March with a preference for the autumn, providing weather and soil conditions are suitable. Plant the young plants carefully, taking care to spread out the young roots, cover with fine soil and firm. The original soil mark on the plant should coincide with the surface of the soil.

Allow 6–7 ft. between the thornless cultivars of blackberry, but 10–12 ft. between the more vigorous thorny types of blackberry and loganberry. When more than one row is required allow 6–7 ft. between the rows.

Supports

Short posts, similar to those required for raspberries, are positioned to support training wires. Three to 5 single wires, placed at 12-in. intervals above soil level, are secured to the supporting posts and made as taut as possible by fitting straining bolts at each end.

Pruning/Training

Newly planted young plants are cut back to 8 or 9 ins. above soil level after planting. This will induce a few strong growths to come from around soil level. Any growths which are made during the first season should be trained on to the supporting wires, and it is at this stage that a definite pattern of training must be started. Each year new growth must be trained in the opposite direction to the previous year's growth. If in the first year the shoots are trained into the wires right of the centre, in the second year the new canes would be trained into the left of the centre. By keeping the younger canes away from the 2-year-old canes, it cuts down the risk of cane spot disease spores passing from the older to the younger canes. Two-year-old canes are removed as low down as possible when they have fruited.

The young canes are tied in to the wires during the course of the growing season using thinnish string. Space out the canes evenly, and thin if overcrowding occurs. Check the young canes at the end of their first winter, and if any dieback has occurred, prune back into healthy wood immediately above a sound bud.

Manuring

To maintain good growth, feed each year with a general fertiliser such as 'National Growmore' at 2 oz. per sq. yd. Distribute the fertiliser evenly in late February or early March to cover the whole area in which the roots have penetrated.

Irrigation

If no mulching material is available to conserve moisture around the base of the plant it may be prudent to apply extra water. Lack of moisture during the growing season can reduce the amount of fruit, and also the number and quality of new canes.

Pests

The two main pests are aphids and raspberry beetle. The damage caused and the methods of control used are the same as for raspberries.

Pruning a young blackcurrant bush to remove old wood.

The resulting crop

BLACKCURRANTS

Blackcurrants have a very high vitamin C content, and although not comparable with strawberries or raspberries for eating fresh, are invaluable for making jam or juice, and for bottling and freezing.

One major problem associated with growing blackcurrants is the virus disease 'reversion'. Infected bushes grow vigorously but cropping ability is seriously impaired.

The disease is very prevalent in gardens and allotments all over the country, but many gardeners are apparently unaware of its presence or its effect. Reversion is spread by the blackcurrant gall mite (big bud mite). This minute insect lives and breeds within the blackcurrant buds causing them to become swollen and rounded.

There is no cure for reversion, and it is very unwise to risk introducing it by planting bushes of doubtful origin, when plants guaranteed free of the disease are readily available under the Ministry of Agriculture certification scheme.

The commonly grown blackcurrant varieties are self-fertile, so only one cultivar need be planted. The use of 2 or 3 will however help to spread the picking season.

Amos Black. Very late. A compact bush with stiff shoots. Commences growth and flowers late, so may on occasion avoid frost damage. Not a very heavy cropper, fruit has a thickish rather tough skin.

Baldwin Late. Early to come into leaf and flower, a small upright bush which requires good land, reasonably heavy cropper, good flavour, very high in vitamin C and hangs well.

Blacksmith. Mid-season. Vigorous bush producing long fruit trusses. Very good for exhibition, fruit thin-skinned, good flavour. Crops are moderate.

Boskoop giant. The earliest to ripen, large bush. Very susceptible to bad weather in the spring, large juicy fruits with a thin skin but only a moderate crop.

Wellington XXX. Mid-season, large bush with rather drooping branches, heavy cropper under widely different conditions. Fruit has rather thick skin and tends to drop quickly.

Soil Preparation

The land should be double dug and manured, well in advance of planting to allow it to settle and break down to a reasonably fine tilth. Add 2 oz. per sq. yd. of general fertiliser such as 'National Growmore' or John Innes base, and work into the top few inches.

Planting

The plants usually supplied by nurserymen are 2 years old, although sometimes one-year-old plants are used. One-year-old plants are not eligible for certification, but providing they have been propagated from certified stock plants they will be satisfactory. Gardeners are strongly advised not to be tempted by advertisements for ready to fruit 3- or even 4-year-old bushes.

Early autumn planting, when the soil is still warm, encourages new root growth, and allows the plants to grow quickly the following spring, but planting can take place any time between the end of October and early March providing soil conditions are suitable.

Bushes are normally planted 5 ft. × 5 ft. for less vigorous types like Baldwin, and 6 ft. × 6 ft. for strong-growing varieties such as Wellington XXX. Cultivation is easier if they are grown in the hedge row system where the bushes are planted 2½–3½ ft. apart with 8–9 ft. between rows. Blackcurrants are always grown as a stool, that is with several stems arising at or below soil level. To ensure there are several buds below the soil level the bushes are planted 1–2 ins. deeper than they have been planted in the nursery. Firm planting is essential, and bushes should be refirmed in the spring if the frost has loosened them.

After planting the shoots should be cut down so that one bud in each stem is visible above the soil. This may seem rather drastic, but it is essential if good crops are to be produced. Blackcurrants fruit mainly on one-year-old wood, and by cutting the shoots right down it gives the bush a complete growing season to establish itself before producing a crop. Pruning can be done immediately after planting or until the end of February. It is a good idea to mark each plant with a cane after pruning down so that it is not trodden on.

Care in First Year

During the first year the plants must be kept free of weeds either by hoeing or with chemicals. Blackcurrants produce a mass of fine roots just below the soil surface, and care must be taken not to damage these by cultivating too deeply. Watering is beneficial during dry weather to help establish the plants. Watch for pest and disease attack and take the necessary action.

Pruning after One Year

After one year's growth the plant should have at least 5 or 6 strong shoots 18 ins. or more in length. These are the shoots which will fruit the following summer, and the only pruning necessary is to cut any very thin weak shoots back to a bud.

If for any reason the plant fails to grow more than a couple of weak shoots in the first year, it is probably best to cut right down again rather than allow it to fruit the following year.

Cultivation in Subsequent Years

Blackcurrants respond to high levels of manuring, and an annual mulch with farmyard manure, after the danger of frost is past, will help to smother weeds, retain moisture, and provide a certain amount of plant food.

This should be supplemented however by an application in late January or early February of 1–1½ oz. of sulphate of ammonia (up to 2 oz. in dry areas), and ½ oz. of sulphate of potash per sq. yd. Phosphate is normally only required if farmyard manure is not used and then 3 oz. of superphosphate per sq. yd. every 2 or 3 years should be applied.

As during the first year, weeds must be controlled, water applied during dry weather, and a careful watch kept for pests and diseases.

Pruning Established Plants

Blackcurrants fruit best on shoots formed the previous year, at or near ground level, i.e. one-year-old wood. These are light yellowish brown in colour, easily recognisable, for as the shoots age they become darker in colour, and although they can continue to produce fruit-bearing side shoots and spurs, the quantity and quality of the fruit will not be very high.

The first stage in pruning is to remove completely any branches growing horizontally. If these are left they will interfere with cultivation, and the fruit will drag on the ground and spoil. The oldest, darkest-coloured branches are then cut back, either to a basal bud, or to a good strong shoot if one is present near the base of the stem. The number of old stems to be removed depends on the vigour of the bush. Where plenty of one-year-old shoots are present, all the old stems can be cut next year, only the oldest should be removed. Finally the thinner weaker shoots should be removed from the centre of the bush.

Pruning must be done every year, or the balance between young growth and fruiting will be upset. If a bush has been neglected for a couple of years, the only way to get it back into shape is to cut it right down to the ground and forego a crop for one year.

Pruning can be done at any time from the end of fruiting until the following February, although the beginner may find winter pruning easier, for when no leaves are present the young wood is easier to differentiate from the old. The sooner after cropping the job is done, the more time it will give the shoots that are left to develop.

One method of growing which is now being advocated, consists of only keeping bushes for 4–5 years, with little or no pruning, and then replacing them.

Picking
The berries are normally picked on the string, i.e. intact trusses, rather than individual berries. It will usually be necessary to pick over the bushes more than once, since the fruit on the outside tends to ripen before that in the middle of the bush. With early varieties, it is best to pick each string before the end berry becomes ripe, otherwise the older berries will become over-ripe and drop. This is not the case however with the later varieties which tend to hang on the bushes much longer.

Pests and Diseases
Aphids. These cause puckering and mottling of the foliage and permanent shoot distortion. Spray with tar oil during December or January to kill the over-wintering eggs, and with malathion or dimethoate as soon as the attack develops in the spring.
Gall Mite (Big Bud Mite). Easily recognisable by the swollen rounded buds. This, the worst pest of blackcurrants, spreads reversion virus. This incurable virus disease quickly reduces the cropping of the bushes to an uneconomical level. It does not affect the vigour of the bush, but causes abnormal blossoms and leaf formation. With practice, reverted bushes can be readily identified. Details of the symptoms are published in the Ministry of Agriculture advisory leaflet No. 277, which can be obtained free from the Publications Department, Tolcarne Drive, Pinner, Middlesex. If however the plant is infected with big bud mite, and fails to crop for a couple of years, it is safe to assume that reversion is present. Therefore dig up and burn the bush.
Always buy certified bushes, and plant them as far away from other blackcurrants as possible.
Spray with 1% lime sulphur plus a spreader as the flowers begin to open, and again 3 weeks later (this may cause slight scorching). Lime sulphur should be used each year as a protection against attack, since once the pest is established in the bushes, they are fairly certain to develop reversion and should be burnt.
Blackcurrant Sawfly. The small green caterpillar will sometimes eat all the leaves in the centre of the bush in the early summer.
Spray with derris or malathion, as soon as the caterpillars are seen.
Leaf Spot. This occurs mainly in high rainfall areas, but is found in most places in wet seasons. Dark brown spots, about the size of a pin head, develop in the leaves, and these become so numerous that the leaves become completely brown and drop early, so weakening the bush.
Clear up infected leaves in the autumn, as these can carry over the disease from one year to the next. Spray with zineb at fortnightly intervals from bud burst until one month before fruit picking begins, and again twice after the fruit has been picked if the disease is very bad.

RED AND WHITE CURRANTS
The cultivation of red and white currants is identical, and they can therefore be dealt with together. They have a distinct refreshing flavour and can be eaten fresh, either alone, or mixed with other soft fruit, or made into jam or jelly. The yield per bush is higher than blackcurrants, a well-grown plant will produce 10–15 lb. of fruit.

Like blackcurrants they are susceptible to frost damage, and since the branches are rather weak at the joints they are also likely to be damaged by wind. Birds are also very partial to the dormant buds of redcurrants, and protection will often be necessary from late November onwards.

Cultivars
Redcurrant – Jonkheer Van Tets. An early cultivar raised in the Netherlands, fairly upright growing, medium vigour, producing heavy crops.
Redcurrant – Laxton's No. 1. Early strong upright grower, very heavy crops.
Redcurrant – Red Lake. Mid-season, moderately vigorous, very large, even-sized berries, heavy crops.
Redcurrant – Wilson's Long Bench. Late, moderately vigorous, semi-erect, good crop, useful because of its lateness.
White currant – White Versailles. Strong grower, very large sweet berries and good flavour.

Soil Preparation
The soil is prepared for planting in the same way as for blackcurrants, by double digging the land if possible and incorporating manure. Then take it down to a tilth, and add 2 oz. of general all-purpose fertiliser just prior to planting.

Planting
There is no certification scheme in operation for red or white currants but plants from a reliable source should always be used. The plants are normally grown on a short stem or leg, rather than a stool, and are sold as 2-year-old plants. Planting is best done in the autumn to give good growth the following year, but can be done at any time from November to February when weather and soil conditions permit. Planting distances are usually 5–6 ft. sq., or alternatively $2\frac{1}{2}$–$3\frac{1}{2}$ ft. between plants and 8–9 ft. between rows. Firm planting is again essential, but unlike blackcurrants, they should be planted at the same depth as they were grown in the nursery.

If there is any likelihood of bud damage the bushes should be protected as soon as they are planted. A 2-year-old bush should consist of 6–8 shoots, and after planting these should be cut back by a half to two-thirds to an outward-facing bud. The object is to build up a framework of 6 or 7 evenly spaced branches, and any that are crossing should be removed, and any weak shoots cut back to one bud from their base.

The plants will not produce a crop in the first year, but must be kept weed-free and well watered during dry spells to encourage as much growth as possible.

Pruning in Subsequent Years
The fruit of red and white currant is produced mainly on spurs on the older wood, and in clusters at the base of one-year-old shoots. The pruning is therefore completely different from that of a blackcurrant, the 6 or 7 shoots which were left when the bush was planted will each develop several side shoots during the first year. The growth on each leading shoot is pruned back to an outward-facing bud about half-way down, and the side shoots are cut back to about $\frac{1}{2}$ in. from the main branch to begin the formation of spurs.

This system is followed throughout the life of the plant, the leader being cut back to about half, and the side shoots cut back to within 1 in. of the previous year's growth. Any strong-growing branches which arise from low down in the bush are normally removed completely, but can be retained where necessary to replace the worn-out branches.

Pruning can take place at any time during the winter, but is usually left until February so that any bird damage can be taken into account.

Cultivation in Subsequent Years
An annual mulch with farmyard manure, after the danger of frost has passed, will help retain moisture and in good soils will produce the food needed by the plant. On the poorer soils however $\frac{3}{4}$ oz. per sq. yd. of sulphate of ammonia can be applied in the spring, if manure is not used. As with blackcurrants 2–3 oz. per sq. yd. of superphosphate every 3 years will be sufficient.

Pest, disease, and weed control, must be carried out when necessary. Watering during a dry spell will also be beneficial, particularly on light soil. Ripening fruits should be protected against birds, and when the crop is heavy it may be necessary to support the branches to prevent them from breaking under the strain.

Picking
Red and white currants are much quicker and easier to pick than blackcurrants, as the strings are much larger. The whole branch or string is picked complete, and some gardeners find it is easier to use scissors.

Pests and Diseases
Aphids. Red and white currants are attacked by several types of aphids, the worst being probably blister aphids, which cause the leaves to become red and distorted during the summer. Control as for blackcurrants.
Capsids. The young green capsids feed on the new growth, puncturing the foliage which becomes distorted and scarred as it expands. The insecticides used for the blackcurrant aphids will also control capsids.
Gooseberry Sawfly. See symptoms and control of blackcurrant sawfly.
Dieback. This can be caused either by botrytis (grey mould), or coral spot. In both

cases branches will suddenly wilt and die back. In the case of coral spot, red spots will appear on the dead wood. Entry of the fungus is through a wound or pruning cut. When pruning, always cut to a healthy bud and do not leave a snag. Paint large wounds with a wound-sealing compound. When a branch wilts and dies, cut it back as soon as possible into healthy wood, and burn the infected material.

GOOSEBERRIES
Gooseberries are the earliest hardy fruit to be ready for picking, green fruits being used for culinary purposes, such as pies, from May onwards. Gooseberries are a valuable source of pectin, and a few will be a great help in getting other jams to set.

They are longer lived than other soft fruits, but take longer to bear a worthwhile crop. If space is limited they can be grown successfully in the shade of top fruit trees.

Cultivars
There are numerous cultivars listed in catalogues, the choice depending mainly on whether the fruit is to be used for culinary or dessert purposes.
Careless. Mid-season. Large green smooth fruit, heavy cropper. Culinary. Moderately vigorous spreading bush.
Keepsake. Early. Medium to large slightly green berries, mainly culinary. Vigorous bush, rather susceptible to frost and mildew.
Lancer. Late. Medium-large yellowish green smooth berries with transparent skin, and very good flavour. Dessert, vigorous, upright bush.
Leveller. Mid-season. Large yellowish almost smooth berries, good flavour, dessert. Bush rather weak on poor soil, needs good drainage.
May Duke. Early. Medium-sized smooth green berries, which ripen red. Culinary use. Moderately vigorous.
Whinhams Industry. Mid-season. Medium dark red hairy berries, sweet when ripe, culinary or dessert. Bush vigorous and spreading, does well on most soils.

Soil Preparation
Double digging and manuring is the ideal preparation for gooseberries. They do not like waterlogged ground, and if the soil is badly drained this must be corrected before planting. If the soil is on the heavy side, Whinhams Industry is the best variety to use.

Prior to planting, 2 oz. per sq. yd. of general purpose fertiliser should be worked into the soil. Gooseberries are tolerant of a fair degree of soil acidity, but lime should be added if the pH is below 6.0. Gooseberries are also much less susceptible to lime-induced chlorosis than, say, raspberries, in an alkaline soil.

Planting
Two- or 3-year-old bushes grown on a 6–8-in. stem are usually planted. If the leg is rather short, it pays to remove a few of the uppermost roots, and to plant slightly higher than the plant was growing in the nursery. Most gooseberries tend to be rather drooping in habit of growth, and without a reasonable length of stem the shoots will tend to trail upon the ground.

Redcurrant bush in fruit

Autumn planting as with other soft fruit is much the best.

Because of their thorns, gooseberries are rather difficult to cultivate and pick, and it is essential to allow plenty of room for this operation by planting 6 ft. × 6 ft. or 4 ft. apart with rows 8–9 ft. apart.

Pruning after Planting
Gooseberries fruit on spurs and on shoots of the previous year's growth. The object of the first few years is to build up a framework of 6–8 well-spaced branches on which spurs can develop. Any badly spaced or crossing branches are removed, weak shoots cut back to about 1 in. and the shoots selected to form the framework are cut back by about half their length. As gooseberries tend to have a drooping habit it is best to prune to an upward-facing bud to keep the bush off the ground.

Cultivation during the First Year
Water during dry spells, to aid the establishment of the plants, and mulch with farmyard manure to conserve moisture. Weeds must be kept under control, but digging around the bushes should be avoided as they are rather susceptible to root damage. A careful watch must be kept for pest and disease attack, particularly American gooseberry mildew and gooseberry sawfly.

Pruning in Subsequent Years
Pruning is very similar to that of redcurrants, except that a few well-spaced one-year-old shoots are often left unpruned to provide fruit. Any suckers or shoots produced from the leg of the bush should be removed, and the centre of the bush kept open to facilitate picking. Where dessert fruit is required, the pruning is harder than where a mass of green berries is the aim. The framework of the plant is maintained by pruning the leaders back by about half their length, while well-placed side shoots are left unpruned for one year to fruit, and are then pruned back. The remainder of the side shoots are cut back to about 1 in. to form spurs, or removed completely if the bush is overcrowded. All worn-out branches are removed and replaced by young vigorous shoots from the middle of the bush. Pruning can be done at any time during the dormant season, but it is usually left until February to avoid bird damage to buds.

Gooseberry 'Careless'

Cultivation in Subsequent Years
An annual dressing of $\frac{1}{2}$–$\frac{3}{4}$ oz. per sq. yd. of sulphate of potash and 1 oz. per sq. yd. of sulphate of ammonia should be applied in February, and 3–4 oz. per sq. yd. of superphosphate every 3 or 4 years should provide the phosphorus required by plants. Mulching, after the danger of frost has gone, will help to conserve moisture, and a good watering will be beneficial during dry weather, particularly from May to July. Weeds, pests, and diseases, must be kept under control. Protection of the buds will also be necessary during the winter, although the fruit of the gooseberry is not often attacked as other soft fruits.

Picking
Half-grown fruit can usually be picked from May onwards, but dessert fruit should be left upon the bush until fully ripe.

Pests and Diseases
Aphids. Several species attack gooseberries and will affect the growth of the bushes. Tar oil wash in winter, and spray with malathion or derris as soon as the attack starts during the summer.
Gooseberry Sawfly. The green and black caterpillars will quickly defoliate the complete bush if not controlled. Attacks usually begin in May. Spray with malathion or derris.
American Gooseberry Mildew. This disease which can be very troublesome affects the leaf, stems, and fruit. The young tips are usually first to be affected. These become covered with a white powdery deposit, which soon spreads to the older stems and fruit. As the season progresses, the white growth turns fawn and finally brown. The disease prevents the plants growing normally, and new growth will be poor and weak.

Moist stagnant conditions are ideal for the development and spread of the mildew, consequently bushes should be kept open by judicious pruning. Soft, sappy growth should be avoided by balanced feeding, with not too much nitrogen. Dinocap and benomyl are the best chemicals to use, and since prevention is better than cure, one of these should be applied as a routine measure 3 times during the season – the first before flowering, the second when the fruit has set, and the last, 3 weeks later.
Dieback. See under redcurrants.

GROWING

YOUR OWN HERBS

Kay N. Sanecki

Herbs surely head the list of undemanding plants, easy of cultivation, accommodating, and at the same time rewarding. The beginner need not be deterred by scant knowledge, and provided that basic horticultural rules are observed, success is assured. Even confined patios, window-boxes, tubs, walls, and pots, can carry worthwhile household herbs, and as so very little of a plant is required for use, a small crop is often adequate.

SOIL
Two essential requirements are:
1) shelter from prevailing winds and,
2) a suitable soil.

By selecting plants that thrive on or tolerate your type of soil, rather than attempting to change the nature of the soil, much time and effort can be saved. Soil or compost required specially for the cultivation of a particular plant, can be made up in a container or confined in an open bed. Clay is the least suitable soil for herbs, supporting mainly mint, angelica, carraway, parsley, and foxglove, but the texture can be lightened and the condition much improved, by the addition of peat or compost or other humus-encouraging material. Once in good heart, and free of perennial weeds, a heavy soil can be expected to support a wider variety of herbs, say dandelion, lovage, chamomile, rose, lavender, and bistort. On the other hand a sandy soil provides only a starved existence for most herbs, unless its condition is ameliorated by the incorporation of moisture-retentive material; then a variety can be grown easily, such as lavender, broom, rosemary, marjoram, thyme, sage, woodruff and alchemilla.

Powdery chalk soils (so untidy in appearance when dry) are beloved of such herbs as rosemary, pinks, verbascum, sage, juniper, chicory, mignonette, and periwinkles, and while it is extremely difficult to change the nature of a chalk soil, the liberal addition of compost does help to improve matters so that pulmonaria, sempervivums, marjoram, lavender, fennel, and elecampane, will flourish. As with most types of gardening, the choice of plant is in no way restricted to a medium moisture-retentive loam in which almost any herb can be grown. Even the banks of a stream or border of a pool may be used as a site for a herb plot, providing the choice is limited to more decorative herbs such as yellow iris, acorus, comfrey, watercress, meadowsweet, purslane, mints, and bergamot.

SHELTER
Herbs are always happiest when protected from prevailing winds, by either a hedge, fence, or building, but the shelter must not plunge the herb border into shade for the greater part of the day. The long-term plan of growing a hedge to confine herbs is justified – the seclusion will enhance the decorative value of the plot and design as a whole, and will prevent drying winds from depleting the aromatic qualities of the plants. The hedge plants themselves should be herbs, informally grown, like rose, lavender, rosemary, cotton lavender, artemisia, or sage.

Walls and fences provide support for scrambling herbs such as summer jasmine and roses. Houseleeks, pellitory, wall germander, thyme and feverfews can be tucked into the fabric of walls.

CULTIVATION
As with any other group of plants, some herbs are annual, some perennial, and others biennial. Most can be started from seed, though it is usual to take cuttings of perennials such as lavender, rosemary, thyme, and sage – or even 'Irishman's cuttings' of mint. Herbs grown as annuals include dill, borage, sorrel, nasturtium, marigold, fennel, purslane, and corn salad. Seed is sown either in seed pans or boxes in March or, preferably, directly into the open ground in April and May. Biennials, like foxgloves, parsley, and verbascum, are sown in summer, and often form good basal plants to wait through the winter to get a good start for a long productive season in the second year, when flowers and seed will be produced. Both annuals and biennials die after flowering, but in some instances e.g. marigolds, fennel, nasturtiums, and angelica, there is always a crop of self-sown seedlings, so the generations overlap and it is often unnecessary to replace the stock.

Perennials are permanent residents that flourish year after year. They are usually propagated by cuttings, struck around the sides of a clay pot or under a light (or plastic cover), or in a cold frame; once rooted they are then planted out into their permanent quarters.

The general rules of cultivation are relevant to growing herbs – to discourage opposition from weeds by hoeing around the plants, to protect the seedlings from the effects of sun and wind, and to remove dead or decaying parts. Otherwise, no plants are easier to encourage and their harvest is so rewarding.

HERBS IN TROUGHS AND CONTAINERS
Several herbs, particularly the culinary ones, are sufficiently accommodating to be grown in confined root space, and will thrive happily in troughs, sinks, tubs, old wheelbarrows, and window-boxes. As with all container-grown plants, good drainage needs to be ensured, and at the same time the compost needs to be maintained in a moist condition. Container gardening is not for the absent-minded gardener! Suitable plants to grow are: chives, borage, balm, catmint, parsley, marigold, nasturtium, sempervivums, corn salad, violets, thyme, rooted cuttings of lavender, rosemary, and sage. The last three named will outgrow most containers and become leggy, straggly, or too floppy in appearance, so fresh rooted cuttings need to be available every two years or so. Bay, started as rooted cuttings, is a favourite plant for porches and balconies, and can be clipped to formal shapes. Provided that it is removed from cold winter winds it will survive several seasons. Mint too, can be contained in a box or trough, in fact it is advisable always to grow mint in some solid container sunk into the herb border to prevent the plant 'trotting' round the corner. Mint is most invasive if left to its own devices.

HARVESTING, DRYING AND STORING
Endeavour and the expense of cultivating herbs can be forfeited completely by incorrect harvesting or careless drying. Knowing when to harvest is an art quickly acquired; obviously, roots are gathered on maturity in the autumn, but where leaves are used, a careful judgement has to be exercised. The best time to gather leaves or small shoots is just prior to flowering, when the plant is buoyant – this is when the active principles are most effective. Flowers or petals are collected when they are first fully open, and particular care needs to be exercised to avoid bruising them.

Drying
Ideally, plant material to be dried is spread out in single layers on trays, cardboard sheets, newspaper, or shallow boxes, and one type of plant kept separate from the others. Put all stems and shoots in the same direction on the trays to facilitate handling later on, and put only a small amount on each tray. Suitable drying places are a warm spare room shaded from sunlight, a very slow oven with the door left open (or even one that has been turned off), or a boiler room (without fuel fumes, which the plant material would absorb once it has been robbed of its moisture). Domestically the airing cupboard usually has to serve the purpose, or a warmed darkened garden shed. In this latter situation herbs can be bunched together loosely, one sort to each bunch, and small bunches hung from a line stretched across the shed. This is a rough and ready makeshift method of drying herbs, to be carried out only in the last resort.

Wherever herbs are to be dried, fresh material must not be introduced once the drying process is started, or the moisture taken from the fresh damp plants will be reabsorbed by the drier ones. Deal with one kind of material at a time and gather no more than can be accommodated. The ideal is to reduce the water content of the plant as much as possible within the first 24 hours, to prevent too much shrivelling and blackening.

To achieve a brisk start, an even temperature of approximately 50°C is required, after which it can be reduced to 35–40°C for the finishing process. The material is dry when stems snap between the thumb and finger; further 'drying' becomes baking when the leaves usually turn black. Remove the dried material from the drying area, cool and take the leaves from the stems, and rub the leaves between the folds of an old dry sheet or linen cloth, crush with a rolling pin, or rub through a coarse sieve.

Storing
Store a small amount in wooden boxes, glass jars, or plastic air-tight containers, labelled and carefully sealed – and in line with most domestic preserves, store only enough for one season – which is a small amount!

RECOMMENDED HERBS

Alecost (*Tanacetum balsamita*)
Alecost, or costmary, to give it its olden name, adds a spicy flavour to beer, and this is probably the reason for its continued cultivation over the centuries. It is a straggly plant, lax of habit, and it likes a sunny spot where the roots can run about just below the soil surface. Pull up parts of it ruthlessly every 2 or 3 years to keep it in check. The leaves are useful against bee stings. When crushed and rubbed on the sting, they will relieve the discomfort and swelling.

Angelica (*Angelica archangelica*)
Angelica, readily recognised by its ribbed hollow stems which are used as a confection after being candied, is a herb for the back of the border. Formerly the plant had a therapeutic reputation for clearing all stomach complaints, and to chew a root was a commonly recommended protection from the Great Plague in 1665. Allow plenty of room for angelica as it reaches 8 ft. or more in height and spreads gracefully. Choose a lightly shaded position in not too rich a loam. Seed sown *in situ* in spring, will produce a crop of stems the same summer. Cut these just before the flowers bloom, to avoid having them coarse and stringy.

Artemisia (*Artemisia* species)
Artemisias are particularly easy to cultivate. Some of the silver-leaved forms enhance the herb garden and should be added to a collection for their decorative value. *Artemisia ludoviciana* is a good felted-leaved form to plant as a foil for many other plants in the decorative herb border. *A. abrotanum*, lad's love, or southernwood, forms a sub-shrub, has velvet-soft silver green foliage which is highly aromatic when crushed. Tuck this one away when grown in the decorative garden, for its winter barren ugliness has gained it the name of 'old man'. *A. absinthium*, wormwood, is a native British plant, intensely bitter in flavour, and formerly used in the preparation of some liqueurs. *A. dracunculus* is tarragon, grown mainly for flavouring vinegar. The shoots should be used fresh for the flavour fades on drying. All the artemisias are perennial, and can be raised from root cuttings or from division. They are accommodating plants, and straightforward in their cultural requirements. The shrubby ones need to be cut back occasionally, especially *A. ludoviciana*, otherwise it swamps its neighbours. Tarragon needs to be divided frequently, preferably in spring.

Balm (*Melissa officinalis*)
Balm is a lemon-scented perennial used mainly for giving flavour to poultry stuffings and sandwich spreads. Sow seed in the spring – it will germinate well even if it is 2 or 3 years old – and once plants are established, they will remain safely below ground in the winter.

Angelica

Artemisia

Bay

Bergamot

Bay (*Laurus nobilis*)
Bay is regarded as being difficult to propagate; it is advisable to buy rooted cuttings in the form of pot plants. These can be planted out of doors in sheltered spots where protection from cold winds can be provided. Once established bay is quite hardy, suffering at worst wind-scorched leaves during the winter. A spray of leaves can be hung in the kitchen, or stored after drying in a box or canister and used sparingly, for only half a leaf adds sufficient flavour to soup, casserole, or blancmange. Bay is a good plant to choose if a small tree is needed for the herb garden, and its evergreen foliage provides the right permanent effect.

Bergamot (*Monarda dydima*)
Bergamot, bee balm, or Oswego tea, has been transformed by present-day cultivars into a highly decorative border plant, and in the herb garden it can provide bold reds and pinks. Introduce it as a division, choosing a moist spot, or a soil rich in moisture-retentive material. Split the clumps every 3 years or so as they tend to become bare in the middle. The leaves, dried or fresh, make a refreshing tisane, and the individual trumpet-like flowers are a pretty addition to fruit cups and salads.

Bistort (*Polygonum bistorta*)
Bistort claims a place in the herb garden for both its economic and decorative value. The black-skinned roots provide one of the strongest vegetable astringents; they wriggle about in an S form earning for the plant the name snake root. The dark green heart-shaped leaves provide salad or a green cooked vegetable early in the year, as they are ready to pull by Easter, hence the vernacular name of Easter-ledges or Easter mangiant. A perennial that thrives anywhere except in parched conditions.

Borage

Caraway

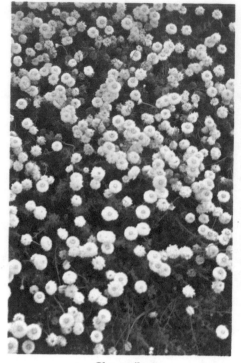

Chamomile

Borage (*Borago officinalis*)
Borage is raised from seed sown out of doors in April, and the hairy blue-flowered plant provides a harvest of fresh leaves all the year round. A winter rosette is often surrounded by seedlings, and provided the old leaves are removed, fresh cucumber-flavoured leaves will always be available. The deep blue flowers are decorative for salads and fruit cups.

Caraway (*Carum carvi*)
Caraway, grown for its flavoured seed, is a biennial, best raised by sowing in late summer. The seed will be ripe for harvesting the following summer. As a flavouring for bread and confectionery, a pinch of caraway seed goes a long way. To collect the ripened seed heads it is advisable to cover them with paper (not plastic) bags because, as with most umbelliferous plants, the seed is scattered and lost at the merest touch.

Chamomile (*Anthemis nobilis*)
Chamomile has become a vague name used to embrace a number of similar plants – mayweeds, feverfews, and anthemis. Accurately it is *A. nobilis* and *Matricaria chamomilla* both of which have a fruity scent, as opposed to the somewhat stale odour of the feverfews and mayweeds. Chamomile tea is made by infusing three or four fresh unbruised flowerheads in a cupful of boiling water. It is said to be an invigorating and refreshing drink, and alleviates many symptoms of disorders of both the digestive and nervous systems. As a hair rinse for fair hair, and as a healer of strains and sprains, the plant has been revered for generations.

A chamomile lawn or path can be made from seed sown broadcast and the resultant seedlings thinned to 4–6 ins. apart each way. Much more uniform and pleasing results will be forthcoming by transplanting seedlings or rooted divisions at about 100 plants to the sq. yd., and using the non-flowering type of chamomile.

Clary (*Salvia horminum* and *S. sclarea*)
Clary, or clear eye, has evolved as the common name because the seeds soaked in water produce a mucilaginous eye bath,

which may be used with safety to rid the eye of foreign bodies. The showy *S. horminum*, increasingly identified as clary, has conspicuous papery bracts, decorating the whole plant with a carnival gaiety. The leaves resemble those of sage and are aromatic. Sow the seed in patches and drifts in spring, where they are to grow, and thin the seedlings 4–6 ins. apart.

Comfrey (*Symphytum officinale*)
Comfrey leaves burst through the ground very early in the spring, and this is the time to break away a division for replanting. The plants grow quickly, making a lot of leaf, and the whole plant is hispid. Leaves can be pulled from early spring for use in hot fomentations or poultices for the treatment of sprained joints. Its country names of 'boneset' and 'knitbone' stem from the former usage by bonesetters as a 'plaster'. It revels in moist conditions with a distinct preference for watery meadows and river banks in the wild – so plant near the garden pool, although it is tolerant of most well-maintained garden soils provided that they are not baked clays.

Coriander (*Coriandrum sativum*)
Coriander seed is possibly best known as a flavouring for pickles, and when mixed with cayenne pepper, ginger, and turmeric, is used in curry powders and pastes. The leaves are parsley-like, less curled perhaps, and the unpleasant odour of the plant changes at maturity to become pleasantly aromatic. Sow seed in spring for a harvest of seed at the end of summer. An interesting plant to include in the herb collection, because the colouring is more interesting than most umbelliferous plants – the lilac flowers of July being followed by pale beige seeds.

Cotton Lavender (*Santolina chamaecyparissus*)
Cotton lavender of old-world garden association, is one of the most useful plants for the herb garden. It does not die down in the winter, its grey foliage is an excellent foil for many less attractive plants, and it is tolerant of clipping. Use it to emphasise the

edges of beds or paths, and clip it in March and July. Yellow button-like flowers are borne in profusion in summer when the plants are not clipped back. Both flowers and foliage when dried, act as a moth deterrent in cupboards and drawers.

Curry Plant (*Helichrysum angustifolium*)
Curry plant is not so called because it might flavour curry, but for its strong curry-like aroma. It is a perennial, with very attractive silver grey foliage above which golden orange flowers appear, resembling everlasting buds. The plant forms a good hummock. Choose a well-drained spot, or it might succumb to the winter climate. If it does, clip back in March to encourage renewed growth. A really good herb garden plant which always arouses interest.

Dandelion (*Taraxacum officinale*)
The dandelion, humble, flamboyant, and unloved, and yet provides both food and medicine. The nutritional value of the plant is high, the leaves contain minerals and vitamins. If the rosette of leaves is blanched by being kept covered by a plant pot or tile in the spring, the tender leaves make excellent salad. Otherwise fresh or dried leaves boiled or infused are an aid to digestion, and are said to clear catarrh and rheumatism. A wine can be made from both leaves and flowers. The seed germinates in three or four days and a row of dandelions may seem a curious adjunct to the herb border but every part of the plant can be used. If the tenacious tap root can be coaxed from the soil, then dried and ground, dandelion coffee can be made.

Dill (*Anethum graveolens*)
Dill is raised from seed sown in spring, but can sometimes be difficult to establish. Ideally a spot that is shaded in the middle of the day is best, and in dry periods the plants will need watering to keep them moving and prevent them flowering too early. The foliage is feathery and an infusion aids the digestion. It has long been used as dill water for infants. The seed remains viable for several years and is used widely in the preparation of dill vinegar.

Clary

Curry plant (Helichrysum angustifolium)

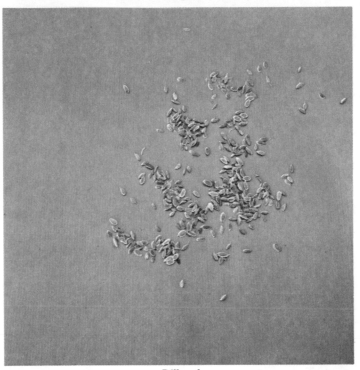

Dill seed

Fennel

Fennel (*Foeniculum officinale*)

Fennel is a fast-growing annual reaching 5–7 ft. in height, and is decked in graceful showers of finely cut leaves. Seeds follow the yellow flowers, and are ready for harvesting in September, but leave a few to scatter around the plant to maintain the stock. If the plants are cut back repeatedly during the summer, a supply of fresh leaves will be maintained from the base of the plant. In the form *F. officinale nigra* (syn *F. vulgare*) the foliage is bronzed, and the plant is a real treasure for the decorative herb border.

Foxglove (*Digitalis purpurea*)

Foxglove is a British native plant, which has been improved to enhance our gardens, but the true herb has the simple one-sided spire of purple-pink bells. The leaves are a rich source of digitalin, and form a basal rosette during the first winter. Once seed has been sown the plant itself will perpetuate the generations, especially in a shaded corner of the herb garden. Sometimes 18–20 months pass before the plant flowers. It can truly be described as a slow-growing biennial.

Henbane (*Hyocyamus niger*)

Henbane is sinister in appearance and poisonous, but is something of a curio in the herb collection. Clammy to the touch, henbane is strong smelling and is raised from seed. Strictly it is a biennial, though sometimes, especially in dry summers, it behaves as an annual, producing its cream flowers daintily veined with purple and then fruits in one season. The leaves are jagged and hispid, and in the past, have earned the herb the name of dwale.

Hyssop (*Hyssopus officinalis*)

Hyssop is shrubby and tolerates clipping, so is a useful plant for edging pathways in the herb garden. The blue flowers appear from July to September and are very attractive to bees. An infusion, hyssop tea, relieves catarrh and is a stimulant. A good clean-growing plant to add to a herb collection.

Lady's Mantle (*Alchemilla vulgaris*)

Lady's Mantle or alchemilla, the plant of the alchemist – the name earned in the Middle Ages – is a real gem for the herb garden. *A. mollis* is the garden plant to grow atop a low wall, or at the paving's edge where the pale green leaves carrying gem-like drops of dew can be appreciated. Used as a wound stauncher and cleanser, the leaves are now sometimes included in herb pil-

Lavender

Lovage

Lungwort

lows. The flowers are yellowish green, tiny, and borne above the foliage in clusters. Introduce divisions to start a colony, and the plant will look after itself for a long time (that is if the flower arrangers do not steal too much of it!).

Lavender (*Lavandula officinalis*)
Lavender is probably the best known of all herbs and takes its name from the Latin *lavandus* 'to be washed'. The Romans flung sprigs of lavender into baths to perfume the water. The gray hummocks of foliage remain attractive all year round, and lavender flower spikes surely need no description. Plant out rooted cuttings of small plants purchased in containers from the garden centre. A low hedge of lavender can be used either as a boundary hedge for the herb garden, or as an attractive internal hedge. To grow such a hedge plants need to be put in about 2½ ft. apart. They tend to be very short-lived sub-shrubs, and often seem to

exhaust themselves after 6 or 7 years, becoming leggy and leaning badly. Clipping back after flowering tends to delay the degeneration.

Lovage (*Ligusticum officinale*)
Lovage is a plant to include in a representative old-world or 'health' collection. It is started from seed, which really needs to be sown as soon as possible after harvesting for good results. The plants quickly reach 5–7 ft., looking like a hybrid between celery and angelica. The good green leaves make attractive salad and aid digestion, the stems may be candied as with angelica, and the seed is tasty sprinkled on baking, in the way that poppy seed is used. Crushed leaves will relieve boils and carbuncles.

Lungwort (*Pulmonaria officinalis*)
Lungwort is a low-growing perennial, reaching perhaps 1 ft. in height, but the stems are lax; once established the plant

forms a good mat of foliage. The flowers are deep pink at first, gradually changing to blue, earning for the plant the country name of soldiers and sailors. The main attractiveness is the leaf, supposedly lung shaped and splashed with milky blotches. Propagate lungwort by division in autumn, to allow it to establish itself ready for its early flowering the following year.

Marigold (*Calendula officinalis*)
Marigolds, today, are bold, gay, double daisy-like flowers, which once sown, are ever present. But the marigold of the herbalist is the simple single daisy, pale yellow, or even apricot, in colour. The petals dried or fresh can be scattered in soup or rice dishes during cooking to impart a yellow colour, as a substitute for saffron. Sow seed at any time of the year, except during snow or frost, and once marigolds colonise a garden they can be found in flower somewhere at any time of the year – living up to their name of calendula, calendar flower.

Marjoram (*Origanum* species)
Marjoram when used in cooking should be added with considerable care, and the plant to use is *Origanum onites*. A highly aromatic plant, it is a perennial which can be grown from seed, or by transplanting rooted divisions pulled from the side of the somewhat sprawling base of the plant. The flowers appear in purplish heads, well above the basal foliage, in July and August.

Mignonette (*Reseda odorata*)
Mignonette, grown from seed sown in May, is generally treated as an annual, although strictly speaking it is a perennial. The herb grows well indoors as a pot plant. Spikes of orange to green flowers will appear in August, so for early flowers to add to the summer potpourri, it is necessary to sow seed in August, and let them over-winter huddled together, and thin out in spring.

Mint (*Mentha* species)
Mint is a pretty general name for a whole group of plants that are mint flavoured, or are aromatic of mint. All are simple enough to cultivate. A rooted division – or Irishman's cutting – needs only to be pushed into

Mint, pot grown to prevent it spreading

Rue

Broad-leaved sage

the ground, and mint is in the garden for ever. In the herb border and kitchen garden it is advisable to control its location by confining the roots in a sunken box or bucket, otherwise the runners live up to their name and move off away from the plant. Moisture-retentive soil suits all the mints best. In fact, they are denizens of marsh conditions. Leaves may be used fresh or dried, but always pick before the plants flower. By chopping back the top growth late in the summer, fresh shoots of young leaves often persist throughout the winter. Several decorative-leaved species and forms are available to add interest to the herb collection.

Monkshood (*Aconitum napellus*)
Monkshood is a poisonous perennial plant, but one that should be included in a representative medicinal collection of herbs. It prefers a rich, cool soil and likes sunshine. Grow it from spring-sown seed, or from divisions made in spring or autumn. The deep blue helmet-shaped flowers have earned the plant the name of helmet flower and old wives' hood.

Parsley (*Petroselinum crispum*)
Parsley has persisted as a culinary herb since the Ancient World, and yet seems not to have gained more around it than a host of myths. It is a biennial with a reputation for running to seed in the spring after sowing, but the flower heads can be removed to prevent this. Fresh seed should always be sown in April or May, and if the drill is soaked with boiling water immediately prior to sowing, a high percentage of germination will be ensured. Parsley is notoriously slow to germinate – it is said to go nine times to the Devil and back before producing a leaf! Well-washed parsley leaves are chopped for adding to sauces and soups, and sprigs are used for garnishing.

Purslane (*Portulaca oleracea*)
Purslane is a somewhat neglected salad plant. Seed sown in spring will provide succulent leaves all summer, and the midribs can be preserved as pickle, flavoured with caraway seed. A dampish border, or even the edge of a pond or stream, provides the right environment for purslane, but it thrives quite happily on most soils, provided that ample water can be given during the summer to keep the plants moving.

Rosemary (*Rosmarinus officinalis*)
Rosemary, symbol of remembrance, is a shrub which can be raised from cuttings. Rooted cuttings may also be potted up for cultivation in pots and containers for the patio, or even for indoors. The grey-green leaves are evergreen, the flowers of soft lilac bloom in early spring, and in mild winters often appear sporadically from January onwards. A good culinary herb, imparting a warm flavour to meat accompaniments, and an excellent herb for incorporating in pot-pourri. A plant shrouded in fable and legend; choose a warm spot for it in the garden where it has space to relax, for it is a sunbather.

Rue (*Ruta graveolens*)
Rue, the herb of repentance, forms a low-growing evergreen shrub with attractive deeply cut blue-green foliage. For decorative effect in the herb garden, it is best in the form 'Jackman's Blue'. A plant to introduce into a collection more for its associations than for its uses. It is very bitter to the taste and a tisane of rue needs to be swamped with sweeteners. Its chief attribute is as a relief for eyestrain, an ancient use to which it has long been put.

Sage (*Salvia officinalis*)
Sage leaves are used to provide a distinctive flavouring to meat and poultry stuffings, and to cheese. The leaves are grey-green, dry very well, and a bush should be in every herb and kitchen garden. Propagated from cuttings taken in summer, and planted out once they have rooted, the bush soon reaches 4–5 ft. in height, and needs quite a lot of space. Shoots can be layered later to renew the stock, as the plants tend to get rather untidy and bare at the base. There are purple-leaved forms and a tricolor-leaved kind, all of which add interest to decorative herb collections.

Thyme (*Thymus vulgaris*)
Thyme is one of the most commonly cultivated pot herbs, and is a first-class plant for tucking between paving stones, or a path or patio, and thrives well in troughs. Its pungent flavour is strong, so a little of the leaves goes a long way. A perennial, raised from summer cuttings, it needs sharp drainage and a non-acid soil. There is a variety of forms with attractive leaves for decorative additions, but the best culinary ones are *T. vulgaris* and *T. citriodorus*, the lemon thyme.

Rosemary

A HOME FREEZER

Margaret Leach

The home food freezer offers a most satisfactory way to preserve high-quality garden produce without undue time-consuming effort. No longer need the gardener be embarrassed by the bounty of his harvest, as the freezer can economically cut out waste, and prolong the use and enjoyment of seasonal crops. This chapter gives general guidance on freezer use, with more detailed instructions for dealing with garden crops, and concludes with a look at the nutritional value of such products.

THE CHOICE OF FREEZER
Freezers are essentially refrigerated boxes, some with a top opening (chests), and some with a front opening (upright or cabinets). The chest type uses current economically and offers flexible storage space with usually a special freezing compartment, but entails a good deal of bending and lifting. The cabinet type offers rather less flexible storage space because of fixed shelves. Prolonged door opening can lead to increased current consumption but apart from these considerations this upright type is very convenient. Both types are made in a wide range of sizes.

The ability of the equipment to freeze food adequately is indicated by the 4 star symbol – a large star preceding 3 smaller

stars. Individual choice is dependent on three main factors:

1) Size
This must be based on the estimated use of the freezer. For vegetable produce, the amount of food packed in the freezer is unlikely to exceed 20 lb. per cu. ft., so that for a family of four, 10 cu. ft. would be the minimum to provide a turnover of frozen fruit and vegetables throughout the year, used, of course, in conjunction with fresh produce. It is unlikely that use will be restricted to fruit and vegetables, and so a larger freezer would be preferable. The cost of basic freezing 'machinery' does not increase in proportion to the size of the freezer, and therefore a larger model can

often be a better buy economically than a smaller one. An added advantage of buying a larger model initially is that ever-increasing pressure is put on freezer space as the many possibilities are realised. Very small freezers are rarely good buys for gardeners.

2) Siting
The location of the freezer must be considered in conjunction with the size required. Chest types take up extra floor space, whereas cabinets are economical in this respect, but may not fit in with wall fixtures. Two-compartment fridge/freezers save floor space, but in most models the freezer section is too small for any quantity of garden produce. The freezer need not necessarily be housed in the kitchen and, in fact, some other dry siting may be better, e.g. utility room. As with cars, rusting is a risk when freezers are sited in a damp situation, or where condensation can be heavy. Freezers sited on concrete floors in garages and out-houses should be on firm wooden stands. The weight of a loaded freezer is considerable, and floor strength should be checked. Space must be allowed for door or lid opening. It is obvious, but

A conveniently compact cabinet freezer

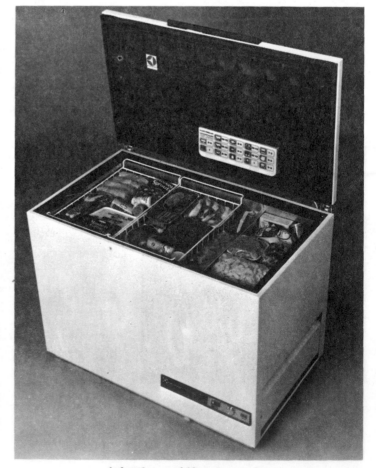

A chest freezer of 10 cu. ft. capacity

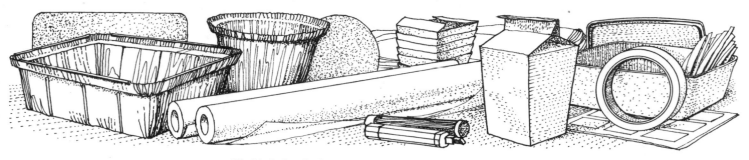

The kind of packaging materials you will need to keep handy.

sometimes overlooked, that a suitable electrical supply will be required, and a lock is advisable for freezers kept in outbuildings.

3) Cost

The purchase of a freezer entails a considerable cash outlay, and the variation in price for similar models can be confusing. Special offers of well-known makes can be worthwhile; but excessive bargains may not be cheap at all in the long run. Always check the arrangements for service before purchase, as these should be reasonably local. The insurance of freezer contents can be recommended.

FOOD FREEZING: BASIC FACTS

Temperature

Domestic refrigeration temperature of 35°–45°F prolongs the storage life of perishable foods for a short time; but a freezer temperature of 0°F, or below, preserves food safely for an indefinite period. *Quality* of food however is not preserved indefinitely at 0°F as some biochemical (enzymic) changes occur, slowly bringing about deterioration in colour, texture, and flavour. It is this quality loss due to enzymic changes, which largely determines recommended maximum storage times for foods. Overstored food will not be a risk to health, but it may be unacceptable in flavour and appearance. To counter enzymic activity, and thus prolong acceptable storage life, special preparation methods are used for some products, for example blanching of vegetables.

As the temperature of 0°F should not be exceeded for maximum quality retention, the purchase of a freezer thermometer is worthwhile. By its use the thermostat dial can be set at an appropriate mark to ensure correct storage temperature, without use of excessive electricity.

Packaging

The cold air in a freezer has a very drying effect, and foods left unwrapped would soon become desiccated. It is therefore important to pack and seal foods in wraps that are 'air tight', i.e. moisture and vapour proof. There is a wide choice of materials which are suitable for food wraps at low temperature, convenient for handling and stacking and economical in price.

Polythene bags, preferably gusseted, give the most economical packs. Gauge 120 is the thinnest recommended for freezer storage. Air can accelerate loss of food quality, so it must always be excluded from freezer packs, and this is easily done with a polythene bag of ample size. With gentle hand pressure the bag is pressed close to the contents, starting from the bottom. When all the pack has been lightly pressed, the neck of the bag is tightly twisted, the twist turned back on itself and secured with a special tie-tite or string. Rubber bands tend to perish at freezer temperature and are not recommended for sealing. The packed poly-

thene bag can be put into a suitably sized cardboard or plastic container until it is frozen, and this will mould it into an even pack for stacking. Rigid waxed cardboard or plastic containers are more costly, but can be re-used several times. A good-quality plastic container can be used almost indefinitely, and the self-sealing lid saves time.

When a pack contains liquid it is important to leave headspace to allow for expansion in freezing, which will otherwise burst the container. Even with 'dry' packs a little space should be left.

Many types of commercial frozen food packaging can be washed and used again in the home freezer. Be careful to avoid using non-food packs, as their formulation may not be suitable for food. With soft fruits, peas, etc., a 'free flowing' pack is often preferred. For this, the produce is spread out in a single layer on a clean metal tray or baking sheet, and placed in the coldest part of the freezer. Once the pieces are firmly frozen they must be bagged and sealed without delay to prevent desiccation.

Labelling and Recording

Once food is packed it should be clearly and simply labelled. With a new freezer it is at first easy to remember what is in the various packages, but soon there is confusion unless they are carefully labelled. Perhaps the simplest type of label is the tie-tite with a 'flag end' broadened out to form a label. Correctly prepared fruits and vegetables will keep their quality for a year, and so exact dating is not so necessary as it is in date marking of commercial foods. The necessary details should be written boldly with pencil or ballpoint pen, e.g. '½ lb. RASPBERRIES sugared 1977', '4 portions FRENCH BEANS; WHOLE, 1977'. The keen gardener may wish to record the variety (cultivar) as well, but too much information can slow down identification. In addition to labelling, a freezer record should be kept. Few people like keeping records, so the simpler the system the more chance there is of its being kept up. A loose-leaf book with a page for each commodity is recommended. For the individual records it is best to mark down packs separately, i.e. PEAS ½ lb. ½ lb. ¾ lb. ¾ lb. 1 lb. 1 lb. rather than PEAS 2 × ½ lb., 2 × ¾ lb., 2 × 1 lb. With the first system, packs can be crossed off as removed, whereas the second entails alterations.

The Freezing Process

When unfrozen food is put into the freezer, considerable refrigeration is required to

freeze it, and because of this the load frozen at one time must be limited. The freezing load limit should be given in the freezer instruction book, and can be taken as about 2 lb. per cu. ft. Thus in a 12-cu. ft. freezer not more than 24 lb. of food should be frozen in 24 hours. Recommended freezing loads should not be exceeded, as overloading slows the freezing rate and this adversely affects the quality of the food. To secure good results the freezer temperature must be as low as possible, and the Fast Freeze or Super Freeze switch should be used. For a full load it should be switched on up to four hours in advance, or a lesser time for smaller loads. It should be left on for 20–24 hours for a full load, and proportionately shorter periods for lighter loads. The purpose of this switch is to enable the compressor to run continuously, instead of cycling as it does otherwise. The maximum refrigeration capacity of the freezer is made available, but there is, of course, no magic increase of refrigeration power! Where there is no fast freeze switch, the thermostat dial can be turned to the lowest setting for the freezing period. Packs of food for freezing should be spread out in contact with the coldest part of the freezer. If packs are stacked tightly at this stage, freezing will be delayed.

Storage of Food in the Freezer

Food can be taken out of the freezing compartment after 20–24 hours, and should then be stored in the main area of the freezer. It is important to have some system to avoid frustration when removing food. Coloured bags for individual packs, or for collecting packs of a kind together, speed up identification. The shelves of an upright freezer provide defined storage areas, but in chest freezers it is necessary to use separators, baskets, or bags, to avoid confusion.

Storage Period

During storage the food should be at a steady temperature of 0°F or below. Interruption of supply is greatly feared by many freezer owners, but test work has shown that food in a well-stocked 12 cu. ft. freezer, situated in the kitchen, will still be frozen after 17 hours without current. This is well beyond the usual breakdown period. It must be realised that the low temperature would not have been so well maintained in a half-empty freezer, or if the freezer had been opened during the cut-out time.

The commonest cause of power failure is due to inadvertently switching off, especially of the main switch, as the family leave

A 'Tie-tite' label

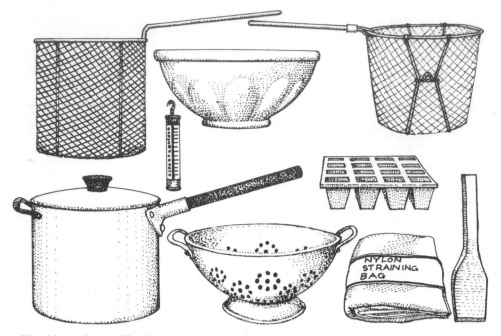

Blanching equipment. Blanching of vegetables (but not potatoes or mushrooms) is advisable to retard the action of enzymes which can cause discoloration and loss of flavour after a time.

for a holiday. A strip of adhesive tape over the freezer switch and a label on the main switch will largely prevent this. Should the fault lie in the freezer itself, the advantage of having a local service agent will be realised. In the course of using the freezer, frost will build up around the opening, and this should be scraped off with a plastic or wooden scraper. If it is not removed once a week the frost will consolidate into ice, and this can only be removed by thorough defrosting. With good management a chest freezer should not need defrosting more than once a year, but it may be necessary to defrost upright freezers 2 or 3 times a year. Ice was once the source of cold, but in the modern freezer it forms a barrier to efficient and economical freezing.

After the general points on the freezer itself, attention must now be given to garden produce.

FREEZING OF GARDEN PRODUCE
The home gardener has it in his power to produce frozen food of the finest quality. His carefully tended vegetables and soft fruit must be picked in prime condition and then frozen as quickly as possible if he is to improve on the best commercial methods. With home conditions it is so easy to eat fresh each successive crop, and only to think of freezing the remainder when family palates are sated. It is not suggested that the fresh crop should be given entirely to the freezer, but that a balance between freezer and home consumption should be maintained. In the text some cultivars are recommended. These have done well in 3-year tests at Long Ashton Research Station, Bristol. However in other regions other cultivars may be more suitable and nowadays, some local seed merchants can give recommendations for their own areas. It must be stressed that, important as is the choice of cultivar, the condition and freshness of the produce is of equal value in food quality.

VEGETABLES
Nearly all vegetables respond well to freezing. Exceptions are salad plants, which would wilt and lose the crispness that is characteristic. Celery can be frozen for use in cooking but not for nibbling with cheese. Instructions are included for tomatoes and Jerusalem artichokes, although not everybody finds them acceptable. Instructions for freezing cabbage do not usually appear, because there is little point in using up precious freezer space for a vegetable that is obtainable fresh for most of the year. There is little point too in freezing mature root vegetables, which store well by other means. The gardener must link his sowing to family taste, but more interest attaches to a good range of frozen vegetables rather than a bulk of, say, peas.

Preparation
Once vegetables are gathered, preparation and freezing should follow as quickly as possible. Preparation is as for cooking, and any exceptions are noted in the instructions below. Wilted or damaged parts are removed, and most vegetables are washed, although this is not inevitably essential with home produce. Where insects and worms may be concealed, a short soak in cold water containing 1–2 teaspoonfuls of salt per pt. will bring them out. Too much salt will kill them in the recesses of the vegetable. Soaking does not improve vegetable quality and should not become a routine of vegetable preparation.

Blanching
With a few exceptions, vegetables lose quality in the freezer unless they are blanched in boiling water. This can be a steamy job, but its value is undoubted in preserving colour, texture, and flavour.
HOW TO BLANCH
1 Put 3–4 pts. of water into a saucepan. The level of the water should be about halfway up the saucepan. Put on the saucepan lid and bring the water to the boil.
2 When the water boils put in ½ lb. of prepared vegetables. For easy removal the vegetables should be in a container, such as a blanching or frying basket, or a bag, e.g. a nylon wine-straining bag. The vegetables will inevitably take the water off the boil, and for good results it must come back to the boil within 1 min. This is important to prevent softening, and if the time exceeds 1 min., then the quantity of vegetables must be reduced for subsequent batches.
3 When the water re-boils the vegetables must be timed carefully, according to kind.

Thick pieces need longer for heat penetration than thin ones.
4 As soon as the time is completed, lift out the basket or bag and place it in cold water containing ice, or in a bowl under a gently running tap, taking care that the flow of tap water does not damage the vegetables.
5 Allow the same period for cooling as for blanching, then remove the vegetables and drain, but do not dry them.
6 Continue with the freezing process without delay.

The blanching water can with advantage be re-used for the same kind of vegetable up to 6 or 7 times. It will be necessary to top up the quantity of water during successive uses.

Packing and Freezing
The vegetables can be packed, sealed, labelled, and frozen right away, or spread on trays for freezing and packed as soon as firm.

Optimum Frozen Storage Period
All correctly prepared and frozen vegetables will keep their quality for 12 months, but it is recommended to use them up within 9–10 months, so that the palate can develop a taste for the new season's crop, fresh from the garden. When any vegetable is available throughout the year, the impact of the new season is lost.

Utilisation
Most frozen vegetables are placed in a small quantity of boiling salted water (¼ pt. of water for ½ lb. of vegetables) in a covered saucepan, and cooked for half to two-thirds the usual cooking time for similar fresh vegetables. Take care not to overcook. If the vegetables are frozen in a block, it should be gently broken up with a fork as it thaws, to ensure even cooking. Free-flowing packs are already separate. When the vegetables are drained, the liquor should be retained for use in gravy as it contains valuable soluble nutrients. A final toss in butter improves all vegetables.

Instructions for various kinds of vegetables are in Table 1.

TABLE I

PREPARATION OF VEGETABLES FOR FREEZING

Asparagus. Scrape off lower bracts. Cut to uniform length. Grade for size, and tie in individual portion bundles. *Blanch* for 2 mins. for thin stalks to 4 mins. for thick ones. Handle gently. Freeze open, and then pack, using a strip of polythene to keep bundles separate. Cook in gently boiling water with heads supported just above water level.

Globe Artichokes. Select succulent, tight heads. Remove coarse leaves and trim stalk close to base of leaves. Wash carefully. *Blanch* 6–10 mins., depending on size, in water containing 2 tablespoonfuls lemon juice per 4 pts. After cooling, invert to drain. Freeze open, then pack, or, if packed before freezing, use a rigid container for protection. Cook gently from frozen for 20–30 mins., until the leaves pull off easily.

Jerusalem Artichokes. These are hardly worth freezing as they can be left in the ground for a considerable time. For making soup, peel and *blanch* for up to 8 mins. in water containing lemon juice, as for globe artichokes (above). Alternatively, slice or dice and *blanch* for 4 mins. Pack, freeze, and use from frozen for soup. To serve as a vegetable, prepare and cook lightly. Put

Chantenay carrots cleaned ready for freezing

Cauliflower 'Polar Bear', another suitable item.

single portions in a 'boil in the bag' container, and add a little savoury sauce, e.g. caper, seal and freeze. To use, reheat bag from frozen in a saucepan of boiling water for 10–15 mins., turn out and serve. Sauce for freezing should be made thinner than for serving at once.

Broad Beans. Recommended cultivars: Aquadulce, Claudia, Giant Four-Seeded, Giant Green Longpod, White Windsor. Broad beans freeze excellently, but must be picked young. Pod and grade to size. *Blanch* 2–3 mins. and cool. Freeze open or packed. Cook in boiling salted water with a little piece of bacon if available. Drain and serve with parsley sauce.

French Beans. Recommended cultivars: Deuil Fin Precoce, Masterpiece, Phenix, Tendergreen. Pick while small enough to be served whole. Cut off ends. *Blanch* 2–3 mins. and cool. Freeze open or packed. Cook in boiling salted water, drain and toss in butter before serving.

Runner Beans. Recommended cultivars: Kelvedon Wonder, Scarlet Emperor. Pick while young and tender. Remove ends and strings. Cut into chunks about ½ in. across. *Blanch* 2–3 mins. Freeze open or packed. Cook as for French beans. Thin slicing should be avoided as it gives a flabby, rather tasteless result.

Beetroot. Recommended cultivar: Housewives' Choice. Full-grown beetroots tend to become rubbery when frozen, and it is better to store them in sand or pickle them in vinegar. Small beetroot up to 2 ins. in diameter freeze satisfactorily. *Blanch* for 5 mins., remove skin after cooling, then freeze. To use as a hot vegetable, cook from frozen and serve with a white sauce. If required for serving with salad, the beetroots can be fully cooked before freezing and, when required, thawed in the bag, sliced and served in vinegar.

Broccoli, Sprouting. Green broccoli (Calabrese) is particularly recommended although all broccoli freezes well. Choose good heads on tender stalks. Cut to uniform lengths. *Blanch* 3–4 mins. Pack, preferably in a rigid container to protect the heads, and freeze. Cook in boiling water, taking care to avoid overcooking.

Brussels Sprouts. Recommended cultivars: Darkcrop, Irish Elegance, Nois-ette, Sanda. Small, tight sprouts are prepared as usual but a cross cut ½ in. deep should be made in the base of the stalk. *Blanch* for 3 mins., cool and freeze open or packed. Cook from frozen. The cross cut allows the boiling water to penetrate the stalk so that overcooking can be avoided. *Blanching* is absolutely essential for sprouts to be frozen.

Carrots. Recommended cultivars: Amsterdam Forcing, Chantenay, Cluseed New Model, Early Nantes. Full-sized carrots store well and are not worth freezer space. It is useful to have a supply of young carrots throughout the year, and it is worthwhile to freeze a few packs. Remove the leaves, *blanch* for 4–5 mins., cool, and rub off the skin. Rinse and freeze. Small carrots for garnishing are left whole, but those slightly larger can be sliced, diced, or quartered lengthways, to make 'spears'. Cook from frozen and toss in melted butter with chopped parsley.

Cauliflower. Recommended cultivars: Improved Snowball, Majestic. Cauliflower heads, unless very small, must be broken up into florets for freezing. *Blanch* florets for 3 mins. or small heads for 5–6 mins. with a little vinegar added to the blanching water to preserve whiteness. Freeze carefully and cook gently. Steaming is better than too fast boiling.

Celery. Only suitable for celery for subsequent cooking. Separate the stalks, clean carefully, and remove strings. Cut into required lengths and *blanch* 2–3 mins. in water with lemon juice, as for globe artichokes. Freeze open or packed and, when required, complete cooking from frozen in boiling water, steam or casserole in the oven.

Courgettes. Recommended cultivar: Early Gem. Use when 4–6 ins. long and do not peel. Leave whole if very small, otherwise cut in half. *Blanch* for 2 mins. or sauté in butter. Cool, freeze, and pack. To use, complete the cooking in a covered casserole with seasoning and a little butter, or in a steamer.

Egg Plant (Aubergine). Choose young plants that feel heavy in the hand. For freezing it is recommended to halve or slice thickly. *Blanch* for 4 mins., and cool in water containing the juice of a lemon to every 2 pts. Freeze and pack. Cook from frozen as for courgettes above, or par-thaw, if to be dipped in batter and fried.

Marrow. Small ones can be sliced and treated as courgette, but large ones treated this way have a rather limited appeal. A mature marrow will store for several months if kept on a shelf or, preferably, hanging in a string bag in a cool place, and turned over once a fortnight.

Onions. There are divided opinions about freezing onions. They store and pickle well, but to freeze non-keeping kinds, they should be peeled and chopped. *Blanch* for 2 mins., cool, freeze, and pack in small containers for use as required. Very small onions can be par-cooked for 5 mins., and then frozen in a white sauce in a 'boil in the bag' container for use as a vegetable. The flour in the sauce should be reduced by a quarter, to counteract the thickening effect of freezing. The packs should be individual size to enable re-heating from frozen within 15 mins.

Peas. Recommended cultivars: Dark Skinned Perfection, Gradus, Kelvedon Triumph, Onward, Peter Pan, Petit Pois, Sutton's Show Perfection, Tall White Sugar Pea, Thomas Laxton. Use really young, pod and *blanch* for 1 min., cool, and freeze before packing. Cook in boiling salted water with a little sugar, and put in a sprig of mint for the last 2 mins., drain, and serve. Surplus lettuce cooks well with peas, and for this, hardly any water is required.

Mange Tout type of peas should be picked when the pods are not more than 3 ins. long, and blanched whole for 1½–2 mins.

Potatoes. Potato croquettes freeze well, but it is not recommended to freeze quantities of this easily obtained tuber. A few packs of new potatoes are appreciated in midwinter. Prepare small new potatoes and cook in salted water until nearly ready, cool and freeze. These lend themselves to 'boil in the bag' methods. To ½ lb. prepared potatoes add 1 dessertspoonful of water, ¼ oz. butter, a little salt and a sprig of mint. Seal the bag and freeze it. To use, put bag in boiling water for 15 mins., turn out contents, remove mint and serve.

Chipped potatoes freeze well. A good chipping cultivar such as Majestic should be used. Peel potatoes, cut into chips, and

Lemon balm. Herbs can be kept fresh in the freezer.

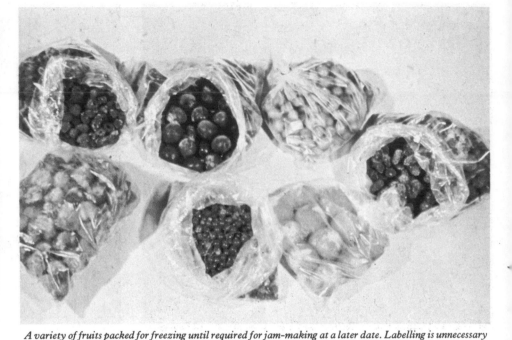

A variety of fruits packed for freezing until required for jam-making at a later date. Labelling is unnecessary with transparent packaging.

soak in cold water for ½ hour. Drain very well and fry in deep fat, until chips look pearly but not brown. Drain, cool, freeze, and pack. To use, allow the wrapped chips to thaw for an hour, if possible, before frying until they are golden brown. Drain and serve. Chips can be fried from frozen, but the foaming and spluttering of the fat is dangerous. A very few chips should be put into the fat at a time and the operator should stand well back.

Root Vegetables. Most of these store well and do not merit freezer space. However it is convenient to have some frozen packs, either of individual vegetables, or a mixture. Prepare the vegetables, cube or slice them and *blanch* for 1–2 mins. keeping different kinds separate. Make up into packs as required, for use in soups, stews, etc.

Spinach. This freezes well whether true or perpetual type. It is very bulky and, it is best to *blanch* in ¼-lb. batches for 2 mins., and to pack in smallish quantities as heat penetration is slow when cooking. The frozen block should be broken up with a fork as it begins to soften. Spinach requires very little water for cooking, but care must be taken until the block begins to thaw.

Tomatoes. All tomatoes are softened by freezing, and they will not be acceptable in salad. Where there is a glut it is worth freezing some. Small, whole, firm ripe tomatoes (2-in. diameter) can be frozen as they are, and slightly larger ones can be halved and frozen. These can both be grilled from frozen with a knob of butter, but collapse is imminent once they have softened. It is best to serve them on the firm side, and to be ready with a slice to remove them intact from the grill at the crucial moment. This method has its supporters, but for less exacting cooking, it is easier to pulp or purée the surplus crop. Any processing of tomatoes should proceed without interruption as delays cause the pulp to lose 'body'.

HERBS

It is well worth picking herbs when they are young and preparing a few packs for freezing.

There are several methods, some adapted to the use of a particular herb. Herbs need

not be blanched, but green colour will turn brown after some months in the freezer if this is omitted.

Frozen Whole Sprigs – *Suitable for unblanched parsley.*
Pick, wash, and drain whole sprigs. Trim off excess main stalk and pack 6–10 sprigs to a polythene bag; seal and freeze. When required, remove from freezer and at once rub bag between the palms of the hands – gloves will offset the cold! When the bag is opened the parsley will be found to be roughly 'chopped', and the stalks can be picked out before using the parsley in sauce or as a garnish.

Frozen Whole Leaf
Pull the leaves off the plant, either blanch for 1 min. and cool, pack, and freeze, or preferably freeze unblanched on a tray, and pack as soon as frozen. This form is suitable for use in stuffings and pâtes, where pieces of the herb should be discernible. If the free-flow frozen leaves are worked into the mixture, they will break up sufficiently to give the desired result. Blanched leaves must be thawed, separated, and roughly chopped before adding.

Frozen Chopped
The easiest method is to wash, prepare, and chop the herbs, and place them in small containers, e.g. egg cups (not valuable china). Pour on enough boiling water to cover and freeze when cold. The frozen portions can be removed from the egg cups if held under the running cold tap, then packed and replaced in the freezer. These portions thawed, soon form the basis of mint sauce with sugar and vinegar added, or parsley sauce, etc. The ice-cube tray can be used, but a very large quantity of herbs is required to provide enough chopped material to make a tray full of herb cubes.

Where a mixture of herbs is required, as in stuffing, a better flavour results from freezing each kind separately, and mixing as required when used.

FRUIT

Fruit adds glamour to the contents of the home freezer. Relatively little frozen fruit is offered for sale in retail cabinets, so the

fruit grower can ensure his own supplies which he can pick in best dessert condition. The 'pick it yourself' centres provide for those without their own fruit.

Choice of Fruit
Most fruits can be frozen successfully, and some emerge from thawing in almost fresh condition. The retention of the texture of the fruit is the crucial test. Raspberries and blueberries retain their texture well, whereas strawberries are disappointing. Fruit is subject to the same loss of quality during freezer storage as are vegetables, but the acidity of fruit slows down the rate of deterioration. However, light-coloured fruits require pre-treatment to prevent undue darkening. The cultivars mentioned in the text have been tested for 3 years at Long Ashton Research Station, Bristol.

Preparation
Final quality depends on initial condition. Fruit should be ripe, but not over-ripe. Medium-sized fruits are preferred to very large or very small samples. Stalks, leaves, etc., must be removed, and the fruit should be quickly washed in cold water if necessary. Some fruit, e.g. loganberries, may contain maggots. If the fruit is gently spread out on a large meat dish and left for ½–¾ hour in a cool place, most of the maggots will have crawled out, so that the fruit will be easier to prepare. Prepared apples and pears should be kept submerged in a bowl of cold water containing 2 level teaspoons of salt per pt., to prevent browning.

White and light-coloured fruit. This includes plums which have light-coloured pulp. All need special treatment to prevent browning, and there are several methods:

1 Firm fruit, such as peeled and cored slices of cooking apples, can be blanched for 1 min. (as for vegetables), and then cooled and packed with or without syrup.

2 Such blanching softens ripe pears, and these are better if the peeled and cored halves or quarters are poached in simmering sugar syrup (8 oz. sugar to 1 pt. water) for 3–5 mins. depending on thickness. Pears for this treatment should be firm ripe, rather than fully ripe, and subsequently packed in syrup (as method 3).

3 To avoid heating the fruit, as for peaches, apricots, and pears, a sugar syrup can be made in advance. To make this, heat 1 pt. of water, add 1–1½ lb. sugar, stir to dissolve, boil for 1 min., remove from heat; cool in refrigerator. To use this for covering, the cold syrup is poured half-way up a rigid container, and the fruit then added. The level of the syrup should not be less than ½–1 in. from the top of the pack. Place a wad of clean crumpled waxed or greaseproof paper on the fruit, put on and seal the lid. The pressure of the lid on the wad should keep the fruit submerged. Syrup made to the foregoing quantities should be sufficient for about 2 lb. of prepared fruit.

4 For added colour protection 500–600 mg. ascorbic acid can be dissolved in the syrup after making. Ascorbic acid (vitamin C), can be bought in bottles of 100 mg. tablets from the chemist, and it has the advantage of adding a little extra vitamin C to the fruit.

5 Fruit, such as plums and gooseberries, can be cooked in minimum water, sweetened, cooled, and frozen.

Other Fruits. These can be prepared as in methods 3 or 4 above, or as in method 5 if to be served cooked.

6 They can also be frozen plain, and this is recommended where bulk fruit is frozen for subsequent jam making.

7 Alternatively they can be slightly dampened with clean water and rolled in caster sugar to coat them.

8 For colour retention, crushed ascorbic acid tablets can be mixed with the sugar, using 2 100-mg. tablets to 2–4 oz. sugar per lb. of fruit.

Freezing
Dry methods of preparation – 6, 7, 8, above – can be frozen while spread on trays, and packed as soon as frozen. They can also be packed and sealed before freezing, as is necessary for methods 1, 2, 3, 4 and 5. It is not advisable to pack soft fruits more than 3 ins. deep, because pressure may damage the lower rows.

Optimum Frozen Storage Period
As with vegetables, correctly prepared and frozen fruit will keep its quality for 12 months, but the palate will be refreshed if there is a break of 2 or 3 months between eating last season's frozen fruit, and the new crop coming in.

Utilisation
All fruit for serving uncooked is best thawed slowly while still sealed in its package. Up to 8 hours in a refrigerator (or overnight) will give a good result. As light-coloured fruit will discolour if left in air, turn out the fruit just before serving. To hasten thawing, the container can be stood in cold running water. This will greatly reduce thawing time, but unless eaten at once, the fruit will soften badly. Frozen cooked fruit can be reheated direct from frozen, or thawed at room temperature for use as cold fruit.

Fruit for jam making should be put in the preserving pan, and heated from frozen as quickly as possible without burning. A little water in the pan will speed the process, even if no water is usually required, i.e. as for raspberry. For blackcurrant and gooseberry jams bring the required water to the boil, and put in the frozen fruit. It is recommended to use a little extra fruit to offset the loss of pectin in freezing.

Instructions for individual kinds of fruit are in Table II.

Two fine selections of produce that will repay freezing. Only perfect fruit should be selected and that should be handled as little as possible. The fruit should just be ripe and no more and should be frozen as soon as possible after picking. Avoid washing the fruit if you can, and keep it in a cool place until you pack it.

211

TABLE II

PREPARATION OF FRUIT FOR FREEZING

Apples. Cooking apples are recommended, particularly Bramley Seedling. For slices, prepare and *blanch* as method 1 above. For pulp, as method 5. For purée, cook as for pulp and pass through a sieve before packing and freezing. Whole apples do not freeze satisfactorily, but dumplings are approved by some. Prepare the short crust pastry and roll it out into circles. Peel and core an apple, roll it in lemon juice, and immediately complete the dumpling. Continue with the batch, putting each dumpling to freeze as soon as it is made. Wrap when frozen. Cook from frozen for 40–45 mins. at 400. Do not store for more than 3–4 months. If the apple colour is not attractive, remember next time to cook the dumplings before freezing, and reheat from frozen.

Blackberries. Recommended cultivars: Himalaya Giant, Ashton Cross, Merton Early. Wild fruit is less acid than cultivated. Berries used must be a good size and juicy. Freeze by methods 6, 7, 3 or 5.

Blackcurrants. Recommended cultivars: Baldwin, Boscoop, Westwick Choice and many others. Can be frozen by methods 6, 7 or 3, but as they are almost invariably eaten cooked, method 5 may be the most practical. For subsequent jam making, *blanch* for 5 mins. to prevent skin toughening during freezing.

Blueberries. Recommended cultivars: Bluecrop (large berry), Jersey. Freeze by methods 6, 7 or 3. This fruit makes a famous American pie. To make a pie filling, weigh and cook some blueberries in minimum water, and allow to cool. For each 6 oz. fruit, stir in 2 teaspoonfuls of lemon juice, and 1 oz. sugar mixed with 1½ teaspoonfuls of arrowroot or cornflour. The mixture can be frozen in the pie case or on its own. The addition of cereal to the sugar prevents a soggy bottom crust.

Cherries. Acid varieties recommended, such as Montmorency. Remove stones if fruit to be frozen for more than 2–3 months. Freeze by method 3 for red cherries, method 4 for white ones (but these are not usually very acceptable), or method 5 if to be served cooked.

Damsons. Choose a true damson, e.g. Shropshire Lad. Freeze by methods 3, 6, 7 or 5. They retain a good deal of true damson flavour.

Gages. Delicious as these are fresh, the texture is usually too soft after freezing for dessert use. Freeze by method 3 or 4 to try dessert condition, or cook by method 5.

Gooseberries. Recommended cultivars: Careless, Keepsake, Lancer and immature Leveller. Dessert gooseberries are not suitable for freezing. Freeze by methods 3, 4, 7, or 8 for use raw or method 5 if required cooked. Raw gooseberries tend to darken if left in the air after thawing.

Loganberries. Must be dark-ripe and juicy. Freeze very well, and retain true flavour. Freeze by methods 6, 7, 3 or 5.

Mulberries. Must be really ripe. If it is possible to spread a clean polythene sheet round the base of the tree, freshly dropped fruit will be in good condition. Freeze by methods 6, 7 or 3. The large core or plug detracts from the enjoyment of this fruit, and a sweetened purée of sieved raw mulberries overcomes this difficulty.

Peaches. When the occasional good crop of ripe fruit is achieved, freezing by method 3 or, preferably, method 4, will preserve the flavour and texture of peeled, halved or sliced peaches.

Pears. This fruit is not easy to freeze. Really ripe pears of good dessert quality become almost slimy in texture if frozen in syrup. For method 4, the pears should be not quite fully ripe, peeled, cored and submerged in syrup right through freezing to actual service. Dessert pears that are still rather firm should be frozen by method 2 and hard cooking pears need thorough slow cooking before freezing. They are not as rewarding as some other fruit.

Plums. A luscious large ripe plum does not carry its quality through freezing. Medium-sized ripe plums should be treated according to colour. Red or black ones by methods 3, 6 or 7, light ones by method 4. Cooking plums can be cooked before freezing or, dark ones, by methods 6 or 7 and light ones by methods 3 or 4. If the fruit is to be kept in the freezer over 4–6 months, stones should be removed.

Raspberries. This fruit freezes very well and there are many good cultivars. Malling Enterprise does particularly well. The fruit must be ripe and can be frozen by any method: methods 6 and 7 are the simplest. Open freezing is recommended. If packed before freezing, use a shallow container. The depth should not exceed 3 or 4 layers of fruit.

Redcurrants. Freeze plain in bulk for subsequent jelly making. Stalks will rub off the frozen fruit, but wear gloves to avoid frozen fingers. A few packs of choice redcurrants prepared by method 7 will provide an attractive decoration for fruit punches.

Rhubarb. Recommended cultivars: Timperley Early, Champagne, Linnaeus. This is a popular 'fruit' for freezing in less favourable fruit areas. Pull young, well-coloured stems before they need peeling, and cut into suitable lengths, about 1½ ins. Freeze by methods 6, 7, 3 or 5. When rhubarb is frozen plain, method 6, the pieces can with advantage be *blanched* for ½–1 min. before freezing. This prevents the drying out appearance that is sometimes thought to be a mould.

Strawberries. Regrettably this delectable summer fruit becomes quite soft after freezing. Very small berries and alpine types keep their texture fairly well, and can be frozen by methods 6, 7, 3 or 4. Larger fruits are better sliced or made into purée before freezing. Thawing should be slow, 8 hours or overnight in a refrigerator, and the pack should not be opened until required for serving. In necessity, packs can be thawed in running cold water, but unless eaten as soon as thawed, the berries will deteriorate quickly.

White Currants. Usually a rare fruit but worth freezing by method 7. Flavour is well retained and the texture is not too soft.

Fruit Salad. Small packs of various fruits will make an attractive addition to a fresh fruit salad in the winter, when choice is limited. Although a mixed fruit salad can be frozen, flavours are more distinct if the fruits are frozen separately and blended when required.

NUTRITIONAL VALUE

At the present time, the main value of garden produce in the diet is its contribution to the body's requirements for vitamin A (carotene), vitamin C (ascorbic acid) and roughage. Other nutrients are present to a varying extent depending on the produce. With present trends, protein from vegetables may well vie with animal sources in the near future.

Vitamin C is the nutrient most easily lost, and its presence in prepared food is taken as an indication of general good nutritional standard. It is soluble in water, and therefore unnecessary soaking, and prolonged blanching and cooking, must be avoided. Cooking water should be kept to the minimum and used in gravy, sauce, or soup. Drip from thawed fruits should be served with the fruit. Blanching is inevitably destructive of some ascorbic acid, but this loss is less than that occurring slowly during frozen storage of similar unblanched produce. Vitamin C is also reduced by exposure to air, particularly warm air, and therefore all delays between picking and freezer, and between freezer and eating must be avoided. Correctly prepared and packaged food suffers little loss of vitamin C, or of any nutrient, while it is in the freezer at a steady temperature of 0°F or below. The preparation of some food for freezing is more elaborate than it would be for eating fresh, but with normal care the final nutritional value is not very different. Fresh food should have the advantage, but can lose it with poor treatment.

It is encouraging that tempting appearance and flavour in a meal, is usually linked with good retention of nutrients. The home gardener and the home cook, working together, can reach high gastronomic and nutritional levels – and economy too!

A GREENHOUSE

Colin Hart

A greenhouse, whatever its size or shape, can add an exciting new dimension to your gardening, because it will enable you to grow a wide range of plants with reliable protection from the weather.

A greenhouse can be unheated, or fitted with automatic equipment that adjusts the temperature, opens ventilators, and supplies water to the plants. Then the environment can be controlled according to your needs. It is not at all like gardening outdoors where sharp frosts, chilling winds, and drought, can quickly spell disaster to plants.

A few years ago a greenhouse was considered a luxury, something that was often bought only when the rest of the garden had matured. The usual decorative pot plants, summer tomatoes, and perhaps a few late-flowering pot chrysanthemums for some autumn and winter colour, quickly filled it up.

Now, with constantly rising prices for vegetables, a greenhouse can be regarded as an essential item for a garden. At little expense it can provide fresh succulent vegetables and fruit all the year round. A seasonal supply of tomatoes, lettuce, cucumbers, capsicums, aubergines, strawberries, melons, peaches, and even rhubarb, radish, beetroot, and carrots, during the early spring months, can mean that a greenhouse becomes an investment rather than a luxury. Even a small greenhouse, about 8 ft. by 6 ft., will provide room for a dozen or more tomato plants, each capable of producing up to 10 lb. of fruit.

Perhaps a greenhouse permanently filled with vegetables does not appeal to you. You may prefer to grow flowers or pot plants, that can be used to decorate the house. This can easily be done with the protection of a greenhouse, as can the raising of bedding plants, and dahlias and chrysanthemums, and dozens of other types of flowers that will put extra colour in the garden during the summer and autumn months.

Even alpines and hardy bulbs, like crocus and tulip species and the larger daffodils and narcissi, in pots and pans, can provide a vivid spectacle of colour in an unheated greenhouse during the spring.

With heating and perhaps other equipment too, you could grow a collection of plants which may come from different parts of the world, but which all enjoy the same conditions.

So, there are some uses for a greenhouse. One plea though, please use your investment wisely. Do not fill it up with the lawnmower, deckchairs, and the children's bicycles. That is not the purpose of a greenhouse. If you had that thought in mind, then you really ought to start thinking about making more room in the garage, or perhaps buying a garden shed, before you purchase a greenhouse.

Planning and Regulations

Planning permission is not normally needed for the erection of a garden greenhouse in England and Wales. The exception might be if you have had extra buildings, such as garages and extensions added to your property. If these exceed a certain size, building approval may be needed before the greenhouse can be erected.

Planning permission may also be needed if the greenhouse is larger than the normal size, or if it is a lean-to type to be positioned against the wall of a house.

Should you be in any doubt, your local authority can give you the necessary advice. They will want to know the length and width of the proposed greenhouse, and possibly its cubic capacity too. This can be calculated by multiplying the length by the width by the average height. The average height is the sum of the height to the ridge, and the height to the eaves, divided by two.

WOOD OR METAL?

Let me say now that the ideal greenhouse that will suit all gardeners does not exist. Everyone will have their own preferences for a wood or metal greenhouse, and the choice of size, shape, and design, may well be influenced by its cost and the amount of room available in the garden. Firstly though, let us have a look at the materials with which they are made.

Wood

Wood is the traditional material for a greenhouse. Natural-coloured wood blends well with the garden, but remember that all woods warp and sag and will rot, despite regular applications of oil or paint.

As most woods used for greenhouses are quite easy to screw or nail, putting up shelves or staging is a simple matter. Glazing however can be a fiddly business, and the linseed oil putty used to bed the glass will need renewing from time to time.

Imported softwood and British Columbian pine are sometimes used for greenhouses but these two woods are not so long-lasting as western red cedar. Although a softwood, cedar is extremely resistant to decay. It will last for many, many years without any attention whatsoever, although it still benefits from a yearly paint of a liquid cedar preservative.

One very good practical point about wooden greenhouses is that they are quick and easy to erect. Often it's just a case of bolting together six main sections, rather than literally assembling the hundreds of pieces that make up the kit of a metal greenhouse.

Metal

Aluminium and aluminium alloy greenhouses have really dominated the gardening scene in the past couple of years. The main reason is that, unlike wood, aluminium simply cannot rot or split, or encourage algae or moss to grow on its surface. It therefore needs no maintenance whatsoever.

Secondly, aluminium is a very strong material, and as it cannot twist or sag, its sections can be quite slender, which allows more light to reach the plants.

Of course, metal greenhouses are not faultless. Puttyless glazing and rustless glazing clips may make it easier to put the glass in, but the pressure of some clips breaks the glass when it is under stress, particularly during windy weather and extremes of temperature.

Erecting shelves or staging can be more

A handsome cedar greenhouse of traditional shape suitable for most gardens.

214

tricky in a metal greenhouse if you have to drill holes in order to bolt brackets to the narrow framework. Fortunately though, most manufacturers provide these as optional extras, but bear in mind that they are usually easier to fit as the greenhouse is being constructed rather than later when it is glazed.

Although aluminium does not rust and therefore does not need painting, it can become corroded on its surface. This still applies even if corrosion-resistant alloys are used. It shows up as a rough, white coating.

Surface corrosion is not normally harmful to the strength or rigidity of the greenhouse but it may spoil its appearance, especially in industrial areas and in the damp and salty air along the coast. To counteract this, some greenhouses can be obtained in a white acrylic finish. The special oven baking following this electrolytic process, ensures that the bonded acrylic will protect the underlying metal for many years to come.

Aluminium greenhouses do not come in large sectional pieces but as a do-it-yourself kit. Some manufacturers send all the parts in one or two bundles, so you have to sort out everything to select the pieces you need for the first section. Others make it easier by sending each section packaged separately.

Even with clearly labelled parts and step-by-step instructions, the erection of a metal greenhouse can still be a slow and tricky job. If you don't feel like attempting it yourself, some manufacturers will provide an erection service at extra cost.

Styles

The span roof type is the most popular shape of greenhouse. It has straight sides and a sloping double span roof that lets the light in from both directions.

The Dutch-light greenhouse is similar to the span roof, except that its sides are sloping. These allow more of the sun's rays to pass through the glass instead of being deflected away. They also give more stability, as the sloping sides present less of an abrupt barrier to the wind.

The lean-to type of greenhouse is not free standing. It is really half of a span roof greenhouse, and must be erected against a sound wall.

Light can only enter from the front, so the back wall is normally painted white to reflect it back on to the plants.

The wall can be used to support training wires for such plants as ornamental climbers, tomatoes, cucumbers, and peaches.

One word of warning. A lean-to, due to its one-sided ventilation, can become very hot during the summer. To counteract this, blinds or a liquid shading material applied to the glass may be essential.

A tunnel house, consisting of tubular steel supports covered with polythene sheeting, is another form of greenhouse. Although the cheapest type of greenhouse available, replacing the polythene every 2 or 3 years makes them expensive in the long run.

Dome-shaped greenhouses are the latest type to appear on the market. Their staging is half circular and the ventilators are sometimes positioned in the apex of the dome. They are more expensive than conventionally-shaped greenhouses, but far more efficient in letting the light through.

Most greenhouses can be obtained either as glass-to-ground or half-clad models.

The glass-to-ground type lets in more light for a border crop, such as lettuce, but clumsy feet or careless handling of tools at ground level can produce costly accidents.

An aluminium frame glass-to-ground greenhouse particularly suitable for D.I.Y. erection.

An aluminium frame lean-to with wooden staging – a handsome adjunct to a house.

An aluminium frame greenhouse of modern design. A green acrylic finish makes it less obtrusive.

Unless guttering is fitted, rain splashes from the ground can quickly dirty the bottom foot or so of the glass. Some glass-to-ground models have integral dwarf walls, which provide the necessary ground level protection against accidents and splashes.

Greenhouses with brick walls, or brick or asbestos cladding, up to a height of about 2 or 3 ft. are really designed for pot plants rather than border crops. Staging fitted at this height puts the plants nearer the light, and makes their maintenance easier for your back. The space underneath the staging comes in handy for the storage of flower pots, seed trays, etc., and the walls or base claddings help to keep in some of the heat.

If you want the best of both worlds, you can obtain greenhouses with glass-to-ground on one side and cladding on the other.

As far as size is concerned, always go for the largest that your pocket can afford, for unless you are going to be absolutely ruthless at times it is very easy to quickly fill a greenhouse to over-capacity. Also, the larger the greenhouse, the easier it is to control its environment.

Although catalogues give a great deal of information they don't usually tell you everything that you want to know. It certainly does pay to see and compare a few types of greenhouses, either on a showground or, better still, in actual use in gardens before you make your final choice.

SITING

The greenhouse should be positioned on a firm, well-drained, level site, where it will receive as much light as possible. An open situation, away from fences, walls, hedges, and trees, all of which can restrict light and create shadows, is therefore desirable, but the site should not be so open that strong and cold winds buffet the greenhouse and keep it cool.

To take full advantage of the available light during the winter, it is often suggested that the longest side of the greenhouse should face east to west. In this position the roof, being angled, can let in more of the oblique rays of the sun.

If you are going to make the most use of your greenhouse during the winter then this position is fine. During the summer though, when greenhouses tend to be more productive anyway, the reverse applies. Then, crops, such as tomatoes and capsicums, should be planted in north to south rows that, for convenience' sake, run along the length of the greenhouse. Rows running this way help all the plants to receive their fair share of even light.

A greenhouse with glass-to-ground one side and a wall or cladding on the other, should be sited so that the all-glass side faces west, to take full advantage of the sun.

For the same reason, a lean-to greenhouse should back on to a south or southwest wall.

In a small garden because of the limitation of available space, a greenhouse may have to be sited alongside fences and walls and virtually be tucked away in a corner. If your greenhouse has to be positioned like this there is no need to worry. Your plants can still grow well, although they may not come into flower or fruit quite so early, or be as large, as if the greenhouse were in a better position.

Preparing the Foundation and Base
A good foundation is as essential to a greenhouse as a good root system is to a plant. The underlying soil or layer of hardcore must be as firm as possible, so that the base

curbs or walls which keep a greenhouse off the ground cannot budge.

Concrete, metal or pressure-treated wood curbs can be purchased as optional extras. This is a good job as far as metal greenhouses are concerned, because their base rails or sills are often designed to be bolted on to shaped curbs. Trying to make these to exacting dimensions can be extremely difficult.

Curbs laid directly on to the soil are often secured in place with long anchor cleats or bolts. If the curbs are to be laid over a trench of compacted hardcore, a bed of mortar will keep them firmly in position.

Single- or double-layer dwarf brick or breeze block walls, are normally laid over concrete footings. This involves digging out trenches about 12 ins. wide and 12 ins. deep, and placing wooden shuttering along their sides. The trenches are then filled with a stiff concrete mixture, such as 4 parts ¾-in. washed ballast, 2 parts sand and 1 part cement. When this is set the shuttering can be removed for the start of the brickwork.

IDEAS FOR THE UNHEATED GREENHOUSE

A cold greenhouse relies entirely on nature for its heat. During the winter the temperature inside could be well below freezing for several days on end, and yet, a few days later with the sun shining brightly and the ventilators tightly shut, the mercury or alcohol in the thermometer could be hovering around the 60°–70°F mark. During the height of the summer with the door and all the ventilators fully open and shading on the glass, the daytime temperature could easily exceed 85°F.

It is the cold rather than the heat that limits the range of plants that will grow all the year round in an unheated greenhouse. This does not mean to say that a cold greenhouse will be as dull as ditchwater or even unprofitable – far from it! There are many hardy plants available to provide colour and interest, particularly in the spring, without the expense of heating.

Pots and pans of early spring bulbs, like the dainty species of crocus, literally burst into colour in February. Other rock or alpine plants like snowdrops, hardy cycla-

men, *Iris reticulata* with its violet-coloured flowers marked with vivid orange can be in flower about the same time, followed by primulas, polyanthus, daffodils, narcissi, and grape hyacinths, to mention just a few.

You could have the satisfaction of picking firm, hearty lettuce in March and April when shop prices tend to be rather high. Varieties like Kwiek and Winter Density, sown in August or September, are tough enough to grow during the winter, relying only on the protection of the greenhouse and the occasional burst of sunlight for their warmth. Carrots and beetroot can also be over-wintered this way, following an autumn sowing, and they can be ready for pulling weeks ahead of an outdoor crop.

Brassicas and lettuces can be sown in pans or trays ready for planting out later on in the garden, and so can hardy annuals like clarkia, godetia, love-in-a-mist, and larkspur.

Tomato plants should settle down nicely in May, although a dull, cool summer may mean that they will not be ready for picking until early August.

Cucumbers will thrive during the summer, as will the more digestible capsicums or peppers and aubergines, whilst pot plants 'loaned' from the house, will show their gratitude by making plenty of new growth for 3 or 4 months.

During the autumn, after the greenhouse has been cleared of its crops and has had a good clean out, the very traditional but useful late-flowering pot chrysanthemums can be brought in from the garden to provide some colour and cut flowers for a few weeks until the really cold weather of the winter sets in.

THE COOL GREENHOUSE

It is not necessary to provide a lot of heat to greatly increase the value of a greenhouse although it must be kept frost-free.

A cool greenhouse has a minimum temperature of about 45°–50°F during the day, and can be allowed to drop to 40°–45°F at night. This will enable plants like geraniums, fuchsias, cacti, and succulents, to be over-wintered as well as all the other plants previously mentioned.

The main benefits from providing a little

Tubular heaters are reliable, long-lasting and economical, and can be thermostatically controlled.

Convenience and complete ease of installation make fan heaters a popular greenhouse heating system.

heat will become apparent in the spring, because an earlier start can be made with seeds and cuttings, and you have the reassurance that they will not come to any harm during very cold weather.

THE WARM GREENHOUSE

A greenhouse kept at 55°F or more, constantly throughout the year, will support the widest range of plants. Here most of the plants, excepting the alpines and hardy bulbs, that grow in a cold or cool greenhouse, will flourish better with extra warmth. But this is not the real purpose of a warm greenhouse – it is more for the enthusiast who will be able to grow several types of temperate and sub-tropical plants for colour the year round.

These might be flowering pot plants like cinerarias or gloxinias, or perhaps plants grown for their decorative foliage, such as coleus, ferns and palms. Colour can also be provided by climbing plants trained along wires or canes. Bougainvillea, jasmine, and plumbago, are just three that can be grown in a warm greenhouse.

If you are more interested in food rather than flowers, then don't just stop at tomatoes, cucumbers, and capsicums. Strawberries, melons, peaches, and grapes, can be grown too, and these are free from the blemishes of the weather and the ravages of birds.

Thermostatically controlled ventilation can greatly reduce greenhouse casualties, as temperature can be kept within acceptable limits in the gardener's absence. This efficient self-contained unit has its own built-in thermostat which also supplies the power needed to operate the mechanism.

TOWARDS AUTOMATION

It is not essential to have any automatic devices in the greenhouse, as heating, ventilation, and watering, can all be controlled manually. For someone at hand during the day these things are easy to attend to, particularly if the greenhouse is conveniently situated. The chances are though that eventually the greenhouse will have to be left unattended for long periods, especially during weekends and holidays.

Under these circumstances some form of automation is most useful, for there is little point in going to the trouble of raising plants only to find that they have suffered from the heat or cold or perhaps from a lack of water.

Heat

A heater is often the first and, apart from staging and a thermometer, sometimes the only extra item of equipment for a greenhouse.

Heating and greenhouse manufacturers' catalogues usually indicate which size heater is needed to maintain a particular size of greenhouse at a given temperature. If in any doubt always overestimate the amount of heat that you think your greenhouse is likely to need during the winter. Outside temperatures can drop to 20°F or below, so your heater must be capable of at least a 25°F lift if you want to maintain a minimum temperature in the greenhouse of 45°F.

It is worth mentioning here two things that can reduce fuel bills. One is to keep the inside of the greenhouse lined with clear polythene sheeting from (about) October to April. If it is stretched tightly across the glazing bars the polythene can help to keep more heat inside the greenhouse. This could outweigh the disadvantages of condensation dripping from the polythene on to the plants, and the poorer light inside the greenhouse.

The second money-saving item is a reliable, rod-type thermostat, if one is not fitted as an integral part of the heater. Thermostats save money by switching the heaters on and off at a pre-determined temperature.

1) Paraffin

The simplest and cheapest heaters burn paraffin but they cannot be thermostatically controlled. Blue flame burners are more efficient in producing heat than the ordinary yellow flame heaters, but both types must burn only a refined grade of paraffin, and have their wicks regularly cleaned and trimmed to minimise the release of unpleasant fumes.

Some models are fitted with tubes that spread the heat over a larger area, and some have humidity trays too. These are filled with water which becomes heated and evaporates into the atmosphere, although a paraffin flame releases moisture anyway, and too much humidity during the winter can increase the spread of fungal diseases.

More refined paraffin heaters can be connected to supplementary storage containers so that they will burn continuously for several weeks, avoiding the necessity of frequent refilling.

A newer type of paraffin heater is actually controlled by a rod thermostat that regulates the height of the flame according to a pre-determined temperature setting.

2) Electricity

This is probably the easiest and most troublefree way of automatically regulating the heat. In view of the damp conditions experienced in a greenhouse, running cables from a domestic power supply and installing and wiring up waterproof sockets, should not be attempted by the amateur handyman, but left in the capable hands of a qualified electrician. Insulated control panels for greenhouse use, fitted with fused 13-amp three-pin switches, make it easy to run more than one electrical appliance at a time.

Tubular heaters, usually 2 ins. or 3 ins. in diameter, with a rating of 60 watts per ft., are reliable and silent. They should be coupled to a rod thermostat. Tubular heaters are connected in banks, one above the other, with an equal number on both sides of the greenhouse. They can be mounted low down on the walls of the greenhouse or, if it is a glass-to-ground model, affixed to metal spikes which are stuck into the ground.

Electric fan-heaters can heat a greenhouse uniformly faster than tubular heaters as their hot air is blown out. They have internal thermostats and adjustable heat settings. One advantage of a fan-heater is that it is portable and needs only to be plugged into a 13-amp socket. During the summer the heating element can be switched off so that the fan circulates the air and this prevents a build-up of excessive heat.

3) Oil

Warm air heaters with integral thermostats are available, that burn second-grade domestic heating oil. The warm air spreads throughout the greenhouse by natural convection or, with the larger models, through polythene ducting, which is perforated to let the heat escape along its length.

Oil heaters are more suited for larger greenhouses, as a flue is needed to vent away the combustion fumes and an integral or external tank is necessary to contain the oil.

4) Gas

Gas heating can be the most economical way to heat a greenhouse. The heaters are of the warm air type and burn only natural gas or propane, because the sulphur content of town gas can harm plants.

A flue is not needed for this type of heater, as one of the by-products resulting from combustion is carbon dioxide, which helps plants to grow during the day.

5) Solid Fuel

External solid fuel boilers usually burn coke or anthracite, which heats water pipes laid inside the greenhouse. These are normally 4 ins. in diameter and, as they are supported just a few inches above the ground, they heat both the air and the soil. Solid fuel boilers need stoking up at least once a day.

Soil Warming

Electric cables can also be used to provide heat in the greenhouse. When they are embedded in soil or sand they are not used on their own but in conjunction with a conventional form of heater that warms the air.

A simple automatic watering system. The plants are stood in shallow trays on capillary matting which is kept moist from a reservoir which serves several trays.

This dual-heating method helps plants to grow better, because it is more important for their roots, rather than their foliage, to be at the right temperature. Running costs are lower, because once the desired soil temperature has been reached, the air temperature can be reduced by several degrees.

The heating cables can be run direct from the mains supply, although it is obviously much safer to connect them to a transformer that reduces the supply to 12 volts.

The wires are laid in the greenhouse border or on the staging in even patterns, avoiding sharp curves, about 6 ins. apart and covered with 6 ins. of soil or sand. Coupling a thermostat in with the circuit will ensure that the operating temperature can be accurately controlled.

Bottom heat, using soil-warming cables, is a great boon when it comes to rooting cuttings and germinating seeds. Propagating cases can be obtained with heating elements fitted in their base. The sides and glass or plastic top covering help to retain both the heat and the humidity.

Ventilation

Automatic greenhouse ventilation can be provided by installing an expansion device to each roof ventilator. They cost nothing to run, and need no maintenance, as the energy is provided by a temperature sensitive mineral substance whose expansion and contraction activates a lever connected to the ventilator.

Each unit can be set to open its ventilator at a given temperature, and models are available for wooden and metal greenhouses.

Where possible the units should be fitted on the most sheltered side of the greenhouse so that unnecessary draughts are avoided.

Ventilation can also be carried out by an electric extractor fan, usually mounted high up on the gable (back) end of the greenhouse. A 9-in.-diameter fan is large enough for a greenhouse up to 500-cu. ft. capacity, whilst a 12-in.-diameter fan is adequate for a greenhouse up to 1000-cu. ft. capacity.

As the stale air is taken outside, fresh air is drawn into the greenhouse through the inevitable cracks and crevices that are always present.

Watering

Watering by hand is an operation that can take a long time in the summer, particularly if there are a lot of small plants involved. Fortunately it can be automated.

The simplest system is to line the staging with polythene sheeting and then to cover it with nylon capillary matting. This is then well soaked – it will absorb about 1½ pints of water per sq. yd. – and the pots are stood on top. The plants are now able to withdraw the water from the matting as they need it, providing it is kept moist.

Plastic and peat pots don't generally require any increase in the size or number of drainage holes to ensure a good capillary contact between the matting and the compost, but clay pots, as they often have only one drainage hole each, may need a wick to aid the uptake of water. This can be made from the matting.

A simple way to keep the matting moist is to let one end of it hang into a container of water positioned about 2 ins. below the level of the staging. The larger the container the less often it will need topping up.

The system can be automated further by connecting a plastic tank fitted with a float device to the mains supply. When the tank is full, the float device allows the water to be released along a plastic pipe fitted with nozzles, so that it can then drip on to the staging.

When this fully automatic method · is used, provision must be made for the excess water to drain away through the base of the staging. The nylon matting can be substituted with 2 ins. of clean, lime-free sand.

A further refinement is to supply the water individually to each plant, whether they be growing on the staging or in the border. This can be done with very small-diameter flexible plastic tubes that are connected to the main plastic pipe supplying the water from the tank.

Lighting

Artificial lighting is useful in the greenhouse, not only as it enables work to be carried out when it would otherwise be too dark to see, but because it can be used to hasten and regulate the growth of plants.

100-watt tungsten filament bulbs – the normal household type – will give a gentle boost to plants and young seedlings if they are kept on for about 12 hours per day. Unfortunately they are not very efficient as only about 7% of the energy they consume actually goes towards the production of light – the rest is given out as heat.

It is this heat which governs the proximity to which they can be suspended over the plants. If they are too close there is the possibility that the plants will be scorched.

Fluorescent tubes are initially more expensive than tungsten filament bulbs and need more fittings. They are cheaper to run though, and more efficient, as 20% of the energy they use is converted into useful light.

They illuminate a larger area evenly all the way along their length, and give off relatively little surface heat, so they can be positioned just a few inches above plants.

In addition to providing supplementary illumination to make plants stronger, lighting can also be used to make plants flower out of season.

Many plants, including chrysanthemums and poinsettias, have been classified into light response groups. Subjecting them to spells of extra light, where the duration and intensity is carefully controlled, can prevent the initiation of flower buds and increase the length of stems. Alternatively, covering the plants with black-out material to exclude all light for a certain number of hours per day, can induce them to initiate and develop flower buds.

These methods are normally outside the scope of the amateur gardener, but should further advice on lighting techniques, equipment, and installation be needed, it can be obtained from your local electricity board.

DAY TO DAY MANAGEMENT

Ventilation and Heat

The most frequent items that need to be attended to in the daily management of a greenhouse are the ventilation and heat. Opening · the ventilators and perhaps the door too, is the surest and quickest way of changing the air and cooling the greenhouse when the temperature rises too high.

It is not necessary and indeed it would be extremely difficult to maintain the temperature of the greenhouse at a steady figure, day in and day out, but large fluctuations should be avoided. A night temperature 10°F lower than the optimum day temperature is quite acceptable to plants, and it could also help save on heating bills too.

When ventilating, the aim is to produce a steady flow of air through the greenhouse without causing any cold draughts. This means opening the top ventilator or ventilators on the leeward or sheltered side away from the wind as the temperature rises. To help retain some heat, the ventilators should be closed as the temperature falls, but well before the optimum greenhouse temperature is reached.

Little, if any, ventilation will be needed at times during the winter, particularly if it's foggy, dull, or frosty. A very slight movement of air though can discourage a build-up of fungal diseases, such as mildew and botrytis. A fan-heater will help to do this, as will slipping a pencil between a ventilator and its frame so that it cannot shut so tightly. This also allows the fumes from a paraffin heater to escape outside.

Spring is a busy time in the greenhouse, and this is when the most care is needed with heating and ventilation, as temperatures can rise and fall very quickly. Young cuttings and seedlings and tomato plants must be guarded against draughts at all times. They really prefer to be mollycoddled as their tender foliage is vulnerable to chills and heat.

During the summer, maximum ventilation may be needed – this will mean opening all the ventilators and perhaps the door too. Side ventilators or, better still, louvres near ground level, really come into their own here. Opening these allows cool air to enter the greenhouse low down. As it becomes heated the air rises up out of the top ventilators creating a moving stream of cooling air throughout the greenhouse.

Watering

One of the hardest things to teach any gardener is when to water plants. It is something that comes only with experience, as all plants must be treated individually for their needs vary considerably.

Plants should only be watered when they need it. This does not mean waiting until they droop over – the signs of dryness are then obvious – but rather in anticipating their needs.

There are several ways of doing this. One is to touch the surface of the compost with the forefinger to see if it feels dry or moist. Another method is to look at the surface because a lighter colour is a sign that the compost is drying out. Pot plants can be picked up and their comparative weights judged. It does not take very long to realise how much heavier a pot is when its compost is wet than when it is dry.

If all this proves to be too difficult, then there are several types of soil moisture indicators available that tell you when water is needed.

During the winter, watering should be carried out during fine, sunny mornings, and avoid splashes. Then the foliage will not stay wet for too long and there is less risk of disease. This is not so important in the summer when the ventilators are open more, and the plants may well need watering more than once a day anyway.

Plants should always be given a good soaking rather than just wetting the surface of the compost, for this tends to bring the roots to the surface and they may die when it dries out.

Tap water is fine for most plants, although if it is on the hard side, the leaves of lime-hating plants, such as azaleas, might show their resentment by turning yellow. If this happens, use rain water whenever possible, as this is slightly acid and soft and promotes better growth.

Using cold water straight from the tap does not appear to be detrimental to large plants. Young seedlings, though, have sensitive roots and they appreciate water that has been allowed to warm up in the greenhouse for at least a couple of hours before use.

Humidity

Some plants, especially sub-tropical and tropicals, relish a humid atmosphere. Moist heat is easy to maintain if the staging is covered with grit, sharp sand, or a synthetic matting, all of which absorb water as well as providing good drainage under the pots.

In addition, damping down the staging and the floor with a fine-rosed watering can in the morning and again in the afternoon or early evening when the ventilators are finally shut for the day, helps to maintain a humid atmosphere.

To help prevent unnecessary fungal troubles, damping down should only be carried out when the temperature is at its optimum or higher, but never when the temperatures are low.

Simple instruments are now available that give a guide to the relative humidity of the air so that corrective action can be taken if necessary.

Shading

Apart from cacti and succulents which tend to have thick, protective skins, most other greenhouse plants, especially young ones, need some protection from the direct rays of the sun in the summer. This is the object of shading. Without it, soft-leaved flowering and foliage plants, and in particular ferns, can quickly become scorched and shrivelled up by the action of the sun on their leaves and stems, and from the high temperatures that build up inside the greenhouse. Shading can also cut down on the amount of watering needed.

Liquid shading materials are mixed with water and sprayed or painted over the outside of the glass. They can be removed quite easily during prolonged dull periods to let in more light, although it is usual to leave them on until the autumn.

A modern method of internal shading is to use roller shades. They are green, translucent PVC sheets, mounted on the sunniest side of the greenhouse. They can be lowered or raised at will as they are fixed to adjustable spring rollers. They will also give some protection from frost.

'Coolglass' is a proprietary mixture for shading greenhouse glass. It is painted on and easily rubbed off.

Feeding

Proprietary composts, such as John Innes, contain enough food to supply plants for several weeks after potting. As plants grow this food is used up and leached away by watering. Unless it is replaced the plants may become weaker.

The easiest and safest way to feed greenhouse plants is to water them with a liquid or soluble fertiliser, as necessary, during their growing season. Specific fertilisers can be bought to suit the specialised needs of certain plants, e.g. tomatoes.

Foliar feeding, i.e. spraying or watering fertiliser over the leaves and stems, can give quicker results. Plants are still able to take up nutrients through their roots, so this method of feeding only supplements the normal fertilisers applied to the soil.

A base dressing is the term used for fertilisers that are mixed into the soil before the seeds or plants go in. A base fertiliser, usually a powdered or granulated compound fertiliser, supplies the immediate and basic nutrients for the plants.

Later on, during the growing season, side dressings will be needed. This is the term used for dry fertilisers that are applied to the top of the soil and then watered in so that they don't scorch the roots.

PROPAGATION

There's nothing quite so satisfying as propagating and growing on plants that you have raised yourself. Once the basic skills have been mastered, all types of plants can be propagated at comparatively little cost.

Seed

The John Innes and the peat-based seed composts are suitable for growing nearly all seedlings.

Fine seed, like petunia and begonia, should not be covered at all but sprinkled thinly and evenly over the surface.

Medium seed, e.g. tomato, can be covered with about $\frac{1}{4}$ in. of compost, whilst larger seed can be covered with a layer of compost equivalent to twice their depth.

After sowing, the compost should be carefully levelled and then gently firmed with a flat piece of wood so that it will not sink when it is watered.

Containers of fine seeds should be lightly watered from underneath by standing them in clean water until the surface of the compost is moist. This avoids the seeds being washed away.

Larger seeds can be watered from above using a watering can fitted with a fine rose.

Following watering, most seeds germinate better if they are covered with polythene or glass, as this keeps the compost moist and warmer. This must be removed as soon as the seeds germinate otherwise they could rot or become drawn up to the light.

For most seeds a temperature of 60°F is satisfactory although some like it cooler and some warmer.

As soon as the individual seedlings are large enough to handle by their leaves, they should be 'pricked out' into pans or seed trays giving each little plant about $1\frac{1}{2}$ ins. of room. The compost should now be stronger, either John Innes No. 1 or a peat-based potting compost.

Seedlings are quite tender and may need protection from hot sun for a few days by shading them with newspaper. At the same time they should be kept out of draughts.

Cuttings

Cuttings always give rise to plants identical to their parents unlike seeds which may give variable offspring. Softwood cuttings are healthy soft stems, about 2 ins. long, taken from recent growth – chrysanthemums and dahlias are propagated this way.

The cuttings are trimmed neatly with a sharp knife or razor blade just below a node – the junction of a leaf stalk and its stem – as this is where most of the roots form. The bottom inch or so of stem should be stripped of its leaves as these would otherwise rot if covered with soil. Hormone rooting powders can give quicker rooting and some contain a fungicide to reduce the risk of rots.

Equal parts by volume of moist peat and sharp sand is an excellent medium in which to root cuttings. John Innes Seed Compost or a seedling peat-based compost can also be used but fertiliser is not needed to help cuttings to root.

Hippeastrum bulbs placed in moist leaf mould and sand to induce root growth.

The cuttings can be inserted in pots, pans, trays or boxes depending upon the number involved. After watering in they must be covered with clear glass or polythene to stop them from drying out.

Bottom heat will speed up rooting – a simple paraffin heater could be used for this – if the temperature of the rooting medium is maintained at about 70°F. Propagators can be bought that have thermostatically controlled heating elements fitted in their base.

New growth from the tips of the cuttings is a sign that they have rooted and once this is seen the glass or polythene should be gradually raised so that they are completely uncovered after about a week.

Semi-hardwood cuttings are prepared in a similar way except that they are taken during late summer when their growth is more ripe. As they will be on the woody side they may not have to be given so much protection to stop them from drying out.

Runners
Some plants, like *Chlorophytum*, and *Saxifraga sarmentosa stolonifera*, send out runners bearing new plants along their length. When they are a convenient size, the new plants can be detached and placed on top of the moist rooting medium where they will quickly become established.

ANNUAL ROUTINE
All greenhouses become dirty, especially the glass, and a thorough cleaning inside and out at least once a year is a good idea.

Plants that are growing during the winter and early spring, lettuce and bedding plants for example, need as much light as possible. Therefore for the plants' sake wash the glass frequently during the winter.

Autumn, when tomato and cucumber crops are being cleared out, is usually the most convenient time to clean thoroughly the inside of the greenhouse. All glass, metal, and wood, should be scrubbed with hot, soapy water, paying particular attention to joints and overlapping glass, where constant moisture encourages mosses and green, slimy algae to thrive. A drop of household disinfectant can be added to the water too, but this is not essential. Finally, rinse with clean water and leave to dry.

Border soil may need treatment. Using the same soil continuously for the same types of plants encourages various root and stem rot diseases, as well as soil pests, to build up. Replacing the border soil to a depth of 2 or more ft. with virgin fibrous loam is one answer, but it is hard work and good soil is just not always available.

The alternative method is to sterilise the border soil *in situ*, with a liquid soil sterilant sold for horticultural use. It works by releasing chemical fumes which kill off many pests, diseases, weeds, and their seeds.

Plants must be kept out of the greenhouse until the fumes have escaped from the treated soil, and a certain interval must elapse before the soil is safe enough for sowing and planting.

Aluminium greenhouses don't need any maintenance as they cannot rust or rot, but softwood structures will almost certainly need some attention.

Areas of thin or flaking paint should be wire-brushed or scraped to remove loose particles before being rubbed down with sandpaper in preparation for painting.

A priming coat should be the first paint to cover wood, followed by an undercoat and finally finishing with one or two coats of good-quality gloss paint.

If panes of glass are loose, re-set them in new linseed oil putty, securing each sheet with six brass glazing sprigs. The top edge of the putty should be painted over to protect it from the weather.

Cedar-framed greenhouses will benefit from a coat of preservative specially made for this type of wood. This will help to repel water as well as enhancing the colour of the wood.

While you are cleaning the greenhouse remember that the staging may need painting or oiling, and that gutters and downpipes and the water butt may need a scrub too, as they can become fouled up with leaves and mosses.

PESTS & DISEASES
Pests and diseases can increase and spread quickly in the warm and sheltered conditions of a greenhouse. Fortunately garden chemicals are becoming more efficient and safer to use all the time, so the control of pests and diseases is certainly a lot easier than it used to be.

In addition to liquid forms, some insecticides and fungicides can also be obtained as smoke generators. These are small tablets or cones which, when ignited, emit chemical gases. Fumigation is a quick way of applying chemicals, although a fairly air-tight greenhouse is needed if the treatment is to be effective.

Some plants are susceptible to certain chemicals. Pirimicarb should not be used on cucumbers and gamma-BHC should not come into contact with hydrangeas or cucumbers, because of the risk of damage.

Pests
GREENFLY: The all-too-common greenfly can be controlled with malathion, derris, formothion, pirimicarb, gamma-BHC and menazon. Because this pest can breed so quickly, spraying should be carried out as soon as it is first seen.

A sticky substance, called honeydew, often appears on the plants following an attack by greenfly and other sucking insects. This natural secretion can attract fungi which feed on it, causing the honeydew to turn black, hence the more common name of sooty mould. It can be removed by washing the foliage with water.

WHITE FLY are very small white insects that feed underneath the leaves, and go up like a cloud of dust when they are disturbed. This sap-sucking pest, a common sight on fuchsias, needs frequent sprays with derris, malathion, or resmethrin, to break the life-cycle.

RED SPIDER MITES are tiny, spider-like insects that congregate on the backs of leaves in such large numbers that they can literally suck them dry. If the infestation is severe, fine webs may be spun over the blotchy, bronzed foliage.

Keeping the atmosphere of the greenhouse more humid, and spraying with malathion or derris, will keep them under control.

MEALY BUG is a small insect that feeds on the leaves and stems of pot plants and climbers. It is protected by a white, wool-like material, and often takes refuge in the axils of the leaves.

Small infestations can be lightly painted with methylated spirits, keeping it off the plants as much as possible, or they can be sprayed with malathion.

SCALE INSECTS resemble scabs on the leaves and stems of many flowering and foliage pot plants, and they can actually be picked off. Malathion is the chemical to use, although several applications will be necessary to penetrate the hard shells of the scales.

THRIPS, like red spider mites, feed on leaves, mainly of freesias, carnations, and roses, causing them to become streaky and discoloured. They also secrete small droplets of red liquid which later turn black.

The chemicals to use are derris or resmethrin.

ROOT-KNOT EELWORM: This is a worm-like pest, invisible to the naked eye, that feeds on roots, with tomatoes one of the main host plants. The symptoms of damage are knobs or galls on the roots, which are the result of the burrowing activities of the eelworm.

Rotation or changing the soil every year is the best way to avoid this pest as it becomes resistant to the chemicals and heat used to sterilise infested soil.

Diseases
DAMPING-OFF: This is a disease always associated with seedlings. It is encouraged by thick sowings and over-watering, and the affected seedlings turn black at soil level and collapse.

Watering with the traditional Cheshunt compound is usually effective.

GREY MOULD (*Botrytis*): Grey mould, or to give it its proper name, botrytis, is a fluffy growth that can appear on virtually all greenhouse plants, especially when the atmosphere becomes stagnant.

Increasing the flow of air through the greenhouse and spraying with thiram or benomyl should clear up an outbreak within a few days.

MILDEW: This grey coating on stems and leaves is encouraged by dry roots and wet leaves. Providing the plants with correct growing conditions will help to keep this disease at bay, failing that, sprays of thiram, karathane, or benomyl, will be needed.

WILTS: Wilt diseases, caused by verticillium and fusarium fungi, invade the roots of plants, such as tomatoes, cucumbers, carnations, and chrysanthemums. Affected plants are then unable to take up so much water and they may wilt during the heat of the day, becoming more turgid again when temperatures fall. Eventually they can collapse altogether.

Shading the glass, or lightly spraying water over the foliage, can give a temporary recovery as can mulching around the roots with fresh compost to encourage the stems to root higher up.

Changing or sterilising the soil in the greenhouse border is the only way to control these diseases, which are largely encouraged by growing the same crops in the same soil for too long.

VIRUS: Viruses are internal diseases that can affect all types of plants, producing symptoms ranging from stunted and distorted growth of flowers and stems, to spotting, mottling, and flecking on leaves.

Greenfly can quickly transfer the diseases from infected to healthy plants, and they can also be spread by propagating from virus-ridden plants.

There is no known cure for virus diseases and infected plants should be burned.

PLANTS FOR THE GREENHOUSE

Tomatoes

The most popular of all greenhouse crops, the tomato, needs warmth, rich soil, and regular watering and feeding to ensure good yields.

Following a February or March sowing under heat, the plants should be ready for setting out in containers or in the border when the first flower truss is formed, from late April onwards. Earlier plantings are possible if the greenhouse can be kept at a minimum temperature of 50°F.

Plants can be spaced 18 ins. apart in the border, or singly, in 9- or 10-in.-diameter pots. Grow bags – polythene sacks containing a peat-based compost – usually take three plants each.

Bottomless bituminised pots or rings can also be used, in which case they are stood on a 9-in. or deeper layer of clean sand, grit, or weathered ashes. Ring culture, the name for this system of growing, entails applying only fertilisers to the pots, whilst the underlying aggregate is kept continually moist with water. With this method the plants are assured of a more regular supply of water, less compost is needed, and the pots or rings are easily removed at the end of the season.

Apart from the initial fertilisers in the compost, no supplementary feeding with a high potash liquid tomato fertiliser should be carried out until the fruits on the first truss have set.

Tomatoes prefer a warm, dry atmosphere and plenty of ventilation should be given when possible, as too much damp air can lead to leafmould disease.

Side shoots should be pinched out when about 1 in. long and the main stems stopped

Tomato 'Alicante'

Splitting like this is generally caused by irregular watering or irregular atmospheric humidity.

when the plants reach the tops of their canes or strings.

VARIETIES: The newer F1 hybrid varieties, such as Eurocross, Supercross, Seville Cross, and Kingley Cross, are easier to grow than the older favourites, including Moneymaker and Ailsa Craig, as they are less prone to disease and they can also give larger yields.

Lettuce

Warm or cold greenhouse lettuces are most useful during late winter and spring when other salads are at a premium.

Sowings from August to early October can mature from November to April depending upon the variety and whether the greenhouse is heated – 55°F is warm enough.

The plants can be spaced as close as 6 ins. sq., so long as every other plant is removed when it is large enough to eat, to allow those remaining to heart up.

VARIETIES: For the heated greenhouse: Kordaat, Kloek, and Delta. For the cold greenhouse: Kwiek, Seaqueen, Arctic King, and Winter Density.

Cucumbers

Cucumbers prefer more heat, humidity, and water than tomatoes, although the two can still be grown together in the same greenhouse.

The seeds should be sown 1 in. apart in pots or boxes in March, keeping the temperature of the compost about 70°F.

The young seedlings should be planted out in the border or in large pots after they have produced their first two true leaves. The greenhouse should be kept warm (minimum temperature 65°–70°F) and humid, and it may be necessary to damp

Peppers make easy greenhouse pot plants.

Lettuces in a Dutch light greenhouse. Note how staggered sowing has spread the crop.

down the paths and borders with water.

As the cucumber is a scrambling plant, it must be trained along horizontal wires spaced about 2 ft. apart. Pinching out the main stem when it is just below the bottom wire will induce the plant to throw out lateral shoots, which can be trained sideways. These can be pinched back just beyond the second fruit, or when they get too long.

Male flowers should be picked off to prevent cross-pollination and seedy fruit. Growing all-female varieties renders this daily task unnecessary.

VARIETIES: Heated greenhouse: Telegraph Improved, Butcher's Disease Resisting, Femspot (female), and Rocket (female). Cold greenhouse: Telegraph Improved, and Butcher's Disease Resisting.

Capsicums and Aubergines

Capsicums (sweet peppers) and aubergines (egg plants), can be sown and grown in the same way as for tomatoes.

Plants are spaced 1½ ft. apart in the border or grown singly in 8-in. pots.

Both will benefit from regular feeding with a liquid fertiliser as soon as the first fruits start to swell.

The peppers can be picked when they are green, or left until they mature and turn red. The egg fruits are ready when they turn dark purple.

VARIETIES: *Capsicum.* New Ace, Worldbeater, Bull-nosed, California Wonder, and Yolo Wonder.
Aubergine. Early Long Purple.

Grapes

Grape vines need to be planted about 4 ft. apart in firm, well-drained soil. Following

Begonia 'Ridler's Yellow'

Begonias, cyclamen, and coleus

A fine selection of Calceolarias

A miniature Cymbidium, one of the easier orchids for the amateur grower.

an autumn or winter planting, the top growth should be cut down to about 2 ft. to build up a strong framework.

During the next year the main shoot should be allowed to grow unchecked with the side shoots cut back to their basal buds in the autumn. It is from these that the fruiting laterals will form in their second or third year. Pinch the laterals back just beyond the bunches of grapes as they form, and in the autumn reduce them further to one or two eyes.

A replacement system of pruning should be adopted where possible, so that old rods are cut out at ground level to allow new, vigorous growths to take their place.

Heat is not needed for grapes to ripen although a minimum temperature of 60°F from March onwards, until the vines have finished flowering, will give an earlier crop.

If the air is too stuffy and dry, vines may fail to set their grapes. Keeping the border moist and spraying the paths with water will help in this respect.

VARIETIES: Heated greenhouse: Muscat of Alexandria (yellow), and Alicante (black). Cold greenhouse: Black Hamburg (white), and Buckland Sweetwater (white).

Peaches

Peaches need a well-drained light to medium loam. Fan-trained trees are the usual form for greenhouses and they can be bought from nurseries.

Horizontal wires about 15 ins. from the glass are used to support the branches which should be spaced at least 6 ins. apart.

The actual fruits should gradually be thinned when they reach hazel-nut size, so that eventually each peach has 9 sq. ins. in which to develop to maturity.

Old fruiting growths are cut out as soon as the peaches have been picked, with the new shoots that will bear the following year tied in to take their place. The shoots should be thinned in the spring if they are too crowded.

Peaches are hardy plants, and the only period when heat is beneficial is from February until the fruits are picked when the greenhouse should be kept at about 60°F.

VARIETIES: Hales Early, Peregrine, and Duke of York.

Carnations

Perpetual-flowering carnations have a useful life of 2 or 3 years during which they flower more or less continuously.

They only need sufficient heat to keep the greenhouse at a minimum temperature of 45°F, and can be grown in large pots or in the border at 7 ins. sq.

Pinching out the tips of the young plants when they have 6 or 7 leaves will encourage them to produce more side shoots which leads to sturdier growth.

Carnations are propagated from softwood cuttings taken from healthy non-flowering shoots during the autumn, winter, and spring.

There are many varieties of perpetual-flowering carnations available, mainly in shades of pink, white, red, and yellow.

Chrysanthemums

Late-flowering chrysanthemums need the protection of a greenhouse during the autumn and early winter, to stop their blooms from being spoilt by rain, wind, and frost.

They are propagated from softwood cuttings taken from the old flowering stools in late winter, potted into 3-in. pots in February, and then into 5-in. pots in April, with a final potting into 9- or 10-in. pots by early June.

To encourage a bushy habit, pinch out the tips of the main stems when they are about 6 ins. high and, in turn, pinch out the resulting side stems when they have made the same amount of growth. After being hardened off in a cold frame, the plants are stood outside, at least 12 ins. apart, from May until September or October.

Chrysanthemum stems are quite brittle and the plants must be securely tied to canes to prevent them from being damaged by winds.

When they are housed in the autumn, ventilate freely and only apply sufficient heat to maintain the temperature at 50°–55°F.

After flowering cut the stems down and reduce the heat until the new growths appear in a few weeks' time.

Cinerarias

The cineraria is a cool-temperature plant that enjoys moist air. Seeds are sown in the spring and the seedlings pricked out into 5-in. pots. During the summer, shade the greenhouse to prevent scorching of their leaves, and stand the pots on slatted staging so that water can drain away quickly.

The cineraria is very sensitive to overwatering and the compost should be kept on the dry side. Humidity is important, though, and damping down will be beneficial during warm, sunny weather. The optimum growing temperature is 50°–55°F.

Begonias and Gloxinias

Both of these plants can be grown from tubers and seed.

Tubers should be set lightly in peaty compost in early spring and kept moist and warm (60°F).

When roots have formed, pot each tuber singly in 5-in. pots. The greenhouse must be shaded to prevent sunscorch.

Feed with liquid fertiliser once the flower buds appear, and gradually withhold water when the foliage starts to yellow in the autumn. The tubers can be dried and stored where there is no chance of damage from frost and planted again in the following spring.

Culture from seed is a slower method. It should be sown in February or March in a temperature of 65°F.

Cyclamen

Cyclamen seed germinates best in a temperature of about 60°F, and the usual sowing times are autumn and spring.

The seeds are large enough to be sown individually $\frac{1}{4}$ in. deep. As they can take a month or more to germinate cover them with a 2-in. thick layer of peat. This helps to keep the compost evenly moist and speeds up germination. The peat must be blown or knocked off the leaves as soon as the seedlings appear.

Prick out into 3-in. pots and later transfer them to their final 5-in. pots in which they will flower.

Young plants can be stood outside in a shaded cold frame during the summer, as high temperatures and direct sun can scorch the leaves.

From September onwards, when the plants are housed again, maintain the temperature at 50°–55°F.

After flowering gradually withhold water so that the corms can be rested until they are started into growth again the following July.

Hibiscus 'Miss Betty', a showy greenhouse subject

Pelargonium 'Lavender Grand Slam', one of the Regal group

Schizanthus, the poor man's orchid, makes splendid pot plants for the cool greenhouse.

HOUSE PLANTS

William Davidson

In recent years there has been a tremendous increase in the popularity of indoor plants, and in line with this upsurge of interest a marked increase in the variety and general availability of more exotic foliage and flowering plants. From the selection available one may choose plants for all manner of situations, be it light or shade, cool or hot, wet or dry. Fortunately most plants have tags attached, indicating the conditions and treatment they prefer.

For many householders the growing of indoor plants has become a fascinating hobby as well as a means of improving the general appearance of the interior of the home.

House plants can bring a welcome suggestion of the garden indoors.

Purchasing

The best advice I can give to the beginner regarding indoor plants, is to suggest that he should not be too ambitious with his initial purchases. It is much more satisfying to learn in the first place how to manage the easier plants, before advancing to more delicate subjects. Always remember that the humble tradescantia, growing with obvious good health, is more attractive than a more demanding croton, that is struggling to survive.

In spite of all that has been written, and all the advice that is freely available, many retailers of plants are still totally ignorant about the requirements of indoor plants, and in particular their needs while on their premises awaiting sale. It is not unusual to see plants of a delicate nature being relegated to a position on the pavement outside the door of the shop, the feeling being, no doubt, that they take up less valuable shop space if they are out of doors. But the would-be purchaser should remember that it can be absolutely fatal for delicate, warm-loving plants, such as African violets, to spend so much as half an hour on the pavement during a cold spell, although it may take a

week or two for such maltreatment to become apparent. Therefore one should purchase from a reliable source, for even though it is more costly, a longer and more satisfying life for one's plants will be the reward.

In cold weather the purchaser should always insist on adequate wrapping for all plants, as it can be permanently damaging to more tender plants to expose them to very cold conditions, even on the short journey from the flower shop to the waiting car.

Finally endeavour to purchase plants with 'care' labels attached. These will give brief advice on watering, feeding, etc.

CONDITIONS FOR GROWING

Temperature
On the whole, indoor plants are rather like people in their requirements in that they object to extremes of temperature. There are exceptions, but the majority of indoor plants do perfectly well in a temperature maintained in the region of 65°F. Wherever possible it is advantageous to keep the temperature at a fairly constant level, as wildly fluctuating temperatures can be more harmful than is often supposed.

Light
Besides reasonable warmth, most plants indoors must have adequate light if they are to do well, so there is little point in purchasing them in order to brighten the darker corners. Some will benefit from a light, draught-free, window position, but it should be borne in mind that all but a few of the plants will require some protection from strong sunlight. Generally speaking, plants with green foliage will fare better in the less well-lit locations, and plants with colourful or variegated foliage will do better in the lighter positions. Almost all indoor plants will benefit from being placed under some form of artificial lighting in the evening, particularly during the more troublesome winter months. Due to possible leaf scorch damage, spot lights should be at a reasonable distance, but other forms of light should be suspended some 6 ft. above one's plants. For this purpose 1000 lux fluorescent warm white strip lights will give good results.

Watering
Watering is probably the most difficult subject on which to offer advice to the indoor gardener, as most plants differ in their moisture needs, and there is an incredible discrepancy in the average amateur grower's interpretation of wet, moist or dry, soil conditions. However, it can be said that for all but a few plants, moist compost conditions should be the aim, as very wet or very dry conditions will inevitably lead to root problems and subsequent loss of leaves. It is quite impossible to say how much or how often particular plants should be watered, as identical plants will vary in their needs according to the growing conditions. Ex-

perience suggests that most plants do better if the compost is well watered and allowed to dry out before repeating, as few plants benefit from permanently saturated conditions at their roots. In winter when they are resting the majority of plants will require less water than during the summer months when they are producing new leaves.

Feeding
When buying your first plant be sure to purchase a properly balanced house plant fertiliser at the same time, and use as the manufacturer recommends, bearing in mind that too much can often be more damaging than too little. The compost should be watered in advance of feeding, and one should not feed sick plants or plants which have been freshly potted.

General Maintenance
Keeping plants in good order entails regular removal of dead and dying leaves. There is nothing that detracts more from the appearance of a foliage or flowering plant than the presence of leaves that are dry, shrivelled, and long past their best. Even in the best-maintained collections of plants it is inevitable that there shall be deteriorating leaves, if only from old age. Tying in unruly growth and trimming away weak or unsightly growth is a job that may be undertaken at almost any time of the year. To keep plants neat and shapely it is best to tie in new growth when it is firm enough to handle.

Vigorous plants may be potted on into slightly larger containers at almost any time during the year if growing conditions are agreeable, but late spring is probably the best time. When plants have filled their existing pots with roots, one should consider potting them into slightly larger pots using a compost made of two parts John Innes No. 2 compost, and one part sphagnum peat. For larger pots, John Innes No. 3 may be substituted.

Central heating is blamed for many plant losses in the home, but one feels that, when properly regulated, the agreeable warmth provided far outweighs the disadvantage of low humidity and inevitable dry air conditions. To counteract the dry conditions it is advisable to provide a container larger than the growing pot, which should be filled with damp peat or moss. Into this medium the plant pot should be plunged to its rim and watered independently as required. Alternatively, the plant pot can be placed on a bed of wet pebbles in a tray or similar container. Here the important consideration is to provide a moister atmosphere in the area where the plant is growing.

PESTS AND DISEASES
Fortunately, these are not too troublesome on indoor plants, and most are simply eradicated by using one or other of the many insecticides available to keep them under control.

It is important to purchase clean, pest-free plants at the outset, and thereafter to keep a watchful eye for pests. If any do appear treat the plant before they become too numerous. Greenfly are usually found on tender young shoots, at the tips of hederas and similar plants, and can be controlled by a number of insecticides available from most garden shops.

The cottonwool-like substance protecting the young of mealy bug makes them easy to detect, and they are usually found in the more inaccessible parts of plants where leaf and stalk join. The time-honoured remedy of methylated spirits dabbed directly on to them is still one of the most effective cures. Mealy bug will also attack the roots of plants and these can be deterred by watering with a solution of malathion.

Red spider mites are minute pests that are mostly found on the undersides of leaves, and multiply rapidly in hot, dry conditions. Dry, brown leaf edges are a sign of their presence, also a multitude of small pin-prick holes on the undersides of leaves. On badly infested plants webs may also be formed. When treating with insecticide the undersides of leaves must be given particular attention.

These are the most common house plant pests, but whatever pest may be attacking the plants it is important that the insecticide manufacturer's instructions should be followed, and that any spraying should be done out of doors in a sheltered corner.

A SELECTION OF GOOD HOUSE PLANTS

Achimenes must be kept moist, in the light, and fed while growing. Keep warm and dry in winter when dormant. Start into growth in February by plunging pot in hot water.

Adiantum. The maidenhair fern should be kept moist, shaded, and warm, in order to do well. New plants are obtained simply by dividing older clumps.

Aechmea rhodocyanea. Has broad, powdery grey leaves that must not be cleaned, and a most exotic pink blush flower that lasts for some 8 months. Keep centre urn filled with water. The compost should just be moist.

Amaryllis. Plant bulbs to half their depth in rich compost. After flowering keep watered and fed until leaves die down naturally. Pot on every third year.

Ananas. The variegated form is by far the most spectacular and needs reasonable warmth and good light. Brilliant plant when producing fruit at fourth, or fifth year.

Anthurium. A. andreanum has large arrow-shaped leaves and brilliant spathe flowers on 3-ft.-long stems, but since it needs high temperature and high humidity, it is best suited to the more tropical greenhouse. Cut flowers last for many weeks. The compact and easily grown A. scherzerianum is much more satisfactory, needing a warm, shaded position and moist conditions. Where possible rain water should be used, and when potting on use a peaty compost.

Aphelandra. There are several varieties of this attractive silver-striped foliage plant, which has the added attraction of producing bright yellow bracts. Compost must be kept moist at all times, as loss of leaves will result if the roots become dry. When bracts die and turn an unsightly green, the plant's main stem should be cut back to a good pair of leaves. New growth will emerge from the axils of the top leaves.

Aralia elegantissima. Thin, almost black, spider-like leaves are most attractive, but

Two fine house plants : (left) Aechmea rhodocyanea and (right) Aphelandra squarrosa 'Brockfield'

plants need shade, good warmth, and careful watering, to succeed. A. sieboldii (Fatsia japonica) has much larger green leaves, is very easy to care for in cool conditions, and is hardy outside. The variegated form is less easy and not hardy, but is a superb plant when well grown. Avoid very wet conditions, as this causes browning of leaf edges.

Araucaria excelsa. The supremely elegant Norfolk Island pine is one of the real aristocrats for use as an individual specimen plant. Keep moderately warm in reasonable light and avoid heavy-handed watering.

Aspidistra lurida. Commonly named the 'Cast Iron' plant, and very durable, needing only moderate conditions. Insignificant flowers appear at soil level. Increase plants by dividing root clumps at any time. No chemical preparations should be used for cleaning leaves.

Asplenium nidus. The beautiful bird's nest fern has attractive pale green leaves arranged like a shuttlecock, and needs warm, shaded, moist conditions. Avoid wetting compost too much, but keep surrounding area of plant moist.

Azalea indica. Still one of the aristocrats among flowering pot plants. It is most essential that the compost should be kept wet at all times. Any drying out will inevitably result in loss of leaves and premature loss of flowers. When watering, the plant pot should be plunged in a bucket of water – rain for preference. Cool, light conditions suit them best, and they may be placed out of doors during the summer months where they should be kept moist and syringed regularly with water.

Begonia. The compact and attractive B. masoniana is a most useful plant for incorporating in mixed plantings. It needs moisture, shade, and regular feeding to do well. Commonly named the Iron Cross begonia on account of a cross-like mark in centre of leaves.

Begonia rex has much brighter leaves in many colours, and requires light airy conditions, as fungus diseases on the leaves will follow a stuffy, airless environment. When potting on, an open, peaty compost is most essential.

Begonias other than the two above are very diverse in their habit and requirements. The most satisfying of the foliage ones for indoor use are the fibrous-rooted cane types, some of which, B. lucerne for example, will attain a height of 6 ft. or more when properly cared for. The majority of these root easily from cuttings, and produce spectacular flowers as well as having colourful leaves. They require light shade and moderate warmth, also moist compost and frequent feeding.

Beloperone guttata. Gets its common name of Shrimp plant from the shrimp-like

Aporocactus flagelliformis or rat's tail cactus

Aralia sieboldii

Aspidistra

Citrus mitis or Panama orange

Crassula argentea, a succulent evergreen

bracts that are freely produced. More robust plants will result if bracts from young plants, and the growing tips of untidy growth are removed. Keep moist, well fed, and in good light.

Bilbergia nutans. An easily grown bromeliad that propagates by means of dividing established plants. Short-lived multi-coloured bracts are pendulous and much admired.

Bougainvillea. Needs full light and airy conditions for success. Climbs freely when well grown, producing spectacular paper-thin bracts in shades of mauve and red mostly. Keep dry and warm in winter and

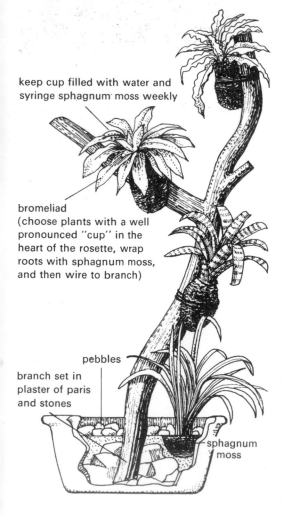

keep cup filled with water and syringe sphagnum moss weekly

bromeliad
(choose plants with a well pronounced "cup" in the heart of the rosette, wrap roots with sphagnum moss, and then wire to branch)

pebbles

branch set in plaster of paris and stones

sphagnum moss

How to construct a Bromeliad tree

moist when in leaf. Check regularly for mealy bug.

Bromeliads. All of these originate from tropical South America, so they need warmth and moist conditions in order to succeed. Most are ideal plants for the home, though many are rather too large for this purpose. Most have exotic foliage, both in shape and colour, and colourful bracts seldom matched by other plants. To make a bromeliad tree can add a new dimension to one's collection of plants. Use an old tree branch embedded in a potful of concrete to provide a simple and secure anchorage. When plants are to be attached to trees, first remove from their pots, and enclose the root ball of the plants in wet sphagnum moss. Tie the moss around the roots with plastic-covered wire, and use similar wire to attach the moss-covered roots to the tree branch. Plants will look more natural and will be more secure if they are placed in a cleft rather than on a straight branch. Moisten regularly and keep reasonably warm and you will find that the smaller bromeliads (cryptanthus and tillandsias in particular) grow much better in this way rather than in the more conventional pot method.

Caladium has the most incredible leaves of almost any plant, being paper-thin (almost transparent) and highly colourful. *C. candidum* has white, paper-thin leaves, and is one of the easier caladiums to care for. Tubers should be started into growth in a temperature of about 80°F in early spring. These are plants that need warm, moist and shaded conditions. Even so they must be considered as only temporary house plants that seldom do well for a second year indoors.

Calathea. There are a number of these that the house plant grower of some ability may consider acquiring; almost all have excitingly colourful and beautifully marked foliage. Not easy to care for, they need constant temperatures in the seventies and require shaded, moist conditions.

Calceolaria. Easily raised from seed, the indoor gardener is advised to purchase young plants of these and to grow them on in the light window of a cool room where plants will enjoy fresh air on warmer days.

Campanula isophylla. Small green leaves and intense white star-shaped flowers give the common name of star of Bethlehem to this lovely plant that is so easy to manage on the light windowsill. Cut back and keep almost dry in winter, water freely in summer.

Chlorophytum. Variegated grass-like

foliage. One of the easiest plants to grow and propagate, the latter from young plants that develop on long stalks which should be pegged down in potting compost, where they soon root.

Chrysanthemum. Professional growers treat these with a dwarfing chemical to keep plants short and compact. They last for about 6 weeks indoors, when they should be discarded, or, planted in the garden to develop and grow to normal size.

Cissus antarctica. Green-foliaged, free-growing climber, that prefers shade and moderate temperatures indoors. Keep moist and feed in the growing months.

Citrus mitis. Dwarf, heavily fruiting orange tree that must have good light and must never be allowed to dry out at the roots, otherwise loss of leaves will be inevitable. Nevertheless, good drainage is essential, as soggy compost is also harmful. In summer, place out of doors in a sheltered sunny spot.

Clivia miniata. The Kaffir lily is a bulbous plant with broad, green, strap-like leaves, that are decorative in themselves. The orange flowers borne on stout stems are an added bonus. An easy-to-manage plant which is more floriferous when the pots are well filled with roots.

Codieaum. For sheer blinding colour nothing compares with the multi-coloured codieaums (crotons), which are available in many varieties. Full sun, temperatures in the seventies, regular feeding, and compost that never dries out, are essential needs of these majestic plants. Dry and cold conditions cause loss of leaves, and insufficient light will certainly result in loss of colour in the foliage.

Coleus also has colourful foliage, but is much less demanding. Coleus may be raised from seed sown annually, or the better sorts may be raised by means of rooting cuttings which give little bother. Keep warm, light and moist.

Columneas. Fine plants for hanging baskets in conditions that offer a minimum temperature of around 65°F. They like a reasonably moist atmosphere and a light shaded position. Spectacular flowers in many shades of orange-red are produced early in the year. Cuttings root easily.

Cryptanthus is among the smallest of the bromeliad family and being slow growing and compact is ideally suited for bottle and dish gardens. Trouble free in moist, warm conditions.

Cyclamen. Among the most popular of Christmas flowering plants, it is essential that these indoors should have a cool, light, window position in which to grow. In a hot room, leaves soon become yellow and eventually drop off. The best plants are raised from autumn-sown seed to flower some 12–15 months later. Avoid saturated compost by allowing it to dry out a little between each watering, and do not water on the flowers or leaves.

Cyperus. Green water-grass plants that bear umbrella-like 'bracts' on stems about 15 ins. tall on small plants. Keep wet at all times, and feed regularly. Pot on every second year.

Dieffenbachia. The compact *D. exotica* is by far the most popular, but there are many exciting plants of considerable merit that are also occasionally available. Temperatures in the seventies are essential, and plants prefer shaded positions and moist atmosphere. The sap is poisonous so must not be allowed to get into the mouth, but this is highly unlikely as the sap exuding from the cut stem has a most unpleasant odour.

Dionaea muscipula. The insectivorous Venus flytrap is a fascinating, but almost impossible plant to grow in the average home as it must have near maximum humidity to do anything at all. Not recommended!

Dracaenas. Amongst these are many fine plants for indoor and greenhouse decoration. All require temperatures in the region of 65°F and protection from strong sunlight. They also need much less humidity in the atmosphere than the average house plant. Many will demand the skills of the experienced grower, but *D. marginata* needs little more than average indoor conditions in order to do well.

Epiphyllum. Succulent plants that produce jointed pads of growth. These are easily managed in reasonable room conditions, but one must avoid overwatering and radical changes in temperature when plants are about to flower.

Fatshedera. Hardy out of doors in many areas, so not difficult in cooler indoor locations. Grows to considerable height, but may be cut back at any time to more manageable size. Moderate watering and feeding.

Ficus elastica robusta. Perhaps unknowingly, the ordinary rubber plant has undergone a number of changes, and we now have this one as the front runner in the field. It is much more durable and attractive than any of its predecessors. Most important requirement is careful watering that allows the compost to dry out a little between each application. This point is of particular concern during the winter months when plants do little if any growing. Clean the leaves occasionally with a damp sponge, and maintain moderate temperature. Of the other varieties there are quite a number, and most are on the whole just a little more difficult to care for. The larger plants include *F. benjamina*, *F. lyrata*, *F. benghalensis* which are green in colour, and *F. schryveriana* which is variegated. Among the smaller creeping green plants there is *F. pumila* with attractive pale green oval-shaped leaves. All the foregoing will require temperatures in excess of 60°F.

Dieffenbachia

Dracaena deremensis

The dainty Cyclamen neapolitanum can be usefully grown in pans indoors.

Ficus elastica robusta, the so-called rubber plant

Cyclamen persicum, the usual indoor cyclamen, brightens February days.

Fuchsia 'Tennessee Waltz'

Pilea repens 'Moon Valley'

Fittonia. For warm, moist, shaded conditions there are three of these low-growing plants with delicately patterned leaves. *F. argyroneura* has veined leaves that are a dull reddish-brown in colour, while *F. verschaffeltii* has attractive silver-grey colouring to its leaves. There is also a newer miniature form of this plant which is especially attractive and easier to care for, needing little more than average room conditions in order to succeed. Warmth, shade, and careful watering, are essential needs for them all.

Fuchsia. For the garden room there can be few better flowering plants, as they are colourful for much of the spring, all the summer, and part of the autumn. Good light is absolutely essential and is one of the reasons for these plants often proving unsatisfactory in the home. Indoors they should enjoy the lightest possible window position. Get them off to a good start and pot on as soon as needed, then maintain by regular feeding. During the winter months keep dry and warm and start into growth in late February.

Gardenia. Difficult plants for the indoor gardener to cope with; even in the greenhouse they are not easy. Maintain reasonable warmth and shade, and when watering it is best to use rain water. Chlorotic leaves result from iron deficiency and should be treated with iron sequestrine.

Gloxinia. Raised easily from seed in heat. Plants eventually make tubers that can be kept from year to year in the same way as those of tuberous begonias. Bought plants are always available. They need reasonable light and warmth, and watering that is not excessive.

Grevillia robusta. Tall, vigorous-growing plant with fern-like foliage. Can be raised from seed and may be grown in the garden during the milder months of the year. Not difficult, needs regular potting and frequent feeding.

Gynura sarmentosa. Attractive purple, nettle-like foliage, and a very rapid grower in most conditions other than cold. Needs frequent trimming back to better shape, and flowers should be removed as they have a most unpleasant smell.

Hedera. There are a great many ivies for indoor use, and all must have a cool environment as they tend to shrivel up and lose their colour in hot conditions. They climb or trail and are perfectly hardy out of doors. Red spider may be the cause of leaves becoming brown at their edges especially in the larger variety, *H. canariensis.*

Helxine. These make attractive hummocks of attractive green leaves and are among the easiest possible of indoor plants to care for. Raise new plants from cuttings and discard older ones.

Heptapleurum. An attractive green plant with palmate leaves, which is reasonably easy to grow indoors, providing watering is not done excessively. Requires light shade and modest warmth for best results. Can be trimmed to shape at any time.

Hydrangea. Still a popular spring-flowering pot plant that can be planted out in the garden when it has outlived its usefulness as an indoor plant. Indoors it must be kept very moist at all times, and will require a light position in a cool room. When planting out of doors they need protection from spring frosts, so should have a wall or wind break of trees to protect them from the north wind.

Hypocyrta glabra. Compact plants with green fleshy leaves, and orange-coloured flowers that are produced on short stalks. Moderate conditions required, care being taken not to overwater. Can be placed out of doors during the summer months.

Impatiens. The busy lizzies are very much the cheap and cheerful plants that do well

Peperomia magnoliaefolia

on a light windowsill where they should be moist at all times. Grown in 5-in. pots they do very much better than in tiny pots.

Kalanchoe. Another very popular plant in the cheaper range, it should be grown in a light window position in a temperature of about 60°F. It dislikes very wet root conditions.

Kentia palm. The supremely elegant palms are among the most costly of all house plants, yet remain popular. Minimum temperature of 65°F is a necessity, and a lightly shaded position – no direct sunlight. Clean the leaves with a damp cloth only, and keep the compost moist, but never totally saturated for long periods.

Maranta. Beautiful plants that do well in small pots. They need warmth, shade, and moisture around them in order to succeed. Some of them fold their leaves together quite naturally as darkness descends, and as a result have become known as the prayer plants.

Monstera. Another plant that has stood the test of time. It seems to become ever more popular with its large green serrated, and often perforated leaves in the more mature plants. Maintain a moist atmosphere around the plant and a temperature in the region of 65°F. Shaded locations are preferred to bright light. Aerial roots growing from the stem of the plant should be directed into the compost when they are long enough.

Neanthe bella. These are slow-growing miniature palm trees that are ideal for rooms of more modest size. Same treatment as for *Kentia*, but they often do better in pots that would seem too large for them; use lots of leaf mould in the compost when potting.

Neoregelia. Rosette-forming bromeliads with leaves that form a natural watertight vase, which should be kept filled at all times. Leaves around centre of rosette become brilliant red when plants begin to develop flowers in their water vases. Very easy to care for, but slow growing.

Pachystachys lutea. Not easy to care for, needing moist shaded conditions and reasonable warmth. Plain green leaves are not very interesting, but golden yellow bracts are a joy to see, and are plentiful on healthy plants during the summer months.

Pelargonium. For indoor decoration the regal pelargoniums are the more popular. They require a light windowsill position and tolerate quite low temperatures without harm. Avoid overwatering and pot on into John Innes No. 3 compost when pots are well filled with roots.

Peperomias. Compact plants that are readily available in a number of varieties. They need reasonable light and temperatures around 60°F. Keep compost on the dry side, and feed during the summer months.

Philodendron. Many superb plants here, but only the smaller-leaved *P. scandens* is freely available. All do better in very moist atmosphere with adequate moisture at their roots. Shaded conditions are also a must, as direct sunlight soon bleaches the dark green colouring from the leaves. For best results, temperatures in the region of 65°F are required. Many philodendrons produce leaves that are much too large for average room conditions.

Pilea. Compact plants that root readily from cuttings – once rooted the growing tips should be removed to encourage more compact habit. These give little trouble if kept moist and lightly shaded in a warm room.

Platycerium. Commonly named the stag's horn fern on account of the antler-like

Tradescantia 'Quicksilver'

shape of leaf. Needs warmth, shade, and a moist situation. The down-covered leaves must never be brushed or cleaned.

Poinsettia. Vast numbers of these plants are now produced for the Christmas trade by new production methods, and chemicals are used to restrict the upward growth of plants. The better varieties are also easier to care for, both indoors and on the nursery. Adequate light is essential, and temperatures in the region of 65°F with moderate watering. To flower for a second time indoors it is essential that from mid-September onwards plants should be subjected to only natural daylight; no artificial light in the evening otherwise plants will continue to grow.

Rhoicissus rhomboidea. Possibly the easiest of all the green foliage plants to care for. Will climb or trail and needs nothing more than average conditions in order to do well.

Saintpaulia. Still one of the most popular of flowering plants. African violets are now very much easier to care for than they were in the past, for the hybridisers have developed better strains. Where specialised conditions are not available, the kitchen windowsill is one of best locations for them indoors. There they will enjoy good light, reasonable warmth and a watchful eye can be kept on their watering needs. Use water that is not too cold, and be especially careful to ensure that water does not get on to the leaves or flowers, as they are easily marked.

Sansevieria. Has tough succulent leaves which hold a lot of moisture, so there is no need to be forever pouring water into the compost. Kept light, warm and dry, these are plants that seldom go wrong. Potting on into John Innes No. 3 is only necessary when plants actually break the pots in which they are growing.

Schefflera actinophylla. Having large palmate leaves there is every chance that healthy plants will develop into tree proportions, but it is a reasonably slow process. Among the most stately of all green foliage plants; treat as recommended for *Monstera*.

Solanum. Attractive berried plants that are normally bought when well developed,

and discarded when no longer attractive. Must have good light allied to cool, airy conditions.

Stephanotis. Climbing green foliage plants with heavily scented clusters of beautiful white flowers. Needs good light with protection from strong sun. Keep moist and well fed while in active growth, and on the dry side at other times. Yellowing and loss of some leaves during the winter months is inevitable, but rapid spring growth soon compensates.

Streptocarpus. The variety *S. constant nymph* with attractive blue flowers for much of the year, is well worth growing, and not at all difficult in agreeable conditions. Many improved sorts have been introduced in recent years, and it is well worth keeping an eye open for them when shopping around for plants.

Thunbergia alata. Has orange flowers with black centres that have earned for this plant the common name of black-eyed Susan. Climbs very freely and flowers for much of the year, but a careful eye must be kept for red spider, which should be treated immediately by thoroughly spraying the undersides of leaves.

Tradescantia. The more common kinds are easily managed and are perfect plants for grouping with other subjects. They root readily from cuttings, and should have a light position in a cool room, with regular watering and feeding while in active growth. To encourage variegation all green shoots should be removed as they appear.

Vriesia splendens. Another impressive bromeliad that is not difficult, and produces a superb spear-like bract from the centre of its rosette. The small tubular flowers are comparatively insignificant. When the bract dies, so does the rosette from which it emerged, but new young plants develop around the base of the old rosette to grow on in subsequent years.

Zebrina pendula. Very similar to the *Tradescantia*, and needing the same treatment. Zebrina makes a super hanging basket plant. Provide a basket with good drainage and put at least five mature young plants, equally spaced, into the container. Pinch out the tips of untidy growth to retain a pleasing shape.

POTS, BASKETS, WINDOW-BOXES

Gay Nightingale

USE POTS OUTSIDE

One of the great virtues of growing plants in pots is, that they can be put in a wide range of situations, and even moved from place to place as the plant and the season changes. Although a raised patio, paved and with pillars, is ideal, even the humble back-yard can be made beautiful with plants in pots, and many of the following suggestions can be adapted to suit terraces of all descriptions, as well as sides of steps or paths.

When carefully placed, pots stood singly or in groups around the garden, often add a new focal point with the additional advantage that you can quickly change them when the flowers fade. Or, you can pop a pot or two anywhere against a background of greenery to put on some instant summer brightness.

If you exclaim in horror at the thought of instant gardening, then consider that many special plants stay in one place in pots all the year round, maturing with the seasons; giving you something to watch and wait for, and ending in results that can only be called a gardener's delight. Such plants are known as collectors' plants.

Choice of Container

Potteries are producing more and more pots to meet the growing demand. Some of them are made in strange and fascinating shapes, and all sizes from the tiny to the gigantic. Some have holes in the sides; some have narrow necks; some are square; some round with smooth sides; and others dented or with pie-crust tops.

A corner of a patio can become a base for a collection of pots of different kinds which will make the display interesting. Or you may favour uniformity, and have a few large containers of the same design. Another idea worth considering is to choose matching pots and window-boxes — say, white pots with white boxes, or black pots with black window-boxes. Where clay pots are pre-ferred, boxes in natural brown wood go well with the terracotta colour.

Planting and Planning

Unless you are willing to carry indoor plants outside, the outdoor pot scene will consist of half-hardy bedding plants, using one-colour schemes or mixed displays. (Half-hardy means they may only be outside during the warm months.) On the other hand many of the plants suggested for indoor decoration can be placed outside during the summer; but you must always be ready with a spray for pests which seem to make a picnic of expensive, exotic specimens. It is a sad sight to see foliage you have nursed through months of winter, munched into holes in one hour.

So outside you may have house plants, bedding plants and collectors' plants. They often have to be re-potted in the spring into individual larger-sized containers, or a number of small plants may be brought together to build up larger arrangements in big pots.

This is how to make up a mixed group: Put a layer of broken crocks at the base of a large pot – 12 ins. or more across – then add a layer of stones or pebbles for extra drainage. (There should of course be a hole at the bottom of the pot.) Fill up to half-way with John Innes Compost mixed with extra peat. The John Innes can be bought ready mixed in a bag, or you can use a good home-made mixture. The John Innes Compost chosen would be No. 2 or No. 3 according to the type of plants being used. I favour No. 2 for mixed groupings of bedding plants. No. 1 is usually preferred for slow-growing subjects, and No. 3 for large specimens, or fast-growing plants like chrysanthemums.

Begin to pack your plants in place, tipping them out of their separate containers or seed boxes, and easing them into the large pot. The number of plants used depends on varieties, so you must always leave space between the plants for root development. Shake more compost between the plants and top up to within 1 in. of the pot rim. Firm gently as you go, but do not ram the soil down hard.

Water thoroughly after re-potting, or making up mixed pot displays, but not so much as to leach (i.e. wash out) most of the plant nutrients contained in the new compost.

Never use tap water straight from the tap. If you must use tap water, at least let it stand long enough to reach the outside temperature; then quite a proportion of the chlorine present in tap water will be lost to the air.

You will find other references to 'hard' and 'soft' water in relation to 'lime-hating' plants. These rules of course also apply to plants in pots. But one point occurs to me: by using pots, you can grow plants in a peaty compost in a garden that is otherwise mostly composed of chalk, and so have some of the 'lime-haters' that you love.

One further complication arises. Some plants seem to abominate overhead watering, while others do well with frequent overhead spraying. Plants with hair or 'woolly' leaves should not be watered overhead.

But above all, the plants in pots that are watered regularly in summer will flourish and flower; while those that are neglected will not. Compost in pots dries out much more quickly than the soil in the garden.

Since a design of colour is a very individual concept, plants should be chosen carefully because colours for grouping can give varying effects. I find it simplest to use the same plants in different varieties.

You may like gay groups in kaleidoscopic designs, or you may find plants in several shades and tints of one colour more stimulating. Even here there is further choice: a one-colour effect can come from, say, a whole pot of red geraniums, or from different kinds of plants all having red flowers. Interest may also be found in the varying shapes and textures of petals and leaves. But there are so very many alternatives. Here are some suggestions:

Summer Pots

MIXED COLOURS: Red geranium (pelargonium), 'Paul Crampel', with blue lobelia, 'Crystal Palace'. A popular arrangement, but still attractive. Choose antirrhinum, 'Little Darling', for a long-lasting display.
WHITE FLOWERS: White Carefree geraniums look lovely on their own in black or terracotta-coloured pots. For a mixed one-colour planting, add white *Campanula isophylla*, the little Star of Bethlehem, and double white petunias.
PINKS AND REDS: Sprinter geraniums are good in groups of three or more in black pots. Or, one large specimen of 'Paul Crampel' will grow over 6 ft. tall, and given some support will act like a climbing plant, sending branches round a window or over a door. To gain this height a plant will have

A selection of useful pots

to be over-wintered indoors (unless you live in the south). But 'Paul Crampel' is the old reliable for outdoor pots in all weathers during summer.

For a pretty pink display, pick out the pink flowers from a packet of mixed Carefree geranium seedlings at the time of first flowering. Or buy the 'Bright Pink' variety. Add pink petunias from the Titan range.

Both red and pink dianthus may be used for small pots.

BLUES AND PURPLES: Double navy blue or shiny violet-purple petals of petunias with blue lobelia, or, the pale blue variety of *Campanula isophylla*.

Ipomoea 'Heavenly Blue' is magnificent arranged in rows to climb up a trellis: a great success is three to a large pot against a sheltered south-facing wall.

YELLOWS AND ORANGES: Splendid arrangements are possible with marigolds on their own. For the English pot-marigold, Calendula, 'Geisha Girl' is a glowing orange, while 'Lemon Queen' is a clear yellow. 'Show Boat' an African/French cross tagetes-type marigold is one of the earliest to flower.

Climbing nasturtiums are suitable where there is a wall or fence; otherwise choose low-growing 'Tom Thumb'.

VARIEGATED FOLIAGE: Try a group of geraniums (*Pelargonium hortorum*) with patterned leaves. 'Mrs Henry Cox' is a well-known variety; and the red, green, cream, and black markings, look attractive in clay pots. 'Mrs Cooper' has yellow and red colour on the leaves and pink flowers. 'Friesdorf' has dark frilly foliage with black rings and red spiky flowers.

Coleus leaves are brightly coloured; and although packets of mixed seeds provide an interesting selection of leaf patterns, remember that if you particularly like, say, the gold or rust-coloured varieties, these may be purchased in separate packets or as rooted cuttings from specialist nurseries.

For a more unusual display try the nasturtium with green and white leaves. A packet of Alaska Mixed seeds will give you round patterned foliage, followed by red and gold blooms.

Fatshedera lizei has rather pretty white margins on green palmate leaves; and it is well worth finding a pot of this foliage for the patio.

Spring Pots

BULBS: After the summer comes to an end in late September, plan your spring bulb show. Even before Christmas some of the green 'noses' will be visible above the compost in pots. And the sight of these early shoots with their promise of spring will cheer you through the darkest days of winter.

It is a good idea to have some of the choice varieties of narcissus outside the door. Try 'Mount Hood' for big yellow blooms bleaching to pure white; 'Cragford' for its rich red centre; *Sempre avanti* for its light wing petals and orange cup. The minute flowers of *Narcissus juncifolius* have a subtle scent which always reminds me of mimosa. The bulbs are suitable for a 5-in. pan.

The first flowers to come out in January or February may be the Cambridge blue *Iris reticulata* Cantab, and all the little species crocus, which open wide in the warmth of the sun to show their yellow stamens.

At the end of the season, white hyacinths, with white violets, are a rare sight which you can easily arrange.

Remember that these pots with their colourful flowers, or exciting foliage pat-

Crocuses in a white polystyrene container

terns, make bold spring and summer displays against walls or a green background of shrubs. But now we turn to some of my favourites for winter and all the seasons.

All Season Pots

The following suggestions are collectors' plants for outdoor pots. There are alternative possibilities of course – there are hundreds of plants which can be grown in an alpine house, a cold greenhouse, or with slight protection (a sheet of glass) outside, e.g. daphne, primula, androsace, etc. But here are three groups especially chosen for the person who simply wants something interesting to grow in a collection of all-the-year pots on a balcony or patio. Most of them are perfectly hardy and do not need any protection.

Sempervivums are strangely attractive due to the fact that there are so many sizes of the symmetrical rosette shapes. They are commonly known as houseleeks. A collection of fifty different species and hybrids is quite easy to assemble: some plants will have reddish rosettes; others are purple tipped, but perhaps the most beautiful is the cobweb houseleek *Sempervivum arach-*

noideum – astonishing to contemplate these tight cushions covered in what appears to be an intricate mathematical design of white hairs: to think they could live unseen for years on the side of a mountain in their natural habitat.

Flowers do emerge on long inflorescence stalks from the centre of mature rosettes during summer, and some of the flowers are fragrant.

Silver saxifrages have similar attractions in that the neat domes of rosettes gradually increase in size over the years. In addition, the leaves are encrusted with silver-white; so that a collection might range from the tiny silver leaves of *Saxifraga aizoon baldensis* through many sizes and leaf variations to 'Tumbling Waters' – a beauty with a silver-wheel rosette, and white flowers in summer that really do look like a waterfall.

Hardy cyclamen make an excellent first choice where space is limited. My enthusiasm for the dainty flowers has been gradually growing over the years. By collecting plants of the various species, it is possible to have plants in bloom for most of the year.

The different shapes of the leaves are

Decorative pots enliven a window-ledge

fascinating in themselves, and the foliage may be marbled in individual patterns of silver on every specimen. But perhaps the greatest satisfaction comes from raising seedlings from your own seed capsules. Watching and waiting for the little leaves to appear is all part of the joy and love of gardening. This is followed by the excitement of the first flowers. (See selection of varieties and suggestions on how to grow them at the end of this chapter.)

These collectors' plants are much smaller than the popular 'bedding' kinds described above. They are suitable for clay pans and half-pots. They require close observation and a taste for the delicate – for the intricate formation of foliage shapes and patterns. Interest may come slowly at first, then, once you are won over, you can't keep away from it!

Dwarf conifers may also be considered. These are natural miniatures, and not to be mistaken for the artificially produced tiny Bonsai trees. However, there is a place, too, for the latter. You may also be interested to know that you can now purchase tree seeds suitable for sowing yourself.

Salads from Pots
We have had success with the following plants by growing them in large-size pots: tomatoes, cucumbers, green peppers, radishes, and herbs. Lettuces are really better in troughs, and so are spring onions and spinach, although they can be grown in pots if necessary.

USE HANGING BASKETS

Choice of Container
It is surprising how many different kinds of hanging basket there are on the market. Grand superstores have green plastic con-

A three-tier hanging basket like this is heavy and needs to be fixed to a beam or similar firm support. It can be put together from chains and baskets bought separately.

tainers, with trays conveniently attached to the base to catch the drips. Wire baskets are becoming more difficult to find; but they are still around in some garden centres. And it is worth looking for the more unusual clay bowls in narrow rope nets, or white wickerwork baskets woven by hand in China.

They come in all sizes: little ones are about 8 ins. across and large ones from 18 ins. across. The choice will depend on where you are planning to hang your basket.

Planning and Planting
Baskets may be hung on black brackets from beams, or on white walls of houses, from the sides of garages, from patio poles, from pergolas, in porches, in greenhouses, and in windows.

Sphagnum moss is placed at the base of the wire container with a little John Innes Compost in the centre. Next, trailing plants are arranged all round so that foliage appears through the wire and the roots lie across the moss and into the compost. Colourful trailing plants which look nice coming through the wire of hanging baskets include: lobelia – blue; small varieties of ivy-leaf pelargoniums – pink; helichrysum – silver, and campanula – white. More moss goes in a ring around the top of the plants, with the trailing stems peeping through. The layers are built up until the top is reached. Into the middle of the basket can go bright begonias, fuchsias, and geraniums. Leave room for watering.

USE WINDOW-BOXES

Window-boxes can be made at home quite easily. The chosen wood should be 1 in. thick, of a length to suit individual windows, and about 12 ins. wide. The box is best painted or varnished on the outside, to seal the surface against weather damage. The inside must be treated with a preservative, but don't use creosote as it harms plants. Remember to drill some drainage holes, and cover them with crocks (broken flower pots) before you fill up with compost, leaving space at the top for watering.

Boxes are fixed to the wall with metal brackets, the brackets being screwed to the wall of the house under the window, so that the top is just below the sill. Wrought-iron brackets can add to the decorative value – there is no need to try and hide them. Some striking effects have been seen where the brackets are black and the boxes white. Imagine red geraniums on top of this in summer, against old cottage walls.

Watering
It is a good idea to arrange a special time every day for watering the plants at the height of summer, otherwise basket and boxes seem to be easy to forget! And wire containers do tend to dry out quickly due to their open surface.

Regular watering can make so much difference between bright blooms and faded flowers. The plants will grow better if you add a little liquid fertiliser to the water about once a fortnight.

The Spring Box
This is planted in the autumn, and it lasts until about May. The following arrangements are usually successful: pink hyacinths with blue grape hyacinths – so pretty. Yellow daffodils are lovely on their own. White daffodil 'Mount Hood' goes well with the coloured primrose 'Mother's Day'. Try bellis daisies with scented narcissus 'Cheerfulness'; or my own favourite mixture – white hyacinths with white violets.

The Summer Box
First consider the length of the flowering season, for if there is only one box you will want plants which come into flower early and stay in flower for 6 months. It is tempting to go back to tried favourites year after year; i.e. geraniums, petunias, lobelia, *Begonia semperflorens*, and marigolds.

The Winter Box
Used sometimes instead of the spring box, or as an extra box. Several shrubs make an interesting group. Try the spotted laurel *Aucuba japonica variegata, Berberis candidula, Elaeagnus pungens aureo-variegata* with ivy. Or there is the delightful sweet box, Sarcococca – don't miss this one – it has scented flowers in February. And pansy winter flowering mixed is useful.

The Solitary Box
Here are examples of planting schemes for a solitary window-box, where maximum eye-catching effect is required throughout the year. We will have to presume that the box is in a semi-sunny situation.

Tulips can go in later than narcissus bulbs, so if you are going to try and fit in an extra seasonal show, plant tulip bulbs in early November. They will flower in April and May.

Follow the bulbs with nicely spaced fuchsias and/or geraniums, or, if you like yellow and orange, mixed marigolds. These will stay in the box June and July until the middle of August.

Construction details for a sturdy window-box. It is most important that all boxes are firmly secured to the wall or to the window-ledge.

For autumn, say late August, September, October to November, have early-flowering chrysanthemums. These must be whipped out to allow for the planting of tulip bulbs by the first week in November.

The arrangement does leave a dull gap in midwinter. You may decide to have a line of dwarf conifers. Bury the 3-in. pots between the bulbs in the compost of the window-box. The conifers can be removed before the tulips flower.

This sort of quick-change gardening should only be attempted with container-grown plants, except for the bulbs, which are placed directly into the soil at the correct planting time.

Selection of Plants

Achimenes. Rest the rhizomes through the winter. Keep them dry and out of the frost. Return them to a light place behind glass and start them off slowly in the spring – placing them in hanging baskets at a later date. Give only a little water until the shoots are growing strongly. Basket varieties include: 'Cattleya' – blue with a white centre; 'Moonstone' – white with a green centre; 'Peach Blossom' – pink.

Agapanthus. African Lily. Tall blue or white flowers. Spectacular in giant pots. Plant deep and place in a sheltered, sunny spot. Variety: Headbourne Hybrids.

Anthemis cupaniana. Don't let the name prevent you from trying this lovely silver plant with divided foliage which stays all winter. It is also covered with short-stemmed flowers like Paris daisies most of the summer. Suitable for window-boxes.

Antirrhinum. Sow seeds in February or March indoors for young plants to be put outside in pots and window-boxes in May. Or plants may be perennial in some districts. VARIETIES: Tom Thumb Mixed or 'Little Darling'.

Aucuba japonica variegata. Spotted laurel for the winter box.

Begonia. Tuberous-rooted kinds make big blooms for summer pots on the patio. Many colours available. Tubers are stored in peat and sand during the cold months at a temperature which will save them from the frost. Start them off again in gentle heat in March. Or tubers may be grown from seed.

Fibrous-rooted *B. semperflorens* hybrids make excellent window-box plants, since plants remain in bloom for long periods, and seed may be sown to produce flowers in the same year.

Choose pendulous hybrids for hanging baskets. These can be grown from tubers. Or if you grow them from seed, begin early in the year and keep the seedlings warm – watering with great care.

Bellis daisies – almost everyone's favourites for spring pots and boxes. And the pretty pink, white, or red flowers have been known to keep on appearing all through the winter and spring. VARIETY: Pomponette.

Berberis candidula. Small shrub for the winter box.

Campanula. Several species are suitable for pot-gardening. But *C. isophylla* is the best choice for hanging baskets. Wide, star-shaped, white or pale blue flowers are produced in summer. It is a hardy alpine and will over-winter outside in most districts, although it is often sold as a house plant.

Chrysanthemum haradjanii – now with the not very popular new name: *Tanacetum densumamani*. But don't miss these white-silver feathery leaves – 6 ins. tall – suitable for permanent pots and boxes. Sandy soil; sunny position.

Coleus have colourful leaves. Much fun

Achimenes hybrids

Agapanthus 'Headbourne' hybrid

Begonia

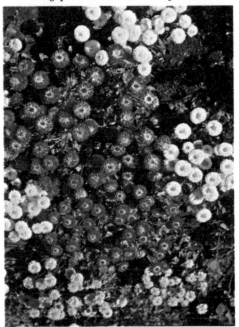
Bellis perennis (double daisy)

Coleus blumei

Cyclamen persicum in variety

233

Dianthus 'Dainty Maid'

Fuchsia 'Ballerina' mixed

Cascade of small-leaved ivies

Hyacinth 'Jan Bos'

Jasminum polyanthum

can be had from a packet of mixed seed. Watch the tiny patterns grow bigger and bigger. Begin early; but keep seedlings warm until May. Can be useful for a semi-shady patio.

Conifers. Choose shapes and colours from a specialist nursery. Dwarf conifers are delightful in winter in window-boxes or permanent pots. My two favourites are: *Cupressus glauco-viridis* (Boulevard), green-grey; and *Chamaecyparis pisifera plumosa nana*.

Cyclamen. Do try hardy species. They can even be grown on a north-east-facing patio. Grow them from seed or corms in John Innes Compost. Use 5–10-in. clay pans or half-pots. A collection will give you flowers almost every month of the year: *C. coum*, December–April; *C. repandum*, April and May; *C. europeum* (scented), June–August; *C. hederaefolium* (the most popular), August–November; *C. cilicium* (hardier than often realised), October–November; *C. atkinsii*, December–March. *C. persicum* is the parent of the indoor pot-plants, but it is only hardy in some sheltered districts. Flowers March–April.

Dianthus do well in the sun. 'Red Brilliancy' is perhaps the best for baskets, as it is very dwarf and continues to flower most of the summer. Or consider Hanging Carnations Mixed. But for pots the old Doris pink is pretty, and for boxes, Dwarf Chez Nous carnations make neat cushions of large scented flowers. Don't forget that the foliage can be attractive too. May I add that I have raised myself a variety with blue leaves for my own pots and boxes. Plants are easy to grow from seed sown in spring, or from cuttings taken in summer.

Elaeagnus pungens aureo-variegata. An attractive green and cream shrub for the winter box.

Fatshedera may be grown out of doors. Useful for training up a pole or the corner of a trellis. Pot on every spring to encourage new greenery.

Ferns are invaluable for the shady site. Try growing some fascinating frond shapes for yourself from a packet of spores. Choose Hardy Ferns Mixed; they can easily be grown at home without a greenhouse.

Fuchsias are fun to raise from seed; and there is always the exciting possibility of a new colour combination that has not been seen before. Begin with Ballerina Mixed for boxes, pots, and baskets. Cuttings may be taken from any plants that you particularly like – these will develop into plants which will be exactly the same as the plant in hand. Over-winter your favourites in a frost-proof place.

For an unusual basket plant, the species *Fuchsia procumbens* is recommended. The pale orange flower tube has green and purple sepals; but the red berries which follow are also attractive. Hardy in most districts.

Geranium (See Pelargonium).

Grape Hyacinths. Muscari. Useful bulbs for early spring. Pot up in the autumn, and keep containers in the sun. Twelve bulbs will fit into a 5-in. clay pan.

Hedera. Ivy. Even the fancy-leaf varieties are hardy, and they can be decorative in all-the-year basket, pot, and window-box arrangements. Enthusiasts might like to consider joining the Ivy Society.

Heuchera. Useful for the shady situation. Suitable for boxes. Evergreen, easy-to-grow, early summer flowering. VARIETY: 'Edgehill' for crimson flowers.

Hosta. Discover the beauty of the young leaves – the bright greens emerging early in the spring; and enjoy the lily-flowers in summer. Species suitable for giant pots in the shade: *aureomarginata*, pale green with dark margins; *albopicta*, yellow and green markings.

Hoya bella. The wax plant makes an unusual display as a hanging plant in a glass extension. Keep above 50°F.

Hyacinths. Bulbs seem happy in window-boxes, the one place where straight lines are accepted as part of a formal pattern. My favourite is white 'L'innocence', which looks well in a white, black or brown box. But other colours are pretty in spring: 'Anna Marie' – baby pink; 'Gipsy Queen' – orange; 'Jan Bos' – red; 'City of Haarlem' – yellow; 'Fairy Blue'.

Hypericum. Low-growing foliage and fluffy yellow flowers, suitable for a box in the shade.

Impatiens – the ever-popular busy lizzie – not so often seen as a window-box plant, but suitable for a semi-shady situation, where the brightly-coloured blooms can be very cheerful.

VARIETY: Minette Mixed or pelleted 'Dwarf Gem'. For flowers the same summer, sow seeds in February at 70°F indoors.

Ipomoea. Morning Glory. We have been successful with seed sown early indoors. Seedlings were planted out into large pots and placed against a south-facing wall in May. The flowers are so beautiful, that it becomes a breakfast-time treat to see how many have opened each day.

VARIETY: 'Heavenly Blue'.

Iris reticulata. If you have never tried these little bulbs in pans, you could be in for a pleasant surprise. The flowers are quite big for their 6-in. stems. Plant them by September and expect the first blooms by February.

FAVOURITE VARIETY: Cambridge blue 'Cantab'.

Jasmine. The yellow winter-flowering species *Jasminum nudiflorum* is useful for the stiff evergreen stems which can be arranged to trail over the top of a large pot.

Lobelia. A summer bedding plant which is neck and neck with the favourite geranium for pots, hanging baskets and window-boxes. Plant seed early and you can raise plants which will be ready to flower outside in May.

VARIETIES: 'Crystal Palace' – deep blue for boxes; 'Rosamund' –red/pink for pots, and 'Pendula Blue Cascade' for baskets.

Marigolds. English Calendula 'Geisha Girl' makes a gay splash of colour in summer. Sow seed in spring or autumn. French Marigolds are not hardy and need to be sown in a temperature of 60°F in February or March for planting out in the window-box in May.

Narcissus bulbs should be planted in the autumn. Yellow or white daffodils are lovely in pots or boxes around an open door. A dozen bulbs go into a 10-in. container without touching each other. Plant so that the 'noses' are below the surface of the compost, and keep well watered.

FAVOURITES INCLUDE: 'Golden Harvest' – yellow; 'Mount Hood' – white; 'Cheerfulness' – scented; 'Cragford' – white with rich red centre. And don't forget the miniature species for patio pans.

Nasturtium – one of the first window-box plants I grew myself. For best results use a not-too-rich compost and a position in full sun. Yellow and orange are the usual flower colours. Why not try all white for a change? Or the cherry-coloured *nanum*. Seed may be planted straight into a box or 5-in. pot in April.

Pansies – may almost be recommended for permanent pots – mine have been in flower

Narcissus 'Geranium'

Nasturtium 'Alaska' mixed

Pansy 'Majestic Giant'

Pelargonium 'Paul Crampel' petunias and violas

Petunia hybrids

235

Polyanthus mixed, here growing outside, are also suitable pot plants.

Tulipa praestans 'Zwanenburg'

Sempervivum arachnoideum

for 10 months. Very often their bonny blue faces are the brightest colour in a shady place. It is easy to raise plants from seed sown in the early spring.

VARIETY: Winter-flowering 'Celestial Queen'.

Pelargonium. This name also covers our ordinary park 'geranium' – still the most popular plant for patio pots and window-boxes. Examples include: old reliable scarlet 'Paul Crampel' for outdoor pots – root cuttings every August to keep your supply going from year to year. These will have to be over-wintered in a frost-free place. 'Sprinter' is an excellent red variety to raise yourself from seed sown in February. Ideal for window-boxes, as they make neat plants which flower early. For hanging baskets choose: 'La France' – double mauve; 'L'Elegante' – white; 'Madame Crousse' – double pink.

Petunias. Thin trumpet flowers for patio pots, sometimes with a velvety appearance. Sow seeds early if you can keep them in a warm light place. Try separate colour varieties for example: 'Red Joy', 'Blue Joy', or pink 'Happiness'. Fading flowers must be picked off regularly for a long summer show.

Pinks (See Dianthus).

Primulas, yellow primroses, multi-coloured polyanthus, or cottage garden 'Wanda' – all are available as plants for the spring box. Or grow your own from seed. This usually means waiting two seasons for flowers; and remember to give the seedlings some shade during summer.

But do try to see the lavender *Primula marginata* – possibly at your local show – even the zigzag-edged leaves are pretty for your little pots. Propagation of this one is by short stem cuttings, which are taken after flowering.

Roses. I still prefer my roses growing semi-wild and tall above my head; but I make an exception for the miniature climbing rose 'Pompon de Paris', when cultivated in a container.

Sarcococca. Compact evergreen shrubs. There are three small species: two with black berries, and one with scarlet. Scented flowers appear in winter and early spring. Good choice for a semi-shady spot.

Saxifrages. A collection of silver saxifrages in pans is intriguing in a semi-sunny corner of the patio or terrace. (Note that semi-sunny is sunnier than semi-shady!)

Surround the domes of foliage with white stone chippings for the best effect. Species include: *Saxifraga grisebachii* – which is the strangest one, since the rosettes invert before flowering, and elongated red inflorescence stems are surrounded by leaves that look like red feathers. *S. a. baldensis* is the smallest with minute rosettes; *S. cochlearis* is collar-shaped in leaf and has lovely white flowers in June. *S. c. minor* has the same-shaped leaves only much smaller; and *S. longifolia* is one of the largest with thin strap leaves radiating out from the rosette centre, covered in silver lime.

To propagate, simply detach rosettes in midsummer and place in a separate pan of John Innes Compost.

Sempervivum. Houseleeks form another fascinating genus for collectors. There are twenty-five species and numerous varieties – so that you can have fifty different plants: some with hairy foliage; some with red-tipped rosettes and so on. Use 8-in. pans and choose a sunny position for the group. Species include: *Sempervivum arachnoideum* – a favourite white-webbed one; *S. octopodes* – covered with criss-crossing stolons; and 'Commander Hay' – a hybrid with reddish rosettes.

Tradescantia and **zebrina.** These two plants are so often mistaken for one another. They are both house plants; both trailers, and both have elliptical leaves. 'Quicksilver' is the popular variety of *T. fluminensis.* Almost transparent green leaves have thin white stripes. 'Quadricolour' is the popular variety of *Zebrina pendula.* The lower side of each leaf is purple; the upper surface deep green and mauve, overlaid with silver stripes.

Both plants trail towards the sun, but light shade is beneficial. Protection from frost is essential.

Viola. I recommend 'Viola Jesse East' for pots, paving, or small boxes. Plants stay in bloom for more than 10 months – purple and yellow petals braving all weather. You can grow a first supply from seed very easily, and after that they self-sow, so that you are never without them. Do try also to obtain white violets.

A PORCH, PATIO, GARDEN ROOM

Fred Loads

THE GARDEN ROOM

There are many reasons why the garden room has become increasingly popular. Some of these are psychological, physical and commercial, but there is also the development of cultivation and the extension of the range of pot plants influenced by the increase in foreign travel.

Our climate usually prevents us from enjoying the outdoor living we find in southern countries but there are many days, even in the northern parts of this country, when the sunshine is warm but the wind is cold, and if we could put a sheet of glass between us and the weather then we could enjoy sitting amongst plants in comfort.

More and more, even in the heart of great cities, we find that balconies are now glass-fronted, not only keeping out dirt and noise, but also providing an area which vastly increases the time we can spend in it because of the protection it affords.

A garden room may be inherited, in that it was attached to the house when you bought it, or if it is your idea, it may be prefabricated. There is nothing wrong with these except that most of them are designed with people in mind and not plants, and because of their unit construction there is the minimum, often inadequate ventilation for plants.

I make no apologies if my introduction seems off-putting rather than encouraging, for I write mainly as a plant lover who has the welfare of the plants at heart. There is no reason why, because a particular plant is suitably ornamental in a place, it should be caused distress and possibly killed. To be brutally frank, if you regard plants merely as ornaments and decoration, then my advice is simply to buy them in at their peak, keep them as long as you can, then dispose of them and buy some more.

On the other hand, with very little trouble it is perfectly possible to grow a very wide range of flowering plants, including orchids, gardenias, *Brunfelsia, Stephanotis*, and even pineapples, on the windowsill of a house or even better, a garden room, which has much more light and very often its own heating.

The Indoor Environment

In the majority of cases, so-called garden rooms or extensions to the house are mainly composed of glass. They may have a glass or a solid top, and are built as an extension to the house rather than for the primary purpose of growing plants. In general, human beings will put up with conditions which are intolerable to plants. The reason is simple. If you find the conditions unbearable in terms of heat, fugginess, smoke, too many people, too draughty, or whatever, you can get up and walk away. Plants cannot. If they are stood in a draught or on top of a radiator or in scorching sunshine during the day, in bitter cold at night, then they have to stay put. They rely on whoever placed them there for water, air, light, and food, in fact their very existence depends on you.

Indoor plants are like children and animals, if you love them you have to look after them, be concerned for them, and often do time-consuming and boring jobs for them.

For example, at different times of the year it may be necessary to move plants out of the sun into the shade, or from the shade into the sun during the winter months. Or they may need warm bright sunshine to initiate buds and growth, and when the plant is in full flower it may need shade so that the blooms last longer. A plant may need bright light to ripen off the wood, or growth for the following season, and of course virtually all plants need a rest, particularly deciduous plants which shed their leaves.

You have to be prepared for falling leaves, for dampness, or the occasional spill with water. You may find too that water with fertiliser in it may cause spotting on polished surfaces. Above all you must restrain the urge to place plants, particularly flowering plants, in an ornamental position if it is seriously detrimental to their well-being. By this I mean if, for example, you have a particularly good specimen of a shade-preferring plant, and you put it in a position of bright sunshine just to enhance the general appearance of the room, then in my opinion, you must accept what might be the unfortunate consequences. But I must confess as a happily married man with a wife who has an eye for the fitness of things, I do concede that for special occasions, or for visitors, the plant may be moved for a few hours to achieve the best effect. Such movements do no real harm because of their temporary nature, but it does involve a few minutes' work.

The other general observation which must be made is that no flowering plant can flower continuously, although many of them do try very hard. They have to have time to make new growth but, even if only because of their willingness to flower for you, they should be given the place that suits them best to recoup their strength and produce the necessary buds to flower again next season.

Unfortunately, when a plant passes out of

A light corridor can be used as a porch.

flower, the tendency is to relegate it to a position of obscurity or even neglect. As with so many other plants the period immediately after flowering is of as great or even greater importance than when it is in bud or actually flowering. For example azaleas and amaryllis need more care and attention after they have passed out of flower, than when actually flowering. And I stress the point that I made at the beginning, that if you are not prepared to put up with this, then turf them out when you have finished with them, and buy some more when they are in season.

This may not be as expensive as it sounds because it is all too easy to have everywhere cluttered up either with resting plants or with plants that are recouping their strength. You must decide whether they are worth waiting for or not, or you may find yourself building another garden room or greenhouse just to nurse plants along.

Of course it all started with the conservatory attached to the house. In my own case, as a professional gardener, in order to supply a conservatory 75 ft. long by 30 ft. wide with flowering plants all the year round, I needed the contents of five fairly large greenhouses.

Conservatories, garden rooms, and house extensions come in many shapes and sizes, ranging from a paved conservatory where spilt water does not matter to a polished floor, often with carpets, to the cast-iron benches covered with gravel. You even use polished windowsills, or even no windowsills at all, or narrow borders at the base of walls up which climbers can climb to ornamental rafters covered with plastic or glass-fibre sheets.

Climbing Plants Indoors

These embrace a wide range from annuals to flowering climbing shrubs to evergreens, but whether you want the evergreenness of ivy, the lushness of grapes, or the colour of

Rhoicissus rhomboidea

passion flowers, the plants have leaves and will inevitably drop them.

Nothing looks more attractive than passion flowers trained over the rafters or on mesh under the roof, or luscious bunches of grapes which you can stretch up to pick, or the cool shade of evergreens; but all these will grow and grow and grow and leaves will cascade down. You can reckon on certain varieties of ivy, particularly the large-leaved varieties, growing at the rate of about 5 ft. a year, while a passion flower will grow at twice or even three times that rate, and a vine will put on anything up to 10 ft. with many side growths.

One way of restricting this exuberant growth is by root containment. For example, if a climber is planted in a border, or with its roots outdoors, then it will grow unrestrained and vigorously. But if the roots are contained in a tub or large pot, then it will grow vigorously in its early stages, until the pot becomes filled with roots and the plant food virtually exhausted. Growth will then slow down and its rate of growth will be controlled by the amount of food you give it.

When using climbers you must also consider the decoration of the woodwork and the ceiling, if it is solid. Glass and plastic need to be cleaned, so although it may be a dream to have a canopy of cool green, it is wiser and more convenient to confine growths to single strands on wires, with controlled laterals, than to let the climber grow at will over the whole of the roof area.

The material from which the structure is made often dictates the type of climber and method of attachment. As an example, I know to my cost that painted wood and plant foliage do not mix. A corner post on a glass-covered veranda draped elegantly with ivy quickly rotted, and had to be replaced at the cost of nearly £100. Where there is foliage there is constant moisture, either exuded by the leaves, by condensation, or by spraying, and air circulation is impeded. Therefore think twice before using a self-clinging subject attaching itself to painted wood, partly because of the danger of rotting, and also because it is impossible to repaint without detaching the established climber.

Red cedar and certain hard woods, when painted, do not seem to decay so quickly as when left unpainted. Metal alloys which do not need to be treated are less vulnerable, but wrought-iron can soon rust especially if foliar feeds containing fertilisers are sprayed on. The old-fashioned cast-iron however, even if painted infrequently, will last virtually for a lifetime. The roving new growths are past masters too at finding openings, and will even push their way through overlapping glass and behave like wild animals trying to escape.

The moral is, therefore, be very careful, and give clear thought to the problems climbers can cause in a garden room.

Containers and Plants

I have deliberately phrased it this way, putting containers before plants, because more often than not the availability of containers determines the type of plants grown. Containers range from large tubs in which plants of tree-like proportions such as *Ficus elastica*, oranges, palms, etc. can be grown, to the smaller ornamental containers of plastic, copper, brass, or earthenware, which will hold the general run of 5- or 6-in. plant pots. These are the outer containers into which ordinary plant pots, be they clay or plastic, are placed.

Every woman will have her own idea of

the way in which containers match the décor of the room, and will want them changed when the furnishings are changed. She may also have ideas on how certain types of container set off the plants themselves. For example plants standing in copper containers give the room a certain elegance, especially when the room is lit by artificial light.

Containers serve two purposes, firstly as ornaments and secondly to serve the more practical purpose of preventing surplus water from draining out of the drainage holes of the plant pot on to painted or polished windowsill, carpets, floors, etc.

Over the years one tends to build up a wide range of these outer containers which will suit virtually any pot, but they should always be several sizes larger than the pot which is placed in them. This is partly to

The outer container should be several sizes larger than the pot.

prevent wedging, and also to accommodate drainage in the bottom, which can take the form of any hard material such as gravel, small stones, or even bits of coal. There should be at least 2 ins. of this material at the bottom of the container, which should of course be deep enough to allow the rim of the pot to come just below the top edge of the outer and ornamental container.

Nothing harms a plant more than standing in water. This is additionally true if it is drainage water which has passed through the soil, carrying with it soluble fertiliser and various organisms, fungi, and bacteria, which feed on the fertilisers, and which soon results in a smelly sort of soup.

Water also prevents air from entering or passing through the soil in the pot. This is particularly so in the case of plastic pots, the sides of which are impervious to the passage of air. Air is just as essential to roots as it is to leaves, and as the water passes through the soil, it drives used air out and sucks in fresh air behind it. But if the base, via the drainage holes, is blocked with foul water, then the plants soon start to die. The first sign of this is the rapid yellowing of the leaves.

This provision is even more important when the room is centrally heated, because water is extracted more rapidly from the leaves, than by evaporation from the surface of the pot soil.

Where plants are standing in full sunshine, particularly during the hottest part of the year, a great deal of water is lost from the leaves and this movement of moisture from the leaves, so essential to the well-being of the plant, is called transpiration. But there is also loss of water from the surface of the soil and where possible this should be prevented by placing a covering of moss or other water-absorbent material over the soil. A layer of pebbles or dry sand or coarse grit will serve the same purpose.

Of course it is not essential that there should be only one plant and pot in one container. If you buy 3 or 4 small orchids in bud in 3-in. plant pots, then these can be arranged on a bed of gravel in a single bowl, packing damp, preferably living, sphagnum moss around the pots so that the sphagnum moss covers all the small pots, and it appears as though the orchids are growing naturally from a bed of damp moss. Certain forms of wild grasses or ferns can also be introduced, particularly sheep's fescue (grass) and small woodland ferns, which give a perfectly natural background, as well as providing the actual conditions of the environment.

If only floor space is available, then metal or plastic trays may be used. The flat shallow trays used by butchers and fish-mongers to display their wares are very suitable. These may be stood on the floor, and covered with a layer of coarse sand, gravel, limestone chippings, or woodland moss. Ferns will establish themselves readily on these materials, and they can be used as a permanent or semi-permanent back-ground. Similarly, trailing plants such as tradescantia can also be used for nesting pots, which will conceal the containers and give a natural appearance.

Two plants which associate extremely well requiring the same sunless positions are *Impatiens* (busy lizzie) and various variegated forms of *Tradescantia*.

Porches and Other Glass Fronted Structures

Although I have spent a lot of time discussing the modern garden room, this should be seen in context as it includes any large or small glazed structure such as a porch, a well-glazed room, corridor, or similar structure.

A structure where there is direct access to the outer air is the least desirable for plants, for this causes draughts if the door is left ajar, and may be chilly if left open. If a structure is only glazed at the front, such as an entrance hall, the back portion will be dark, and may be cold or even extremely hot, but even so there are very few places where some sort of plant cannot be grown. The list of plants at the end of this chapter, and their required conditions, should help here.

PATIO OR TERRACE

Only usage has given us the word 'patio' to denote what is really a terrace or sitting-out place, either paved or grassed. In actual fact a patio is to all intents a roofless room. In Spanish it is simply a word meaning a court of a house, a glorified backyard in effect. It is a word I feel which must have been dreamed up by an astute estate agent.

Paved areas are a comparatively new innovation for the ordinary house, and are literally smaller versions of the terraces fronting the great houses, where chairs, tables, etc. could be brought out into the sunshine without sinking down to the cross-bars on wet grass.

The essence of a terrace is that it should be adjacent to the house, either connected by a doorway or french window, and open to the sunshine, but protected from cold winds. Portable screens can be used to protect the sitters-out, but something more permanent is required for plants, and if the paved area can be arranged in the angle of a building, so much the better.

Tubs or Containers

Unfortunately most of the sitting-out places, except on rare occasions, can be very draughty indeed for plants, and during the period when the areas are not actually in use, the poor unfortunate plants or shrubs

A pool and a patio can be successfully combined.

The kind of pot that looks well on a patio or terrace.

Urns can be decorative in their own right.

in tubs are left to suffer from drought in summer, or, during the winter months are frozen solid for days on end.

Containers of wood should be not less than 1 in. thick and lined with aluminium foil. Concrete or cement containers should be 2 ins. thick, and thin plastic containers should be insulated with 1 in. of polystyrene. A double layer of ceiling tiles will effectively insulate plastic containers, and can be inserted at the same time as they are filled with soil.

All containers should be well drained, with drainage material such as stones, chippings, or broken pots covering the drainage holes. The container should be raised slightly off the ground so that air can pass underneath. Where a manhole, as so often happens, forms part of the paved area, it can either be painted to match, or a tub can be stood on top of it. Stone dust mixed with paint is available, and makes an effective camouflage.

Bulbs and annuals are usually more satisfactory for furnishing tubs and containers than permanent subjects, for very few shrubs can survive the alternation of hot and dry with cold and wet, which is the lot of most containers.

Spaces can be left between flagstones in which you can plant permanent subjects or bedding plants, and from the point of view of the plant, beds are much more satisfactory than flimsy containers, which roast the roots during the summer and freeze them during the winter. It is human nature to water and look after plants when in full leaf or flower, but they are apt to be overlooked during the months when they are either bare, leafless branches, or drab evergreens.

Growing in the Soil

The soil in any bed should either be below the level of the paving (otherwise it will splash out), or alternatively there should be a raised edging so that the soil is above the general level. Personally I favour this, and it is even more advantageous if a low wall can be built round the area in which trees or shrubs are to be planted, as this allows for top dressing and soil renewal. If the little wall is topped with 6-in.-wide slabs of stone or slate, then these can be used for occasional seats.

The most important thing to remember about a terraced area is that it is used only

Making a tiered bed

occasionally in this country, when time allows, and when weather conditions are right.

After continual exposure, natural stone or artificial flagstones will inevitably become green with algae. Caustic solutions may be used to kill these. Mercuric preparations, as for treating moss on lawns, household bleach, or even winter-wash, may be used for clearing off the green algae from the paving, which may become slippery and dangerous. If there is a little wall round the planted area, this prevents any chemical used from soaking into the soil, as would happen if the soil was below the level of the paved area.

Obviously, if the area is large then it should slope away from the house very slightly to drain off excess moisture, which is necessary when the paving has to be scrubbed.

Another idea is to treat the whole area as crazy paving and plant low-growing plants such as thyme in pockets specially left between the slabs. These plants, once anchored in a pocket, will spread over a wide area and thrive quite happily on dust which is washed or blown under them. Cushion saxifrages, rock roses, as well as dwarf geraniums are also very happy under these conditions.

A Homemade Container

A technique which I have used for many years and which my wife has christened

Hyacinths in a tiered bed

'wedding cake flower beds' is ideal for decorating paved areas, or for setting on tarmac drives, or around the front door. The beds can be filled with bulbs, spring bedding, a wide range of summer bedding, as well as herbs, which could be both useful and decorative.

These beds are made from strips of plastic mesh 6 ins. wide enclosing an area up to 1 yd. in diameter, and look much more attractive than flat beds as they can rise to a height of 2 ft. or more, depending on what is planted in them.

Construction and preparation is simple. Decide on the diameter of the bed and cut a circle of polythene sheet to cover the paving. This is merely to prevent discoloration, particularly if the stones are coloured and ornamental. Cut a length of plastic mesh which can be diamond shaped and has a small mesh (about $\frac{3}{4}$ in. in diameter). The strip needs to be about three and one-seventh times longer than the diameter.

Join the ends with plastic-covered wire to form a circle. This is then stood on the circular plastic sheet, and lined with black polythene which is held in position with spring clothes-pegs – very much like lining a cake tin. Soil is then placed in the enclosure. The compost can be of John Innes No. 2, or similar soil that one would mix for potting up tomatoes or chrysanthemums. Firm this gently with the hands. Then make a smaller circle of mesh some 5 or 6 inches less in diameter than the first one. There is no need

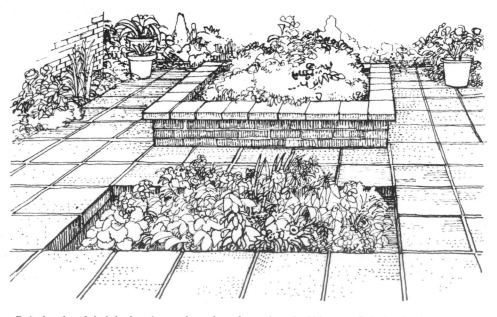
Raised and sunk beds lend variety to the surface of a patio and add interest. Raised beds, if they are not too large, can make weeding and planting somewhat easier.

Remember to make use of odd corners, especially sunny ones.

An impressive tiered bed of tulips

An insecticidal tile is a handy aid.

for another layer of plastic underneath, simply sit this circle on the soil of the bottom tier, and line the second circle and fill with soil. Now make a third circle. Place it on top of the second circle and line and fill as before.

Planting is simple as bulbs, forget-me-nots and polyanthus can be planted in any sort of mixture in the beds. When these finish flowering the plants can be removed, and any soil lost in removing the roots can be replaced with fresh soil. Summer bedding plants can then go in including perhaps a fuchsia on the top. Begonias and lobelia are two suggestions, but in fact the variety is as wide as the plants available.

Watering is no problem because there is a considerable volume of soil to hold the moisture, and there is no need for any attention to be paid to drainage as excess water seeps through. Feeding is seldom necessary as the compost is topped up twice a year when the old plants are removed.

PESTS

Pests readily attach themselves to indoor plants, or plants grown under sheltered conditions, where they find a convenient and congenial home. As the temperature is much to their liking all the year round they can breed and live in comfort twelve months out of twelve. Not for them the rigours of a British winter; in fact the drier winter atmosphere of a heated room suits the pests better than the plants.

The three most persistent pests of pot plants grown under the conditions found in garden rooms and similar structures are, greenfly (aphids), red spider, and scale. White fly sometimes puts in an appearance, as well as various forms of thrips.

Fumigation with a good insecticide is the ideal method of control, but not very prac-

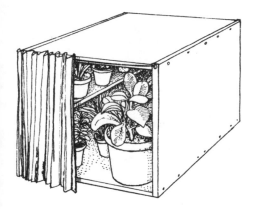

If you have numbers of potted plants, it may be worthwhile to make a fumigating box.

ticable, unless the whole business of growing is taken very seriously. If so, a gas-proof cabinet, lined with plastic-coated paper, can be made. Shelves can be arranged to accommodate various plants but the shelves should be easily removable, so that a single large plant can be accommodated along with a number of small plants. A suitable container would be a tea chest laid on its side, with a heavy curtained entrance. The infected plant(s) could then be put into this mini-gas-chamber and the insecticidal fumigant pumped or blown in.

Alternatively you can spray, using a small hand-pressure sprayer which holds about 1 pint, or you can use an aerosol.

Where plants are too large or too inconvenient to move, then a screen of plastic material may be placed round them, so that there is no damage to soft furnishings or polished surfaces when spraying.

Probably one of the most effective and convenient methods of controlling pests on pot plants is the impregnated ceramic tile. This gives off a vapour and will kill most pests in a matter of hours. It is aptly named Floragard, and is contained in a plastic case, the top half of which is removed, and the stem of the case is merely stuck in the soil avoiding direct contact with the leaves.

If the plant is bushy, then the tile can be hung by another hook from the top of the pot. This material must not be wetted otherwise it loses its efficiency, but if kept dry, it remains effective for at least 6 months, so after use replace the cap and store in a cool room. To make this device more effective encircle the plant to be treated with a sheet of newspaper in the form of a cylinder, so that an air current can carry the vapour upwards and through the foliage of the plant.

Incidentally, if the plant infected is standing on a polished surface and it is not desirable to move it, then stand the container on a sheet of paper to collect the dead bodies as they fall off the plant. Brown scale is very persistent as it builds a little igloo of a varnished material, and the female and her brood are as secure under this as a limpet on a rock.

Systemic insecticides may be used. These are absorbed by the leaves of the plant, and will give literally weeks of protection. They are particularly useful on succulent plants such as busy lizzie.

If fungi appear in the form of moulds such as botrytis, then dust with a fungicidal powder, or even flowers of sulphur, or, spray with a systemic fungicide such as Benlate.

A considerable folk-lore has grown up over the treatment of leaves, particularly of the stiff polished variety such as *Ficus*. All

sorts of weird and wonderful specifics are used, ranging from milk to cold tea and coffee. There is even available an aerosol containing leaf shine, which literally varnishes the surface of the leaf.

None of these concoctions is necessary, and any wiping or washing that is required can be done with clear water, to which a few drops of insecticide can be added. This provides an insecticidal wash. Soap may also be used, but not a detergent, as the detergent will remove or break down the natural protective coating found on the leaves of most plants.

FEEDING

There are of course several forms of liquid feed available, perhaps too readily available, because feeding is often used to counteract any and every ill, when perhaps the best thing would be to leave the plant severely alone – not even watering it. Most house plants suffer from over- rather than under-watering. Never feed a plant when the soil is dry, but always wet the soil first, and leave it for at least 12 hours before applying soluble plant food. Feeding once a month from April to September is sufficient. Over-feeding, especially in winter, can be more disastrous than under-feeding. Where plants can be removed from the room, then spraying with a foliar feed, which is absorbed by the leaves, is very effective as the modern foliar feeds contain all the essential elements of plant growth.

WATERING

Perhaps this is the biggest problem of all as it takes experience and skill to assess when a plant requires water. Plants differ considerably in their water requirements. For example an *Aeonium* could easily go 2 months without a drop of water, similarly the mother-in-law's tongue (*Sansevieria*) could probably go 3 months without showing any ill effect, but would die within a month from over-watering.

There are electrical devices available which when pushed into the soil will indicate whether the plant requires water or not but, generally speaking, touching the soil with the fingertips is as effective as anything. If the plant is in a container or a plastic pot, tapping, as gardeners used to do, is not feasible.

Soil should be kept moist, but how wet is moist? The nearest definition I can get to this, which will perhaps appeal to the ladies, is that the soil should be just as moist as a woollen garment which has been squeezed, and had all the excess moisture removed.

Generally the active period of a plant's growth is from April to October, but with artificial heating it often happens that the room is warmer in winter than it is in summer, because there is usually less ventilation.

General guide-lines are, deciduous plants need to rest during the period of low light, and the leaves may even fall off, as in the case of fuchsias. Foliage plants, on the other hand, can be kept growing right through the winter months, so only water if there are living leaves on the plant.

SUITABLE PLANTS

It is really not practicable to grow a range of plants together, with differing temperature, humidity, and light requirements, and expect them all to do well. There are many books available to the keen and specialist grower, giving encyclopedic lists and true and factual descriptions of the plants, but unfortunately 75% of these plants are not available through ordinary channels such as markets and florists, so I will confine

Giant solanum

Poinsettia can be stood out-of-doors in the summer.

Epiphyllum cactus flowers readily and is easy to keep if given winter protection.

myself to those plants which *are* available at various times of the year.

In general, flowering plants are bought when in flower. They need good light, often all available sunshine, but must be rested or fed after flowering to prepare them for their next cycle. The alternative is to throw them away and get some more.

Non-flowering plants which rely entirely on the size, shape and colouring of their foliage can be regarded as permanent or semi-permanent subjects, and if doing well, it is often the sheer size that forces you to get rid of them.

Starting in the months running up to Christmas the most likely available plants are:

Amaryllis or **Hippeastrum.** Dry bulb. Start into growth at a temperature around 75°F. Flower spike produced first, when this fails leaves form. Keep leaves growing to plump up bulb. Ripen off in summer. Disappointing if you do not give it the full ritual treatment after flowering.

Azalea. Will bloom for 2 or 3 months. After blooming if you wish to save the plant, remove the blooms, feed, stand outside during the summer months, continually water, do not repot. Life 10–15 years.

Campanula isophylla. Excellent long-lasting, long-living, trailing pot plant, colours blue and white, the white one more amenable to indoor culture. Treat as tradescantia, the variegated trailing plant. Shady position, ordinary soil, will stand quite low temperatures provided it does not fall below freezing.

Chrysanthemum. Dwarf kind. The lower the temperature the longer they last. Buy in bud, keep them until the flowers fade, then discard. They are artificially dwarfed, as are poinsettias, and will revert to tall ones if attempts are made to grow them on or propagate.

Cyclamen. Will last until the following April. Allow them to dry out occasionally to the point where the leaves wilt, then water thoroughly. Do not keep consistently wet. To save, grow on in best possible conditions then allow to dry out, repot in fresh soil in July, otherwise discard.

Erica hyemalis. A lovely plant of the heather family, virtually impossible to keep for more than a few months. Do not attempt to grow on.

Hedera. Ivies. Varying leaf shape and colour, require no sun and even poor light.

Kalanchoe. Member of the sedum family, usually available after Christmas. Do not over-water, easily propagated, will flower virtually all the year round. Sun or good light.

Pelargonium. Zonal and Regal geraniums.

(Zonal are the ordinary geraniums, while the Regal are the more colourful varieties.) Available all the year round, sunny position, minimum water, prune hard back each spring, propagate from pieces cut off.

Poinsettia. Will last with a minimum of attention until the following June. If you wish to propagate then they must be cut back in April.

Primula. Invariably bought in flower, *P. malacoides* will last several months then discard. *Primula obconica* can be grown on, keep out of sun, will last for years.

Pteris. Ferns. Good in bowls of bulbs. Can be potted and kept in the shade; last for many years – peaty soil.

Rhoicissus and **Cissus antarctica.** Climbing evergreen plants. Under favourable conditions produce small flowers and berries, but this should be discounted. Will thrive in very dim light.

Solanum. A shrub with little cherry-like fruits. Leaves may fall off if not treated, keep attractive by sticking sprigs of evergreen in the pot. Prune and repot if you wish to keep, otherwise discard.

Zygocactus. Christmas cactus. Will go on virtually for a lifetime, easy propagation by inserting portions of the plant round the edges of pots in April. No sunshine.

Although not a complete list, all these plants are easily available and will be quite happy in a room where the temperature suits *you*. All should be protected from frost, and if the temperature at night drops, insert 2 or 3 sheets of newspaper between the glass of the window and plant, allowing it to fall inwards over the plant. If curtains are used, then place the plants on the room side of the curtains. This applies particularly to cacti and other succulent plants. If reed or venetian blinds are fitted, then regard these as curtains and lower during frosty periods.

From late spring and early summer, other plants are available, such as *Fuchsias*, which require good light, and my favourite, *Brunfelsia*, a non-stop almost continuously-flowering shrub. If repotted (no lime in the soil) and the leaves turn yellow, then treat with chelated iron compound available under the name Sequestrene.

Citrus. Miniature orange trees. Will produce miniature, edible, oranges and can be potted on into larger pots, when they will make quite bushy plants carrying blossom, green, and ripened fruit. Spray regularly with clear water and the odd drop of foliar feed.

Clivia. A bulbous plant with strap-shaped leaves and orange lily-like flowers. It should be treated as a continuous-growing plant, so do not ripen the bulb by drying.

Ficus elastica. The rubber plant. These are bought as young rooted cuttings and are literally branches of trees, or rooted leaf bud cuttings. These will grow to a height of 12 ft. in the house, and plenty of room should be available for their development. Best stood on floor after they reach the height of the windowsill.

Passiflora. A climber, which like *Stephanotis*, *Jasminum* and *Hoya* should be grown round a wire frame to use as many of the young growths as possible.

Oleander and **Hibiscus** are prolifically flowering, virtually evergreen shrubs, but will eventually need quite a lot of room.

Sansevieria. Mother-in-law's tongue. One of the potted plants that thrives on neglect. Plenty of light, temperature not below 50°F but if higher presents no problems. Keep on the dry side, soak it once a month, and keep free from frost. Plant will rot if kept too wet.

Pansy hybrids grow well in pots and make a colourful splash.

Petunias and Mesembryanthemum do well in the sun.

Slightly more unusual is the Sempervivum garden which can provide interest all the year round.

GARDENING ALMANACK

Alan Gemmell

PERENNIALS

Achillea filipendula (Fernleaf yarrow). 36–48 ins. Flowers yellow all summer. Propagate by division in spring 15 ins. apart. Very easy border plant which cuts well and is at best in full sun. *A. millefolia* (Yarrow). 30–36 ins. A good red variety is Cerise Queen. Otherwise as above.

Aconitum napellus (Monkshood). 48 ins. Blue flowers in summer. Sow seed in spring or propagate by division in Sept/Oct. 12 ins. apart. Prefers a moist soil and partial shade.

Alstroemeria ligtu hybrids (Peruvian lily). Flowers of pink, red, yellow, in summer. Sow seeds as soon as ripe in cold frame and plant out in spring in sunny sandy border. Can also be divided in autumn. Is often slow to establish and may need a little protection in frosty areas.

Althea rosea (Hollyhock). 60–100 ins. Flowers red, yellow, pink, white, from mid to late summer. Sow in open in June/July and transplant in autumn or early spring to 24 ins. apart. Prefers a sunny well-drained soil. Only lasts a few years and since it does not divide well, should be raised from seed about every third year.

Alyssum saxatile. R*. 3–12 ins. Yellow flowers Apr/Aug. Plant in spring in sunny well-drained soil 21 ins. apart. It grows profusely and will drape walls or fill crevices in paving. Cut back after flowering.

Anchusa azurea (Alkanet, Bugloss). 36–72 ins. Flowers blue in May/July. It is propagated from root cuttings 1½ ins. long in cold frame in autumn and planted out at 18 ins. in spring. Prefers sun but has no soil preference.

Anthemis tinctoria (Chamomile). 24–36 ins. Yellow flowers like very large daisy in summer. Propagate by cuttings in Aug. or division in spring in well-drained soil.

Aquilegia hybrida (Columbine). 18–36 ins. Long spurred flowers red, blue, yellow, white, in early summer. Sow seed in spring and transplant about 12 ins. apart in autumn. Not very long-lived.

Armeria maritima (Thrift). R. 4–6 ins. Cushions covered with pink flowers from May/July. Prefers a sunny well-drained situation and can be planted by division at 12-in. stations in spring or early autumn. Can be used for rockeries, walls, crazy paving, etc.

Aster novae-belgii (Michaelmas daisy). 36–48 ins. Flowers blue, red, violet, yellow, white, etc. in autumn. Propagate by division

in spring using shoots from edge of clump at 12-in. stations. Does well in ordinary soil. If clumps become too big mildew is usually severe.

Astilbe arendsii (Meadowsweet). 24–36 ins. Flowers crimson, white, pink, in summer. Divide in Dec/Mar. and plant at 12-in. stations in a shady moist soil. Very good for edge of stream or pool.

Aubrieta deltoidea (Aubretia). R. Trailing plant with blue, purple, pink, flowers in Apr/May. Sow seed in spring, or take cuttings in summer. Space at 12 ins. and will be very decorative in wall, rock garden, or any well-drained spot.

Campanula glomerata (Clustered bellflower). R. 12 ins. Flowers blue in May/July. Propagate by division in Mar. about 12 ins. apart. Invasive in a rich soil, but does well in crazy paving.

Campanula species (Bellflowers). There are many species all about 12 ins. high with blue or mauve flowers in summer. Practically all can be divided in spring and planted at 12-in. stations.

Carnation. See Dianthus.

Cheiranthus cheiri (Wallflower). 12–24 ins. Scented yellow, brown, red flowers in spring. Sow in June/July in frame or pots, plant out in Oct. at 12-in. stations. Prefers sunny well-drained soil containing lime. Although a perennial it is often treated as a biennial and discarded after flowering.

Chrysanthemum maximum (Shasta daisy). 24–36 ins. An easy plant with large white daisy-like flowers in summer. Propagate by division in autumn or spring at 15-in. stations. A good border plant with some cutting varieties, e.g. Esther Reid.

Convallaria majalis (Lily-of-the-Valley). 6–12 ins. White sweetly-scented flowers in spring. In a shady, moist soil, crowns can be planted in Aug., 1 in. deep and 12 ins. apart. Will spread rapidly and can be invasive.

Delphinium elatum hybrids (Delphinium). 60–80 ins. Blue, white, often with coloured 'eye' in mid-summer. Plant in Nov/Mar. in a deep rich soil about 18 ins. apart. Feed heavily with compost and split and replant young shoots in Mar/Apr. Very attractive to slugs and requires staking.

Dianthus caryophyllus (Carnation) and **D. plumarius** (Pink). 12–15 ins. Shades of pink and red in summer. Sow seed in cold frame in March and plant out in autumn at 12 ins. apart. A very good border plant and needs well-drained sunny soil, preferably with some lime. Can also be propagated by

cuttings (pipings) in early summer. Beautifully scented.

Dictamnus albus (Burning bush). 24–36 ins. White flowers in summer. Plant in autumn or spring in ordinary soil 10–12 ins. apart. Produces an oil from stalks which can be lit on a hot day.

Doronicum caucasicum (Leopard's bane). 12–20 ins. Yellow flowers in Apr. Easy to grow in any soil by planting autumn or spring 12–14 ins. apart. Can be divided in autumn. Stays in bloom for many weeks.

Erigeron hybrids (Fleabane). 18–36 ins. Pink, mauve, purple, flowers in July/Sept. Plant in spring at 12 ins. apart and divide old clumps then. Not fussy about soil, but likes sun.

Gaillardia aristata (Blanket flower). 24–36 ins. Yellow, red, daisy-like flowers in July/Sept. Plant at 12-in. stations in spring in light soil. Propagate by division in spring. Does not like heavy wet soils.

Gentiana species (Gentians). A very large number of species each with special requirements. Have probably the most striking blue flowers of all, and are suitable for rockeries, walls, screes, etc. The most common are *G. acaulis* which flowers in spring and *G. sino-ornata* flowering in summer and autumn. Both are easily propagated in spring, but are fickle in establishing themselves.

Geranium cinereum (Cranesbill). R. 12–15 ins. Pink, red, white, flowers in summer. Easily grown in well-drained sunny position. Plant in spring at 12-in. stations. Can start from seed in pots in cold frame in spring.

Geum hybrids (Avens). 20–30 ins. Red, scarlet, pink, flowers in June/Aug. Sow seed in summer in nursery bed and plant out at 12 ins. in spring. Divide in spring.

Gypsophila paniculata (Baby's breath). 36–48 ins. Large sprays of white flowers in May/July. Sow seeds in Apr. in light, well-drained limey soil. Alternatively cuttings can be taken in mid-summer. A very good border plant.

Helianthus rigidus (Perennial sunflower). 48–60 ins. Yellow flowers in Aug/Oct. Grows anywhere in ordinary soil. Plant in spring 18 ins. apart. Useful because of lateness of flowering.

Heuchera sanguinea (Coral bells). 18–24 ins. Red, pink, heart-shaped flowers in sprays in summer. It also has attractive foliage. Ordinary soil and will tolerate shade and some drought. Plant at 12 ins. in spring

* R = plant suitable for the rockery.

244

Alyssum saxatile

Aubrieta deltoidea, mixed

Phlox douglasii 'Eva'

and divide clumps every 3 or 4 years in spring.

Iberis sempervirens (Candytuft). 12–15 ins. White rounded heads in spring/summer. Plant at 12-in. stations in ordinary soil, or wall. Easily spreads by seed.

Incarvillea delavayi (Chinese trumpet). 30–36 ins. Red and rose flowers in June–July. Divide in spring to 12 ins. apart and leave to spread. Requires full sun and good drainage. Sometimes called Hardy Gloxinia.

Kniphofia uvaria (Red hot poker). 36–72 ins. Bright red and orange flowers in July/Sept. Plant and divide in spring in groups 12 ins. apart in a sunny light soil. Can tolerate dappled shade especially if leaves are tied together in winter to protect the crown.

Limonium vulgare (Sea lavender). 6–12 ins. Flowers purple in July/Sept. Plant in spring when divide to 9-in. stations. At best in a loam but will stand lighter soils.

Lithospermum diffusum (Lithospermum). R. 6–9 ins. Bright blue flowers in May/July from an almost prostrate shrubby plant. Plant in late summer in a peaty soil (avoid lime) and will cover areas of rockery or trail over a wall. Very beautiful plant.

Lupinus hybrids (Lupins). 36–50 ins. Red, blue, yellow, flowers in June/Aug. Plant in spring at 18-in. stations in light sandy sunny soil. Many varied varieties of Russell lupins and can propagate these by cuttings in frame in spring.

Lychnis coronaria (Dusty miller). 18 ins. Rose, pink, flowers in July/Aug. A standard border plant. Divide and plant in spring at 12 ins. in a sandy, sunny area.

Monarda didyma (Bee Balm, Bergamot). 30–40 ins. Red, pink, flowers in July/Aug. Plant in fertile, moist soil at 18-in. stations. Spreads quickly and has scented foliage.

Oenothera missouriensis (Evening primrose). 9–12 ins. Yellow flowers from June/Sept. usually best in evenings. Plant in spring 12 ins. apart in a sunny well-drained spot. Can sow seed in spring in a cold frame and transplant.

Pelargonium species (Geranium). 6–12 ins. Red, white, pink, flowers from May/

Aug. There are many species of this fine garden plant which are usually grown for bedding and require winter protection. Usually cut back after flowering and taken indoors. Cuttings can be made of the prunings. Overwinter in a 'dryish' state and water and feed in spring. Bed out when threat of frost has gone.

Penstemon hartwegii (Penstemon). 20–30 ins. Red, scarlet, flowers in June/Aug. Take cuttings in Sept. and overwinter in frame. Put out when frost is over. *P. fructicosus* (R) is a shrubby hardy species.

Phlox species (Phlox). R. 4–9 ins. There are many rockery species with pink, purple, white, flowers in May/July. Most prefer a sunny well-drained site and are planted in spring. Can be propagated by division, seed, or cuttings taken after flowering has ceased.

Polygonum bistorta (Bistort). 12–24 ins. Pink, red, flowering spikes in June/Aug. Divide and plant in Oct. or Mar/Apr. at 12-in. stations. Not very demanding and will tolerate partial shade. Also *P. amplexicaule* (Knotweed). 36–48 ins. Deep crimson spikes otherwise as above.

Primula species (Primrose, Polyanthus). 3–36 ins. A very wide range of colours in spring/summer. They can tolerate a wide range of soils and light intensity, but on the average prefers damp, shaded places. These are most versatile and beautiful plants demanding little care and for details of species and varieties a good catalogue is recommended.

Pyrethrum roseum (Feverfew). 24–36 ins. Red, pink, flowers in May/June. Plant and divide in Mar/Apr. in sunny light soil. *P. parthenium* is a white flowered species.

Rudbeckia purpurea (Cone flower). 24–36 ins. Purple, crimson, flowers in July/Aug. Plant and divide in spring or autumn in any soil. Prefers full sun.

Salvia superba (Sage). 18–36 ins. Violet, purple, red, flowers in late summer. Plant and divide in spring or autumn in light shade in any garden soil.

Saponaria ocymoides (Soapwort). R. 3–6 ins. Spreading mats of red, pink, flowers in summer. Very easy to grow from division in spring or autumn at 12-in. stations.

Saxifraga species (Saxifrage). R. 2–12 ins. A large number of species very suitable for rockeries. Most flower in early spring/summer in white, pink, red, yellow, etc. but there are autumn species. Most prefer full sun and well-drained soil such as rock garden, crazy paving, wall crevices, etc. Consult specialist catalogue for species.

Scabiosa caucasica (Scabious). 24 ins. Blue flowers in July/Sept. Plant and divide in Mar/Apr. in light soil at 12 ins. apart. Prefers a little lime. Usually lasts 3–5 years and then should be divided or cuttings taken in spring.

Sedum spectabile (Stonecrop). R. 18 ins. Large flat heads of rosy purple flowers in July/Sept. Divide in Mar/Apr. to 12-in. stations. Very attractive to butterflies. There are many species of sedum but all are best in a poor dry soil, rock crevices, walls, paving, etc., and the sizes range from 2–18 ins.

Sempervivum montanun (Houseleek). R. 2–12 ins. Flowers pink, purple, in June/Aug. Divide and plant in spring every 3 years at 6-in. distances. A sunny position in a gritty soil is preferred. The family of sempervivum is large and most members make excellent rockery or wall plants.

Sidalcea malvaeflora (Prairie mallow). 36 ins. Flowers purple, red, in June/Aug. A twiggy plant divided in spring at 12-in. stations. Prefers sunny moist soils.

Statice. Now called Limonium.

Thymus serpyllum (Thyme). R. 2–4 ins. A spreading rockery species with purple flowers in summer. Plant and divide in spring at 12-in. stations. A very good ground cover plant at its best in full sun. Foliage is aromatic and is used as a herb.

Trollius europaeus (Globe flower). 24–30 ins. Yellow flowers in May/June. Plant in spring at 12-in. stations in a rich soil, preferably moist. Likes full sun and does well by a pool.

Verbascum olympicum (Mullein). 36–48 ins. Yellow, pink, flowers in June/Aug. Rather useful for back of herbaceous border so plant in spring at 18-in. stations. Can be propagated by root cuttings taken in autumn. Divide root into 2-in. portions and make them horizontal at top and slanting at base. Insert with slanting cut down in cold

245

Viola 'Market White'

Iris reticulata 'Joyce'

Narcissus 'Sun Chariot'

frame in good compost. Should be ready by spring to put out.

Veronica prostrata (Speedwell). R. 2–6 ins. A matted rockery plant with blue flowers May/July. Plant and divide in spring at 6-in. stations. Good for walls, paving, etc.

Veronica (shrubby). See Hebe (p. 247).

Viola hybrida (Viola). 4–10 ins. Blue, yellow, purple, white, flowers in May/Sept. Divide in spring or by cuttings in autumn. Plant out in spring or autumn 9 ins. apart. They prefer a moist, partly shaded soil and are useful for edging and underplanting.

BULBS, TUBERS, CORMS

Allium maly (Golden garlic). Bulb. 12 ins. Golden yellow flowerheads 3 ins. across in May/June. Plant in autumn 3 ins. deep and 9 ins. apart in light, sunny soil. Spreads quickly and is very vigorous.

Anemone coronaria (Florist's anemone). Tuber. 9–12 ins. Flowers in many colours from Mar–July. Soak overnight and plant 2–3 ins. deep and 9 ins. apart in autumn for spring flowers, and Mar. for summer, in light humus rich soil in full sun. Excellent cut flower and St Brigid and de Caen varieties are very good. In mild areas can be left to overwinter, otherwise lift in autumn, dry and store.

Begonia multiflora (Begonia). Tuber. 15 ins. Flowers many colours from Jan–Sept. For summer bedding plant in late spring with concave side up and barely cover, 12 ins. apart. Soil should be rich with leaf mould. Lift after frosts and store cool and dry. There are many greenhouse species and varieties which require special treatment, e.g. *B. rex*, *B. tuberhybrida*.

Chionodoxa luciliae (Glory of the snow). R. Bulb. 6–10 ins. Blue flowers. Plant in autumn 2 ins. deep and 4–6 ins. apart. Almost any soil and prefers full or dappled sun. Will naturalise from seed.

Colchicum speciosum (Autumn crocus). Corm. 12 ins. Lilac/red flowers in Sept/Nov. Plant in Aug/Sept. 4–6 ins deep and same apart. Will increase, but large green leaves which are ugly must be left on all summer. Does well in front of shrubs

where the large summer leaves are not out of place.

Crocus, spring. Corm. 4–6 ins. Flowers of many colours from Jan–Mar. There are numerous species and varieties but in general plant in Aug. 2 ins. deep and 4 ins. apart. Likes full sun and if undisturbed in a quickly draining soil will spread. Let leaves stay on all summer.

Crocus, autumn. Corm. 6–9 ins. Lilac and pink. Plant in Sept. 4 ins. deep and 6 ins. apart. Will tolerate semi-shade. Prefers a damp soil. Try *C. speciosus*.

Cyclamen neapolitanum (Cyclamen). Tuber. 4–5 ins. Flowers white, pink, purple, in Aug/Sept. Plant 1–2 ins. deep and 4 ins. apart in June/July. Ideal for rock garden or carpeting between shrubs or even under trees. Likes mulch in July/Aug. If left alone will self-seed. *C. persicum* (House cyclamen). Tuber. 6–8 ins. This is the florist cyclamen described on p. 226.

Dahlia. See p. 110.

Eranthis hyemalis (Winter aconite). Tuber. 3–4 ins. Golden-yellow flowers in Feb. Plant tubers Sept/Oct. 1–2 ins. deep. Prefers a moist soil where it will spread and naturalise.

Erythronium dens-canis (Dog's tooth violet). Tuber. 5–6 ins. Pink, purple or white flowers in Mar/Apr. Plant in Sept. 3 ins. deep and 4 ins. apart. Will tolerate shade but prefers a humus-rich well-drained soil. Has attractive foliage.

Freesia species (Freesia). Corm or seed. 15–24 ins. Many colours in April or Sept. depending on variety. Essentially green-house with corms planted in Aug/Sept. for spring flowering. Seed may be sown in Mar. in pots, put outside in summer to flower.

Fritillaria imperialis (Crown imperial). Bulb. 24–36 ins. Flowers Apr/May lemon yellow, red, purple, in rosettes round stalk. Plant in autumn 4 ins. deep and 18 ins. apart, in shady borders, grass, or rockery. Prefers well-drained soil. *F. meleagris* (Snake's head). Bulb. 15–20 ins. Selection of colours in Apr/May. A beautiful flower especially in moist soil where it will naturalise. Makes a pleasant pot plant.

Galanthus nivalis (Snowdrop). Bulb. 4–6 ins. White flowers in Jan/Feb. Plant

2–4 ins. deep and 3 ins. apart. Easy in any soil and will spread and can be split. Sun or shade.

Gladiolus nanus (Gladiolus) and *G. primulinus* (Butterfly gladiolus). Corm. 30–40 ins. Many species and varieties of all colours from June–Sept. Plant corms in Apr. 3-5 ins. deep in groups of 5 or 7 about 6 ins. apart. Soil should be well-drained or with peat and sand put in planting site. Lift corms after leaves die down, dry and store in frost free shed or room.

Hemerocallis hybrids (Day lily). Rhizome. 30–40 ins. Yellow, pink, red, flowers all summer. Plant rhizomes 6 ins. deep in humus-rich soil in early spring. Will tolerate shade or full sun. Spreads and can be divided in about 5 years in the autumn. Does well beside water.

Hyacinthis orientalis (Hyacinth). Bulb. 6–10 ins. Flowers blue, pink, red, white, in late spring. Plant Sept/Dec. outside in groups 5 ins. deep and about 8 ins. apart. Avoid wet ground and should be protected by mulch in well-drained soil. After flowering let leaves die down, then lift, dry and store in a frost-free place. May naturalise in mild areas.

Indoors can grow in fibre filled bowls. Plant in Sept., water, and leave in cold dark place until buds are well through. Bring into heat and light and will flower in Feb/Mar. Very heavily scented.

Iris hybrids. There is a very wide range of English, Dutch, bearded, etc., iris varying from water-loving flag iris to rockery and herbaceous species. There literally are species or varieties for every purpose. Some are bulbous, e.g. Dutch summer flowering, some have a rhizome, e.g. bearded iris. For selection consult a good catalogue.

Iris reticulata (Dwarf iris). R. Bulb. 6–8 ins. Lovely blue-purple flowers in Dec/Feb. Plant 3 ins. deep and 3 ins. apart in late summer. Warm, sunny well-drained spot. One of the loveliest and most reliable.

Lilium auratum (Golden lily). Bulb. 60–80 ins. Flowers white or crimson flecked, heavily scented in July/Aug. Plant 6–8 ins. deep in full sun or semi-shade. Is a lime hater.

Lilium candidum (Madonna lily). Bulb. 40–80 ins. Flowers white in mid-summer. Plant 1–2 ins. deep 12 ins. apart in well-drained humus soil in late summer. Helpful if you can shade the root run. Leave undisturbed, but if they deteriorate, lift and replant in early autumn.

Lilium martagon (Martagon lily – Turks cap). Bulb. 40–72 ins. Flowers deep blue/red in June/July. Plant 4–6 ins. deep in light shade, 12 ins. apart. Likes a lime-rich soil.

Montbretia crocosmiiflora (Montbretia). Corm. 24–36 ins. Flowers orange and yellow in July/Aug. Plant 3 ins. deep in spring and 6–8 ins. apart. Naturalises easily and can then be separated in mild areas. Otherwise lift in autumn and store. Tolerant of shade and poor soil.

Muscari botryoides (Grape hyacinth). R. Bulb. 4–6 ins. Blue or white flowers in Mar/Apr. Plant 3–4 ins. deep and 4 ins. apart in autumn. Ordinary soil but sunny spot.

Narcissus species (Daffodils). Bulb. 12–20 ins. Flowers white, yellow, orange, in spring. A very varied group with something for every taste. Plant in early autumn about 1–1½ times the size of the bulb deep and the same apart. Will tolerate all soils but prefers rich and well-drained. Many will naturalise if the foliage is left to die down naturally, otherwise lift and heel in a spare piece of land, then when leaves are dead, lift, dry, and store the bulbs.

Puschkinia libanotica (Striped squill). R. Bulb. 6 ins. Flowers blue in Apr. Plant in drifts 3 ins. deep and 3 ins. apart in autumn. Likes a sandy soil and spreads quickly.

Ranunculus asiaticus (Persian buttercup). Tuber. 12 ins. Flowers yellow, red, blue, in May/June. Plant autumn or spring with claws downward at 2–4 ins. and 5 ins apart. May need a little protection in winter. Sunny, well-drained position.

Scilla sibirica (Squill). R. Bulb. 4–6 ins. Pretty blue flowers in Feb/Mar. Plant 3 ins. deep and 4 ins. apart in ordinary soil. Prefers sun. Will increase naturally.

Tulipa hybrid (Tulips). Bulb. 15–30 ins. Many gaily-coloured species in Apr/May. Plant in late autumn 4 ins. deep and 6–8 ins. apart. Not fussy about soils or shade, but must leave foliage to die down naturally. Bulbs can be lifted, dried and stored.

Tulipa species (Species tulips) Bulb. 6–15 ins. A wide range of white, yellow, red, flowers, in late winter/early spring. Many are useful rock garden species and will spread and can be divided in late autumn. Beautiful species and useful for naturalising.

SHRUBS

Azalea. See Rhododendron.

Berberis darwinii (Barberry). 10 ft. Red flowers in Apr/May. Also *Berberis thunbergii* grown for its foliage and berries in autumn. Very undemanding of soil and can be pruned to shape in winter (deciduous) or spring (evergreen). Can be layered.

Buddleia davidi (Butterfly bush). 15 ft. Purple, white, flowers in July/Sept. which are very attractive to butterflies. Ordinary soil and a sunny position suits them best.

Needs little pruning but can take out flowered wood in spring. *B. globosa* (Orange ball tree). 15 ft. Orange golden balls of flowers in June. Can take cuttings in July/Aug. when pruned.

Camellia japonica (Camellia). 3–20 ft. Beautiful flowers in Feb/Mar. which are often destroyed by frost, so frequently grown in tubs indoors and put outside in summer. Avoid lime and thin hot dry soils. Constant peat mulch and ample water supply essential.

Ceanothus dentatus (Ceonothus). Wall shrub. Long branches with blue flowers in May/July. Needs support in a well-drained sunny spot. Prune immediately after flowering. *C. hybridus* varieties can be pruned in early spring. Propagate by cuttings in Aug/Sept.

Chaenomeles speciosa (Cydonis, Japonica, Quince). Wall shrub at 12 ft. Very early red flowers in Feb/May, and should be pruned immediately flowering stops, unless you want the fruit for quince jelly. Hard wood cuttings will root, but natural layers or suckers are best.

Cistus laurifolius (Rock-rose). 6–10 ft. White, red, pink, flowers in June/July. Prefers a light, well-drained soil and is useful on walls or rockeries. There are much smaller hybrids, e.g. × *pulverulentis*.

Clematis species (Clematis, Old man's beard). Scrambling over walls and trees. Different species flower from spring (*C. montana*) until Aug/Sept. (*C. jackmanii*) with white, blue, purple, or red flowers. Likes moist shaded soil containing lime and should be liberally mulched. Prune according to flowering time: 1) spring flowering – when necessary by cutting out old or dead wood, and 2) summer flowering – cut back to old wood in early spring.

Cornus alba (Cornel Dogwood). 5 ft. Grown for red bark on young shoots in winter, so should be pruned back each spring. Almost any soil or situation but prefers humus-rich.

Cotoneaster salicifolia (Cotoneaster). 6 ft. A graceful spreading shrub with long pointed leaves. The flowers are inconspicuous, but good red berries in winter. Any soil will do and requires little or no pruning. Also *C. horizontalis*, a good ground cover shrub. Propagated by cuttings of half-ripe wood in July.

Cytisus scoparius (Yellow broom). 6 ft. Yellow, red, purple, and multicoloured varieties flowering in May/June. Should be planted in spring in permanent site in a reasonably drained soil. Propagate from seed. They can be pruned after flowering but only live about 10 years.

Daphne mezereum (Mezereon). 5 ft. Purple, red, or white flowers before leaves in Feb/Mar. Usually propagate from self-sown seed. Likes lime. Also *D. odora*. Lovely white flowers in early spring. Fragrant but only suitable for mild areas.

Deutzia gracilis (Deutzia). 6 ft. White, red, or purple flowers in June/Aug. Prefers a rich soil. Prune immediately after flowering. Propagated by cuttings in June/Aug.

Erica carnea (Heath, Heather). 1–2 ft. Low spreading shrub with flowers of white,

red, purple, pink, etc. Dec/Mar. There are so many varieties of this species that they suit all gardens and will even tolerate lime. Should be clipped over after flowering and propagate by tip cuttings in summer.

There are many other species including *E. arborea*, the tree heath, *E. vagans*, the low spreading Cornish heath, and *E. cinerea*, the Scots heath. All the latter are lime haters.

Escallonia hybrids (Escallonia). 10–15 ft. Evergreen shrub with attractive glossy leaves and red or pink flowers in June/Aug. They are slightly tender but will stand salt spray so are useful around the coasts. *E. macrantha* with large red flowers makes a good wind-break hedge against winds coming off the sea.

Forsythia intermedia (Forsythia). 6–9 ft. Yellow flowers in Apr. before the leaves. An attractive easily grown shrub which does well in any soil. Sometimes birds may attack the buds and this is the commonest cause of non-flowering. Should be pruned as soon as flowering is over. *F. suspensa* is a winter and early spring flowering species which can be grown against a wall.

Fuchsia hybrids (Fuchsia). 3–6 ft. A beautifully flowered range of hybrids with red, purple, white, trumpet-shaped flowers in summer. Most are frost tender and have to be given protection inside in winter. They are therefore best grown in pots and put out in summer. They can be allowed to dry out in winter and started again the following spring, or can be raised by cuttings of soft wood. *F. riccartoni* and *F. magellanica* will overwinter in mild areas where they may be cut back in winter but will throw new growths in spring.

Genista hispanica (Spanish gorse). R. 3 ft. Small spiny shrub with bright yellow flowers in summer. Good ground cover in rockery in a sunny position. *G. lydia* is a very good trailing species for a low wall.

Hebe speciosa (Veronica). 6 ft. Purple, red, lilac, sprays of flowers in summer usually in seaside areas. Evergreen and useful in sandy soils. Away from the sea they can be frost tender. Require no pruning and propagate by cuttings in July/Aug.

Cytisus hybrid

Rhododendron 'Willem Hardijzer'

Hedera helix (Ivy). An evergreen climbing shrub, with a number of golden or variegated-leaved varieties. The green varieties will do well in shade but the others prefer better light. No soil preference and can be propagated by summer cuttings.

Helianthemum chamaecistus (Rock rose). R. 1 ft. Flowers yellow, pink, white, red, in June/Aug. A dwarf shrub which forms spreading mats in rock garden or borders. Plant and propagate by cuttings in Aug/Sept. in well-drained soil in full sun. Can tolerate lime.

Holly. See Ilex.

Hydrangea macrophylla (Hydrangea). 2–10 ft. Blue or pink flowers in massed heads in July/Aug. A semi-tender shrub which will lose its flower buds in severe winters. Prefers a humus rich soil and will tolerate shade. A good house plant which is suited to outdoor cultivation in mild areas or if given protection. Propagate by cuttings in July. *H. petiolaris*, a climbing self-clinging plant which does not have the showiness of *H. macrophylla* but is tolerant of shade and north exposure.

Hypericum calycinum (Rose of Sharon). 1–3 ft. A spreading ground cover plant with large yellow/orange flowers in June/Aug. It has no special soil demands, will tolerate sun or shade and can be pruned in early spring to keep compact. There is a very good variety called Rowallan hybrid. Many have attractive fruits.

Ilex aquifolium (Holly). 20 ft. An evergreen grown for foliage and Xmas berries. It has male and female trees and Golden King has beautiful leaves but is female and so requires a male nearby of which Golden Queen is a useful supplier of pollen. Undemanding of soil or light and is usually propagated from self-sown seedlings.

Jasminum nudiflorum (Winter jasmine). A wall shrub. 10 ft. Bright yellow flowers in Dec/Feb. One of our best winter-flowering shrubs which prefers a well-drained soil.

Prune after flowering to shape and can take shoots for flowering indoors. Is *not* self-clinging so must be tied up.

Lavandula spica (Lavender). 2–4 ft. Very fragrant purple flowers in June/July, which can be dried and stored. Should be clipped in early spring and can be shaped as a low hedge. All leaves and stems are scented when crushed.

Lonicera periclymenum (Honeysuckle). Climber. Strongly-scented cream flowers in July/Aug. Prefers a humus-rich soil and part shade. Are very good scramblers among other taller subjects. Prune after flowering or in winter when it can be cut back very hard. Propagate by cuttings in July/Aug. *L. nitida* is a small-leaved hedge species.

Mahonia aquifolium (Oregon grape). 4–5 ft. Sprays of yellow flowers in Feb/Mar. followed by little purple 'grapes' in summer. An evergreen spiny-leaved shrub, hardy and spreading by suckers. Not demanding and requires no pruning.

Paeonia lutea (Tree peony). 5 ft. Large yellow flowers May/June. Prefers rich well-manured soil with lime and should not catch morning sun. Propagate seed.

Philadelphus coronarius (Mock orange). 10–12 ft. White fragrant flowers in July/Aug. Grows in light soils and good light. Propagate by cuttings in July and prune in winter to shape.

Pieris formosa or **forrestii** (Flame of the forest). 6–11 ft. Slightly tender shrub with bright red young leaves in spring and long sprays of lily-of-the-valley-like flowers in May/June. Prefers a humus-rich soil and some shade. Attractive when grown well.

Potentilla fruticosa (Cinquefoil). 2–4 ft. Yellow, white, orange, flowers in May/Aug. Does well in well-drained soil in full sun. Divide in spring or take cuttings in Sept. A very popular easily grown shrub.

Pyracantha coccinea (Firethorn). 15 ft.

Grown for many berries in autumn/winter. Useful on a north-facing wall and is tolerant of soil and shade. Can be pruned hard in early spring.

Rhododendron. This is a very large and varied group of plants and is possibly the most popular shrub in Britain. They range from 1–50 ft. and the colours are white, yellow, red, purple, etc. It is impossible to do them justice here, but a few general directions may be useful.

They hate lime and since they are surface rooters they require deep surface mulch to protect against drought. Dead flowers should be removed by snapping them off, and they require no pruning. Most are grafted on the wild purple *R. ponticum*, and if pruned hard suckers are encouraged.

Every garden should have some azaleas or rhododendrons which flower mainly in late winter/spring although there are summer-flowering species.

Ribes sanguineum (Flowering currant). 6–8 ft. Pink, red, flowers in spring. Easily grown in full sun and any soil. Propagate by cuttings in July. Cut branches taken indoors in Feb. will usually flower early.

Rosa species. See chapter on *Making a Rose bed*.

Skimmia japonica (Skimmia). 3–6 ft. White flowers in large heads in Apr. but is usually grown for scarlet berries in winter. Plants are male and female and so need at least two to obtain berries. Likes a humus-rich soil and semi-shade. Evergreen.

Spiraea arguta (Spiraea). 4–8 ft. Sprays of white flowers in Apr/July. Grows in most soils but prefers chalk. Propagate by cuttings in Aug. or by division. Prune to old wood in Feb.

Syringa vulgaris (Lilac). 10–20 ft. White, purple, deep red, sprays of flowers in May/July. Prefers lime soils with much humus. Most are grafted and sucker freely. Propagate by layers or cuttings in July/Aug.

Veronica. See Hebe.

Viburnum species (Guelder rose). This genus contains many beautiful shrubs with pink or white flowers from *V. bodnantense* and *V. tinus*, *V. fragrans* in winter and early spring to *V. opulus* and *V. tomentosum* in summer. Some are evergreen (*V. tinus*) but others are deciduous (*V. tomentosum*) and many (*V. hupehense*) have berries in winter. Only prune if necessary and propagate by cuttings in June/July.

Vitis vinifera (Vine). 50 ft. Usually grown as climber for its attractive (esp. in autumn) foliage. Does best with roots in shade in rich soil. *V. coignetiae* is a very colourful and vigorous autumn species.

Weigela hybrids (Weigelia). 6–10 ft. Free flowering shrub, crimson or pink in June. Easily grown in sunny position and propagated by cuttings in July or Sept. Not demanding of soil.

Wisteria sinensis (Wisteria). 10–100 ft. A vigorous wall climber which makes a marvellous show of long purple sprays of fragrant flowers in May. Should be pruned hard in autumn or winter, cutting new shoots back to 2 or 3 buds. Prefers a rich sunny position and is best propagated from layers.

GLOSSARY

Activator. Material added to a compost heap to speed up the decay of the plant remains and the formation of humus. Activators usually contain nitrogen in the form of dried blood, sulphate of ammonia, urea, or a proprietary compound. Some activators may contain helpful bacteria but this is not always necessary.

Alga(e). Non-flowering plants which live in the sea, in fresh water, or in the film of water on overwet soils, tree trunks, etc. Algae are usually green, but can be red or brown also.

Alpine. A general term for plants which in nature grow at high altitudes (not necessarily in the Alps).

Annual. An annual is a plant which, grown from seed, will flower, set seed, and die in one growing season.

Anther. That part of the stamen (q.v.) which produces the pollen (q.v.), the yellow dust which contains reproductive cells necessary for fertilisation and seed production.

Antibiotic. A substance produced by one living organism which reduces the growth of another or even kills it. For example, penicillin is produced by a fungus, *Penicillium*, and acts against the growth of bacteria.

Auxin(s). Chemical substances which affect the rate and the type of growth of plants. Unequal distribution of auxins on opposite sides of a stem or root can produce curvatures and so directional growth. Thus plants grow towards light because there is more auxin on the shaded side of the stems than on the lit side, which inevitably produces a curvature towards light.

Axil (leaf). The axil of a leaf is the junction it makes with the stem. There is usually a bud in the axil which only grows when the leaf is dead or removed on ageing (see Axillary Bud).

Axillary Bud. The dormant bud in the axil of the leaf. If this bud grows it develops into an 'axillary shoot' which is usually removed by tomato or chrysanthemum growers, as it diverts food materials which otherwise would go towards swelling the fruit or flower.

Bark Ringing. The practise of removing a narrow strip of bark to induce or increase fruiting in fruit trees. This can be done (a) by ringing half the trunk on one side of the tree and then ringing the other half a few inches higher or lower. Alternatively a simple form of ringing (b) may be done by simply running a sharp knife round the trunk. This does not remove bark but does interrupt, and reduce the flow of sap. Usually done in March/April.

Bastard Trenching. A system of digging in which the top spit (q.v.) is removed, the second spit is dug over and the trench is then filled with the top spit of the next row. The last row is filled with the top spit of the first. Digging is therefore progressive.

Batter (Wall). When building a retaining wall, it is advisable to build it at a slight angle from the vertical, inclining towards the area to be retained. This angle is called the 'batter'.

Bed, Bedding. (a) Using a single species of flower in mass plantings. (b) In rockeries it is good practice to make the natural planes of the large rocks run so that they appear to come naturally out of the ground. These are called 'bedding planes'. (c) Flagstones are said to be 'bedded' when they are finally settled on sand and will not rock when walked upon.

Biennial. A plant whose seed germinates and grows in one season, overwinters, and then flowers and fruits in its second year of growth. Many vegetables e.g. carrots, lettuce, celery are biennials.

Blanching. (a) Covering the base of growing celery or leeks with a light-proof material in order to keep it white. (b) Before deep-freezing many green vegetables such as peas or sprouts should be put in boiling water and brought back to the boil. This helps to retain the green colour.

Bleeding. When a plant is wounded accidentally or by intention, as in pruning, it may exude sap from the cut surface. It is then said to be 'bleeding' and at one time it was thought it could bleed to death. This is now known to be very unlikely.

Bolting. Under stress conditions a biennial plant may flower in its first season. It is then said to 'bolt'.

Bordeaux Mixture. A mixture of copper sulphate and lime used in plant disease control.

Boss (Foliage). A solid dense compact mass of foliage usually circular and dome shaped.

Bract. A leaf-like structure at the base of the flower or a true leaf. The bright red 'leaves' of Poinsettia are bracts at the base of a group of rather insignificant flowers.

Breast Shoot (Wood). A branch growing at right angles to the desired plane of growth; thus in a shrub against a house the breast wood should be removed to encourage growth up and along the wall.

Bromeliad. A member of Bromeliaceae, a family of succulents used widely as house plants. The best known are pineapple, Bilbergia, *Aechmea bracteata*, and are usually characterised by tough leathery leaves closely overlapping, so that they form a water-tight trough in the centre of the plant.

Bud Burst. The time when the tightly shut flower buds of fruit trees begin to open. This is usually followed by other ill-defined stages such as 'pink bud' or 'petal fall'.

Budding. The technique of implanting a bud of a desirable variety, of, say, rose, on the base of a plant of a freely rooting variety, say, brier. Once the bud starts to grow the top of the brier is cut away and the desirable variety will then grow on the good rootstock. This technique is really a variety of grafting but is much more economical of plant material.

Bulb. Used for any swollen underground plant part, but should really be restricted to swollen leaf bases, e.g. onion, tulip.

Calcifuge(s). Plants, such as rhododendrons and azaleas, which will not grow well in a soil which contains lime.

Calyx. The outermost whorl of parts which make up a flower. These are usually green, as in roses or salvia, but may look like petals as in daffodils and tulips. Each segment of the calyx is called a sepal (q.v.).

Cambium. A layer of continually dividing cells in the stem. In trees and shrubs they produce the bulk of the woody tissue and it is by the action of the cambium of stock and scion that grafts unite.

Cane. (a) A bamboo stem used for staking. (b) The main shoots of fruit such as raspberry, blackcurrant, etc.

Care Label. A label which besides bearing the name of the plant carries instructions for its general growth and maintenance. Usually supplied with house or pot plants.

Carpels. Together they constitute the central female part of the flower and contain the ovules which when fertilised produce the seeds. Each carpel consists of a basal swollen part (containing the ovule) topped by a slender style with a broader top, the stigma, on which the pollen lands or is deposited.

Caustic Lime. Also called quicklime, because of its burning properties when wet or mixed with water. It is calcium oxide.

Cellular Respiration. See Respiration.

Cheshunt Compound. A fungicide containing copper sulphate and ammonium carbonate which is useful as a mild soil disinfectant, especially against damping off.

Chimaera. A plant which contains layers of cells of different genetic constitution, e.g. many variegated plants such as Tradescantia.

Chlorophyll. The green colouring material found in leaves and occasionally in stems which is active in the chain of chemical reaction (photosynthesis), which cause carbon dioxide and water to interact and be converted to sugars, starches, etc., in the presence of light.

Chloroplasts. The small structures in plant cells which carry chlorophyll and in which the first capture of light energy takes place so providing energy for photosynthesis.

Chlorosis (Chlorotic). A yellowing of leaves mainly produced by the shortage of iron in heavily limed or limestone and chalk soils. The colour is due to a lack of chlorophyll and leads to a poor development of the plant.

Chock Stone. (a) A stone placed under one end of larger stone to support it clear of the ground. By using successively larger chock stones a large stone can be levered in short easy stages into a vertical position. (b) A stone placed under a wheel of a barrow to prevent it rolling downhill. (c) A wedge.

Clone. A number of genetically identical plants. These are usually produced by vegetative propagation, e.g. cuttings, of a chosen individual.

Cloves (Garlic). Young bulbs produced under an outer skin.

Collectors' Plants. Usually rare or exotic species which are grown more for their unusualness than for their decorative or useful qualities.

Columnar. Erect with branches growing nearly parallel to the main stem, not spreading.

Compatible. When the pollen of

one fruit tree variety will fertilise and so produce fruit on another variety, the two varieties are said to be compatible. It is very important for growers of apples, cherries, pears, and plums, to plant either self-fertile or compatible varieties.

Compost. (a) The brown humus-rich material produced by the rotting down of plant materials. (b) The mixture of peat, soil, and sand, in which pot plants are grown, e.g. John Innes, Levington, Arthur Bower's, etc.

Contact. Herbicide or insecticide which kills immediately the weed or insect which comes in contact with it.

Cordon. A plant usually planted at an angle of 45° against a wall or along a wire frame which is pruned to produce one stem. Could be called a 'flat' tree.

Cotyledons. The seed leaves. Usually of simple appearance as opposed to the 'rough' or normal leaves.

Crocks. Bits of crockery, stones, or old pots, placed in the bottom of a plant pot to ensure that the drainage holes do not get blocked up by the compost or soil.

Crown. (a) The heart of the plant containing the apical bud. Sometimes applied in chrysanthemum growing to the flower buds on lateral branches. If the first crown bud is removed, second crown buds will develop, so the number and size of flowers can be controlled. (b) The branches of a tree.

Crumb. Particles of soil held together by fungi or other micro-organisms or by humus. A good crumb structure is essential for a fertile soil.

Cultivar. Usually varieties or local variants maintained in cultivation. They often vary a little from the original variety.

Cuticle. The outermost waxy covering of leaves or tender stems.

Dead Heading. Removing fading or dead flowers to ensure that plant food will not be spent in seed production.

Deciduous. Shedding all leaves, usually in the autumn. Opposite of evergreen.

Decumbent. Growing prostrate on the ground, usually with the tips turning up.

Deficiency Disease. An unhealthy diseased condition caused by a shortage of an essential element in the soil, e.g. iron deficiency. Such diseases are often induced by overliming or a chalky soil.

Dibber. A blunt-ended piece of wood pushed into the soil to make a hole when planting brassicas, leeks, etc.

Dieback. The gradual death of a shoot or branch from the tip backwards. It often follows bad pruning.

Dip. (a) The angle made by the planes of a series of rock strata with the horizontal.

(b) A fungicide in which plants or plant parts (e.g. tubers) are dipped to control pests or diseases.

Dormancy. A state of inactivity common in seeds and in over-wintering trees and shrubs.

Double Leader. A bush or tree in which there are *two* leading or main shoots and not one.

Draw (Leek). Blanch, or elongate by withholding light.

Draw Hoe. A hoe used to form drills.

Drift. An area of irregular outline covered with one flowering species, e.g. a drift of bluebells.

Drill. A narrow furrow in the soil.

Drilled. Sown or planted in drills.

Dry Set (Tomatoes). A failure of fruit to set, usually the result of extreme dryness of the atmosphere.

Dutch Hoe. A hoe used for weeding, whose blade is nearly in the same plane as the handle. Used with a to-and-fro action.

Edaphic. Pertaining to the soil, e.g. 'edaphic factors which affect growth are pH, moisture, nitrogen content, etc.'

Embryo. The result of fertilisation of an ovum by a male cell. A very young plant still in the seed.

Environment. All the factors which influence the growth or behaviour of an organism. It includes man, weather, soil, other organisms, etc.

Enzyme. A chemical whose presence either speeds up or causes the interaction of other two substances. The enzyme is not changed in the process.

Espalier. A method of training fruit trees along a system of horizontal wires, or a tree so trained.

Evergreen. Does not shed all its leaves in one season of the year, e.g. holly, pine, etc.

Family. (a) One of the larger categories of classification (see p. 33). (b) A 'family' tree is a fruit tree, especially apple, with a number of different varieties grafted on the one rootstock. By this technique the same tree may bear cooking and eating apples both early and late.

Fan-trained. A fruit tree pruned and trained in such a way as to produce a fan shape.

Feathered. (a) When applied to a young tree it implies having young side branches from the main stem. (b) With a fine edge or a different colour to the petals as in some tulips.

Fibrous Rooted. Possessing a mass of fine roots as opposed to tap rooted or tuberous rooted.

Flocculate. To cause smaller particles to come together in larger aggregations. Lime flocculates clay particles and so helps to create a crumb structure.

Foliar Food. Plant foods sprayed or watered on the leaves and taken

up by them. Useful for applying trace elements, e.g. iron in a lime soil.

Fomentation. A hot liquid used to bathe injured areas such as cuts or sprains.

Frost Pocket. Because cold air is denser than hot air, the coldest air will drain downhill and may collect in a small valley or glade. In frosty weather this area would be a frost pocket and suffer more frost and lower temperatures than ground higher up the slopes.

Fruit Setting Hormone. A chemical which can replace one of the actions of pollen in that it can cause fruit to set and swell but cannot produce seeds.

Fumigant. A gaseous chemical used to kill pests, etc. in confined spaces.

Fungus. One of a very numerous group of flowerless plants, many of which cause plant diseases. Examples are rusts, mildews, blights, mushrooms, toadstools, etc.

Genetic Barrier. A block against the crossing of two plants which arises from their hereditary constitution.

Genus. A term used in plant classification. Thus a potato is given the Latin name of *Solanum tuberosum* where 'tuberosum' is the species name and 'Solanum' the name of the genus. A closely related plant (in the same genus) is *Solanum nigrum*, the nightshade.

Glaucous. Blue grey or covered with a waxy bloom.

Globular. Shaped like a drop or globule.

Grafting. A technique for joining parts of two separate plants together so that they grow as one. This is done for plants such as roses, apples, rhododendrons, etc. where the above ground part of one plant is grafted on the rootstock of a less desirable but maybe stronger growing variety. There are many types of grafting, e.g. splice graft, whip and tongue, cleft, etc. Budding is a refinement of grafting.

Graft Union. The point on a grafted plant at which the tissues of the two different plants are in contact. Often the weakest part of the combined plant.

Green Bud. When the tips of young leaves are showing in new opened buds.

Grouted. Filling the interstices of rocks or paving slabs with fine mortar or cement.

Growth Hormone. See Auxin.

Guard Cells. The two cells either side of a stoma, whose movement controls the width of the pore.

Half Hardy. A plant which must be started growing under protection but will withstand a light or moderate frost.

Hardening-off. Acclimatising a plant to outdoor or colder conditions. Thus a plant reared in a cold frame could be hardened off by leaving the lights off the frame for

an increasing period each day until the plant was sufficiently hardy to be planted outside.

Hard Water. Water containing lime in some form usually as calcium bicarbonate.

Hard Wood Cutting. A cutting, usually taken in late autumn, of fully ripe wood.

Heart Wood. The wood usually hard and dark in colour forming the central area of a tree trunk.

Heel (Cutting). When a small shoot is torn from a tree or bush, it usually brings with it a ragged piece of bark and stem. This is the heel, and after trimming neatly it is often the area where roots are emitted.

Heel In. A temporary planting made by cutting a narrow slit in the soil and inserting the plants in it. It is then closed with the heel. Heeling in is a useful device for preserving plants alive when conditions are too bad to put them in their permanent sites.

Herbaceous. Usually green and non-woody plants.

Herbicide. A chemical, such as a weedkiller, which is used to kill plants.

Hispid. Covered with dense hairs.

Hormone. See Auxin.

Hormone Powder. A powder containing a hormone which is often used to stimulate rooting in cuttings.

Hot Bed. A layer of decomposing manure produces heat, and if such a layer is covered with soil and planted up, growth is much accelerated.

Humus. The dark brown or black mixture of materials formed during the decomposition of organic waste. Humus has very important physical and chemical properties which help to make soils fit for plant growth. It is also used as a food by bacteria and fungi so that unless constantly replaced it will gradually disappear from the soil.

Hybrid (F1). A plant produced by crossing two pure strains. Those hybrids show unusual vigour and often earliness and enhanced colour.

Hydrated Lime. Chemically, calcium hydroxide. A safe and effective form of lime for improving soil drainage and pH.

Infusion. If leaves are boiled in water and the whole then passed through a strainer, the resulting liquid is the infusion.

Inorganic. Has never been part of a living thing, or alternatively a chemical whose structure is not based on carbon.

Insect and Suck. Insects (as aphids) possessing a sharp, hollow tube which they push into the leaf of a plant, thereby injecting infected material and, at the same time, sucking food out through the tube.

Insectivorous Plant. One which derives some of its food material by trapping and digesting insects.

Inter-compatible Groups. Groups of plants (usually fruit) which can fertilise each other between groups, but plants belonging to the same group cannot cross-fertilise.

Ionic Form. When many chemicals are dissolved in water they break down into electrically charged particles called ions. The substances are then said to be in the ionic form.

Irishman's Cutting. Part of a plant bearing a root which is separated from the main growth.

John Innes Compost. A series of composts carefully formulated, used in growing pot plants and in other situations where careful control is required.

King Fruit. Usually the fruit which terminates or dominates a cluster.

Larva. A stage in the life history of an insect which corresponds to a caterpillar.

Lateral (Root or Shoot). A side shoot (or root) borne by a main branch.

Leaching. The removal of nutrients from the soil as a result of their being dissolved in rain water and washed away into drainage channels or down beyond the reach of plant roots.

Leader. A main branch of a plant. Usually refers to fruit trees.

Leg. Some fruit bushes, such as gooseberries, are normally grown with a single stem. This single stem is called the 'leg'.

Legumes. A group of plants which includes peas, beans, clovers, sweet peas, etc. They are important by virtue of the fact that they contain nitrogen-fixing bacteria.

Lights. The sliding glass windows used to cover cold frames.

Lime-induced Chlorosis. A yellowing of the leaves of plants usually due to a shortage of iron, brought about by excessive applications of lime to the soil.

Macro-nutrient. A plant food required in relatively large quantities. The usual ones are nitrogen, phosphorus and potash.

Manure Water. If a sack of horse or cow manure is suspended in a tub of water, the water will become pale-straw coloured and will contain some plant foods derived from the manures.

Meristem. An area of a plant where growth is either actively taking place or where it could potentially take place, e.g. the stem apical meristem, and the cambium.

Microclimate. The climate in a very restricted area. For example, among a crop of potatoes there will be a microclimate differing in terms of shade, humidity, possibly temperature, etc. from that in a crop of peas.

Micro-nutrient. A plant food required in very small quantities, e.g. boron, iron, manganese, etc.

Mist Unit. A device which will spray fine water droplets over an area when the humidity drops. It will therefore maintain a high humidity and is useful in rooting cuttings.

Mulch. An application of rotted or rotting organic matter, such as compost or peat, to the surface of the soil around the base of plants.

Mycorrhiza. The association of a fungus with the roots of a plant. This is very common in trees, ericaceous shrubs, orchids, etc. and is beneficial to both partners.

Nectar. The sweet fluid exuded from nectaries in flowers. It is attractive to insects, which pollinate the flowers in its collection.

Nitrogen Fixing. Having the ability to use the N_2 in the air and combine it in amino acids, protein, etc. Usually applied to specific bacteria which have this power.

Nodule. (a) A swollen area.
(b) Commonly used to describe the swollen areas produced by nitrogen-fixing bacteria on the roots of leguminous plants.

Occlusion (Wound). Material which stops up a wound, or plugs a hole.

Offset. A young plant bulb often produced by starving the parent, (onion, shallot), or a small bulb produced by larger bulbs, or even a plantlet produced in the flowering head.

Organic. (a) Made from materials which have once lived, e.g. wool as opposed to nylon. (b) Chemical based on carbon.

Outcrop. The point where a stratum of rock breaks through the soil surface.

Ovule. That part of the female reproductive structures which contains the ovum.

Ovum. The female reproductive cell.

Parasite. An organism which derives part or all of its food from another organism, thus caterpillars may be parasitic on cabbages and apple scab on apple trees.

Pectin. A substance commonly found in cell walls, which is useful for thickening jams and jellies.

Perennial. Growing over a large number of years, or coming up every year.

Petals. Usually the brightly coloured part of a flower. Are situated immediately inside the sepals or calyx (q.v.).

Petiole. The leaf stalk.

pH. A scale used to measure the acidity or alkalinity of a soil. pH 6·8 is regarded as neutral, a lower figure denoting an acid condition and a higher figure an alkaline condition.

Phloem. The food-conducting channels within a plant stem.

Phyllotaxy. The arrangement and order of leaves around the stem of a plant.

Pilaster. A stone column usually associated with a wall.

Pillar Tree. Used for a tree growing over a vertical structure or used to designate a columnar-type tree.

Pinching. When applied to buds or small shoots, signifies nipping out with the fingers.

Pink Bud. A stage in the development of a flower bud of an apple tree in which the tips of the pink petals are just seen.

Plunge Bed. A deep bed usually of ashes or sand in which pots containing plants can be sunk during the summer.

Plutonic. Derived from a volcano.

Pollen. The yellow powder produced in the anthers (q.v.) which carries the male reproductive cells.

Pollination. The transfer of pollen from the anthers of one plant to the stigma (q.v.) of another.

Pot Bound. A plant which has been in a pot for so long that the roots are forced to grow around the inside, is said to be pot bound. This is usually an undesirable condition and such plants should be re-potted to a larger pot and the roots carefully teased out.

Potion. A liquid medicine or draught.

Poultice. A soft mass of material made usually with boiling water and then spread on an infected or inflamed part. The material is very often covered with lint or muslin.

Pot-pourri. A mixture of dried fragrant leaves or petals kept in a container and used to perfume a drawer or a room.

Predator. An organism which feeds on another, e.g. a ladybird is a predator because it eats greenfly.

Primary Branch. A branch which rises directly from the main trunk.

Radiation Frost. A frost which is the result of the ground absorbing warmth so that the impression is given that coldness is coming up from the soil.

Radicle. The first root to emerge from a germinating seed.

Re-cycle. To use again and again as in the re-cycling of nitrogen.

Regenerate. (a) To be revigorated as a result of pruning.
(b) To develop small young plants from some part of the parent.

Rendered. Covering with mortar or cement as in the case of rendering a wall.

Residual Herbicide. A weed-killer which stays in the soil for some time, thus having a prolonged action.

Respiration (Cellular). The sequence of chemical events which results in the liberation of energy from food materials.

Reversion. A return to a more simple or primitive state.

Rhizome. An underground stem.

Rhizomorph. The bootlace-like filaments of fungi such as *Armillaria* which spread disease from one plant to another.

Root Cap. The very tip of a root which, as it is pushed through the soil, is constantly worn away on the outside and continually replaced from the apex on the inside.

Root Hairs. Small extensions of the epidermal cells of roots which constitute the main absorptive part of the plant.

Root Nodules. The swollen parts of the root of leguminous plants which contain nitrogen-fixing bacteria (q.v.)

Root Run. The space in which roots can and do grow.

Rootstock. The underground part of a grafted plant.

Rotation (Crop). A system of gardening which avoids growing the same crop in successive years in the same soil. This prevents the build-up of pests and diseases and the depletion of the soil of specific elements.

Runners. Above-ground stems which spread out from the main plant and take root at their tips where new plantlets are produced, e.g. strawberries.

Sap Wood. The light coloured ring of wood which surrounds the heart wood (q.v.) of a tree.

Scale. (a) A hard outer case.
(b) A type of insect.

Scandent. Climbing.

Scarp. A steep slope.

Scion. A short stem which is grafted on a rootstock (q.v.).

Scree. A steep slope covered with stones. Screes are made in rockeries and can carry a fairly unique series of plants.

Sedimentary. Rocks which have been formed by the compression of sandy deposits on the sea bed.

Self-fertile. A plant whose pollen can fertilise its own ova.

Sepals. See Calyx.

Sequestrene. A type of chemical compound which contains a metal, such as iron, in a form which can be assimilated by the plant, but will not be 'fixed' by chemical action in the soil.

Shore. A piece of timber used to prevent a structure, e.g. a wall from falling. A prop.

Shuttering. A wooden framework used to contain or shape cement or concrete.

Sick Soil. A soil which has grown the same crop for a number of years in succession and has now built up a high concentration of pests or diseases.

Slow Release Fertiliser. A fertiliser formulated in such a way that the food only becomes available gradually during the season.

Soakaway. A pit usually filled with

stones into which water will drain and so gradually soak away.

Soft Water. Water containing no calcium salts, e.g. rain water.

Softwood Cutting. A green non-woody cutting of the current year's growth.

Spawn. The spores of a mushroom, or compost which is penetrated by fungal growths.

Spit. The depth of the blade of a spade.

Spore. The reproductive bodies produced by flowerless plants such as ferns, fungi, etc.

Spur. A short branch on a fruit tree which bears flowers and fruit.

Stamens. The whole male structure in the flower consisting of the filaments (stalk) and the anther (q.v.).

Stations. Planting sites.

Stigma. The sticky part where the pollen lands on top of the style (q.v.).

Stock. See Rootstock.

Stoma. The tiny openings in leaves through which gases and water vapour pass.

Stool. The basal part of a plant (e.g. chrysanthemum) from which new young shoots will arise once the top is cut off. These shoots are used as cuttings, thus from one parent plant many cuttings can be derived.

Stopping. Pinching out an apical or lateral bud.

Style. The structure which terminates in a stigma (q.v.) and leads in its base to the ovules.

Sucker. A shoot arising from the rootstock of a grafted tree.

Symbosis. The association of two organisms often with benefit to both. The classic example is the bacteria in leguminous root nodules (q.v.).

Systemic. Penetrating all parts of the plant's system.

Tamp. To plug or block with clay.

Tassel. The silky long anthers and stamens of maize.

T-budding. A method of budding in which a T-shaped cut is made in the bark of a young shoot. The corners are then bent back and a bud inserted. The flaps are then replaced and the bud will grow under the protection of the outer layers of the parent plant.

Tipping. Removing the tips of raspberry canes to stop continuous growth.

Tilth. The texture of a seed bed.

Tisane. An infusion, such as tea.

Trace Elements. Elements which are needed by plants in very minute quantities.

Transpiration. The loss of water from the leafy parts of a plant. This loss can be regulated by movements of the guard cells of the stomata (q.v.).

Tuber. A swollen underground stem.

Tufa. A coarse rather porous rock.

Turbulence. Not moving in any one direction.

Turgid. Full of water and so erect.

Understock. See Rootstock.

Umbelliferous. Belonging to the family Umbelliferae, e.g. carrot, parsley, gout weed, etc.

Variant. A departure from a recognised variety of plant.

Virus. Agents whose presence produce disease of plants and animals.

Volcanic. Derived from a volcano.

Ward Case. A glass case in which plants can be grown.

Weed Killer. A chemical which will collectively kill weeds. In some cases these are selective and in others they may be general.

Wind Break. A hedge, group of plants, or single trees, planted on the windward side of a garden to protect and shelter more tender subjects.

Worked on. Grafted on.

INDEX

July

August

September

Vegetables

Sow beet, carrot and lettuce.
Plant out broccoli, winter cabbage, leeks, sprouts and kale for winter use.
Treat brassicas with calomel dust.
Protect summer cauliflowers by bending leaves over the curd.
Lift shallots.
When early crops are lifted and used replace with winter vegetables.

Fruit

Prune currants and raspberries after fruiting.
Clear strawberry beds of straw and weed thoroughly.
Train cordons, fans, espaliers etc.
Prune any new blackberry canes.
Summer prune apples.
Continue spraying against pests and disease.

Flowers

Remove faded flowers.
Plant out biennials, such as wallflowers.
Take cuttings of pinks, hydrangeas.
Divide polyanthus, arabis, etc.
Water gladiolus and sweet peas generously.
Carnations can be layered.
Cuttings taken of pelargoniums, violas and pansies.

Shrubs

Prune deutschia, weigela.
Clip evergreens.
Can layer shrubs of all kinds including shrub roses.
Divide spiraea.
Order for autumn delivery.

Lawns

Cut grass regularly and weed.
Trim edges.

Greenhouse

Most indoor plants should be planted outside.
If flowering is over cut back, rest and then water.
Pot up fuchsias.
Sow auriculas for inside use.
Pinch out the tops of tomatoes.

General

Weeding, watering and hoeing are essential to keep the garden tidy.
If cut flowers are being brought into the house they should be cut as early in the morning as possible and plunged up to the neck in water for an hour or so.

Vegetables

As early crops are used, dig and fertilise the ground for replanting.
Sow spring cabbage, winter lettuce, onions, spinach, etc.
Plant any winter green crops.
Earth up kale, leeks etc.
At end of month lift onions and expose to sun to dry.
Feed asparagus beds.
Green manuring can be carried out with mustard or rape.
Remember to pick vegetables regularly.

Fruit

Continue training apples and pears.
Cut out fruited wood on peaches, nectarines and blackcurrants.
Spray late varieties, and early varieties should be picked and eaten immediately.
Strawberries can be planted.
Pinch back gooseberries.
Reduce raspberry canes to 5 or 6 per plant.
Support branches of heavily laden plums.

Flowers

Dead-head.
Plant early spring bulbs outside.
Continue spraying roses against greenfly, mildew and blackspot.
Larger single chrysanthemums should be disbudded.
Lift, divide and replant irises.
Cut and dry herbs.

Shrubs

Semi-ripe cuttings will root for next spring.
Prune rambler roses and wisteria.
Continue mulching.
Evergreens can be layered and hedges trimmed.
Take cuttings and layers of shrubs.

Lawns

Continue cutting and edging.
Dig over land on which a new lawn will be sown at the end of the month.
Turf diseases are prevalent in autumn, so buy in fungicide.
Last feed should be applied about the middle of the month.

Greenhouse

Watch for low night temperatures and condensation as this encourages mildew, keep ventilation good therefore.
Pinch out tips of tomatoes and stop watering and feeding them.
Paint frames and woodwork and at the end of the month wash down and sterilise benches.

House plants

Bring in plants from outside.
Feed and water for winter growth and keep in a cool, shady place.

General

A good month for cutting hedges.
Continue weeding and hoeing.
When on holiday ask neighbours to use your vegetables in return for keeping an eye on the garden.

Vegetables

Lift and store root vegetables before they start to lose quality.
Leave roots of pea and bean plants in the soil to increase fertility.
Sow main crop or Japanese onions.
Trim parsley to encourage fresh shoots.
Earth up celery and winter greens.
Break up new soil for next year's crop.
Plant spring cabbage.
If there are signs of slugs or wireworm lift potatoes.

Fruit

Tidy up and plant strawberries.
Cut out old fruited raspberry wood.
Prune peaches after harvesting the fruit.
Blackcurrants can also be pruned and cuttings taken.
Prune off and burn mildewed tips of gooseberries.
When the fruit is ripe, apple pips are black.
Clean and tidy the fruit store.
Order new trees and bushes.

Flowers

Bulb planting can be started.
Perennials and biennials sown earlier can be transplanted.
Lift summer bedding for over-wintering.
Sow sweet peas and hardy annuals in pots.
Seed collecting can be begun but be sure that the seed is ripe and that it is stored dry.
Weeding is very important this month.
Clear away withered annuals.
Divide any layered plants, such as carnations, and plant layers in the frame.
Divide saxifrage, sweet williams flag irises.
Lift and store dahlias and gladioli.
Plant Christmas roses in a cool, deep soil.

Shrubs

Plant conifers and evergreens.
Trim ramblers and hedges.
Shrubs can be moved at this stage if you take a large root ball.
Hard wood cuttings of hardy shrubs can be taken.

Lawns

Continue killing weeds and aerate with a hollow tine if possible.
Top dress with coarse sand and compost.
If any signs of disease treat with a lawn fungicide.
De-worm.
New lawns can be sown about the middle of this month.

Greenhouse

Plant bulbs and put in a cool place.
Pot plants should be brought indoors.
Sow godetia, larkspur, phlox drummondii and early vegetables.
Begin to withhold water from gloxinia and begonia.
Feed house plants which you are growing for decorative foliage.

General

Finish all concreting operations before the frosts come.
Start collecting leaves for compost heap.